THE BRECKINRIDGES OF KENTUCKY

THE

BRECKINRIDGES OF KENTUCKY

1760-1981

James C. Klotter

THE UNIVERSITY PRESS OF KENTUCKY

Copyright © 1986 by The University Press of Kentucky

Scholarly publisher for the Commonwealth,
serving Bellarmine College, Berea College, Centre
College of Kentucky, Eastern Kentucky University,
The Filson Club, Georgetown College, Kentucky
Historical Society, Kentucky State University,
Morehead State University, Murray State University,
Northern Kentucky University, Transylvania University,
University of Kentucky, University of Louisville,
and Western Kentucky University.

Editorial and Sales Offices: Lexington, Kentucky 40506-0024

Library of Congress Cataloging-in-Publication Data

Klotter, James C.
  The Breckinridges of Kentucky, 1760-1981.

  Bibliography: p.
  Includes index.
  1. Breckinridge family. 2. Kentucky—Biography.
I. Title.
CT274.B75K56   1986   929′.2′0973   85-17983
ISBN 0-8131-1553-1

To Freda, with love

Contents

Illustrations

Preface

Onwardness lost, at last, its imagined attractions, only
inwardness remained to be explored. Only the human soul
remained terra incognita. . . . What were people like in olden
times, with their souls as yet unexplored?
Kurt Vonnegut, Jr. *The Sirens of Titan* (1959)

"IN KENTUCKY the name of Breckinridge is held in special veneration."
So proclaimed an 1860 campaign biography of a presidential candidate
who bore that surname. Statistics supported the claim, for in half of the
sixty-eight years of Kentucky statehood a Breckinridge had served in
either the state or the national capital. A quarter of a century later, a
correspondent wrote to a Breckinridge who would be in Congress for the
next decade: "The name of *Breckinridge* seems to fill the minds of the
people." By the beginning of World War I, a Washington, D.C., newspaper noted, "Of course, everyone knows about the Breckinridges of
Kentucky; they have been in American public life ever since there was an
American public life." Another reporter concluded six years later that "the
name of Breckinridge is eminent in Kentucky." Of a Breckinridge who ran
a state race in 1955, an editorial pronounced, "We believe he will make a
record worthy of a name with which Kentucky's fame for statesmanship
began." And as recently as 1979 a congressman proclaimed that the name
Breckinridge "is synonymous with service to the state."[1]

Why has this clan, generation after generation, produced state and
national leaders? How did the family become—and remain—one of
America's outstanding dynasties?[2] Why have no other Kentucky families—and few, if any, American ones—approached the Breckinridges'
record of achievement across the years?

Amateur writers, journalists, and historians have long examined the
history of particular families. Some address a few or even all of the crucial
questions involved; all too many do not. As a result, past studies have
rarely received a favorable hearing among scholars. One work, for example, was termed merely an "annotated genealogy," which as scholarly
history was "worthless." Others have been criticized as mere biographies
of the outstanding members, with no unifying themes or search for the
dynamic element in family continuity. They frequently have not probed
the "innerness" of the family's experience or its internal process of
change. Thus, what might be termed "old style" family history—a surface

study of a particular family—is viewed as some sort of antiquarian curiosity, a forgotten eddy far from the historical mainstream.[3]

More highly favored at present is the examination of the history of the family through what are called "New Social History" techniques. Over the last two decades there has been an outpouring of such studies. Historian Christopher Lasch has termed this deluge virtually "an academic industry." By concentrating not on great families but instead on the masses, by using chiefly quantitative evidence over literary or manuscript materials, by depending on statistical measures rather than individual ones, by focusing on the macro rather than the micro—this approach almost completely reverses the older style. Demographic matters previously ignored, such as longevity, marriage order, family structure, and age at marriage, are now crucial indicators. Applications of such measures have provided important insights into American life.[4]

Yet, if the "old style" histories were elitest and did not ask the "right questions," the newer ones go to the other extreme and cannot answer all the questions posed. As one author noted, the intergenerational history of a continuous family "is more sensitive than quantification studies to the impact of change on a wider range of human experiences," and Edward Pessen has pointed out that "the historian needs to know all he can about both the masses and the classes, about groups and individuals."[5] In short, the idea behind the old family histories should not be discarded completely. With an awareness of "New Social History," the historian studying an individual family may find new answers to the old questions of value transmittal, leadership patterns, and generational change.

This work examines several of those areas, but the focus is on the development and evolution of (1) political philosophy, (2) racial and social attitudes, and (3) intrafamily relationships. The book is a study of eight family members about whom enough information exists to examine and portray in detail their lives, attitudes, and actions. To minimize selectivity and focus on the influence of change in a fixed environment, the study is limited to those who were born Breckinridges and were active in Kentucky.[6] Thus, only one chapter is devoted to Sophonisba P. Breckinridge, whose public career centered outside of Kentucky, and none to Henry Breckinridge, who had only limited contact with the state. Studying only those who were Breckinridges from birth and who grew up in that environment of expectation and demand allows a more detailed exposition of all the family questions vital to understanding these patricians. Looking at the relationship of family to home and society, at community sociology and local pressures, and at changes in family and cultural influences can lead to a fuller understanding of family life-style, identity, and continuity.

Obviously the Breckinridges were not typical. What selected family would be? The picture seen through one family's eyes, as Harold D.

Woodman has noted, is always distorted.[7] But studying a single, select group allows us to go beyond the statistical family to show motivation, illustrate change, and demonstrate emotions. Individuals emerge more clearly as fascinating and complex people, rather than remaining abstractions modifying and shaping other abstractions.

The Breckinridges provide an excellent vantage point for understanding America and its history over two centuries. Not among the earliest immigrants (they arrived around 1728), they typified the later wave of Europeans who came to claim the opportunities offered by a new world. Their migration routes—Pennsylvania to Virginia to Kentucky—followed the pattern of many settlers. Breckinridges built new homes and governments, all the while fighting the elements, the frontier, and, sometimes, each other. In Kentucky they rose to prominence and were caught up in those issues important to the new nation—the question of sectionalism, the Louisiana Purchase, forms of government, and all the rest. Slaveholders, they, like the nation, could not peacefully solve the problems of the peculiar institution; they became involved in political controversy and, finally, fought in a civil war that deeply divided them. The family, rebuilt, again claimed national office and then reflected the national divisions that disrupted the 1890s. A new century brought new Breckinridge faces and new orientations—again, ones typical of the time. Reformers, they questioned their own beliefs in the twenties and emerged, changed, into the New Deal era. Through World War II, the Cold War, and into the 1970s another generation faced old global questions and new domestic ones.

Throughout all this, the family remained vital and complex. The Breckinridges' history, like that of the Lowells, is in part "a history of the heart, mind, imagination."[8] It is a study of unexplored souls.

Acknowledgments

THIS PROJECT began when I, as a naive young graduate student, asked my dissertation director for suggestions for a topic. Enthusiasm for the one chosen—the Breckinridges—temporarily overcame what soon became a very sobering fact: research involved reading some eight hundred volumes and boxes of family papers, while interpretation required delving into several disciplines.

Numerous people were especially helpful in my research. At the University of Kentucky Library, William J. Marshall, Terry L. Birdwhistell, Anne G. Campbell, William Cooper, Jr., Claire McCann, and several others aided far beyond what any researcher could expect. So too did members of the Kentucky Historical Society in Frankfort: William R. Buster, Robert B. Kinnaird, and Hambleton Tapp supported my research efforts and provided encouragement, while Mary Lou Madigan and Anne J. McDonnell and her staff in the library assisted ably and often. Aiding also were Cathy Dalton, Jane Turner Censer, and James Larry Hood. James R. Bentley and Nelson L. Dawson of the Filson Club in Louisville, Elaine M. Harrison and others at the Kentucky Library at Western Kentucky University, Charles C. Hay III of the Eastern Kentucky University Archives, Gerald F. Roberts of the Berea College Special Collections, William J. Morison, Thomas L. Owen, and others at the University of Louisville, together with librarians and archivists at other institutions mentioned in the notes—all provided insights into both their collections and this subject. Generous in allowing me to use material in private collections were Katherine C. Breckinridge and John Marshall Prewitt of Mt. Sterling, Kentucky, Robert Breckinridge Warfield of Lexington, Dorothy Breckinridge of Summit Point, West Virginia, and Lyssa Chalkley Harper of Richmond, Virginia. Permission to use material which first appeared in article form was granted by *The Historian*, *Reviews in American History*, and the Kentucky Historical Society.

Historians owe a greater debt to those who precede them than is usually acknowledged. I am no exception, but do wish to note specifically unpublished works on deposit at the University of Kentucky Library:

Alfred B. Sears, Robert W. Miles, Will D. Gilliam—all now deceased—contributed in this way. Excellent published works on the Breckinridges have greatly aided my efforts as well, especially the fine books by William C. Davis, Lowell H. Harrison, and the late Frank Heck. Valuable assistance came also from those who saw a very different version of this work as a dissertation. Charles P. Roland, James F. Hopkins, George Herring, Carl Cone, and the late Holman Hamilton all offered valuable suggestions.

Perhaps the greatest obligation of any author is to those who listen to ideas, then read and analyze them in printed form. In that regard, I owe a particularly large debt to Thomas H. Appleton, Jr., and John David Smith. They not only supplied leads to materials and criticized with both verve and insight, but did so with humor and good will. They have served Clio well. I wish to acknowledge also the excellent aid provided by Cheryl Conover and Scott D. Breckinridge, both of whom read the entire work. Commenting on various chapters were Nancy Schrom Dye, Helen L. Horowitz, Robert Seager II, Daniel Blake Smith, and George C. Wright.

"A complete history of the family would be a contribution to history and a service to future generations," a relative once wrote to editor Desha Breckinridge. But, he added after further reflection, "I know that unless it is done by friendly hands it will be done by those assiduous recorders of history from New England. . . . How will the Breckinridge family fare when they get to it?"

That question remains to be answered, but I do know that members of the Breckinridge family with whom I talked or corresponded have been both kind and informative. A few certainly did not reveal all they knew; some held back a few family letters. But no one attempted to dictate what was written. Knowing and working with people like Scott D. Breckinridge and Helen Breckinridge, as well as numerous others related to the Breckinridges, may have biased my views. If that is the case, then so be it, for I treasure the insights gained and the friendships given.

But the greatest acknowledgment goes to my wife. After reading a draft chapter on one Breckinridge, she said she was truly sorry to read of that person's death. Her empathy should be a historian's first tool. I thank my wife and children for allowing me to bring strangers into their lives and trust that they too have profited from it.

Cast of Characters

PRIMARY

JOHN BRECKINRIDGE (1760–1806). Grandson of the clan's founder in America. He served in the Virginia House of Delegates, moved to Kentucky in 1793, and became that state's attorney general and then Speaker of the House. John introduced the Kentucky Resolutions, sat in the state's 1799 constitutional convention, and represented the commonwealth as U.S. senator and attorney general under Thomas Jefferson. Husband of Polly (later called "Grandma Black Cap"), and father of Robert Jefferson Breckinridge (below).

ROBERT JEFFERSON BRECKINRIDGE (1800–1871). Son of John (above) and father of W.C.P. (below). After a stint in state legislature, he turned to the Presbyterian ministry, wrote religious works, and became moderator of that church's General Assembly. A Whig antislavery leader in the state, Robert supported Know-Nothings in the 1850s and Republicans later. Called the father of Kentucky's public school system, he was also temporary chairman of the 1864 convention that renominated Lincoln.

JOHN CABELL BRECKINRIDGE (1821–1875). Grandson of John (above), son of Joseph Cabell, nephew of Robert J. (above), and first cousin of W.C.P. (below). After serving in the Mexican War, he was elected to the state legislature, then to Congress two terms, then to the vice-presidency as a Democrat in 1856. Defeated four years later for president, John C. represented Kentucky in the U.S. Senate until entering the Confederate Army, where he rose to the rank of general. Secretary of War at the conflict's end, he fled overseas, returning only in 1869.

WILLIAM CAMPBELL PRESTON BRECKINRIDGE (1837–1904). Son of Robert J. (above) and father of Sophonisba and Desha (both below). A lawyer by training, he fought for the Confederacy in the Civil War, edited the Lexington *Observer and Reporter*, served a decade as a Democrat in Congress (1885–1895), then became editorial writer for the Lexington *Herald*. Known as the "silver-tongued orator from Kentucky," he saw scandal mar his public career.

SOPHONISBA PRESTON BRECKINRIDGE (1866–1948). Daughter of W.C.P. (above), sister of Desha (below). Admitted to the Kentucky bar, she later received Ph.D. and J.D. degrees from the University of Chicago, where she taught for many years. Author of many books and articles on social problems and civil rights, she was vice-president of the National American Woman Suffrage Association and was active in other reforms.

DESHA BRECKINRIDGE (1867–1935). Son of W.C.P. (above), brother of Sophonisba (above), and husband of reformer Madeline McDowell. Publisher and editor of the Lexington *Herald* from 1897 to 1935, he was a leader of the Progressive movement, was actively involved in politics as an independent Democrat, and was instrumental in establishing and keeping parimutuel betting in the state.

MARY BRECKINRIDGE (1881–1965). Daughter of Democratic Congressman Clifton Rodes Breckinridge and granddaughter of John C. (above). A nurse by training, she served in France during the post–World War I recovery period, studied nurse-midwifery in England, and set up the Frontier Nursing Service in Appalachian Kentucky in 1925.

JOHN BAYNE BRECKINRIDGE (1913–1979). Son of physician Scott Dudley Breckinridge and great-grandson of Robert J. (above). A lawyer, he served in World War II, returned to begin practice, and won two terms as state legislator and two as attorney general. Twice defeated in attempts for the office of lieutenant governor, he served three terms in Congress, before a primary election defeat in 1978.

SECONDARY

(In order of appearance. Italics refer to those mentioned in previous section.)

ALEXANDER BRECKINRIDGE (died 1744). Founder of the clan in America, he moved from Pennsylvania to Virginia, where he died. Father of Robert (below).

ROBERT BRECKINRIDGE (died c. 1773). Son of Alexander (above), he served as sheriff and justice of the peace in Augusta County, Virginia, and in other posts in Botetourt County. His marriage to Lettice Preston brought further family connections. Father of *John*.

ROBERT BRECKINRIDGE, JR. (1754–1833). Son of Robert (above) by his first wife, he fought in the Revolutionary War and then migrated to Kentucky, where he became the state's first Speaker of the House and a trustee of the city of Louisville. Half-brother of *John*.

JAMES BRECKINRIDGE (1763–1833). Son of Robert (above) and brother of *John*, James remained in Virginia, where he served as militia officer, representative in the House of Delegates, Federalist candidate for governor, congressman, and member of the Board of Visitors of the University of Virginia.

MARY HOPKINS CABELL "POLLY" BRECKINRIDGE (1769–1858). Called "Grandma Black Cap" after her husband *John's* death, she managed a large estate for over half a century and influenced numerous family members.

JOSEPH CABELL BRECKINRIDGE (1788–1823). Son of *John*, married to the daughter of Princeton's president, he served as Kentucky Speaker of the House and secretary of state. Father of *John C.*

JOHN BRECKINRIDGE (1797–1841). Son of *John*, brother of Joseph Cabell (above), *Robert J.*, and William (below), he was a renowned Presbyterian minister who became a professor at Princeton Theological Seminary and was president-elect of Oglethorpe University at his death.

WILLIAM LEWIS BRECKINRIDGE (1803–1876). Son of *John*, brother of Joseph Cabell, John (both above), and *Robert J.*, he too became a Presbyterian minister and served as moderator of that church's General Assembly, later William was president of Centre College and Oakland College.

ROBERT JEFFERSON BRECKINRIDGE, JR. (1834–1915). Son of *Robert J.* and brother of *W.C.P.* and Joseph Cabell (below), he served the Confederacy as colonel and representative. After the war, Robert resumed his law practice, became a judge, and was state attorney general briefly.

JOSEPH CABELL BRECKINRIDGE (1842–1921). Son of *Robert J.*, and brother of *W.C.P.* and Robert J., Jr. (above), he fought for the Union and then made the military his career, rising to the rank of general and serving as inspector general of the army.

CURRY DESHA BRECKINRIDGE (1875–1918). Daughter of *W.C.P.* and sister of *Desha*, Robert (below), and *Sophonisba*, she overcame dyslexia, served in various philanthropic positions, and became a nurse, going overseas in World War I.

ROBERT JEFFERSON BRECKINRIDGE (1870–1944). Son of *W.C.P.* and brother of *Desha*, *Sophonisba*, and Curry (above), he encountered early personal problems, and a long absence caused the family to believe him dead. On his return, Robert worked with the *Herald* and was involved in other activities.

MADELINE MCDOWELL BRECKINRIDGE (1872–1920). Wife of *Desha Breckinridge*, she suffered from tuberculosis of the bone but became active in numerous reform causes. A leader of Progressivism in the South, "Madge" served as president of the Kentucky Equal Rights

Association and vice-president of the National American Woman Suffrage Association.

HENRY BRECKINRIDGE (1886–1960). Son of General Joseph Cabell (above), he started his career as a Lexington attorney, then became U.S. assistant secretary of war under Woodrow Wilson before entering the army in World War I. A member of two Olympic fencing teams, Henry was Charles Lindbergh's counsel and ran as a conservative third-party candidate in the 1930s.

CLIFTON RODES BRECKINRIDGE (1846–1932). Son of *John C.* and father of *Mary*, he entered the Confederacy, then turned to planting and trade in Arkansas. After a decade in Congress as a Democratic representative, he was appointed minister to Russia.

SCOTT DUDLEY BRECKINRIDGE (1882–1941). Father of *John B.* and son of General Joseph Cabell (above), he was a respected gynecologist and obstetrician. Scott, a member of the 1912 Olympic fencing team, wrote about and briefly coached that sport.

JOHN BRECKINRIDGE

1760-1806

Good and able men had better govern than be
govern'd, since 'tis possible, indeed highly probable,
that if the able and good withdraw themselves from
society, the venal and ignorant will succeed.

John Tyler to Thomas Jefferson, 1782

Americans

JOHN BRECKINRIDGE did not contemplate his coming journey with any great joy. In 1789 the trip across the mountains, through Cumberland Gap, and over the Wilderness Trail to the Kentucky Bluegrass was dangerous and arduous. He would leave behind a loving wife and a son only recently recovered from a nearly fatal illness, his law practice, and a promising political career in his friend Thomas Jefferson's home county of Albemarle. Yet he would go despite the dangers, for although "a Violent Effort will be necessary to start me," Breckinridge had in mind the well-being of his family, "whose Happiness is my greatest object."[1] Faced with a secure life in Virginia or the unknown possibilities of Kentucky, he had chosen the future, determined to seek a better life and greater prestige for unborn generations of Breckinridges.

In the spring of 1789, he started west to seek out and purchase good land. Left behind, his wife wrote to her mother-in-law that "the Lord only knows whether I am ever to lay my eyes on him again." She would trust in her God, as had past members of the family, and pray that her John, "all my happiness . . . on this earth," would return safely to the Old Dominion.[2] A letter in May calmed fears, for John had completed the journey without danger or difficulty. He was pleased with the rich, cheap, available land and purchased a six-hundred-acre tract on the waters of the North Elkhorn. This rolling, fertile stretch of soil—and the almost thirty thousand acres he eventually claimed elsewhere in the state—gave promise that his descendants would live as he desired.[3]

Four years elapsed, however, before Breckinridge moved his family to their new home. Finally, by August 1792, only two months after Kentucky became the nation's fifteenth state, he had made his decision. "Nothing terrestial" would now stop him from leaving Virginia in the spring, for the Breckinridges were ready to start anew. "As fixed as fate" in his resolution, he admitted to a friend that reconciling his family was difficult. Behind lay his old plantation, "The Glebe," his wife's relatives and his own, and his past. Ahead lay Kentucky and an uncertain beginning.[4]

The new state already displayed the contradictory elements that would characterize it for the next two centuries. For explorers and trappers it offered plentiful game; for small settlers, easily attainable land of their own; for wealthy easterners, large tracts of unclaimed acreage; for merchants, new untapped markets and monopolies; for the persecuted, freedom from surveillance; for them all, new homes and new dreams. Stories from the mountains had filtered back to eager men and women in the East, telling of this land of giant cane, tall sycamores, extensive grasslands, massive animal herds, and untold fertile acres. A young George Rogers Clark proclaimed that "a richer and more Beautiful [country] than this I believe has never been seen in America." Tales became so fabulous in their description that one overexuberant preacher described heaven as "a mere Kentucky of a place."[5]

But the "Kentucky myth of plenty" had dark shadows. This land of milk and honey at the same time fully merited its Indian name of a "dark and bloody ground." The first decade of settlement was one filled with death and sorrow. Few families did not lose a loved one. Violence was commonplace, peace the exception. Bloody and spectacular acts of cruelty by both red man and white seemed almost the norm, and years became known for their death toll, with 1777 infamous as the year of the "bloody sevens." By 1790 an estimated 1,500 had been killed over the past seven years.[6]

This dualism, this contrast between beauty and wealth, and death and fear, faced each settler, as the poet William Gilmore Simms recognized when he wrote, "Beauty came . . . with Terror looking over her shoulder. The wilderness was charming to the senses and the mind, but its thickets of green concealed the painted and ferocious savage." Yet the lure of land overshadowed the dangers, and great migrations resulted. Peace finally came to the commonwealth, and the state-of-seige mentality passed as the threat of death lifted. Men and women intent on erecting and protecting homes in the wilderness could now turn to building a new commonwealth.[7]

The old pioneers became men out of touch with their era, unwanted and unhonored. In their place came a new elite, one which included John Breckinridge. With this change came a further contradiction, for the democracy of the frontier would now fuse with the more hierarchical society coming over the mountains. Other contrasts would arise in this evolving land—such as Kentuckians' ability to reconcile religion, racing, and red-eye—but that mattered not to the young emigrant ready to leave Virginia in 1793. He knew only that Kentucky had sent forth a siren song to which he eagerly responded.[8]

"Advancing with fear & trembling," Breckinridge chose the sometimes safer northern route of the Ohio River on his second trip west. The family proceeded up the Shenandoah Valley to a port on the Monongahela, where they boarded boats. "Comfortably fixed" and provided with necessities, they had a reasonably pleasant eight-day journey down-stream to Limestone (now Maysville), then the gateway to Kentucky. Although Indians had attacked boats on the river only weeks before, the Breckinridges sighted no red men, and on the last day of April, the party left behind the boats and the river.[9]

While John knew what the interior held, the rest of the family did not face an encouraging first view of their new homeland. With houses haphazardly located on high, uneven banks, Limestone was an un-distinguished town, even for the frontier. But the winding road leading out of the area soon led the newcomers to the kind of land that had attracted eager thousands—a rich, black soil covered with rye, clover, and tall, sturdy stands of cane. Only a few years before, travelers on the same route had remarked that the howling of wolves kept them awake at night. Now settlements were rapidly driving such wild animals from the more fertile areas.[10]

But as if to warn of the inconsistencies of the state, the calm, rolling lands soon gave way to steeper hills. Worsening roads signaled a greater threat of Indian attack, a danger of which John Breckinridge was well aware. His half-brothers, Alexander and Robert, had migrated to Ken-tucky a decade earlier, and their letters had given frequent news of Indian raids. In August 1792 a friend who was looking after John's Kentucky lands wrote of the deaths of two neighbors in such raids. Only a month before the family landed at Limestone, and within thirty miles of their present location, nineteen women and children had been captured by Indians. Kentucky was not yet free of its bloody past, if indeed it would ever be.[11]

Soon, however, the rough, unsettled areas, the forbidding hills, the dry and dusty roads yielded to the lushness of what was becoming known as the Bluegrass. After three days of travel from the Ohio, thirty-two-year-old John, his twenty-four-year-old wife, and their four children arrived in Lexington. Breckinridge's choice for his new home in Kentucky could not have been better. Still in a transitional stage between wilderness and civilization in 1793, Lexington had been founded only fourteen years earlier. But growth came quickly, and from 835 people in 1790 Lexington doubled its population within six years. By 1790 it served as the county seat of a political unit containing 25 percent of Kentucky's total population and 30 percent of its slaves. Although it was no longer the state capital, the burgeoning town already had a two-story stone courthouse, a bookshop, and a newspaper, all vital to the educated gentleman and aspiring attor-ney. Horses and lawsuits, as well as real property, dominated con-versation, and Breckinridge took advantage of the interest. The writer who noted that a Kentucky purchaser "buys a law-suit with every plot of unoccupied land he pays for there" was describing a muddled title situation that offered ample opportunities for advancing fortunes. Kentucky became a happy hunting-ground for lawyers as well as Indians.[12]

John Breckinridge was clearly pleased with the outcome of his gamble. Situated in the cultural center of the young state in a town soon praised as "the Athens of the West," he told his brother-in-law of this happiness: "I am satisfied with this country better than the old. . . . 1. Because my profession is more profitable; and 2ndly Because I can provide *good* land here for my children & insure them from want, which I was not certain of in the Old Country." Even the children loved the land, he wrote; they never had been "so fat & healthy." Later the family moved some six miles from their temporary Lexington quarters to a two-story double log cabin on their plantation, which they named "Cabell's Dale." The trek had ended.[13]

The Breckinridge family had long been restless.[14] Much earlier, as Scottish yeomen in the Ayrshire region, they had been covenanters during the English Civil War and Interregnum, and on Charles II's return had departed for safety in the highlands of Braedalbane. Sometime later, probably in the late seventeenth century, they had migrated to Ulster.[15]

New lands across a wider sea promised more than Ireland, and in 1728 elements of the family came to America. While one branch settled in New England, Alexander Breckinridge—"the Ancestor"—made his first home in Bucks County, Pennsylvania. Caught up in the sweeping flow of Scotch-Irish migrants, the Breckinridge clan moved southward to Virginia's Shenandoah Valley, where by 1738 they were building log cabins. Two years later Alexander Breckinridge, large family in tow, appeared in court and "made oath that he imported himself . . . from Ireland to Philadelphia, and from thence to this country, at his own charges." Satisfying the justices that he was indentured to no man, Alexander obtained further land titles and purchased 245 acres near present-day Staunton. Granted little time to fulfill America's promise, he died in 1743, probably in his forties.[16]

The lack of a will meant that Alexander's land went initially to his oldest son, but within five years a younger offspring, Robert, purchased the land and added it to the four hundred acres he already held. During the next quarter-century he would expand his holdings to over three thousand acres and make the Breckinridge family locally prominent. His rise among Augusta County's local gentry came steadily: under-sheriff in 1747, sheriff six years later, then justice of the peace. Each step increased his status and brought obligations. Very early, certain Breckinridges accepted the idea that they must be active members of their society, not self-centered patricians concerned with only their own brief generation. They acted for their children's future as well as their own.[17]

In the midst of defending his own property by fighting in the French

John Breckinridge, circa 1780. Courtesy Christina Willcox

and Indian War, Robert made a decision that would prove vital to his descendants. He married Irish-born Lettice Preston, the thirty-year-old daughter of John and Elizabeth Patton Preston and sister of his friend William Preston. Bonds that stretched across the sea to the British Isles had long allied the two families. The ties brought by Robert's marriage to a Preston would further connect the Breckinridges to leading families of the Old Dominion.[18]

While that marriage brought a prestigious name into the fold, it did not bring harmony. Lettice Preston had to fill the difficult position of stepmother to Robert, Jr., and Alexander, children of her husband's first marriage, which had ended with his wife's death. "Much disagreement" with her stepsons caused Lettice to accept her brother's suggestion to apprentice the boys to his brother-in-law, a carpenter. After leaving that trade to serve in the Revolutionary War, the two young men were re-united by 1783 in Kentucky, where Robert, Jr., shortly rose to political prominence. He sat in the first constitutional convention and was elected as the first Speaker of the Kentucky House of Representatives. His financial well-being enabled him in one instance to lend the hard-pressed state treasury £475—at an appropriate 5 percent interest—to help keep the infant commonwealth solvent. While active later in numerous civic activities, the stern, reserved Robert never reached further pinnacles of political power, due in part to "habits of intemperance."[19]

Alexander's actions may have caused part of his brother's problems. There are two versions of his story. In one account, Robert returned from a business venture in Virginia to discover his sibling married to his fiancée. Another, more charitable, version recounts that Robert was believed killed by Indians and Alexander consoled and then married the grieving fiancée. In the latter version, told by a relative in 1845, the woman was pregnant by Robert when Alexander married her, and Robert later was "more intimate with the woman than he should have been," given the fact that she was then his brother's wife. From the marriage— and from whomever the father was—came Louisville congressman James Douglas Breckinridge.[20]

That all lay in the future. In Virginia in the 1760s, Lettice supervised a growing household. She and Robert reared their own six children— William, John (born 2 December 1760), James, Elizabeth, Jane (who died young), and Preston. Concerns over this family probably stimulated Robert's search for more land, wealth, and prestige. Early in the 1760s he moved his brood southwest into what soon became Botetourt County. Active politically, Robert was commissioned one of the first justices of the peace; the first county court met in his home in February 1770. Positions as road surveyor, lieutenant colonel in the militia, and constable followed.[21]

Sometime in this period Robert made another decision that would shape the lives of his descendants: he became a slaveholder. Very probably there was little decision involved. By this time black slaves were a long-accepted work force, and, with hemp crops of more than a half ton, Breckinridge needed laborers. Nevertheless, the question of racial control may not have been far removed from his thoughts at the time. Robert left little evidence of his feelings toward blacks, but he did sit on a court in 1769 that acquitted a slave of raping a white woman. Less than six months later, with four other justices present, and three of the five (including

Breckinridge) who had ruled on the case earlier now absent, the Negro was convicted and ordered hanged. Yet any leniency Breckinridge may have indicated in this instance must be balanced by his purchase of slaves and the fact that one of his bondsmen was hanged for stealing guns.[22]

In the early 1770s Breckinridge continued to hear cases as justice of the peace, but by the summer of 1772 he was reputed to be "very unwell" and soon died, probably in 1773. To his wife and seven remaining children he left an estate of over 1,600 acres, a "plantation," and eleven slaves. To the most promising (although not eldest) son, John, he left some three hundred acres of land (or money from its sale), one slave, and a half-share in another. More than that, John's father left him the memory that Breckinridges were important members of society.[23]

Barely a teenager at his father's death, John earned money to supplement the family income by working in a surveyor's office and by teaching. As he grew to maturity the Revolutionary War raged around him, but John was determined to attain further education. With the assistance of his wealthy uncle William Preston, he secured a position as a surveyor for Montgomery County, probably to help to raise money to attend college. Finally, in 1780, he determined to enter the College of William and Mary, a move that delighted his cousin John Brown. Future United States senator Brown wrote Preston that Breckinridge's "genius is such that if assisted by the advantages" Williamsburg offered, "I am well convinced that he would not only become an important member of society but that he would do honour to his Connections."[24]

The opportunity to "do honour" soon came Breckinridge's way. While at the college in 1781, he learned of his election to the Virginia House of Delegates. George Washington, Thomas Jefferson, James Madison, James Monroe—all were elected as burgesses before they turned twenty-six; although John Breckinridge was not yet twenty-one, his ability—plus "Connections"—had impressed his peers. The frank, open young man confessed to his uncle that his pride in accepting the post, "and imagining myself Capable to serve my Country in that Capacity, is great. The Confidence my Acquaintances were pleased to repose in me, tho' unsolicited, does me the greatest Honour and raises no small Ambition in me to endeavor to serve them as well as I am capable of."[25] That outlook would serve as an articulated family goal for the next two centuries.

For the neophyte legislator of 1781 such service became difficult amidst the chaos of wartime. The college closed, and enemy troops disrupted the legislative meeting at Charlottesville in June; the lawmakers fled just ahead of the invading forces. Despite the sobering aspects of the whole experience, Breckinridge found himself in an exciting and distinguished company that included Patrick Henry, George Nicholas—later "father of Kentucky's first constitution"—and John Taylor of Caroline. Of the delegates who represented the few counties of that Virginia area then called Kentucky, two stood out: Benjamin Logan and Daniel Boone had founded two of the three original settlements in the western lands, and their stories of the rich—though still dangerous—region may have kindled an interest in young John.[26]

But financial problems tempered Breckinridge's "no small Ambition." In 1782 another man represented Botetourt County at Richmond, for that winter John traveled along the edge of the mountain area of Virginia, seeking to raise money. The young surveyor found "every farthing" already collected by others, but persisted. Although still pressed for funds, he was again chosen to represent his constituents at the capital, and, notwithstanding "very great uneasiness" over his finances, he determined to serve—a course in which George Wythe, former tutor of Jefferson, encouraged him. Breckinridge made up his mind not to spend life to a "poor purpose"; he would go to Richmond. At the same time he decided to reenter William and Mary as soon as the House rose, for John Breckinridge fell short, so far, of the requirements he had set for himself.[27]

Despite previous hesitations and his uncle's death, Breckinridge by March 1784 indicated a strong desire to hold his seat. Unable to campaign because he was away at school, he feared that lack of political solicitation might be looked upon "as a species of Pride & Ostentation," or even indifference. Appearances, Breckinridge recognized, often outweighed actions. He was returned, however, and he gained some important assignments and served on committees that included future jurists Spencer Roane and John Marshall, as well as Nicholas and Taylor. As important, he made valuable allies and long-lasting friends.[28]

These future leaders shaped and influenced the young representative's developing political philosophy. Although many of his attitudes would change as years passed, the Revolutionary ideology of Jeffersonian Virginia dominated. In speeches probably prepared for the session, John Breckinridge portrayed government in Lockean terms. According to his view, people surrendered some of their natural rights when they agreed to live in a society. The government they created, then, existed to protect and guarantee the happiness of mankind. The citizens could institute whatever form of government they desired, and the best form of government simply conformed to whatever the people ruled. Harking back to the "lost liberties" that hastened the Revolution, he declared that where citizens grew corrupt an inevitable dissolution of government resulted. Education—the "most sacred, the most useful and at the same time, the most neglected thing in every country"—would solve America's problems of instability.[29]

On one specific question Breckinridge stressed his devotion to a stronger central government than that favored by some of his contemporaries of the Confederation period. His conservative bent led him to fear the dangerous temper of the times, only accented by financial difficulties, and he thus favored the controversial impost duty as the "least objectional" method of discharging debt. Pointing to a common interest, stressing more than regional concerns, he called for a national, uniform collection of revenue. Too much jealousy of a state's powers could be a dangerous as too little. Trust the people, for "the greatest of virtues," said Breckinridge, "is a Conformity to the *General Will*."[30] The makings of a Jeffersonian Republican were evident in part, but so was a contradictory theme that when planted in the soil west of the mountains would develop into a unique outlook.

His beliefs led Breckinridge to the Constitutional Society of Virginia, another group that both influenced his still-changing political philosophy and united him further to state and national leaders. Including Madison, Monroe, Henry, Roane, Taylor, and John Brown in its membership, the society pledged to keep a "watchful eye" over the people's rights. Breckinridge seldom wavered, at this time, in his support of the general government, a living body "no part of which can be wounded or injured without causing a painful sensation to the whole." Still a nationalist in the 1780s, he would not remain one.[31]

Influential relatives, an environment that pushed the talented into politics, the tradition of service in his family, familiarity with Enlightenment philosophy, educational advantages—all had instilled in him, as they would in his descendants, a sense of political responsibility. But after the 1784 session Breckinridge left politics to concentrate instead on acquiring land and fortune through the law practice he entered in 1785. Another factor encouraged him to build up his holdings: on 28 June 1785 John and the sixteen-year-old Mary Hopkins Cabell ("Polly") were wed at her father's home. As a gift, Joseph Cabell, who served in the Senate when Breckinridge sat in the House, presented the couple with a four-hundred-acre farm in Albemarle County. In their new home the first child, Letitia (a variation of Lettice) Preston, was born on 14 June 1786. Other children came—in 1787 a son named for Polly's father, in 1790 a daughter named for the woman who bore her, and in 1793 a second son, Robert, namesake of John's father. The practice of naming the children for relatives and in-laws predated the clan's arrival in America, and would be continued in the new land, a reminder of past glories to be emulated, of men and women to be honored.[32]

The new husband, despite the dowry, had not yet gained financial independence, at least not the kind the wildly speculative Virginia society demanded of its leaders. By 1786 John and Polly held fifteen slaves, and between 1787 and 1789 the family added 850 acres to the holdings these bondsmen worked.[33] Certainly not poor, and recognized as a member of the dominant gentry, Breckinridge still had not accomplished all he sought. A good lawyer, he saw Albemarle filled with fine attorneys; a rising politician, he knew Virginia had abundant talent in that field; a promising farmer, he found many of the good lands already gone or accelerating in price; a young father, he foresaw an uncertain future for his children. The concerns that would culminate in his first trip to Kentucky had begun.

John's half-brother Alexander, already in that part of Virginia beyond the mountains, reported holding land warrants for two hundred thousand acres. His letters stressed the desperate paucity of trained lawyers and the advantages for someone like John, who held slaves. By 1785, both Alexander and Robert received appointments as trustees of the new town of Louisville, located at the strategic Falls of the Ohio. Brother William had also made the journey and confirmed the innumerable law disputes. For a man struggling in Virginia, the new region promised much, and in 1789 John made plans to move west.[34]

Then, at almost the eleventh hour, Virginia voters selected John Breckinridge to represent them in the Congress of the United States.[35] The decision to leave was hard enough without this, for it meant uprooting an insecure wife in her twenties, their young children, and some twenty slaves. But Kentucky beckoned, for there lay the promise of the future.

Two

Kentuckians

OPPORTUNITY welcomed the newcomer in 1793 and John Breckinridge eagerly grasped the outstretched hand. The new master of Cabell's Dale soon realized that Kentucky offered greater chances for community leadership than did the overcrowded and talented environment of Virginia. The young commonwealth presented fewer barriers—for the time at least—to inhibit natural abilities. A frontier spirit that judged a man on how he performed, not on the prestige of his ancestors, still lingered to make the Bluegrass, if not a valley of democracy, at least a fertile glen for that outlook. Yet a respect for social position crossed the mountains also. Aided by family alliances, connected to important men by friendship, Breckinridge combined those advantages with his considerable talents to rise rapidly, both economically and politically, in Kentucky society.

The promise of economic betterment had been a major motivation for the move to Lexington. Landholding indicated wealth and status, and John warned his mother-in-law that the "moment you give up your property, you give up your independence, your happiness, your comfort." He apparently held tightly to all of these, for his holdings passed twenty thousand acres in 1796 and peaked at thirty thousand half a decade later. The financial security sought when he left Virginia was his.[1]

But if Breckinridge sought land for many of the same reasons that motivated his Virginia friends, for the most part he used it differently. The Old Dominion owed its early economic existence to the "filthy weed" of tobacco, but John refused to grow a crop that so exhausted a soil not yet commonly enriched by fertilization. Instead, he favored hemp for the Bluegrass. With its dew-rotted stalk yielding the fiber for rope or cotton bagging, hemp became the chief cash crop of central Kentucky, outdistancing tobacco for decades. Furthermore, hemp's dependence on tariff protection from outside competition would be a factor in shaping Kentucky's response to the national government. In the hemp stalks that John Breckinridge grew lay the roots of future problems.

Other, less controversial, crops, such as corn, wheat, and rye, complemented his hemp and allowed the gentleman farmer the opportunity for barter in a money-poor state. Four hundred bushels of rye, for instance, would be traded for four hundred gallons of "good, proof" whiskey. With Breckinridge's sheep, cattle, and hogs producing food and clothing, with sugar from maple trees and fruit from an orchard, the family became nearly self-sufficient.[2]

But not completely. Another form of livestock attracted the agriculturalist's attention, and to improve that breed required aid from afar. Horses held great appeal for John Breckinridge, as they did for many Kentuckians, for if the limestone under the soil reportedly improved the horseflesh, it seemed almost as though something in the very air made citizens yearn for the thrill of the race and the satisfaction of a winning bet. Nearly a century would pass before the region could rival eastern stables, but the Bluegrass quickly became an established entrepot for the thoroughbred.

Despite a slow beginning (eight horses in Virginia in 1786 and nine in Kentucky in 1793) and some problems with thieves, Breckinridge increased his herd to 128 by 1806. To improve the stock, John secured George Banks's stud Speculator, an English-bred seven-year-old bay with a good racing record. After being brought though the still-dangerous wilderness to become the twentieth stud horse in young Fayette County, Speculator stood at Cabell's Dale and other nearby farms for a ten- to twelve-dollar fee. His owner joined a fledgling Jockey Club. By the time Virginia-bred Bald Eagle joined his stable in 1805, John had begun to achieve the high-quality stock he sought. In this self-contained world of rich land, varied crops, and purebred horses, John Breckinridge personified the rural ethos. None of his descendants ever abandoned it completely. It did not, however, prove the sole belief guiding them. A brief venture in an ironworks represented one aspect of John's nonagrarian side, but more typical was his interest in nearby Lexington, the increasingly urban area where he practiced law and, in time, invested his own future.[3]

Because Breckinridge, like others of his era, believed education was a prerequisite to successful democracy, he focused on that aspect of Lexington life. "Tis education alone that makes a man," he had proclaimed, and he sought to make certain that life's higher purposes would not be ignored in a still-frontier atmosphere. John's warning to his brother James in 1790—that he should avoid spending so much time riding and so little in reading—reflected his philosophy.[4] As a result, Breckinridge actively supported efforts to found a college, and his efforts succeeded when Transylvania University opened its doors in 1798. For four years he served as its trustee, aiding the school's growth. In his children's time, Transylvania would be the one institution more responsible than any other for giving Lexington its sobriquet of "the Athens of the West." Breckinridge, recognizing that education extended beyond formal schooling, also promoted successful efforts to fund the Lexington Library. His work in both endeavors bettered the city's cultural standing.[5]

John Breckinridge aided education in other ways as well. As a teacher of the law, the attorney trained students in his office and, more important, gave them full use of one of the most extensive libraries in the new West. Plutarch, Cicero, Shakespeare, Bacon, Milton, Locke, Rousseau, Burke, Hume, Gibbon, Franklin, Jefferson, Swift, Adam Smith, and the multi-volumed *Debates in Parliament* graced his shelves. These represented, in his day, standard fare for the educated. Within a short time, the community had accepted John Breckinridge as lawyer, farmer, man of culture, and person of stature. He had attained goals thought worthy of a gentleman. Yet the very process of gaining these aspirations had involved him in other spheres. He was also John Breckinridge, politician.[6]

Just as the new state lured talented newcomers with the promise of land and wealth, it also offered another, almost irresistible, enticement—the promise of political office. A void occurred with the passing of those who had molded the state: of thirteen original justices of the peace in Kentucky, five had been killed by Indians; George Rogers Clark, so responsible for the safety of the commonwealth, now stood unappreciated, virtually deserted by the government, and broken in health; the greatest of Kentucky scouts, Simon Kenton, barely eked out an existence; Boone left for Missouri by 1799; and James Harrod, founder of the first settlement, had disappeared, reportedly murdered. Men such as these—violent, brave, indifferent to convention, contemptuous of artificial ethics—had secured the land, but the frontiersman's day had passed by the 1790s. Their outlook seemed as passé as their rough clothes in increasingly fashionable Lexington.[7]

Into the void stepped a new breed—planters, attorneys, physicians, merchants, professional men—all bent on developing an increasingly stable land. But how? The debate on Kentucky's turbulent course to statehood had continued without resolution for almost a decade before Breckinridge arrived in the Bluegrass, and it almost brought the area to independence—not from Virginia, but from young America. Although Virginia understood and sympathized with the Kentuckians' desire for self-rule, its terms created debate, confusion, and delay. So, too, did Kentucky's own uncertainty, for the Confederation Period left many citizens unsettled about the future of the United States. Thus it was that nine statehood conventions met and argued before the final decision was made and the government formulated.[8]

The problems lay in geography, economic needs, and sectionalism. As the most-developed region west of the mountains, Kentucky faced the problems of a minority whose needs seemed secondary to those of the eastern majority. The Bluegrass could best find a market for its goods by shipping them downstream to New Orleans, then by sea to eastern or European markets. Alternative transportation routes across the mountains or upstream proved costlier and slower. The Mississippi thus loomed as Kentucky's economic lifeline, but Spain controlled New Orleans, at the river's mouth. Citizens saw the national government attempt to barter away river rights in exchange for concessions to the larger United States system, and with New Orleans closed to American commerce, Kentuckians faced grave economic woes.[9]

In this atmosphere of distrust, some Kentucky leaders, led by the young General James Wilkinson, covertly agreed to work with Spain to try to persuade the region to break away from the East. Formation of this "Spanish Conspiracy" in the 1780s made real the dangers of separation. When the Kentucky members voted at the Virginia ratification convention, they opposed the new Constitution ten votes to three. As James Breckinridge told brother John in 1788, Kentuckians feared that "a combination of the northern states" would render the opening of the vital Mississippi "entirely impractical." When the last Confederation Congress refused a Kentucky statehood petition, John Brown warned Jefferson, "There is every reason to expect that immediately on hearing that Congress have refused to receive them they [Kentucky] will assume their Independence."[10] But such expectations did not come to pass; despite some covert actions, the final suggestion was never made. Anglo-Saxon ties, a new and realistic Virginia agreement, the strength of the new federal Constitution, a fresh Congress and a new president, and stronger nationalistic feelings overcame—for the time—the doubts and the sectionalism. On 1 June 1792 the state of Kentucky entered the federal Union.

Less than a year later John Breckinridge, aware of most of these occurrences, arrived. Already factions were forming into what would eventually become the Federalist and Republican parties. But in Kentucky the divisions never really became so clear-cut as in other places: while the factions (and later the parties) had basic differences, these differences remained more apparent than real, and the ambiguity made John Breckinridge's political decisions even more difficult. Brothers Robert in Kentucky and James in Virginia followed their consciences to the Federalist party. John, however, chose the Republicanism of his old Virginia friends. In so doing he did not reject completely his opponents' creed. For if in the roughness of a developing state Breckinridge's public statements gave democracy free rein, the liberalism of his Virginia days faded as he became a wealthy landowner and slaveholder. Even as he voiced sentiments of the small farmer, he moved to limit their applicability. As he cried out against a central government that inhibited or threatened the various states, Breckinridge at the same time called for more oligarchical control in Kentucky and resisted liberalizing political reforms. And all of this did not indicate deceit; it simply reflected the paradox of Jeffersonian Republicanism.

In this highly charged political atmosphere, Breckinridge could not long avoid the political world. A new and uncertain state, still seeking leaders, still distrustful, still searching for some order, would welcome the experience of a former Virginia legislator who had given up a congressional seat to come to Kentucky. Rewards came quickly, for in but thirteen years he rose to serve the commonwealth as attorney general, Speaker of the Kentucky House, United States senator, and first member of the cabinet from west of the mountains. His meteoric political ascendancy indicated the strength of family ties, the traditional social attitudes of the area, and, at the same time, the people's ability to recognize and impart power to a responsible person. Indicative of this, Breckinridge gained a post of some prominence less than four months after his arrival in Kentucky: on 28 August 1793 members of the newly formed Lexington Democratic Society chose him as their chairman.[11]

Nationally, the more than forty Democratic Societies had grown out of American sympathies for the French Revolution, then raging in Europe. Attacking "aristocracy" in the United States, organizing to support friends and punish enemies (almost always Federalist), they seemed to more conservative citizens to be hotbeds of sedition, fomenters of impending insurrection. "If these self-created societies cannot be discountenanced," President George Washington predicted, "they will destroy the government of this country."[12]

Breckinridge and other founders of the Lexington Democratic Society feared that without their efforts government as they envisioned it would be destroyed. John Breckinridge wanted the new nation to survive. Yet he also wanted protection for his land, for his slaves, for his new state's prosperity, for his rights, for his future. Could the East guarantee that? Convinced of benign neglect by eastern states, and encouraged by Jefferson's own challenges to authority, Breckinridge supported a potentially revolutionary group. For a conservative, it would be a test of conscience.

The immediate issue, once again, was the old one of Mississippi River navigation and the right to deposit goods at Spanish-controlled New Orleans. The Democratic Society, though it never attracted a large membership, did include Kentucky's secretary of state, chief justice, and most prominent editor, and leading this distinguished group and drafting many of its resolutions, John Breckinridge—as planter and as politician—shared fully the society's aims. In November 1793 he wrote that navigation on the river "is the NATURAL RIGHT of the inhabitants of the counties bordering on the waters" and declared that westerners had a right "to expect that the present Federal Government would before this time have taken effectual measures" to obtain free navigation. An even bolder resolution asserted the West's "good cause" to suspect that the administration's efforts had been "feeble" and that the opening of the river "is not wished for by part of the United States." Finally, the Democratic Society demanded more forceful steps, adding that—though strong enough "to obtain that right by force"—respect for authority would commit Kentuckians to a peaceful course.[13]

The following month, in a signed address to "Inhabitants of the United States West of the Allegany and Appalachian Mountains," Breckinridge called for unity to secure what was a "right of Providence"— the navigation of the Mississippi. Again he questioned the motives of easterners, and he appealed to his fellow citizens' sense of history, asking them to make certain that posterity would not look back and point to his generation's "neglect and supineness" as the cause of their lack of river rights.[14]

Peaceful appeals were combined with threats of violence. The new French republic, at war with Great Britain and Spain, seemed a suitable ally for those Kentuckians who cast a hungry look at the Mississippi. Citizen Edmond Genêt, France's minister to America, did nothing to discourage such alliances, despite the United States' avowed policy of neutrality. He spoke to Secretary of State Jefferson, who, according to Genêt, "gave me to understand that a little spontaneous eruption of the inhabitants of Kentucky" would hasten action against Spain. Then, formulating semisecret plans for an expedition—organized in American territory—to seize Spanish Louisiana, he got Breckinridge and other members of the Democratic Society to promise financial aid. George Rogers Clark, troubled by debt and disgruntled over his "notoriously ungrateful" treatment by the government, even agreed to lead a proposed army. In 1793 the "French Conspiracy" was born.[15]

Whether this so-called conspiracy involved some plan of separation from the eastern states is uncertain, but actions contrary to the stated national policy of neutrality were openly contemplated. The Spanish governor of Natchez was told that western Democratic Societies sought to cause the region "to think, & act, independent of, the eastern States." A worried President Washington queried John Randolph: "What if the government of Kentucky should force us either to support them in their hostilities against Spain or disavow and renounce them? . . . The lopping off of Kentucky from the Union is dreadful to contemplate, even if it should not attach itself to some other power." But Genêt's deficiencies in diplomacy and tact soon alienated even loyal supporters. Following his removal and Washington's proclamation forbidding any proposed expedition, the dispute died—temporarily. Virginians cautioned Breckinridge to be more moderate in the future: "Your old friends, to the Eastward," one wrote, "condemn you a little for your warmth, while they approve of your republican dispositions."[16]

Once committed to his course, however, Breckinridge continued his criticisms of the government. A letter written in September 1794 clarified his feelings: "The Miss. we *will* have. If Government will not procure it for us, we must procure it for ourselves. Whether that will be done by the sword or by negotiation is yet to scan."[17] At the same time that challenges to federal authority came from Kentucky, protesters in western Pennsylvania expressed their dissatisfaction with the excise tax upon distilled whiskey. Some leaders foresaw the Union's destruction if such defiance of the national authority went unchecked. The crushing of the Whiskey Rebellion, Genêt's decline, and the fall in popularity of the transmontane Democratic Societies again diluted the threat from Kentucky, but early in 1796 Breckinridge wrote to James Monroe telling of anger, resentment, and disappointment still extant in the West. The federal government had not answered their needs: "Without the free use of the Mississippi, our posterity in one generation more, will be content to parch meat . . . & become as uncivilized as the savages which surround us." Kentuckians had no confidence in the government, and, Breckinridge warned, *"something will be done."*[18]

The implied threat went unfulfilled, for federal action finally defused the explosive situation. In September 1795 American plenipotentiary Thomas Pinckney had signed the Treaty of San Lorenzo, which secured the grant (not the right) of navigation of the Mississippi River and the right of deposit at New Orleans. Ratification came two months after Breckinridge's outburst. The West, at last, had secured an important goal. The problem, like the river, lay deceptively calm and placid, always poised to rise to flood stage and disaster.

The whole affair strengthened Breckinridge's distrust of the Federalists and of a central power whose majority largely ignored Kentucky's interests. He grew more convinced that if the federal government failed to meet a state's need, some method of recourse—perhaps even an independent one—would be required. That method he had not yet defined.

His political activities were bringing Breckinridge more formal rewards. In December 1793 he was appointed Kentucky's attorney general—after less than a year's residence. Joining half-brother Robert Breckinridge, then Speaker of the House, in the new government, John found his post did not demand a great deal of time or even a Frankfort office; conversely, it offered few financial rewards. But for four years he remained, representing the commonwealth as lawyer and adviser until his resignation in 1797. A month later, Fayette Countians chose Breckinridge to fill a vacancy in the state House of Representatives, and the regular elections in May 1798 returned him. The results indicated, however, that the patrician could not expect automatic victory in the new state: two of the defeated candidates of the previous year surpassed his vote, and the incumbent finished seventh in the field—the last of the delegates chosen from Fayette. A shift of eight votes would have defeated him and perhaps ended a career.[19]

The barely elected representative moved quickly into activity. His first concern centered on national affairs, where political factionalism had developed into party feelings. Growing Federalist intoleration of opposition resulted in passage of the Alien Enemies Act, the Sedition Act, the Alien Friends Act, and the Naturalization Act—all congeries of threats to the Jeffersonian Republicans. After a few convictions under the Sedition Act, the volume of protests against the administration of John Adams increased. The fears of a tyranny, the perceived dangers of an uncontrolled, distant majority reappeared as they had before the Revolution. In Kentucky, Breckinridge and his ally George Nicholas led the movement for repeal of the Alien and Sedition laws. With the heavy-set, balding "Old Nicholas" providing the oratory, Breckinridge began drafting resolutions expressing opposition to such "despotism." The Woodford County resolves, probably written to him, called recent governmental actions "direct violations" of the Constitution and "outrages against our most valuable rights." The resolutions also stressed the now threatened freedoms of speech and of the press as "inseparable rights of freemen."[20]

While the attacks continued to come from Kentucky, Breckinridge, bothered by poor health, left for Virginia to "take the waters" at the springs. When he returned home, he brought with him an important draft document prepared by Jefferson, expressing opposition to the Alien and Sedition Acts. From these thoughts evolved the famous Kentucky Resolutions of 1798. Precisely how Breckinridge received the original draft is uncertain. Some two decades later Jefferson recalled that he met the Kentuckian at Monticello and gave him the draft there. In a letter to Jefferson in October 1798, however, Wilson Cary Nicholas, future Virginia senator and governor, wrote that he had handed Breckinridge a copy of the manuscript "that you sent me." The question of whether a conference occurred between Breckinridge and Jefferson is of less importance than the fact that the vice-president had approved the choice of his friend to introduce the resolutions, probably with the understanding that Breckinridge could alter them if he wished. The whole affair was so cloaked in secrecy that the Kentuckian's family and many friends long believed that he had written the resolutions.[21]

In fact, Breckinridge made crucial changes as he and Jefferson faced the question of minority rights in a democracy. What if the ruling powers were blatantly wrong? Or unfair? What then was the solution? In answering such questions, Breckinridge copied Jefferson's draft, omitted one section, and made significant alterations in another. Then on 8 November 1798 he introduced the nine resolves in the Kentucky House. They passed with only three opposing votes, went through the Senate without amendment, and were signed by the governor. As enacted, the first seven resolutions read almost exactly as Jefferson had written them, with a few minor exceptions. They affirmed the right of each party in the envisioned compact to be an "equal judge" of the constitutionality of congressional enactments, and they also declared that seizure of undelegated powers— something his opponents thought President Adams had done—provided sufficient cause to declare the federal laws "unauthoritative, void, and of no force."

More crucial, however, were the omissions. Breckinridge had not included a part of Jefferson's proposal that read: "But, where powers are assumed which have not been delegated, a nullification of the act is the rightful remedy; That every state has a natural right in cases not within the compact . . . to nullify *of their own authority*—all assumptions of power by others within their limits." No references to the word "nullify" appear in the final version. Breckinridge inserted instead a fifty-word section that more cautiously called for the resolutions to be sent to congressmen, who would then seek repeal of such "unconstitutional and obnoxious acts." The Kentuckian saw the resolves as a means of expressing disapproval, a way to cause Congress, not individual states, to "nullify" laws by repealing them. Breckinridge also modified the last resolution, which presented the views of one who feared unbridled power. Those who would govern not by laws but by "a rod of iron" sought to sweep away "the barrier of the Constitution," wrote Jefferson in his draft. Only more limited government could resist this tide. Breckinridge omitted a section which said that a state should "take measures of its own" to nullify unconstitutional acts. His draft as passed by the legislature simply invited all states to unite with Kentucky in requesting their repeal.[22]

In this second crucial test of his conscience and his conservatism, Breckinridge had begun to modify his views. He now advocated more realistic, if less forceful, protest methods. John had significantly modified the intent of the resolutions, but it is an exaggeration to claim, as some have done, that he was "the responsible author," or that he "had more to do with them than any other man." Rather, as James Morton Smith has pointed out, Breckinridge made "fundamental alterations." As revised, the Kentucky Resolutions did not completely satisfy Jefferson. Had they declared the Alien and Sedition laws "null, void, and of no force," he wrote Wilson Cary Nicholas, "I should like it better." That they did not do so was John Breckinridge's work.[23]

Writing to United States Senator Henry Tazewell of Virginia a few weeks after passage of the Resolutions, Breckinridge said he hoped they would silence any talk about the state's "disposition toward disorganization or disunion." He made it plain that disunion was not sought: "We have but one object, & that is, to preserve the constitution inviolate, & that by constitutional efforts. —No people in [America] are more sensible of the importance & necessity of union . . . than the people of Kentucky."[24] Strange words, considering the commonwealth's actions. But perhaps the state's very history made Breckinridge more sensitive than Jefferson to the possibility that the state would be accused of disunion sentiment, in the light of the Spanish and French conspiracies and the earlier strong words of his Democratic Society.

On 14 November 1799 Breckinridge introduced the single Kentucky Resolution of that year. Now Speaker of the House, he guided the Resolution through without a dissenting vote, and, after a Senate fight, it was accepted nine days later. Much briefer than those of the previous year, the 1799 resolution (its author is unknown) began by stating that Kentucky could not be silent and thus be interpreted as acquiescing in the principles and doctrines of the Sedition Act. Kentucky was "unequivocally" devoted to Union, and, if limits set by the compact of states were transgressed, a consolidated government—built upon the annihilation of state governments—would result. The remedy (as states had the "unquestionable right" to judge infractions) was nullification. Kentucky declared the sedition laws unconstitutional but took no stronger action.[25]

In tone more radical, the 1799 document did not depart from the spirit of the earlier resolutions. It retained the statement that Kentucky's opposition followed "a constitutional manner."[26] (The question remained of how a state could declare a law unconstitutional and remain within the boundaries of the Constitution it professed to follow.) The Resolution of 1799 attracted less attention than its predecessors, added little substance, and became only a corollary to the philosophy presented in 1798. That theory would form a stepping-stone to John C. Calhoun's thoughts on nullification and give a southern minority in 1861 a theoretical basis for its actions. Kentucky's own views were slowly evolving from the sectionalism of earlier days to a viewpoint more favorable to the idea of an indissoluble Union. In that environment, John Breckinridge had changed also. The nationalist of 1784 had been susceptible to disunionist thoughts in 1793, but now, a half-decade later, he had moved to a more moderate, though still Jeffersonian, outlook. The Kentucky Resolutions reflected that change.

Breckinridge's reputed authorship of the Resolutions propelled him to the leadership of Kentucky Republicanism, but his next actions would show the contradictions inherent in that party: his role in the formulation of Kentucky's second constitution was that of an aristocrat more than a democrat.

Three

Politician and Parent

A PERSISTENT and perplexing problem shadowed John Breckinridge's political and social world, calling out for a solution. Negro slavery had built much of that world and furnished much of the labor for its continuance, but like others of his generation and class Breckinridge recognized some of the problems inherent in the institution. In a time when white Americans threw off the shackles of what they called "political slavery," they maintained and even tightened the bonds that held black Americans in human slavery. Coming out of a frontier culture where slaves at times had fought and died beside their masters, Kentucky developed harsher relationships as "civilization" advanced westward. Educated and knowledgeable men, including Washington and Jefferson, had been unable to solve the paradox; nor could John Breckinridge.[1]

When John came to Kentucky in 1793, the decision for slavery had been made only a year earlier, and its continuance remained in doubt for much of his lifetime. Slaves had long been on Kentucky soil; early explorers had brought slaves with them, and founders like Boone and Logan had at various times been slaveowners. Within two years of its permanent settlement, the population of Harrodsburg, the first town in Kentucky, was one-tenth black. By 1790 whites outnumbered blacks in the state by only five to one; a decade later the declining ratio was four to one.[2]

While such rapid growth in black population usually heralded stronger restrictions on slaves as racial fears intensified, there were elements in the commonwealth that did not accept slavery without protest. In 1791 John Bradford's influential *Kentucky Gazette* had published a proposed constitution that included provisions for slave emancipation. Significantly, the Kentucky constitution of 1792, while legalizing slavery, mandated no restrictions of free suffrage by race or color. The inclusion of slavery in that document had, in fact, engendered serious debate. Led by Presbyterian minister David Rice and five other preachers, the opposition to slavery gained sixteen votes to twenty-six for its proponents. By that margin of ten, Kentucky went slave.[3]

Coming to Kentucky shortly after that decision had been made,

Breckinridge supported it wholeheartedly. He had confessed to his mother in 1792 that he was "somewhat afraid of the Kentucky politicians with respect to Negroes," but despite such fears would send at least twenty of his slaves to Fayette County to prepare land for the family's arrival. A few months later John underscored his estimation of the value of slaves, advising her to leave all her other property behind in Virginia, but "your negroes I would endeavor to keep."[4]

Having hired out most of his own slaves to Kentuckians, Breckinridge brought the remainder with him when he moved permanently to the state in 1793. He owned twenty-five slaves that year—up from fifteen in 1786—and, convinced of their profitability in labor-poor Kentucky, he increased the number to thirty-eight in 1795, sixty-five in 1799, and almost seventy in 1806. The last figure made him one of the largest slaveowners in a young state whose slaveholders averaged fewer than seven slaves per family. Throughout these years his attitude on the economic value of slaves apparently never wavered, for four years after settlement in Kentucky he advised his brother William "to purchase all the negroes you possibly can bring here. They are of very great value here either to hire, or farm with, they also sell high. It would be an important thing to you if you could turn your goods into slaves."[5]

Breckinridge's own increasing number of bondsmen had dictated the hiring of an overseer, a rarity in Kentucky. Over a thirteen-year period, he employed five men to supervise his slaves. Few overseers satisfied for very long. The first, an illiterate, agreed to supervise eleven blacks in return for 10 percent of the earnings, plus pork, salt, and "Bread Corn." In August 1795 John advertised for his replacement, an overseer "capable of managing ten or twelve hands. . . . None except such as have been accustomed to the management of Negroes need apply." As managers came and went, the terms binding them varied. George McDonald's 1801 agreement gave him, among other provisions, the right to breed three of his mares to Breckinridge's stud horse. Five years later, overseer John Payne agreed to supervise fourteen blacks (the rest were hired out to hemp factories or worked as domestics). In return he would receive seven hundred pounds of salt pork, sufficient milk and meat for his family, and "a small Negroe for a nurse to his children."[6]

Breckinridge's treatment of his slaves remains generally unknown, but a few clues exist. As early as 1786 he wanted a runaway returned to him, even if the slave had to be handcuffed. In instructions to an overseer twenty years later he warned him to "keep good authority among my negroes, & keep them close at home. . . . Visit their houses frequently at unseasonable Hours of the night." While skilled bondsmen, such as his carpenters, were given more freedom, Breckinridge told the overseer to make them work or punish them accordingly. Yet nothing suggests that as a master he ever prescribed extreme punishment, as did some contemporaries. He probably never sold a slave, although he did purchase them. Overall, Breckinridge personified neither of the extremes in his actions toward his slaves. He simply reflected the attitude of many men of his region, his era, and his environment—men of paternal, patrician outlook who viewed Negroes as an inferior race rightfully enslaved. Slavery, to them, might even be wrong in the abstract, but present realities could not be quickly solved. Slavery thus remained, with contradictions of which John Breckinridge was well aware: brother James had written that all were healthy in "my family, both white & black," while another correspondent stressed not human but property aspects when he informed John that "your Blacks and Stock are well."[7]

It was Breckinridge the proslavery property-owner who came under attack in the late 1790s. This man, whom a recent writer has extravagantly characterized as "one of the most effective promoters of the expansion of slavery the nation was ever to see," now saw fellow citizens demanding constitutional revision, and some included emancipation in their cries. Under the existing constitution an electoral college, not voters, selected both governor and state senators. Judges on the state's highest court likewise remained free from the influence of the citizenry's vote. As a more democratic spirit spread across the state, elitism did not serve. Voters wanted a stronger voice in the commonwealth's affairs.[8]

John Breckinridge, the Republican, opposed this upsurge. On the last day of January 1798 he spoke against a bill designed to speed up the constitutional process; such a change would arouse "the halcyon dogs of anarchy." Let man repose, as at present, in "tranquil security under his vine and his fig tree." Do not, he counseled, "raise up in the imagination dangers which do not exist." Clearly, John Breckinridge distrusted what the people—or at least some of them—might do. Earlier he had branded the poorer inhabitants of the newly settled Green River country as nothing but "hunters, horsethieves & savages." Only "wretchedness, poverty & sickness" characterized their region, and, even worse, these people favored the "dangerous" changes.[9]

Writing to former Governor Isaac Shelby in March 1798, Breckinridge outlined the favorite targets of these partisans of change. They wanted abolition of the Senate, House selection of officials, and "a speedy emancipation" of slaves. Those who had "little to risque," the "discontented & disorderly," also wanted a convention, which Breckinridge definitely did not desire. The present government adequately protected property, persons, and lives, according to Breckinridge, who underscored his fear of change: "It is the dangerous examples such things afford, which I most dread. If the envious, the discontented, or the needy, can, at any time, they may take a fancy to any of the property of their fellow-citizens . . . & wish to reduce them in point of property to a level with themselves, produce a ferment & assemble a convention, & under it perpetuate acts of

Injustice. . . . If they can by one experiment emancipate the slaves, the same principle pursued will enable them at a second experiment to extinguish our land titles; for both are held by rights equally sacred." This Jeffersonian Republican did not believe the people incapable of evil and did not intend to defer to their will.[10]

In the hope of directing the public will to accord with his own beliefs, Breckinridge participated actively in the campaign for convention delegates. A satire on emancipation, written by him, appeared in the papers and in pamphlet form. Under the pseudonym "Algernon Sidney" he acknowledged the possible desirability of emancipation but warned Kentuckians not to liberate "at the probable expense of our own freedom" and called for action at a less passionate time. An organized group headed by Breckinridge and George Nicholas (called the "Bryan Station ticket" from their mass meeting at that location in 1798) vigorously defended slavery and criticized their rivals as landless, *"beardless boys."*[11]

The strong organization of the landed, proslavery group, together with his own efforts in recent political affairs, brought Breckinridge victories in elections for both the convention and the legislature. In June he wrote privately of what he hoped the constitutional convention would accomplish. In line with his conservative ideas, he sought direct popular vote for House members, but the senators and the governor would be chosen by electors. The chief executive would serve a three-year term with no immediate reelection. To fill a need not covered in the earlier constitution, he also proposed that an office of lieutenant governor be provided. Satisfied with the Virginia system, where the gentry dominated local affairs, Breckinridge suggested that justices of the peace be recommended by county courts and commissioned by the governor. Sheriffs and coroners, he thought, should be selected from court personnel and commissioned by the head of the commonwealth. To insure what he considered more responsible voting, he proposed a return to the old *viva voce* method, still used in Virginia, in place of secret balloting. In addition to all these safeguards against the "discontented," Breckinridge also wanted the Assembly given more control over slave immigration.[12]

When the constitutional convention assembled in late July 1799, many expected Breckinridge to dominate it. Most of the delegates were receptive to his ideas: all but one owned slaves and nearly half held over ten of them; these were men of property, planters still acquiring land and wealth. Yet the ideas of Breckinridge and the Bryan Station ticket did not prevail without challenge. For nearly a month, the debates continued, and the resulting document represented a spirit of compromise and accommodation rather than any specific theory of government.[13]

The articles that were approved reflected both Breckinridge's suggestions and the independence of the delegates. The matter of restricting voter eligibility to whites brought little discussion and was adopted, but

Breckinridge's proposal that the legislature be given the power to prohibit slave importation met a 14–37 defeat. His position was motivated not by emancipation sentiment but rather by his desire to prevent blacks from immigrating to Kentucky from states where slave revolts raged. Breckinridge also failed in regard to indirect election of the governor and state senators; both offices would be filled by the vote of the people, not by electors. After protracted discussion, his *viva voce* proposal won adoption, however, as did the creation of the office of lieutenant governor. The county courts returned to a more oligarchical, self-perpetuating system of government. Generally, however, his victories did not outnumber defeats. He failed to secure the Senate, the executive, or the representation he desired; in fact, he had barely avoided the destruction of the Senate and of the executive's veto power. Despite all this he voted in the 53–3 majority when delegates approved the document. Not submitted to the voters for ratification, the constitution of 1799 became effective on 1 June 1800 and remained in effect for half a century.[14]

Breckinridge received credit as the principal leader of the convention, but his power has been overemphasized. The conservative, wealthy landowner and slaveholder, seeking retrenchment and not reform, had helped frame a new constitution which mollified popular discontent while leaving power basically with the group that had opposed the convention at the beginning. Only in this general sense had Breckinridge succeeded.

If Breckinridge's attitudes on slavery and his role in the constitutional convention placed him firmly in the intellectual company of the conservative elite, that did not mean that he ignored reform issues. His objections to such Federalist initiatives as the Sedition Act, for example, came not only from fear of a strong central majority, but also from devotion to the idea of free speech. Unlike many other aristocrats, he actively supported public education. His clearest advocacy of reform was his effort to revise the state's outdated penal code.

As early as 1793 Breckinridge had incorporated attacks on the old law into the Democratic Society's position. Under the then-existing statute some twenty-seven offenses, including forgery and horse-stealing, were punishable by death. Public hangings—such as one of a counterfeiter in Lexington in 1794 that drew seven thousand witnesses—did not improve society's morals, he felt. Breckinridge pledged to change the system and in a January 1798 speech asserted that the death penalties, as they stood, were "a scandal to reason and to humanity." Confinement to prison would reform the offender because he could be taught a trade and reenter society as a useful citizen. Death solved nothing. Heeding his call, the General Assembly in 1798 adopted a new criminal code that abolished the death penalty except for first-degree murder, slaves being excepted. Despite provisions for prisoners that dictated shaven heads, clothes made of "coarse materials," and "inferior food," the new law served as a model for other states.[15]

This penal reform again showed Breckinridge's dominance in the General Assembly. A fellow legislator recalled that "none thwarted his plans, none attacked his position, or dared to enter with him the arena of debate." By 1800, then, the name John Breckinridge carried with it many positive connotations for Kentuckians. Since his arrival seven years before, Breckinridge had kept his name before the public, and Kentucky assemblymen now selected him to be their United States senator.[16]

Almost eight years earlier Breckinridge had spurned national office in his move from Virginia to Kentucky; not so this time. For a man who had objected to sections of the federal Constitution years before, especially to the "inequality of Representation in the Senate," now Breckinridge seemed happy to be a part of that "inequality." The day after his election John could not resist telling his Virginian brother James (only recently defeated as the Federalist gubernatorial candidate against James Monroe) that he was pleased to see that normally Federalist Botetourt County, his old home, had recovered its senses and gone Republican. Leaving several unsettled lawsuits in the hands of rising attorney Henry Clay, John Breckinridge left for Washington to share in the victory of the Jeffersonians.[17]

An opportunity to express himself came for Senator Breckinridge on 8 January 1802. The man who spoke that day was still young, just a year over forty. His tall, spare, muscular frame stretched over six feet. Long chestnut-brown hair and hazel-green eyes enhanced his attractiveness, while a courteous and gentle manner contrasted with a grave, almost austere temperament. Excellent in debate, he could devastate with sarcasm, overwhelm with reason, and then conciliate with moderation. His eloquence was revealed as he addressed the question of repeal of the Judiciary Act of 1801, in the first major battle of Jefferson's administration. The law in question—a last-minute measure of the Adams administration to appoint deserving Federalist judges—did provide some needed reforms, but Republicans viewed it as mainly partisan. In a polished and statistical speech, Breckinridge, who introduced the repeal resolution, attacked the legislation as unnecessary, a move to set up sinecures and waste public money. As the debate developed, Breckinridge began to amplify his remarks, and the philosophy he presented essentially served most of the family for the next century. On 14 January he answered New York Senator Gouverneur Morris's assertion that Congress could legislate in wide fields, to protect the weak. Meeting argument with argument, Breckinridge denied that Congress possessed authority to wield this "extensive legislation" power. He stood—as in the past—for a limited concept of the Constitution. Unless checked, he declared, such motions as those supported by Morris would end in a "consolidated sovereignty" erected on the ruins of state government.[18]

Encouraged by the praise of Monroe—"Believe me, you have nothing to fear from any opponent"—Breckinridge continued to urge repeal. As the final vote approached, Federalists argued that the courts would declare the Republican repeal unconstitutional. In response, Breckinridge insisted that the judiciary did not have the constitutional power to annul laws. After further debate the bill to repeal the Judiciary Act passed by a 16–15 vote and on 8 March 1802 was signed by Jefferson. Breckinridge's philosophy of strict construction had combined with partisan politics to provide a successful conclusion.[19]

When the Seventh Congress reassembled in December, the troublesome question of Mississippi River navigation arose again. In late 1802 the Spanish announced the closure of the right of deposit at the port of New Orleans, and Kentuckians reacted as expected. Some who had supported the earlier French Conspiracy now prepared for an armed expedition to open the river, while the state legislature requested its two senators to present resolutions condemning the Spanish move. Later word of French control of the region did not diminish the bellicosity that prevailed. Breckinridge's past criticisms of governmental actions on the question had been under a Federalist regime, one he thought unfriendly to the West. Now, with an administration controlled by fellow Republicans, he moved more cautiously.[20]

Calls for reason and temperate words, came from the senator. Writing to a Kentucky friend, he expressed confidence that the government would take measures to insure free navigation. His moderation helped hold the West firm for the Republicans, and on his return to Kentucky in July 1803 Breckinridge found fellow citizens "in the most profound tranquility." That calmness turned to exuberance when word of the Louisiana Purchase reached the West. Breckinridge quickly wrote Jefferson expressing his complete surprise and great happiness over "one of the most important events we have ever witnessed." The annals of no country, he proclaimed, could furnish a parallel expansion of such magnitude, accomplished without bloodshed. The pleased master of Cabell's Dale exulted that the Mississippi River was finally American.[21]

In his letter to Jefferson, Breckinridge said nothing about any possible constitutional conflicts in the transaction. The president in his own communication had already counseled the senator that Congress must ignore "meta physical subtleties" in ratifying the purchase. But he recognized the problems in such a course for Republicans devoted to a strict constructionist interpretation of the Constitution. "I pretend no right to bind you," said Jefferson, who told the Kentuckian he could disavow his leader, if he so wished. Returning to Washington, the senator faced the issue of treaty ratification, and then authorization of a temporary government, allocation of funds for the purchase, and creation of a territorial government. Since no serious constitutional questions arose on the vote to ratify, Breckinridge did not need to offer his thoughts on the issue.[22]

A more difficult debate arose when the question of funds came up. After hearing several opposition arguments, Breckinridge on 3 November 1803 answered his party's critics. Would the gentleman who thought this too expensive prefer to risk an even costlier war? The argument of the senator from Delaware—that vast acres would destroy the Union as men knew it—was, said Breckinridge, but "an old and hackneyed doctrine." "The Goddess of Liberty," he asserted, knew no geographic bounds. Then, finally and almost reluctantly, he turned to the objection that the purchase was unconstitutional without an amendment to the Constitution. Had the purchase taken place before 1801, under Federalist rule, the matter might have been more difficult for Breckinridge, torn between the economic and sectional needs of the West and his own constitutional fears of Federalist consolidation of powers. But in this 1803 fight with his conscience—another major test of his theories—his fears were diminished and economics won. To the Senate he declared that the Constitution's treaty-making powers covered this case. The essential argument lay in Louisiana's importance to America, and national honor required the purchase. Rejection would drive the West—his West—beyond the point of endurance. At that stage, "I shall begin to tremble for my country." Passage of the bill by a 26–5 vote dispelled any such fears.[23]

Breckinridge would continue to hold true to his abstract ideals of government, but he would not ignore the forces of change in his maturing world. A compromise of ideals would result. As new generations came to power in the next few decades of the nineteenth century, however, the ability to reconcile the forces of pragmatism and philosophy faded as part of a politician's character. Unlike John Breckinridge, some of his descendants would hold fast to the limited-government philosophy he had expressed in 1798 and overlook his later actions. They would become more inflexible, and by midcentury that stance would lead them down the path of tragedy toward civil war.

Jefferson had entrusted Breckinridge with the task of providing for the government of the Territory of Orleans. Stating that he perceived in the senator "a dread of the job," however, the president sent his own draft bill to his former Virginia neighbor. That outline formed the basis for the Breckinridge Bill. Under the final proposal no slaves could be imported from abroad, and only those taken to Louisiana by masters who settled there could remain. Debate on the slavery aspect of the territorial constitution crossed party lines and even became sectional at times. It foreshadowed what would follow in the next half-century.[24]

Breckinridge, delivered three speeches during January 1804 in an effort to influence recalcitrant northern Republican senators. He interpreted his bill as one actually aiding slavery's eventual extinction and expressed a hope that the time was "not far distant" when the peculiar institution would be eliminated. Pointing to the danger of a slave revolt, he argued that by sending slaves to Louisiana Congress could free the southern states of some of their black population, and thus weaken and disperse the incipient peril. Nor, he said, should his opposition ever forget that the Constitution recognized and protected slavery. Liberty and slavery, the Kentuckian avowed, could exist together.[25]

Once again the slaveholder had dominated the antislavery man within Breckinridge. It was as an owner of property, as a southerner shocked by actual slave revolt in the Caribbean and a thwarted one in his native Virginia, that he spoke. And the senators accepted the message. When the question arose of ending slavery on a gradual basis in Louisiana, a 17–11 majority defeated the proposal. Slavery would advance into the territories, and in doing so would eventually create a situation that could not be mended by compromise.

Breckinridge's role in working for president and party had now made him a major political figure, and men began to envision him in higher office. As early as July 1803 he was mentioned as a vice-presidential candidate to replace Aaron Burr. John Randolph thought the Kentuckian wanted the office badly. "You would never recognize our friend," he told Monroe. As the only western man "of any pretension," Breckinridge—according to Randolph—displayed "great anxiety" over the outcome. If so, the Kentuckian's letters are silent on the question. As John Taylor told W. C. Nicholas, a ticket pairing a Virginian and a Kentuckian who had been born in Virginia was simply not good politics—and Breckinridge probably realized this. In the nominating caucus New York's George Clinton gained sixty-seven votes and the nomination. Breckinridge gained the support of twenty, while an almost equal number scattered their ballots among four other hopefuls.[26]

Across the mountains, Kentuckians did not accept Breckinridge's loss quietly. At a May gathering, toasts were drunk to "John Breckinridge . . . our next vice president." The *Kentucky Gazette*, as was its custom, printed stories both favoring the senator and criticizing him. Finally, in a public communication to the rival *Palladium*, Breckinridge explained that no one should cast ballots for him. To reassure party chieftains of his loyalty, he told Monroe that "malevolent rascals," chiefly those opposed to his slavery stance in the 1799 convention, were behind the whole affair.[27]

While the whole tempest passed rather rapidly, the talk of a westerner in the executive branch may have influenced Jefferson in his decision to offer Breckinridge the vacant post of attorney general. Or it may have been simple recognition of his friend's ability. Whatever the motive, on 7

August 1805 Jefferson made the request, "as your geographic position will enable you to bring into our councils a knowledge of the western interests & circumstances for which we are often at a loss & sometimes fail in our desires to promote them."[28] Breckinridge accepted.

In retrospect, it can be argued that Breckinridge erred in his move from the legislature. His senate leadership would be missed, and as attorney general he occupied a relatively minor office with no department to administer. He was "an officer without an office, a legal advisor without a clerk, a prosecutor with no control over the district attorney." The frustrations became evident when, in early 1806, he argued six cases before the Supreme Court, winning only one. If he had hoped to influence Jefferson, Breckinridge faced a difficult task. The man from Monticello often kept his own counsel, and rumors spread that Jefferson's confidence in his appointee was waning. Only in his function as liaison between the executive and legislative branches did Breckinridge find satisfaction, as various senators, as well as the president, sought his aid in drafting bills.[29]

In the spring of 1806, Breckinridge left for Kentucky, with an undistinguished career as attorney general behind him. More important cases could be expected in the future, and the young lawyer might yet fill a valuable niche for his president, his party, and his country. Now, at Cabell's Dale, a large and affectionate family waited.

The four children (Letitia, Joseph Cabell, Mary, and Robert) who had accompanied their parents from Virginia in 1793 had been a major motivation for that move. "Let them be preserved," John had written, "and I am contented. My happiness shall not depend on the amount of property. But it certainly will upon the prosperity and happiness of my family."[30] Those hopes were quickly crushed. A smallpox epidemic raged through central Kentucky in the winter of 1793-94, and, although family members received inoculations, they came too late. Breckinridge's wife and three of the four children were stricken. Polly, son Cabell, and daughter Letitia survived; the two youngest children did not. John Breckinridge was not emotionally demonstrative and did not often express his deepest feelings on paper, but his children were the one part of his life that caused him great joy and had spurred him to take risks. To brother James, John expressed his despair in March 1794: "The only objects of my toils, my wishes, & my affections, have been brought to the brink of the grave & two of them actually torn from me." The death of the son named for John's own father bore down particularly hard, for, to John's eye, Robert was "the finest child we ever had."[31]

Never particularly devout, Breckinridge—unlike his wife—did not turn to religion for solace. He seldom mentioned the dead loved ones again, perhaps because such memories came too painfully. New additions to the family helped assuage somewhat the losses of Robert and Mary. In 1795 Cabell's Dale welcomed Mary Ann to the family; in 1797 came John, in 1800 Robert Jefferson, then William Lewis, and finally in 1806 James Monroe—the seventh living child of nine born over a twenty-year period. A weary father remarked of the son James, named for his Virginia friend: "I hope he is the last." In 1804 eighteen-year-old Letitia married Alfred W. Grayson, son of a United States senator. (Her dowry included eight slaves, sixty-four farm animals, and various household goods.) Joseph Cabell, the oldest son, next left friendly Kentucky environs for further schooling at the College of New Jersey, at Princeton.[32]

But the most distressing separations, and ones that most strained the familial ties, were caused by John Breckinridge himself. His Washington duties meant many winter and spring months far from Polly and the children. As a result, the task of childrearing fell heavily on a woman also expected to inform John of the farm activities, the overseer's success or failure, and the activities of the slaves. The father's influence on his children, while still important, declined. Subordinate to her husband in many things, Polly Breckinridge displayed a strong will that grew stronger as distance added to her responsibilities. She cared deeply for John, worried about his health, and feared for his safety. Her dissatisfaction came more from love than from anger. She had, from the beginning, opposed the move to Kentucky. John's first exploratory trip to the area had moved his very young wife nearly to hysteria, especially since Letitia had almost died (she had gone "out of her senses" said the mother) in his absence. But when the time came for the move, Polly went with her husband. One traveler who had met the couple on their journey to Kentucky recalled later that John had asked him to "tell my wife your funny stories, it would keep up her spirits, for she has not even smiled since we set out on our journey." "Mrs. Breckinridge," the observer recollected, "was a Cabell of rather a serious and desponding disposition though a very intelligent and fine woman."[33]

John's frequent absences from home intensified the loneliness of his wife, near the attractions of Lexington but confined on the farm. Worrying often about her "Johnny's" health, Polly expressed her usual frame of mind during such times when she signed herself "Your ever Affect. tho Miserable Wife." Although present in the District of Columbia in the winter of 1802-03, Polly and the children remained at Cabell's Dale or in Virginia for the other sessions, partly because of her pregnancies and the inadequate and expensive housing in Washington. Letters passed almost weekly between husband and wife, usually concerning the children and Congress but also hinting at intimate disagreements. On 30 December 1803 a usually calm John exclaimed, "It gives me much disgust that you make yourself so unhappy on account of my absence." Characteristically, after such an outbreak, the two would resume a normal correspondence that made it evident they both regretted their words and actions.[34]

John's anger derived in part from his own feelings of guilt, for he loved his family and the separations pained him. His departure in 1804 was especially difficult. At the gate of Cabell's Dale, seven-year-old John had stopped his father, and that farewell, Breckinridge wrote Polly, "shook what little fortitude I had left after parting with you. I did not suppose I could be so [moved] by the tears & affecting sensitivity of a child. Take care of my dear Boys." The fact that Breckinridge found it difficult to communicate these emotions to his wife caused much of the fleeting anger that passed between them. His frustrations burst out in a February 1806 letter to Polly: "I think I have the most reason to complain of any detached situation from you & my family. You have the children around you, the greatest of all comforts, you are under your own roof; & are not perplexed with the concerns & affairs of others. . . . I have not the cheering sound of a single member of the family to comfort & relax my mind. But I trust it is the last winter, that either of us will make a similar complaint." He told her that in the fall of that year he would take the family with him to Washington. Then there would be no tearful farewell from the children.[35]

Two weeks later John, not Polly, worried about a spouse's health, for spasms, pregnancy complications, and "your complaint" caused John to advise her to fear only the present, not some unknown future. "It is as much as we can do," he wrote, "to bear up under affliction when it actually [assails] us. We ought never to anticipate it, because by doing so, we increase our unhappiness, by adding imaginary distresses, to those real ones, which all are doomed in one period or other of their lives, to experience." With a promising future, she should "view the bright side of things."[36]

But her pessimism reflected the future more accurately. Illness struck John during the summer, and a visit to Kentucky's Olympian Springs did not give relief. Still plagued by a persistent cold, John wrote his son Cabell in late August that he had nearly regained "my former Health," adding that he hoped they could meet in Washington by November.[37] They never saw each other again.

Somewhat recovered by late October, John determined to make the trip to the capital, but on the day of his leaving Cabell's Dale, as his horse was being made ready, he grew seriously ill. For two months he struggled to fight off what was probably tuberculosis. His then ten-year-old daughter Mary Ann years later still could not forget the horrible memories of her father's "tall thin form, weak, sunk breast, and pale visage" during those days. Death came early on Sunday morning, 14 December 1806.[38]

Only forty-six years old, John Breckinridge never realized many of his dreams. His driving desire to insure his children from want was frus-

trated when he died intestate. Court struggles over land and other property dragged on for seemingly endless years. But if he did not live to see
his children grown, and to observe with pride their achievements, John
did leave his descendants the memory of a man who, in a short career,
accomplished much in state and national affairs. Similarly, he bequeathed
to them a philosophy that would serve the family for a century, and a
model of how a national figure should conduct himself. His example
powerfully motivated later members of the family to emulate what they
perceived as the very best features of a real and ideal leader. Firmly
established in the state before John's death, the Breckinridges of Kentucky
continued to reflect his legacy of activism. Thus, through the persistent
involvement of his descendants, the dreams of John Breckinridge lived
on.

TWO

ROBERT J. BRECKINRIDGE

1800-1871

As the nation was rent apart, so was the
Commonwealth; as the state, so was the county; as the
county, the neighborhood; as the neighborhood, the
family; and as the family, so brother and brother, father
and son.

John Fox, Jr.

Four

The Jaws of Death

THE DEATH of John Breckinridge left his still-youthful wife devastated. According to family tradition Polly's almost incessant crying so injured her eyes that she lost her sight "and for nearly fifty years sat in darkness awaiting her call." In later years loss of hair caused her to don the apparel that gave her the family's loving and respectful name—"Grandma Black Cap." All the elements of a life of pathos seemed present in the Widow Breckinridge: the young bride dependent on a husband now gone forever; the proud daughter of an aristocratic family, now alone and broken; the child of Virginia, who opposed the move to Kentucky, now isolated in a house in that commonwealth. Yet Mary Hopkins Cabell Breckinridge was not typical of her time. Unlike many of her contemporaries who quickly remarried to escape the problems of widowhood, Polly did not. The reverence she had for John's memory was transmitted to her children, who learned from Polly the glories of their dead father's life. By all accounts she was a remarkable person who grew intellectually, spiritually, and emotionally after the tragedy. Forced either to live a life of dependence or to rule her own destiny, she chose the latter. In so doing she did not always ingratiate herself; at times sharp-tongued, stubborn, and vindictive, on other occasions she displayed to her children and relatives the kind of warmth and love she had once shared with her husband. She became a nexus, a connection that stretched from just after the French and Indian War to just before the Civil War. At her death in 1858 "Grandma Black Cap," nearly ninety years old, had been a widow for over half a century.[1]

A factor compelling Polly's metamorphosis from quiet, dutiful wife to strong-willed businesswoman was concern for her children's future, and a sustaining force was her religion. Unlike John, who had never been religious, she had become increasingly devout, and after the great revivals that swept Kentucky just before her husband's death and then continued beyond, her faith in a higher being found support all around. These two forces joined with Polly's own strong personality to produce men and women of outstanding ability.

The mother's aspirations first focused on the two oldest sons. Joseph Cabell quickly rose to positions that matched his father's early achievements—as a respected attorney, Speaker of the Kentucky House of Representatives, and secretary of state for the commonwealth. But promise again was cut short. On 1 September 1823 Cabell Breckinridge, father-image to his younger siblings, was taken from them in death. He had lived but thirty-five years.

Polly's attentions turned to her second son, John, who also furnished his mother ample reason for pride. Nine years old at his father's death, John graduated from the College of New Jersey at Princeton and then turned to the Lord rather than the law. Three years' study at the Theological Seminary at Princeton brought him a license to preach in 1822, and for the next two years he served as chaplain of the United States House of Representatives. He then settled into two important pastorates, and by 1836, his eloquence and fame impelled his theological alma mater to call him back as professor. He served briefly as general agent for the Presbyterian Board of Foreign Missions, and when Oglethorpe College, Georgia, offered him its presidency in 1841 he accepted. His death intervened, however, on 4 August 1841. The second John Breckinridge died at age forty-four, two years younger than his father had been at his own death.[2]

Three sons, including the last-born James, and two daughters had now died young, but Polly continued to give heart and soul to her family. Another son, William Lewis Breckinridge, did not disappoint his mother's attentions, nor die early. Educated at Lexington's Transylvania University, William turned to his family's church at age fifteen and, like his older brother, achieved fame as a minister. From his First Presbyterian Church pulpit in Louisville he influenced the course of both state and nation, serving as moderator of the Presbyterian General Assembly in 1859. His emphasis on education brought him the presidencies of Centre College, Kentucky, and Oakland College, Mississippi. Throughout his life, he remained devoted to his mother and presented her with twelve grandchildren, four of whom died before reaching maturity. In naming them, he continued the family pattern: two Cabells, a Robert, a Letitia, and a William, Jr., honored his own generation; John and a Mary Hopkins confirmed his devotion to his parents. Urbane and polished, yet open and unafraid to offer opinions, William Breckinridge, when he died in 1876, ended a life that had presented few opportunities for criticism.[3]

Long lives did not come to Polly's daughters. The oldest, Letitia, had left home to marry before her father's death, but within four years she too was a widow, with two children. Letitia remarried after eight years, but that union (to Peter B. Porter, later secretary of war under John Quincy Adams) ended with her death in 1831, when she was forty-five. Sister Mary Ann Breckinridge Castleman had died fifteen years earlier, at age

Mary Hopkins Cabell Breckinridge. Attributed to Matthew H. Jouett

twenty-one, shortly after the birth of her only child. Of the nine children of John and Polly Breckinridge, only two outlived their mother.[4]

The one of Polly's offspring who seemed to challenge his forceful mother most would, in the end, emerge as perhaps the family's strongest intellect and certainly its most controversial figure.

Robert Jefferson Breckinridge "was born on Saturday the 8th of March 1800," according to the simple entry in the family Bible. His proud father called him "superior to any of the rest," but—fatherless at the age of six—

Robert soon displayed a personality that led to conflict. On one occasion he poured salt in a blind cousin's coffee; when his enraged brother John berated him for the action, Robert drew a butcher knife. That fight ended in defeat for the younger sibling (John "beat him, and stamped him & kicked him"), and later, at age fourteen, Robert received a "tremendous whipping" from his mother for beating an old slave.[5]

Such incidents may have been exceptions, or may have not differed greatly from the norm for young gentlemen in a still-violent world. His family apparently saw little reason to alter his course from that followed by his brother. After schooling by tutors at Cabell's Dale came a stint under Dr. Louis Marshall on his "Buck Pond" farm in neighboring Woodford County. The family's physician, an educator who would later serve as president of Washington College in Virginia, a duelist, and a younger brother of Chief Justice John Marshall, Dr. Marshall was also a relative. Robert, bearing the name Jefferson and son of a leader of the Jeffersonian Republicans, thus combined in his early life the influence of the two men Henry Adams later called the most aristocratic of democrats and the most democratic of aristocrats. Like his father, Robert Breckinridge would face a difficult political choice: the influence of one man's spirit and the day-to-day teachings of another would struggle for supremacy within.[6]

But that struggle would not be decided for some time. Further education beckoned, and in 1817, like brothers Cabell and John earlier, Robert entered the College of New Jersey at Princeton. Scholastically an average student, he enjoyed extracurricular life so much that he incurred expenses of over twelve hundred dollars in one year. Nor did he overcome his personality problems. In one instance his "profane and abusive language" to a senior instigated a fight that ended in a brief suspension. Other outbursts of temper, some gambling, and attention to several young women did not enhance his academic standing. After transferring to Yale for a three-month stint, he turned to Union College in Schenectady, New York, where he graduated at age nineteen. He had surmounted intellectual obstacles but not personal ones.[7]

In poor health, and "in no very good feeling toward my family" because of quarrels over expenses, Breckinridge went to the springs in Virginia in 1820 to recover from what he called "a very shattered constitution." That pilgrimage initiated what would become another and more maturing form of education. Traveling to Philadelphia and New York, Robert tarried in the District of Columbia, listening to the Missouri Compromise debates; he visited Virginia and North Carolina, and in April 1821 returned home. After recovering from a bout with "lake fever," he spent most of another year away from Kentucky, traveling more than three thousand miles. During these months he read widely, finishing Adam Smith's *Wealth of Nations,* Homer's *Iliad,* William Gordon's *History of America,* ten volumes of Shakespeare, a four-volume history of France,

Blackstone's *Commentaries*, Dante's poetry, and Byron's *Don Juan*. Despite "the most excruciating bodily pain," he continued to study: "I have been smitten with such an ardent desire to acquire information as nearly to lose my senses."[8]

Breckinridge had also been smitten in ways other than intellectual. After favoring several young women with his love poems, Robert focused his attention on a girl he had met two years earlier when visiting the Virginia spas. Daughter of John Breckinridge's first cousin—former Congressman Francis Preston of Abingdon—Ann Sophonisba Preston met "Bob" again when she visited her sister in Kentucky. His courtship of this dark-haired girl who dressed plainly and wore her hair simply soon began in earnest, and on March 1823 the two were married at the home of the twenty-year-old bride. A generally happy union, like that of his grandfather to another Preston, this marriage would produce eleven children over the next twenty-one years. It also solidified existing Preston-Breckinridge ties, ties that allied the groom's family to many leaders of import.[9]

"Sophy" Preston was herself a grandniece of Patrick Henry, and her siblings included her brother William Campbell Preston, United States senator from South Carolina; Susan, married to cousin James McDowell, a Virginia governor; Sarah, wife of John B. Floyd, another chief executive of the Old Dominion (and another cousin); and Margaret, wed to Wade Hampton, Jr., South Carolina senator and governor. Like Sophy, Robert Breckinridge was a great-grandchild of John Preston and could also call "Cousin" William B. Preston, Zachary Taylor's secretary of the navy; Elizabeth McDowell, wife of Missouri Senator Thomas Hart Benton; Kentucky Congressmen Thomas F. and Alexander K. Marshall; and Francis P. Blair, Sr., confidant of Andrew Jackson and editor of the *Globe*. Obviously, Robert Breckinridge had important relatives to whom he could appeal in any future endeavor.[10]

Robert had initially chosen to pursue the law. He received his license to practice in 1824, but his first case—a murder trial—was interrupted by "violent attacks of spasms." His career as an attorney would prove financially unrewarding, inauspicious, and brief. Burdened by debts and the desire for a landed estate of his own, Robert soon sold some of his father's Jefferson County land and used the money to purchase the Fayette County estate he called "Braedalbane." The political arena, however, soon lured him away from the land, and in 1824 he began his canvass for a seat in the Kentucky legislature. Barely a year had elapsed since Cabell Breckinridge's death had removed the family name from Frankfort politics.[11]

Robert J. Breckinridge's political views were already formed and had been made known to the electorate. Two years earlier, in a speech on "The Formation of a National Character," he had revealed the details of his

Young Robert Jefferson Breckinridge. By an unknown artist; courtesy
Kentucky Historical Society

philosophy. History to him was but a record of man's depravity to man, but in it could be seen "stars that glimmer thro' the horrors of the Egyptian darkness, which may guide us along the dazzling pinnacle of fame." He sought to emulate that fame, his family's fame. "What they achieved," he had declared, "it is ours to maintain." He must transmit unimpaired the heritage that was his.

What did that require in the 1820s? First of all, according to Robert, it demanded an end to sectionalism and an emphasis on the "most intimate" state interdependence; local prejudices must be overcome by a system of internal improvements. Second, slavery—which breathed corruption and tyranny into America—must cease. All who loved liberty and respected the rights of man must agree that emancipation was the only answer. And, third, historical darkness must be overturned by the light of education. Poets, historians, orators, all should now commemorate America's deeds as did citizens in Roman times. "Let us not," he pleaded, "be content to dwell in the middle regions of renown," but instead advance to new elevations, "hitherto unequaled, hitherto unknown."[12]

At age twenty-two, then, Robert emphasized education, as had his father; but his words on nationalism and emancipation struck a discordant tone. Youthful optimism further separated him from the outlook of the patriarch. Why? What caused the man who called for children to "transmit unimpaired" their heritage to turn away from parts of his past? Throughout his life, Robert continually accentuated his devotion to family, but yet the philosophy of the 1790s would not be his philosophy. A partial explanation for Robert's metamorphosis lay in his schooling, under Louis Marshall and then in the North, and in the influence of "Grandma Black Cap," who apparently taught her son the realities of her husband as well as his ideals. Robert realized that his was a different age with new problems.

A changing environment had more to do with Robert Breckinridge's outlook than any other factor, however. Kentucky had matured. In John Breckinridge's time, it had been a frontier state, a western state, unsure of its position in the new union. John Breckinridge had sought to protect a young economy and to ensure that new states would receive equal rights in an emerging federal (and Federalist) government. Now, however, the problems were different. Agriculture thrived and the Mississippi River was American; the question of sectionalism still raged, but it focused now on North and South more than on East and West. The matter of the rights of new states seemed settled, and Kentucky was assuming its place as one of the most important of the states. The period from 1820 to 1860 would be filled with capable statesmen from the commonwealth; wealth increased; culture grew; population soared. As the state developed, it grew more attracted to what Henry Clay would call "The American Plan"—including internal improvements and protection for American industry. Changing transportation routes required that Kentucky compensate for its position behind the mountains; canals, roads, and railways were built. A growing hemp rope and bagging industry meant that many Kentuckians supported high protective tariffs to ensure survival of that aspect of their economy. The new transportation routes and the support for a high protective tariff kept Kentucky from becoming solely a southern state in its outlook; on the other hand, the existence of slavery and of a way of life that was basically southern ensured that the commonwealth would not become northern either. While some locales, such as Louisville and Covington, followed a pattern similar to that existing north of the Ohio, others, like Breckinridge's Lexington or the lands to the west, differed only in degree from the South. Combined with the state's continuing westernness, the result was a mixture of contrasts and contradictions.

In the period when Robert J. Breckinridge grew to maturity, his state continued its turn from sectionalism to Unionism. The spirit of the Kentucky Resolutions had vanished. Conflict—the War of 1812—stimulated the change. Much of the fighting in the western theater of that conflict was done by Kentucky troops, including Cabell Breckinridge. The state's casualties were high, and Kentuckians were determined that the Union they had fought for must be preserved. The words of Henry Clay counseled compromise and preservation of the Constitution. Other strong voices supported him, including that of Zachary Taylor, who lived much of his life on a plantation near Louisville. Not until the 1850s would equally strong leaders give the states' rights argument full display. By then it was too late: a generation of Kentuckians, either Democrat or Whig, had as their heroes western men—Jackson, Clay, Taylor—and even slavery would not overcome their Unionism. Thus in 1825, when Robert Breckinridge initially stood before the electorate, the intensity of forces within Kentucky produced outstanding political leaders but also divisions that would plague the state for years.

Such forces and divisions proved the impetus for Robert's decision to continue his campaign. Torn between "love & duty," between a sick child and the canvass, he explained his choice to Sophy: "Do not consider the results for which I struggle as merely the gratification of a vulgar ambition—but look on them as tending to save & restore my distracted & degraded country."[14]

The most divisive issue raging in 1825 threatened Kentucky with civil war, though it involved neither slavery nor sectionalism. Instead, it involved class feelings and the question of wealth versus poverty—dangerous matters for the young patrician politician. The "Old Court–New Court" controversy grew out of financial problems resulting from the panic of 1819. Sympathetic legislators had passed replevin laws favoring debtors, but a conservative Court of Appeals declared such laws unconstitutional. The next year, as Breckinridge began to campaign, the General

Assembly responded to the judicial decree by abolishing the entire court. A new court, with four different justices, was established. Utter confusion reigned. Neither judicial body would recognize the other, and respect for public authority wavered. Political feelings intervened as well, for New Court supporters tended to evolve later into Jacksonians, while Old Court adherents generally drifted into the Whig party of Clay.[15]

Despite the heated times, Breckinridge won his race easily. But once in office he had to take a stand on the explosive issue. With families dividing, with class conflict resurfacing, with party feeling intensifying, his course of action would prove an important indicator of sentiment. Would the son of John Breckinridge, the man who bore the name Jefferson, follow the New Court route to Jacksonian Democracy or the Old Court road to Whiggery? Robert, displaying class feelings and fears of unconstitutional change, went with the established and the "orderly." His vote supported the Old Court, as he joined those who would dominate Kentucky politics for the next quarter-century. Kentuckians' support for the constitutional way overcame other appeals, and Old Court supporters controlled the 1826 Assembly. With abolishment of the New Court, tempers cooled somewhat and quarrels abated.[16]

But they did not disappear: running for reelection in 1827, Robert encountered again the lingering bitterness. As the legislator's former law partner, Charleton Hunt, told Andrew Jackson, a "very animated" canvass had taken place: on election day, Old-Court advocates tried to place their hemp stalk symbol over the courthouse door; Jacksonians sought instead to put up their hickory bough. A "brick-bat fight" broke out. Finally, Robert and a member of the opposition coolly walked together into the midst of the flying bricks and called for peace. Only then did the election proceed.[17]

After a calmer canvass the following year, Robert Breckinridge turned away from the constitutional questions of the judiciary to issues concerning the place of states in the national scene. South Carolina based its 1828 declaration of the right of a state to nullify laws, in part, on the philosophy of the Kentucky Resolutions of 1798 and 1799. Through memorials to other legislatures, Carolinians requested support for their interpretation of the Constitution. On the committee chosen to draft Kentucky's response sat Robert Breckinridge: he had now to support his father's words or reject them. He revered John and held him up as an example to others, but he faced the matter squarely, stood firmly for what he believed to be correct, and supported the majority resolutions that rebuffed South Carolina's position. "Any forcible resistance by the states," they said, "tends to anarchy, and a dissolution of the compact between the states." Kentucky—and Robert Breckinridge—went for the Union. While one would later waver, the other never would.[18]

Robert Breckinridge did not devote all his attention to politics in the

1820s. Earlier in the decade, serving as adjutant of a Kentucky regiment, he had a brief fling with the military spirit so popular not only in the South but in the nation. The same year he followed Cabell into the Masonic Order, in which he eventually rose to the office of Grand Orator for Kentucky. Later members of the family would continue that alliance.[19]

Robert also injected himself into the controversial issue of academic freedom and religion in Kentucky higher education. Transylvania University had selected Horace Holley as its president in 1818, in a move to realize Thomas Jefferson's words comparing Kentucky to Virginia: "Rational Christianity will thrive more rapidly there than here. They are freer from prejudices than we are, and bolder in grasping the truth." Holley's presidency had brought about the institution's "golden age," as it became the leading western university and rivaled those to the east in attendance and perhaps even in quality. Well-read, liberal in his religious outlook, and talented in various areas, Holley angered some by his deviation from established patterns and religious orthodoxy. By 1825 the attacks on the president had become furious, and leading them was the Reverend John Breckinridge, whose father had been one of the founders of the school and a supporter of its library. Just as the institution seemed to be reaching its promise, the Reverend John Breckinridge began to attack its proud foundations. Robert Breckinridge took a more moderate course; the religious conservatism of his brother's Presbyterianism was not yet a part of Robert's make-up. He resisted pressures to join John and at times supported Holley. But the opposition was too strong, and Holley resigned in 1827. Enrollment immediately dropped, and Transylvania never regained its prominence. Another of the first John Breckinridge's dreams had died—and the catalyst had been one son's attacks and another son's relative inaction.[20]

Despite involvement in such turmoil and great personal conflicts on philosophical matters, the youthful, ambitious politician seemed well on his way to a public career that would rival his father's. Robert Breckinridge had won elections, had chosen the victorious side in the bitter judicial controversy, and had impressed his peers. His future seemed to lie in the political realm. But the winter of 1828-29 changed all that.

Though only twenty-eight, Robert had lived for some time in nearly constant pain. His career as an attorney had been interrupted by serious health problems, and while attempting to reopen his practice in 1825, he again was "attacked with pain." In 1828 his worried wife, visiting Virginia relatives, wrote back to ask if his severe headaches had gone. Robert could scarcely respond: he had been confined to bed in Frankfort for some two months, near death. "A fever, more violent than any I had ever experienced," almost ended his life. Large doses of calomel, "blue-lick water," and coffee, plus shocks from a powerful battery, had—not surprisingly—

done little to quicken his recovery from typhoid. Finally, by February 1829, Breckinridge had regained most of his strength,[21] and only then could he be told that his daughter had died in Virginia the previous month. His own near-death, then the news of this death of the second of his children, caused Robert to pause and reevaluate his life.

Earlier, when Cabell died, a niece had written to the grieving brother, "I hope you will get ready for you do not know what day or what hour you may be taken from this world." Apparently, he had given little thought to her counsel. He understood theology and attended church, but the rebellious youth in him had kept him from the religious commitment of those around him. His mother, surrounded by death, maintained her religious intensity, and in 1824 his wife joined the church. Brothers John and William were already ministers; the dead Cabell had been very active in religious matters. Robert's illness during the winter of 1829 awakened him to the vision they embraced.[22]

Other elements within—perhaps ones even he did not openly recognize—were possibly present as well. His earlier decision to electioneer instead of visiting his ill son probably left feelings of guilt when the child later died. Robert's own tumultuous youth could have created internal doubts as the boy matured. The open break with some of his father's basic tenets—in effect, a repudiation of a past he wanted to emulate—left Robert Breckinridge filled with doubts. Aware of his own vanity but unable to overcome it, experiencing a brush with death, feeling guilty perhaps, he believed that his life was spared so that he could remedy the errors. Soon after his illness he recorded the process that resulted in a crucial decision: "My restoration from the jaws of death, was a direct answer to the prayers of his saints put on my behalf. . . . Broken in health by long & unremitted disease for a period of almost ten years—bowed down by domestic afflictions—embarrassed by my pecuniary affairs . . . I resolved to withdraw from political life—to abandon my profession. . . . God had helped me—at ease in my married affairs—happy in my family—at peace with men. . . . I see not clearly before me, what my master would have me to do . . . but, his grace helping me, I am . . . to obey him unto death."[23] Breckinridge's decision to abandon politics was not immediate or absolute (he ran again the next year), but it began with the winter illness. He made a public profession of faith in spring 1829, and in December he wrote his wife that he still had "a deep sense of heaviness at my heart." Yet by that time he felt "a deep sense of God's merciful dealings toward me." By the fall of 1830, Robert Breckinridge was prepared to embark on a new journey. He would enter the world of religion.[24]

Camp meetings that attracted as many as twenty-five thousand people; preachers of various denominations exhorting their flocks about the glories of Heaven and the evils of Hell; participants falling deathlike to the floor, or joining in uncontrollable singing, or rolling, or even barking—this was Kentucky's Great Revival of 1800–01. It had triggered a reaction that swept across the South and gave that region its own "Great Awakening." The greatest of the camp meetings, at Cane Ridge, attracted huge crowds. "The noise was like the roar of Niagara," remembered one participant: "The vast sea of human beings seemed to be agitated as if by a storm." Amid sermons and songs, surrounded by thousands who simultaneously cried out, groaned, and pleaded for salvation, the people became part of an emotional tide that few could resist. There were "hundreds moving to and fro, with lights or torches, like Gideon's army; the preaching, praying, singing and shouting, all heard at once . . . was enough to swallow up all the powers of contemplation." In this atmosphere it seemed that the "godless" forces of the Kentucky frontier would be overcome. The president of Washington University found Kentucky "the most moral place I had ever seen. . . . A religious awe seemed to pervade the country."[25]

Many of the increasingly large upper class—men like John Breckinridge—had resisted the forces of the revival. Some of the frontier spirit remained, not yet overcome by the religious zeal. Conservative churchmen stood firmly for their own doctrines and creeds; others appeared wary of the forces of change. Out of this came a great upsurge of religious spirit, but also great confusion. The Great Revival stressed emotionalism, not an educated ministry; individual spiritual welfare, not communal reform; otherworldliness, not material concerns; the letter of the Bible, not the spirit. And if the Great Revival became a civilizing factor to the rural South, if it made frontier society less barbaric and resulted in some religious diversity—the Shakers found Kentucky hospitable and the Disciples of Christ gained a firm foothold—it also created new problems for religion. Revival emotionalism invoked denominational retreat into increasing rigidity, as churches sought to repress any threat to their orthodoxy. Foremost in this category stood the Presbyterian Church, Robert Breckinridge's choice as an avenue to his God.[26]

In April 1832 Robert received a license to preach. After brief preparation at Princeton Theological Seminary, he succeeded his brother John in November as minister of the Baltimore, Maryland, Second Presbyterian Church. Over the next four decades Robert served in many capacities: for thirteen years he was a pastor in Baltimore; he then served as president of Jefferson College, Pennsylvania, for two more. Returning to Kentucky in 1847, he held the pastorate at the Lexington First Presbyterian Church for six years, then resigned to head the Danville, Kentucky, Theological Seminary. The church honored him with its highest position—moderator of the General Assembly—in 1841. Through writings in three quarterlies he edited and in several books, Robert Breckinridge presented his theology to a church in change.[27]

He was not uncertain of his course. Accepting the philosophy of John Calvin, he believed wholeheartedly that the Lord chose certain men, solely through His grace, without regard for human works. Only the predestined, the elect, the godly, could receive eternal salvation. Religion was "the only parent of virtue—as God is the only source of all good." Calvinism also stressed Biblical authority, and only through that infallible book could answers be found. Because of this, Robert had little use for what he perceived as frivolous trappings in God's church. "A church of music, and architecture, and titles, and dress, and forms," he insisted, "is beneath the consideration, we will not say of a Christian, but even of a philosopher." So strongly did he feel on this issue that he opposed his brother William's use of a pipe organ in his own church—a move that brought an angry sibling's threat to leave the state.[28]

Robert's acrimonious debate with his brother on the point of organ music typified his actions. He believed that God chose certain men for eternal life and had little doubt of his place with the Divine. When he spoke, he believed God approved; when his opponents differed with him on issues he considered important, he felt equally certain that they were thwarting the Lord's course. Acting in the belief that he was one of God's company, Breckinridge, in Will D. Gilliam's words, "may have confused what he wanted with what God desired; he may have more often battled for himself than for the Lord; he may have too frequently assumed that Satan supported his opponents." Many contemporaries saw him as a conceited man too sure of his own infallibility and of his superiority over them. In his own mind, Breckinridge was simply accepting the challenge of molding the world according to God's will.[29]

These beliefs intensified some of the conflicts within Breckinridge. Self-assured and lacking humility, he could yet state after one sermon, "I preached to my fellow worms"—words which, for a man proud of his ancestors and defiant of democracy, could seem to be spoken for appearance only. And at times they were. But as a man deeply devoted to his religion, Breckinridge may have expressed feelings that at the moment reflected his outlook. The two forces struggled for supremacy—humility sometimes dominant, pride often winning. And was his course always the Lord's approved one? Was he always right in his stands on issues? Could the opposition *ever* be correct? All these questions would be posed as his life unfolded. The answers could be troubling.

Five

It Is a Great Thing
to Be a Kentuckian

THE TIME between his ordination in 1832 until the stirrings of conflict in 1860 was Robert Breckinridge's most productive period. It was a tumultuous time. Politically, as the nation divided further along sectional lines, a strong party emerged as an older, major one died. Commercially, a spirit of enterprise dominated, as busy entrepreneurs used canals, railroads, and coastal routes to spread their influence and garner their wealth. The urban ethos began to intrude further on the agrarian mind. Territoriality, expansion, and talk of "Manifest Destiny" brought a brief conflict with Mexico but also yielded more land. A vision of an unlimited future intruded into the realities of the present and was accepted with little question. In religion, in class attitudes, in manners, in education, a transformation of society occurred, as the forces of reform struggled violently with the forces of reaction.[1]

Robert Breckinridge apparently recognized no conflict within himself. His outlook explained his actions as consistent and, to his mind, forward-looking. Convinced that America provided an asylum for the world, that it served as a great experiment, he held optimistic views about the power of American institutions over the individual. God's favored nation, His chosen church, and His minister—Breckinridge—all had a mission. Here in the United States the world would see the emergence of the purest of nations. Here the best form of government would grow, free of the Old World's vices.[2]

In 1837, speaking on "The Formation and Development of the American Mind," Breckinridge revealed in clearest form the sentiments that would shape his future. This new land of wonders, he told his Lafayette College audience, had been peopled by the strongest and most resolute of Europeans. Stressing a kind of political Darwinism, he explained that these newcomers had room to try the weaknesses as well as the strengths of their theories, and that by trial and error "great truths" had emerged. The founding fathers had turned these truths into political reality; now his generation must transmit "untarnished and undiminished" this grand inheritance.

"We offer to mankind the light of our example," Breckinridge proclaimed. An almost limitless future awaited: "This vast continent is . . . to be crowded . . . with a free, educated, and virtuous population; and the banner of our republic wave over an empire unparalleled in the greatness of its extent, as unequalled in the wisdom, justice, and humanity of its institutions." This strong Americanism and devotion to the Union shaped Breckinridge's antebellum actions. Sharing the nation's faith in the idea of natural laws, he worked to ensure the victory of destiny over the forces of darkness.[3] His adversaries would be many.

Robert's initial foes were American Catholics. Early in his ministerial career, he became convinced that the "Roman Church" threatened not only the promise of America but even the Union he had grown to support. He renewed the religious wars of his Scottish ancestors, although his faith in America's power to transform kept Robert's nativism from becoming completely fanatical. To him, Catholicism stood as the "most corrupt of all superstition—most debasing of all tyrannies—and most hateful to God, of all apostacies." This Old World religion with its hierarchies, forms, and authority had no place in the American republic, he argued. It was but a plot that threatened both civil and religious liberty.[4]

To oppose this "hostile" religion, Robert Breckinridge sponsored and edited the *Baltimore Literary and Religious magazine* and later the *Spirit of the XIX Century*. As "thoroughly protestant" journals, both openly attacked Catholicism and the conspiracy their founder saw before him. He left little doubt of his attitude.[5] Nor did his brother, the Reverend John Breckinridge. Until his early death John served as an even stronger spokesman for anti-Catholic thought. In 1836, the year that Robert's anti-Catholic "Address to the American People" was printed, John's acrimonious public debate with John Hughes (later a bishop) came out in book form under the title *A Discussion of the Question Is the Roman Catholic Religion . . . Inimical to Civil or Religious Liberty?* Displaying the harsh debating tactics his brother Robert later would continue to use, John attacked the "coarse and ill-bred impertinence of a priesthood" that frequented nunneries that were *"prisons to the inmates, and generally brothels* for the priests." John's widely noticed book gave the Breckinridge family much of the early national leadership in the movement.[6]

While all this was occurring, Robert was visiting Great Britain and western Europe as a delegate to the Congregation Union of England and Wales. Leaving New York City in April 1836, he and Sophy spent a year abroad—a period during which Breckinridge sent back to his magazine articles based on his observations and opinions. (These pieces and additional material formed the basis for his later two-volume work, *Memoranda of Foreign Travel.)*

Focusing on some of the evils that he encountered, while overlooking positive aspects of continental Europe, Breckinridge gave his readers a gloomy travelog. He explained, for example, that Savoy's poverty came from Catholicism's deplorable superstitions, and that priests throughout the Italian peninsula never preached or wrote books. All of this convinced him that American society could never complete its development until the papal system was defeated, and he returned to the United States even more certain of his correctness in attacking Catholicism. Travel did not broaden Robert Breckinridge.[7]

Another vehement anti-Catholic tract followed soon after his return. In 1841 Breckinridge published some of his articles as *Papism in the XIX Century in the United States*, in which he repeated standard propaganda of the era: a convent was but a prison which nuns could not leave; Catholicism, this "religio-political heresy," threatened the Union by priestly control of the immigrant vote; these unfit, dangerous newcomers should not have the franchise, for no more degraded and brutal white population existed anywhere. According to Breckinridge, these words of warning to America placed him in great danger. Should he disappear, he warned, citizens should search for him in secret cells in Catholic chapels, for there people disappeared. As for himself, he feared no one: "Oh! How willingly, would I become their victim, if that be the means of making my country feel that every sentiment of patriotism . . . [impels] us to suppress, by all lawful means, this unparalleled superstition." Strangely, considering his availability, he was not called to martyrdom.[8]

Robert Breckinridge could offer his life so easily partly because he fully expected to be on this earth only briefly. Since his early health problems, matters had not improved. Very ill in 1834, he suffered facial pain prior to a crucial debate two years later. Writing to Sophy in 1838, he complained of biweekly attacks of "dreadful" headaches, and other real or imagined sicknesses plagued him during the 1830s. In 1843 he described his health as precarious, broken. Three years later his close friend James Thornwell of South Carolina observed that Robert's health was "still precarious." Writing to Thornwell in March 1849, Breckinridge reported: "I have been very much of an invalid for some months past. . . . The malady became gradually more concentrated, in a sort of spasm of the whole contents of the chest or some of the more vital of them, after violent speaking."[9]

The physical ailments did not abate in the next decade. In 1850 he wrote of having experienced "a very bad winter and am good for nothing." His lungs bothered him in November 1851; in 1852 he was confined to his room for over two months; in 1854 he did not leave his house for twenty days because of illness; and two years later he concluded: "My health is wretched; my deafness almost total; my confinement to the house constant . . . and my prostration—complete." The next year his eyes troubled him. Yet, despite all this, he lived an active life and took an important part in state and national affairs. Discomfort may have strongly influenced his life's pattern and his reaction to events, but it seldom proved a barrier. He continued his work, at peace with himself, for he no longer feared death whenever it might come: "There is a deep and enduring consolation at the bottom of my heart. . . . The good spirit of the master is upon me."[10]

Robert Breckinridge, however, was not at peace with the terrestrial world. His continued attacks on Catholicism incited further conflict. He probably deplored the actions of a mob which, after he spoke to them, threatened to destroy a Catholic convent in Baltimore, yet his writings and speeches increased religious hatred in the city.[11] An indictment for libel followed a particularly bitter attack on a Catholic who worked in the county almshouse. On 10 March 1840 the trial opened, and after an eight-day trial the jury (which included no Presbyterians or Catholics)—reported a 10-2 deadlocked vote for acquittal. The judge discharged the twelve jurors, and the case never came to trial again. But the fact that he had not been declared innocent irked the defendant. Breckinridge publicly proclaimed that he was ready to endure "a thousand times more" for poor and oppressed Baltimore Protestants. Privately, though, he asked rhetorically: "Have I not been indicted like a felon? Would I not rather have been burned at the stake?" The man who promised martyrdom found it difficult to accept mere indictment.[12]

Robert's concern that he would not leave his growing family a worthy reputation increased his anger. By 1840 his oldest child, Mary Cabell, was twelve and approaching an age when a father's every action seemed crucially important to her happiness. The other children—Sarah Campbell, Robert, Jr., Marie Lettice, William Campbell Preston, Sophonisba Preston—had not yet reached that stage, but their future concerned him as well. Despite the father's distress, the Breckinridge household remained a generally contented one. The love between Robert and Sophy had apparently deepened as years passed: in 1837, the romantically inclined Breckinridge had proclaimed, "Oh! my Sophy, how deeply, tenderly, sweetly, is your image bound up in all that is good & noble in my nature! After sixteen years of ardent love—the heart satisfied, & confiding." Four years later he admitted that "I love you too tenderly for my own peace." With the births of two more boys—Joseph Cabell in 1842 and Charles Henry in 1844—Sophy's childbearing semed to be ended and the couple prepared to enjoy one another's company into their old age. But in December 1844—three months after the birth of her eleventh child— Sophonisba Preston Breckinridge died after a painful illness. Writing to his dead wife's brother, Robert could convey only a measure of the pain he felt within. "As for the future," he wrote, "I have no heart to look into it." While her death had to be "in some wondrous way" intended for good, he could not discern it in the depths of the despair he felt.[13]

Sophy's death brought about more than the usual changes in such cases. Besides the loss of a soothing influence on an intemperate soul, her death caused Robert to end his connection with his Baltimore pastorate. This move had been in the making for several years, for he had discovered a "restlessness of mind & heart" after his court trial. He told his friend Thornwell in 1842 that he felt like one condemned, "for having not only done nothing, but attempted nothing, worthy of my master, or my age. I am sure I am capable of better things." Writing to a Virginia minister, Breckinridge described "a kind of restlessness" that had taken him over recently. His wife's demise left too many memories in Maryland, and all these factors combined to bring about his departure, four months after Sophy's death, and eventual return to his home state.[14]

But the trek homeward to Kentucky was not immediate. Offered the choice of the Second Presbyterian Church in Lexington or the presidency of Jefferson College in Pennsylvania, Robert surprisingly chose the latter, against the advice of his brother William. Part of the reason lay in difficulties with his brother Cabell's widow and with other relatives. It did not yet seem to be the time to return. Instead Robert moved to the school, located seventeen miles from Pittsburgh. Inaugurated on 27 September 1845, he never found the happiness there that he expected. Separation from his children added to the void left by Sophy's death. By November, seventeen-year-old Mary and one-year-old Charles were sent to live with a Kentucky cousin, Virginia Hart Shelby. Nine-year-old Marie stayed with her Uncle William, while Joseph (three) and "Puss" (Sophonisba, who was six) lived with Mercer County, Kentucky, relatives. Thirteen-year-old Sally attended school in Virginia, and only the oldest boys, Robert, Jr. (eleven), and "Willie" (eight), remained with their father.[15]

The college presidency was neither tranquil nor stimulating. A student uprising in December 1846, against both president and faculty, made Robert's decision to leave the school easier. In February 1847 Lexington's First Presbyterian Church called and Breckinridge accepted the pastorate. He resigned his presidental post in June, after being awarded an honorary LL.D. degree by the school. Dr. Breckinridge returned to the land which made him feel almost young with its "delicious atmosphere." The happy native had only a few months earlier proclaimed, "Oh! me it is a great thing to be a Kentuckian, & to be loved by Kentuckians." He was going home—finally.[16]

Robert Breckinridge's decision to leave Pennsylvania did not come solely from his desire to return to preaching or from an unhappy presidency. Other attractions now made Kentucky more appealing. Among them was his thirty-six-year-old widowed cousin Virginia Hart Shelby in Danville. Breckinridge's letters to her had soon included more than advice about his daughter Mary, in Mrs. Shelby's care. He and Virginia began a confusing, complex, and strange courtship. By November 1845, he was writing love poems, with such titles as "My Dear, Dear Cousin," "Our Star," "Too Late—too late," "I *do* love thee—and I *will* love thee," "My Betrothed One," and "A Ballad of My Lady Love." Virginia's letters openly questioned the wisdom of their mutual devotion. "Oh that we had been wise, that we had guarded our old hearts," she replied. By January 1846 she had agreed to marry him, to his "unspeakable happiness," but this marked only the beginning of his matrimonial effort.[17]

The next month, the widow Shelby was being asked by her betrothed whether her feelings had changed. "I do not fully understand your letter to me," Breckinridge admitted. In March she wrote that "since the days my faith was plighted I have been miserable, wretched." Love was certain, but she wondered if love alone could make them happy. Less than two weeks later, she confessed a "wild, confused tumult of feeling, sometimes ardent and impassioned, but always distrustful of its own strength." Trips to Kentucky by Breckinridge in April and September reassured both Virginia and him. They repeated mutual vows "of true and constant love." But she continued to be unsure. Once widowed and aware of Robert's health problems (of which he constantly complained) Virginia feared for him. "Almost frenzied" after receiving no letter for ten days, she threw herself on the bed and wept for hours. "Cousin," she told him, "you love me I know you do ardently, fervently, wildly, blindly I may almost say but also you know not . . . half the feelings and emotions that fill my heart." On Christmas, Virginia reminded him how he had explained in his last letter "about things (some very haughty) and then you love me so tenderly," but later she confessed that she wished she never had been born "or that the grave would cover me over." Virginia asked Robert to pray for her, "a rebellious, sinful and unbelieving woman," and she informed her "noblest work of God" that she doubted she possessed the needed self-denial, wisdom, or meekness. She questioned whether their offspring could live together harmoniously, especially since his Mary and her son Isaac were romantically attracted. Mrs. Shelby's sisters counseled her to avoid the marriage, citing Breckinridge's "violent" temper as their reason.[18]

All these tribulations resulted in a serious strain upon her. With the approach of their wedding date—in April 1847—the physical manifestations of Virginia's emotional qualms increased. In the "spells" she described to Robert, she felt possessed by "an evil spirit." "I live as one dead to all around me." Her head was often full of "discordant and horrid sounds." Less than two weeks before their marriage, she reported that

she had slept only thirty minutes in the past thirty-six hours and complained of "spells of darkness, of doubt and despair." On the announced
day, nevertheless, Robert Breckinridge and Virginia Shelby were married.
Before her marriage she had correctly described her nature as "naturally
quick, impatient, irritable, and long indulged." The two temperaments
did not complement each other, and the marriage, as might be expected
from the courtship, brought neither partner the happiness each desired.
Virginia seldom found in Robert the disposition to ease her dissatisfaction. She had earlier opposed his taking the church in Lexington, for she
viewed it as "an old dilapidated edifice" whose congregation was composed of "ignorant unpolished and poor people—unable to understand
and appreciate my cousin's precious preaching. . . ." A Lexingtonian by
birth, Robert may also have disagreed with his wife's characterization of
that city's citizens as "great gossips—empty headed, purse proud, wor-
shippers of men and mammon." It was more than symbolic that the
Breckinridges maintained two homes, one in Danville, one in Lexington.[19]

Tragedy added to the already existing tensions. Of the three children—Virginia Hart, Nathaniel Hart, and John Robert—that Virginia bore
her second husband, only one survived childhood. The strain increased
in 1848 when two of Virginia's sons by her first marriage died within three
weeks of each other. It was little wonder that Robert noted, "She seems
hardly herself any more." Nor could the couple fully solve the problem of
children by previous spouses. The new Mrs. Breckinridge never really
replaced Robert's daughter Mary, who had been almost a mother to her
younger brothers and sisters. Ill will grew. Virginia continued to experience what she described as "sleepless nights and distracting dreams
driving me almost to derangement and despair," and by February 1856 a
divorce seemed imminent. In September Robert wrote that he had been
"abandoned" by "this deluded woman" and would allow her to live
separately from him. Mrs. Breckinridge told her son-in-law John Warren
Grigsby that she would seek a separation, based "upon a full review of all
the circumstances and after the most mature consideration." But the next
day, Robert informed his nephew that he had done all possible "to avert
the shame & misery of such calamities." For eight months he had been
denied "every marital right," but he had now written her a letter such "as
every good man will approve." Reconciliation followed, but family life
remained unsettled until Virginia's death in 1859 ended the unhappy
alliance.[20]

Ironically, Robert Breckinridge's domestic turmoil coincided with his
greatest reform work. Within months of his return to Kentucky, he accepted an appointment by Governor William Owsley as state superintendent
of public instruction (although he had voted against a common school

system almost two decades earlier). In September 1847 he became the sixth superintendent in the commonwealth's history. Prospects for achievement seemed dim. While Kentucky had created the office in the 1830s (the third state to do so), little had been accomplished since that time. Five previous superintendents had quit the post, which offered a meager $750 salary. Since 1840 at least thirty counties had received no state school funds; in 1847 only one of every ten eligible children ever went to school; average attendance fell even lower; a three-month school with fifty pupils could expect to receive a total of fifteen dollars in state aid; the system was a "mockery."[21]

As his father in an earlier age had fought for education, so did the son take up the cause. If he could enable all children to attend school, Robert said, he would "die satisfied." By the end of his six years in office, he had virtually reached his goal. Within a year he had lobbied successfully for a measure imposing a two-cent property tax for educational purposes, subject to voter approval. Breckinridge vigorously publicized the bill, and in 1848 it received endorsement by a popular vote of 74,628–37,748. The amount of money spent on schools rose from a paltry $6,000 in 1847 to $51,000 in 1849, and $144,000 by midcentury. Working surprisingly well with four of the five governors he served under, Breckinridge won his only serious fight with a governor when John L. Helm, a conservative critic of state-funded education, saw his veto of Breckinridge-backed legislation overridden by the General Assembly. Financially, the school system was sound.[22]

The superintendent's greatest contribution lay in his publicizing the needs, pushing legislators to action, and arousing public sentiment favorable to education. His influential annual reports to the General Assembly were scholarly and readable, and by 1850 only one of ten children did not attend school. "The first great work is done, the ground plan is broadly and deeply laid"; now "it remains that we should perfect what we have achieved." By the next year Breckinridge saw a strong desire by the people to sustain the system; public opinion had been transformed. When his office changed from an appointive to an elective one, following adoption of a new constitution, Breckinridge questioned whether he should run: not for twenty years had he faced the electorate. But he felt that his work must be vindicated by popular support. In a Democratic governor's year, 1851, the Whig Breckinridge won over five candidates.[23]

Yet within two years of the election Breckinridge resigned. Reasons were many. His support for parental selection of textbooks, his call for more compensation for his office, his opposition to ending tuition charges (because of financial reasons), all had been rejected in the revision of laws following the adoption of the new constitution. Breckinridge's proposal that the Bible, "the cheapest and the best of all books," should be the chief reading material in school angered some, as did his disagreement with fellow Whig Governor Helm over financial matters. With the prospect of more bitterness before him, Breckinridge submitted his resignation in 1853.[24] His educational accomplishments were, in some ways, his most significant contribution. In the South, only North Carolina could equal Kentucky's record. Statistics verify the state's success: School attendance rose from 24,000 in 1848 to 195,000 four years later; the number of school districts increased from 170 in 1847 to 3,112 in 1853. He had fought for some state-supported system of teacher-training—half a century before it was actually adopted in Kentucky—and had given the state "a public principle, fixed, general and earnest, . . . settled in the heart of our people, that the work can be done and shall be done."[25]

With some truth, Robert Breckinridge could refer to the system "which I have administered, may I not say almost created." In his farewell report he affirmed: "There is a glory, greater than the glory of wealth, and power, and arms, and conquest—the glory of loving, getting, cherishing, diffusing, perpetuating knowledge."[26]

While out of public office, Robert did not long remain out of politics. Having again tasted its temptations, his spirit found resistance difficult, especially in the 1850s. The Whig party was disorganized, its last great leader—Henry Clay—now dead; splinter parties thrived in the sectional atmosphere that grew stronger daily; the time was opportune for a new political force. By 1854 the young American or "Know-Nothing" party had supplanted the "unsatisfactory" Whigs in Kentucky. Breckinridge eagerly joined the organization, hopeful for its future, blind to some of its faults. Backing for the nativist group came from diverse sectors—men who firmly disliked Catholics and immigrants, those who feared the result of increased sectional feelings, and voters who saw the party as a building force that could skirt the divisive slavery issue. Some old Whigs, never willing to vote for the party of Jackson, simply supported the Know-Nothings because they had no place else to go. Breckinridge's own support came from all these reasons.[27]

Kentucky in 1850 had a small foreign-born population that comprised only 4 percent of its citizenry. But Robert's fears exceeded the logic of numbers. His European trip had sustained his low opinion of foreigners and Catholics. When the Louisville Union of Germans platform in 1854 supported woman suffrage, social equality for blacks, and immediate abolition of slavery, his fears of foreign radicalism were strengthened.[28]

As usual Robert Breckinridge quickly made his views plain. In the spring of 1855 he told editor Albert G. Hodges that his "irresistible" party would protect the country's most vital inheritance, its Protestant civilization. He and his ancestors, Breckinridge declared, had an "unsettled account" with Catholicism, and "a great conflict" must soon result, for *"Americans must rule America."* He emphasized the same points to family:

Writing to his nephew John C. Breckinridge, Robert praised the new movement and its aims in a long letter that read in part, "The movement itself demonstrates the final escape of society, from its old party leaders & tests; and it is, in itself, the most profound excitement, of the actual civilization, nationality, and religion of the nation. . . . For thirty years, I have seen, & urged forward public sentiment, in the *general* direction of this movement—so far as it is, *national, protestant* and invariably devoted to the killing off, of all men & organizations—which tolerate, a papal, a foreign, or a disloyal power in the bosom of society."[29]

Whether Breckinridge's view was shared by other Kentuckians would be tested in the 1855 governor's race. Already Massachusetts had a Know-Nothing governor, and the party would soon carry other parts of New England as well as Maryland. In Kentucky, election day became "Bloody Monday" in Louisville as mobs roamed the streets, burned buildings, and left over twenty dead in their trail. Statewide victory by the nativist party was tainted by the violence, and it proved to be the zenith of the party's success. The next year, rumored brass-knuckle beatings and stonings of opposition candidates by Know-Nothing partisans caused Democrat John C. Breckinridge to call on his Uncle Robert to stop them. But their tactics and internal weaknesses did that for him, and by 1859 only a vague group labeled "the Opposition" confronted the Democrats. Partyless, disappointed, confused over his own political faith, Robert Breckinridge could only wait—not an attractive course for an impatient man.[30]

Defeated once more in his struggle with Catholicism, the minister turned to other areas that were more rewarding: service on the board for the Louisville Institute for the Blind, from 1852 to 1866; Masonic Lodge activity; directing both the Kentucky Agricultural and Mechanical Association and the Kentucky Racing Association (which also numbered him among its founders). In these ways Robert served his community and functioned as a part of it. But his greatest efforts in the 1850s, after his resignation as superintendent of schools, came in the field of religion. In 1853 he left his Lexington pastorate and founded the Danville Theological Seminary. Affiliated with Centre College and approved by the Presbyterian General Assembly, after a bitter fight led by Breckinridge, the seminary was expected to be the church's dominant educational outpost west of the mountains. Breckinridge, installed as professor of exegetical, didactic, and polemic theology, served as the seminary's guiding spirit, financial advisor, and outspoken leader. He also used the time to refine and publish his religious views.[31]

His labors produced two massive books, the first in 1857, the other two years later. *The Knowledge of God Objectively Considered, Being the First Part of Theology Considered as a Science of Positive Truth, Both Inductive and Deductive* was followed by *The Knowledge of God Subjectively Considered* (1859). In the initial work, Robert described his pathbreaking efforts, claiming that no previous theologian had ever conceived the subject or the method he now pursued. All theology, he argued, could be placed in his rational, almost mathematical, system. Indebted to European thinkers Gottfried Wilhelm Leibniz, Christian-Wolff, and Johann Friedrich Stapfer, Breckinridge stressed a metaphysical explanation of evil in a rational world.[32]

Reaction to the first book came quickly. *The Biblical Repertory and Princeton Review* predicted that the book would greatly increase "the already high reputation of its author"; Chicago's *Presbyterian Expositor* in its initial issue called the work the first system of theology from that church's American ministers, "and as the product of a mind so gifted, so peculiar, and of so varied attainments [it] . . . will be much sought after"; Thornwell in another religious journal termed the study a masterpiece. Not everyone shared these sentiments. The Reverend Robert L. Dabney, a conservative professor at Union Theological Seminary in Virginia, disliked the effect "Breckinridge's undeserved glitter and prestige" had among young Presbyterians. In the *Southern Presbyterian Review*, he labeled Breckinridge a plagiarist who followed antiquated scholarship.[33]

Robert, predictably, responded angrily to these charges in his second book. In *The Knowledge of God Subjectively Considered* he explained that the "utter shortcoming of man" in every previous condition showed mankind's depravity and insensitivity "to all that is evangelically good." Thus only the elect of God could be saved, he repeated. Other familiar ideas followed in the book's 687 pages of difficult text. Reviewers' response to the second volume was similar to the earlier reaction: most, like Thornwell, agreed on the work's value but a few expressed dissatisfaction with its reasoning. Measured by a financial criterion, the books proved reasonably successful, selling together over 5,700 copies by 1860.[34]

By that year Robert had become an acknowledged leader of his church and, as a professor at a seminary that he had virtually founded, he could inculcate young scholars with his ideas. His work as "father" of the educational system of Kentucky had allowed even younger students a new opportunity for schooling. But in one major area to which he had devoted considerable attention in recent decades, his record had been less clearly defined. That area concerned the great controversial question of his age.

Six

Ultimate Rather than Present Glory

THE "CURSE of slavery" demanded Robert Breckinridge's attention, as it did his nation's. It had long been so. The 1799 Constitution had protected slavery in his father's time. Since then, the peculiar institution had become even more firmly established, as men of wealth paradoxically broadened their power in an era of expanding democratic government. As the slave system became a more widely accepted way of life than in frontier times, it proved increasingly difficult to uproot. To attack slavery was to assault all society, property, class, science, all security.[1]

Comprising 18 percent of Kentucky's population at Robert's birth in 1800, slaves accounted for 24 percent thirty years later. Although the 1830 figure represented Kentucky's antebellum peak, the institution still held an important place in the midcentury commonwealth. For every hundred whites in 1850, there were twenty-eight slaves; more than one in every four white Kentuckians were concerned in some way with the ownership of blacks. Many more citizens had relatives or friends who were slaveholders, and even greater numbers sympathized with the system.[2]

Kentucky's economic structure scarcely seemed to necessitate the existence of slavery, however. Only hemp—and, to a lesser degree, tobacco—required a large labor force, a fact that has led a careful historian to suggest that "without hemp, slavery might not have flourished in Kentucky." Even with the crop, few large farms existed: the commonwealth ranked only thirteenth of fifteen slaveholding states in the average size of slaveholdings. In Kentucky, no large cotton crop demanded chattel labor; no harsh, oppressive climate existed as an excuse for using blacks rather than whites in the fields. Kentuckians nevertheless embraced the system. Slavery was ingrained and convenient, and small slaveholdings became commonplace. By 1850, the Bluegrass State had more families that owned at least one bondsman than any other southern state, except for Virginia and Georgia. And even among those citizens less sympathetic to slavery there remained the difficult questions of how to end it, and what would happen to freed blacks—as well as whites.[3] Unable or unwilling to confront these queries, many Kentuckians comforted themselves with the assertion that theirs at least was the mildest form of slavery in America. They wrote and spoke of faithful servants who moved in a system based on mutual understanding and little punishment. As evidence of their liberality, Kentuckians pointed to the relative void in absentee ownership, to the small, family-size holdings, to the less restrictive laws, and to the continued presence of slaves, even with free territory nearby.

Whether their perceptions matched reality is, in some ways, not particularly important. Whether mild or harsh, slavery, in the end, was still a system of complete control over another being. Exceptions to the rosy picture of slavery certainly existed. One Kentucky slave, for example, remembered that "most" masters had treated bondsmen cruelly, beating them often. Another, a mulatto, recalled seeing a "light colored" girl tied to the rafters of a barn, then whipped, "until blood ran down her back and made a large pool on the ground." After a failed escape attempt, a former slave explained, he had been severely beaten for three hours and then chained every single night thereafter. Lewis Clarke, a successful runaway, said there were few days when some slave did not receive a beating or severe abuse from his owner's wife. Advertisements for runaways tell a story filled with burns, brands, cropped ears, whip marks, and other punishment. The one very extreme example of a black servant being literally chopped to pieces and tossed in a fire overshadows less sensational murders that took place. The records suggest that physical punishment was more than an occasional occurrence.[4]

In addition to physical abuse, the system also inflicted mental anguish on the enslaved. Even with the best of treatment, slaves were still subject to their owners' orders and whims, always told of their inferiority, and usually severely limited in their level of advancement. Added to this were the other evils of the system—the separation of families, the slave sales, the subordination of will. One former slave concluded that his Kentucky treatment was worse than at any other place, and another told of being "brought up, or rather whipped up, in Kentucky."[5] Others remembered a different situation in the commonwealth, one more akin to the white image. A very young bondsman held that he never saw a whipping on his twenty-slave farm, while an elderly black minister who fled to Canada said that he never "met with any rough usage" in Kentucky slavery. The mutual affection which often existed was later recalled in a number of the bondsmen's recollections, both during antebellum times and later. While such accounts also included memories of slavery in realistic and considerably less rosy terms, many called Kentucky the "best" of slave states.[6]

The often-repeated antebellum assertion of the benign quality of Kentucky slavery suggested to some that the state offered fertile ground for the growth of emancipationist societies. Former college roommate to

Cabell Breckinridge and later abolitionist James G. Birney, when he returned to Kentucky in 1832, wrote, for example, "I looked upon it as the *best site in our whole country for taking a stand against slavery.*" Three years later, Birney told ally Lewis Tappan that emancipation occupied the mind of his Kentucky community, and favorable sentiment was fast growing there. The Reverend John Rankin, at nearly the same time, claimed that the peculiar institution wore its "mildest aspect" in the Bluegrass State. James Freeman Clarke, no friend of slavery, served as a Louisville minister in this period and recalled later that he learned his antislavery there: "Slavery *mild*. People said 'all wrong, inexcusable; Kentucky will emancipate,'" he noted. Public sentiment in 1835, Clarke wrote, was "almost unanimous" against continuance of the system. Even William H. Seward at one time concluded that, in Kentucky, slavery was seen in its least repulsive form. But perhaps the most astute assessment came when one observer wrote a friend that "Kentucky, no doubt, exhibits slavery in its mildest form, but even here there is enough to cause the very heart to sicken."[7]

Within this context, Robert J. Breckinridge faced the slavery issue and the difficult questions it posed. It was to be one of the decisive periods of his life. By the 1830s Robert had already strayed far from his father's political philosophy. Now he looked around him and saw a different aspect of slavery than had his father decades earlier. He became an antislavery spokesman in Kentucky, and the Breckinridge name he bore ensured that, no matter how unpopular his message, he would at least be given a forum.

Other antislavery Kentuckians had been making their sentiments known for some time. The initial organizations—and the first west of the mountains—appeared in the state in the 1790s, and a Kentucky Abolition Society formed in 1808. Shelbyville's *Abolition Intelligencer*, although destined for a brief life, was reputed to be one of only two antislavery publications in America in 1822. Five years later some eight local societies kept alive discussion of the question of freedom for black Americans.[8] Breckinridge's church had added its support to the movement, although its policies were contradictory and at times uncertain. Presbyterian minister David Rice had led opposition to slavery in the first state constitution; two years later the Transylvania Presbytery had ordered its members to instruct their bondsmen, to "prepare them for the enjoyment of freedom" (slaves were allowed instruction in reading and writing in the state, unlike most of the South). In 1800 the Presbytery of West Lexington labeled slavery a moral sin in its call for approval to exclude slaveowners from its places of worship. The plea was denied, but the 1818 General Assembly of the entire church did term the willful enslavement of one race by another

"a gross violation of the most precious and sacred rights of human nature
. . . utterly inconsistent with the law of God."[9]

Breckinridge was determined to fight slavery—despite being a
slaveholder. In 1825 he owned nine blacks, all inherited or purchased
from a relative's estate; five years later he had seventeen, worth five
thousand dollars; in 1860 he held more than twice that number, and a
slaveholder he remained for most of his life. This obvious contradiction
between his antislavery beliefs and his holding of slaves was one which
Robert apparently did not view as a serious discrepancy. Many of his
generation believed that black freedom without preparation would be an
injustice to both races. Some, recognizing the racism around them, came
to believe that bondsmen could not find opportunity in such an environment. Still others disliked slavery but feared a world without it. Their own
racism bred talk of amalgamation and race warfare. Yet all these voices
spoke against slavery, sometimes sincerely and often forcefully.[10]

For men like Breckinridge the choices in the 1830s were between
dichotomies—slavery or antislavery, colonization or noncolonization,
gradual emancipation or immediate freedom. Robert chose what he considered the more pragmatic mode of ending slavery, one with some hope
of success in a slaveholding state. He called for gradual, compensated
emancipation, coupled, if possible, with colonization. Certain of God's
will, for thirty years he never modified and seldom questioned his decisions.

His first major public attack came in an election year, as he placed
before voters his views on a potentially damaging subject. In seven
articles entitled "Hints on Slavery" that appeared in the *Kentucky Reporter*
between 21 April and 9 June 1830, Robert Breckinridge displayed attitudes
unusual for his time and place. Unlike many of his generation, he did not
fear the black nation of Haiti, for he believed it exhibited more knowledge
of the principles of free government than most white countries. The
candidate held high hopes for blacks—as long as they lived beyond the
United States—and questioned slavery's profitability, portraying it as "an
ulcer eating its way into the very heart of the state." And he proposed a
specific plan for eradicating the disorder: levy a luxury tax on slaveowners
and end "in a few generations" the institution in the commonwealth. The
General Assembly could then declare that all unborn black persons would
"remain as they are born—free."[11] Slavery, Breckinridge declared, could
not exist forever. Fellow slaveholders must realize that "it may terminate
in various ways; but terminate it must. It may end in revolution. . . . It
may end in amalgamation. . . . Or it may be brought to a close by
gradually supplanting the slaves" by colonization. Breckinridge's predictions did not evoke sympathetic answers. Victory in the election went to
others. Abolitionist James G. Birney reported Henry Clay's assessment of
the effect on Breckinridge of the antislavery identification: "He spoke of

Mr. Robert J. Breckinridge," said Birney, "having put himself down in popular estimation by his having advocated emancipation and that he and Mr. John Green—two gentlemen of great worth—had disqualified themselves for political usefulness by the part they had taken in reference to slavery."[12]

Blocked in political circles, Robert joined his brother John in an effort to gain support for antislavery elsewhere. As early as 1824, John published articles critical of slavery in his *Western Luminary* magazine. He served as a manager of the Colonization Society of Maryland and sent regular contributions to the Kentucky branch organized in 1829. William Breckinridge also advocated the aims his brothers proclaimed. They made a strong trio in the cause of antislavery.[13] The most outspoken and vigorous of the three, however, was Robert. In January 1831, addressing the Colonization Society of Kentucky, he praised the "stupendous" plan they advocated. Like many antislavery men who supported colonization, Breckinridge saw it not just as a means of removing blacks from America but also as a part of the Lord's plan for spreading His will throughout the world. In the minister's view, colonization would regenerate Africa as exslaves became missionaries overseas. A continent once prosperous could recapture its past. Just as white Americans had a particular destiny in their new world, so too did black Americans in the world they had left. Those who worked for the end of slavery, of whom he was one, could expect the Lord's rewards, he predicted. "Their counsels will be heard. When the day comes, and come it surely will, when throughout this broad empire not an aspiration shall go up to the throne of God, that does not emanate from a freedman's heart, they will live in story, the apostles of that hallowed reign of peace."

Breckinridge followed this appeal with a powerful passage that sought to awaken white men to the evils of the system. Imagine your child condemned to the tragic life of black youths taken by the slave trade, he implored white parents: "Let the father look upon the dawning intelligence of the boy that prattles around his knee, the pride of his fond heart . . . and then, if he can, let him picture him in distant bondage, . . . the light of knowledge extinguished in his mind, his manly and upright spirit broken by oppression, and his free person and just proportions marred and lacerated by the incessant scourge. Let the husband . . . picture [his loved ones] basely exchanged for gold, like beasts at the shambles, bent down under unpitied sorrows, their persons polluted, and their pure hearts corrupted—hopeless and unpitied slaves, to the rude caprice and brutal passions of those we blush to call men. . . . He who can preserve the even current of his thoughts in the midst of such reflections, may have some faint conception of the miseries which the slave trade had inflicted on mankind."[14]

The son of a man who had done much to continue slavery, Robert J.

Breckinridge accepted the responsibility of dismantling the institution. In a March 1831 letter to the *African Repository,* the organ of the American Colonization Society, he emphasized that any means "which will be at once prudent and effectual" should be used to eradicate the enormous evil. Speaking before the Pennsylvania Colonization Society the next year, he reminded listeners that the goal was the entire abolition of slavery. At that time Breckinridge—unlike some colonizationists—advocated the end of the slave system first.[15] While a minister in Maryland, he sought to put into action the ideals he had uttered in words, outfitting eleven slaves and sending them to Liberia. In 1835 he signed a deed promising gradual emancipation of his remaining twenty slaves—some within three years, others by age twenty-one. (If he carried out these plans—evidence suggests that he did not—he remained a slaveholder, for his marriage in 1847 to Virginia Shelby brought her slaves into the household, and he did not free them.)[16]

Breckinridge continued to spread the antislavery gospel. His "Hints on Slavery and Abolition" appeared in 1833 in the influential *Biblical Repertory and Theological Review.* Social equality and amalgamation were not the goals, he wrote, but only "equal privileges and rights" for the black race. Slavery could be ended. Justice to blacks would result in a better world and the "just, and generous, and enlightened hearts and minds of those who own the slaves will not allow the system to endure."[17] The erstwhile lawyer and new minister was at that time moving toward a fairly strong antislavery position. His published addresses between 1830 and 1833—while illustrating selfish motives, a paternalistic attitude, and some insincerity—exhibited attitudes increasingly unusual for a southerner. Breckinridge's outlook could have developed into a more extreme antislavery position; it did not. His belief that moral appeals could end slavery represented, in fact, the high point of his reform spirit. The wealthy slaveholder, the southerner under attack, would eventually dominate the emancipationist within the same mind and heart.

The rising clamor for immediate abolition hastened Robert Breckinridge's conservatism. On 30 July 1834 Robert and John spoke for the antislavery and colonization cause before a Boston audience that included William Lloyd Garrison. To his *Liberator* readers, Garrison reported that the brothers had opposed social, political, and legal equality for blacks and had attacked his programs. The abolitionist followed with a series of editorials on the "Maryland Scheme" of emancipation and colonization. The "blasphemous" Robert Breckinridge, said Garrison, spoke for "the spirit of negro hatred" and evidenced "a most unchristian feeling" toward blacks. From Breckinridge's speech to the 1833 meeting of the American Colonization Society, the editor selected one section which, claimed the *Liberator,* showed him to be a friend of slavery. The Massachusetts radical abolitionist became a bitter critic. Breckinridge, in turn, called Garrison's immoderate principles "false, pernicious, and immoral," as well as impractical, unreasonable, "stupid and shocking." The spirit of the abolitionist movement would, he predicted, lead to insurrection, war, or disunion—all threats to the American mission in the world. Breckinridge's inability to find common ground with Garrison abolitionists symbolized the larger national divisions and meant that the small number of antislavery southerners would be further fragmented before a strong opposition.[18]

His was more than just a paper quarrel with abolitionists. While Breckinridge was in Great Britain in 1836, George Thompson offered to debate any American clergyman who would answer the charges that the American clergy were apologists for southern slaveholders. Thompson, an agent for the British and Foreign Society for the Abolition of Slavery throughout the World, had recently visited America under Garrison's auspices. With an eye to America (and particularly Boston), Breckinridge accepted the challenge.

For five evenings in June 1836 the two men addressed an overflow audience of twelve hundred at the Reverend Ralph Wardlaw's chapel in Glasgow. The American's dislike of abolitionists led him almost to defend an institution—slavery—that he in reality wanted to end. On the other hand, Thompson portrayed the United States as a "nation of slaveholders," a nation that was "the vilest and most culpable" on the face of the earth. "The aristocracy of the skin" ruled America. Criticize the abolitionists as he might, Breckinridge surely must know that those who love liberty "are always odious in the eyes of tyrants."[19]

So spoke the Englishman. Noting that his adversary had been in America but fourteen months and in the South not at all, Breckinridge appealed to his auditors—and to a larger British public—to hear him as one who knew and understood slavery. Colonization—not immediate abolition—was the only answer. A "good, wise and benevolent" movement, colonization would benefit the Negro who could find "comfort, freedom, and peace" in Africa. If Thompson so wished to begin a system of "leveling" and universal equality, why did he not begin in Britain among the poor? If racial equality came to the South, "a revolution more terrible and revolting would immediately follow." To stress equality and amalgamation was, to Breckinridge, to fight against the "purposes of Providence, the convictions of reason, and the best impulses of nature." There were but two ways to end slavery—by violence, or by the consent of the masters. Rejecting the former, Breckinridge sought to convince the slaveholders of the errors of their ways. "The persuasive power of truth" could rid the land of the system. Breckinridge portrayed abolitionists as men advocating war. They would grab a slaveholder by the throat, call him "a great thieving, man-dealing villain,"—and then ask him to accept their beliefs. That was hardly the mode "a prudent man" would follow;

trusting God, men should ask His guidance to do what was right.[20]

Breckinridge's quarrel with the abolitionists continued. He claimed that he had been attacked in Boston by a mob "stirred up against him, by placards written . . . by William Lloyd Garrison." An angry Garrison responded to these "false and dastardly" charges with an edition of the Scottish debates with his own "notes" added. At various points, he inserted such remarks as "What insolent behavior!" and asserted that the Kentuckian's entire hostility to slavery was "insincere or delusive." Garrison's words ensured that Breckinridge's attitude toward abolitionists would not change.[21] After these mid-1830s fights Breckinridge grew increasingly conservative in his racial outlook. Although he never abandoned his quest for slavery's end (unlike some colonizationists), he did tie emancipation more closely to deportation of the freedmen. Blacks, in his later speeches, were presented as a people whom American institutions could not transform. His optimistic Americanism did not extend to them. He began to see "this unhappy race" as God's instrument to bring "a great Hamite Commonwealth" to Africa. Increasingly, Breckinridge blinded himself to the fact that more and more American blacks had no desire to go to a land they had never seen.[22]

Robert Breckinridge did not follow early southern emancipationists into the proslavery camp as the years passed. He never accepted the "positive good" theory of slavery, nor did he abandon his basic moral, humanitarian stress—one with which abolitionists could actually find much common ground. Instead, his conservatism grew with his gradual acceptance of the idea that the two races could not coexist in America without serious consequences—race warfare, black degradation, or amalgamation among them. His increasing racial conservatism, however, never submerged his abstract antislavery attitude.[23]

Four years after the Thompson-Garrison-Breckinridge exchange, another debate occurred. The vitriolic Wickliffe-Breckinridge affair made it clear that in slave states individuals publicly had to be either for or against slavery; no compromise course existed. The debate furthered in Breckinridge's mind the idea that immediate abolitionism could not end slavery peacefully, and while it showed him that all antislavery men should unite, it also told him that they, in clear conscience, could not.

On 10 August 1840 Robert Wickliffe, called "the Old Duke," attacked the state's 1833 law that forbade most slave importations. One of the wealthiest lawyers and largest slaveowners in the state, Wickliffe had once been sympathetic to colonization and antislavery. But as his very cautious views were discarded and as the fight became more heated, he embraced slavery fully and completely. Wickliffe's flashing blue eyes and reddish hair, together with a booming voice, made him an impressive orator. Now in his mid-sixties, he seldom allowed his opponents whatever moderation they thought they deserved.[24]

Speaking to his fellow Lexingtonians, the influential Wickliffe predicted the butchery of whites and "the surrender of the country to the negroes" if abolitionists were permitted to spread their insidious slander. Slaves would become thieves who would murder their masters or burn their barns. Kentucky slavery, he intoned, was slavery "in its mildest and most mitigated form," but if abolitionists enacted emancipationist legislation, "a war of extermination" would follow. Wickliffe then uttered words best left unsaid, for they were the catalyst for Breckinridge: "The Old Duke" called Cassius M. Clay and Robert J. Breckinridge "your abolitionists in disguise."[25]

Breckinridge soon delivered his "defense," the first of three responses to Wickliffe. A large audience gathered at the Fayette County courthouse and saw before them a slender man, weighing about 150 pounds, with long, thick, black hair and small facial features except for a long and pointed nose. His "brilliant and clear" eyes could be troubled or thoughtful, bitter or bright. Nearly six feet tall, Breckinridge was acclaimed as "the best stump speaker in Kentucky" and as "The Napoleon of the pulpit." A friend like Thornwell could describe a private side of Breckinridge, one not evident to most men: "The more I see him, the more I love him. . . . He is exceedingly affectionate, kind, and affable in his family and among his people [in Baltimore]. . . . He loves to sleep in the morning, to smoke cigars, to sit up at night, and to tell funny stories. He is a very industrious and laborious man." Thornwell's version—the "affectionate, kind" Robert J. Breckinridge—was not evident at the courthouse yard in Lexington.[26]

In a direct style, Breckinridge vehemently denied that he supported either "race mixing" or immediate abolitionism. Amalgamation—*"a base, spurious, degraded mixture, hardly less revolting* than revolution"—horrified the speaker. He was an emancipationist and proud of it: "I have the sanction of an obscure man, of whom Mr. Wickliffe may possibly never have heard—named Thomas Jefferson—and of an instrument of no repute, which may have escaped his learned researches, called the Declaration of American Independence."[27]

Stung by the sarcasms, Wickliffe grew increasingly bitter. Speaking before an audience that included Breckinridge, Wickliffe called him a "biped . . . instigated by the devil," "a wicked Doctor," a *"Hots-pur* of a preacher," a being "who never never opens his mouth but he raised a *stench of slander."* Comparing Breckinridge with Oliver Cromwell, Wickliffe pronounced both "excellent hypocrites," both great gamblers in their youth, though Cromwell later had returned *his* money. Departing at last from personal attacks, Wickliffe concluded by warning merchants of the possibility of arson, now that slaves had heard emancipationist speeches.[28]

Arguing that Wickliffe's speech discredited its author, William and John C. Breckinridge both advised their kinsman to remain silent. Combative, Robert could not accept their counsel. After consulting Henry Clay, John J. Crittenden, and others, he was certain he could put Wickliffe "out of the pale of civilized warfare. He is a pirate . . . and should be treated accordingly." In his "second defense"—largely a factual presentation of his past life—Breckinridge seldom lowered himself to the depths of Wickliffe, who had called him "a baron of a brothel." Yet he did observe that "slanderer" Wickliffe's soul was "consumed with the very lust of gold." In a sixty-four-page pamphlet filled with minute legalistic arguments supported by documents, Wickliffe answered the "filth" of his opponent. Breckinridge was a "foul-mouthed blackguard," a coward, a man "essentially selfish and brutish."[29]

Once again, Breckinridge felt compelled to answer Wickliffe. This time his defense covered nearly ninety pages and was not restricted to factual rebuttals: "You have allowed yourself to descend so low, have displayed in a manner so humiliating, your want of feeling, of honor, of truth, have displayed so palpably, those degrading passions which even the vilest of our species are ordinarily ashamed to exhibit." As a minister of the gospel, he found Wickliffe so ignorant in his discussions of religious questions that they deserved no answer: "pearls are not for swine." In closing, Breckinridge warned that "the dealings of God are often pregnant with a fearful retribution."[30]

Wickliffe discarded any remaining moderation in his pamphlet entitled *A Further Reply . . . to the Billingsgate Abuse of Robert Judas Breckinridge*. This "miserable wretch [was] playing the game of his great prototype and namesake, Judas Iscariot." His "stench" still poured forth, "until he foamed at the mouth like a fretted viper," with his "sneaking and stealthy looks, and his blue china artificial teeth, rattling and shaking in his mouth like the dry bones." Wickliffe could not respect a man who joined emancipators in order "to render himself famous." Breckinridge— "a counterfeit Christian, a reckless liar, a calumniator, and a shameless braggert [sic] and coward"—was only "a brothel debater." "*A more selfish, cold-hearted being exists not upon the earth.*"[31]

Not satisfied with that, Wickliffe entered into another volatile field— interracial sex. As a young sixteen-year-old, "Libertine" Breckinridge, said "the Old Duke," had owned a slave named Milly. "I do not wish to be understood as intimating that I believe that Judas [Robert] had any hand in siring the boy Alfred [her mulatto child]." But, he added, "I do not pretend to say that Judas is a stranger to Miss Milly," for she had once made up Breckinridge's bed "while *he was in it.*" Thus, said Wickliffe, although Breckinridge declared against amalgamation and said he preferred whites, it should be noted that "men acquired their preferences by practice." Showing a side of his own nature, Wickliffe then noted that one of Breckinridge's slaves named Louisa, who lived at Braedalbane, had two "almost white" children. Only thinly disguising his intimation, he described Louisa as "a beautiful mulatto" with "a heaving *bosom,* and *lips,* a little too thick to be sure, but panting most amorously." Breckinridge had left "his mulatto breed" to die, declared Wickliffe, calling his foe "this *Boca-Negra.*" Wickliffe's most truthful statement came when he said he would "cease to nauseate the reader further." A disgusted Breckinridge, finally, did not continue the useless debate.[32]

Aside from illustrating the personal attacks typical of the period, and exemplifying the type of rebuttal that Breckinridge would continue to evoke from his opponents, the debates are important in other ways. Wickliffe's assertions would not be forgotten by Breckinridge's opponents, and Robert was a man who made many enemies. Wickliffe's use of these tactics is also indicative of the associations brought out by even moderate antislavery statements. Opposition to slavery, in the eyes of Wickliffe and the class he represented, meant support for amalgamation. Antislavery of any sort was becoming synonymous with abolitionism; and, although Breckinridge deplored both amalgamation and immediate abolitionism, he was grouped with all abolitionists. The middle ground he sought was eroding quickly, as Kentuckians' attitudes changed.

In 1835 a forceful abolitionist position taken by James G. Birney resulted in a local committee's warning to that erstwhile Alabama resident that he could not publish his proposed *Philanthropist* in Kentucky. Three years later the Lexington postmaster refused to send American Anti-Slavery Society materials through the mail. In 1845 citizens of Lexington suppressed Cassius Clay's *True American.* Such instances corresponded with the increasing proscription of antislavery views throughout the South, but in Clement Eaton's estimation Kentucky remained "the most liberal state in the South" during the 1830s and later. Many prominent leaders continued to voice their opposition to the peculiar institution, and slaves continued to enjoy more privileges than in most other slave states. Breckinridge believed that the commonwealth's antislavery forces could elect enough delegates to influence the 1849 constitutional convention. Here—not in Virginia in 1832, as some have suggested—lay the last major opportunity for slave reform in the South. Emancipationists were confident they could include a provision for gradual emancipation in a new constitution.[33]

Adding to their prospects in 1849 was the unity achieved by all four branches of Kentucky antislavery—conservative, moderate, liberal, radical. The very conservative emancipationist views of Senators Henry Clay and Joseph R. Underwood had become so carefully stated and qualified as to become innocuous and almost without influence. The relatively liberal antislavery stance, as represented by the tall, forceful, aristocratic Cassius Clay, could still gain a respectful hearing, but it gathered few adherents, even with "the Lion of White Hall's" stress on economics and distaste for the idea of black equality. The so-called radicals, those who favored immediate abolition of slavery, had almost no statewide support. The earnest words of racial equalitarianism came from such men as the Reverend John G. Fee, the tiny, balding son of a slaveholder, or from editor William Shreve Bailey of the *Free South*. Both would attract violence as a result of their outspoken views.[34]

Thus it was that the two extremes of antislavery made little progress in changing Kentucky's course regarding slavery. Only the moderate course of men like Breckinridge retained significant, articulate support while remaining forceful in its opposition to slavery. While someone like Cassius Clay could not win elections in the commonwealth after 1840, and while Fee's followers were driven from the state in 1859 by a mob, Robert Breckinridge remained in statewide office as late as 1853. So it evolved that this patrician, born to the old order, owner of slaves, led the attack in 1849 on slavery, the cornerstone of a way of life. He challenged the social and political order, and powerful allies assisted him. Judge Samuel Smith Nicholas, son of the "Father of the First Constitution," also aligned himself in opposition to his ancestor's actions. In February, Henry Clay's famous Pindell letter announced his support for some constitutional provision for gradual emancipation, compensation, and colonization. But was that a realistic hope? Breckinridge wrote an Ohio friend assessing the prospects in Kentucky: there were three basic groups in the state, he explained—the proslavery, the emancipationists, and the "party hostile to both." The latter group, *"perhaps"* supported by "the bulk of the state," wanted neither an increase of slavery nor any emancipatory action; both political parties and most newspapers supported the proslavery group because they feared controversy. Breckinridge himself certainly had no such misgiving. In 1843 he had written of slavery that "my only fear is that I have not said enough about it. . . . I have kept too near to the outer edge of that question." Six years later he was attempting to rectify the error, if error it was.[35]

Throughout the late winter and early spring, the Friends of Emancipation held gatherings across the eastern half of the state, electing delegates, attacking slavery, preparing for the fight. On 25 April 1849 some 150 men assembled in Frankfort for the association's state convention. Members represented one-fourth of Kentucky's counties; ministers made up about one-tenth, and slaveholders over one-half, of the delegation. Delegate Breckinridge, for example, held thirty-seven slaves; fewer than a thousand Kentuckians owned more. In attendance also were the Reverend John G. Fee, Cassius Clay, the Reverend Dr. William Breckinridge, the Reverend Dr. John C. Young (the president of Centre College),

Louisville *Courier* editor Walter N. Haldeman, and other prominent leaders. When Clay yielded to a moderate course, saying that *"We fanatics* are willing to take your compromise," then harmony reigned.[36]

Robert Breckinridge gave two spell-binding talks. "Never have we listened to addresses of more thrilling eloquence, or more transcendent power," wrote a reporter. "At times, while he spoke, the silence of the house was like the stillness of the grave. At other times his words roused and agitated his hearers almost beyond their powers of self-control." Calmly, then passionately, Breckinridge told his fellow delegates that they must convince all citizens that emancipation would aid both them and the state. Cautioning them to be patient, he at the same time pronounced slavery a "great evil, that is weighing down my country, and I will sacrifice all but honor, to rid my country of it." "We must look to higher aims. We must look to ultimate rather than present glory." Inspired delegates went home to fight their antislavery battles.[37]

On 12 May 1849, a Lexington meeting nominated Robert as a delegate to the constitutional convention, to oppose a strong proslavery slate of both Whigs and Democrats. Still seeking the middle ground, he gave his major campaign speech in late June, and the Whig *Observer and Reporter* reprinted it in its entirety. Aiming his rhetoric at both slaveholder and laborer, he proclaimed that emancipation should come "only gradually" and only with colonization. He emphasized that "poor men" must keep Negroes out of Kentucky and end slavery, "or move out of it themselves." Their rights, the minister stressed, were as sacred as any property rights. To his view "the just rule" of the greatest good for the greatest number should apply. Appealing also to slaveholders, Breckinridge emphasized that emancipation without compensation would be "an act of robbery." Although slaveowners had a legitimate claim for protection of their property, they had no justification for increasing and perpetuating slavery. They too should desire an end to this evil. Breckinridge then turned to his more familiar moral and religious arguments. Kentuckians, he said, should trust in their God for He would lead them: "What is just, what is right, what is good—let them do these, and they will fail no more. . . . When the day has come for mankind to break their chains and burst open their prisons, [Kentucky] will not select that day to consecrate her soil to eternal slavery, and dedicate her children to eternal wrong. . . . Every one of these human beings [slaves] was, like us, created in the image of God; has, like us, an immortal soul, is, like us, capable of joy and sorrow. . . . They are property; but still they are our fellow men."[38]

The desire for a rational, calm campaign proved hopeless. In Paducah two convention candidates argued, a judge drew his pistol, and a death resulted. At the Madison County hamlet of Foxtown, two sons of proslavery candidate Squire Turner fought with Cassius Clay. Clay killed one and was himself seriously wounded. Disease accompanied violence, for 1849 was a cholera year. Speakers canceled engagements. Breckinridge wrote that "my friends and neighbors are sick and dieing around me. . . . From eight to twelve persons die every twenty four hours." As a minister, he temporarily abandoned the canvass to aid the sick, noting in a newspaper "card" that for this reason he could not campaign. At the same time, he assured readers that emancipation would triumph: "Our generation hears our voice; our children will take up the echo of it; and God will not let it die in silence." Breckinridge, secure in the righteousness of his cause, was perhaps not surprised that locally only he of the convention candidates was not stricken by cholera. Candidate Aaron K. Wooley, son-in-law of Robert Wickliffe, died from the scourge.[39]

In August, the cholera abated and voting began. Whig James Dudley and Democrat Robert N. Wickliffe won convention seats with 997 and 903 votes, respectively, while the two Emancipation party candidates— Breckinridge and Samuel Shy—trailed with 738 and 465. Although anti-slavery advocates may have had a forum in Kentucky, they lacked the support of a majority or even a very large minority. Not one of the emancipationists was elected statewide, but their twenty-nine candidates polled a total of ten thousand votes. Breckinridge, who had run best of the emancipation nominees, told his wife that he had done his duty. Their noble hopes would triumph yet, "next cause—or next—or next."[40]

In the 1850s, Breckinridge himself seldom challenged slavery, as he became heavily involved in his educational work, in his seminary labors, in his marital problems, in his book-writing, and in his Know-Nothing crusades. Troubled by ill health and by a disruptive home situation, he never again fought for the cause with the same spirit. A defeated man looked at the sectionalism around him and grew fearful. His increasing racial conservatism intensified as new northern forces gained victories. Addressing the Kentucky Colonization Society in 1851, for example, he referred to the black race as a "feeble parasite"; the black man's problem, however great, should never compromise "the far higher and more important interests of the white race." In public letters in 1855 to Senators Charles Sumner and William H. Seward, Breckinridge continued his sad retreat. He insisted that the power of the gospel was making slavery more "endurable" in the South. Would these abolitionist politicians jeopardize the lives of seven white Americans over the interest of "one black African?" Their inflammatory speeches and actions, he feared, would lead to the "most direful of all diseases"—civil war. One Lexington paper praised his "brilliant defense of the question of slavery."[41]

Breckinridge the politician, the preacher, the author, the educator, the father, now gave particular attention to his land. Because of frequent absence, he used an overseer to supervise his six-hundred-acre Fayette County farm. The most trusted and loyal of these, Christopher "Kit"

Keiser, served for some sixteen years. But soon after financial strigency caused Breckinridge to cut Keiser's pay from $500 to $350 and use of a servant, the man who addressed his employer in letters as "Dear Robert" left. The next overseer signed on for a salary of three hundred dollars, plus a house for his use, nine hundred pounds of pork, corn meal, and wheat flour, vegetables for his family, firewood, a horse, and two slaves, to be clothed by the employee. Similar terms were made for other managers. Robert's overseers supervised a profitable farm. In 1850 Braedalbane included 150 sheep, 80 hogs, 73 mules, 40 horses, and 29 cattle. Agricultural diversity ruled production, which included 40 tons of hay a year, 10 of dew-rotted hemp, 1,000 pounds of butter, 600 of wool, 200 of beeswax and honey, and 100 of hops. The farm also yielded over 7,500 bushels of corn annually, 300 of potatoes, 250 of oats, 100 of wheat, 100 of rye, and 50 of sweet potatoes. All this placed Breckinridge among the twenty wealthiest men in a wealthy county.[42]

Braedalbane was a haven, a place to rest amid all his troubles. The name itself a region in Scotland—suggested the return to the past that Braedalbane offered its owner. It was there that many of the letters to and from family told of his preoccupation with their lives as they grew to maturity. As he wrote one son in 1853, "My great & last worldly interest lies in my children. . . ." His daughters gave him no great occasion to worry. The expressive, loving Mary had married horse-breeder and physician William Warfield in 1848; Sarah's union in 1856 with the Reverend George Morison and Marie's marriage to the Reverend William C. Handy in 1857 brought ministers into the fold but also some problems of finances; Sophonisba joined Dr. Theophilus Steele, Jr., in wedlock in 1858. The succession of marriages—all when the women were either nineteen or twenty years old—had been fairly good unions, and the father was pleased. His sons' conduct was another matter. Robert, Jr., the oldest, had been troubled by drinking problems and had been expelled from three schools (disgracing "your name and your race") before John C. Breckinridge had finally secured for him a patronage position in the Coastal Survey. Willie, perhaps Robert's favorite, had done well at Centre College but then quit the seminary, saying that God had rejected him. Angry, Robert replied: "It is you who are rejecting his service." Filled with anguish, the father "would a hundred times rather have died . . . than to have this trial." Three other sons—Joseph Cabell, Charles Henry, and young John Robert (born in 1850)—still had further schooling before them.[43]

All this occupied Breckinridge's attention as the decade neared its end. Yet there was always the peace of the farm—its quiet comfort, its solace. Robert would drive the six or so miles from Lexington to his estate, enter through a gate into cleared woodlands, and continue down a slope, past his springhouse, then up a short hill to his plain but spacious dwelling. There some of the twenty-one slaves (the rest were "hired out") would welcome him home again. Around him the land and livestock showed the careful attention he gave them and demanded of his workers as well. One-third of the farm lay in woodland pasture, where trees stood but from which—by using three laborers for three months each year—all weeds had been removed. These forest-parks, often inhabited by deer, gave the countryside a unique, almost English atmosphere. Around them Breckinridge grew his crops and pastured his livestock. It was a prosperous, well-run farm that pleased the pocketbook as well as the eye. Travelers would arrive to find chickens being fried, biscuits being beaten on marble slabs, hams, rich in cloves and brown sugar, being sliced, ice cream being turned in tall, "stove-top," freezers, and coffee being ground. By 1860 Braedalbane offered all that the fifty-nine-year-old Breckinridge sought, and he wrote from there on 6 January, "I need repose—and am no longer fit for the incessant care & toil that fall on me." Upcoming events, however, precluded any rest; his toils were to begin again.[44]

Seven

The Last, Cruel Decade

THE INSCRIPTION on the marble block Kentucky furnished to the Washington Monument in 1850 proclaimed, "Under the auspices of Heaven, and the precepts of Washington, Kentucky will be the last to give up the Union."[1] But would it? By 1860 that Union was threatened and talk of secession filled the air. John Brown's raid at Harper's Ferry a few months earlier had stirred up long-lingering fears of slave insurrection. Rumors of similar plots had swept the commonwealth, adding to the distrust of the North. And now the "Black Republicans" seemed on the verge of gaining the presidency. Could Kentucky—a southern state in its devotion to slavery, in much of its lifestyle, and in many of its sentimental ties—accept Abraham Lincoln? Or would the state support another native seeking the post, Vice-President John C. Breckinridge? Many of John's southern supporters seemed to support secession. With the northern ties of Ohio River cities such as Louisville and Covington, with the links of land investments and the railroad, and—most important—with the devotion of the commonwealth to the idea of Union, could the Bluegrass State bring itself to give John C. Breckinridge a majority? In 1860, Kentucky wanted both Union *and* Slavery.

Robert J. Breckinridge, John C.'s uncle, faced a similar problem. As an ex-Whig and Know-Nothing, he opposed the political creeds of Democratic presidential candidates Breckinridge and Stephen A. Douglas. As an increasingly conservative emancipationist and owner of over thirty bondsmen, Robert feared the abolitionists' influence on Lincoln, but he deplored any talk of breaking up the federal Union. While a plurality of voting Kentuckians went for John Bell, the Constitutional Unionist, Robert Breckinridge did not. His vote, the vote of a self-acknowledged "Clay Whig—a steadfast Know-Nothing," went to nephew John C. Breckinridge—not because of his platform, for no man was more devoted to the Union than he, said Robert, but simply because of their "common blood and common name."[2]

Kentucky's vote showed its lack of sympathy for the incoming president—the state gave Lincoln less than 1 percent of its vote—but also indicated that it did not seek to separate, nor to wage war on either North or South. Yet as South Carolina's secession forced the issue, some decision would have to be made. Kentuckians would have to answer the question, "Who am I, rebel or yankee?" Breckinridge answered clearly. He told his son, "I am utterly opposed—and will resist to the utmost of my ability—a confederacy of the fifteen slave states." Such a confederacy would destroy God's vision for America. Determined to influence Kentucky's course, he became an untiring spokesman for the Union, and his 4 January 1861 speech, claimed the *Princeton Review*, became at once the "acknowledged view of all the supporters of the Federal government" in the border states. Copies of the speech appeared in pamphlet form for distribution from Louisville, Cincinnati, and Baltimore, and James G. Blaine called Robert "the strongest and sturdiest champion of the Union cause South of the Ohio."[3]

Breckinridge pictured the chaotic results of secession: bankruptcy, the downfall of constitutional government, the threat of foreign invasion, and death. "If we desire to perish," he told his Lexington audience, "all we have to do is to leap into this vortex of disunion." Breckinridge counseled Kentucky to ignore the South's course. "Do you want the slave trade reopened? Do you want some millions more of African cannibals thrown amongst you?" The commonwealth must stand by the Constitution; to do otherwise would be treason.[4] But the costs would be high. In Kentucky the term "the Brothers' War" had more meaning than elsewhere. Some one hundred thousand soldiers fought for the North and as many as forty thousand for the South, and indeed brother did fight brother and father, son. An Indiana recruiter noted that he never saw anything like the situation in Louisville: "The division of 'house against house' foretold by our Lord was never more complete and utter." Mediator John J. Crittenden saw his attempts fail and one of his sons fight as a Confederate general, another as a Union one. A son of the great protector of the Union, Henry Clay, became a Confederate sympathizer. First Lady Mary Todd Lincoln, a Lexington native, saw many of her family support a different cause from the one her husband led: a brother, three half-brothers, and the husbands of three half-sisters went to the Confederacy.[5]

The divisions tore apart Robert Breckinridge's family as well. His namesake was the first to go. Writing on 4 July 1861, Robert, Jr., explained that he left without telling anyone, for "I have no money, no business now and few friends. I have in twenty-six years done what a man should live a century without doing. I can . . . but to try and commence life anew. Be if you please sir as lenient as possible in your thoughts of me." The son went on to sit in the Confederate Congress before returning to the battlefield. An angry father told Willie that his brother "hopelessly ruined himself—every way." Hesitating for a year, Willie too joined the southern cause at last. "Whatever may be in store for me," he wrote his father with some sadness, "I shall never forget your kindness to me." Three months later, after facing danger and death, he wrote that he deeply regretted their political differences but even these could never erase his "unchanged love & gratitude." Adding to these great disappointments for the senior Breckinridge, son-in-law Theophilus Steele became a major under Confederate leader John Hunt Morgan, while a step-daughter's husband served the South as a colonel. To his eyes, all of these men were traitors, yet they were family. In partial balance, Robert's son Joseph enlisted in the Union army, and Charles transferred from Princeton to West Point, later to be commissioned in the federal forces. Three sons-in-law joined Breckinridge in supporting the North. But the anger and sadness he felt for those who fought for the opposite cause affected him much more than the pride he demonstrated for the others.[6]

Such differences of opinion in the family did not cause Breckinridge to hesitate for even a moment. Through the pages of the *Danville Quarterly Review*, which he edited, Robert called for the triumph of the Union. The "anarchy . . . of secession" would fail, he predicted, and in failure would ruin southern agriculture and business, leave the land in the hands of the military, and destroy the propertied class. A man like Confederate General John C. Breckinridge "was not equal to his destiny." Old friend B. M. Palmer, writing in the *Southern Presbyterian Review* in 1861, fairly summarized the differences between Robert's philosophy and that of the South: "He affirms the people to be one, divided into many; we, that they are many, united into one. He ascribes sovereignty to the Union; we, to the States. He regards the Constitution as creating a government which is over the States; we regard it as a common law, established between the States." Only war's end would decide whose philosophy ruled.[7]

Meanwhile, however, the war began raging in earnest. Kentucky's brief four-month fling with official neutrality could not endure in a war-torn world, and the Confederate seizure of Columbus, Kentucky, prompted the state legislature's proclamation of loyalty to the United States government. In the summer of 1862 Confederates briefly captured Lexington and inaugurated a provisional governor in Frankfort, but the ensuing southern retreat after the Battle of Perryville ended large-scale military activity in the state. Raids by men like Nathan Bedford Forrest and John Hunt Morgan only temporarily interrupted federal control. The military forces in the state, however, committed blunder upon blunder as they sought to control a loyal state alive with southern sympathizers. They faced an almost impossible task, for who was friend or foe, who was ally or spy? Each decision, if the wrong one, could mean battleground deaths. Wholesale arrests of suspected sympathizers were not always prudent; the imprisonment of an old and ill former governor was unwise; closing prosouthern newspapers, while necessary in war, proved unpopular. In short, all the evils of military rule soon accumulated, almost

Robert Jefferson Breckinridge in later life

entirely on the northern side. All this began to turn sentiment slowly away from the Union. By 1862 the Union adjutant-general wrote with some trepidation, "We are daily losing ground in Kentucky and what it is to end in God only knows."[8]

The fires of Unionism across Kentucky began to flicker and die as federal actions dampened the people's enthusiasm. Robert Breckinridge saw this gradual transformation in 1862 but did not fear it. He agreed with the necessity of military action in a wartime situation and believed that this would not effect a major change of sentiment. But then came the Union victory at Antietam Creek in Maryland. President Lincoln's ensuing announcement of his preliminary Emancipation Proclamation shocked Breckinridge as nothing else had. What should he do? Even though the proclamation did not immediately affect Kentucky, it sounded the death knell for involuntary servitude. In late 1862 a majority of the Kentuckians who wanted an end to slavery favored a gradual, compensated emancipation, coupled with colonization. Lincoln's plan suggested none of this. And because some Union soldiers from Kentucky owned slaves, their conflict was obvious and their reaction quick. A member of the Union 7th Kentucky emphasized that "If Abe Lincoln's proclamation don't stop at what its at it will break our regiment to pieces. We all say we volunteered to fight to restore the old Constitution, and not to free the negroes. And we are not a going to do it." Union soldiers resigned their commissions; in many of those who stayed, the will to fight lessened. Reflecting Kentuckians' anger, in March 1863 the General Assembly protested the proclamation, calling it "unwise, unconstitutional and void"— words a secessionist might use.[9]

Throughout the conflict Robert Breckinridge, a leading spokesman for the North in wartime Kentucky, had stressed that the issue in the Civil War was the Union, not slavery. In 1861 he had even said that the threatened extinction of slavery might be a legitimate cause for secession in some circumstances. The federal government had no jurisdiction over slavery in the states, he had averred. Now came this proclamation. Breckinridge agreed with almost nothing in the president's course, except the long-term end. How could he best serve the Union, his paramount objective, while serving his own conscience? It was probably the greatest intellectual crisis of his life and would take many months to resolve.

Breckinridge's first formal reaction to the proclamation came in an essay entitled "Negro Slavery and the Civil War," in the December 1862 *Danville Quarterly Review.* In his opinion, the president's actions would only delay peace, for southerners would fight harder than ever. Who could guarantee the safety of white women and children if blacks received freedom? Was it worthy of his people to inflict such a fate on themselves, "for the supposed benefit of an alien and inferior race"? Would not God, "in his own time," free the Negro race? It would be folly, if not a sin, to frustrate the course of Providence, as he thought the proclamation was doing. As a friend, Breckinridge publicly warned the president not to enforce his plan.[11] In the March 1863 issue he continued his plea to halt the "absurd" policy now in force; by December his attention focused on the question of using black soldiers, a move he considered even more dangerous and unwise.

Kentucky's sentiment was changing. Friends of the Union, like George D. Prentice of the Louisville *Journal*, began to turn away. Old

Congressman Crittenden announced, in the last speech before his death, that he could not support a war waged for the Negro. The president's policy had cost the Union "the heart of the people." A Union man who owned twenty-five slaves asked the governor in a public letter, "How do you suppose that it is possible for men to fight in a cause which they know and believe will ruin themselves?"[12] The questions of slavery and the use of black troops were tearing the state apart. In this highly charged atmosphere, Robert Breckinridge published "The Loyalty Demanded by the Present Crisis" in the March 1864 issue of the *Danville Quarterly Review*. "However distasteful" the Emancipation Proclamation, he asserted, it served to ward off foreign intervention; it aided the Union cause; it should be supported. The choice still came down to submission and loyalty, or resistance and disloyalty. As usual, no middle ground existed: "Those who are not for us in the struggle are against us."[13] Breckinridge had not substantially altered his convictions. He still believed the president to be wrong, and privately he vented his feelings to Congressman Brutus J. Clay. "Full of sadness" and bewailing "the terrible evils around and before me," Robert would stand by his country and shut his eyes to its errors. But publicly he asked readers of the *Review* to back Lincoln. Yes, Kentucky preferred to retain slavery, but more than that it wished to preserve the Union. Even if the administration followed an unconstitutional course (as he believed), should the people destroy themselves by forcible resistance? No, "let us submit to what we can not avoid." As Breckinridge now saw matters, God had "permitted" the enslavement of the Negro, to elevate the race, but now the Lord willed slavery's end.[14]

If slaveholder Breckinridge did not resist his Lord's will, neither did he enact it quickly. By May 1864, four of his male slaves had fled with their families to nearby Camp Nelson, the center of black enlistments in central Kentucky. Their owner agreed to let the men join the army but wanted the women and children returned to him. By July, the straggling to Camp Nelson had become a veritable exodus. Going there himself, Breckinridge left General James B. Fry a list of seventeen of his slaves in the encampment. Those in the army could remain, but he desired the return of the rest. Since living conditions were extremely poor in the camp, benevolence may have dictated his request, but that is a very charitable view. More likely, he—like so many other citizens of the state—could not relinquish slavery under the stated conditions.

But once committed to a public policy of support for the Union, he emerged more uncompromising and unyielding than ever. As the core of Union allies declined in Kentucky, Robert again rose to a position of leadership. Rumors branded him the mover behind a secret cabal that controlled the armed forces. His ties to military commander General Stephen G. Burbridge gave him a ready and sympathetic audience, and his friendship with President Lincoln enhanced his influence on policy-making.[15] The first challenge came in March 1864, when black enrollments began. Former Union Colonel, now Governor, Thomas E. Bramlette angrily wired, "If the President does not upon my demand stop the Negroe Enrollments, I will." At nearly the same time Colonel Frank L. Wolford, hero of the Union 1st Kentucky Cavalry, called Lincoln a "tyrant" and suggested that "interference" with slaves "would not for a moment be tolerated."

Calling together a half-dozen of the leading Unionists, including Breckinridge and General Burbridge, Governor Bramlette read a proclamation he intended to issue. According to one participant's recollection soon afterward, Bramlette "was disposed to resist the action of the Federal Government." Only after a seven-hour, late-night session at Frankfort's Capitol Hotel did those present persuade him to drop his original plan and accept black enrollments. The ensuing proclamation eased tensions, but had Breckinridge and the others not acted, armed warfare against federal forces could have resulted. Again, Robert's influence had been important in preserving Kentucky for the Union.[16]

The issue of blacks remained volatile, but official policy did not threaten this. As the fall elections approached in 1864, Breckinridge began opposing the so-called Conservative Union Democrats, led by Governor Bramlette, editor Prentice, former soldier Wolford, and Lieutenant Governor Richard T. Jacob, a relative and son-in-law of Senator Thomas Hart Benton of Missouri. In speeches across Kentucky, Robert called them weak and spineless leaders whose seditious words showed their intent to cause a mutiny among the people. In one such talk, Breckinridge showed a less serious side of himself than was usual in his speeches. Speaking to a friendly Fayette County audience, Robert recited a little story about one of his granddaughters, whose father rode with Morgan. The child's mother tried to make the youngster "secesh," but the child was confused. When he asked her if she was Union or Confederate, she said she was neither, she was "Abolish." Later, when he questioned her again, this time she replied she was "Conservative Union." Robert told her that was fine, "for it is as near being nothing as anything can be."[17]

Such moments reveal the Breckinridge who held such great appeal to his supporters; this was the popular side of the man whom Unconditional Unionist delegates chose to represent them at the Baltimore convention that renominated Lincoln in 1864. In a move indicative of his national stature, Breckinridge was selected as the convention's temporary chairman and delivered an extemporaneous address that was enthusiastically received. His body now bent by age, his voice weak, Robert was still impressive. The long, full, gray beard, the thick gray hair that had not receded, the steel-rimmed glasses gave him the appearance of a stern but loving grandfather. James G. Blaine, who was present, long remembered the "tall figure, strong face, and patriarchal beard." To him, the Kentuckian's speech proved the most inspiring talk at the convention.[18]

Breckinridge told the delegates that principle was the issue before them. They must maintain the Constitution and "with undoubted certainty" put to death anyone "who undertakes to trample it underfoot." Then, in an even harsher tone, he declared that the only "imperishable cement" of free institutions had been the blood of traitors. This "fearful truth" must be recognized, for every blow struck, every rebel killed, every battle won helped insure the life of the government and the freedom of their children. This man whose beloved nephew and two sons fought for the South sought no quarter. The Union superseded all.[19]

Widely acclaimed at Baltimore, Breckinridge found his popularity at home considerably lower; his acrimonious words denouncing anti-Union Kentuckians would not be quickly forgotten. He was reported to have said, "When Simon de Montfort was slaughtering the Protestants in the south of France, he was appealed to by certain persons—declaring that his men were mistaken, that they were killing many who were good Catholics. To which he replied, 'Kill them *all*; God knows his own.' And this is the way we should deal with these fellows; treat them all alike; and if there are any among them who are not rebels at heart, God will take care of them. . . ."[20] Such unrelenting words only engendered more bitterness. Governor Bramlette called Breckinridge "a weathercock in politics and an Ishmaelite in religion," who hoped to enact harsh military measures and create rebellion. He and Honest Abe—astride the "'wooly horse' Miscegenator"—would destroy Kentucky government. George Prentice concurred. His Louisville *Journal* roundly criticized Breckinridge's "unsatiated and insatiable" soul. This "sort of Rev. tiger, a saintly hyena, a holy wolf . . . will raise a wild cry for blood." Robert's former allies had become more severe critics than his consistent enemies.[21]

Convalescing at Braedalbane from injuries received in a fall from a horse, Breckinridge made his home a meeting place for the select group of Union leaders that their opposition branded "the Secret Inquisition." Saddened but not surprised by Lincoln's failure to carry Kentucky (where he received the lowest percentage from any "loyal" state), Breckinridge was gratified that the president triumphed elsewhere. Soon after the election, General Burbridge, acting commander in Kentucky, arrested Lieutenant Governor Jacob, who had been a bitter critic of Breckinridge, and exiled him to the South. A month later, writing from the capital of the Confederacy (where he stayed with John C. Breckinridge), Jacob asked Lincoln to allow his resumption of official duties. Burbridge advised the president that Jacob's "treasonable and seditious speeches" had prompted his arrest, as advised by Dr. Robert Breckinridge. On 18 January 1865, after studying the case, Lincoln granted Jacob's request, and a month later Burbridge was relieved of his command, a further blow to Breckinridge's prestige. The president's actions, however, did not mean that he completely rejected Breckinridge's advice. Lincoln's desire to keep the Kentuckian's counsel was reflected in the favors he continued to bestow. In July 1864, Robert based a request on "the old friendship" between himself and Mrs. Lincoln's father, as well as his "public relations" with Lincoln himself. Shortly, he found occasion to use that avenue for more serious favors.[22]

Some writers have taken Breckinridge at his word, assuming he did nothing to help Confederate members of his family when they needed aid. That was not the case. Willie's wife, who almost despised her father-in-law, requested a pass through Union lines to visit her Confederate husband. Lincoln wrote back that he would grant the request "if Dr. Breckinridge sees fit to ask it in writing." She refused to take the letter to Robert. It is not certain that Breckinridge asked the aid of his friend Burbridge, but soon his son's wife received a pass "as requested by Gen. Burbridge" and signed by "A. Lincoln."[23]

Similarly, when soldiers seized his son-in-law, Theophilus Steele, and charged him as a guerrilla, Breckinridge wrote Union General Hugh Ewing that for "personal & public" reasons he was interested in the case. Denying that the Confederate should be tried for his life, he thought newspapers were trying to hurt him through Steele. His "single wish," he told Ewing, was that his son-in-law be jailed as a prisoner of war. Fellow Kentuckian and United States Attorney General James Speed eventually wrote Breckinridge that the outcome should please him: Steele was imprisoned, not hanged.[24]

Other favors came when his sons Joseph (a Union officer) and Robert, Jr., (a Confederate colonel) were captured near the end of the war. A special exchange quickly freed Joseph, while Robert, Jr., became the only prisoner of war in the Columbus, Ohio, penitentiary. Unlike other Confederates, he did not go to such camps as Johnson Island or Camp Douglas. Secretary of War Edwin M. Stanton told Ohio's governor that it was "inadvisable" to put striped clothing on Breckinridge, and the son remained a special prisoner until at war's end he returned safely to Kentucky.[25]

In an often quoted remark, Lincoln reportedly said that "to lose Kentucky is nearly the same as to lose the whole game." The president nearly lost the state when the "game" was almost won. Actions by the military, together with the Emancipation Proclamation and black enlistments, caused a change in sentiment by war's end, and Robert Breckinridge's role in those developments hastened the very shift in opinion he desired to prevent.[26] Before the end of 1865 many of the men of the party that had fought successfully to preserve the Union were engulfed by southern sentiment. Men who only months before had been military enemies joined to become political allies. What the Confederates could not win in four long years of fighting came to them almost freely after the peace. The "lost cause mystique" reigned supreme. Those who had waged war on the Union—not the majority who fought for its preservation—became the idols: Morgan's men, the Orphan Brigade, not Morgan's captor or hard-fighting federal units such as the Union 1st Kentucky Cavalry. The vanquished ruled the victor, totally and completely.

Breckinridge could not understand such madness. His world seemed upside down. At the moment of triumph, as he neared the end of a long life, he should be receiving rewards and honor. Instead, a majority of his fellow citizens labeled him a black abolitionist, a bloodthirsty Radical Republican, an outcast. Angry, confused, yet somehow still certain of his course, this leader of those who were becoming Republicans in Kentucky advised continued use of force to suppress "violent & irresponsible" men. His advocacy of stationing more black troops in the state added to his unpopularity.[27]

The two years following Appomattox were, to Breckinridge, still part of the war. Lawlessness seemed the norm in many counties. The state legislature rejected all federal amendments directed to it for approval. Blacks could not testify in courts, and their schools became the focus of violence. The 1865–66 General Assembly repealed acts concerning rebellion and expatriation. By the next year the trend had become overwhelming and the Cincinnati *Gazette* reported that the rebellion had not yet ceased in Kentucky. On election day 1867, the Democratic candidate gained almost 66 percent of the vote, bringing the Lexington *Kentucky Statesman's* response: "What Bragg failed to do in 1862, with his army and banners, the people of Kentucky, five years later, have done; they have given the state over into the hands of those who are and have been the enemies of the Union."[28]

Nor did religious affairs give Breckinridge victories. The issue of slavery and wartime allegiance had so divided the Kentucky Synod of the Presbyterian Church that it split into two factions in 1866. Quarrels over ownership of church property and over control of Centre College continued to alienate the two groups. Rapidly outstripped by its prosouthern rival, Breckinridge's branch numbered only some five thousand members. In church affairs, too, Kentucky had waited until after the war to secede. All that Breckinridge believed right—the cause of the Union in Kentucky, the "loyal" course of state Presbyterians, and so much else—lay around him in ruins. Little honor had come to this prophet.[29]

Added to his public problems were private woes, for daughter Sally died in April 1865 and son Charles two years later. Five sons had survived the war, but the death of his daughter came as "a great blow." Robert felt suddenly "very much alone" on his estate. Family members who had served the South during wartime found their father ready to forgive them.

Some did not feel, though, that their convictions or sacrifices needed forgiveness. Issa, the wife of Willie Breckinridge, had refused, during her husband's three-year absence, to allow Robert even to see his grand-daughter Ella. "I assure you," she wrote coolly, "that neither I nor our child expect or desire anything from you." In only one unexpected instance had he seen the youngster, accompanied by a servant, on a Lexington street. He placed her on his lap and said, as perhaps only a grandfather could, "God bless the child. She is the prettiest thing I ever saw." Then he returned her to the servant, never to see the child again during the war.[30]

While he and Willie saw each other frequently after the conflict, Issa— like many southern women—could not easily forget and forgive. The birth of Willie's third child induced Robert to write, in August 1867, that the third one was born "without my ever having been allowed to see the second one." Only several months later did Willie finally persuade his wife to relent. The grandfather at last would be welcome in their house-hold. Robert's now feeble scrawl on the envelope told of the significance of that communication. He wrote, simply, "Important." After five years, he could only now become acquainted with three grandchildren. The wartime hatreds died slowly.[31]

His children also became a monetary strain on Robert Breckinridge. Generous in assisting both the married and the unmarried ones, he found frequent financial worries. At Princeton, youngest son John, dependent on Kentucky for monetary support, received bitter criticism from his elderly father because of his activities at college. Marie and Sophonisba were, by Breckinridge standards, impoverished. Attorney Robert, Jr., had not prospered since 1865. In addition to other debts, lawyer and editor Willie owed his father a large amount of money. Of the seven surviving children, only Mary and army officer Joseph Cabell Breckinridge were relatively free of indebtedness.[32]

Plagued by these concerns along with the bitterness of postwar events, Breckinridge lived his last half-decade in much anguish, both physical and mental. In a gloomy letter written soon after the war he told Willie that the people of America had become so contemptuous of the Lord that "delusion and destruction" would soon visit them. His vision of America's future was waning. In March 1867 the minister resolutely wrote to his son at college that people "sometimes, outlive their day." Yet he continued to be active. Typically, when not teaching, he would read the Bible, newspapers, and magazines daily, and an occasional book. He admitted that he disliked historian Edward Gibbon's "shallowness, . . . bombast, . . . disgusting vanity and pretension." Old age had not mellowed him a great deal.[33]

Infirmities did not preclude yet another marriage. On 5 November 1868 Robert repeated vows with his third wife, the widowed and younger Margaret Faulkner White. She helped him in many ways and by August of the next year was composing letters for her husband, who suffered too greatly to write. Health problems forced Breckinridge's resignation from the seminary in October 1869, and a little over a year later he confided to a son that his decline daily became "more decided & more rapid." On the evening of 27 December 1871 he died—"fully dressed, quietly waiting, unafraid to meet the ultimate test of the faith by which he lived for forty years."[34]

The essential contradictions of his character and actions complicate any analysis of Robert J. Breckinridge.[35] His devotion to the idea of America's mission and destiny, for example, caused him to support the Union, yet the same beliefs drove him to lead anti-Catholic and Know-Nothing crusades. His loyalty kept him from taking the final, important step toward abolitionism, for he feared that movement would destroy the Union and frustrate God's plan; but his sense of destiny told him at the same time that slavery itself could not be a part of the nation's glorious future.

Similarly, Breckinridge's religion created conflicts for him. It was a moral outrage growing in part out of his spiritual feelings that made him an antislavery advocate in the first place, but that same force supported prejudices toward other religions and immigrants. His desire to educate all Kentuckians came partially from the minister's belief that universal education would encourage greater Bible-reading and more enlightened leadership. Religion, however, also led to his decision to resign as super-intendent of public instruction, bringing to a premature close a very important educational career at a time when much work was left undone.

Similar patterns occurred in other areas. As an individual, Breckinridge could be generous and hospitable, yet at the same time he aroused the deepest of hatreds in public debate. The Reverend Dr. John C. Young best explained this aspect of the man in a remarkably frank and knowledgeable "homily" to Robert: "You cudgel persons unmercifully often for differing with you when they would really like to agree with you, if they honestly could. . . . You attribute the opposition to personal feelings." Within his family the devoted father placed family pride ex-tremely high, yet he bitterly alienated sons and daughters by his wartime actions. Breckinridge's own words reflected the conflicts, as did his actions. Humbly, he said on one occasion that "there is probably no man whose opinions have less weight with me than my own." But on another instance, he acknowledged: "I am a wonder to myself."[36]

This man who could not be silent in the face of perceived error, who believed that time and individuals but not principles changed, who trusted his Calvinist religion and the certitude that history would support his actions—this man gave an evaluation that posterity can accept: "I am full as near being what men call a radical—as what they call a conservative.

I am neither the one nor the other. I do not believe that all that exists is good—nor yet that all is good which does not exist." It was this man who had ended his will, written several months before his death, with the words, "I have done what I could for [Jesus Christ's] blessed cause, for my generation, and for my country. My best wish for my children who survive me is that they do more and better for all three."[37]

THREE

JOHN C. BRECKINRIDGE

1821-1875

Some of them have gone quietly to rest, in the tombs of their fathers, leaving behind them a name, at the sound of which their children may rise and call them *blessed*. Such has been the fate of Nicholas, of Breckinridge.

Frankfort *Spirit of '76*, 14 April 1826

Eight

A Son of Fortune, Destined to Rise

AT CABELL'S DALE the young boys watched a familiar scene as a slave girl helped the venerable Mrs. John Breckinridge from the house. A widow now for almost half a century, Mary Hopkins Cabell Breckinridge was simply their "Grandma Black Cap." They observed quietly and respectfully as the blind woman was led to the nearby family cemetery, where she would sit alone, except for the silent, ever-present servant, surrounded by the four high walls. On some of these occasions she asked some of her young relatives to go with her. Sitting on the stone slab that covered her husband's grave, she told them of the man buried there—how he wrote the Kentucky Resolutions, how he framed Kentucky's Second Constitution, how he helped secure Louisiana. Mrs. Breckinridge, a woman of powerful intellectual force, did not hesitate to remind them of John's greatness. Often she invited them to accompany her to his old law office, and again she would tell of the famous men who had learned their law there. Then "Grandma Black Cap" would return to the house, to linger with her memories a little longer.[1]

Memories were almost all that was left for Mrs. Breckinridge. Her oldest son, Joseph Cabell, the one of such great promise, had died when but thirty-five years of age, on 1 September 1823. As a young man, Cabell had learned of his father's death while at Princeton, in 1806. "From this time forward," he wrote a relative, "I consider my life dedicated to my mother's ease." Remaining in college for the time, Cabell soon encountered a situation that revealed his independence. Suspended for involvement in a student "rebellion" over certain rules, and required to issue an apology for readmittance, the proud Breckinridge vowed never to retreat from his "equitable and just" stand: "I spurn their college . . . as they do truth. I lament that men who are incapable of a proper exercise of power, should ever possess it for the detriment of others." The substance of his stand would remain in the mother's memory, to be imparted to his children later.[2]

Despite the independent words, Cabell recognized the need for education and reentered school in the fall of 1808. He courted Mary Clay Smith, the president's daughter, and a year after his graduation in 1810 the handsome Kentuckian and young Mary exchanged marriage vows. In the next twelve years the union produced six children, five of them daughters. The only son, born 16 January 1821, was named John Cabell Breckinridge. "Grandma Black Cap" wrote of her new grandson: "Oh that he may inherit all the virtues of the one he is called for [,] that he may be a John Breckingridge [sic] in every whit."[3]

After returning from "a foolish & ineffectual brace of campaigns" in the War of 1812, Joseph Cabell Breckinridge became an attorney. Head of his father's family and beginning his own, Cabell impressed those around him with his decisiveness, prudence, and maturity. Friends soon urged his entrance into the political arena, and in 1816 he won the first of three one-year terms in the Kentucky House of Representatives. Fellow members selected him Speaker before his thirtieth birthday.[4]

The year 1820 proved portentous for Cabell. Governor John Adair appointed him secretary of state, and in February Cabell delivered a widely distributed oration on George Washington. A new age had now dawned, he said, for "amid the night of terror, from the tempestuous ocean of the passions, the redeeming spirits of the age break forth to illuminate the world and calm its agitations." His nation's glory would extend through the ages and rise above past civilizations. This optimism led him to fear the future less than had his father or, as it turned out, than would his son.[5]

To have his beloved family nearer to him, Breckinridge moved them to Frankfort from their Lexington home—a move that displeased his mother very much. But as a contemporary noted later, "his plans were extensive and his hopes high," and he had selected Frankfort as the location where his plans could mature.[6] In the autumn of 1823, however, the family returned to Cabell's Dale because of an epidemic in the capital. Mary and Cabell remained behind to nurse sick relatives, and in late August he contracted the fever. Within a week he was dead. Mary, pregnant with their sixth child, was shocked, tearless, almost numb with grief. Her brother-in-law found her "the nearest object of hapless woe, I ever saw." The family feared she might lose all reason, so greatly did the bereavement affect her. With five children already and another born in February, Mary Breckinridge received little encouragement from the status of her husband's estate. Debts totaled some $15,000 in a depression time. Their one slave, Cabell's large library, and some land might all have to be sold to meet the obligations. Before the estate was settled, the two-year-old baby died in July 1826.[7]

In disaster, the two Marys came closer together. Cabell's widow joined her mother-in-law at Cabell's Dale, in a move that had important consequences for the young John C. Breckinridge. Had his father lived, it seems likely that the son would have learned from and emulated a man whose political path could have paralleled his brother Robert's, a path that led to Whiggery and, eventually, to the Union. But Cabell's death meant that John C. Breckinridge would hear his grandfather's philosophy as well as his father's. Indeed, by the time the youngster grew to an impressionable age, "Grandma Black Cap" was living more in the dead past than she had been when rearing her own children. Endowed with a superior memory and a vigorous mind, this woman who had known many of the founders of the Republic could tell also of the men her father had known. These recollections spanned two centuries and two continents. In a delightful, racy way, "Grandma Black Cap" used her wit to entertain and educate both visitors and family. As the only son of her oldest and perhaps dearest child, John C. Breckinridge received full attention from his grandmother. Through her, the world and philosophy of the earlier John Breckinridge subtly crept into the experience of the youngster, and once there, it would not leave.[8]

The informal education that John C. Breckinridge was acquiring from his mother and grandmother was interrupted when the two Marys quarreled. The imperious younger woman left Cabell's Dale, an action some Breckinridges never forgave. A proud, haughty woman of inflexible will, Mary Clay Breckinridge could at times be particularly intimidating. As a grandson remarked, "She was never known to be humble except to God." After leaving Fayette County for a sister's home in Danville, Cabell's widow was never completely reconciled with her mother-in-law or with Robert J. Breckinridge, her brother-in-law. John C., partly isolated from all this, would remember his schooldays as the most pleasant of his life and, unlike his mother, would remain close to the mistress of Cabell's Dale. But both he and his sister Caroline continued to find their mother very difficult to deal with. In 1843 Caroline wrote that the matriarch "takes fire in an instant" if her absolute authority over the children was questioned. John C. even directly chided his mother and advised her to act in a more Christian spirit. Bitterly, Mary refused to accept his letter, wrote of "unrequited love," and told her son not even to mention her name again. Quieter times did not fully heal the divisions.[9]

Continuing his schooling at Centre College in Danville, John C. was welcomed by friendly faces: his Uncle William served on the faculty and Dr. John C. Young, the president, had married John's sister Frances Ann. Her death in 1837 was a shock. Only two years before that, another sister, Mary, had died. The happy days of youth were steadily interrupted by the specter of death.[10]

After graduation in 1838, John C. prepared for a career in the law. He studied for six months at Princeton, then returned to Kentucky to work under Judge William Owsley, a future Whig governor. The youngster wrote an uncle in February 1840 that he had yet no cause to regret his disposition toward law. Though not in good health, he read Blackstone "twice with attention" and by that spring understood "the great principles which govern the system." He slowly formed an appreciation for the shape and symmetry of law, but it did not come easily: he studied law for seven or eight hours a day, then history or literature for three more. "My mind accumulates as much as it can manage and becomes exhausted."[11]

After completing study under Owsley, Breckinridge began receiving tutelage from the excellent legal department of Transylvania University. A fund left by his grandfather almost depleted, he had financial support from his Uncles John and Robert; the latter became a close confidant and father figure for the next two decades. As his graduation in February 1841 grew closer, John C. Breckinridge told Robert, "As soon as I procure a license it will be proper that you should discontinue the contribution which you have made to my support in several years past." The day after graduation, he had that license—before he was old enough to vote. But where to use it? Would John begin his career in Kentucky, home of two generations of Breckinridges? Or, like his grandfather of a half-century before, would he strike out into a new area as so many Kentuckians were doing?[12]

In several ways Lexington attracted him. The town's handsome, pleasant, and lively appearance impressed many observers. "Few towns in the West, or elsewhere," an enthusiastic traveler recorded, "are more delightfully situated. Its environs have a singular softness and amenity of landscape, and the town wears an air of neatness, opulence, and repose." The locust trees and small gardens charmed one English visitor. Several writers stressed the "rural beauty" of the city's shaded streets and many flowers. The dwellings of Lexington and the "beautiful villas" of the surrounding country gave the whole area an air of wealth and comfort.[13]

Commercially, the town offered much to a prospective lawyer. Seven turnpikes—one macadamized for over sixty miles—ended in the city. Six stage lines and a railroad connected Lexington with those outlying areas that a lawyer would visit. The city boasted rope and bagging factories, cotton and brush factories, cigar manufacturers, hatteries, carriage-makers, silversmiths, bookstores, printing shops, banks, and merchants. Though nine lawyers already practiced in Lexington, a skillful young lawyer with ties could still expect to earn a good living.[14]

There were cultural, social, and educational advantages as well. Transylvania University's library of over eight thousand volumes, the university's many debating and scientific societies, and the Lexington Lyceum gave citizens a variety of reading and listening activities. For lighter moments, parties and dancing prevailed. "The People are addicted to giving parties," a traveler commented, and a newcomer to Lexington discovered a "waltz-mania." Making a good impression at such affairs, as John C. Breckinridge usually did, generally resulted in more opportunities: "If you attend one and do not displease people, you are sure to be invited to all." It would be difficult for John C. Breckinridge to abandon his hometown.[15]

Lexington did not, however, resemble the Elysian Fields, by any means. While streets might be bordered with shade trees, they also were often lined with garbage. Odors of dead animals, open privies, tanneries, and slaughterhouses mingled with the sweeter fragrances of nature. The homes of the wealthy sometimes obscured older and more unsightly wooden or even abandoned dwellings. Main Street was overgrown with grass and largely unused over two-thirds of its distance. Once the commercial center of the state, Lexington had long since lost that title. A cholera epidemic in 1833, followed by the Panic of 1837, slowed growth, and in the two decades since John C. Breckinridge's birth Fayette County had not gained in population. The state's population, meanwhile, nearly doubled.[16]

Even in the field of education, where Lexington had once stood unrivaled in the West, doubts now existed. The internal feuds and religious attacks that had forced Transylvania University's President Horace Holley out in 1827 resulted in an immediate and substantial decrease in enrollment. In the late 1830s Lexington newspapers described the university as a "languishing institution," whose library contained only outdated books of an "ancient and soiled appearance." By the Civil War, Transylvania would lose its medical and law schools as well.[17]

For a time following his graduation, Breckinridge remained uncertain of his future. A brief romance faltered, after which a sympathetic young friend invited John to visit the St. Louis, where the beauty of the women surpassed the "black-eyed nymphs which look their lovers into ecstasies in Mahoumet's Paradise." Despite the temptation, Breckinridge somehow remained in Kentucky. Though already better trained than most beginning barristers, he borrowed books liberally from John J. Crittenden's library to continue preparation for his chosen profession. The chance to distinguish himself arose on the Fourth of July, 1841. John C. Breckinridge, only twenty years of age, had been chosen to deliver the main address to the Frankfort Light Infantry.

On a hot, dry day people filled the hall of the House of Representatives. A speaker read the Declaration of Independence, and then young Breckinridge came forward to address the gathering.[18] Well proportioned and erect, the orator impressed audiences as a tall man, but face to face, people found him not nearly as tall as they had expected. When speaking, he seemed "to dilate to yet larger proportions." He was clean-shaven at this time, but would much later grow a distinctive mustache that drooped nearly to his shoulders. The firm jaw, the raven-black hair, and the unusual blue eyes enforced the feeling that here stood a special man. A

John Cabell Breckinridge. Courtesy Kentucky Historical Society

mere glance from those large, almost fierce eyes would elicit wild cheers. All combined to produce an individual "handsome almost to the verge of beauty." Champ Clark wrote later that Breckinridge "was the handsomest man I ever saw or ever expect to see."[19]

"John C. Breckinridge had no peer as a stump speaker in Kentucky," stated Basil W. Duke. Few disagreed. Every attribute of the orator was present, and a resonant, sympathetic voice carried to the full limits of the large audiences that would hear him in years to come. His clearly spoken words projected lucid, expressive, illustrative images. So attractive a speaker as Breckinridge caused crowds to gather and listen for the simple pleasure of savoring excellence.[20]

In smaller gatherings, the more private Breckinridge was equally impressive. Editor Henry Watterson remembered him as "the Beau Sabreur among Statesmen" and knew of no one more winning in manners. A foreign visitor found in Breckinridge one of the rarest—to him—of American characters, "a perfect gentleman." Charming, cordial, chivalrous, he offended few. One friend, a young boy close to the family, recalled that when in his company "you were in the presence of true greatness, and yet no one felt abashed for his manner was so charming and so natural that you liked him at once." Another, in a somewhat sarcastic yet friendly overstatement, came near the truth: "Never . . . do I recollect to have met with a person who, for brilliancy of parts, readiness of wit, happy force and luxuriance of imagination, as a gentleman, scholar, statesman, or companion, could in any manner, or with any justice be compared to your lordship." He was "a fine-looking man, universally esteemed and respected, deemed and taken to be a son of fortune, destined to rise."[21]

In Frankfort on that Fourth of July, the youthful, already charismatic speaker began his talk with a vehement defense of liberty of the press. He cautioned those present not to follow men who filled the land with "their lamentations and dark forebodings of the destruction of our liberty." Liberty may exist "in one bosom—in a thousand or in the hearts of all men, but it cannot die. There is a sure guarantee of the final triumph of the cause of man." Enlightened knowledge, virtue, an educated citizenry ("in whom all political sovereignty is vested")—these would protect liberty and hurry that final victory. Choose an industrious man to lead, he advised, "but above all let him be an honest man." He who betrays a private trust may likely betray a public one. An educated, honest leader of strong convictions, free of demagoguery, certain of the people's right to rule, was Breckinridge's ideal. Like some of his Calvinistic relatives, he emphasized that all men are born with greater or lesser propensities to error and vice. Still, he added, early training, for the most part, dictated a man's final destiny.[22]

Breckinridge's own destiny remained unclear. A Frankfort paper praised his Independence Day speech, "characterized alike for its chasteness of diction, its patriotic sentiment, pure morality and sound philosophy." Despite the laurels, however, and despite his uncle's counsel to stay "where your family are known & renowned," John C. Breckinridge left Kentucky in October. Like so many young, energetic men "on the make" in Kentucky, he joined the exodus that contributed to the state's decline. Now an established commonwealth, Kentucky found itself in the same position as those states that had furnished its own settlers some three generations earlier. So many of the talented moved on to leadership elsewhere that Kentucky eventually earned the label of "Mother of Governors." Lawyer Breckinridge settled in Burlington, a town of some two thousand in Iowa Territory. His letters praised the new country but also noted the competition of twenty other attorneys. In spite of this, he still thought the prospects good "for a young man who desired to acquire honour and position."[23] In May 1843 he returned to Kentucky for what he expected to be a brief visit. Worried about the health of his sister Laetitia, he found that other family problems had not subsided. His mother would not speak to Robert or visit other Breckinridge relatives. John then suffered an influenza attack and decided that the cold climate of Iowa required him to stay at least for the summer in Kentucky. His decision not to return owed more, however, to seventeen-year-old Mary Cyrene Burch, than to Iowa rigors; by September the twenty-two-year-old bachelor had promised to marry Miss Burch. "The only objection I have to the lady," he wrote, "is her name, and that of course can be changed." On 12 December 1843, that transformation took place and John, realizing that he could best build a career in Kentucky, decided to remain in his native state. His hopes for quick distinction, won on merit and without the aid of the family name, and in a land far from Kentucky, had vanished before the workaday reality of life as a struggling attorney in the Midwest. Now his future would be tied to Kentucky.[24]

After a brief and unrewarding stint as a lawyer in nearby Georgetown, John moved his growing family to Lexington and reentered the society he had left behind five years earlier. Once there his fortunes soared. By the 1850s he could write of his "fine practice" and command a hundred-dollar fee simply to argue a final summation before a jury. In 1846 the Breckinridges moved into a new house near South Broadway, and for the next decade that would be home for their growing family, symbolizing the permanency that Breckinridge seemed at last to have found.[25] The birth of the first child, Joseph Cabell, in 1844, almost cost Mary her life, but over the next eight years she gave birth to five more children—Clifton Rodes (1846), named for Mrs. Breckinridge's father, Frances (1848), John Milton (1849), John Witherspoon (1850), and Mary Desha (1854). Child-rearing was a task that increasingly fell to the mother alone, since John was often absent as legislator, congressman, lawyer on the circuit, and soldier.[26]

The Mexican War did not at first disrupt the family's life. Remaining aloof from the conflict, John finally agreed to give a speech, in July 1847, in memory of Kentuckians killed at Buena Vista. A crowd estimated at ten to twenty thousand heard an impressive, patriotic talk that reportedly inspired attorney Theodore O'Hara to write his famous poem, "Bivouac of The Dead." Aging Henry Clay, whose most talented son had died in the battle, was so moved by Breckinridge's eloquence that he wept openly. Struck by the effect he had on the audience and the emotions displayed, the speaker seemingly talked himself into the fight. Shortly afterwards, Governor Owsley rewarded his former student with a military commission.[27]

Major Breckinridge's Third Regiment left Kentucky on 1 November 1847 on a Mississippi steamboat; over two weeks later they arrived in Vera Cruz. The war John tardily sought had already passed him by—a situation that brought a friendly exchange with his uncle. Robert pointed out that "the Mexicans heard my young nephew was coming and straight-away they made peace." To his combative relative, John replied, "That is more distinction than I deserve, but of this I am sure, that if my uncle had been in my place, and could have had his way, the war would be going on yet." Despite the banter, John learned some of the realities of war, even while stationed in Mexico. Of the thousand men in the regiment, over one hundred died of sickness. By July 1848, it was over, and he returned after a nine-month absence to see his month-old daughter, the other children, and Mary. John C. Breckinridge had experienced war and would not forget.[28]

Wartime comrades, impressed by their leader's strengths, asked him to run for political office. Accordingly, in June 1849 the local Democratic committee endorsed John C. Breckinridge as one of its choices for Fayette County's two seats in the Kentucky House of Representatives. The decision surprised some, for the nominee's Uncles William and Robert supported the Whig ticket, and John C. had studied under the Whigs Owsley and Crittenden. But his grandfather's spirit led him to the Democrats, who captured his allegiance. His mother was reconciled to Breckinridge's identity as a "loco-foco" but Uncle William sent news that he felt as would one whose daughters had been dishonored.[29]

Several factors complicated the canvass. Voters were also to select delegates to the constitutional convention, and in that race Robert J. Breckinridge sought support on an Emancipation party ticket. His nephew was part of a proslavery, bipartisan opposition. Then, in the middle of the campaign, cholera struck Lexington, and John's law partner died in the epidemic. The personal loss and Democrat Breckinridge's opposition to his uncle distressed the young candidate, but after the second day of balloting it became clear that the novice would win his seat. His count of 1,481 outdistanced two competitors by over four hundred votes.[30]

An impressive victory in what was considered a strong Whig district focused more attention on Breckinridge. On the first ballot for Speaker of the House, the freshman legislator's thirty-nine votes exceeded those of two other nominees. A majority required only eight more votes. But after the third ballot, with a deadlock in prospect, he withdrew his name in favor of another Democrat. A Whig eventually obtained the post, but Breckinridge received appointments to the Judiciary and the Federal Relations committees and settled into the legislative routine.

On his birthday in January 1850 John C. Breckinridge rose and read a resolution addressed to the issues then before the country, issues that would dominate the next decade. Slavery in the territories, "being [a] wholly local and domestic" question, should be decided by the people of each locality, he declared. He opposed abolishing the institution in the District of Columbia on the grounds that such a move would be unconstitutional. Property, that is, slaves, must be protected. Declaring loyalty to the Union, he also stated that Kentucky did not advocate disunion as a remedy for any "of the evils that threaten our peace." The Constitution and patriotism would settle in "a *just* and *equal*" manner all questions that disturbed the country.[31] Less than a month later Breckinridge signed a minority report of the Committee on Federal Relations. Largely his work, the report further clarified his belief that Congress had no power to legislate on the subject of slavery. Powers were specifically delegated, and nowhere were federal legislators granted authority to control slavery. Slaveholders and nonslaveholders had composed the document that governed the nation, and, John held, duty required that both groups should now maintain it. The Kentuckian's stand for the next, crucial, decade would not change.

Breckinridge's son John Milton died soon after adjournment of the House, and Breckinridge declined to run again for the state legislature. But in January 1851 he sought office again. Higher honors beckoned— Henry Clay's old seat in the U.S. House. The Ashland district was the cradle of Whiggery, a party bailiwick since that party's foundation. History did not promise a Democrat hope, nor did the formidable opposition. Aging general Leslie Combs was favorably identified in voters' minds with the War of 1812, Texas, and Clay. His long service included a state legislative seat and a record of party activity. Defeat for Breckinridge seemed all but certain.[32]

John campaigned as if ignorant of the odds. He studied economist Adam Smith again and again, finally formulating his course. "Free thought needed free trade"; government interference slowed national progress, but internal improvements "of a *national character*" were permissible. Breckinridge's speeches stressed such themes, but the real key lay less in what he said than in the way he said it. After a strong speech, he mingled with the audience, and admirers remarked that he seemed to know everyone. Not only did he call voters by their first names, he also asked them about their personal affairs: "His memory of faces & names was phenomenal always."

Whigs worried, Combs among them. The latter's lack of eloquence contrasted starkly with Breckinridge's oratorical prowess. The older man, tiring at the end of the campaign, proved no match for the thirty-year-old Breckinridge, who attacked at every opportunity in this friendly but fierce contest. Robert J. Breckinridge turned some of his Presbyterian Church's support to his nephew, and many observers felt that other Whigs increasingly favored the young Democrat. On election day Breckinridge's majority topped five hundred votes. He carried only three of the seven counties, owing his success to a two-to-one majority in Owen. The narrowness of the victory justified some fear for the future, but a triumph for any Democrat was striking. On the state level, Democrat Lazarus W. Powell became the first of his party to win the governorship since 1832.[33]

Such success did not sit well with leading Whigs. John C. Breckinridge's victory in 1851 and Henry Clay's death the next year symbolized the course of events for their party. When reelection time came, two years later, the effort to defeat the young upstart assumed national scope. Whigs chose an able candidate, former governor and congressman Robert P. Letcher. If the large-bodied, dark-skinned "Black Bob" did not seem a good campaigner at first glance, his short arms and legs, black eyes, and almost neckless body could be misleading. Humor and anecdote flowed freely when Letcher spoke in his expressive manner, and even political foes admitted he could spin a fine story to entertain.[34]

Greatly outfinanced, the Democratic incumbent was not outargued. Once again platform performance decided the contest. An observer found in Breckinridge "nothing theatrical, nothing inefficient. His look, his attitude, his gestures commanding. His enunication clear, distinct and emphatic. His facts, deductions and inferences are logically made—and with an earnestness and animation which have much effect upon his hearers." By contrast "Greasy Bob" was older (sixty-five), much less attractive physically, and much more theatrical. It became obvious that Letcher was no match for the talented, youthful Democrat.[35]

A typical confrontation of the two candidates occurred in the Woodford County courthouse on court day. A Whig partisan who was present remembered that the "motley crowd of long-haired, unkempt rustics" sat on benches, on the floor, or simply stood. They smoked, swore, and chewed tobacco in prodigious amounts. The observer, like other Whigs, was not satisfied with Letcher's performance that day. Breckinridge, "very handsome and gracefulness itself," spoke fluently; "the way he slaughtered all my previous notions of Whig doctrine utterly astounded, confounded, and put me to flight." The Democrat's pleasant smile and winning ways "stole the senses captive." One of Letcher's weak points, his uncontrollable temper, betrayed him on this occasion as on others. "Breckinridge played with him," and the madder "Greasy Bob" got, the more the crowd shouted. "It was a game of fence between an accomplished and elegant swordsman and a heavy, blundering dragoon, with a saber like a weaver's beam." Letcher would rain down his fiercest blows, not always in the choicest debating terms. Breckinridge's replies were calm, courteous, and deadly in their rapier-like precision. As his opponent made his closing talk, Letcher kept interrupting. "He was quite an old man, and to be thus foiled and handled and harried by a mere boy—a boy, too, who was so perfectly cool and self-possessed—made him furious." The former governor accused his adversary of unfairly denouncing the Whig party. Breckinridge answered that all present knew his remarks to be perfectly parliamentary. "Oh! Confound your parliamentary language, Major Breckinridge, and you too," answered the angry Letcher. Crittenden pulled on "Black Bob's" coattails to hold him down, a move that delighted the Breckinridge partisans, who promptly dubbed Letcher "Coat-tails."[36]

Desperate, the Whig candidate, like so many southerners, fell back on the slavery issue in an attempt to win votes. Letcher sought to portray himself as "a Simon pure pro-slavery man" and his opponent as an abolitionist. Using arguments of guilt by association (John's uncle was Robert J. Breckinridge) as well as claiming that Cassius M. Clay supported John, "Black Bob" hoped to use racial fears to win votes. His opponent counterattacked by suggesting that Letcher, not he, was the abolitionist. At that level, the contest closed. On a rainy election day, 1 August 1853, seventeen hundred more voters turned out than two years previously. As a national audience waited, the results again centered on Owen County, where an 875-vote majority gave Breckinridge the race by over five hundred votes. A happy Breckinridge nicknamed young son John Witherspoon, "Owen." In a district that had gone Whig by over six hundred votes in the presidential election of the previous year, Breckinridge had reversed the results and almost the margin.[37]

In the years that John C. Breckinridge served Kentucky in the United States Congress he introduced few important bills. Rather, working behind the scenes, advising others, speaking in support of or in opposition to bills before the House, he made valuable contacts. An appointment to the Committee on Foreign Affairs placed him with Georgian Robert Toombs. Fellow legislators included Andrew Johnson of Tennessee, Alexander H. Stephens of Georgia, Thaddeus Stevens of Pennsylvania, Joshua Giddings of Ohio, Joseph Lane of Oregon, and William A. Richardson and Stephen A. Douglas of Illinois. After a brief disagreement, Senator Douglas in particular became Breckinridge's ally.

State responsibilities received much of Breckinridge's attention. On the first day of the session he voted with the majority for Kentuckian Linn Boyd as Speaker. Important committee assignments did not result, however, as Boyd and Breckinridge remained factional enemies. In the second term John C. sat on the Ways and Means Committee, but he still did not head a committee, as many had expected. Recognizing that he owed his election to Whig voters, he trod a careful path. He fully backed Whig hemp growers of his district, and, on Clay's death, the young Kentuckian, whom many viewed as Clay's successor in national prominence, delivered an able eulogy. Less than a month later he offered an amendment to a river and harbor bill, asserting that Kentucky should derive more funds from it. While favoring improvements of a national character, he asked for a share of the spoils for Kentucky too. The aid Breckinridge sought was rejected, and he blamed the defeat on sectionalism.[38]

A typical Breckinridge congressional speech included factual, detailed information; in print his celebrated oratory was muted. But on rare occasions, when personal clashes developed in the fury of debate, the cool, dispassionate approach that Breckinridge had used to silence Letcher disappeared. When Francis B. Cutting of New York was thought to have killed a particular bill, Breckinridge rose to protest at the "stab aimed" at the bill by a "professed friend." Here, the Kentuckian charged, was the kind of man who threw his arm around a friend and then fatally stabbed him; "the heart of the gentleman may be for the bill, but his tongue is the tongue of an enemy." Congressman Cutting responded that the "unprovoked and unjustifiable" assault centered on "facts" that were not true. Angered, Breckinridge expressed his outrage at the flagrant manner in which the New Yorker had attempted to twist his words in a style of debate which suited "a bad action in a court" rather than a speech in the halls of Congress. What a spectacle—a person "governed on great questions by the low ambition of thwarting others instead of the high rule of the general good." Breckinridge declared that his vote would be dictated by conscience, not by outside pressures: "Clothed with the majesty of the people I represent, I stand here in my place to-day the peer of Presidents and of Cabinets."

"The peer of Presidents," Cutting sarcastically emphasized.

"Yes, sir; and the peer of the gentleman of New York; fully and in every respect, his peer."

As the applause died down before Boyd's gavel, Cutting called the speech "one of the most violent, one of the most inflammatory, one of the most personal assaults that has ever been known upon this floor." Furthermore, the individual who attacked him "skulked" behind others' bills. Breckinridge quickly asked Cutting to withdraw his last remark.

"I withdraw nothing."

"If the gentleman says I skulk, he says what is false, and he knows it."

The answer to such remarks, said the New York representative, belonged to a different arena. He would not "desecrate" his lips by answering it "in the manner it deserves." Instead Cutting challenged Breckinridge to a duel. The Kentuckian chose rifles at sixty paces. His opponent insisted on pistols at ten. Seconds finally satisfied both men and avoided a violent confrontation.[39]

The increasing sectional feelings that had fueled the Cutting-Breckinridge exchange would not die, within or without Congress. Harsh words, full of vitriol, matched equally strong ones by opponents. The question of whether to allow slavery into the territories called forth such debates. Working with his Kentucky colleague Senator Archibald Dixon, then with Douglas, and finally with President Franklin Pierce, Breckinridge aided in the eventual success of the controversial Kansas-Nebraska Act. Rejecting the restrictions on the expansion of slavery that had been set up by Clay and others in the Missouri Compromise of over three decades earlier, the bill left the issue in the hands of territorial voters through the process called popular sovereignty. It angered many northerners, who felt betrayed, and pleased southerners who supported the spread of slavery. Breckinridge's role ("Few contributed more," said Representative Stephens) had placed him closer to the cause of the South.[40]

No one should have been surprised. His record already indicated such support. He had spoken of devotion to Union, true, but such devotion coincided with actions favoring one part of that Union. A fixed philosophy dictated past stands and future ones; with his interpretation of government, Breckinridge could not avoid sectionalism. The earlier John Breckinridge had argued, half a century before, the philosophy his grandson now held: the states were supreme; complete, self-sustaining political communities, they had created the federal government, and the whole system rested on the foundation of state equality; a limited, fixed "perfect" compact had emerged from the convention at Philadelphia in 1787.[41]

Not only did his strict construction views bring John C. Breckinridge to the southern viewpoint; so too did his stance on slavery. Even though he had been greatly influenced by emancipationists—especially his uncles—as he grew to manhood, even though he shared Robert J. Breckinridge's vision of America, even though he held few or no slaves himself, he had become a forceful supporter of the peculiar institution. Although he on occasion voiced humanitarian sentiments, his actions spoke louder for continuance of the slave system. But why? What turned the Kentuckian to his course, one that ended in as much tragedy for him as it did for his uncle?

Part of the answer lies in the fact that John C. grew to maturity just as the immediate abolitionist's attack came to the forefront; Robert had experienced a far different influence early in life. Nor was the nephew imbued with the religious and moral outrage his uncle displayed. He considered the issue less a moral one than a constitutional one. Though voices within told him otherwise, he regarded slaves as property, first and foremost. Attacks by northerners on slavery were, by his definition, attacks on rights protected in the Constitution, "the supreme law for us all." He placed the blame squarely on certain groups in the North; they reacted to his words by consigning him to a southern bloc. If Congress violated the Constitution by shutting out the property of half the states, he maintained, then a despotism, erected in the name of outraged liberty, would result.

A situation similar to that existing before the American Revolution threatened, Breckinridge told fellow congressmen. If he admitted that Congress could legislate on slavery's end, he must concede it could interfere on other matters not specified in the "perfect" Constitution. Surrender on this one point would lead "into the very lap of arbitrary power." The whole theory of a flexible Constitution "is a libel on our institutions." In Breckinridge's view, the government as it existed in 1789 needed no change.

For John C. Breckinridge, moral arguments did not override legal ones. Ohio Congressman Joshua Giddings declared that, despite the law, he would never return fugitive slaves to their masters. "Against the impotent raving of his baffled fanaticism," answered Breckinridge, "I place the plain words of the Constitution."[42] This attack on antislavery extremism—two years before the Kansas-Nebraska Act—would be repeated again and again. The Union he sought to support must function on his own and his ancestors' terms; the Union his opponents desired must serve their needs. It all boded ill for the future.

Nine

A Lucky Steed Falters

IN KENTUCKY, the Whigs sought new ways to unseat Breckinridge. Unable to defeat him in elections, they finally outflanked him through state legislative action. Their party reapportioned the Ashland District so that "Sweet Owen" County would no longer serve Democrats. The normal Whig majority, twice overturned by Breckinridge, would be increased by some five hundred votes in the new arrangement. Given this realignment, John C., who had not yet lost an election contest, decided to forgo an attempt at reelection. It proved a wise decision, for the fall canvass ended in the expected Democratic defeat. Breckinridge's political acumen on this occasion had served him well.[1]

The Kentuckian, now out of public office, devoted more time to the law and to the land. Seemingly little interested in acquiring a large estate, he happily farmed his twenty-six acres, which produced ample oats and potatoes. More central to John's leisure concerns, however, were his two horses. As president of the Kentucky Association for the Improvement of the Breed of Horses, he took an active role in furthering racing in the Bluegrass. The private citizen enjoyed life away from the political arena.[2]

But politics would not long ignore Breckinridge, nor he it. As his mother feared, "having tasted political life, he will never be willing to return to the monotonous Tread to and from his [law] office." As 1856, a presidential election year, approached, that political life beckoned again. John's friend Stephen Douglas was one candidate. The ambitious Illinois senator projected an image as a man of action rather than intellect, the personification of young America. Another seeker of the office was the more staid incumbent President Franklin Pierce, and a third was James Buchanan, only recently returned from a stint as minister to Great Britain. As a delegate to the Democratic national convention in nearby Cincinnati, Breckinridge first backed Pierce (who had earlier offered him several appointive posts) and then, as the president's hopes declined, Douglas. When both men's combined strength could not secure enough votes for "The Little Giant," Douglas withdrew, and Buchanan emerged with the nomination.

Meanwhile, Kentucky-born Representative Richardson of Illinois pushed Breckinridge for the vice-presidency, arguing that his selection would help mollify Douglas and the South. Buchanan's managers agreed, and the fight for his nomination began. It was not, of course, a surprising move. In January 1856 H. M. Rice had advised the Kentuckian to "stay behind [,] smoke yr. cigars & *steer too.*" A cousin, in the same month, had asked if John would allow Louisiana to present his name for the vice-presidency. The private citizen had been active in those preconvention months.[3]

One item complicated matters considerably. Kentucky already had a favorite son—Linn Boyd, still a bitter Breckinridge opponent. When Louisiana nominated Breckinridge for vice-president, John rose immediately and said he could never consent to have his name in competition with Boyd, a fellow Kentuckian; he thus declined the honor. J. Stoddard Johnston, John's cousin by marriage, was deeply impressed by this tall, poised kinsman with the simple delivery and rich voice: "That speech was irresistible and though sincerely declining made him more votes on the first ballot than . . . Boyd secured after a year or two's active electioneering and wire pulling." The talk reminded one commentator of Caesar's refusing the crown.[4]

When balloting began, states continued to vote for Breckinridge, despite his supposed disavowal. At the end of the first count he stood second to John A. Quitman of Mississippi, and ahead of Boyd. The second ballot turned into a Breckinridge stampede. "Such enthusiasm and admiration for a man," said Johnston, "I do not think I ever saw." The grumblings of Boyd and Tennessee's Andrew Johnson, who felt the Kentuckian's lack of a national reputation would hurt the party, were drowned out by the cheers of the young and the oratory of the candidate.[5]

Once selected, Breckinridge—unlike many candidates of the time—campaigned fairly actively. Themes in his speeches seldom varied. Preservation of the Union required Democratic victory; the Republican party—the "Black Republican" party—only fomented sectional hatred. Democrats tested every question by the Constitution, Breckinridge emphasized, and did not follow "heedless fanaticism." Not a proslavery man, he insisted, he only defended the constitutional right of a people to form their own territorial laws, while the Republicans sought to array one state against another. "The only bond of the Union" was his party. His state did not seek to be the dark and bloody ground of a civil war, "and yet if this new party should succeed, how could Kentucky longer remain in the Union?" If his listeners accepted what Breckinridge said, and if the Republicans triumphed, then his counsel could have but one meaning—secession.

When the final test of the ballot came in 1856, a campaign song proved to have gauged accurately the Democratic mandate:

Oh! Buck and Breck are bound to win—
No power can stop their coming;
The Pennsylvania steed is lucky,
And so [is] the one from Old Kentucky
Pennsylvania's safe and lucky
So's the hoss from Old Kentucky.[6]

When he took the oath of office on 4 March 1857, John C. Breckinridge became the youngest vice-president in the nation's history.

Buchanan was not impressed by that fact. His letter of congratulations to Breckinridge after the nomination gave only very formal assurances of good will. After all, Breckinridge had supported both Pierce and Douglas over Buchanan in the convention. John C. thus entered the vice-presidency under suspicion and "wholly ignorant" of the president's plans. In fact, throughout the term he had little or no influence on Buchanan's actions. A cold reception in his first formal call on the chief executive was followed by only rare return visits. Friends received few appointments. By 1859 a newspaperman reported that "as the Administration falls lower every hour in prestige and political consequence, the star of the Vice-President rises higher." Such comments increased Buchanan's displeasure with Breckinridge. In a post with little power, under a president with no inclination to change the situation, the vice-president's sole compensation (such as it was) lay in presiding over the Senate.[7]

In November 1859, as his vice-presidency neared its end, Breckinridge was in Kentucky awaiting the result of his state legislature's vote for the United States Senate term that would begin in March 1861. Breckinridge, with eighty-one votes, gained the seat over Joshua F. Bell, with fifty-three. Now senator-elect as well as vice-president, the victor thanked the General Assembly in a speech on 21 December 1859. Not coincidentally, he addressed a wider audience as well, for within months presidential candidates would be chosen. Speaking neither for moderation nor for compromise, he accepted the Supreme Court's proslavery Dred Scott decision: "It accords with my own convictions." Slaves were property, and property must be protected in the territories under the Constitution. With William H. Seward's "irrepressible conflict" speech and John Brown's raid fresh in his memory, Breckinridge painted Republicans as seeking either complete surrender to "the doctrine of negro equality" or else violence. Brown's "ignorant and fanatical" forces had invaded a southern state; this was the forerunner of a "blazing border war" in which Kentucky would bear the brunt.[8]

Not only did Republicans approve Negro equality, Breckinridge maintained, but they also wanted to repeal the Fugitive Slave Law, to abolish slavery in the District of Columbia, and to emancipate all slaves immediately. The Democrat claimed such positions resulted in "alienation, discord, and finally hostile collisions." Resistance in some form is inevitable. . . . Resistance, I repeat, is certain." Though briefly alluding to the dangers of southern secession, he continued to advocate defeat of the Republican party, lest awful evils follow. Extreme proslavery men could not yet count Breckinridge as one of them, but if it came to a decision between two extremes, his course seemed already charted.[9]

The economics of slavery, however, would not determine John's choice. In the critical presidential election year of 1860, John C. Breckinridge probably held no slaves. That had not always been the case, and circumstance, more than anything else, made it so in 1860. Emancipation occasionally tugged on his conscience. In 1841, for instance, he had told his Uncle Robert that "ignorant, foolish men" were alarmed "by the cry of abolition." Reasoning people, he wrote, saw the correctness of Robert's emancipationist views. Yet such a belief did not keep him from buying slaves himself. In 1850 he owned five, ranging from eleven to fifty years of age. Following his vice-presidential election, Breckinridge moved his family to the capital, and the sale of a black woman and her six-week-old baby (for $1,100) in November 1857 probably liquidated his holdings.[10]

Influenced by emancipationists, yet a slaveholder—what did Breckinridge feel toward the institution? At one time he had been viewed as an ally of antislavery men: in 1850, as legislator, he aided the Kentucky Colonization Society; the next year a northern friend found in him a dislike of slavery; in his 1856 race he came under attack for allegedly abolitionist views. Former slaves, now free, received his loans and legal aid. Yet, throughout his career, his speeches and public actions gave little indication that he deeply desired to alter the status of slaves. John C. had strongly opposed the Wilmot Proviso concerning slavery in the territories; he had voted against his uncle when Robert ran on an Emancipation party ticket in 1849; he had favored the continuation of slavery in the 1850 Kentucky Constitution and supported both the Kansas-Nebraska Act and the Dred Scott decision; and, by 1859, he had called for protection of slave property in the territories. At no time did he ever characterize slavery as any kind of moral or economic albatross around the neck of the South. He simply ignored the slavery question except as a constitutional issue. Many of his fellow southerners used the same constitutional stance to cloak a defense based on several possible factors: racial fears, economics, or life style. The Kentuckian rarely indicated any of these hidden motives in his public or private thoughts. Instead he continued to defend the institution on abstract legal grounds. His veneration of the Constitution caused him to view emancipation as unconstitutional, since such a power was not specified in the document. Granting freedom to slaves thus would open the door to future dangers. Slavery would continue, and he would support it.[11]

As he entered the presidential year of 1860, then, John C. Breckinridge's views on what action should be taken in the slavery dispute remained publicly obscure—a fact that could gain him support from both North and South. But was he a candidate? Senator James H. Hammond of South Carolina told fire-eater Edmund Ruffin in early 1859 that Breckinridge was actively pursuing the nomination. President Buchanan, later in the year, said the same thing. In January 1860, however, John C. told both his uncle and a friend that he did not expect nomination: "I have neither said [n]or done any thing to encourage [such talk]—and am firmly resolved not to do so." Douglas believed otherwise. Convinced that the vice-president sought to advance one rung further up the political ladder, "the Little Giant" saw Breckinridge as his chief Democratic rival. The Kentuckian's lukewarm support in Douglas's 1858 senate race, the backing he received from the senator's opponents, and his recent endorsement of a federal slave code split the two former friends. In January 1860 it was reported that Douglas very much opposed Breckinridge. When Buchanan, somewhat reluctantly, used presidential patronage to support his vice-president, matters did not improve.[12]

Breckinridge's own actions that crucial spring and summer of 1860 were those of a man caught between conflicting forces. There is little question that he desired the presidency. But, like Douglas, he wanted to avoid appearing ambitious. Still young, Breckinridge always could run later; defeat in a factional battle might damage such a prospect. Seriously worried about the possibility of disunion, however, the vice-president was confident in his own ability to avoid that danger, if nominated and elected. He, then, chose to pursue a cautious course, thwarting no one and appearing as a logical second choice.

When the Democratic convention opened at Charleston, Breckinridge remained on correspondents' lists of possible nominees. Former governor Lazarus F. Powell, Kentucky representative and kinsman William Preston, Henry Clay's son James, and Breckinridge's law partner (and future U.S. Senator) James B. Beck acted as agents for the senator-elect. He told the latter that "under no circumstances" should his name be offered. As in 1856, another Kentuckian sought office, and Breckinridge openly pledged to support him. James Guthrie, Louisville and Nashville Railroad president, received the commonwealth's vote as the balloting began on 1 May 1860.[13]

For thirty-five ballots Douglas led by a wide margin but failed to gain the necessary two-thirds. Guthrie ran a consistent but distant second. On the next ballot, Arkansas cast its ballots for Breckinridge, but Beck rose and asked that the vote be withdrawn in accordance with the vice-president's wishes. Twenty-one further ballots changed the results only slightly. Deadlocked, the delegates adjourned. Baltimore was chosen as the site for the next attempt to nominate a candidate.[14]

Throughout the rest of May, Breckinridge acted and sounded more and more like a candidate. The Charleston proceedings would produce "great calamities, unless there is wisdom and forbearance . . . to redeem error at Baltimore," he predicted. To James Clay he disclosed Buchanan's position: "The President is not for me except as a last necessity, that is to say not until his help will not be worth a d_n." Turning to the forthcoming "caucus," Breckinridge told Clay not to present his name—unless it was evident that his strength and chances exceeded Guthrie's. "I have some hope," the vice-president added. That optimism proved well founded. After the "National Democratic Convention" met on 18 June and selected Douglas, the so-called "Seceders" met five days later. They quickly nominated Breckinridge. The candidate later maintained that his friends had presented his name "against my expressed wishes," and in his letter of formal acceptance and in later months he stressed that he had not sought the nomination.

In one sense, he was correct: a united party's support had been his hope at Baltimore. Now, if he accepted, he would split the party and probably ensure the election of a Republican.[15] In another sense, he was being less than candid, however. Nomination had been sought, under certain circumstances. Those circumstances never presented themselves fully, but Breckinridge now accepted the challenge of beating the "Black Republicans." If he did not run, someone else probably would, leaving the party still divided. Douglas, he declared, could not unite the Democracy. In his mind, he could. John C. explained to an intimate that the strength of both Douglas and himself would force both to withdraw, leaving the way open for a compromise candidate. One of Alexander Stephens' friends suggested another reason why Breckinridge did not refuse: "Mr. Toombs induced Breck to accept—asserted that he would carry the whole South like a storm, and that in less than 40 days he would have the field clear to himself—Douglas being withdrawn." Whether his motive was a noble effort to reunite the party through his sacrificial candidacy, or a more selfish one to drive out Douglas, Breckinridge was in the race to stay, opposing three candidates—Lincoln, Douglas, and John Bell of the Constitutional Union party.[16]

When it soon became clear that Douglas had no intention of dropping out, some form of compromise seemed the answer. In August reports circulated that the two Democratic candidates "are off the track and a new ticket in." Another observer felt *something in the wind*," and expected a Breckinridge withdrawal. Behind some of these rumors lay Jefferson Davis's quiet attempt to get Douglas, Breckinridge, and Bell all to withdraw in favor of a fourth person. But the bitterness of Douglas's friends toward Breckinridge, and Douglas's strong stand—"*We can have no partnership with the Bolters*"—made such a move impossible.[17]

Though young—not yet forty—Breckinridge was an experienced politician, and he realized that chances of victory were not promising. He knew that he must carry some northern states, yet Lincoln seemed strong in that region. To gain northern support Breckinridge would have to muffle talk that he represented secession and extremism. On the other hand, if he rejected his southern ties too strongly, the South might prefer Bell's candidacy to his. He never really solved this dilemma. Wags wrote that the candidate of the South "is chiefly noted for his eloquent silence on all public occasions." When he did speak, the opposition, with some justification, found his sentiments vague and hollow. Campaign addresses repeated old and familiar themes. Speaking at Frankfort in July, Breckinridge answered the increasing attacks upon him: "Pour on, I can endure." A just cause gave him strength, for he knew that the "pure Constitution" had state equality as its fundamental principle. "Men are nothing, principles are everything. Come Kentucky! Prove you are not degenerate sons of the men of '98. Assert the equality of your Commonwealth." Following the speech, a *New York Times* reporter wrote that John C. and Robert J. Breckinridge shared similar sympathies but the nephew could not resist "the fatal tide." Though not a friend of the southern extremists, John was "tainted with sectionalism and Disunion. His skirts smell of secession and treason! There is a spot and a wrinkle on his fame." The writer added: "His birth and aristocratic relations cannot save him."[18]

Under attack on two fronts—as both an emancipationist and a proslavery secessionist—Breckinridge decided to make one final, major speech, at Henry Clay's old "Ashland" estate in Lexington. He would try to rid himself of both labels. "If there is an individual here," he asked, "who ever heard or knew of my sympathizing with the doctrines advanced by Rev. R. J. Breckinridge, let him now speak." Silence answered him. Never an emancipationist, he had campaigned in 1849 "to the best of my ability in opposition to emancipation." With less force, the vice-president turned to his supposed disunionism. The platform he ran on was a constitutional one, one that would "preserve the equality and restore the harmony of the States." To him the goals of the disunionists were clearly visible:

> See yourselves environed and closed in upon with steady and relentless steps. State after State enacting laws, making it penal in the people to assist the officers of the United States to execute the laws which protect your rights; armed mobs making rescues from the Marshal and refusing to surrender prisoners; a thorough anti-slavery opinion maturing and taking the form of political action in the Northern States; inroads in every direction—at Harper's Ferry; arsons in Texas; the South environed and beset; the Constitution thrown with contempt into her face; the purpose avowed to exclude her from all the vast common domain of the Union, and thus to begin that "irrepressible conflict" which must end in the abolition of slavery in the States.

In a sense, Breckinridge had surrendered to the emotionalism of the campaign.

Friends expected John to answer the "Norfolk Questions." If Lincoln was elected, Douglas had been asked at Norfolk, Virginia, would the South be justified in seceding from the Union? Douglas answered no. If the South did secede before Lincoln committed an overt act, would you advise resistance by force to that secession? Douglas answered yes. Breckinridge sidestepped the questions, and this "dodging," as the opposition press called it, did not satisfy some Breckinridge Democrats. Emancipationist Cassius Clay's earlier prediction that Breckinridge's "star has set—that his destiny is fixed," now seemed closer to the truth.[19]

Breckinridge had not increased his slim chances of victory. He had recognized at the time of his nomination what might occur. "I trust I have the courage to lead a forlorn hope," he told Mrs. Jefferson Davis then. Her husband, as well as Toombs and other southern leaders, assumed a fatalistic attitude as election day neared, and results did not surprise them. The electoral majority went to Lincoln with 180, followed by Breckinridge with 72, Bell with 39, and Douglas with 12.[20]

Portrayed as the candidate of the slaveowning, landed aristocracy, how then did Breckinridge run? In Kentucky, which he lost, his strongest support came from the eastern Kentucky mountains, an area of small farmers and few slaves. (Johnson County, where he ran best, was the third smallest slaveholding county in the state.) Most of those counties supported the Union cause later. They did not vote for John C. Breckinridge as secessionist or slaveholder. A more accurate indicator of voting patterns than slaveholding in Kentucky was the party voting pattern of the recent past. Men voted for John C. Breckinridge, Democrat.[21]

In the rest of the slave states of the border and Upper South, with a few exceptions, and in all the Lower South, urban areas preferred Douglas or Bell over Breckinridge. The Kentuckian polled his greatest majorities and pluralities among rural, native-born southerners. The fewer the number of slaves in a county, the more likely it was to back Breckinridge. He carried two of every three counties that had a low slave population. In counties where large numbers of slaves lived—counties that might be expected to be dominated by large planters—his vote declined comparatively. Constitutional Unionist Bell did much better than Breckinridge in black-belt counties, for example. Though a majority of counties carried by Breckinridge were secessionist in sentiment later, when broken down further the picture changes. The areas of the Lower South where he gained his greatest support (generally, the counties low in slaves) did not favor secession. Douglas's contemporary assertion— that, while all the Breckinridge men in the United States were not disunionists, there was "not a disunionist in America who is not a Breckinridge man"—has been widely accepted. But if secession sentiment is carelessly tied directly and only to secession and slave ownership ("slaveholders supported Breckinridge"), then Breckinridge's vote suggests that a reevaluation is in order. Other factors—such as party feeling and economic conditions—must also be considered.[22]

Breckinridge returned to Washington after suffering his first, and only, political defeat. As vice-president, he still had a service to perform. On 13 February 1861, it was his task to announce the presidential vote. A little pale and nervous, but in an unfaltering voice, Breckinridge declared that "Abraham Lincoln, of Illinois, having received a majority of the whole number of electoral votes, is elected President." Already seven southern states had seceded, setting up a provisional Confederate government and withdrawing most of their representatives from Congress. Like those men, he would have to make a decision. On 4 March the vice-president wished his colleagues prosperity and happiness, thanked them for their courtesy, swore in Hannibal Hamlin as his successor, then adjourned the Senate *sine die*. Hamlin quickly ordered a special session and turned to the swearing-in of new senators. John C. Breckinridge took the oath of office and joined fellow Democratic senators Powell, Douglas, and Johnson. On the Republican side sat Charles Sumner and Henry Wilson of Massachusetts, Salmon P. Chase and Benjamin F. Wade of Ohio, William P. Fessenden of Maine, Zachariah Chandler of Michigan, and others. Representing the seat that compromisers Clay and Crittenden had filled, Breckinridge would find compromise all but impossible.

Within a month the new senator uttered prophetic words regarding his future course. Supporting "the theory contained in the Kentucky resolutions of '98," Breckinridge told the state legislature that commonwealths must, in the end, be the final judge. Before them were "radical, uncompromising" abolitionists in control of the government, a future that held the promise of slavery's end, and the approaching "political and social curse" of free blacks on the face of the land. To Breckinridge, constitutional liberty and national principles seemed on the verge of destruction. Kentucky must expect to leave a government that offered no protection and enter a "sanctuary" where pure principles would remain untainted. He did not mention the Confederate States, but few doubted what sanctuary he meant.[23]

His course in the next few months remains perhaps the most inexplicable of his life. His sympathies obviously lay with the South, yet he stayed in the United States Congress for a long period after the fighting erupted. Increasingly he fought his fights alone, against almost the entire Senate. The question is not why Breckinridge finally joined the South, but rather why he waited so long to do so. Kentucky's brief neutral course could have influenced his delay, but when he finally united with the southern cause, the state's sentiments still furnished no clear course to follow. The specter of war haunted him. He acknowledged the rights of the southern states to secede but wanted desperately to avoid fraternal war. "Some of us came to this session of Congress," Breckinridge told the Senate, "with a lingering hope that something might yet be done to avert war." Hoping for words of peace, they had been disappointed: "The man who speaks of peace is looked upon with suspicion." Let the Confederacy alone, and "all those sentiments of common interest and feeling . . . might lead to a political reunion founded upon consent." War would bring nothing but "ruin, utter ruin" to all sections. Now two confederacies existed. With war, in a year America would have three confederacies; in two years, perhaps four. Foreign nations would prey on them all. America, as men knew it, would disappear like Atlantis. As late as August 1861 the Kentucky senator still believed the war he earlier sought to avoid could be stopped. "I infinitely prefer to see a peaceful separation of these states," he told his audience, "than to see endless, aimless, devastating war."[24]

Breckinridge feared the conflict on two counts—its effects on both the Constitution and civil liberties. In March he had talked of his theories and outlook: "I believe, administered according to the true principles of the Constitution, [this government] is the best on earth; and for myself, neither in public nor in private life, will I ever consent to sacrifice the principles of constitutional freedom, of municipal liberty, and of state equality, to the naked idea of Federal Unity." Republicans had "perverted" the Constitution, he declared. By refusing to recognize property in slaves, by refusing to give slavery equal protection in the territories, the Republican party had forced an "impassable gulf" between the two sections. The compact was being broken, and Kentucky would not accept that: "She will exhaust all honorable means to reunite these States; but if that fails, she will not lay her bright and beaming forehead in the dust." Turning to its "southern sisters," Kentucky would unite with them "to found a noble Republic, and invite beneath its stainless banner such other states as know how to keep the faith of compacts."[25]

By July Breckinridge, convinced that this was a "War of Subjugation," a "War of extermination," declared that the Constitution was being "deliberately trampled under foot." By what authority had the President proclaimed a blockade? Was not the act of Lincoln enlisting men for three years "an unconstitutional and illegal act"? Did not suspension of the writ of habeas corpus harken back to the actions of English monarchs long dead? Who had declared war—Congress? Had Congress, as the Constitution specified, appropriated all the money used by the Republican leader? Were the people exempt from unreasonable search and seizure? With an executive assuming legislative and judicial powers, "we are rushing, and with rapid strides, from a constitutional government to a military despotism." Breckinridge saw all around him a tendency to establish a government "without limitations of powers," a government that proposed to change radically the character of the republic. He would fight that tendency, hoping that "this flash of frenzy may not assume the form of chronic madness, and that . . . Divine Providence may preserve for us and for posterity, out of the wreck of a broken Union, the priceless principles of constitutional liberty and of self-government."[26]

By this time the Kentuckian stood almost alone in Washington. He still opposed the war. On a resolution pledging "the entire resources of the Government" to the fight, only Breckinridge voted no. Fellow senators scoffed when he remarked that never did he utter one word "or cherish one thought that was false to the Constitution and Union of my country." Edward D. Baker of Oregon responded to a Breckinridge speech by saying: "Sir, are they not words of brilliant, polished treason, even in the very capital of the Confederacy?" When the session ended in August 1861, John C. Breckinridge returned to Lexington.[27] If he had gone to Washington that year to prevent a war, he had failed. If he had sought to register a protest against unconstitutional actions, he had seen few results. Should he go on serving a nation that—to his mind—was destroying all he cherished? Could he justify, on the other hand, abandoning the Union? Events in Kentucky soon made the decision easier.

Rumors that Lincoln was sending arms to pro-Union Kentuckians strengthened Breckinridge's belief that the president sought something other than peace. The news that General John C. Fremont had published a limited emancipation plan confirmed his predictions. The invasion of the state by Confederates in September, followed by the Union forces a few days later, did not change his feelings. Neutrality could still remain the commonwealth's course. Speaking in Mason County, Breckinridge gave young men no vision of glories to be won in battle. He talked instead of "grim war, with death and devastation in train, with ruin for every interest, and sable for many a hearthstone. The thought of it makes my heart ache." In this year at least, Breckinridge did not want to fight, but he was too prominent a public figure to be ignored. His public statements placed his loyalties in a questionable position. When Kentucky abandoned neutrality, Union men arrested former governor Charles S. Morehead and shut down the prosouthern Louisville Courier. Word reached Breckinridge that Union Colonel Thomas E. Bramlett sought his arrest next. He prepared to flee. At the Phoenix Hotel in Lexington, Breckinridge smiled sadly as son Clifton eagerly helped his father pack. It was an adventurous time for a young boy, but Breckinridge did not share the youthful excitement. What lay ahead, he knew, would not be pleasant.[28]

Ten

Mount and Away

ON 8 OCTOBER 1861, in Confederate-occupied Bowling Green, Kentucky, John C. Breckinridge explained his recent actions to the people of Kentucky. In a printed manifesto he told them that southerners no longer had any place in Washington councils. Despotism and executive usurpation had buried constitutional rights beneath the heel of the military. Kentucky's "new protectors" likewise had swept away all vestiges of public and personal liberty so that "mobs and anarchy rule the hour." Then, harking to Revolutionary War themes, Breckinridge asked if Kentucky would allow Lincoln's "German mercenaries" to imprison the children of founders of the commonwealth. As for himself, he intended to resist. Dramatically, the new Confederate concluded, "I exchange with proud satisfaction a term of six years in the United States Senate for the musket of a soldier."[1]

The former Major Breckinridge of the Mexican War soon received a commission as brigadier general, under the immediate command of Simon Bolivar Buckner and overall command of Albert Sidney Johnston—both native Kentuckians. While with the army he learned that in early December the U.S. Senate had expelled "the traitor Breckinridge." The politician had now been fully transformed into the soldier. As William C. Davis notes, a "curious paradox" resulted, for Breckinridge had "a character and intellect naturally adapted for leadership in the profession of arms, but a heart and soul whose revulsion for war's bloody work would leave him wandering down another path, toward great sadness."[2] The bloody work of war would occupy the man of peace for three and a half long years. Most of the first years he spent as a subordinate commander in the Army of Tennessee. As commander of the reserve division at Shiloh, he performed well, in the judgment of General P. G. T. Beauregard. But of some seven thousand men in his unit, the dead numbered 386, the wounded 1,682. The retreat left Breckinridge to hold back the enemy; he accomplished the task despite limited rations, bad weather, and "worn-out" troops. President Davis soon promoted him to major general.[3]

After going to Vicksburg in expectation of an attack which did not materialize, Breckinridge moved his four thousand men southward toward Baton Rouge, which had been captured by the Union forces in May 1862. The march turned into disaster as heat, sickness, and lack of shelter left him with a thousand fewer effectives when he reached his destination. Unhesitatingly he attacked and pushed the federal forces back, but he had to retire when Union gunboats made his position untenable. Over 450 of his men were killed, wounded, or missing. After the battle, the dead could not be buried because of too few picks and shovels. Half of the surviving soldiers had no coats; hundreds wore no shoes; shelter, water, and food were unavailable or "indifferent." When Breckinridge returned to Vicksburg, less than half the troops who had left with him could be considered available for duty.[4]

When Confederate forces invaded Kentucky in the fall of 1862, Breckinridge received orders to join them. At last he would see his home state and once there could attract recruits. With a motley division of "exchanged prisoners and unarmed regiments," he marched to within twenty-eight miles of his home state, then heard the news of Braxton Bragg's retreat after the Battle of Perryville. Kentuckians in the ranks received the news quietly. Tears fell. As they turned toward Knoxville, the tattered troops shouted, half in defiance, half in desperation. At Murfreesboro, Tennessee, on a cold January afternoon in 1863, Breckinridge followed Bragg's orders and commanded some of those same soldiers to charge across a deadly open space. Initial success, at a price, was followed by increasing Union artillery fire, "heavy, accurate, and destructive." Confederate forces abandoned the captured positions, and the entire army eventually retreated. Breckinridge lost nearly one-third of his command.[5]

The cold of Murfreesboro was followed by the dry, choking dust of Mississippi. Sent to aid in Vicksburg's defense, the command marched and countermarched, but the city fell. Rejoining Bragg, Breckinridge fought at Chickamauga, again suffering heavy casualties. Victory there brought the army to Chattanooga, where Breckinridge's forces retreated before the federal assault that gave Ulysses S. Grant his last western victory and Bragg his last western defeat. The latter requested relief from command soon after, criticizing Breckinridge before he did.[6]

Significantly, such criticisms seldom came from Breckinridge's troops. They noticed, for example, that he played no favorites. Cabell, an aide to his father, was seldom protected; at Shiloh his horse had been killed. The general, in ordering his oldest child to the midst of dangers, remarked that, with the sons of widows in battle, "I must not shield my son from the dangers of his comrades." At Chickamauga, Theodore O'Hara asked Breckinridge not to send Cabell on a dangerous mission. "With great emotion," he refused the request. Lieutenant Breckinridge was captured at Missionary Ridge on 25 November 1863; he was later exchanged and rejoined his father.[7]

The general also shared the trials of his troops. On the many occasions when it seemed impossible to provide subsistence for the command, somehow he did so. After the battle of Chattanooga, he took time to tell a courier to whom he had spoken harshly in the heat of battle that he had done him a great injustice. Soldiers received inspiration from the mere sight of the general. With his heavy slouch hat and blouse of Kentucky jeans material, the commander at first might not impress observers, but usually they realized their mistake. A staff officer at Shiloh thought Breckinridge "the most impressive-looking man I ever had seen." One officer remembered him as the finest-looking man in the saddle that he had observed. After watching the army's general officers ride by, a foot soldier noted that when it came to looks, *"that Breckinridge of ours ranks them all."* Astride a beautiful bay horse at Chickamauga, the Kentucky general seemed to one observer to be as indifferent to the shells falling around him as if he had been on dress parade: "I never saw a more godlike hero than Breckinridge at that moment." On another occasion General Basil Duke, too, emphasized this quality: "I have never, I think, witnessed an indifference to danger so absolutely calm and imperturbable as I have seen him display under very extraordinary exposure to personal peril." Similarly, General John Echols termed him "a very Chevalier Bayard, without fear and without reproach," a man who inspired enthusiasm and confidence in his men. Even-tempered and self-controlled, Breckinridge seldom exerted authority harshly. He cared deeply for his men. After a festive evening in Richmond, Virginia, amid gaiety and laughter, he was asked whether he had enjoyed himself. "I do not know," he replied. "I have asked myself more than once tonight, 'Are you the same man who stood gazing down on the faces of the dead . . . ?' The soldiers lying there, they stare at you with their eyes wide open. Is this the same world?"[8]

Breckinridge did not have to live always in the world of dead men, amputees, the wounded, and the sick. Fortunately, his wife remained near, and escape from the war—albeit a short and temporary one—could be found with her. Owen, Fanny, and little Mary had remained with relatives near Georgetown, but after staying with them for a time John's wife, Mary, had moved southward. Wherever her husband went, she followed as closely as possible. At Murfreesboro and Chattanooga she waited, ready to aid John should he be injured. "I feel I must go to you—I cannot stay away." "I do not mind privations and trials if you and my children are spared." In the silent hours of night unhidden tears stole down her cheeks, at the thought of John and sons Cabell and Clift. Her constant prayer was that they would survive. If John should wish her presence, all he had to do was to say the word, for she kept a trunk packed and ready.[9]

The hours alone, the time apart from John, Mary spent in the work of a dutiful wife of a Confederate general. She made bandages for the wounded (sometimes at the expense of her clothing), oversaw the making of hospital soap, and sewed a flag for a regiment in John's division. For her family she made or repaired jackets, pants, slippers, flannels, collars, and linens. Malarial fever in October 1863 left her for a time without hearing and almost blind, but she recovered. John's own health remained good, with some minor exceptions. At Shiloh, he alone in a group of officers emerged unscathed. On one occasion he was struck by two spent bullets; several horses were shot from under him in battle. Despite his lack of precaution, the wound Mary feared never came to Breckinridge.[10]

Away from his family, in battle, Breckinridge performed well overall. By his example, by his unfailing courage, he inspired his troops, and at Baton Rouge and Chickamauga the general commanded the forces as well as he motivated them. In some other battles, however, his record was more debatable. Courage at Shiloh did not overcome a failure by Breckinridge to supervise his entire command. And before his attack on that disastrous January morning at Murfreesboro, Breckinridge had not moved his troops as he perhaps should have. Throughout his stint with the Army of Tennessee he failed to use his cavalry to best advantage. While Breckinridge may not have stood "without peer" among division commanders of the Army of Tennessee, as a political general and a non–West Pointer, he certainly commanded as well as, and in many instances better than, his fellow generals. The Kentuckian's chief asset lay not in his strategical abilities but in his remarkable rapport with the soldiers. General John B. Gordon saw in him "in a marked degree the characteristics of a great commander" because he inspired troops with enthusiasm and ardor. If not a masterful tactician, he was a natural leader.[11]

The admiration for Breckinridge did not extend to Braxton Bragg. Sickly, sour-tempered, and stooped, Bragg looked older than his years; his cold eyes beneath dark brows did not move men in the way that the sight of Breckinridge did. Nor did Breckinridge's ties to powerful blocs in the army help the Bragg-Breckinridge association. Related to many commanders (Joseph E. Johnston, Wade Hampton, John B. Floyd, William Preston, and others), Breckinridge held strong allegiance to what has been called "the Kentucky bloc." Outcasts in a sense, serving a state occupied consistently by Union troops, the congressmen and generals from Kentucky kept close connections with their comrades from that state. As one of the unifying forces of this group, Breckinridge served as symbol. Bragg's dislike of Breckinridge surfaced when the Kentuckian failed to reach his home state in the 1862 invasion. The blame lay elsewhere but was put on Breckinridge. Following the Murfreesboro fiasco (for which Bragg indeed had much responsibility), Bragg sent to Richmond and had published a report very critical of Breckinridge. Remarks by O'Hara and Preston, members of Breckinridge's staff, added to the fires. Bragg virtually dismantled Breckinridge's Kentucky division, so that not a single brigade that served under him in the spring was retained by autumn. Envisioning a conspiracy against him, Bragg reacted against Breckinridge as a leader of a clique.[12]

The supposed leader did not take it all quietly. In a letter to the adjutant general of the army, Breckinridge answered that Bragg's report on Murfreesboro "fails . . . to do justice to the behavior of my Division." Such "injurious statements" must be refuted. In fact his troops had been ordered to do the impossible. Bragg, not he, should be censured. Breckinridge requested but did not receive a court of inquiry. Kentucky congressmen criticized Bragg and asked that their comrade's report be published.[13] His attack on Breckinridge and criticism of the Kentuckians' fighting ability, as well as his own failure to retake Kentucky, made Bragg generally unpopular among the Kentucky bloc. Enlisted men and some Kentucky officers called on Breckinridge to resign and challenge Bragg to a duel. The commanding general's report rankled among soldiers already angered by Bragg's actions just before Murfreesboro. At that time a young corporal who had left the army to care for his wife and children in Kentucky was arrested as a deserter, court-martialed, and sentenced to die. He pleaded that he was in fact returning to his unit when captured, but despite calls for mercy from Kentucky officers Bragg refused to reconsider, citing a need for an example. With the incensed Kentucky Brigade watching, the soldier was executed. Breckinridge, "seized with a deathly sickness," dropped forward on his horse and required help from his staff. Bragg's conduct after Murfreesboro increased an already smouldering anger within Breckinridge.[14]

The battle of Chattanooga ended Bragg's career as commander of the Army of Tennessee. Angry, certain that Breckinridge was in part responsible, he blamed the defeat on the favorite of the Kentucky bloc. Drunkenness had incapacitated the Kentuckian at a crucial time, Bragg charged. Some historians have accepted the accusation or have pictured Breckinridge as a hard drinker. A recent biographer, in a lengthy defense of Breckinridge, refutes the allegation, calling him only a "moderate drinker." The Kentuckian certainly enjoyed a reputation as a man who liked one of his state's best-known products, and admirers and friends sent him whiskey as a favorite gift. Bragg's charges, though, have little foundation, except in Breckinridge's reputation as a man who liked to drink but who could handle his liquor well.[15]

It was not out of character for Breckinridge to react as he reportedly did in 1865, when arranging surrender terms with General William T.

Sherman. General Joseph E. Johnston told the story to a friend, and it was later published:

"You know how fond of his liquor Breckinridge was? . . ." added General Johnston as he went on with his story. "Well, nearly everything to drink had been absorbed. For several days, Breckinridge had found it difficult, if not impossible, to procure liquor. He showed the effect of his enforced abstinence. He was rather dull and heavy that morning. Somebody in Danville had given him a plug of very fine chewing tobacco, and he chewed vigorously while we were awaiting Sherman's coming. After a while, the latter arrived. . . . Some one suggested that we had better take up the matter in hand.

"'Yes,' said Sherman: 'but, gentlemen, it occurred to me that perhaps you were not overstocked with liquor, and I procured some medical stores on my way over. Will you join me before we begin work?' "

General Johnston said he watched the expression of Breckinridge at this announcement, and it was beatific. Tossing his quid into the fire, he rinsed his mouth, and when the bottle and the glass were passed to him, he poured out a tremendous drink, which he swallowed with great satisfaction. With an air of content, he stroked his mustache and took a fresh chew of tobacco.

Then they settled down to business, and Breckinridge never shone more brilliantly than he did in the discussions which followed. He seemed to have at his tongue's end every rule and maxim of international and constitutional law. . . . In fact, he was so resourceful, cogent, persuasive, learned, that, at one stage of the proceedings, General Sherman, when confronted by the authority, but not convinced by the eloquence or learning of Breckinridge, pushed back his chair and exclaimed: "See here, gentlemen, who is doing this surrendering anyhow?"

Sherman sat for some time absorbed in deep thought. Then he arose, went to the saddlebags, and fumbled for the bottle. Breckinridge saw the movement. Again he took the quid from his mouth and tossed it into the fireplace. His eye brightened, and he gave every evidence of intense interest in what Sherman seemed about to do.

The latter, preoccupied, perhaps unconscious of his action, poured out some liquor, shoved the bottle back into the saddle-pocket, walked to the window, and stood there, looking out abstractedly, while he sipped his grog.

From a pleasant hope and expectation the expression on Breckinridge's face changed successively to uncertainty, disgust, and deep depression. At last his hand sought the plug of tobacco, and, with an injured, sorrowful look, he cut off another chew. Upon this he ruminated during the remainder of the interview, taking little part in what was said. . . .

General Johnston took occasion, as they left the house and were drawing on their gloves, to ask General Breckinridge how he had been impressed by Sherman.

"Sherman is a bright man, and a man of great force," replied Breckinridge, speaking with deliberation, "but," raising his voice and with a look of great intensity, "General Johnston, General Sherman is a hog. Yes, sir, a *hog*. Did you see him take that drink by himself? . . . No Kentucky gentleman would ever have taken away that bottle. He knew we needed it, and needed it badly."[16]

Such accounts of Breckinridge's fondness for drink contained only a modicum of truth but would be the basis for many later assertions—generally unfounded—that would support Bragg's excuses for his own failings.

In Richmond in the winter of 1863–64, the Kentuckian, according to one observer, paced "like a caged lion," rarely sitting down. Although a favorite of the capital's society, he still longed to redeem his name and honor, besmirched by Bragg's charges. On 15 February 1864 Breckinridge received orders relieving him from command in the Army of Tennessee. Soon, however, he was given command of the Trans-Allegheny or Western Department of Virginia, a vast but valuable territory known as the "graveyard of Confederate generals." Relieving his predecessor in March, Breckinridge found a state of "*social* war" existing in the more mountainous part of his command and began to plan and consolidate for the attacks that must come. The troops reacted positively to their new leader. An aide wrote that Breckinridge's impressive bearing in the "sober garb of a civilian" would excite a stranger's admiration. But in the uniform of a general, superbly mounted "as he always was, he was the very embodiment of manly grace." The soldiers soon would hail "the new Jackson."[17]

The clash of arms restored Breckinridge's prestige. In a "brilliant" battle at New Market in May, he faced an enemy superior in numbers and won decisively in what has been termed "the finest day in his military career." Using his artillery well, displaying the courage of earlier battles, Breckinridge forced a federal retreat. Richmond again talked of the "dashing commander" in the Valley. Moving to aid Lee in his struggle with Grant, Breckinridge narrowly missed death when a cannonball struck his horse, pinning him beneath it. Temporarily disabled, the general left his sickbed (on Lee's urging) to return to the Valley when the Union forces again advanced. Joining his good friend General Jubal A. Early, Breckinridge marched northward. Successful in turning back the federal army in the area, Early invaded Maryland. Breckinridge got close enough to Washington to see the dome of the capitol he had left three years earlier. General Early joked that he would let Breckinridge lead the column and invited him to sit in the vice-president's chair once more. Such light moments did not last long. The army retreated and, after the battle of Winchester, never threatened to advance again.[18]

The aftermath of one of those rare triumphs left more bitterness than did a defeat. Confederates repulsed Union General Stephen G. Burbridge's Kentucky forces at Saltville on 2 October 1864, and the fleeing federals left behind many wounded, a good number of them black soldiers. The next morning, gunfire filled the fog-covered valley. Wounded blacks were being killed, and a young Confederate later wrote, "We surely slew negroes that day." Kentuckian James B. Clay, Jr., wrote his mother two weeks afterwards: "I assure you it was a great pleasure the next morning to go over the field & see so many Lexingtonians of the African decent [sic] lying mangled & bleeding on the hills." Not in the fury of battle, but in a cold-blooded massacre, soldiers killed about a hundred of the wounded. A boy of not more than sixteen lined seven or eight blacks along a wall and then shot them. No orders had been given; the men, said one participant, simply could not be restrained. Breckinridge heard the firing, and "with blazing eyes and thunderous tones," ordered the massacre stopped. To the long nightmare of war another haunting chapter had been added. The horrors Breckinridge warned of in 1861 had visited him once again.[19]

A weary Breckinridge left all this behind when he went to Richmond in January 1865. Rumors that he had been offered the portfolio of the Confederate War Department vied with other rumors that Congress opposed this because Breckinridge had joined the Confederacy so late. Yet the popular general had been given the privilege of the floor of the Senate, and President Davis knew Breckinridge from their congressional days. Thus it surprised few when the Kentuckian was appointed secretary of war. On 7 February 1865 Breckinridge took over the affairs of the War Department, to operate in that capacity until the Confederacy died.[20]

Breckinridge served admirably in difficult times. William C. Davis even suggests that he proved to be the "most capable and efficient" of all the secretaries of war. For, unlike other secretaries, Breckinridge would be his own man—not President Davis's. Well qualified by service in all commands except the Trans-Mississippi, he received the confidence of the Confederate Congress, which backed him in his actions. Eventually he assigned officers, recommended promotions, advised Lee and Johnston on strategy, and generally strengthened his office. While not impressing one of his subordinates initially ("the new secretary is evidently not a man of papers") Breckinridge soon immersed himself in the ocean of orders. "Overwhelmed with work," he told a friend, he stayed up past midnight working at the new job. Assuming his duties under different circumstances than those of his predecessors, the last Confederate secretary of war took advantage of the situation to function more independently.[21]

Breckinridge's duties ultimately included organizing the evacuation of Richmond as Grant's armies drew near. One of the last leaders to leave the city, he ordered the James River bridges burned. Clifton Rodes Breckinridge resigned as acting midshipman and joined his father in flight. By 23 April 1865 the secretary of war had reached Charlotte, where he and other cabinet officers advised President Davis. With the ports closed, foreign supply sources lost, urban areas captured, and armies decimated, reasonable hope of success had disappeared. General Johnston, Breckinridge pointed out, should be allowed to surrender. If such suggestions were ignored, the contest would probably "lose entirely the dignity of regular warfare." He concluded: "The situation is anomalous and cannot be solved upon principles of theoretical exactitude." Preparing for the possibility that Davis might reject the advice, Breckinridge asked Johnston to send some cavalry and artillery to the fugitive Confederate government.[22]

Pressing southward, the small contingent appeared to be aiming for the Trans-Mississippi theater. Trouble erupted over $150,000 in gold specie in the Confederate treasury. Some soldiers in the escort demanded the money, and mob action seemed likely. Dressed in an old hunting jacket, Breckinridge told them that they were gentlemen, not highwaymen, and must live honorably, not in disgrace. Each would, in time, be given his share. A soldier recalled of those days: "I believe General Breckinridge was the finest-looking man I ever saw." His eyes—"clear, penetrating, magnetic and commanding"—searched the recesses of their souls. The men dispersed.[23]

When Davis was finally captured at Irwinville, Georgia, Breckinridge was already moving southward in Florida, attempting to escape from the United States. In company with John Taylor Wood (the grandson of Zachary Taylor and former commander of the raider *Tallahassee*), several other soldiers, and his body servant Tom Ferguson, Breckinridge began the trek. His fears for personal safety were real ones. General Sherman had personally advised Breckinridge to flee, explaining that the North felt especially bitter toward the former vice-president who took up arms against the government. The atmosphere following Lincoln's assassination increased the bitterness, and the *New York Times* suggested that "the leading traitors" should die on the gallows. By June three former Confederate cabinet members, Vice-President Stephens, and President Davis were all imprisoned. Breckinridge determined early that he would not suffer such a fate.[24]

What followed enhanced the Breckinridge legend and surrounded an already appealing figure with even more romance. Here was a dashing, charismatic Confederate leader fleeing from Union pursuers. Swarms of mosquitoes, ticks, sand-flies, and other insects of every description tormented him as he fled through Florida. In a boat too small to lie down in, the party rowed along the rivers of the area for days. Alligators surrounded them; rain soaked their food; hunger reduced them to eating turtle eggs, sour oranges, green limes, and coconuts. A federal steamer stopped them for questioning but "by dint of looking stupid" they quieted suspicions by posing as hunters.

Needing a larger boat to cross to Cuba, the "sailors" commandeered at gunpoint a larger craft. Still without food and drinking "blackish" water, they chanced stopping at an old fort peopled by a motley group. Seeing Breckinridge's gold, these scavengers attacked the boat, but after some ineffective gunfire a truce was arranged and food secured. Almost

General John C. Breckinridge. Painted in 1899 by E.F. Andrews; courtesy
Kentucky Museum, Western Kentucky University

as quickly, all was thrown overboard so the fugitives could again flee a Union steamer. By pulling their boat over a reef to shallow water, they escaped the deeper-drafted ship as its cannon fire fell short. Finally, after over three days on the ocean, the sloop *No Name* sailed into Cardenas, Cuba, on 11 June 1865. General Breckinridge—bronzed, unshaven, his feet swollen by salt water but the long mustache still intact, wearing a blue flannel suit open at the neck and an old slouch hat—was welcomed as a conquering hero.[25]

Two weeks after his arrival in Cuba newspapers glorified Breckinridge's escape. A reporter at Havana wrote that the episode "may yet form the groundwork of an exciting novel or thrilling drama." Meanwhile a wealthy merchant put his purse at Breckinridge's disposal, and a hotel offered to board him without a charge. The robust frame that men remembered had suffered from the deprivations of the escape, and, an observer noted, the general "is frequently lost in fits of abstraction." Moody and taciturn, he spoke only to intimate friends.

John had earlier expressed his hope that the time was "not far distant when he could, and would return to his old Kentucky home."[26] But not for almost four more years would he go back to the state he had not seen since 1861. After leaving Cuba for England, he sailed back across the Atlantic to Canada and asked for asylum. In Toronto he was reunited with Mary and all the children except Clifton. To the absent offspring, Breckinridge advised, "Always select the best, most well bred and instructive society you can find—avoid low company, and vulgar cant, and ungrammatical expressions—*don't drink.*" The father, while in better health, still looked older than his forty-four years and needed frequent rest.[27] On 8 August 1866, the family sailed to Great Britain, and the next year and a half was filled with tours throughout Europe and the Near East. Breckinridge attended debates in the House of Commons, dined with William Gladstone and Thomas Carlyle, saw the French emperor, attended the races, and renewed friendships with former Confederates in exile. A British member of Parliament found the Kentuckian "among those who had most irresistibly struck me with a feeling of ability and ready power." In November 1867 Breckinridge began a tour of Europe, the Near East, and particularly the Holy Land. For three months he wandered, finally arriving in Naples in February 1868 for a reunion with Mary. They went to Rome, enjoyed riding, observed a fox hunt, and attended balls; the nephew of three anti-Catholic clergymen even had an audience with Pope Pius IX. At last the family left Italy for England; from Liverpool, they returned to Canada in June. At their Niagara home, the Breckinridges were reunited with Cabell, Clifton, and Mary—all together for the first time since the war.[28]

John C. Breckinridge could not yet cross the boundary that separated him from the United States. Influential men sought to remove the indict-

John C. Breckinridge with family and friends in Canadian exile; son Clifton is the youngest male. Courtesy Kentucky Historical Society

ments for treason. Kentucky editor George D. Prentice in 1865 asked both Robert J. Breckinridge and General John M. Palmer (commander of the federal forces in the state) to allow the absentee's return. Both advised against it. In 1867 Horace Greeley thought it "a pity" that the former leader in Kentucky could not be among his people to give them wise counsel. Soon after the reunion with his children in 1868, Breckinridge received a letter from a correspondent who had spoken with President Andrew Johnson, a former colleague. No apprehension should exist, said the letter, for Johnson promised to intervene in any difficulties. Perhaps realizing the president's political impotence, Breckinridge remained away. In November and December 1868 the calls for Breckinridge's repatriation increased. James Beck, now representing the Ashland district in Congress, told his former law partner that Johnson promised to sign any request Breckinridge might make for pardon. Other friends talked with the president and relayed the same information. A proud man, Breckinridge made no request. He would not admit error, if convinced that error it was. But on Christmas Day Johnson granted an amnesty that affected Breckinridge. The years of exile could now end.[29]

Kentuckians had not forgotten Breckinridge. Two years earlier, amid the "wildest enthusiasm & cheering," Democrats in one Kentucky county had made him their nominee for governor. In the spring of 1868, a story in a Cincinnati paper told that Breckinridge, during his escape, read Bulwer's *Athens, Its Rise and Fall*. At one stop the general gazed westward, then turned to his men and recited thirty lines of verse praising the South. "We remained almost spell-bound by the grandeur of the occasion," one remembered. The silence was broken when Breckinridge called to them, "Mount and away." Such memories kept the Breckinridge name alive and brought with it pleasant associations and past glories.[30]

Kentucky newspapers now followed his progress as he moved to Washington, to Virginia, then to Cincinnati. On 9 March 1869 John left Ohio, bound for Lexington. Though publicly expressing a desire for no demonstrations, he found crowds all along the route. The mustache was longer now (reaching the lapels of his coat), the hair a sandy gray, but the man had changed little. The face that women called handsome and men called strong remained the same. But new emotions came as the distant years forced themselves on his mind. Twice Breckinridge said, seemingly to no one but himself: "Nearly eight years ago." He fell silent as he approached Lexington, and quickly leaving the large crowd at the station he went to the house of a cousin. At half past ten that night, while rain fell, men waiting outside cheered their hero; finally Breckinridge relented and spoke briefly, ending with the statement: "I no more feel the political excitements that marked the scenes of my former years than if I were an extinct volcano."[31]

If extinct politically, Breckinridge soon glowed with activity as business matters developed. Things had come easily to him before. When they had not—as in Iowa—he gave up and returned to his hometown, where his name mingled with his own strengths to yield rewards. But now in 1869 John was tired of it all. He had had great ambitions and had come very near his greatest goal, the presidency. He had been part of what seemed a true cause, but its death left him a political outcast. He could still make a living as a lawyer, and opponents would feel the point of his "keen and resistless lance," but even that seemed too great a task at times. It proved easier to lend name and voice to insurance or railroad companies, as so many of his former fellow generals in gray were doing. He managed the Piedmont and Arlington Insurance Company and served as president of the proposed Elizabethtown, Lexington, and Big Sandy Railroad. And so he took the least taxing way out of his economic dilemma. He was too weary to do otherwise.[32]

Breckinridge's most controversial postwar activity began in the summer of 1869, when he became general counsel for the proposed Cincinnati Southern, a line that would link the northern city to the South through Lexington. Louisville, long a rival of the central Bluegrass city, bitterly opposed the plan, since it would break the Louisville and Nashville (L&N) Railroad's virtual monopoly on the southern trade. Retaining Breckinridge had been a shrewd move, as Louisville's Henry Watterson recognized: "It was certainly stupid in Louisville to allow Cincinnati to engage your services; and I regret this the more because I do not relish the idea of making a fight against you or the odds which you will throw in favor of the other side." The L&N's sectional arguments lost much of their force when Breckinridge allied with the North.[33]

On 25 January 1870 the Kentuckian presented the Cincinnati case to a joint session of the Senate and House railroad committees, and to a larger audience. Breckinridge's arguments showed his utter devotion to the New South ideal of railroad growth, with little thought of restriction. Kentucky lagged behind all other states in railroad mileage, he claimed. Tying railroads to progress, the advocate told his auditors that the new road would yield additional taxes, attract new immigrants "of the right origin—of the white race," and would make the land around the line bloom like a garden. Never could there be too many railroads; reject sectional and selfish appeals and support the line, he concluded. While defeated in 1870, the Cincinnati Southern was approved two years later. Breckinridge had been a winner again.[34]

In the main, the years following John C. Breckinridge's return to Kentucky were quiet ones, the Cincinnati Southern fight notwithstanding. His opposition to the lawlessness of the Ku Klux Klan stirred up some controversy but mostly garnered praise. Similarly, in the struggle over whether black testimony against whites would be allowed in courts, Breckinridge supported the new order. Meanwhile, his family prospered:

young Mary attended a New York school, Fanny helped her mother in Lexington; Owen began a California law practice; and Clifton and Cabell tried their hands at growing cotton in Arkansas. As owner of five thoroughbreds, the father enjoyed his position as president of the Lexington racing society called the Kentucky Association.[35] But the early 1870s were also unhappy years. The life insurance company did not prosper; the Big Sandy line was almost bankrupt; the panic of 1873 hit hard. Moreover, John C.'s health grew worse. In a trial he showed unmistakable signs of sickness, and a newsman reported that the "manly form and face and noble carriage" were weakened by persistent illness. An attack of what Breckinridge described as "pleuro-pneumonia" forced him to the New York seashore in an attempt to recuperate. A journey to the Virginia mountains brought no relief. For nearly two years he remained almost an invalid, looking like "a dying lion, sad but majestic."[36]

Gray, thin, pale, coughing blood, this "magnificent wreck" of a man suffered from cirrhosis of the liver. In an effort to relieve his pain, doctors tried to drain a lung two-thirds full of liquid. Following the operation, the patient made out his will. He seemed near death, his voice barely audible. The next day he became speechless but remained conscious. The devoted Mary, their children Clifton and Fanny, and a few others gathered around him. At 5:45 P.M. on 17 May 1875 John C. Breckinridge died at the age of fifty-four. His metallic coffin was similar to the one in which "Grandma Black Cap" had been buried, only seventeen years earlier.[37]

The magnificent physique, the attractive personality, the winning voice that had stirred thousands were gone, but memories of John C. Breckinridge continued long after his death. Together with Henry Clay he stood as one of the best-known Kentuckians. The charisma and the spirit of the man did not die with him. The philosophy that guided his actions, like that lighting the way for many Americans of his era, was a concept transmitted almost directly from his grandfather. The key phrases in the grandson's principles were "state equality" and strict construction of the Constitution. If a "flexible" Constitution resulted from assaults on its property provisions by antislavery forces, he feared for his country. Even though imbued with the spirit of "Young America," even if allied to a growing, changing nation through business and railroad interests, Breckinridge could never place his trust in constitutional evolution. A sensitive man of deep emotions, especially in regard to war, he distrusted those emotions and calmly, cautiously made his decisions. Such a process convinced him of his correctness.

Certain that the Republican party sought through a centralized government to destroy slavery and overturn civil liberties, Breckinridge reacted accordingly. Jealous of states' rights and of the constitutional rights of citizens, convinced of the sacredness of the Constitution, he saw all these under attack when Fremont and Lincoln spoke of limiting slavery's expansion. Fanatics, he asserted, guided Republican councils and must be defeated. Although he seldom used the arguments of a race war as other southern leaders did, Breckinridge depicted other "horrors" and portrayed a despotism in the making. The victory of Lincoln in 1860 gave him the choice of supporting an administration he had predicted would destroy all he held dear, or joining a southern Confederacy, which at least promised a better future. He left behind a republic he had served as soldier, representative, vice-president, and senator—all by the time he was forty years old. Later, all that he had seen and experienced in the war he hated so much destroyed his desire to reenter the heated political arena of Reconstruction.

In calmer times and with different issues, John C. Breckinridge might have pursued a still more successful career. In the turbulent 1850s, he reached for such a destiny, but it remained a fingertip away. Slavery blighted his promising prospects, and the public man never recovered. As in his early fifties he resigned himself to his impending death, so Breckinridge had earlier resigned himself to the reality that the son of fortune would rise no more.[38]

FOUR

W.C.P. BRECKINRIDGE

1837-1904

I do not altogether fancy the words "New South." . . .
In all essentials it is the same Old South.

W.C.P. Breckinridge, 1891

Eleven

The Ready Kindling
of the Spirit

ON A BRIGHT AND CLOUDLESS MAY morning in 1865 William Campbell Preston ("Willie") Breckinridge, late colonel of the Confederate cavalry, came back to Kentucky as a defeated man. His decision to join the South had deeply wounded his Unionist father, Robert J. Breckinridge, for Willie was the patriarch's favorite son. On several occasions the Reverend Dr. Breckinridge had bitterly arraigned the Confederacy, even to the extent of calling for the "blood of traitors."[1] Throughout the Brothers' War, Willie had tried to maintain the close family ties of quieter times. He sent letters through the lines and penned a few words to his father each birthday, revealing divisions at one level, love at another. "I would I could have acted differently," he wrote on 8 March 1864. "I pray God that we may both survive this war long enough for you to know that I loved you as a son ought." To a wife who bore the wartime hatreds longer than her husband, Willie explained that Robert's harsh speeches mattered little: "Nothing he can say or do can make me forget that he is my father, & was a loving, kind, indulgent father, to whom I owe more than I can repay." In the same year, the devoted son, then but twenty-six, acknowledged paternal affection:

I was a delicate child—he was as tender as a mother—I was an obstinate boy— he was patient; I was sensitive and proud—he was . . . indulgent; I was quick-tempered—he was forbearing; I was an eager questioner—he was a willing & oh! how lucid explainer; as I grew older, he stirred up my ambition, was lenient towards my faults, was generous in my extravagance, pleased & gratified at my successes, encouraging me even in my failures, interested in my most trivial plans: in short a . . . friend, teacher, guide, companion—all in one. He is old—his life has been a most laborious one—a very great part of it full of suffering—much of it very full of sadness; and my precious, loving darling, my heart goes out to him in his old age.[2]

But when Willie made his way back to his ancestral home would his father return the affection? Could Robert forgive the errant son who had opposed his—and, to his mind, God's—will? Doubts proved groundless. The prodigal's welcome was "without reproach or censure; without patronage or evidence of triumph—the welcome of one who was gentleman as well as father." As novelist John Fox, Jr., would write, "When the war was over, the hatchet in Kentucky was buried at once and buried deep. Son came back to father, brother to brother . . . and the sundered threads, unravelled by the war, were united together fast."[3]

Postwar reunification renewed intimate ties that had existed between father and son in antebellum times. Born 28 August 1837 during Robert's ministry in Baltimore, W.C.P. Breckinridge had felt his father's influence early. The mother's death when the boy was seven left the burden of child-rearing solely on a grieving husband. Robert's professional uncertainty, in turn, resulted in a less-than-stable childhood for Willie; after Maryland, he attended school both in Pennsylvania and at Pisgah Academy in Woodford County, Kentucky. At the latter place, according to a classmate's recollection, "Billy would sit astride of a puncheon bench all day and read an old novel, and when we came to say our lessons, if Billy didn't know more about them than any of us the teacher was afraid to tell him so, for Billy would beat him in the discussion any time."[4]

Robert recognized his son's abilities and very early introduced him to the duties expected of his station. As a fourteen-year-old, Willie gave "important aid" in arranging the reports of the superintendent of public instruction; to the father, he was "confidential friend" as well as son. Otherwise the childhood seemed fairly typical: farm work, but also play in the nearby Indian mounds; school, but also time to flirt with "Miss Emma," or Ann Shelby, or "Miss Mary," or "Mr. Dixon's daughter," or numerous others.[5] Departing from the example of his father's generation, whose members attended college outside the state, young Breckinridge first entered Transylvania University, then the Presbyterian-sponsored Centre College of Kentucky. With a cousin's husband as president and (after 1853) his own father as a professor in the seminary, Willie was carefully supervised. Nevertheless, he established a rebel Literary Society, assisted a friend to elope and engaged in a pistol and knife fight with classmate and future governor John Young Brown. The small and remarkable student body included such future politicians as Kentucky Governor James B. McCreary, Senator J.C.S. Blackburn, Missouri Governor Thomas T. Crittenden, Vice-President Adlai E. Stevenson, and Kentucky gubernatorial candidate Thomas Z. Morrow. At graduation in 1855, Willie Breckinridge received several honors, but, in an appropriate culmination of a somewhat stormy college career, graduation "broke up in a sort of row, in which several of us sided against the faculty."[6]

His life's contrasting aspects continued during the next few years.

Uncertain of a career, Willie vacillated between the law and theology. After receiving a law degree in 1857 he attended the Danville Seminary but, to his father's great disgust, left in less than a year, saying that God had rejected him. Willie rejoined his brother, Robert, Jr., as a Lexington attorney and wrote a prize-winning essay on agriculture and education.[7]

More settled now, with firm ties already to many prominent Kentucky families, the twenty-one-year-old W.C.P. Breckinridge strengthened them when on 17 March 1859 he married attractive Lucretia Clay, the young granddaughter of "the Great Compromiser." That union celebrated but one anniversary. On 29 April 1860, four days after giving birth, Lucretia died; the baby, Lee Clay Breckinridge, survived for only two months. The young widower lived alone for some fifteen more months, then on 17 September 1861 wed seventeen-year-old Issa Desha, granddaughter of a Kentucky governor. His life would now be focused on his profession and his new wife—but the creeping shadow of war darkened his future, as it did for thousands of others of his generation.[8]

The two most influential people shaping his philosophy now pulled him in different directions. His father's loyalty was unalterably to the federal Union, but first cousin John C. Breckinridge represented prosouthern sentiment in Kentucky. Though Willie loved and respected Robert Breckinridge, at the same time he so believed in the words of his younger kinsman that he had supported the Breckinridge Democrat cause in the 1860 election (as did Robert, Jr.). From Whig roots, the younger Breckinridge generation had grown into Democratic timber. Yet while brother Robert, Jr., made his decision early and entered the Confederate army, Willie hestitated. Both son and father seemed to realize the eventual outcome, but neither wanted it. Robert tried to persuade the errant youth to remain at least neutral. Willie, in turn, sought to make the break as painless as possible and continued to delay his decision. First he visited the capital of the Confederacy, where he discussed the conflict with Secretary of War John B. Floyd (a relative), with several generals, and with Kentucky-born Jefferson Davis; then he heard from Robert E. Lee the details of the Battle of Bull Run. After viewing that battlefield the Kentuckian wrote, sadly, "Oh, God! That brothers should do this. . . . If it is only a bloody repulse as I fear, . . . another battle will soon follow." More bloodletting proved his prediction all too correct.[9]

As the war intensified, Breckinridge still hesitated to join the cause he so obviously supported. He was, after all, almost a newlywed, having been married only ten months by July 1862. Moreover, he was the father of a month-old daughter, Ella. Could he separate so soon from the young woman he had promised to guide, counsel, and support, "alleviating pain with love, driving away care with tenderness?" The couple had stood before an open door on a stormy night, listening to distant church music, and had pledged their eternal love. A worried young man had told Issa then that "I know not what the future has in store for me—but nothing can take out of my heart the memory of your love & trust & confidence."[10]

Soon the matter was decided for him. After being threatened with arrest by Union authorities, Willie wrote to his father on 15 July 1862 that, while he had intended to remain "entirely aloof" from the action, events forced him to fight. He added, "I shall never forget your kindness to me." The next day Robert tried a last time to dissuade his offspring, but just before dawn on the seventeenth W.C.P. Breckinridge, guided by a servant, slipped away on a thoroughbred fitted with his Union brother's "borrowed" cavalry saddle. He looked back at his home, wept, prayed briefly, and then rode off to join the command of fellow Lexingtonian John Hunt Morgan. A proclamation bearing the young Breckinridge's signature quickly appeared, asking Kentuckians to join him in driving the oppressor from their soil. "I have sacrificed so much already," he concluded, "that life itself can add but little to the sacrifice." That same day the recruit, still outfitted in a linen duster, low-quarter shoes, and striped socks, fought his first battle. In December his troops elected the twenty-five-year-old Willie colonel of the Ninth Kentucky Cavalry.[11]

For Issa, the eighteen-year-old mother and wife back in the Bluegrass, the war made great sacrifices necessary. She and her husband would not see each other again until hostilities ended, nearly three years later. Issa's and Willie's letters revealed the sadness of separation and the love they shared. After a year apart, the wife lamented that "each moment has added to that deep confiding love which I gave you long ago. . . . How you are loved you will never know." He wrote of their postwar dreams and called on her to join him in the South. She answered with a pledge of love for "the fearless *man* and humble, trusting Christian that united form the noblest man on earth." A sorrowful Issa told Willie, "All I care for is just once more to be near you."[12] Actions by Union authorities did little to ease tensions within the sensitive, proud, and even haughty woman. "Very, very bitter and unforgiving" to those who warred on her husband, Issa Desha Breckinridge portrayed the federal-occupied commonwealth as a place of "persecution, woe and misery." She felt degraded in any place where "Yankees" resided, and she eventually joined other wives of prominent Kentucky Confederates in their Canadian exile. Little Ella, left in the care of Desha grandparents, soon learned that "Mama way up in Tanada" while "Papa down in Dissie." A victim of the physical and emotional separations inherent in war, the child told her mother, "Mama I lub Papa," although, as Issa said, "she can't understand who or what Papa is."[13]

During those hard years apart, Breckinridge fought for the Confederate cause with little surcease. The ordeal passed in almost endless raids, skirmishes, and battles, interrupted by the harshness of winter and the tedium of camp life. Names of the campaigns meant less than the memories they left. Breckinridge joined Morgan in many of his fast-paced Kentucky raids; the Ninth Kentucky fought across Tennessee and into Virginia, where it participated in the Saltville affair; their colonel led them in the exhausting struggle around Atlanta, and finally he commanded several harassing forays against Sherman's army as it marched to the sea, then across South Carolina to the north.[14]

The cost in lives was high. While the conclusion of one survivor that only one in ten of the original unit survived is exaggerated, nevertheless the Ninth Kentucky suffered heavy losses. Breckinridge estimated that only one in three did not suffer capture, wounding, or death. The adjutant general's report, usually a staid account of each unit, departed from the norm and described the regiment's service as "constant, arduous and hazardous." The colonel received "several" wounds and had two horses shot from under him, but, like two brothers, several cousins, and a brother-in-law, he survived. Nearly one-third of all Kentuckians who fought were not so fortunate.[15]

In the midst of the slaughter, events constantly reminded soldiers of the contradictions of this so savage yet so humane conflict. During a truce period in Tennessee, Colonel Breckinridge greeted a Union soldier he had helped nurse to health during a Kentucky cholera epidemic in 1849. They met as friends, and the federal trooper relayed a message to Willie's wife. Operating on the flank of Braxton Bragg's army, Breckinridge's unit became so "acquainted" with an opposing Ohio regiment that the two agreed to exchange captured troops immediately after battles. As one major recalled, "we were passing them backward and forward every few days." Following the clashes soldiers resumed a "lively little trade" across the lines, until it came time to fight and kill again.[16]

Yet the sometimes faceless men in the Union lines that opposed Breckinridge could not always conceal the reality of fighting one's friends and relatives. In the Atlanta campaign of 1864, hearing that his Union brother Joseph had been captured, Willie rode twelve miles in the dark to locate him. The colonel gave the prisoner some precious gold coins, and the two passed the July night, as General Joseph Wheeler related, "with as much warmth of fraternal affection as though visiting each other from neighboring armies engaged in the same cause." The Reverend Robert J. Breckinridge, writing "*almost* without tears," thanked his son in gray for the kindness; Joseph, freed by a prisoner exchange, told President Lincoln of Willie's material help and active aid.[17] His own soldiers, as well as his superiors, also testified to Breckinridge's kindness. Major J. P. Austin found his leader "a gentleman of marked ability" who had inherited the noble qualities of his ancestor. General Wheeler, Willie's commander in the last months, praised his subordinate's "brave and faithful" actions. The colonel's troops would seek him out and renew old ties for years after the conflict.[18]

But long-deferred defeat finally came. Escorting Jefferson Davis in his attempted escape, Colonel Breckinridge obeyed Secretary of War Breckinridge's order to divert pursuing Union troops and, having done so, to surrender at last. With a longer beard, a few gray hairs, and a "more reserved and grave" spirit, Willie came home to Issa's embrace and his father's welcome. Fighting for liberty, he declared in his oddly eloquent way, "has softened & warmed my heart."[19]

For men and women of Breckinridge's class the postwar world seemed utterly chaotic. Black emancipation meant modification of a long-prevailing labor system; mass migrations of former slaves to cities produced housing and employment problems; some returning soldiers found farms destroyed and businesses wrecked. The rich antebellum promise of prosperity now mocked Kentuckians. Their proud prewar educational system lay in shambles, one-fourth of the population was illiterate, and now a whole new group—blacks—demanded education. An earlier, diverse agricultural base increasingly turned toward one-crop dependence with declining demand for hemp and increasing cries for the new burley tobacco. And particularly bitter guerrilla warfare, especially in eastern Kentucky, contributed in no small measure to a violent ethos that resulted in the feuds and assassinations that plagued the postwar commonwealth.

The chaos extended to Kentucky politics. Since the death of the Whig party in the early 1850s no party had dominated the state. By 1865 various groups still wooed these wandering former Whigs, as well as the returning Union and Confederate veterans. Republicans, as Robert J. Breckinridge had quickly learned, failed to overcome their wartime identification with black emancipation and military rule; they received but 24 percent of the votes in the 1867 gubernatorial race. Only when Kentucky blacks received voting rights three years later did Republicans even mildly challenge the controlling Democrats. Split into Union and "peace" factions during the war, infused with a group of former Confederates afterwards, and finally mixed with prewar Whigs of both armies, the Democratic party was hardly likely to become or remain a stable coalition. Factionalism would be the party's price for dominance. Democrats, united at election time, could seldom agree on concerted policies once in power. For three decades the fragile combination held together, but continued stress would eventually break it apart.[20]

Willie Breckinridge faced a political path with two forks—his father's Republicanism and John C. Breckinridge's Democracy. But, as before the war, grandfather John and Thomas Jefferson's brand of political theory prevailed. He became a Democrat and found himself initially in the minority wing of his chosen party. One faction, opposing any moves that favored former slaves, dominated early, defeated all attempts to ratify the

William Campbell Preston Breckinridge

three Reconstruction amendments, and fought black voting and court testimony by Negroes. More realistically, a second, probably younger, faction realized that the battle could not be won and that opposition could not halt what seemed inevitable. Led by the talented, vain, and controversial editor Henry Watterson, and by rank newcomer Willie Breckinridge, this second group called for a "New Departure." Their views ultimately triumphed, but only after a bitter struggle. One casualty would be Breckinridge.[21]

Such an outcome seemed unlikely in the first few years after the war. Southern soldiers were welcomed as heroes, and angry Republican papers protested their ascendancy. The Lexington *Kentucky Statesman* complained of the "open defiance of unregenerate traitors"; the Cincinnati *Daily Gazette* cried out that Kentucky was "more deeply imbued with the heretical doctrine of states rights than even South Carolina was." After the Democrats' victory in 1867 one editor claimed that 90 percent of all state offices were held by former Confederates or their wartime sympathizers. A visitor to a party nominating convention said it seemed "as if all the Confederate troops in Kentucky had been concentrated there." As one of these former Confederates, as a former officer, Breckinridge assumed a leadership role in the party, and his position as editor of the powerful Lexington *Observer and Reporter* from July 1866 to July 1868 added to his influence. Generally, his stands echoed accepted Democratic policy. Critical of Reconstruction, he warned of a military despotism and accused the North of betrayal. Had not the South accepted defeat and met conditions for resuming a role in government? Now new conditions were being imposed, in violation of the "compact." Surely another war would result if these Radicals did not taste defeat.[22]

Breckinridge opposed not only specific Reconstruction policies but also the opposition's very philosophy of government. "Liberty is the true spirit we worship," an editorial proclaimed." We are no advocate for license—for unbridled red Republicanism—but for that true constitutional, regulated, law-fearing liberty won by our ancestors." Government had no duties requiring regulation of the people; that doctrine was as false as it was dangerous. While recognizing certain areas requiring legislation (such as asylums), the editor declared that Republicans should remember that governments must not be "the guides, or fathers, or school masters of their citizens. They are the protectors." It was John Breckinridge and Thomas Jefferson reborn.[23]

But not entirely. While many Kentucky Democrats still looked wistfully to their antebellum world as their ideal, while a significant part of the leadership refused to give up the agrarian ethos, while many regulars sought to reenact the slave regime as closely as possible, Breckinridge did not. He advocated a rebirth of the region, a "New South." As one of the earliest spokesmen of this movement that would eventually sweep the region, W.C.P. Breckinridge sounded a philosophy that departed in spirit from family tradition. His ancestors, though professional men, had still remained tied to the soil. Even John C. Breckinridge, with little in the way of an estate, had proclaimed the same ethos. Willie, in the chaos of Reconstruction, gave his energies to the urban, industrial ideal, though he never departed in significant ways from the background that shaped him. His New South and his political philosophies reflected the contradictory forces of this past—his Whig father, his Democratic cousin, his Jeffersonian grandfather. Such contradictions proved hard to resolve.

Willie Breckinridge's New South vision came through clearly to his newspaper readers in 1867. Proclaiming that in climate, in wealth, and in people, no area was as blessed as the South, Breckinridge called on it to develop these resources. Extend your railroads, open up your rivers, mine your mineral wealth, erect mills "with zeal and energy." Do all this, he suggested, and political rights will be secured. A rebuilt South, equal to the rest of the country, could then claim its rightful place in national life. Reunion on terms of equality would be the most healing of remedies for sectionalism. Then the states, united at last, could move forward to the untold promise America held. Breckinridge had little opportunity to develop his creed through formal political channels, however. One issue overrode all others, and on that he departed from the majority of his party. The question of the role of the former slave in a free society dominated political matters. Answers were neither easy nor popular.[24]

When a Confederate soldier, Breckinridge had told his wife that he did not believe slavery inherently good: "God forbid I should thus believe." But, like so many, he could not accept the presence of millions of free blacks. The role of editor now allowed him to offer his thoughts on the issue to a wider audience. He told his readers, initially, little they could not accept. If blacks received the ballot, they would either vote as their employers dictated, or else be "exterminated in the terrible war of races that ensue from any effort upon their part to become the rivals . . . of their late masters." This ignorant, inferior, dependent race "without any developed capacity for any higher toil than manual labor" must be controlled; "We . . . are irrevocably determined to fight to the bitter end for the imperial white race," he wrote. The editor's January 1868 declaration spoke for Kentuckians of his race: "We want a white man's State and we intend to have it."[25]

Yet, gradually, Breckinridge's editorials emphasized another goal to be sought—justice. Blacks might not need special rights, he suggested, but they did have the right to demand "fairness, justice and protection." "The Colonel," as he was called for the rest of his life, asked Lexingtonians if they had been equal to their duty, as Christians, as charitable citizens, as enlightened people, to the blacks among them? His was a racial paternalism; of that there is little doubt. He did not consider the black citizen his equal. He grew over time, however, to become a staunch supporter of Negro rights at a time when few were—and he did it at the cost of his own career.[26]

A bitter question for Kentucky politicians in the late 1860s concerned black testimony. Commonwealth legal codes still would not allow Negroes to offer testimony against Caucasions in state courts; cases involving blacks went to federal jurisdiction instead. New Departure leaders such as attorney Breckinridge joined Republicans in protesting the continuance of such a system. His paper cried out that blacks paid taxes and supported the government. Did it not follow that the race was entitled to just protection? "To do justice, the truth and the *whole* truth, must be made known to the arbiter. . . . How can this be done when one-fourth of a community are not allowed in many cases to enter the witness box?" The answer was obvious to Breckinridge; it was less clear to other Kentuckians.[27]

This issue confronted the editor when he decided to run for common-wealth (district) attorney for the tenth circuit court. County attorney since 1867, he now determined to set out on a course that for earlier family members had led to steady political advancement. The opposition was strong: former Confederate general and later United States Senator John S. ("Cerro Gordo") Williams; relative Edward C. Marshall, son of Robert J. Breckinridge's old teacher; and J. Lawrence Jones, a former Confederate captain. Others of his family had overcome such odds—John C.'s victory in a Whig district, for example. But John C. had been—like his state—proslavery. In the postwar period Willie Breckinridge's racial stands more closely followed his father's minority view, and the result was similar.[28]

On the inflammatory question of black testimony, Willie made his attitude known. At a Madison County gathering in 1868 a man in the crowd denounced the Colonel, accusing him of supporting the black man in the controversy. Breckinridge's response was clear: "Fellow-citizens, the charge my opponents urge against me is true. I am aware that this avowal will most likely defeat me in this canvass, for you are not ready to view this question calmly and dispassionately. Your prejudices blind your judgment. . . . In the after days, when the passions of this hour shall have cooled, when reason shall assert her sway, when the nobler feelings of your nature shall rule your hearts and judgement—in that hour you will approve though now you condemn me.[29]

On at least one count, Breckinridge's analysis was correct. Support for him declined in the hard-fought race, and he withdrew when the nomi-nating convention met. As Willie told his father, "a very little dodging on that question would have inevitably secured . . . the nomination." But he could not do that. He had earlier explained to a leader of the conservative wing of his party that if his "honest convictions" defeated him, "it must be so, for I will not eat my words to be President and much less to be Attorney for my district." A year later an editor in analyzing the race again pointed to Breckinridge's crucial stand as the sole cause of his defeat. An unfriendly Cincinnati paper even lauded the candidate's "manliness" in taking such a forceful position. Praise for his statesmanship, however, could not overcome the bitterness of defeat. Not for another sixteen years would he seriously test the political waters of his district.[30]

Breckinridge sold the *Observer and Reporter* in July 1868 and redirected his energies to his law practice, his family, and his local concerns. As an attorney he prospered at last, but only after early financial difficulties. His practice gradually grew and with it his reputation. In 1872 Willie's "masterly efforts" in the circuit court attracted attention; that same year the governor selected him to be one of three lawyers who represented the commonwealth in a case that went to the Supreme Court; in 1874, he argued for academic freedom for Kentucky University (Transylvania University) before a joint legislative committee. In this case, he called for the removal of political and ecclesiastical influences: legislators should think of the people, not a certain religious sect, and make laws "not for to-day only, but for the future." Later, in the 1880s, Breckinridge made such a "clear, forcible and logical" argument for the state university that an opponent admitted that it "shook my confidence in our case to the foundation." The attorney had gained respect, attention, and a reasonably secure financial base.[31]

Strains came with success. A typical work week might find him taking the train to Georgetown on Monday, Winchester on Tuesday, Paris the next day, Danville on Thursday, and Frankfort the following morning. In one year, a case in Louisville necessitated a stay of some months there. The demands of his career did little to ease family tensions already made taut by stress between his wife and his father. It would be two years after war's end before Issa would tell Willie that her bitterness and unpleasant feelings were "*now* all gone & *for ever*." Letters between the two told of their devotion, despite the distances and frequent absences. From Elizabethtown, Willie wrote that "never was a wife so loved" as she by him. Issa, in turn, poured out her feelings to her "own idolized husband," the man she loved with "all the earnestness of my heart." "My soul bows down in worship of you & added to this love is the fervent, unutterable gratitude I owe you darling for all the tender, thoughtful, patient love you have given. . . ." Issa admitted that when she thought of how she "worshipped" him, she feared and trembled, "but I love you Willie with all my soul."[32]

Love could not overcome all obstacles, however, and the couple changed as years passed. Their joy in the five healthy children—Ella, Sophonisba, Desha, Robert, and Curry—was dampened by deaths of one-year-old Campbell in 1870 and one-year-old Issa Desha in 1872. With neither spouse very careful in money matters (Issa had six servants in 1870), finances remained a constant concern. Their personalities clashed more frequently now, and Issa openly recognized the changing relationship in October 1884: "I have loved you Willie—twenty-four years—loved you at the first with the love of a whole heart. . . . I fear some times . . . that I will grow less lovable—more cold in manners as I grow older." Her fears were justified. In a fourteen-page letter the next May, Breckinridge angrily attacked Issa. Ella had showed disrespect for him, and her mother had refused (according to Willie) either to criticize the daughter or to allow him to. His wife had "deeply wounded me—painfully & apparently intentionally" and he held her directly responsible. For years he had been uncomfortable at their house and, unable to control Ella, hesitated to invite friends because of family friction and household economics. Yet he loved Issa, he repeated, and (injecting a note of self-pity very much in his father's manner) told her that a sense of duty to their children tempered his remarks. But husband and wife would remain together, and he continued to close his letters to her, "with a heart full of love."[33]

Despite family strains, W.C.P. Breckinridge did not reduce his outside activities. He served as chairman of the Alumni Association of Centre College, helped organize the Kentucky Historical Association in 1878, and answered the calls for financial aid by blacks who had migrated from Kentucky to Kansas. He assisted in the organization of the Lexington Cemetery in 1879, joined the fledgling American Historical Association in 1884, and for a time held a councilman's seat in the city.[34] Try as he would, Breckinridge could not escape politics. Still ambitious, he worked within the party, served on committees, stood as a presidential elector, went as a delegate to the 1872 and 1876 national Democratic conventions, and—most important—made speeches. At the 1875 state convention his impromptu, "soul-stirring" talk earned him great praise. Afterwards, the party's official organ, the *Yeoman*, enthusiastically proclaimed that "all the elements of a solid and substantial popularity of the highest order seem to meet in him—purity of life and character, a lofty and chivalrous bearing, a matchless eloquence, and a cherished Kentucky name. . . . Perhaps no public man that the Commonwealth has produced for many years has possessed more of the ready kindling of the spirit so indispensable to his highest triumphs." Four years later, Breckinridge's midnight speech nominating his wife's kinsman Joseph Desha Pickett for superintendent of public instruction won acclaim as the most eloquent address of the Democratic party's proceedings. A Republican paper admitted that Willie "made only a speech as he can, . . . full of feeling and warmth. . . ."[35]

Breckinridge did not, of course, confine his speechmaking to the convention floor. He had become a sought-after orator soon after the end of the Civil War and had made the most of his abilities. While using the podium at times as a platform for furthering his political views, the

Colonel chiefly praised the Confederacy and at the same time proclaimed the New South vision. To large audiences across Kentucky, Breckinridge relived again the glories of the antebellum past. In 1861 two civilizations had existed, and the choice lay between submission and separation. "A peaceful and pastoral people" had been threatened by northerners, "the most warlike people in the world." He and the South had fought for personal liberty, for state sovereignty, for "the dear old freedom of our fathers." Slavery was not mentioned as a cause, but Willie knew it represented more than economics to the South, for the institution had "become interwoven into the social fabric of the State in a way hard now to explain. . . . It made race and color, not condition and wealth the distinction. It gave habits of domination and caused a form of pastoral life that was peculiar and influential. If the slave had been white the problem would have been easy of solution."[36]

Breckinridge contributed to the growing myth of a world of moonlight, magnolias, and mint juleps, and his version often pictured a civilization that never existed. Yet he, unlike some others, recognized that the cause was dead. Now he counseled the South to accept "new thoughts, other traditions, other customs, other hopes." To the students at Washington and Lee University he spoke words of optimism: "You are the heralds of a new day—the advanced guard of a new and mighty army— the army of the future." His words revealed much of his own transformation. Breckinridge told the audience that all countries must pass through a trial. America had survived its "fires of adversity"; out of the flames came change and they must now meet the new world face to face. "Tolerate no second-hand thinking," he advised, "nor be content to receive as maxims the party cries of the past, or the sayings of the fathers." His own philosophies had been modified (and would be more changed in the future) and students should remember, he warned, that "each age has its own questions to answer . . . and it is a real, though disguised slavery, to receive unquestioning the teachings of the past." Do not tear down the temple of previous wrongs, as blind Sampson did, but rather drive out the impure from the temple, as did Jesus. Test ideas and theories, and only then reject or accept them. The Kentuckian spoke for an intellectual challenge, for an evolving—not static—philosophy. John C. Breckinridge's world was being left behind.[37]

Speech-making, the lawyer's trade, dreary political work—this was not enough. In 1884 Willie Breckinridge decided to seek the congressional seat in his district. Although earlier mentioned as a possible choice for several important positions, he had not made a serious effort since his campaign sixteen years before. Now with the incumbent taking a senate seat, with the race issue in the background, with his long work for the party, it seemed the moment to try again. First he wrote to prominent local politicians to seek their aid. Then, satisfied with the response, he announced his candidacy in February 1884, quickly picked up more support, and began organizing "Breckinridge Clubs." Barbecues and burgoo, and talk of tobacco, taxation, and tariffs, marked the campaign; Breckinridge had no fears, for he was unopposed by the Republicans. Both he and his party triumphed in the fall. Grover Cleveland entered office as the first Democratic president since the war; William Campbell Preston Breckinridge's election marked the reappearance of the family in national office for the first time in that same period. The representative and his party shared a long-deferred return to power, and both sought to make the most of their opportunity.[38]

Twelve

A Man of Passion

THE NEW congressman brought with him tremendous advantages. Breckinridge's oratorical powers could—and would—win over foes in speeches and debates. Speaking in a southern, ministerial drawl, the "Silver-Tongued Orator from Kentucky" had a mellow, winning voice that was clear, resonant, and "melodious." Newspapers across his home state proclaimed his ability without reserve: "He is the finest orator we ever heard," a Hopkinsville paper reported in 1879. "No one who has listened to him has ever professed to have heard his superior," exclaimed a Midway correspondent five years later. "The Lexington Demosthenes" when he spoke in Frankfort was deemed the best speaker heard in that political town in years. Journals outside the commonwealth, while somewhat more restrained, nonetheless left little doubt of his talent. A Philadelphia newspaper called him one of the best orators in Congress: "He is quick, he is ready, he is keen, he is well informed, and, above all, he is dignified and of even temper." After a tariff debate featuring Breckinridge and future president William McKinley, a Washington paper called the Kentuckian "a speaker of marvelous powers. His language is rich, . . . his diction chaste, and his voice as musical as a woman's; but it is a man's voice and it fills a hall like an organ tone." A decade after Breckinridge had been elected to Congress, the Washington *Post* reported that he had made, "as usual, a brilliant speech."[1]

Individual writers praised him as well. Thomas Crittenden remembered a campaign speech when the words "rolled from his mouth smooth and musical, charming all who came under his spell," and John S. Sherman, who served at various times as cabinet officer and member of both houses of Congress, recalled that the Kentuckian was the greatest natural orator he had encountered. Historian and contemporary E. Polk Johnson termed Willie Breckinridge simply, "the most eloquent of Kentuckians, past or present." The Colonel's old wartime comrade Basil Duke had been involved in public life for almost half a century after the war when he wrote, "I have sometimes thought Breckinridge was the most gifted and attractive orator I ever heard. He was very brilliant, but there was nothing of grandiose declamation or ostentatious ornament in his speech and it was replete with reason and argument. His eloquence, even when impassioned, flowed like a river, bank-full but limpid, and bearing a rich and abundant freight."[2]

Not all, of course, agreed. While the ability to influence with words was still highly valued in America, the trend toward more issue-oriented speechmaking had begun. For those who disliked what they considered long, flowery, meaningless talks, Breckinridge held little appeal. The political opposition, especially acrid Republican editor Sam J. Roberts of the Lexington *Daily Leader*, did not spare him. In an October 1888 satire that paper described the congressman's speech at a typical rally, where he "bares his white head . . . and talks of the bright and beautiful moon, the men that fought for the 'lost cause,' the green sward that separates the beloved dead in our own beautiful country, your fathers, and my f-a-a-a-thers . . . . " But even the *Leader* had to admit two years later that the "eloquent" Breckinridge gave the most sensible speech at another election gathering. In a period that rewarded a talented orator, Willie won wide acclaim.[3]

An impressive physique added to his oratorical attributes. While not so tall as many of his family's men (he fell three inches short of six feet), Willie compensated with a robust frame dominated by a large head. A thick growth of silver-gray hair, a long beard, and large, "brilliant" blue-gray eyes gave him the appearance of a silver-maned lion. Moreover, the Kentuckian was a witty conversationalist, an excellent dancer, and had few apparent vices in an age when some public figures had many. The minister's son seldom drank, smoked, played cards, or even bet on Bluegrass thoroughbreds. With such a physical presence and such a personality, the freshman representative seemed to have unlimited promise in 1885, when he joined the Forty-ninth Congress.[4]

The institution Breckinridge entered functioned as the most important part of the postwar government, but increasing complexity and confusion marked its councils. Lack of longevity was one problem, for member turnover was high. Woodrow Wilson in his book *Constitutional Government* (which appeared the year Breckinridge took his seat) remarked that a representative who served many terms was "a curiosity." English observer James Bryce said that ability counted in the long run in Congress, although instability in that body meant "there is, for most men, no long run." Democrats won control of the House in 1874, fell from power a half-dozen years later, regained the majority in 1882, lost it in another six years, and were victorious again in 1890. With such precarious political balance, both parties carefully avoided most issues of controversy.[5] Members recognized the quagmire in the House. The number of resolutions and public and private bills introduced by legislators rose steadily, from eleven thousand in the Forty-ninth Congress to fourteen thousand in the Fifty-first; and, given the labyrinth of the rules, it is surprising that much legislation occurred at all. As a history of the House of Representatives notes, Breckinridge's entry into Congress coincided with a time when that body "had been reduced to a condition of legislative impotence by abuses of its then existing rules of procedure. . . . The use of dilatory motions combine with the disappearing quorum and a series of filibusters to make the House an object of public ridicule and condemnation." In 1888 a Washington paper observed "that no other body in the world takes up so much time and spends so much money doing nothing." The national legislature ground slowly forward, consumed in minutiae and in the morass of parliamentary procedure.[6]

Congressional morality did little to improve members' stature before the public. A newspaper reported that prostitutes had been admitted to the private gallerys of House members in the 1880s; rumors of liaisons were fed by enough reality to ensure their survival and growth. In 1888, for example, Breckinridge's Kentucky colleague, Congressman Preston Taulbee, was discovered "in a compromising way" with a young woman who worked in the model department of the Patent Office. His career ruined, Taulbee did not return the next session. Novelists had already picked up the theme, for Henry Adams' anonymous *Democracy* had told of a senator who "had made love to every girl with any pretensions to beauty that had appeared in the state of New York for fully half a century." The implication was that the practice was not confined to that Empire State congressman, nor to the Senate.[7]

Lobbying activities did not strengthen reputations, for men with money and influence and women with other persuasive powers challenged a congressman's ethics at almost every turn. Dinners, entertainment, blatant bribery—all were employed. One correspondent wrote that the most successful of the lobbyists might have been those he sneeringly called the "vampires" of the lobby, the "lobbyesses" who used "the lever of lust" to influence both the naïve and not-so-naïve members. Public assessment of Congress was not high.[8]

The era, then, was characterized by all the images the term "Gilded Age" suggested; it appeared to be "a huge barbecue"; it displayed ostentatious vulgarity and frequent corruption; it seemed peopled, in John A. Garraty's words, by "inefficient Presidents, narrow-minded legislators, parties that existed for the sake of winning and holding office, [and] a Congress weighted down by antiquated procedures." But it was also a period when the national debt was lowered significantly, when the cost of living declined, when various parts of American life became more interdependent and united, and when the nation squarely (if slowly) faced the dual problems of the effects of the Civil War and the Industrial Revolution. Corrupt congressmen of dubious moral fiber and questionable ability certainly existed, but other members represented a different political world.[9]

According to Woodrow Wilson, a first-term congressman of the 1880s received little notice. "He finds his station insignificant, and his identity indistinct." The future president's analysis did not fit the case of W.C.P. Breckinridge. Not only did he carry with him a name familiar to members, but the Kentuckian also had kinship ties with some representatives, military ones with others, and bonds of recognition (as a result of his speechmaking) with still more. During his years in Congress, he sat at various times with Clifton Breckinridge of Arkansas, a second cousin; Champ Clark of Missouri, who had been born and educated in central Kentucky; Joseph Wheeler of Alabama, Willie's former commander; John H. Reagan of Texas, who as Confederate postmaster general had served in the cabinet with John C. Breckinridge; George Craighead Cabell of Virginia, another distant relative; Tom Loftin Johnson of Ohio, who had been born in Kentucky; and others who knew him earlier. Included among his close senatorial friends were Wade Hampton of South Carolina, who had visited the Breckinridge home shortly after the war, and Kentucky's James B. Beck, a former law partner of John C. Breckinridge. Kentucky-born Adlai E. Stevenson filled the vice-presidential post for part of Breckinridge's time in the House. With such allies, the new congressman expected (and received) support and favors. His most important ally, however, turned out to be neither relative, ex-Confederate, or leader from another state, but rather a member of his own delegation. The selection of the somber, intellectual John G. Carlisle as Speaker of the House meant that all-important committee assignments would be in the hands of a southerner, a Democrat, and a Kentuckian.[10]

Committee work increasingly determined both the outcome of legislation and the relative success or failure of members. Woodrow Wilson even suggested that committees deserved to be labeled "miniature legislatures," since they performed the basic work. The selection of first-termer Willie Breckinridge and cousin Clifton to the Ways and Means Committee placed them in key positions in the power structure. Ties to the Democratic President Cleveland strengthened Breckinridge's power base in Congress, for the two men shared common traits as sons of ministers, as Presbyterians, and as men with similar views of the nature of mankind. They agreed not only on the importance of law, doctrine, and principle in preserving the order of the universe, but on many specific policies. Breckinridge supported the more inflexible Cleveland throughout his career and received patronage and other rewards for such support.[11]

But if Willie Breckinridge entered Congress in 1885 with many positive attributes, other representatives in the past had done so and had squandered any advantages they had held. Family and political ties, important assignments—all this meant little without talent and ability. Breckinridge quickly surveyed the growing complexity of American government, and he adjusted rapidly. Through the maze of privileged motions, amendments to amendments, and other confusing procedural matters, the Kentuckian moved smoothly. Indeed, he seemed to enjoy his congressional years immensely. Active in debate, he could be either winning in style and charm, or critical in manner. His humor could not be hidden, even in the dreary and serious debates on the tariff. After one congressman's smooth discussion of the olive oil duties, the colonel noted that "I knew the gentleman was not an oil-maker, except on the floor of Congress." When William McKinley praised the effect of his 1890 Republican tariff as "very favorable," Willie rose and agreed with the Ohio representative, "because it has turned out the present Republican Congress and put in a Democratic Congress." As time expired for a colleague who was reading from an earlier Breckinridge speech, the silver-tongued orator quickly won the floor and asked that, since "that seems to be a very good speech the gentleman is reading from . . . I hope the House will allow him to proceed." It did.[12]

Not only his wit but also a quick mind, a thorough knowledge of the rules, and a devastating sarcasm made debate with W.C.P. Breckinridge particularly risky. When a usually silent member, for example, remarked that he disagreed with the Kentuckian, Willie generously gave the representative "my admiration for the modesty that has kept his light under a bushel for so many years that we never heard of it before."[13] Such tactics had their risks, of course. When Representative John T. Heard of Missouri asked the House on one occasion to refuse Breckinridge the opportunity to make a critical, "buncombe" speech, tempers erupted.

"You are a dirty pup," Willie instantly shouted.

"You are a d——d liar," replied Heard.

The stocky, muscular, red-faced former colonel stormed toward the frail, slender, pale man from Missouri. Another congressman held Breckinridge's arm while the Speaker of the House pounded his desk and called for the sergeant-at-arms. Only after the head of the Speaker's gavel flew off and hit a nearby page did the shouting have some effect. Finally both Breckinridge and Heard were led to the Speaker's stand. They refused to apologize but later that day retracted their remarks and shook hands.

"Billy," said Heard, "when men's beards get as gray as yours and mine they ought to have more sense than to quarrel like boys."

Breckinridge replied: "Yes, John, but it sometimes seems to me that the grayer we get the less sense we have."[14]

In quieter and more typical times, Breckinridge returned to the traditional congressional pursuits of lawmaking. His legislative output was small—of his bills to incorporate the Red Cross, to regulate commerce, to enlarge the Department of Agriculture, to declare trusts illegal, and to lower tariff barriers, none passed under his sponsorship. But his real strength lay as Democratic spokesman, for, although he and his party differed on several issues, in many more ways Breckinridge represented perfectly the philosophy of the Democratic majority of his era. As Morton Keller has pointed out, the tensions of late nineteenth-century America repeated the long-existing struggles "between equality and liberty, because the desire for freedom and the need for social order, between dependence on government and hostility to the state, between localism and nationalism." For W.C.P. Breckinridge and his party the choice on many of these alternatives was very clear-cut.[15]

The congressman offered solutions based on a natural-rights philosophy. As a Jeffersonian Democrat, Breckinridge constantly stressed that maximum individual rights balanced minimum state interference. "Home rule" stood as the cornerstone of American institutions. Since people had surrendered certain rights to the state, it, as trustee, returned to them rights to liberty, property, and fair, legal administration. If evils arose, abuses would be confined locally. Commonwealths free from central-government encroachment represented the Kentuckian's ideal. Members of the present generation, he believed, were drifting away from that ideal, and he fought what he saw as a growing tendency to accept federal control of private and economic life. Since the end of the Civil War, "every form of paternalism" had been adopted; the trend must be reversed. A paternalistic government, he told the House, interfered with the progress of civilization "by putting its hand . . . into that progress." Each step in this direction made citizens more likely to seek a temporary legislative remedy rather than some lasting "philosophic solution" to problems. Paternalism was dividing the nation; class legislation separated rather than united. Capital and labor should not seek special laws, Breckinridge argued, for citizens should think of themselves not as members of one class or another, but simply as Americans. The only legislative remedy must be "equal laws" and "free and equal rights to all." Government's duty was to protect these rights, not to promote the people's happiness—"this is [as] false as it's dangerous."[16]

Breckinridge oratory presented the plight of working people, those whom he said bore the burdens of paternalism. He pictured Congress debating the lot of poor laborers with statistics while life away from Washington was filled with the pathos of men "embarrassed by debt and unoccupied by labor" and women full of "gloom and distress." There were those who preyed on these laborers. Congressmen who prospered in the late war had gained seats in the name of patriotism. Rid the land of them; rid America of the idea that businessmen can buy votes, bribe Congress, and corrupt judges; rid it of class legislation and favoritism.

Then American can return to the ways of Jefferson, where all could advance without "unnatural" burdens placed on them.[17]

Congressman Breckinridge proclaimed the American dream that all were born with equal opportunity to advance to the top, but all around him he saw evidence of a dream betrayed. His answers to the contradictions and problems were simple, perhaps too simple. Give the states more power, and interference would be ended. Give the federal government more strength, on the other hand, and the corruptness of "American sharks" would divide the country and revolution would follow. Only state sovereignty could heal class divisions and bring reform. While such themes and theories, when applied to nineteenth-century problems, have been criticized as "negative and simplistic" and the party has been characterized as "clinging to outdated ideals of states rights, retrenchment, and limited government," Breckinridge recognized few of these criticisms in his own time. He declared his party and its philosophy to be protectors of the best of the past and advocates of the future.[18]

All these threads of policy were woven into the fabric of the tariff issue. It came to represent the battleground for these conflicting views of America, as Democrats found that a low tariff expressed well their laissez-faire ideology. Republicans viewed protective tariffs as a legitimate function in government's efforts to promote growth. Deeply interested in the question, Breckinridge carefully studied the dry and seemingly endless tariff schedules, read about the matter, and, properly prepared, became one of the leading Democratic voices in a debate that stretched across many Congresses. His stand was simple. Believing in equality of opportunity, convinced that nature dictated American expansion and that governmental favoritism was unwise, Breckinridge saw the Republican idea of a protective tariff as the ultimate evil that slowed the progress of America. "We are being strangled," the New South leader cried out, "by the limitations put upon our market." Not until the "wealthiest, the largest, and the most powerful combinations in the land" were shackled could there be remedies. Their lobby in Washington must be destroyed. A reduced tariff was the solution for the representative of Henry Clay's Ashland district.[19]

Free trade would open opportunities to United States shipping and allow America to dominate. "With our labor, with our skill, with our credit," we could produce cheaper and better goods than anyone else in the world, Breckinridge predicted. Motivated more by Adam Smith and the English example than by constituent interest, he joined in the Democrats' struggle to lower tariffs. His statements on the raising of wool duties typified his views: A high tariff would result in the use of inferior substitutes and allow men using "dishonest" materials to make a profit. If wool was on the free list, on the other hand, lower-priced clothing, better-quality goods, and a higher standard of manufacturing would all result.[20]

If Congress failed in its duty Breckinridge envisioned further excesses. In earlier sessions he had seen the duty on "costly goods" go up 5 percent while duties on products "such as poor peope have to buy" increased 78 percent. Why were only certain duties raised? "Is a statement of a manufacturer of an article that the increase of duty up to a certain per cent will allow him to take possession of the American market a sufficient reason to justify the writing into a tariff bill the duty which that manufacturer asks?" Breckinridge was not blind to the depressed conditions of the farmer and the laborer. His solution to those issues was neither revolutionary nor unique to the age, but it was a solution he believed in, as he asked the people to look to the rising sun of greatness: "If we can do no more we can lift our eyes toward this east of new hopes and resolve that from this hour our steps shall be in that direction."[21]

W.C.P. Breckinridge's own future seemed bright. Rumored as the next Speaker of the House if that body became Democratic, or as a cabinet-level appointee, or as a candidate for the vice-presidency, he had achieved national fame as a rising politician. Speaking requests came to his office almost daily. Accepting many (for financial as well as political reasons), he lectured widely on diverse topics: at a revenue-reform meeting in Philadelphia he supported tariff modification; at the celebration of the Pilgrim Society at Plymouth he advocated Canadian unity with America; at the festival of the New England Society of Pennsylvania he spoke on the responsibilities placed on America by "the divine economy"; at the Young Men's Democratic Association of Philadelphia he toasted the New South; at the Union League Club in Chicago he traced political history; at Princeton University he praised the Cleveland administration; at the Place Baptist Church in Brooklyn he considered the "Southern Problem."[22]

In addition to his talks on politics, imperialism, religion, and race relations, Breckinridge also discussed morality. He had proclaimed, in an address to the Bourbon (County) Female College in 1872, that female "chastity is the foundation, the corner-stone of human society." On it rested the stability of human government. Though "our passions mislead us," we must hold true to principle, for "pure homes make pure governments." At Sayre Institute, a girls' school in Lexington, he repeated his advice some ten years later. Speaking as a "gray bearded and prosaic" man, Breckinridge gave fatherly counsel. The girls should not be "staid and prudish old women," but neither did he want them to have rumpled hair or rub their cheeks with a flannel rag. They must be able "to look every living being in the eyes, and yourself also, without conscious guilt." Women must be pure and should avoid "useless hand-shaking, promiscuous kissing, needless touches and all exposures."[23] If Willie Breckinridge had confined himself to handshaking or even "promiscuous kissing," he might have been better able to look at others without guilt. The man who seldom drank or smoked or played cards or bet on horses did have one weakness.

Her name was Madeline Pollard. In 1893 this woman petitioned a Washington, D.C., court that she be given fifty thousand dollars because W.C.P. Breckinridge had promised to marry her but did not. On 1 April 1884, her petition claimed, when she was a "maiden of the age of 17 years" and the defendant "a married man of 47," they had met, and by August he had "completed his seduction" of her. From that time and until only recently, she had been his mistress—giving birth to two children. In 1893, after his wife died, she once again was pregnant, miscarried, but received a promise of marriage. The defendant secretly married another woman. Thus Madeline Pollard pled for a judgment of breach of contract in the District of Columbia. Breckinridge, after apparently failing to buy Pollard's silence, decided to contest the suit. Although an attorney, he chose not to conduct his own defense and instead depended on his talented Lexington law partner John Todd Shelby, his young, hot-tempered son Desha Breckinridge, and four other attorneys under the direction of Benjamin Butterworth of Ohio, a former Republican opponent in Congress who now had a Washington law practice.[24]

Attention quickly centered on the plaintiff. The unknown Madeline Valeria Pollard certainly was not considered beautiful. Breckinridge described her as "about five feet four inches tall, with a very full suit of brown hair, turned up nose, long upper lip, and a rather peculiarly long-strided walk." When she entered the courtroom she was dramatically dressed in black, but the most widely circulated picture of her showed a young girl in a high-necked collar, her long hair bound in a knot. Her dark eyes, narrow face, and wide mouth made her look rather plain. Quiet and thin, she would attract little attention on a crowded street. She seemed ordinary.[25] On the witness stand she described, in a soft voice, her initial chance encounter with Breckinridge on a train. She then told the jury of meeting him at Wesleyan College in Cincinnati, with chaperones in abundance, and of his request for a more "confidential" conversation. They had left in a closed carriage, on a hot summer night. Later the Colonel asked her to accompany him to Lexington. Persuaded by his silver-tongued oratory, she said, she agreed. Breckinridge took her to an appropriately located assignation house, where, after returning from an evening meal at home with his wife, he completed the seduction. They would meet there at least fifty more times in the three years the girl was in Lexington. Entering Sayre School at his suggestion (two years after his speech there), she received funds from Breckinridge. In April 1885 she went to a foundling asylum in Norwood, Ohio, "to have Willie's baby."[26]

Continuing the account, Pollard said she left the baby at the asylum and went to Washington in September 1887 to be closer to the con-

Madeline V. Pollard when a schoolgirl

gressman. Soon she was pregnant again, and in February 1888 a second baby was born. When she told of that child's death, the mother dramatically fainted. The next day she resumed her testimony: She had continued to meet Willie three or four times a week in Washington, where he secured her a position at the Department of Agriculture. (As a congressman he had supported enlarging that department's staff.) After his wife's death in July 1892, she said, Breckinridge promised marriage, in the presence of Mrs. Luke P. Blackburn, widow of a Kentucky governor. Pollard saw him more often now—"once a day, sometimes twice a day, and during the evening": when rumors reached her that his offer was not sincere, she almost committed suicide; then, after learning of her Willie's secret marriage to his cousin, the widowed Mrs. Louise Wing, Madeline decided to seek revenge.[27]

Before the trial Breckinridge had written a long letter to his son, trying to explain what had happened: "My recollection is that all that was done was she asked permission . . . to go out with me, she having asked me as I got up to go if I was going to stay in Cincinnati that night and if so, whether I could not take her to hear some music on one of the hill-tops . . . . It is all a lie about my having anything to do with her leaving that school and going to Sayre Institute in Lexington . . . . I never saw her [from November 1885] that I can recollect, until March [18]87. . . . There must have been some bad behavior during that long period." His defense, then, would be that she was not "unspoiled" when he met her, was not as innocent as she proclaimed, had willingly agreed to his suggestions, and had lured him as much as he lured her.[28]

Memorandum after memorandum supported some of Willie's contentions. One man wrote, "She schooled herself in that sin for the love of it, and . . . is now trying . . . to place herself on the open market." The owner of a store in her hometown, "knew the plaintiff to be a lude [sic] girl—always fast and forward and improper in her behavior with young men." He had caught her and a man in a "compromising position," after which the man admitted that it was not an infrequent thing and anyone who could pay could have done the same. Another man had been caught on a bridge with her "in a compromising position." But in several unfavorable rulings, the judge would not allow the introduction as evidence of much of this hearsay material, calling it "too filthy and obscene."[29]

A successful defense would depend largely on how well Breckinridge presented his story. Taking the witness stand, he explained in a soft, soothing voice that he had met Pollard—at her request—that first time, but it was she who suggested a closed carriage. When he made advances in the carriage she had not resisted, and he had given her ten dollars as they parted. When he left for Lexington she followed him and on the second night there they had slept together: "She was a woman of passion;

I was a man of passion. We yielded ourselves to each other. That was all."[30]

"The Plaintiff" (as he always referred to her) had not been an inexperienced, pure young maiden, but rather an experienced woman who yielded to him as she had to others. Looking back, he could see now that she was ambitious and had used him to gain prominence. Breckinridge denied knowledge of any of the children except the last, stating that none could have been his. When she followed him to Washington, he had given her some money and tried to get rid of her, but she clung like a parasite. She threatened to ruin him completely, to kill him or herself, if he would not marry her. Weak enough to fall into her trap he had been coerced into a vague promise. Yes, he had visited the plaintiff seven times one day in Washington, had recommended her for a governmental position as a person of "good moral character and of good repute," had given her large amounts of money, and had told certain acquaintances that she was his daughter. He deserved condemnation but "there is but one punishment which I have not deserved, and that is to marry the woman who was concerned with me in the act."[31]

Pollard's attorneys in their closing arguments stressed her "spoiled" pureness, and Breckinridge's hypocrisy. "I stand here for womanhood," one proclaimed, while "Grandpa Breckinridge" had lived a lie. In return, one of Breckinridge's lawyers called Madeline a "self-acknowledged prostitute" who had been very good at "stage acting."[32] The outcome was predictable. The jury found for the plaintiff in the sum of $15,000 (three years' salary for a congressman). Accompanied as usual by a nun, Madeline Pollard left the room, while Breckinridge quickly moved for a new trial, pulled his slouch hat over his eyes, and walked out of the courthouse to the carriage in which his third wife awaited him. They casually drove home, stopping to buy vegetables on the way.[33]

When Willie had first contested the suit, he publicly stated his purpose to be "the moral effect of a verdict of vindication." The result of the trial was far different. As historian Hambleton Tapp wrote, "The fall of Breckinridge was like that of an archangel." Books on the trial had as their theme that it "will be a warning to the millions of boys and girls in our country whose characters are just being moulded." Further gossip surfaced, alleging that Pollard was not the only woman who had received Breckinridge's attentions. A Republican paper in Lexington concluded that Breckinridge was no longer useful and was but "a picturesque ruin."[34]

Breckinridge himself was not so certain, and he chose to run for reelection to Congress. The response to this announcement proved even more vocal and critical than that following the trial. For one thing, the incident came at a time of heightened public interest in morality. Those whom David J. Pivar calls "the new abolitionists" sought moral revolution during the late nineteenth century, demanding equal standards of morality for the sexes and calling for high personal morals, not only at home but in politics. Purity reform gained mass-movement status and by the mid-1890s, says Pivar, "the American public was well acquainted with the new social morality." The congressman faced an increasingly hostile world.[35] A Lexington paper noted that he was under attack by everyone from "preacher to prostitute." The National Christian League for the Promotion of Social Purity asked that he be removed from office and implored his new wife to leave her husband "if she has a spark of womanhood." The Union League Club of Chicago prepared to expel Breckinridge as an honorary member. Members of the New York Methodist Episcopal Conference attacked the Kentuckian as a "self-confessed libertine," but the resolution failed to pass. In Boston, the Women's Rescue League condemned him.[36]

In his hometown, attacks proved even more vehement. Professor James B. Jones of Hamilton College for Females asked that this "fallen and gifted man" be rejected, and his party as well, because of its own "inherent rottenness." "An insult to every pure woman, a menace to every virgin," Breckinridge followed the examples of Aaron Burr and Lord Byron, said Jones. Writing again a week later, he grew more specific: Breckinridge was a depraved man of "beastly lusts," a serpent, a "lust fiend," "a wild beast in search of prey." "Let the rapist die," Jones concluded. All this led Breckinridge to write John T. Shelby: "Who is this J.B. Jones . . . who seems to be acquainted with the purpose of God, as I see he speaks of there being 'A remote possibility' of God's pardoning me?"[37] Others were more moderate than Jones but stressed similar themes. The Sunday after the trial ended, Lexington sermons included "Moral Standards" and "The Christian Church in Politics." Forgive the sinner, the preachers said, but do not reward him. Even Democrats should not vote for such a "filthy man." A prayer at the Methodist State Conference called for his defeat. Evangelist Sam Jones of Georgia spoke in opposition to him. Then Breckinridge's own Presbyterian Church, founded by his uncle, expelled him for four months. The congressional campaign would be conducted, as the Lexington *Kentucky Leader* had predicted, on "the lowest plane" of any political race in Kentucky.[38]

Since his initial race for Congress in 1884, election and reelection for Breckinridge had never been difficult, but during that first campaign he had listed those possibly opposed to his election. One was "Mr. Owens of Scott."[39] Ten years later, in 1894, William Clayborne Owens, still in opposition, sought Breckinridge's House seat. Younger than Willie by fourteen years, a Columbia Law School graduate, protégé of Henry Watterson of the *Courier-Journal*, and past Speaker of the Kentucky House, Owens was a formidable opponent. Over a decade earlier he had unsuccessfully challenged incumbent J.C.S. Blackburn, who called Owens "a

A W.C.P. Breckinridge campaign poster in Lexington, 1894. Courtesy
Kentucky Historical Society

low-bred vain, imperious blatherskite." Two years later he had been the
strongest candidate behind Breckinridge. Many voters, including Breckinridge, believed Owens gave Madeline Pollard the financial backing
needed for the 1894 trial; an Owens organizer was one of her lawyers. A
Frankfort attorney warned Willie, "I am satisfied that politics lie at the
bottom of this suit." While the case progressed in Washington, Owens
campaigned in the Seventh District, promising to "return to the people
their banner unsullied with dishonor."[40]

A third candidate also sought the 1894 Democratic nomination. Evan
Evans Settle—forty-six years old, tall, his hair and mustache streaked
with gray—was a former legislator from Owen County. Now he was
attacked by Will Owens as entering the race only to pull votes from him
and thereby aid Breckinridge. Settle denied the charge. Handsome and a
good orator, "Van" Settle would develop into a strong candidate.[41]

Both Owens and Settle had already campaigned vigorously when
Breckinridge gave his first speech in the district on 4 May 1894, at the

Lexington Opera House. Many in the almost totally male audience were openly hostile. His reelection hopes could be destroyed if he faltered. With tears in his eyes, in a quivering and low voice, he quietly began the one-hour talk by telling how his father had taken him over the same route that John Breckinridge had followed to Kentucky and that he had then determined to remain a Kentuckian. He then reviewed past elections, his years in the House, his attacks on a protective tariff, and his national standing in the party. Then, near the close of the speech, Breckinridge focused on recent problems: "I knew the secret sin; I tried to atone for it." Trying to spare his supporters, but "entangled by weakness, by passion, by sin, in coils which it was almost impossible to break," he had failed. If there were men better qualified, let them be chosen. Select "someone whose life has been stainless," he declaimed, "whose nights have been sinless, whose ability is ample, whose experience is wide. For a hundred years this district has been represented by men. They have not always been sinless men." He stood back and brushed away a tear.

The effect was magnetic. Both talk and candidate were enthusiastically received. In the bold and almost arrogant speech, the old eloquence still remained and won victories. An admirer later recalled that it was "one of the most remarkable scenes I ever witnessed. His audience was completely at his command, wild with enthusiasm, and ready apparently to rend his accusers." Another supporter noted that many who had "come to scoff remained to pray."[42]

Breckinridge still had an excellent chance for success. He encouraged the circulating reports that suggested Owens' morals were suspect as well, while Settle admitted that he once had been "the victim of drink." This, plus a divided opposition, would aid Breckinridge. In addition, a powerful voting interest remained generally loyal to Willie. The only former Confederate in the race, Breckinridge did not play down his old ties. Everywhere he went, the Colonel praised the old Confederacy and kept close connections to fellow veterans who attended the Morgan Men reunions. Before a speech in Athens, Kentucky, in August 1894, he was escorted to the site by 180 cavalrymen riding two abreast while some 350 "rebels" proceeded on foot in column formation. Breckinridge rewarded the faithful by castigating opponents unmercifully. His Confederate background made it possible that the sectionalism he attacked in his national speeches might bring him local victory.[43]

He had other supporters as well. Ten years of recommending patronage choices had gained him some friends. Most blacks voting in the Democratic primary gave him their support. Nor did all ministers oppose him: evangelist George O. Barnes spoke for him, and the Reverend William E. Knight took the position that the sinner had confessed and should be forgiven. A man of "rare personal charm," who was "like a gentle summer wind," Breckinridge, in Knight's judgment, deserved reelection.[44]

For a few of the men who continued to oppose him Breckinridge could use private persuasion effectively. He had in his possession information that could prove damaging to two prominent Lexington families. To a man who had just attacked him in the Lexington *Kentucky Leader*, Willie warned that further criticisms would bring a public statement: "I know what your relations with Miss Pollard were when you had her as a guest of your own daughter under your roof . . . . You know that there was a living child born to Miss Pollard on Feb'y 3rd 1888, in all probability it was your child. My sincere kindness for you and yours has been conclusively demonstrated by my decision to risk my case without your testimony. There are persons . . . who will bear me witness if need be to the truth of these assertions. It will be intensely painful to some of them to do this, and it will give me pain to require it of them. *But they will do it.* . . . I respect your wife and would fain spare her pain. But there cannot be any misunderstanding between us. . . . There are those who are very dear to me; and he who wounds them by these attacks must be ready to take the consequences."[45] The criticisms ceased.

Many of the members of the opposite sex, however, continued to find fault. Communications to newspapers warned that young men supporting "Papa" Breckinridge should discontinue visits to the writers' daughters. Merchants who favored the Colonel reported being ostracized by women shoppers. Other women used the opportunity to appeal for a woman's ballot to insure defeat of the man "who has plunged the poisioned stilleto [sic] into the heart of virtue." A friend informed Breckinridge that "strong-minded women are doing their utmost to defeat you." John Shelby reported, "The women are very bitter against you and intensely active and stirred up." A protest meeting at the Opera House drew over a thousand women, and an Owens barbecue sponsored by Lexington women attracted even more. Resolutions proclaimed that the election of Breckinridge "would be a disgrace to Kentucky, a shame upon manhood, an insult to womanhood, a sinful example to youth, a menace to both society and home." Susan B. Anthony expressed her hope that "exposed & confessed unchastity won't win." Breckinridge's former sister-in-law Mary Desha, one of the three founders of the Daughters of the American Revolution, persuaded that organization to oppose him. All this brought an outburst from Willie: "I have been and am a consistent friend of the advanced notions of permitting women to win their bread. . . . It seems a travesty of justice that I should be the victim of unscrupulous women who have taken advantage of these benefits."

The campaign involved the women of Kentucky in politics to an unprecedented degree. The *Kentucky Gazette* reported that "women who never took the slightest interest in politics in their lives have become active politicians." Unquestionably, Breckinridge was aiding the woman suffrage movement, though hardly in the manner he would have wished.[46] Censure came from other sources as well. Breckinridge's free-trade views and his opposition to tariff protection for hemp also hurt him. In Congress he had consistently supported Democratic bills lowering hemp duties; since Kentucky produced over 90 percent of the nation's hemp, largely in his electoral district, those had not been popular votes. His role in formulating tariff policy on the Ways and Means Committee brought a local newspaper attack on a record "directly contrary to the interests and of course the wishes of his constituents." In 1888 the Blue Grass Hemp Trust (supporting Owens) had failed to block his renomination: popular and virtually unopposed then, Breckinridge could sidestep the obstacle; in 1894 it would be more difficult.[47]

The effects of the Pollard trial still constituted the key to the election. Willie had to defend himself against the charge that "courtesans" traveled on his campaign train, and that he had once visited Madeline after teaching a Sunday School class. His own band defiantly ended a rally by striking up a provocative air—"The Girl I Left Behind Me."[48] The voter turnout was the largest ever for a primary election in the district. Reporters from New York, Washington, Cincinnati, Philadelphia, and many other cities came to record the results. Breckinridge was defeated. Owens received 8,074 votes to Willie's 7,819. Of Settle's 3,406 votes, almost half came from his home county. Defeated by 255 votes out of some 19,000, Breckinridge received evidence of fraudulent voting in several counties and of ballot-buying in others. He asked for a recount, especially in Owens's home county of Scott, where Owens received over a thousand-vote majority, but the appeal was rejected. In November Owens defeated Republican nominee George Denny by only 101 votes. As Breckinridge had received a majority of about six thousand in 1892, it was evident that the Democrats were split.[49]

Breckinridge's near-victory was remarkable. The national press recognized the uniqueness of the race. The Washington *Post* declared that the campaign "had no parallel in our history. In intensity of feeling it was like civil war. It divided neighborhood, churches, and families." Closer to the commonwealth, the Cincinnati *Enquirer* proclaimed it "the most remarkable campaign in the political history of any country," and reluctantly praised the "brilliancy, audacity and eloquence" of the loser. "The most famous political fight in the history of the United States" was the New York *Herald's* summation. Most of the press admitted to a "brilliant personal canvass" by Breckinridge but expressed their joy over the outcome. Typical headlines read, "The Silver Tongued and Moral Leper Defeated"; "Kentucky Redeemed"; and "The 'Kentucky Rosebud' is Blasted."[50] And most reporters agreed on why Breckinridge lost. Had it not been for the ladies, the Los Angeles *Times* claimed, Owens could not have won. Other papers noted that women "almost to a unit" opposed Breckinridge. Never before had "the fairer sex" played the leading role, but Breckinridge's race offended their morals and sense of rightness. Though without the vote, women exerted tremendous influence, and some of those who tasted politics first in this race would turn to seeking the vote for women. Ironically, the woman most responsible for furthering the women's rights movement in Kentucky two decades later would be Willie's own daughter-in-law, Madeline McDowell Breckinridge. An opposition editor, though glad of Breckinridge's defeat, acknowledged his achievement: "We cannot conceive of another man in public office who would have dared appeal to his constituents for a renewal of their favors under such unparalleled conditions." The loss by less than 1 percent of the vote revealed that despite his human errors people still loved their "Billy Breck."[51]

Thirteen

Rising Suns and Lengthening Shadows

RETURNING to Kentucky after his lame-duck period in Congress in the early months of 1895, Breckinridge found a political world as chaotic as the one he had entered after the Civil War. In 1865 several parties and factions had sought votes, rapid shifts of power had taken place, and fundamental alignments had occurred that shaped state politics for the next three decades. Similar and equally important movements transpired in the 1890s, and Willie Breckinridge strove to regain his accustomed place in the center of the turmoil. By 1895 Democrats had ruled the commonwealth for thirty years. Removal of the issue of black rights had partially healed party factionalism, and the party found election unity and won impressive victories. But throughout that period various third parties questioned that rule. Once-silent agrarians began to voice their discontent more openly, and as Breckinridge's party faced this angry electorate it provided few new answers.

Threats to Democratic hegemony came from within and without. Unquestioning devotion to New South industrialization angered many. More important, the party, in power for so long, simply went stale. In election after election, the same themes surfaced—war stories, low taxes, aid to railroads, race, the tariff—and the same faces appeared before impatient voters. Specific events also stimulated dissatisfaction. News of the disappearance in 1888 of popular state treasurer James W. "Honest Dick" Tate, for example, was followed by an investigation that revealed shortages of some $247,000. "Tateism" quickly became a byword for corruption, further tainting the party's image. Republicans reveled in Democratic distress. As memories of the war faded, as the race issue decreased in importance, as businessmen gained importance in an increasingly urban age, the "outs" began to be viewed by some as the reform element. Kentucky Republicans gained an increasing share of the vote.

All of this came together in 1895, the year Breckinridge reentered the state political picture. Agrarian defections from the Democrats, increased party factionalism on the money issue, Republican inroads in Louisville, and a skilled gubernatorial candidate led to a Republican victory. A stunned and shattered Democratic party suffered deep wounds that did not heal quickly, and the last five years of the 1890s would see some of the most bitter political infighting in the state's history.

Breckinridge's place in the controversy was clear. He now represented the older generation, the so-called Bourbon Democrats, the financial conservatives. Where did that leave him, with his party dominated by agrarian influences, devoted to inflationary "free silver" finances, and committed to increased regulation of railroads? To the silver-tongued orator it seemed that he and his allies voiced the true creed of the party; the others did not. They must be purged, and the doctrines of Jefferson restored. "Redeemers" once during Reconstruction, his generation must again redeem the South, now from itself.

The nomination of William Jennings Bryan in 1896, the platform he supported, and the Populist party's endorsement of the Nebraskan left Breckinridge even more convinced that his own party had lost its way. It must turn its back on the cross of gold and worship old principles. Guiding the party of pilgrims were important Kentucky Democrats, for the opposition to "boy Bryan" included many of the earlier leaders: editor Henry Watterson, United States Senator William Lindsay, former governor Simon B. Buckner, constitutional convention president Cassius M. Clay, former United States senator and secretary of the treasury John G. Carlisle, several former congressmen, and a score of other politicians, including W.C.P. Breckinridge.[1]

As a delegate to the National (Gold) Democratic Convention in September 1896, Breckinridge eloquently told the assembly why he joined this third-party movement. He opposed those "radicals" who sought to destroy his vision of a fraternal society that was blind to classes. By stressing—according to Breckinridge—division and hostility between business and labor and by supporting strikers, Bryan preached the doctrine "of hate and of discord." The Kentuckian stood for order, for law, and for peace. Bryan Democrats represented chaos, lawlessness, and class warfare—in short socialism or communism, not American principles. Applauded once more by a national audience, Breckinridge stood proudly with the party's nominees, Kentucky-born, former Union general John M. Palmer of Illinois and former Confederate general Buckner of the Bluegrass State.[2]

Willie Breckinridge returned from the convention to become the Gold Democrats' candidate for Congress. Seeking to regain his old seat, fusing with the Republican party, he hoped to draw enough votes to defeat Bryan and "free silver," if not to win himself. As in 1894 the race was bitter, and on several occasions hecklers disrupted his campaign addresses.

Such tactics only confirmed Breckinridge's view of the opposition. For the rest of his life he would attack what he perceived as a real danger to America—these leaders who sought to enlist class against class, who fought for further governmental intervention, and who, according to his view, would use any means to gain their ends. Breckinridge held fast to a visionary society, one that he believed could exist, and in doing so he often ignored the reality of the present. Two crusades and two political worlds—one declining, the other rising—now met in combat. Breckinridge, in the smaller army (as in 1862), only fought that much harder.

His regular Democratic opponent in 1896, old foe Evan Evans Settle (Owens too had turned Gold Democrat), was not Breckinridge's primary target. "Bryanism" was. "Wandering Willie" of Nebraska, Breckinridge maintained, advocated policies that encouraged men to tear down privately owned toll-gates, to "shoot at women," and to destroy property. These "lewd fellows of the baser sort" received support for their unlawful actions when men like Illinois Governor John Peter Altgeld pardoned convicted "anarchist" murderers, and when Bryan condoned him. Such "incredibly poor," foolish, and reckless leadership made it evident that "the skimmings have been thrown to the top." Not only had "incompetents" taken over the Democratic party but, even worse, they advocated policies that were anathema to Breckinridge. The speeches of Bryan contradicted his every view of the political world. Freedom of commerce, cried out Breckinridge, not governmental control; open markets to labor, not unions; "impartial" legislation by a "just" government, not class actions; "natural and normal" progress on laws, not statutory experiments—these alone could bring prosperity and the dawning of a new day.[3]

Instead of the rebirth he sought, the darkness of defeat was Breckinridge's political fate. Settle won the election by some 1,800 ballots. Victory of a sort rewarded the Gold Democratic candidate, however, for Republican William McKinley's narrow win in Kentucky was commonly credited to Breckinridge's attraction of normally Democratic voters to the cause he led.

Bryan was defeated, but so was Breckinridge. No more would he actively seek office, but he could never abandon politics either. As the opportunity to influence through oratory lessened, Willie and his son Desha turned to the printed page. Purchase of the new Lexington *Morning Herald* in 1897 gave the family an outlet for their political views, and over the next seven and a half years the elder Breckinridge wrote about 95 percent of the editorials—some 2,500 pieces—as well as occasional regular stories. He also kept up a reasonably successful law practice.[4]

Busy in these endeavors, the Colonel did not neglect politics. His fight had not yet been won, for if Bryan had lost, followers of his philosophy still ruled Democratic councils. Should he rejoin the regular organization and try to work with men he despised? Fellow editor Watterson, faced with a dwindling newspaper circulation, would take that course. Or should he instead go with the Republicans, the party of high tariffs and of a different "paternalism"? Writing to an influential northern Kentuckian, Breckinridge answered these questions. Unalterable principles must be upheld so that in time the Democratic party would again be "the party of tomorrow, . . . the party of progress, the party—not of negation—but of affirmation." No surrender could occur. Breckinridge fought for a future based on theories of the past.[5]

A rising politician from northern Kentucky, William Goebel seemed the antithesis of Willie Breckinridge and his world: whereas the Colonel boasted of his British heritage and four generations of American ancestors, Goebel, the son of German immigrant parents, could claim only one generation; while Breckinridge used his forensic skills to attract votes, Goebel, not a good public speaker, depended more on organization, backroom alliances, and an urban machine to win; while the New South spokesman advocated continued corporate and railroad growth, Goebel used the issue of increased railroad regulation as his chief avenue of power; whereas the old warrior stressed his Confederate ties, so popular with Kentucky voters, the young challenger could make no such appeals, for his father had fought for the Union; as Breckinridge stood for the aristocracy, Goebel symbolized the laboring class from which he rose; while the former congressman had felt the shame of scandal, the young, ambitious state senator had not, for he never married and had few, if any, romantic attachments with the opposite sex; as the central Kentuckian supported the gold standard, so the Pennsylvania-born northern Kentuckian went with "free silver" and Bryan. In 1898, the sixty-one-year-old editor viewed this forty-two-year-old rising star of Kentucky, this new political type, and quickly placed him in the camp of political enemies. Each man saw the other as the embodiment of the forces of evil he sought to destroy. The two men, and their two political courses, were converging toward a turbulent and explosive January day in 1900, when the struggle would reach its bloody climax.[6]

Breckinridge's *Herald* first turned its full attention to Goebel in 1898, when the state senator pushed through a bill that set up a central, three-man election board with authority to decide contested races. The so-called Goebel Law gave its sponsor, who virtually selected all three members, tremendous potential power. The *Herald* warned the public to fear this "third-rate leader" who sought office by any means, for his law was the medium chosen for self-advancement. Honest men should have defeated such a corrupt, unconstitutional measure in the legislature, Breckinridge declared; strong men would have attacked its evils. Instead the measure had been passed by "poor weaklings . . . whose backbone is mush and whose liver is white; who know what is right . . . but who are too cowardly to stand up for their convictions and cower behind the hypocritical pretense of caucus and regularity." They deserved only contempt.[7]

"Strong-willed, intelligent, cold, and ambitious," Goebel aroused more hatred than any other late nineteenth-century Kentucky politician. Machine methods of "Boss Bill" seemed alien to the state's older politicians, and his stringent attacks on railroads led conservatives to call him "communistic." Opponents associated dictatorship, anarchy, and lawlessness with "King Goebel," while to his many allies he stood as the rational voice of overdue reform. He stirred deep passions in an already turbulent age, and his actions in 1899 at the Democratic state convention confirmed conservatives' fears. After trailing in a field of three entering the contest, Goebel emerged on the twenty-sixth ballot with the gubernatorial nomination. Both of the defeated candidates and many of their supporters cried out that they had been fraudulently deprived of votes. The convention at Louisville's Music Hall ended in bitterness and discord.[8]

Seeing an opportunity to defeat the Goebelites and Bryanites he so opposed, Breckinridge called on these disgruntled Democrats to unite and form a third party. This they did and selected former governor John Young Brown as their nominee. These voter defections, coupled with opposition from some former Confederates, old Bourbon leaders, and those progressives who disliked Goebel's methods, meant that regular Democratic nominee Goebel faced a divided party. Republicans did not capitalize fully on Democratic distress, however; their nominee, forty-five-year-old William S. Taylor, was not their strongest or most attractive candidate. Breckinridge, in surveying the 1899 gubernatorial field, found little promise in any stable. The party he wanted to support, the "Honest Election League" or Brown Democrats, no longer appealed to him, for their candidate supported the hated "free silver" heresy; additionally, Brown and Breckinridge had been cool to each other since their Centre fight in the 1850s. Goebel, clearly, could not be considered, even with Willie's brother Robert J. Breckinridge, Jr., on the same ticket as attorney general. That left only Taylor, a man who aroused little enthusiasm in the editor.[9]

If restrained in his support for the Republican, Breckinridge left no doubt of his opposition to "Goebelism." That disease, that madness, that "moral aberration" threatened the commonwealth. People must not be duped by false issues raised by the Democrat, the railroad lawyer warned, for Goebel's attacks on the L & N were only "irrelevant hellabaloo"; he was fighting windmills and raining blows on straw men. Such demogoguery masked the frauds of the Music Hall convention, the evils of the Goebel Law, the machination of the "most expert political schemer, trickster and charlatan" in Kentucky. Goebel, who had killed a man four years earlier, not only practiced lawlessness, said the editor, but encouraged his obeying followers to do the same. They were but Hessian mercenaries led by their German general.[10]

The close of a canvass, in which each side perceived and publicized the opposition as evil incarnate, brought quiet relief to nearly all involved. With election day came the *Herald's* elated response: "Goebel Beaten!" Democrats, however, proclaimed their candidate victorious in the contest. As reports of corruption by both sides filtered in, the Goebel-approved election board finally made its decision. Surprising almost everyone, it declared Taylor the victor with 193,714 votes to Goebel's 191,331. Brown's 12,140 ballots meant that a third party had once again deprived Democrats of victory. Taylor, the commonwealth's second consecutive Republican governor, was inaugurated, but Breckinridge watched the proceeding carefully, for he feared the Democrats might still march forward to "the ultimate crime"—the theft of the governorship.[11] In fact, Democrats had one last opportunity for victory, and they took it. They decided to contest the results before the General Assembly in its January 1900 session. That decision infuriated the editor. The legislature had no right to decide the matter, he thundered, and this unconstitutional move only underscored Goebel's determination to win by whatever method. Breckinridge agreed to serve as one of Governor Taylor's attorneys before the legislative contest board that would recommend a course of action to the Democratic-controlled General Assembly. The presence of only one Republican on the eleven-man board made the outcome clear, however, and Breckinridge complained bitterly of a sham hearing. Most observers predicted that Goebel would be recommended and that the House and Senate would then agree to it (as had happened recently in Tennessee).[12]

This must not occur, said the editor. Such a move would result in political confusion, even violence and bloodshed: "Force will be met with force." Breckinridge's prophecy edged toward reality when Republicans moved to counter the Democratic majority by bringing to Frankfort over one thousand armed men, chiefly from eastern Kentucky, in an attempt to pressure undecided solons. Tensions rose as both sides prepared for a clash. Breckinridge, who had not been consulted, quickly criticized the Republican action "in measured terms," calling it unwise and dangerous. His counsel, along with others', resulted in the departure of most of the "mountain Army," but the damage to the party's cause had been done. Civil War memories of militarism resurfaced, and a Breckinridge prediction written almost two years earlier moved closer to fulfillment: he had then foreseen that "we may have two distinct legislatures, two rival Governors . . . each claiming recognition."[13]

Violence shocked Frankfort with tragic suddenness. On 30 January 1900 an unknown assassin shot William Goebel. As the senator lay dying, the contest board met and, despite Breckinridge's fervent protests, proclaimed the wounded man entitled to the gubernatorial chair. The Democratic legislators—a majority of each house—met secretly, accepted the board's report, and declared Goebel governor. He took the oath but survived only four days after the shooting, dying on 3 February. Young Lieutenant Governor J.C.W. Beckham was then sworn in as his successor. Republican Taylor had countered all this by calling out the militia (on Breckinridge's advice), adjourning the General Assembly to the Republican stronghold of London, Kentucky (against Willie's counsel), and ignoring the Democratic actions. Two governors, two legislatures, two different militias now existed. Brothers Willie and Robert represented opposite sides, as the dangers of civil and fraternal war again threatened the commonwealth.[14]

W.C.P. Breckinridge stood confused in the midst of chaos. He denounced the assassination, but at the same time he told readers that the murder should not obscure the facts—Taylor, not Goebel, had won. Believing that the legal system would uphold the Republicans, he counseled them to hold fast and avoid compromise, while he continued to be troubled by the chief executive's order adjourning the legislature, a move he believed unconstitutional. And as his faith in Taylor's ability to govern declined, so too did his enthusiasm for the cause. When the Republican governor refused to appear in public and walk with Breckinridge to show his fortitude (in a display reminiscent of Robert J. Breckinridge's walk in the "brick-bat fight" of 1827), Willie displayed rare anger. A little more than a week following Goebel's death, the Colonel privately described Taylor as "an irresolute, unstable and indecisive man—incapable of either making up his mind or keeping it made up. . . . He is patriotic, well meaning and perhaps with physical courage; but wholly unfit for leadership in times like these."[15]

His heart was no longer in the struggle, but W.C.P. Breckinridge could not admit that to himself or others; he fought on. As Republican attorney, he argued the contested election before a lower court and the state Court of Appeals, only to lose. He had based his entire course of action on his belief that the law supported him. Now it did not. Confused, he voiced his anger over the "theft of the Governorship." One "unalterable and vital fact" still remained: Taylor had won. Under the heading "Kentucky—Crowned Mistress of Liars," the editor saw a state with "Judas, the high priest, the Pharisees and the mob in the saddle." On 21 May 1900 the United States Supreme Court reaffirmed the lower-court decisions, thus defeating Taylor and ending the dual governorship that had existed for three months. Goebel, even in death, had won.[16]

To Breckinridge, "Goebelism" seemed at first to live on in the person of Governor Beckham, but Beckham's administration bespoke a more conservative stance, and when Beckham ran for a full term three years later Breckinridge felt he could support him, if begrudgingly. Nationally, Bryan's loss in 1900 had caused Breckinridge to rejoice openly over defeat of "the prophet of evil." Now the Democratic party could spread the gospel of brotherhood, common interest, national unity, and "class intra-dependence," instead of the heresies preached by Bryan. The once-powerful war horse of the Democrats, recently termed a "traitor" and a "wandering lamb," supported his party again: after almost a decade of defections and shifting coalitions, Breckinridge now believed that the party had rejoined him at last.[17]

Politics did not occupy all of Breckinridge's time, nor fill all his editorial columns. During this period he devoted equal attention to other causes which, if not creating the same fervor, still represented beliefs he strongly supported. His politics did not follow in detail the course of some of his ancestors, but his views on America's place and destiny did. "God meant us to rule the world," he blandly asserted. The controlling spirit of the world he identified with Anglo-Saxonism. America's mission required that its "armies of civilization" spread new thoughts, customs, and traditions everywhere. Imperialism would reform the world. More than moral victories were to be won, however, for expansion promised economic success as well. Both manifest destiny and economics thus demanded that the nation acquire Hawaii and Cuba, and form a political and "organic union" with Canada. With an English-speaking empire from the Gulf to the Arctic, with South America and the Pacific shores open as markets, Breckinridge said, America could prosper and benefit the world as well.[18]

The Spanish-American conflict in 1898 brought these matters to center stage. Surprisingly, the *Morning Herald* was not jingoistic, for its editor argued that Cuba could be conquered peacefully. Even after the sinking of the *Maine* in February, Breckinridge advised patience. A rare front-page *Herald* editorial asked Kentuckians to refrain from threats, insults, and bravado. But when the Colonel read Senator Redfield Proctor's analysis of the Cuban situation, he too declared that duty required intervention. But the former soldier emphasized that war "is always brutal, always fierce and . . . inhumane." Soon after the war formally began, however, he wrote patriotically that no country had ever entered hostilities with such pure motives, prompted only by "disinterested and lofty sentiments of humanity."[19]

More worldly motives also operated, however, and Breckinridge candidly acknowledged "self-protection—self interest" as causes of intervention. America needed Cuba because it guarded the Gulf, "our *mare clausum*." American victories were "the natural . . . fruit of our races," all part of the "irresistible currents of human history." Imperialism and the fruits of war gave the nation a promising future. Through the Philippines America had a stepping stone to China, the location of "our true 'home markets.' " The United States must receive its share of that "huge and valuable carcass . . . to be sliced up and divided." Breckinridge predicted that in a few years the Philippines would be like other American territories, "contented American Commonwealths." His words supported imperialism, and they also implied that Asiatics could be assimilated into the nation's fabric as full citizens. Other southerners of his generation argued against both of the Kentuckian's stands. Once again, his racial views differed from the prevailing pattern of the South.[20]

One major hindrance to sectional reconciliation and southern industrialization still remained, and its solution seemed more distant than ever. In Breckinridge's view, "this terrific race problem" meant life or death, extermination "or wonderful progress" for the region, indeed, for America. It must be solved. Breckinridge did not deal in abstractions. Although Kentucky had a small and declining black population (13 percent) in 1900, the editor's hometown did not. In that same year blacks made up 38 percent of Lexington's population; the city ranked twelfth nationally in the percentage of Negroes (ahead of Richmond, Virginia, and New Orleans). Despite a state law segregating railroad cars, which Robert J. Breckinridge, Jr., supported and Willie opposed, black citizens in Kentucky still retained voting rights in the 1890s and suffered less legal persecution than many southern blacks. But that decade witnessed increasing segregation, disfranchisement, and lynching throughout America. Could blacks in the commonwealth turn back the prevailing climate of proscription?[21]

Breckinridge assisted them in that endeavor. Through actions and through the pages of the *Herald*, the editor and attorney, like some other southern conservatives, opposed the rising spirit of racism. Still, he was no racial egalitarian. In Breckinridge's view, slaves had been the foundation of a great civilization, but that way of life had passed, leaving slaves as freedmen. Deprived of "discipline" and training, the Negro race faced great problems, the editor believed. Uneducated and without property, blacks made progress "beyond what its best friends hoped." Those "prudent, thrifty, frugal" and docile members of the race who had closest contacts with the superior white race had advanced furthest. Yet blacks still had a long way to go, in Breckinridge's eyes. "For some time" yet they would generally serve as manual laborers, as domestics, as the lesser race. "Evolution may be certain," the Calvinist proclaimed, "but it may be very slow." If patient, if treated fairly by whites, blacks would progress as the years passed. Through the vocational-school emphasis of men like Booker T. Washington (whom Breckinridge admired greatly), Negroes would be better prepared for citizenship. The Colonel's support of Washington, and his acceptance of black inferiority (at least at present), typified the aristocratic, conservative southern reaction.[22]

Yet if Breckinridge's evolutionary view of the race allowed him to consider blacks to be his present-day inferiors, that did not mean that he did not support them in their struggle to retain rights. After all, the patrician viewed a great many people around him—black and white—as less than his equal. Even if Willie sympathized with states that disfranchised Negroes, for example, he could not condone such actions. Blacks were American citizens and had fought heroically in America's wars. They deserved full political and civil rights. When demagogues like the "blackguard" Ben Tillman sought to use the race issue to solidify power, they only made Negroes "a hopeless, irritating, hostile race" instead of a hopeful, contented, and friendly one. Worse, to the New South spokesman, these self-proclaimed progressives sowed reactionary seeds of class dissension which would grow to disturb social and industrial life. You could not rid the South of blacks by depriving them of the vote; they could not be legislated out of existence. Negroes must be recognized as a part of southern life and must be treated as the citizens they were. The sooner the people rid the region of cruel racists, said Breckinridge, "the sooner they will realize that their institutions are in no danger, their civilization is not at stake, and that their permanent and practical undisputed sway can not be overturned." He opposed literacy tests and other paraphernalia of disfranchisement, in the hope that someday, "all races might enjoy a common liberty secured by an impartial law."[23]

In further contrast with many white southerners of his time, Breckinridge approved not only the efforts of Booker T. Washington, but also the much more militant ones of black leader W.E.B.DuBois. In an editorial comparing Washington's *Up From Slavery* with DuBois' *The Souls of Black Folk*, he called both books "remarkable contributions" to literature and termed *Souls* "the most significant and remarkable utterance yet published by a negro." He recommended both books and both men to his readers. As an attorney, he represented blacks in court. When a Franklin County Negro was convicted of murdering a prominent citizen who had led a mob to seize him, Willie fought to obtain a pardon. Through editorials and speeches, he advocated equal protection for all. A young black lawyer offered aid to Breckinridge during his 1894 problems, noting that the congressman helped many "young colored men" in their law careers. Representative Breckinridge had asked the commissioner of labor to retain in the Census Office a black worker who feared he would be fired because of his color. Ever optimistic, the editor continued to predict a better day for race relations: "Barriers will be removed, prejudices will die, class distinctions be obliterated. Not at once, not in our day; not without fierce contest; not without heroism and sacrifice, but yet slowly, surely, the day grows stronger; the sun rises higher toward the better noon and the glad twilight." Echoing his father, he wrote: "The negro is a man and the race in its essential unity is one race. Of one blood were all men made."[24]

Even if racially paternalistic, even if he believed Caucasians the superior race and Negroes an inferior one that must be elevated by white contacts, even if something of a racist by later standards, Breckinridge was nevertheless an ally of the Negro at a time when the race had few white friends. Advocating political and legal equality, he had supported blacks even though it hurt him politically, as in 1868. As Carl Degler has noted of another southern politician with similar views, "It seems certain that if [William] Mahone's views had prevailed, limited as they were, the future of black people in the South would have been considerably brighter than it turned out to be during the years of lynching, disfranchisement, and legal segregation that followed." Breckinridge publicly voiced the thoughts of an all too silent minority, the "liberal" wing of the New South movement. He spoke for the southern conscience.[25] Additionally, he lent voice, pen, and action to various progressive causes of the late nineteenth and early twentieth centuries. Neat labels and stereotypes are always dangerous, particularly so in the case of W.C.P. Breckinridge. He was, despite the contradictions, a progressive Bourbon.

Devotion to the New South and its railroads, for instance, did not blind him to the perils of unlimited corporate wealth. This attorney, whose firm earned well over a thousand dollars annually from the L & N and Chesapeake and Ohio railroads, and who fought Goebel's form of regulation, at the same time attacked as menaces to liberty the "oppressive trusts" whose wealth went to the favored few. Only months before he began criticizing Goebel, Breckinridge in an editorial agreed that opposition to monopolistic trusts was "just and intelligent." An economic system that produced both multimillionaires and paupers seemed to him "radically wrong." Unchecked progress, he said, crushed "under its remorseless wheels" both human hearts and human lives. In a frank appraisal of his own mental and philosophical struggle, Breckinridge wrote in March 1897, "It is just along here where the conservative statesman finds difficult problems. He does not believe in communism or socialism; he is reluctant to regulate the acquisition of wealth by statute. . . . And yet he recognizes the danger that may arise from the unlimited power of organized and corporate wealth, and must find some remedy for this impending evil."[26]

Like his ancestors, the Colonel also criticized Kentucky's school system. Calling for better facilities, higher teacher salaries, day nurseries for children of working parents, and a practical compulsory attendance law, Breckinridge was no reactionary or financial conservative in that milieu. Given his stress on liberty, it is not surprising that he championed freedom of speech and discussion in schools: "ancient dogmas" should be attacked, and the classroom should become "a field of battle where thought contests with thought. . . . Out of this comes only good." The professor must teach his pupil to think, free from censorship, "even though he teach heresy, rebellion and schism."[27]

Other calls for action came from the Breckinridge pen, as he supported rural free delivery, expanded library facilities, improvements in eleemosynary institutions, prison reform, sanitary sewers, party primaries, reorganization of the army, and an improved judiciary. ("Cheap judges," he intoned, "are far more expensive than cheap doctors, who ought never to be employed except by impatient heirs.") The editor also envisioned a "Republic of Republics" made up of federated nations all united in "some organic order." Based on equal representation, such a unit would be the best hope for world peace, his most fervent desire.[28]

Yet despite his support for change, Breckinridge could not modify his basic tenets beyond a certain point. Much earlier, he had advised students to test their philosophies, and his own had differed from his father's. Now, as an older man, Willie could not change, while party and world changed around him. The sense remains, however, that he knew a modification must come. Breckinridge recognized the complexities of modern life and advised his children to follow their own beliefs in this new age— though ever mindful of family traditions. He constantly spoke of the possibilities of the future, but some prospects hurt more than he could bear. Repudiation of his party came hard enough, but that only required rejection of men, not principles. Even though his own words, especially in private, betrayed laissez-faire doctrine in many ways, whenever the proud patrician was tested publicly and forced to a stand, the old Colonel could never retreat from the ground he had fought so long and hard to hold, even though much of its worth was now gone.

By 1904 Willie Breckinridge's fights lay behind him. The sixty-seven-year-old Kentuckian now settled into old age and a life that he hoped would be freer of distractions. In Lexington, he lived among friends and in comfortable surroundings. The town of over thirty thousand had changed little in recent years. Devoted more thoroughly than ever to the horse, it still retained an older, country-like air. No longer a rival of Louisville, which had far surpassed "the Athens of the West" in both size and importance, Lexington was still home to a landed aristocracy and an upper class that offered the old Colonel good conversation, earthy humor, educated repartee, and solid stimulation. The sleepy town, retaining "fragrant memories of fugitive greatness," stood for an unchanging, stable past. For Breckinridge, that was important.[29]

The attorney and editor had hoped to make his home, near the corner of Third and Limestone streets, the happy center of family activity. But both sorrows and joys intervened. His wife, Louise, suffered "hysterical," nervous attacks (perhaps drug-induced), during which she became very abusive to those around her. Husband and children helped when they could, but the stress grew almost unbearable for some of the children. Of Willie's own seven full brothers and sisters, three had already died. His brother Joseph Cabell had succeeded in his military profession. Advancing from an artillery captain in 1874 to brigadier general, then commander of the inspector general's office by 1889, Joseph had entered the Spanish-American War in a position of some prominence. After action in Cuba he had returned to organize Camp Thomas, which was in what has been described as "a condition close to anarchy." Now a major general, Breckinridge succeeded in his task, but his criticisms of army inefficiency embroiled him in internal controversy with the service. Finally, in 1903, an angry and weary general retired to his estates in Kentucky and Canada. The two brothers corresponded and remained close. The relationship between Willie and Robert Breckinridge, Jr., remained more strained, due to Robert's identification with the Goebel faction, but the brothers maintained civil relations.[30]

Willie Breckinridge's children presented a more mixed pattern in 1904. Of the five surviving offspring, three gave their father genuine joy. Desha, now thirty-seven, had married and worked daily with his father on the *Herald*. Daughter Sophonisba ("Nisba") had broken the typical pattern for Breckinridge women and moved into professional life. Educated at Wellesley College and then at the University of Chicago, the intelligent, bright, and loving thirty-eight-year-old had already become the first woman admitted to legal practice before the Kentucky Court of Appeals. Her future seemed secure and her father was proud. The first-born, the witty and charming Ella, had followed a more traditional pattern, as the wife of attorney and teacher Lyman Chalkley. Although beset by serious family financial problems, she too gave her father little concern.[31]

Matters did not go so well with the two youngest children. Twenty-nine-year-old Curry Desha Breckinridge was quiet, sensitive, generous, uncertain of herself, and handicapped by dyslexia. Working with kindergarten children, with Kentucky mountaineers, and with the sick gave her some satisfaction but did not quench the strange fires that burned within. Willie confessed to Nisba that Curry's "somewhat morbid feeling" gave him much unhappiness, but he could not alleviate her pain. Trouble between the daughter and her father's third wife probably only marked the surface tensions of a deeper malady, one perhaps left by Willie's scandal, for Curry had been the most impressionable at that time. Her future worried Willie.[32]

When the name of the remaining son, Robert Jefferson Breckinridge, was mentioned, feelings of regret and guilt surfaced. Difficult to discipline, not as inclined to education as the others, the hot-headed young

Robert had created many problems and had been in numerous scraps. (After one, Willie telegraphed a friend, "Keep Bob locked up until I get there.") Finally his father had apprenticed him on a ship in a futile attempt to create maturity. Bob had promptly jumped ship in Savannah, hopped a freight bound for New Orleans, and had been kicked off and arrested in Georgia. He returned penniless, went west, then journeyed to India, from where, it is said, on hearing of his father's upcoming trial in 1894, he mischievously wired: "Lock father up and keep him until I get there." Three years later Robert returned briefly, but he again could not overcome intemperance and left once more. For some time thereafter the family received no further word, except that he was fighting in the Boer War in South Africa. By 1904, years had passed without a communication of any kind. The family believed him dead, and the father blamed himself for much of what had occurred.[33]

Breckinridge's editorial tasks helped to dispel some of his worries. Working without pay, twice offered positions on larger papers "at a salary that would tempt most men," he remained in Lexington as a kind of unofficial spokesman for the city. Now called the man with the silver pen and praised by numerous fellow editors, he had told the Kentucky Press Association in 1902 to "be true to yourselves and be true to Kentucky." Above all, he counseled, "be brave and independent and courageous like a knight of old." They should remember, he concluded, that "a paper can be a gentleman." He saw his course as that of a gentleman knight.[34]

Still bothered by recurring financial problems, Breckinridge continued to go on speaking tours. On one such outing in September 1904 he caught cold on the Great Lakes and "suffered very much from my ears and eyes." A month later he regretted that he could not redecorate a room for Nisba's visit, but confessed that illness had prevented him from earning his usual fees. In early November he voted, and by mid-month he felt strong enough to invite Nisba to come for a holiday visit. Five days later, on the night of 20 November 1904, William Campbell Preston Breckinridge died.[35]

Many newspapers eulogized him, and his funeral, according to accounts, surpassed all previous ones in the city, save Henry Clay's. The tributes that Willie would have perhaps most enjoyed came from the black community. The *Kentucky Standard* praised the old Colonel, saying that "when others faltered and hesitated he stood firmly by us." An editorial in the black paper concluded: "He was one of the best friends the negroes of Kentucky ever had. . . . When he took a position he stood like a stone wall."[36]

For over half a century Breckinridge had stood solidly for his beliefs, but because he lived when he did, many of his recommendations had been rejected. Comparatively, Kentucky and the South had not advanced in industrialization. High tariffs remained. Demagogues dominated more than one southern state. Blacks received fewer, not more, rights. Needed reforms in education, in politics, and in many other areas had not been enacted. Like Henry Adams and others of his era, Breckinridge could have despaired of it all and retreated into safe obscurity, but he was certain that history would prove him correct and that the future would be better than his present. He remained a public figure and, even after controversy, was at his death one of the most respected and loved men of his state and nation.

Throughout his lifetime, but particularly in the testing last decade of his life, Breckinridge retained an impressive and inspiring optimism. One friend called Willie "the most perfect Optimist I have ever known"; Breckinridge himself pitied "the poor unfortunate pessimist who walks backward . . . and sees only the lengthening of shadows." He turned instead to the "rising sun of unnumbered days of liberty and happiness for our children and our children's children." This absolute faith in the coming of a better day contrasted more sharply with previous family philosophy than any other facet of his public make-up. John, Robert, John C.—all, to various degrees and at various times, had feared the future. Not so with W.C.P. Breckinridge. At the time of his defeats, he could still write that "no matter how dark the hour may seem, the Sun is shining in some part of the universe, and day will dawn even to those who are in the deepest gloom." For those who knew Breckinridge, this outlook made their friend the kind of man they wanted to meet daily.

Breckinridge believed that his was the life of the future: "I live not in the past. I live in tomorrow," he told a cheering Georgia audience in 1900. And although occasionally recalling the glory of an antebellum vision, he decried any thoughts of those being Utopian days. While some spoke of "the great old days as though there could never be other great days," that was not his way: "I myself envy the boys and girls playing in the streets of Lexington, for they will see greater and grander things than their fore-fathers ever dreamed of." To his children, this optimism was his greatest legacy. Mankind had a high calling: "He who follows truth for truth's sake as it is given him to see it will follow Duty, be accompanied by Honor, and crowned by God."[37] Believing that he followed both truth and duty, Willie Breckinridge, like his father before him, died unafraid of the ultimate judgment of either the Lord or of history.

FIVE

SOPHONISBA BRECKINRIDGE

1866-1948

DESHA BRECKINRIDGE

1867-1935

A progressive . . . is one who stands on the past that
he may reach further into the future, but does not try
to take the past with him.

The Nation, quoted in Aaron, *Men of Good Hope*

Nisba

IN THE half-century after his death historians accorded W.C.P. Breckinridge a major role in state and national affairs. But over time historians' perspectives and evaluations change. By the second half of the twentieth century, a daughter of Willie Breckinridge began to receive recognition as an equally important force in America's recent past. Increasing attention to women's role in society soon placed Sophonisba Preston Breckinridge ahead of her illustrious father in new historical dictionaries and encyclopedias. All of this was supremely ironic, for the silver-tongued orator's example spurred his daughter's ambition, and she desired to follow her father, not supplant him. Had Willie lived, it seems likely that he would have been proud of his offspring and would have approved her success, for, in her, his spirit lived on.

Sophonisba Breckinridge—or "Nisba" as family and friends called her—lived a life that amply justified history's favorable evaluations. Thirty-eight years old at her father's death in 1904, she had already exhibited that her way departed from traditional patterns of the Breckinridge women. A decade earlier Nisba had been the first woman admitted to the Kentucky bar; in 1901 she received a Ph.D. from the University of Chicago; three years later, Dr. Breckinridge earned a J.D. degree from the same university's law school. After that, her career was kaleidoscopic, and even a brief outline of it indicates just how varied were her interests and actions.

As an educator, for example, Nisba became an assistant professor in the University of Chicago's department of household administration and, for a time concurrently, taught at the Chicago School of Civics and Philanthropy. Succeeding Graham Taylor to the deanship of the latter school, she led its transformation into the Graduate School of Social Service Administration at the university. She served as assistant dean of women, dean of the college of arts, literature, and science, and, finally, dean of undergraduate social science students—all the while continuing as a professor of social economy and public welfare administration. As teacher and administrator, Dr. Breckinridge remained involved even after retirement.

Active outside the classroom, the Kentuckian spent numerous summer vacations as a social worker at Jane Addams' Hull House in Chicago. She also served for a time as that city's health inspector, as first secretary of Chicago's Immigrants Protection League, and as a member of the executive committee of the Illinois Consumers' League. Aiding a garment workers' strike and campaigning for a federal child labor law were but two more such activities. Long an advocate of civil rights, Nisba was elected vice-president of the National American Woman Suffrage Association (NAWSA) in 1911 and held membership very early in both the National Association for the Advancement of Colored People (NAACP) and the Urban League. During the First World War she helped found, and was the first treasurer of, the Woman's Peace Party, and in 1933 she was the first woman to serve as an official United States delegate to the Pan-American Congress. No danger of academic isolation existed for her.

Somehow, amidst these activities, the teacher, social worker, and advocate found time to write. Dr. Breckinridge's many scholarly books and articles covered such varied topics as a history of legal tender, child delinquency and truancy, state poor laws, woman's rights, and a biography of her sister-in-law. For two decades, she also served as managing editor of the *Social Science Review.* Judged as teacher, interested citizen, or scholar, Sophonisba Breckinridge receives high marks for her concern, achievement, and quality. But if her accomplishments are clear, the reasons for them are less so. What forces shaped the young southern lady into a forceful, mature leader of the Progressive Era? Was her family's influence positive or negative? And why did she follow the path she did?[1]

Answers to those questions lie in her pre-Chicago years, for the most part. To understand her motivation and behavior requires an evaluation of her formative years, her Kentucky environment, and most of all her family life.

Nisba, born 1 April 1866, eleven months after her father returned from the Civil War, was the second surviving child and the first that Willie could be with from birth. She received much love from a father who had, by his account, built up a surplus of that emotion during wartime. Sister Eleanor (Ella), already four when Nisba arrived, seems to have been her mother's favorite, having received Issa Desha Breckinridge's full attention while the husband and father was away. Sibling rivalry and perhaps some jealousy may have resulted, judging from a reflective Sophonisba's autobiography, written just before her death. She recalled then how Ella, who "was not entirely frank" always, was also "much cleverer, really cleverer, but she had many distractions. She had great charm and very early became attractive so that boys and young men flock[ed] about her." Decidedly unattractive, the thin and sad-looking Nisba reacted in a di-

Sophonisba Breckinridge. Courtesy Special Collections, University of Kentucky Library

ametrically opposite way from Ella. When their father, for example, told the two that they could have either one dollar or a "little party" if they got perfect marks, Nisba took the money, Ella the party. Indicative of her later philanthropic pursuits, Nisba saved her dollars until a missionary from the Orient told of Chinese poverty. Then, "I gave her my savings. My mother never forgave me for taking my little savings. . . ." Ella, though a sister, was not a close companion.[2]

Three other children completed the Breckinridge household. Desha, only fifteen months younger than his "Nim," remained a kind friend and in later life defended her as she did him. As young adults, the two argued and disagreed over women's rights, but still expressed sentiments indicating real affection for each other. Brother Robert, on the other hand, was a loner whom the family could never quite control or understand. Sister Curry, some years younger, was Nisba's closest female companion in the family, but the younger girl's sufferings and outlook created a gulf neither could fully bridge, though both tried. While handicapped by dyslexia, Curry had an active mind, a talent for making friends, and, like Nisba, a concern for helping others. Yet the way her older sister remembered Curry reveals much: "She was a strange person, much more interesting than I and much more fundamentally honest," recalled Sophonisba. "One day she looked at me quite seriously and said, 'Of course, Nisba, you do mean all right, but you never had any common sense.' Especially I regret my treatment of her when we were abroad in the Early Nineties. That was when I was horribly [,] wickedly pious, concerned for my own soul, and I made Sunday a dreadful day, even in Paris."

Guilt and jealousy, friendship and affection—these characterize Sophonisba Breckinridge's relationship with her brothers and sisters. While she felt a "very real weakness" in dealing with them, and while she even stated that none had any real affection for her, that emotion and that assertion both seem overstated. And while her sibling interactions contain many elements important in shaping the mature person, they are in themselves not the key.[3]

Parental influences were. Nisba's guide, her motivator, her example, her idol was clearly W.C.P. Breckinridge. For if she loved her mother, she adored her father. To the end of her life, in the last days, she still judged others—and herself—by his image and memory. She did so, not in a thoughtless, wistful way, but as an intelligent person who recognized what she was doing. Sophonisba filled her manuscript autobiography with revelations of Willie's influence on her, beginning, "I have wanted to write an account of my father, but I seem unable to make a beginning of a biography of him, while I cannot speak of myself without speaking at length of him." Later, when describing (as she did often) her "dullness," she said that one of the two things that "saved" her was her love for her father and her desire to please him. In assessing her childhood as a good one generally, Nisba recalled, "I was anxious to please my father. He was wonderfully patient and kind." At college she sought high marks, "because it pleased my Father to have me make good grades."[4]

Quite evidently, Willie Breckinridge's counsel to his wife when his daughter was but five months old—"Don't let Nisba forget me"—had been taken to heart. The mother tried to teach all the children, she said, to be just like their father. Willie, for his part, took a particular interest in this young daughter, who reminded him of his first wife's child, his "little boy in heaven." Learning her letters from her father's law books, Nisba apparently comprehended quickly, for by the age of seven she was already getting perfect scores. Moreover, she learned from him the unconventional idea that women did not have to be bound to traditional patterns of behavior.[5]

It was a strange lesson from a surprising source at an unexpected time. Women, after all, were still expected to conform to an ideal image. The southern lady on her pedestal should, the stereotype said, be educated in "womanly" pursuits, be refined, modest, and virtuous. Compassionate, emotional (rather than logical), and submissive, women should, as one author suggested, "love, honor, obey, and occasionally amuse her husband, . . . bring up his children and manage his household." Never did she feel sexual stirrings or passion. In Margaret Ripley Wolfe's words, "If the literature were taken seriously, readers might logically conclude that the South had been populated by a massive outbreak of virgin births."[6]

Most Kentuckians honored this image of southern womanhood. A reporter in 1879 declaimed that woman's sphere was that of mother and wife, and nothing further. The next year a state senator made his feelings clear (and his options few) when he exclaimed, "Give me a wife that can love, honor and look up to me as her lord and master, or give me separation and death." Legal restrictions supported the established pattern. As late as 1890 the state had no property law for married women, no law permitting a woman to make a will without her husband's consent, no law giving women full rights to their own earnings, no law allowing them full voting privileges. As Paul Fuller notes, "Kentucky laws in the rights of women were among the most backward in the country."[7]

Despite all these attempts to shape a society to honor an ideal, the image conflicted harshly with the reality. Kentucky women on the frontier, from the state's beginning, had fought and died; had, like "Grandma Black Cap," managed large estates; had sometimes prospered when men were absent. They had spoken out on issues, overcome the destruction of war, and survived. In the 1880s, when Sophonisba Breckinridge was in her teens, this conflict between image and reality was erupting in full force. A more favorable environment now existed. By 1867 Kentucky had its first suffrage organization; in 1879 aging suffragist Susan B. Anthony spoke in the state; in 1881, when Nisba was fifteen, the American Woman Suffrage Association (AWSA) met in Louisville, the first such gathering in the South; that same year leaders founded a Kentucky branch, also the first in the region.

Mary B. Clay, Cassius Clay's daughter, was elected national president of the AWSA in 1883; two more of Clay's daughters were writing columns on women's activities in Kentucky newspapers; and in 1888 still another Clay offspring, Laura, became president of the new Kentucky Equal Rights Association. The large, commanding, strong Laura Clay, who, like her sisters, had been influenced in her activities by the divorce of their parents, soon led the equal rights movement in the state and the South. Her Lexington home and aristocratic prominence made her an appealing model for young Nisba.[8]

An even closer physical and emotional model, however, was her father. When a youngster at Centre College in the 1850s Willie had seen women compete with men. Three of his cousins studied there but because of their sex could not receive degrees. W.C.P. Breckinridge witnessed his grandmother's control over her own life, and he recognized the abilities of other women in his talented family. Sophonisba concisely summarized her father's outlook: "My father was never a suffragist, but as he had favored the development of facilities for the education of women and negroes he was always for fair play."[9]

Actually, Willie Breckinridge may have been more supportive than his daughter remembered four decades later. He favored coeducational colleges and praised women who voted in local school elections. An 1898 editorial admitted that he saw no reason why women should not vote in all elections, although he hedged on that stand at times. His own thought process and his own reasons for supporting and encouraging his Nisba in her course were revealed in a frank 1902 editorial worth quoting at length. Under the title, "The Problem of the Daughter," he wrote:

It is only when the rare girl, who in spite of all her hereditary instinct to submission and to filling her alloted place in that "sphere" of life (which someone else has assigned her to), finds the virtue of her college life working in her; when she begins to think a little of what she is doing; and after a season of irresolute and uncomfortable protest, comes to the conclusion that artificial activities are not as interesting as real ones. It is only when this unnatural daughter begins to murmur against the usual order of things, . . . that the father is forced to pause and examine. And if he be open-minded, as many such fathers are, moreover, who has maintained a comradeship with his daughter since her childhood, he begins after a little to agree with her. . . . Later on he begins to wonder why this daughter, for whose intellect and character he, after some years of acquaintance, has a distinct respect, should, in case she does not marry, have no apparent place in life to fly: why, when so many jobs are lacking the doing because of the inadequate supply of intelligent and capable doers, the custom should close the door of activity in the face of a person young, vigorous, intelligent, and with a perfect passion of interest in all the realities of life. . . . He begins to feel with her the troublings of the new "social conscience.". . .

As a result of all these reflections and awakenings, the father at length begins to question the system which in his circle of society prepares a daughter exclusively for marriage and to be a costly and pleasing plaything in her father's or her husband's home. . . . He wonders if perhaps the system which differentiates so sharply between the activities of a man and a woman is not a perverted one. . . . He begins to comprehend that some of the strange new demands made by women are but the outcome of an unrepressed individuality, are but a part of the development of the new social conscience in which women, as well as men . . . have become the heirs. . . . He becomes rather more sympathetic than disapproving.[10]

After four years as one of the first women students at Lexington's State College, Sophonisba Breckinridge departed for the unknown: in 1884 she entered Wellesley College in Massachusetts as a first-year student. The school's motto, *Incipit Vita Nuova* (the new life begins), accurately reflected her future. This eighteen-year-old daughter of a former Confederate who would soon preach the South's cause in the halls of Congress found herself in a women's school in the center of Yankeedom. The opportunity for loneliness, despair, and alienation was obvious, and, like many freshmen then and now, she experienced some of these emotions. But she overcame them and matured both emotionally and intellectually.

Her parents gave strong support. Writing separately, and frequently, they kept her informed of current Kentucky gossip or Washington happenings, and of their own lives. Issa's letters frequently focused on the trivial and traditional interests of women of her generation but occasionally on more personal matters as well. Telling Nisba, "You know . . . that you are *your father's idol*," Issa implied that Willie loved his second-born more than any of the other children. The mother told Nisba that, if strong and healthy, she could do *"all that God ever wanted women to do!"* She had birth and breeding already; only maturity was required. Privately, Issa Breckinridge wrote to a friend that her freshman daughter differed little from her classmates and was subject "to like troubles to other girls who are not wise." A particularly motherly worry was that all the girls wore their hair drawn back in the "modern" fashion.[11]

A more worrisome concern arose when Issa and Willie first took their daughter to Wellesley and encountered black students. This troubled Mrs. Breckinridge, who asked soon afterward if Nisba was "thrown with them in any way." Issa wrote that she could not treat blacks as equals, "but they can do you no harm, and I can trust you to treat them properly." Willie responded more directly. When a friend asked whether he would allow his daughter to be enrolled with blacks, he answered firmly, "She got on all right with the boys; I think that she will get on all right with the colored." Nisba later recalled, admiringly, that Frederick Douglass, who visited the Wellesley campus while she was there, "often said that my father was the white man with whom he could most freely and without consciousness of racial differences discuss problems of public concern." The young Kentuckian, however, needed some time to adjust. Nisba noted that she disliked Douglass's "pitiful" story about the harshness of slavery and recalled that when sitting at a dining table with blacks she could serve them all right, "but my own food I could not swallow." Time and experience helped overcome many of her prejudices.[12]

Willie Breckinridge continued to encourage and counsel his daughter in this new environment. Writing to Nisba just after she entered school, he discussed her homesickness and, almost harshly, told her that she had been too sheltered for too long. Now she must conquer the emotions within. Study the Bible, "a wonderful book," he advised; avoid "the needle, the school-room & the story" and aim instead for chemistry and the sciences, a more profitable field for women. Do your own shopping, Willie suggested, and rely on your own tastes, for self-control and self-mastery came from self-dependence. Since a "feeble will" created much unhappiness, he had wanted his child "from the hour of your birth," to be strong. Her happiness had long been his chief desire, even when he criticized; as his loving, dutiful, "pure," daughter, his Nisba had always known of his love and of his belief that all would turn out well. By May 1885 Willie's concerns had apparently vanished. He was comforted, he wrote, by the awareness that this daughter could make her own living, should he die suddenly. "I have loved *you*," Willie confessed, "all these years; and I know that it is inevitable that you will drift away from me, and I will make no complaint at it." He would be happy if only she remembered that "Duty is the noblest pursuit & compatible with the highest attainment." He added, "You don't know how glad I am that you are not a genius; but a hard-working, dutiful, trained intellect, capable of doing anything because you are willing to undergo the necessary labor and submit to the request [ed] discipline."[13]

Sophonisba enjoyed school, performed well, and left her mark. Fellow students three times selected the southerner to be class president. Grades matched high expectations. Social life flourished. Life seemed good. The attractive Massachusetts countryside, the nearby lake, the New England autumn colors—all were new and delightful experiences for the young southerner. Her small room had a bureau, a table, red cheesecloth over the door, and the family picture on a washstand. The slender-faced, dark-eyed, dark-haired student would sit in the quiet of her room, look out her window, and work, at peace with herself and her school. Wellesley agreed with Nisba and she with it. Schoolgirl letters reveal both a young, naïve, and impressionable girl and a mature, serious, and studious woman. College days were ones of transformation, and, more often than not, the student won out over the socialite. Early in her Wellesley career, after describing in some detail a costume party outfit, Nisba added that such affairs would be missed, because "things like these take so much time and don't pay." By that semester's end, in a mood rarely experienced by students, she felt so exhilarated after exams that she wanted to take them again: "They have been so very lovely and I have enjoyed every one." As a sophomore in 1885, she made her first public speech, entered a reading club, tried her hand on the rowing crew, and described herself as being in a "very blissful state."[14]

Sophonisba as a junior was even more ambitious. Sunday-school teaching, a public address at a temperance meeting, a debate on her father's favorite topic, the tariff—these combined with usual study to make a school year full. The young Kentuckian began to think seriously of her world, her life, and her future. Early in the term she wrote Issa, "I am trying very hard this year to make my life as even as possible, that is, to eliminate all the nervous, hurried element & take things calmly. And I hope I am succeeding." Several letters passed between mother and daughter concerning Nisba's desire to wear the looser and freer clothes of "a working woman." The younger sister also wanted Ella to stop wearing "those heavy dresses and things tight about her waist" that give backaches, and turn instead to the freedom of the "new" style. The surface issues symbolized the daughter's deeper change. By March 1887 restlessness mixed with uncertainty. "I ache to get out and work," Nisba explained to her mother. To her father she wrote, "Nothing extraordinary ever happens here   That, I suppose is why the days are so happy. And they are happy. I some times wonder how it will seem to go out and fight when all has been so easy here. And yet I shall be glad to go fight—glad to feel some times the delight that must come from doing something hard." She added later, "Sometimes, I think if the Lord wants to make me perfectly content in Heaven He will give hard problems that I can at least solve. But then I suppose all things are really just that are they not?"[15]

Despite her personal progress and successes, despite Willie's words to the contrary, Nisba approached graduation still dependent on her parents in many ways. Earlier she asked her father what he wanted her to do after school: "I know it will be decided for me, but if I knew what I thought I was working towards it would make it easier. . . ." Three months later Nisba indicated her own hopes when she asked Willie if he would let her work for him. "I will be a 'good girl,'" she promised. A proud father delivered the Wellesley commencement address in late spring 1888, while a satisfied and equally proud daughter received her long-sought diploma. Yet Sophonisba Preston Breckinridge left college still uncertain of her future.[16]

The Wellesley graduate may have been questioning her worth, her intelligence, and her abilities, but others recognized her extraordinary talents. Alice Stone Blackwell, the sensitive editorial writer for the *Woman's Journal*, told a Kentuckian, for example, to recruit young Miss Breckinridge to the Woman Suffrage Association: "She would be a valuable acquisition, I think, being a bright girl & a college graduate." Noted Blackwell also, "Her father's commencement oration is very highly praised—& he said something friendly about woman suffrage, too."[17] But Nisba's potential remained yet unfulfilled, and ahead lay a turbulent decade that nearly destroyed that promise.

Sophonisba Breckinridge remembered the years immediately following graduation as muddled ones that formed part of "confused life." She had "pretended" that she would follow in her father's footsteps and study law, but few schools admitted women. Additionally, her mother continued frail and the family, as usual, lacked money. Nisba did just what she and her father did not want—she secured a high-school teaching job in Washington. From 1888 to 1890 she taught mathematics, with little apparent love for her work. Still very religious, she also seriously considered joining an Episcopal sisterhood.[18]

Teaching had certain benefits, of course. She would remain with the family and help her ailing mother financially and in the housework. Probably during this time, also, Susan B. Anthony spent the winter as a guest of Congressman Breckinridge's family. The women's rights leader used the opportunity to enlighten Nisba on suffrage matters, "to the amusement and sometimes discomfiture of her modest little victim." It was still a learning time, even after college. But in the spring of 1890 a serious attack of what she called the "grip" ended Breckinridge's school-teaching career in the capital. Returning to Lexington with the rest of the family in the fall, Nisba recovered sufficiently to begin sampling once again the social life she had largely forgone at Wellesley. She enjoyed horseback riding and the races, and there were friends' dinner parties that attracted the talented of the city. At one such gathering women in formal evening gowns joined their male guests in rooms ablaze with pink candles in silver candelabra. In the flickering light the state's nationally known literary figures, the serious-looking James Lane Allen and the younger John Fox, Jr., read portions of their works, and men and women mingled and talked. Despite the romantic atmosphere of that and other parties, however, the twenty-four-year-old Sophonisba developed no firm attachments. She later admitted to having been in love twice in her youth, but "neither really loved me though. Each for the moment thought he did. Both married women who were cleverer than I was and both made happy gracious homes." Although Nisba mentioned no names, one beau was Thomas Hunt Morgan, the brilliant Lexingtonian who would win a Nobel Prize for his work in genetics. But Nisba remained single.[19]

Still plagued by health problems, Sophonisba soon joined sister

Curry for a sojourn in Europe. Travel, combined with further study, renewed her determination to become a lawyer. Again she went to her father's law office, this time to study his books, not just learn the alphabet from them. In helping Willie prepare cases, his daughter left little doubt of her abilities. Then almost by accident Nisba accompanied her brother to Frankfort one day in August 1892 and, while there, asked the chief justice of the state's highest court if he would examine her for the bar. A wartime comrade of Willie, the judge agreed and assembled two other justices. It was a tense, unprecedented occasion, and the examination dragged on for over three hours. The decision was favorable—Sophonisba Breckinridge was deemed qualified to practice and was admitted to the bar, apparently the first of her sex so honored in Kentucky. In 1897 this woman whom the *New York Times* described as quiet and unassuming, with a clear voice and some of her father's eloquence, was qualified further to practice before the state's highest judicial body.[20]

While one goal had been achieved, happiness did not follow. Emotional peaks and valleys continued to characterize Nisba's post-Wellesley years. Joy over entering her father's firm was tempered by the small number of clients. Her mother's death in 1892 and the need to accomplish something more satisfying led to the young attorney's decision to return to school, with hopes, perhaps, of finding whatever it was that could give meaning to her life. But just as she began to make that move, events occurred that shook Sophonisba's confidence to the foundations and tested her emotions to the utmost.

Initial rumors in 1893 of her father's sexual involvement with Madeline Pollard were easily dismissed as vicious lies. Then came the lawsuit, the trial, and Willie's admission of the affair. Here stood her idolized father, publicly acknowledging that he had been unfaithful to the mother Nisba loved, unfaithful because of a woman so young that she had passed as Willie's daughter. Here stood the man Nisba had modeled her life after, the man whose praise she sought above all others, the man who had advised development of a strong will and who had stressed the importance of duty and self-control. Here stood her honored father, in disgrace.

Everything could have combined to produce her total repudiation of him. She could easily have rejected Willie Breckinridge and—like Laura Clay—devoted her attention to the equal rights struggle with increased ferocity. She could have struck out at him for all the pain and embarrassment he had caused. She could, with justification, have turned her back on her father. Yet she could not—and did not—do any of this. The evidence suggests a continuance of love and an outpouring of understanding. She did not allow his action to destroy the image, or, for that matter, the reality she called her father. She remembered instead Willie's devotion to the dying Issa, calling his aid "endlessly kind." She wrote of all the love and affection her father had given the family, of his deep interest in her own life, of his frankness with her. Nisba apparently accepted Willie's transgression as a single flaw that did not destroy his shining armor, and she continued to function as a devoted daughter.[21] But if on the surface she displayed no scars, the whole affair may well have left deeper, hidden emotional marks. It would be too much to claim that the scandal sparked Nisba's reform spirit to action, for she had already long shown an inclination to her later course. The change, if change there was, appears to have been more subtle.

Nisba did not abandon many of her father's deepest faiths—his optimism, his sense of America's promise, his devotion to continuing certain traditions—but she did impose modifications after the Pollard trial. Her father's imperfections seem to have caused her to be more tolerant of the weaknesses of others. If he was not perfect, then she did not have to be either. Unlike those charity workers who held to the "Victorian ethos" that blamed the condition of the poor on individual shortcomings of the "unfortunates," she began to stress instead environmental causes for poverty. As her earlier deep religious feelings declined in intensity, Sophonisba turned to social welfare work as her outlet for enacting basic Christian values into reality. Rather than follow a conservative path, she chose to be an innovator who challenged many beliefs of the day. After the scandal Sophonisba Breckinridge remained very much her father's daughter, but it was a transformed woman he now knew.[22]

Throughout the remainder of the 1890s Nisba faced difficult situations. When Willie asked her to return from the University of Chicago to take care of his third wife, the daughter did not refuse. She found a woman suffering from serious hysterical attacks; through "sheer will power" Nisba sometimes could control her, but if not, as she wrote, "the results were quite dreadful for she became very abusive, especially about my father. His patience was incredible and he and I would go through these experiences together." Adversity strengthened already close familial bonds, and on her return to Chicago classes Sophonisba continued to receive evidence of an aging father's devotion and support. In April 1899 Willie reminded her that on each Easter Sunday morning he thanked God that she was such "an unalloyed blessing and comfort" to her family. Four months later, the father expressed his happiness over his daughter's preparation for "independent life-work." Letters and reports told of the daughter's advancement—a master's degree in 1897, the Ph.D. four years after that, an instructorship, an assistant deanship, then the law degree (with the highest class average) in 1904. After the last honor, a joyful Willie wrote, "I am growing quite famous as your father; a fame very dear to me." In November the proud patriarch looked forward to Nisba's arrival at Thanksgiving. Then, on 20 November 1904, W.C.P. Breckinridge died. The bond that held Sophonisba so close was now broken.[23]

With her father's death, Nisba severed most close ties to Kentucky. She now sought to leave the past behind. Still, she could not forget the commonwealth entirely. Through her brother Desha's investments she drew income from state businesses. Appeals to her to speak were not always refused, as she returned to plead with the legislature for full suffrage, or to talk on "Women in Industry," or to dedicate a school, or to promote some other cause. As editor of the *Herald*, Desha Breckinridge sometimes called on Nisba to write editorials or signed stories for the paper. She obliged, and he reciprocated by reprinting stories favorable to his sister and keeping citizens of the central Bluegrass informed of her activities. One 1911 account from the *World Today*, for example, praised the good legal mind and varied interests of Dr. Breckinridge, and concluded: "People say that Miss Breckinridge is like her father in many ways, and that she inherited from him her keen mind, her social insight, her unfailing sympathy, and a rare personal charm. But Miss Breckinridge adds to these qualities a genuine humility, a great eagerness to serve, and a willingness to serve in humble ways." Family and Kentucky remained important to Nisba, but it was in Chicago that she would make her most notable contributions.[24]

Chicago in the 1890s represented many facets of American life. The city contained both reactionaries and radicals, and saw them clash in open warfare. It included luxurious sheltered mansions on Prairie Avenue or Lake Shore Drive for the McCormicks, Fields, Armours, Pullmans, and other wealthy families, as well as dirty, ill-constructed frame houses for workers near the infamous "Back-of-the-Yards." Both the elite and the forgotten could smell the stench drifting from the stockyards—the manure, the hides, the slaughter refuse, the street garbage, the pollution of Bubbly Creek. Chicago, Carl Sandburg's "Hog Butcher for the World," inspired Americans by its ability to rebuild from the fire of 1871, and impressed them with its Columbian Exposition of 1893, but it shamed them with its unpaved streets, corruption, and class differences. Chicago was unlike anything Sophonisba Breckinridge had known.

The paradox of poverty amidst great progress made Chicago a place that required reform and understanding, a testing ground for both ideas and people. When Nisba arrived she had seen European cities of similar size, but she knew few large urban areas in America. Now she found herself in a metropolis whose population had increased almost six-fold in three decades, an urban area where three of every four people were foreign-born or whose parents were, a city of exploding transportation, supply, and merchandising businesses, pulsating with human energies. Tragedy was a part of Chicago life in those years. At the end of the exposition came the assassination of the former Kentuckian Mayor Carter Harrison, then the full effects of the panic of 1893. The Pullman strike of the next year reinforced the bitterness between workers and owners.

Children suffered malnourishment and disease. Hope for the future contributed to the city's psyche as well, however. Intellectuals saw in the reborn University of Chicago an example that could save the nation and educate its citizens. From its opening in 1892 the school attracted an excellent staff and became a positive symbol of Chicago. Some first-rate cultural institutions added to the image of the "White City." This combination of failures and successes, of despair and hope, was a magnet that attracted a remarkably talented group of reformers who sought to bridge the gap between the privileged and nonprivileged. Making an organized, path-breaking attack on urban poverty, they sought to correct this ugliness beneath the American dream. And in some ways they succeeded.[25]

Progressivism was emerging, and its currents swept Sophonisba Breckinridge into the mainstream. Like many other reformers of the period, she was young, unmarried, college-educated, and from a well-to-do family. Many of her allies and their counterparts across America combined a sense of responsibility with a sense of mission. They infused the movement with a strong, moral, almost evangelistic, will, but their realism accepted the government's role as vital. Progressives placed their faith in social democracy, in institutionalized change, in method and technique. Their idols had traditional roots; their principles suggested an "old-fashioned" concept of humanitarianism and morality; their ethos harked back to personal responsibility; but they went further than any before them in their direct efforts to better the lives of the city's poor.[26]

Among this group of reformers in Chicago were several women who would influence Breckinridge, as she would them. Sharing a similar philosophy and goal, generally, this first generation of professionals in social work formed a tightly knit core that was not always united, not always right, but was seldom inactive. Dean of women and close friend Marian Talbott, for example, gave Breckinridge her fellowship to attend the university and was credited by Nisba as one who clarified her thinking. At Hull House, where Nisba spent her summers, the magnetic, yet bashful and sometimes remote Jane Addams had already begun the work that would win her a Nobel Prize in 1931. Joining Addams' work among the immigrants was Julia C. Lathrop, congressman's daughter, Vassar graduate, and the first woman admitted to the Illinois bar. The plain, mournful-looking Lathrop would eventually teach with Nisba, work on similar projects, and then head the United States Children's Bureau in 1912. Another Hull House occupant, Mary E. McDowell, moved "Back-of-the-Yards" and began settlement work there. Joining the group later from Wellesley College, Edith Abbott was the daughter of a Nebraska lieutenant governor and sister of the equally well-known Grace. Both Abbotts would form a long and close association with Breckinridge, as would others. Like many of her associates, Nisba had been drifting, confused, purposeless. Now, prepared by her background, family, college, and Kentucky experience, she at last found in Chicago the niche she had sought.[27]

By the first decades of the twentieth century, these reformers had overcome obstacles, attracted support and achieved so much that they became almost heroines, models for new generations of women. Sophonisba, not a radical in her stands, was more extreme than many of her fellow reformers. More supportive of blacks and less fearful of immigration than many, she went beyond those who sought to improve conditions simply by inculcating the poor with the mores of work, thrift, and abstinence. In time she transcended the desire simply to improve institutions and sought instead to redo them.[28]

In practice Breckinridge's philosophy centered on three areas of concern—blacks, women, and the poor generally. Negroes received less attention in her publications than the other two groups, but she still emerged as a leading white advocate of black rights. Her stress on environment allowed her a deeper understanding of the difficulties of Chicago blacks than some other reformers achieved. Through books, through efforts on the advisory committee of the NAACP, and through work with the Association of Black Women, Breckinridge sought to transform public opinion so that blacks could claim their place in a pluralistic society. More central to her concerns was the women's rights movement. Aside from her father's interest and the influences of Laura Clay and Susan Anthony, Nisba had a further motivation. Her aunt, Mary Desha, had been one of the founders of the Daughters of the American Revolution in 1893. Mary at that time intended to create an organization devoted chiefly to benefit womankind, and Nisba, supportive of her aunt's goals, later wrote that if she had been at Washington at the time she probably would have been one of the founders, too. As it was, Nisba did serve on the first executive committee.[29] But her interests turned to other organizations as the Daughters of the American Revolution moved away from suffrage and equal rights issues.

In 1911 Sophonisba Breckinridge was elected as a vice-president of the NAWSA. She accepted, however, only after an exchange of letters with Laura Clay. Alienated more and more by the association's stress on a national suffrage amendment, Clay had begun to inch closer to the states' rights argument of the South. Breckinridge did not want to anger her friend by accepting an office she had not even sought. "I know nothing, absolutely nothing of it!" Nisba protested. The older woman responded with assurances that Breckinridge would aid the movement by her political sagacity and her "ability to seize upon and utilize political situations to help the cause which very few women possess." She should accept the post, counseled Clay.[30]

Breckinridge furthered the woman's rights cause not only by action but also by the printed word. An early article advocated stricter laws regulating women's work, in order to protect "mothers . . . of the coming generation." Eight years later, in 1914, an article on "Political Equality for Women and Women's Wages" indicated that her views had intensified. She noted that females' wages averaged one-third to two-thirds those of males. Admitting the natural barriers in some jobs, she questioned why exclusion existed in others. She pointed out that of 824 school superintendents in larger cities, only six were women. Obviously, a change was required and Nisba offered an answer—political equality. Self-confidence and "a very real new spiritual power" would result. But after passage of the Nineteenth Amendment the millennium did not come. In 1923 Breckinridge turned to the argument that women should be paid less because they were not the primary breadwinners. Men's wages were not determined this way, she contended. And what of single women (like her)? A decade later, Nisba's important study *Women in the Twentieth Century* surveyed the entire array of women's work, concluding that the emancipation of wives had been completed legislatively, but not in reality. But the book's overall tone was hopeful and reasonable: successes had been achieved, but some victories still had to be won.[31]

Breckinridge's concern for the plight of the poor overshadowed her efforts for blacks and women. Of over a dozen books she wrote, edited, or coauthored, at least nine dealt with some aspect of that problem, whether it be the delinquent child, welfare work, housing, or juvenile-court legislation. Her edited works, in which she compiled documents and case studies totaling over four thousand pages, continue to be used, and at least two of them are still in print. Throughout these works and in her articles, Breckinridge, like others of her "factual generation," stressed figures and data. When writing about poor housing, she would practically stagger a reader with statistics, noting for example, that 1,100 people lived in a one-block area of Chicago.[32] But the professor stressed that such statistics must be the basis for social action. At times she also offered her readers some forceful prose and even some morality amid the figures. Breckinridge and Abbott, in examining Chicago's housing, discussed the evils of the "furnished room" where "people of loose habits" met. They explained part of the overcrowding in housing as a result of an "un-American standard of living." The two authors, however, offered more angry words than moral judgments. They repeatedly criticized the poor ventilation, the bad or nonexistent plumbing, the dismal halls, the ever-present fire hazards. They accused a city that enforced few ordinances and substituted "the shadow for the substance" of the law. "We still find the same overcrowded areas, alley tenements, dilapidated houses, oppressive density of population, families in outlawed cellar apartments, in dark and gloomy rooms, and in a condition of overcrowding which violates all standards of decency and health." State appropriations were "little short of ridiculous," and the housing code was inadequate. Their solutions for these evils did not differ greatly from those of their progressive counterparts, however: thorough studies of the problems, better laws and strict enforcement of them, an adequate staff, more appropriations, and, finally, an altering of industrial conditions by business, so that "decent" living standards could be maintained. These solutions sometimes "sidetracked" rather than advanced reform; they placed too much faith in legal answers to social conditions; and they simply did not have the expected effects. Nevertheless, a confident and pragmatic Breckinridge labored to improve the existing situation. She tried new answers and rejected old ones in an attempt to fulfill the dream the immigrant sought in the New World. That was more than most were doing.[33]

Nisba studied not only immigrants' housing, but almost all conditions of their lives. In a paper read to the American Home Economics Association in 1919, she told of poor wages, gang labor, crowded homes, and discrimination based on the assumption that immigrants were inferior. Such assumptions, she declared, would result in a great loss of the "rich contributions" immigrants could make. In such speeches and in her books Dr. Breckinridge showed a sympathy and understanding of immigrant life that completely reversed the xenophobia of her grandfather, Robert J. Breckinridge.[34] But Nisba's strongest words, her boldest suggestions, came when she discussed the welfare and future of children. In a distinct departure from her father's philosophy, she advocated strong state intervention in child-rearing. If children in their homes were surrounded by immorality, obscenity, and "low associates," then they should "be lifted out bodily at the earliest possible moment." She made a distinction between the "destitute home," where private aid would suffice, and the "degraded home," where the "strong hand of the state" should interfere. Like other reformers of her era, Nisba pressed this point hard, for in the children lay the future. Remove them from their bad environment (or correct it), expose them to new ideas, and the next generation would have few of the evils of the present one, in Breckinridge's vision. Thus most of her reform activity—in housing, among immigrants, in the court system—focused on the children she never had, but cared about nonetheless.[35]

In the classroom Professor Breckinridge influenced many future social workers and reformers. Operating out of the University of Chicago's Green Hall, she formed one part of a triumvirate of pioneer social workers completed by the two Abbott sisters. In the quiet surroundings of the college, Edith and Nisba would walk together, their long skirts sweeping the sidewalk, and would become completely absorbed in some common problem; the sprightly Kentuckian in her floppy Panama hat and sheer dress contrasted with the somber Nebraskan in her black hat and dark dress.[36] In teaching, Nisba did not entrance the class with flowing oratory or overwhelm them with a forceful presence. A slight woman, five feet, four inches tall who looked as if a breath of wind might blow her away, the professor possessed a "clear treble" of a voice that was precise, expressive, and effective. Teaching for the most part by the case-study method she introduced at the school, she stressed facts, the law, and a social-welfare approach to her auditors. According to Edith Abbott, Breckinridge respected and had confidence in the young, "in their courage and their ability to right the old wrongs," and displayed this respect in the classroom. Students labeled her liberalism, her activism, her advocacy of the oppressed simply "the Breckinridge point of view."[37]

Outside the halls of learning, friends knew a different Breckinridge. They saw a woman who liked music and who said that "with a little practice I probably could sing worse than any one else in this country." Acquaintances recalled Nisba's fine, "southern" manners, noting that she displayed such simplicity and such a "genuinely democratic spirit" that few could guess her aristocratic background. A gracious personality, a gentle presence, a dry wit, a vibrant spirit, a creative mind—this was the private Sophonisba. Beneath the "beguiling softness," behind the gentle Kentucky voice with its trace of an accent, also lay the potential force of an iron will. Energetic and independent, Breckinridge sought what she considered practical, concrete, and attainable aims. Those adults whose minds were not as creative or disciplined as hers, or who questioned her aims, received little sympathy if they disagreed. A very private person, Nisba chose to keep secret many individual acts of kindness. At one time, for example, a Green Hall student mentioned that the upcoming Christmas would be her first away from home. Later, when Breckinridge quietly handed the student an envelope containing a round-trip ticket home, she told the youngster that her sole wish was that no one else should know. Other, similar recollections of her thoughtfulness attest to the difference between the sometimes impersonal spirit of her lectures and writings and the deeper concern she felt within.[38]

Retirement in 1942 ended some of Nisba's closest associations. The college had been virtually her life since her father's death, and she continued as a part of its community, even if not on the active staff. But as time passed, colleagues, friends, and relatives died, and loneliness increased. Her scholarly output declined. She grew old. Working now in the family papers and on her autobiography, Breckinridge turned to the years before Chicago, and recalled the great happiness and the equally great sadness of that time. Labor on the autobiography had ceased by the spring of 1948, for the eighty-two-year-old Sophonisba had by then suffered a serious illness. By June her condition had so worsened that her old friend and emotional partner Edith Abbott stayed with her almost daily, and on 30 July 1948 her life ended.[39]

In the lifetime of Sophonisba Breckinridge America had changed from a generally laissez-faire, individualistic civilization to one that placed more responsibility on state and society. The Kentucky of her youth, the Chicago of her maturity, the nation of her entire life had each changed dramatically. Not all the changes had pleased Breckinridge, but to the end she apparently remained convinced that her adult world, with all its imperfections, had greatly improved the one she had encountered as a young, eager Wellesley graduate. If her analysis was correct, Sophonisba Breckinridge could take pride in the fact that she had been an important force in that improvement.

After the usual honors for one of her stature, burial took place in the family plot in the Lexington Cemetery. The green coffin was placed in the brown soil of the Bluegrass, and Nisba once again was near her father.

Fifteen

The Patrician
As Progressive

DESHA BRECKINRIDGE was Sophonisba's closest sibling, in years, in outlook, and in affection. Nor was that surprising, for next to Nisba, he had received Willie Breckinridge's closest attention. The son, like the daughter, adored the father. In Desha's judgment, W.C.P. Breckinridge had been "the greatest in brain and heart," a man above reproach. Trying to act as he thought his father would wish, Desha acknowledged that he often longed for lost paternal guidance in times of stress and trial: "His wisdom and foresight and courage have been more and more emphasized and vindicated by the course of events. More than any man of his day . . . he foresaw the future."[1] Desha accepted wholeheartedly the transitional philosophy of his father and molded it, as Willie had counseled, to fit his own life's peculiar problems. Year after year, until his own death, he reprinted Willie's editorials celebrating special occasions. He fought his father's fights and seldom spared his father's enemies. The son long remembered the past, yet at the same time did not ignore the present.

Awareness of his Breckinridge heritage came early in life. Born on election day, 4 August 1867, this third child and first son was nearly named for the Democratic governor elected that day. But Willie changed his mind: he thought his son deserved more and was capable of higher honors. Thus came the family name his mother had brought to the marriage.[2] On his father's side, an imposing figure briefly influenced the youngster: years later, Desha still recalled how his grandfather Robert's fierce eyes had seemed "to look clear through us and strike terror to our childish heart." He remembered also how he would sit on the Reverend Dr. Breckinridge's knee, listening as Willie and the old clergyman discussed with both affection and frankness their divergent political views. Desha also had a source of family history that stretched even beyond his grandfather's era. A former slave who had once belonged to the first of the Kentucky clan, John Breckinridge, still lived; when she was over one hundred—three years before her death—Desha talked with her and learned firsthand of events that had occurred almost a century earlier. More recent history came to Desha as congressmen, governors, and other notables visited the Breckinridge home. As a boy of nine, for example, he heard his father and South Carolinian Wade Hampton talk over important political questions. At other times relatives visited and the family would gather for dinner. "Campaigns were planned; candidates appraised; points of law debated; new books reviewed." Then they would retire to the parlor, where his mother would play the piano, his maternal grandmother would sing the old tunes, his father and aunt would dance, and all would enjoy themselves, until a servant took the reluctant children to bed. From such gatherings of family and other notables, Desha came to feel that the Breckinridges had numerous peers, but few superiors.[3]

Learning also took place outside the drawing room. In 1875, the family traveled the rough roads to Cumberland Gap, on the way witnessing a hanging that left bitter memories for the youngster. Two years later the boy visited the Gap again and spent six weeks in the tents of noted Harvard geologist Nathaniel Southgate Shaler and his state geological survey team. Two years after that he and his father journeyed on horseback to West Virginia, where Desha spent some of the happiest days of his youth.[4]

Less pleasant experiences awaited him at Lawrenceville School in New Jersey. After tutelage in Lexington by novelist James Lane Allen, and then a stint at State College in 1880-81, Desha entered the eastern preparatory school. In poor health, bothered by the eye problems that would cause him to wear glasses thereafter, low on money, and concerned over his grades, the student did not find the experience totally enjoyable. Exposure to certain new ideas troubled him, and he complained when one teacher concluded that Alexander Hamilton equaled two Thomas Jeffersons—an idea Desha found very "queer." But grades and social life improved, and the Kentuckian left the school better informed than when he entered.[5]

Armed with four volumes his father had given—the Bible, Milton, Shakespeare, and *Don Quixote*—Desha Breckinridge found himself at his grandfather's old school, the College of New Jersey. His many problems at Princeton nearly rivaled those of Robert and Cabell years earlier. Low grades continued to plague him: "Every Prof. seems to be trying to see how hard he can make it for us now & they succeed pretty well." Nevertheless, Desha told his mother, he was doing "steady work, though not brilliant." More alarmingly, Breckinridge predicted that he might be suspended for his hazing activities. He managed, however, to escape that fate.[6]

Athletic pursuits attracted the student more than academics. At Lawrenceville earlier Desha had served as treasurer of the tennis club, captain of the football team's second eleven, and "director" of the first. He described to a sister his enjoyment of a football game there, though he "got broke up worse than I ever did before. . . . I can hardly move a finger to-day." Weighing less than 150 pounds, Desha, in abandoning the sport at Princeton, showed latent intelligence, although as spectator, bettor, and avid fan, the young Kentuckian concluded after a Harvard-Princeton match that this "grand" game represented "a battle between giants." Work with the United States Geological Survey occupied Desha's summers, and in 1886 he and his brother Robert camped for five months in the Carolinas, where they climbed mountains and hunted quail and wild-cats.[7]

Back at school as an upperclassman, Desha finally devoted more attention to academic pursuits, though his job as editor of the college paper took much time. While writing an essay on Kentucky's role in the building of the nation, he read Woodrow Wilson's *Congressional Government* and wrote to the young author at Bryn Mawr. Wilson permitted Breckinridge to visit him and, as Desha later recalled, "gave lavishly of his knowledge and advice." He labeled Wilson "an intellectual aristocrat and a social aristocrat." Aid from such men as Wilson and his father furthered Desha's attempt to gain scholarly respectability.[8] After graduation from Princeton in 1889, Desha studied for the bar, spending two years at Columbia University and a summer at the University of Virginia. During part of 1891 he worked as superintendent of an isolated West Virginia lumber mill. His father encouraged this "experiment," despite its harshness, for he felt there was "a great deal of manhood in Desha" which he thought the job would develop. Willie wanted his son to become a lawyer, but he told a daughter that he would not push his children into a calling that was not congenial. Desha left West Virginia the next year, "greatly improved in looks by his beard and sun-burn." Failing to secure a position as assistant paymaster of the Navy, he returned, almost reluc-tantly, to pass his home state's bar exams. Lawyer Breckinridge, like Nisba, joined his father's law firm.[9]

Immediately the son's attention centered on Madeline Pollard's breach-of-promise suit against Willie. That searing episode welded the once-restless Desha to Lexington. He determined to remain and fight, and would thereafter become inseparable from the Bluegrass. The affair also indicated his strong sense of family honor and his devotion to his father. Desha worked under an obvious strain before, during, and after the trial, but courtroom reporters noted that the twenty-six-year-old was well known in the "swell set" as a punctiliously neat dresser, an accom-plished athlete, and a good conversationalist. Having worked as every-thing from cowboy to surveyor, Desha was called "the hero of a hundred fights."[10]

The count soon increased. Earlier, Desha had warned *Leader* editor Samuel J. Roberts to stop publishing items reflecting adversely on his sisters' honor or he would "feel compelled to do my-self the pleasure of thrashing you." On his father's advice, he withdrew that impetuous threat five days later. Then, in June 1894, the young attorney called his father's chief opponent, Will Owens, "by nature a coward, by instinct a traitor, by practice a liar, and by profession a gambler." When the two men met at the Phoenix Hotel in Lexington some months later they glared at each other, and a fight was barely avoided. A reporter present noted that the son possessed the same complexion, same eyes, same white hands with delicate fingers, and same "patrician bearing of form" as his father, and he found Desha's devotion one of the contest's most notable features. Young Breckinridge told why he supported his father, openly and strongly: "I loved him, I do love him, as I have loved no other man. I approve nothing he has done. I pass judgment upon nothing he has done. He has given me pleasure, for that I thank him; he has given me pain, for that I forgive him. . . . I know there are no depths to which I could sink that he would not put his arms around me and shield me with his love."[11]

On primary election day, as his father was going down to defeat, the son's emotions and frustrations exploded. First, Desha challenged one man to fight, because he had said no decent woman could entertain W.C.P. Breckinridge. Later he met another critic, who questioned Willie Breckinridge's integrity, and who, after being called "a one-horse Scoundrel," hit Desha and knocked off his glasses. Breckinridge quickly drew a knife and bloodied his assailant's hand. The attacker fled. Victorious in one fight, however, Desha and the family lost the larger struggle. His idol had been defeated.[12]

Like Willie, he rebounded quickly. Both moved into a new profession, although the father also kept his active law practice. Desha took up the editor's pen and never put it down. In January 1897 he leased the newly formed Lexington *Herald* for twelve months and then purchased it outright the next year. Willie would have advised otherwise, but he had not been consulted. Besides, as he said, wanderer Desha "may make a success out of it and find his vocation." In his role as managing editor, and as editoral writer after his father's death, Desha did in fact find the profession he enjoyed. Through this medium, not in the uncertain world of politics, he would attempt to carry on paternal traditions.[13]

Desha Breckinridge's view of family history became very important. After Willie's death in 1904, it would be the son who perpetuated the past through newspaper editorials and through repeated contact with the historians who would write the volumes that would dominate for almost a half-century. To Desha, his great-grandfather John still represented the voice of the reformer (in penal legislation), the voice of free speech against tyranny (in the Kentucky Resolutions), and the voice of leadership (in the Senate). More than that, John Breckinridge stood for an image of pastoral opulence in a serene setting. Grandfather Robert was more troubling, for his image projected extremism—in anti-Catholicism, in abolitionism, in Unionism. Yet through Desha's own recollections and those of his father he knew also a Robert of vast intellect, a man of much learning, a reformer. While he might not receive as much of Desha's praise as did others, Robert would not be ignored, either.

And then, of course, there was Willie. Desha left no doubt of his feelings for his father. Love and admiration—even adulation—marked almost every utterance by Desha concerning W.C.P. Breckinridge. The son presented readers with his version of Breckinridge defeats (never mentioning Pollard) and even modified his own stands to avoid conflicts on specific issues. While he departed frequently from Willie's philosophy, Desha did so with the patriarch's lingering counsel still dominant. Change, Willie had advised, if the change was warranted. That Desha Breckinridge would do, but his devotion to the family he had shaped in his consciousness would always condition that change. While sister Nisba became in almost all respects a twentieth-century person, the editor never could break away completely from the world of his forefathers. He moved between two centuries, representing reform causes in one, but looking backward with a sigh toward the other.[14] Desha's upbringing and reading strengthened his wistful vision of the first two-thirds of the nineteenth century. By the time he was thirty-five the son had gone beyond his father's temperate view of the antebellum South. To Desha, it appeared to have been a place of simple, carefree, and genteel pleasure. Contrasting it sharply with the complex, sometimes corrupt, and often distasteful industrial and political world of the 1890s, he accorded the prewar plantation a way of life that even Willie Breckinridge had rejected. Desha was not alone; friends and acquaintances supported that vision of history.

Desha's former teacher, James Lane Allen, gave the nation an image of Kentucky he may have implanted in his young pupil. To the novelist, the world before the war represented hospitality, honor, and heroism. It had a graceful landscape, harmonious citizenry, rural gentleness, elegant culture, and mellow beauty. His portrayal of postwar society included both a continuation of that idealism and a realism that dealt with contemporary currents. In *Kentucky Cardinal* (1895), for example, Allen pictured an idyllic, romantic love, while in a book such as *The Reign of Law* (1900), he dealt with the more forbidden topic of evolution. Desha, too, would be both idealistic and realistic.[15] The literary current in Kentucky and the South in the first decade of the twentieth century moved mostly with the sentimental tide, however. Near Louisville Annie Fellows Johnston wrote of the "Little Colonel," while Alice Hegan Rice gave her readers a smiling and hardworking Mrs. Wiggs in her slum, the Cabbage Patch. John Fox, Jr., another Allen follower, presented the clearest image of the warmth with which the old regime was embraced. His *Little Shepherd of Kingdom Come* (1903) told of that Kentucky: "It was a land of peace and of a plenty that was close to easy luxury—for all. Poor whites were few, the beggar was unknown. . . . If slavery had to be—then the fetters were forged light and hung loosely. And broadcast, through the people, was the upright sturdiness of the Scotch-Irishman, without his narrowness and bigotry; the grace and chivalry of the Cavalier without his Quixotic sentiment and his weakness."

Fox described antebellum Lexington as the site of the proudest families, the broadest culture, and the finest courtesies in the state's entire history: "There were as manly virtues, as manly vices, as the world has ever known." This land that never existed was what Desha Breckinridge sought. He wanted his twentieth-century state to regain past—imaginary—glories, and he doomed himself to frustration. At the same time, his search brought that vision closer to reality.[16]

Willie Breckinridge's death removed paternal counsel, but the void was gradually filled by Desha's wife. Without her the editor might never have moved as far down the reform road as he did. She led him away from his misty vision of the idyllic past toward the clear progressivism of the present. In a sense, Madeline McDowell was a strange companion for Desha Breckinridge. Her Republican father, the former Union officer Henry Clay McDowell, had almost run against Willie Breckinridge in the 1894 race, an act that had alienated the two families. Worse, Madeline, too, opposed the congressman's reelection. But, in other ways, she and Desha had much in common. A granddaughter of Henry Clay, "Madge" had grown up surrounded by many of the same kinds of family influences as had Breckinridge. Her friends included poet-artist Robert Burns Wilson and author Fox, as well as numerous others in Lexington society. This tall, slender woman with a thin face, sparkling eyes, and light brown hair exuded a reserved graciousness and a controlled lightness that made her an attractive partner.[17]

Madeline McDowell's educational route, from Miss Porter's School in Connecticut to State College, differed little from the experience of hundreds like her. Her sheltered background presented few hints that she would depart from the expected pattern and be anything more than the refined wife of some member of a conservative, well-established family. Yet by the time she began to see Desha regularly, Madge had suffered deeply. This young woman, once eagerly engaged in hunting, dancing, and other social activities, contracted tuberculosis. The disease affected both lungs and bones, and would result in the amputation of a leg. Emotionally, she was no longer the same person.[18]

Madge and Desha, then, both bore hidden scars—she, an illness, and he, his father's scandal. Both represented leading families. Both believed in the need for reform, though not certain in exactly what form. They

seemed completely devoted to each other, and in May 1898 their engage-
ment was announced. The move gave Desha's father little joy. Willie wrote
to Nisba of the "tremendous risks" involved, but he admitted that Madge
was intellectual, gracious, and attractive; if she was his son's choice, then
as a father he would treat her with affection and respect. On 17 November
1898 the marriage took place between the dapper, socially-minded, thirty-
one-year-old editor and the more somber, crippled, twenty-six-year-old
budding reformer. These two very different personalities together would
become leaders of Kentucky Progressivism.[19]

The groom was a short, thin man who had long been attractive to
women and who enjoyed parties immensely. Usually witty, he could also
be severe at times. On one occasion, a woman laughingly asked if it was
true her face would stop a clock. He drew out a timepiece used to clock
races, pressed a button to halt its movement, and—saying not a word—
held it up to her. The party crowd roared. Not particularly tolerant of what
he considered "chit-chat" at such affairs, in another instance a casual
compliment on a recent editorial brought from him a quick question:
"What *exactly* did you like about it?" Yet throughout his life, an overwhelming courtesy, good manners, and dapper dress caused people to
remember Breckinridge most often as "gentleman." His marriage did not
alter this earlier lifestyle.[20]

Madge would on occasion entertain or visit their friends, or go to
parties, but most often she concentrated instead on those public issues
she considered important. Work became an outlet for her unhappiness—
over her health, her childlessness, her father's death within a year of her
marriage—and she used that work to achieve much good. "An orator in
the best sense of the word," Mrs. Breckinridge spoke with a well-pitched
fluency. Her forceful, sarcastic speeches could win converts to the cause
even as they sometimes embittered enemies. Coworkers found her tolerant; opponents had a decidedly contrary reaction. Through her work, she
involved Desha, shaped his views, and influenced him. In 1899 and 1901
Madge made long trips to the eastern Kentucky mountains to assist in
social reform work there. As charter member and then president of the
Lexington Civic League and as founder of the public and privately supported Associated Charities, she encouraged activities similar to those
Nisba supported in Chicago. Besides organizing the Kentucky Association for the Prevention and Relief of Tuberculosis, Madge also served as
the mainstay and chief fundraiser in the construction of the Lincoln
School for children, in a slum section of Lexington. Public health concerns, a new compulsory attendance law, establishment of a juvenile
court, abolishment of child labor, improved playground facilities, better
race relations—these too received attention. She had few tranquil moments.[21]

In one area, Madge's influence on Desha was particularly important.

Her activities in the women's rights movement shaped and modified her husband's views, and as a result the *Herald* became the chief spokesman for the movement in Kentucky, and one of the leaders in the entire South. As Melba Porter Hay has observed, "Perhaps the most influential convert Mrs. Breckinridge made to the cause of woman suffrage was her husband." One of Desha's main contributions during his lifetime was to give the suffrage cause a forum in his paper. For a time Madge wrote for the new woman's page of the paper. She had access to the editorial page as well, with results not always pleasing to Desha. The editor, in fact, was at best a reluctant reformer. He remembered when, as a five-year-old, he had told his grandmother, "men always know better than women." Later, in early manhood, Desha expressed his disapproval of Nisba's growing independence and even of her purchase of a bicycle. Before his marriage he openly opposed the women who were operating in the reform arena.[22]

Desha Breckinridge's attitudes changed, but slowly. Nisba's outstanding work, his father's own support for limited suffrage, and then Madge's influence all "helped educate us" to the need for equal rights. In 1905 he predicted that while his opposition to suffrage remained, it might soon dissolve. By November of the next year the treasurer of the National American Woman Suffrage Association told Laura Clay how delighted she was with Mr. Breckinridge's apparent conversion. Desha saw that women did not get a fair hearing before some legislators, and in 1907, after telling readers he regretted his earlier inaction, he added, "Confidentially, the more we see of men the more firmly we are convinced of the superiority of women." Breckinridge in 1909 warned politicians to support suffrage, for it would come "as sure as the day follows the night."[23]

When the Kentucky House Committee on Suffrage and Elections met the following year, both Madge and Desha spoke before it in favor of school-election suffrage for women. The chairman's illogical arguments in opposition, his contention that the arguments would be stronger if the speakers were mothers, and his high-handed manner pushed Desha Breckinridge into a final, full advocacy of unqualified suffrage. A year later Madge could banter: "A Kentucky man for whose opinion I have considerable respect—in spite of the fact that he is my husband—has recently stated his opinion that Kentucky would get full suffrage for women inside of ten years." Desha answered in kind: "We are her friend in spite of the fact that we are her husband."[24]

Madge Breckinridge traveled and lectured widely supporting the suffrage cause, and Desha reported it sympathetically in the *Herald*. The question was not whether women were fit for suffrage, Madge explained, "but whether men are fit for it." Asking for the governor's aid in 1915, she pointed out, "Kentucky women are not idiots—even though they are closely related to Kentucky men." Her humor served her well, for disappointments abounded. Pleas to various governors and congressional leaders resulted in encouragement—sometimes—but little else. By 1914 the state press recognized the eloquent Mrs. Breckinridge as "one of the brainiest women in the state." Already president of the Kentucky Equal Rights Association, vice-president of the NAWSA in 1913-14, and mentioned as possible successor to Anna Shaw, the national president, Madge saw an increasing possibility that what she and Desha were fighting for might become reality. But just as those hopes rose, so too did the forbidding image of factionalism in the movement, as two groups argued over how best to achieve suffrage—through state initiative or federal action. By 1918 the split was completed. Feminist leader Laura Clay resigned her post in the Kentucky Equal Rights Association. Both Breckinridges, through a series of public letters and editorials, opposed Clay's approach.[25]

The growing sentiment for suffrage could not be halted by splits such as this, however. Madge observed the proceedings in early 1920 as Kentucky approved the woman suffrage amendment by legislative votes of 30–8 and 72–25. Celebrating that event a month later at a Chicago banquet, she joyously turned songwriter:

> The sun shines bright in my old Kentucky home,
> 'Tis winter, the ladies are gay,
> The corn top's green, prohibitions in the swing,
> The Colonel's in eclipse and the women in the ring
> We'll get all our rights with the help of Uncle Sam
> For the way that they come we don't give a ——
> Weep No More, my lady, oh, weep no more today,
> For we'll vote one vote for the old Kentucky home,
> The old Kentucky home, far away.[26]

By 1920, then, Madeline McDowell Breckinridge had achieved many of the reforms she and her husband had long sought. For twenty-two years she had encouraged Desha in his reform programs; without her counsel his stands might have been far different. Their collaboration had put Desha Breckinridge at the forefront of the Kentucky reform movement.

"We are a Kentuckian," declared editor Breckinridge over and over. He loved the state above all else and wanted it to regain the prominence it once held; but, looking critically at the commonwealth early in his career, Desha sadly concluded that it lagged behind other states. He sensed what the 1910 census showed: only two states had lower population growth in the previous decade. Feuds, the Goebel assassination, and other violence had given the state an unenviable reputation. Internal political infighting did little to dispel that. Bourbon-drinking, goateed aristocrats and moonshine-producing, gun-toting mountaineers became Kentucky caricatures representing the entire South. The commonwealth, said Desha, "has retrograded in the opinion of the world, and deteriorated in the judgment of those whose judgment is not tempered with mercy."[27]

What, then, could be done to reverse the process? His answer—a change in outlook and a dedication to reform—required a major philosophical shift. Desha Breckinridge recognized that the laissez-faire philosophy generally followed by his ancestors would no longer meet his generation's needs. This did not warrant abandonment of the ideas of private property, rewards, or competition, but it did mean, to him, that railroad arrogance and financiers' ambition had gone too far. Social reformers, preferably from the propertied classes, should take the lead in bringing about a change. He never completely rejected the idea that state aid was preferable to federal, but "the truth is, there is not much left of the old idea of state's rights." Nor should the Constitution be strictly interpreted, for it was an elastic creation, "pulsating with life." Only when his state accepted this, only when it saw that human rights were more important than property rights, only when the commonwealth abandoned the "cruel and extravagant" theory of laissez-faire, only then could it recapture past glories. To triumph, then, Kentucky must repudiate many of the theories of John, John C., and even Willie Breckinridge.[28]

The words came hard, for Desha Breckinridge would not allow his past to be rejected out of hand. Duty, he proclaimed, required that future improvement must be accomplished only with the recollection and guidance of the past. Whatever good existed in his time resulted from that "all compelling" instinct to obey the traditions of forefathers. It was that sense of duty to the past, ironically, that allowed him to reject philosophical parts of it, for the father's advice had been for Desha to change in a way Willie never could. That the son tried to do, but Desha Breckinridge's view of mankind confused the change. His father had been overwhelmingly optimistic about the future, despite his Calvinist beliefs, but his grandfather had usually spoken words of doom and disaster. Many progressives of Desha's generation placed their faith in progress and in removal of evils through either moral persuasion or governmental intervention. Breckinridge could never take that final step. There was too much respect for both father and grandfather for him to move completely into one position or the other. Such conflicts tormented an already troubled soul.[29]

Still, they did not cripple his advocacy of reform. By 1904 Breckinridge was calling for a juvenile court system in Lexington. The next year, his *Herald* advocated state aid in upbringing of children, arguing for central control should parents fail in their duties. Similarly, the paper advocated a child labor law to prevent exploitation of youth and to ensure their proper physical and mental growth. The state also should take the leadership in striking down the disease that affected his wife and others, tuberculosis. After several disappointing starts a tuberculosis commission was finally set up and several sanatoriums established. Like many progressives, Breckinridge placed great faith in education, and he fought hard for increased funding. No state or country, the editor wrote, could spend too much on such a vital cause; the results would be worth every dollar.[30]

Crime and criminals were a part of Kentucky's present and, like his great-grandfather, Desha found an unfulfilled need in that area. Prison reform was desperately needed. From the time he spent three nights in an "indescribably filthy" jail in the 1890s while protecting a prisoner from a mob outside, Breckinridge had seen the need for change. The state penitentiary in Frankfort he correctly called a breeding place for crime, since many of the three-foot-wide and seven-foot-long cells housed two prisoners. At times tuberculosis and other diseases swept through the prison population almost unchecked. Such a "rotten" system could never accomplish society's goal of reform, he prophesied; it could only remain "an abomination in the sight of the Lord, [and] a disgrace to the State in the sight of men." Again, the answer was proper funding: "We cannot escape from this natural and inevitable tendency to increase expenses . . . unless we are ready to leave undone many of those things which can be done only by the public authority."[31]

Various other reforms, usually associated with the progressives of his era, also found a willing sponsor in Breckinridge. He pronounced himself a "firm believer" in a state-supported direct primary system and supported Lexington's continuing attempt to institute a commission form of government. Kentucky's already outdated 1890 constitution received frequent criticism for its "archaic" provisions. The lack of a good highway system came under attack as well. On the local level, Desha found equally numerous areas that required action. The "smoke nuisance" needed an antipollution ordinance; the snow-covered sidewalks required strict enforcement of the city laws; the explosion of fireworks, the playing of slot machines, the sale of liquor on Sunday—all meant to Breckinridge that local officials were failing to enforce the laws. After observing a public execution in the city, he called for private ones—if there must be such. Breckinridge had serious doubts whether the death penalty ought ever to be inflicted. Part of the problem, he believed, could be solved by a law forbidding the carrying of concealed weapons. A longer-range solution could be to stop the propagation of criminals or those of a "defective race." Sterilization, he once told the Kentucky Press Association, "is a duty one generation owes to the next generation." His numerous stands attest to his place in the Progressive Era.[32]

Another problem that attracted the attention of progressives would prove more troubling. Like his forebears, Breckinridge had to deal with the "Negro problem" that so divided his age and his region, and at first he chose the moderation displayed by Robert and Willie. When the film "Birth of a Nation" first appeared in Lexington, the editor attacked its appeal to prejudice and passion. He supported a black in an application for a governmental position, despite political repercussions. Criticism of black school facilities came more than once, and the Negro press praised several noteworthy editorial stands, particularly those against governmental segregation. In both 1905 and 1915 the black New York *Age* recommended Breckinridge's paper to its readers, concluding, "More courage and truth to the *Herald* and the Southern thought it voices." Black writers in the A.M.E. *Church Review* and in the *Crisis* gave similar praise. Desha also joined the call for a national conference on lynching. Later, when a white man assaulted two Negro girls within days of the hanging of a black man for a similar crime against a Caucasian girl, Breckinridge pointed out that "in the eyes of justice there can be no difference in the punishment inflicted."[33]

Despite these stands the Kentuckian did not predict significant black progress. Indeed, a serious doubt existed in his mind, as in the minds of many southerners, whether blacks of his generation were as intelligent and "amenable" as those who had lived under slavery. Several generations would pass, he predicted, before the race would be anything more than servants of the master class. Seeking order and stability, Breckinridge stressed that the "deterioration" of blacks must be slowed; manual training schools on the Hampton/Tuskegee model provided one answer he favored. Until such long-range plans matured, controls might be needed, but what kind? Desha Breckinridge had little sympathy for answers given by "Dixie Demagogues" such as James K. Vardaman of Mississippi. Their race-baiting held no more appeal for him than it had for W.C.P. Breckinridge. In 1908 Desha called recent laws disfranchising blacks in the South a serious mistake. But in the North, progressives were reacting to boss control of the immigrant vote in much the same way their southern brethren did to black voting, turning to some form of restriction in order to "purify" politics. In 1909 Desha reconsidered his position and suggested that citizens seriously consider eliminating the vote of "the ignorant, the venal and vicious." Not only was the black vote corrupt and purchasable; worse, it was solidly Republican.[34]

Following the November 1909 election Breckinridge explained: "We have doubted the wisdom of the enactment of election laws similar to those enacted in the Southern States. But neither this community nor this State desires, nor does it intend to have it possible by one-fourth of the white voters combined with the solid negro vote to elect its officers and control its destiny." Three days later he advocated a constitutional amendment to eliminate the black vote. When that race broke its shackles of bondage to one party and voted for reason rather than prejudice, then, he stated, he would propose a restored franchise. Racist political cartoons appeared in his paper, and although declaring himself the friend of Negroes, Breckinridge warned that they themselves were responsible for his disfranchisement pronouncements. Like others of his class and his era, Desha supported the prevailing climate of restriction—a climate that kept the South solid and segregated.[35]

This course was far removed from the program and stands of Robert and W.C.P. Breckinridge. How could the loving son move so away from them? Desha certainly had no desire to repudiate his past, but the racial future his father had predicted was not the one Breckinridge now saw. It would be simplest, of course, to say that he yielded to the era's racial climate and its attendant pressures, but Desha seldom indicated any predilection to surrender to popular opinion on any issue, if he thought his view correct. More central is his understanding of the past and of his father's counsel. The Lexingtonian viewed his ancestors as reformers—of prisons, schools, politics, and other institutions—and he saw himself in that mold. Yet each generation had realized that what was reform in one era might not be in the next, so they had slowly and gradually transformed family philosophy. All this created conflict within Desha Breckinridge. He respected the "all compelling" instinct to obey the traditions of his forefathers, but he also recognized weaknesses in parts of their philosophy. His turn from laissez-faire had resulted in a reform orientation; the change in racial philosophy would end far differently.[36]

In facing the race question, Desha was imbued with the idea that he could modify family tradition and still remain loyal to familial duty. His paternalistic beliefs, after all, did not upset previous family traditions, nor did his individual aid to blacks. His views about the regression of blacks since slavery did not depart so much from the past either: Robert had opposed immediate black suffrage and Willie had voiced his own concern over black advancement by the late nineteenth century. But Robert had tempered such feelings with a strong moral support for blacks, and Willie had been ever-optimistic. Desha Breckinridge shared neither attribute. It seemed to him that further regression of the black race had taken place since his father's death, and Desha at times feared the future. Adding to his latent fears was the role blacks played in elections. Voting almost continually with Republicans, blacks were an important bloc in electing four Kentucky Republican governors between 1895 and 1919. Significantly, Desha Breckinridge's harshest words against blacks came in election years. These two forces—fear of a "savage," regressive race and the recognition of their rising importance in state politics—combined to bring a call for proscription. That science and progressives called this a reform only made it that much easier.

One further element—in some ways perhaps the most vital—made this course more acceptable. Desha Breckinridge was never particularly religious. His grandfather, the Reverend Robert Breckinridge, had been honored with his church's highest position, while W.C.P. Breckinridge's speeches to the Presbyterian General Assembly had strongly praised the Calvinistic spirit. Both men's sense of moral outrage, first over slavery, then over white injustice to blacks, can be traced in part to their religious backgrounds. Neither the eighteenth-century Deist and proslavery advocate John nor the twentieth-century Desha was imbued with such a strong religious sense of morality and justice. Thus Desha Breckinridge's religious outlook, his pessimistic view of blacks, his political fears, his interpretation of his own past, his father's counsel, and his era's definition of reform united to create racial views that were typically progressive, southern, and probably national. Only an examination in the light of four generations' past philosophy and actions explains this evolution fully. As Desha wrote, by his desk was a portrait of his grandfather, "who suffered social ostracism, political oblivion, physical mutilation because of his devotion to the cause of emancipation," and in his memory was a father who "sacrificed public office for his conviction that the negroes were entitled to equal justice." The words were Desha's, as he wrote editorials calling for further restrictions on blacks.[37]

As Breckinridge's stands on racial issues indicated, politics shaped his actions and his outlooks. Although he never made a formal race for political office, his interest in that sphere remained acute. Desha could never extract himself from the political world, nor apparently did he want to. He, like his father, faced difficult choices. A Democrat (he once trained his dog, when asked, "Would you rather be dead or a Republican?" to roll over and play dead), Desha had followed W.C.P. Breckinridge into support for the Gold Democrats. Too, he aided a fusion ticket in 1896 and Republicanism for a time following that. In the Goebel affair the young editor's allegiance unreservedly went to opposition of the "Kenton King," and the martyred governor's successor—the tall, aristocratic, thirty-one-year-old John Crepps Wickliffe Beckham of Bardstown—received similar Breckinridge criticism. But Willie's death in 1904 freed Desha of any loyalty to his father's politics.[38] He could now return to the Democratic party.

Party factionalism complicated the decision, however. By the time Governor Beckham left office in 1907 he had built an organization that exceeded Goebel's. Percy Haly, a former campaign secretary for Goebel and a Catholic, compensated for the handicap of his religion in Protestant Kentucky by becoming a behind-the-scenes boss, and the two became the center of party fights. Failing in a 1908 senatorial contest, Beckham won that seat in 1914, then lost it six years later. A "dry" on the prohibition issue (even though he himself drank), an opponent of woman suffrage, and a man of moralistic reforms, "boy Beckham" found opposition in his party to many of those stands. Divisions resulted, so that Kentucky's

Desha Breckinridge, 1920

political scene over the next three decades would compare favorably with the machinations of the Byzantine empire.

Breckinridge's dilemma was that he wholeheartedly supported neither Beckham's faction nor its opposition, led by witty, "wet," western Kentucky congressman Augustus Owsley Stanley. Desha remained outside the circles of power and could stand aloof from bitter party battles, but at the same time, he had no political base, should he desire office. Throughout the first two decades of the century, he charted a political course that amply indicated his independent spirit, but one that only occasionally endeared him to a victorious candidate. In what amounted to a three-party state—Beckham Democrats, Stanley Democrats, and Republicans—the editor at times backed each group. In 1907, for example, Desha praised the well-educated Republican gubernatorial candidate Augustus E. (Gus) Willson as "a gentleman of character and ability." Four years later, though, he backed the Democratic ticket without reserve when the elderly former governor James B. McCreary won the race. In the 1915 race, defeat of McCreary's candidate in the primary left Breckinridge the choice between Democratic factional leader Owsley Stanley and Republican Edwin P. Morrow. While a progressive in the southern context, Stanley opposed woman suffrage and, in Breckinridge's eyes, gained his support from "the vicious elements" of the liquor interests. Republicans included the *Herald's* critical description of the Democratic platform in their campaign handbook, but Breckinridge editorials ignored the race completely. Stanley won by fewer than five hundred votes. But four years later, in 1919, when Morrow again ran for the governorship—this time opposed by James Black, who had been Stanley's lieutenant governor— he did not gain the *Herald's* endorsement. Breckinridge had mixed feelings about the Stanley administration, but he disliked Republican Morrow's promise to reduce expenditures and his silence on the League of Nations. A Republican victory in 1919 left Desha again on the losing side.[39]

Nationally, he had done little better. Grudgingly supporting Parker in 1904 and Bryan four years later, Desha cared little for either Democrat. On the Republican side, he vacillated between complete disgust with and partial admiration of Theodore Roosevelt. Desha supported railroad regulation completely, for example, but feared T.R.'s bombast and vanity. He saw William Howard Taft as a man with his eyes glued on the past. But one man, a Democrat, did attract him as the 1912 election approached. As early as 1906, the Lexington *Herald* had praised Desha's former term paper adviser, Woodrow Wilson. When nominated for the New Jersey governorship in 1910, Wilson was described in a *Herald* editorial as one of the great men in America—"great alike in intellect, in character and in learning." During a 1911 trip to Kentucky Wilson was Desha's houseguest. The same year, the Kentuckian pushed hard—and unsuccessfully—for Wilson's endorsement by the Democratic state convention. As the Democratic national convention drew near, however, Breckinridge called for the nomination of Alabama congressman Oscar W. Underwood, a Kentucky native. Neither Wilson nor Kentucky-born Champ Clark of Missouri could command the two-thirds vote needed, Desha believed. But with Wilson's victory at the national convention, the *Herald* immediately came out for the ticket. Victory that fall brought a Democrat with strong southern ties to the White House for the first time in sixteen years.[40]

Breckinridge, despite friends' advice, thought it an excellent time to ask for a patronage appointment. Always an independent Democrat, he could make but a weak claim to the post of collector of internal revenue. His support of Democratic nominees had been anything but consistent, and that did not bode well with a president devoted to the idea of party support. But Desha had powerful friends, including Kentucky's millionaire national committeeman John C.C. Mayo, state campaign committee chairman Johnson Camden, cousin Henry Breckinridge, now assistant secretary of war, and the chief of the Democratic Bureau of Publicity, Kentuckian Robert M. Woolley. All gave Breckinridge their support. But he also had powerful enemies: Stanley allies Kentucky Senator Ollie M. James and Congressman J. Campbell Cantrill had felt the stings of Breckinridge editorials—and after their opposition would do so again. The president generally turned the patronage over to the organization in control of the state party, and in faction-ridden Kentucky many Wilson men were excluded from patronage posts, Breckinridge among them.[41]

Defeat did not subdue the erstwhile renegade. While Breckinridge openly supported Wilson's domestic programs, the president received little but criticism from the *Herald* on foreign affairs. "Jekyll and Hyde are no more contradictory characters," wrote the Lexington editor, than Wilson as domestic leader and foreign policy leader. After violence broke out in Mexico, Breckinridge demanded that an army be sent to protect American property and to wipe out the "Mexican cancer." The death of one leader, the rise of another, and the ensuing revolt against him left Mexico confused and unstable. Desha had thoroughly absorbed the imperialistic teachings of his father. Having taken half of Mexico in another war, why not complete the conquest now? he asked. "Do we not fall short of our mission if we withhold from so ignorant and ill-trained a people those blessings which race superiority alone can give?" Outrages and insults of the past year required redress. Exasperated with his father's old devil, Secretary of State Bryan, and with President Wilson, Breckinridge declared that "sooner or later" all territory north of the Panama Canal must be American. "Heirs of a manifest destiny," Americans must conquer the half-breed savages and carry the blessings of trade and government to them.[42]

Acceptance by Mexico and the United States of a mediation offer in 1915 made the war Desha desired more remote, but raids by Francisco "Pancho" Villa on American border towns convinced him that "Nero fiddles while Rome burns." His animosity toward Wilson increased. Again and again he called for war. Future historians writing of the events in Mexico, he predicted, would find them "the most humiliating chapter in our history." To a friend, Desha summed up all his frustrations with Wilson: "I am so disheartened and, to use the mildest possible term discouraged by the prospect of affairs in relation to Mexico. . . . I firmly believe that unless President Wilson does something definite and conclusive in regard to Mexico he will be beyond hope of redemption."[43]

Wilson's European policies drew equally strong language. Seeing Germany as early as 1906 as a threat to progressive ideas, Desha quickly supported the Allied cause after the outbreak of World War I in 1914. His ancestral ties to Great Britain, his belief in Anglo-American superiority, and his view that Germans were fighting an uncivilized war brought him to that conclusion rather easily. Even before the war actually began for America, Breckinridge proposed an increase in military force in preparation for expected events. Preparedness would be his watchword for the next three years, and he could not understand Wilson's logic. "Shall we as a nation remain passive," the editor cried out, "while an outlaw nation wreaks its will on whomsoever it may please to destroy?" Too many pacifists found forums, Breckinridge believed, and their words made them enemies to their country. "If it be our purpose to commit national suicide we have certainly selected the right course to pursue." He did not exclude Wilson from the "pacifist" ranks.[44]

Throughout 1916 Breckinridge's anger mounted: "Has reason fled? Have we been doomed to destruction by supine inertia?" The Kentuckian confessed that he did not accept "as sound, or even tolerable" the views of Washington leaders; what was needed was "real nationalism." The *Herald* called for a "little more fire under the melting pot." Apathetic indifference must be overwhelmed by a "red-blooded Americanism." The "craven or vacillating" policy of those for whom he had campaigned in 1916 invited national insult. An extremely proud man—whether it be for family, state, or nation—Breckinridge reacted accordingly when that honor, as he perceived it, was threatened. As American participation neared in mid-March 1917, he wrote to the sister who had seen the struggle firsthand: "It looks as if we were drifting toward war or being dragged into war; whatever it may be called, and I hope with all my heart we are. I have thought from the first we should be in the war." Though the conflict he sought with Mexico did not come, in April 1917 Desha and his nation were at last at war.[45]

Before the American involvement began, the editor promised that "a little blood letting" would be good for the health of the nation by establishing a national unity. Now, in his opinion, some of the blood-letting should begin at home. While rival Henry Watterson won approval for his "To Hell with the Hapsburgs and Hohenzollerns" editorial, Breckinridge proclaimed in similar fashion, "Scotch the Snakes, Kill the Vipers." Convinced that spies lurked everywhere, he advised death to them all. Almost as dangerous were those who did not purchase war bonds: for anyone in the United States who did not, the mildest punishment should be deportation. Breckinridge also advocated setting up volunteer organizations in every county to punish those not loyal to the cause.[46]

The fierceness of his attitude may have been affected by his sister Nisba's wartime activities. His editorial attacking the American Union Against Militarism considerably embarrassed her in early 1917. Nisba politely informed her brother that she belonged to the organization. Her brother publicly relented—to a degree. Still, he expressed regret at the organization's "apparent purpose" to prevent actions he deemed necessary to preserve not only national honor but national integrity. Adamantly defending Nisba's actions after the war, however, Breckinridge more quietly suggested, "Her one thought was to bring peace with the least suffering to humanity. We disagreed as to the methods by which this might be done."[47]

To the conflict's end Breckinridge remained critical of Wilson's conduct of the war. The president's call for a world league, "a parliament of man," prompted the Bluegrass editor's response in 1917 to this "dream of a dreamer": Such a feeble parliament, he predicted, would meet Japan's demands for free immigration into the United States. America must act "to protect the purity of the white race against Mongolian contamination"; the United States must demand reservations prior to its entry. Two years later, however, Breckinridge defended the League of Nations against all opposition. At least partially responsible for this change of heart was a growing fear that only through a League could Bolshevism be halted. As *Herald* headlines exclaimed "Bolshevik Contagion Spreading Over Eastern Europe," Breckinridge supported a total intervention by American forces in Russian affairs. Lenin, "the Russian butcher," had declared war on civilization, the editor wrote, and was attempting to overthrow the social order of the world. As part of that order, Desha came to think that the United States' "obligation" to civilization required its entry into the League—"a barrier against Bolshevism."[48]

News stories in Breckinridge's paper pictured a world going to hell at an alarmingly fast rate. Conflict seemed inevitable, whether it be a race war with Japan, or a class war between Russia and the world. With the steel strike and hundreds more, bombings and rumors of bombings, race riots and lynchings, chaos seemed everywhere and stability nowhere. The League offered at least a few years of peace. When that idea met defeat in its first test, Breckinridge saw the vote as one that humiliated, betrayed, and dishonored the American people. After a later defeat, his nation had descended to the "very depths of the valley of humiliation." America now stood, not as moral leader of the world, but as the most selfish and most sordid of all nations.[49]

Yet even at that moment, Breckinridge's fear of Russia, and his belief in the need for the League, lessened. The future destiny of the two nations would be intertwined, he now predicted. America must win the confidence of Russia, but for reasons he earlier had supported (the American troops on Russian soil among them) the opposite was happening. Prosperity demanded trade with Russia; events were making that impossible. "The key to the future history of the world," Russia must unite commercially with English-speaking races to insure that the "yellow races of Asia" did not dominate the world. In 1920 Breckinridge had traveled a long way from his opinions of only a year before. Now he strongly opposed the deportation of "radicals" to Russia. It was "inconceivable" that officials would do such a deed. Recognition of Russia soon held no fear for him, and when recognition finally came much later, it was men with motives like Breckinridge's who made it possible.[50]

Editorial work, of course, did not consume all of Breckinridge's time during the first two decades of the twentieth century. Besides successful business ventures—organizing a telephone company, investing in a land company near the University of Kentucky, speculating in eastern Kentucky coal properties—Desha's attention focused on enjoyment of those hours away from the newspaper office. Breckinridge automobile parties periodically toured the state, much to his wife's pleasure. In Lexington, the couple enjoyed a reputation as charming hosts. At their house or the newly opened country club, they entertained with bridge and—somewhat surprisingly—dancing. On quieter evenings guests worked puzzles, roasted popcorn, or simply talked. On special occasions parties lasted far into the morning hours. And though a prohibitionist in his editorials, Desha served guests and himself Kentucky bourbon. As he once remarked of his vices: "During the infrequent intervals . . . when we do not ourselves use tobacco or drink any alcoholic liquors, we wonder at the patience and power of endurance of those who never use either. . . . The only protection we have ever been able to find against the odors of tobacco is to use it ourselves."[51]

Guests at such gatherings included members of the immediate family. Sister Ella, whose husband taught for a time at Transylvania and at the university's law school, joined Madge Breckinridge to support women's rights and other reform movements. Nisba returned on many occasions to speak on topics of interest to her, and to renew friendships. But the most welcome family member may have been Robert Breckinridge, Desha's wayward brother. No one had heard from him for almost two decades; all apparently thought he had died, a forgotten man, in a self-imposed overseas exile. Then, in 1914, he came back—much changed but alive. Desha noted that his brother's face showed the hard life he must have experienced in those clouded years, for he had lost several teeth and had a prominent scar on his cheek. He told of jaunts to Africa, racetrack ownership in Australia, ranching in New Zealand, being a cook in South

Madeline McDowell Breckinridge. Courtesy Kentucky Historical Society

America. After his homecoming he worked for a time in the eastern Kentucky mountains, married a young girl who bore him three children, then made his home in Lexington. Desha offered Robert a job on the paper, and shortly a humor column appeared under his by-line. Robert entered the Lexington society he had earlier scorned, but he never completely shook off the old problems; drink, divorce, debts, and uncertainty marked some of the next years.[52]

If Robert's return brought some joy to Desha, his relationship with sister Curry did not. Youngest of the children, she had perhaps suffered most from the Pollard affair. The images of a young, intelligent, friendly, carefree girl playing golf at the country club, visiting a mountain resort, or reading a paper before the Lexington Art League, contrast with the brooding melancholy of a woman bothered by physical problems and an outlook that caused siblings to worry constantly about her. She too went to the mountains of eastern Kentucky and for a time became an extremely well-liked settlement worker. Very independent, however, Curry told none of the family when she broke arches in both feet while away studying nursing. She completed her training and worked with the mentally ill, but depression and overexertion continued to plague the extremely pious Curry. Throughout, Desha counseled his "Monkey" (as he addressed her in letters) to take better care of herself. When war broke out in Europe she rushed to France as a volunteer nurse. Tired and recognizing her need for further medical training, Curry returned to America in 1917. In January she wrote, "Isn't life a wonderful adventure—and Death more wonderful than life?" Within two months, she suffered a severe heart attack, and after an agonizingly long and painful illness, Curry Desha Breckinridge died on 23 June 1918, at the age of forty-two. A tragic and sad figure, she left Desha convinced that he had not helped her enough. Now nothing could be done.[53]

The Progressive movement in the postwar period was in decline. Would the editor become a "tired progressive," and sever his reform ties? Were his intellectual roots deep enough to hold, at a time when progressivism appeared perilously close to extinction? Wilson's reforms, the war, the later disillusionment, the prosperity—all had either satisfied the reformers' desires or shaken their idealism. In some cases the movement had triumphed too well, as woman suffrage, prohibition, participatory democracy, and other aims had been achieved. In other instances the prewar innocence had fallen before the many postwar fears over labor, radicalism, communism, and other perceived threats. In this atmosphere many progressives found it increasingly easy to turn their backs on reform. Breckinridge's progressive commitment would now be tested.[54]

Sixteen

The Transformation
of Desha Breckinridge

IN THE fall of 1920, when the chaos and confusion of an election year and
the still-lingering debate over the postwar world combined to create
uncertainty, Desha Breckinridge's personal problems overshadowed any
national ones. His wife's declining health continued to trouble him, for
Madge had always worked too hard and rested too little in their twenty-
two years of marriage. During the winter of 1903 she had been forced to
go to a Denver sanatorium and, while there, had suffered temporary
paralysis of one arm. In 1908 and from 1915 to 1918 she had visited similar
institutions. As her husband wrote to his sister while staying at a New
York state retreat, "We eat and sleep and then sleep and eat, and then
reverse the process." Such inactivity grated on them both. Invariably, she
returned to her work, despite Desha's attempts to dissuade her.[1] Madge
sailed to Geneva in May 1920 as a delegate to the International Woman
Suffrage convention. In October she returned and began speaking for the
League of Nations, but on 25 November Madeline McDowell Breckinridge died. Eight years earlier, she had visited Rock Creek Cemetery in
Washington to view Augustus Saint-Gaudens' statue of Grief. Her companion later recalled that visit: "I thought, as I saw her absorbed, quiet
gaze into the mysterious face, that for a large part of life she had thus
looked Death in the face—calm and unafraid."[2]

Desha Breckinridge was now alone in the house they had built on
Linden Walk, near the University of Kentucky. His tribute, "She is Dead,"
remained his most eloquent editorial. Madge, he later wrote, "was the
inspiring and dominant factor in all the Herald did for good." Now that
inspiration was gone. The shock of Madge's death had come only two
years after his sister Curry's death, and in the same year as his stepmother's. These personal losses, when combined with the general decay
of the reform movement, with the lack of a driving national spirit, with the
disillusionment, could have—perhaps should have—caused Desha
Breckinridge to slip quietly into the background and join the retreat from

progressivism. But they did not.[3] His progressive spirit survived, though it would be transformed over the next decade. Desha had never shared with some progressives their complete faith in progress, nor did he think there was nothing left to do. At the state level, Kentucky's earlier hesitancy toward reform actually helped keep Breckinridge in the reform camp. He saw a state that stood like a giant, yet was "hampered and bound by the pride and prejudice and ignorance of the past generation." His counsel was needed still.[4]

Breckinridge did not retain all his earlier stands, however. Prewar reforms designed to bring government closer to the common man no longer appealed to him. By 1923, for example, he favored a return to the convention system of nomination, away from the primary system he had advocated earlier. Like his grandfather he opposed bills for popular election of school superintendents. His demands for corporate regulation dimmed. Along with many southern progressives in the twenties and early thirties he concentrated instead on public service reforms and, unlike most, on social justice reforms also. While his brand could be called a "business progressivism," Breckinridge made it clear that it was not progressivism led by businessmen: "A 'business man' who places 'business' above human rights, who values the dollar more than human happiness," he declared, ". . . is not, as a rule, a particularly desirable public officer."[5]

Like many progressives, Breckinridge saw education as the first demand of the new decade; the second must be a "liberal and scientific" understanding of the problems of the penitentiaries and eleemosynary institutions. "The one-room school in a box house, a starved university, under-equipped normal schools—shall these go longer in hunger and nakedness?" he asked. When politicians advocated taking money from the school fund to reduce Kentucky's debt, Breckinridge criticized their "false economy." Would they pay the money debt while defaulting on the debt owed to the children? If they would, they were blinded by the magnified importance of a dollar over a human being.[6]

Editorials entitled "The Glory of the Past and the Shame of the Present" and "The Glory That Was and the Shame That is Kentucky" stressed the sad condition of state prisons. Noting that John Breckinridge's 1798 code of laws was a model for the nation at that time, he rhetorically asked where the state now stood. Did it lead or trail? Self-interest, niggardly economy, and political cronyism dominated the system. Breckinridge himself had seen the blood-covered bull-whip used on prisoners. He wanted the disgrace of such a "hell-hole" as the Frankfort penitentiary destroyed. Prisons, mental institutions, and institutions for the blind were seriously overcrowded, and Breckinridge advised state leaders to construct new buildings, pay higher salaries to attract better workers, and stop playing politics with the state Board of Charities and

Corrections. The *Herald* continued its advocacy of a child labor amendment, minimum wage legislation, and a strong state-supported effort to eradicate tuberculosis.[7]

Despite his emphasis on "Americanism" during and just after the war, Breckinridge repudiated the Ku Klux Klan of the twenties. Founded on racial and religious hatred, the new Klan threatened liberties Breckinridge held dear. Though not historically accurate, he praised John Breckinridge for drafting the Kentucky Resolutions defending free speech, and he presented John's son and grandson as opponents of the Know-Nothings (ignoring Robert's stance). Like them, he declared, Kentucky should not tolerate bigotry and prejudice. To insure that Klan and other violence would be curbed, Breckinridge again advocated the establishment of a state police force. His earlier call for a concealed weapons bill was repeated, like his demands for restricted gun production. Desha wanted the police to possess a record of every revolver sold, its owner, and its serial number. With these moves, he said, the violence that had long plagued Kentucky could finally end.[8]

Conservation—a particular concern of twenties progressivism—also captured Breckinridge's attention. The chief issue was a proposal to construct a dam and power plant at scenic Cumberland Falls. Though he wanted hydroelectric power, Desha did not desire it if it meant destruction of "those things which can never be replaced." T. Coleman du Pont's offer to purchase the area and then turn it over to Kentucky for a park seemed the logical and wise course, and the Republican governor's opposition to this move angered the Lexington editor. When the chief executive bargained with Samuel Insull to develop the falls as a power plant, Breckinridge called on the Democratic legislature to take a firm hand in the matter. In non-partisan votes the General Assembly backed Breckinridge's position, accepted du Pont's offer, and then overrode the governor's veto. In part because of Desha's efforts the hum of electric generators would not be heard at Cumberland Falls. With good reason Virginius Dabney concluded in his *Liberalism in the South* that the liberal leadership in Kentucky journalism had passed to Breckinridge's *Herald*.[9]

After 1920, Breckinridge allowed himself to enjoy life more fully. A long-time interest blossomed, at first taking him away from the political arena. "Since my youth I have been devoted to racing [and] ever since my young manhood I have owned race horses. I have never owned many at a time. . . . I have always had as many as [my] newspaper would support." The twenties were prosperous years for the *Herald* and Breckinridge's stable grew. As early as 1897 he had bought and sold horses. The will he prepared before he left for the Spanish-American War gave to "Her who would be my wife" interest in two race horses. The provisions of the will made it clear that these were his most valued possessions. It was well that Breckinridge viewed racing as a sport, an enterprise advancing a community's agricultural interest, a means of improving the breed of horses, for, on the business side, racing would seldom prove profitable for Desha.[10]

Only a few of his horses ever exhibited consistently outstanding form. Lady Madcap, a four-year-old brown mare, won Latonia's 1922 Inaugural Handicap. The next year, she finished in the money in some minor races but never regained her previous form. Helping Breckinridge to the best racing year of his career in 1922 was his sprinter Braedalbane. By June of that year, Breckinridge stood as the leading owner at the Latonia meet and among the top twenty horsemen in the country. His most successful thoroughbred was Kentucky Cardinal, a chestnut son of North Star III. Wearing the Braedalbane Stable's blue and gold, Kentucky Cardinal proved frustratingly inconsistent but pleasantly profitable. His overall performance in 1924 made him the sixth leading money-winner among two-year-olds. Breckinridge had his Kentucky Derby candidate at last, but only two days before the race he sold the horse for a reported thirty thousand dollars. Running poorly on a sloppy track at Churchill Downs, Kentucky Cardinal finished ninth in the Derby. On the surface it looked like a good bargain for Breckinridge. But other arrangements had been part of the sale, as Desha reported to his cousin Henry. Had the horse won, he bitterly noted, "it would have made a great deal of difference sentimentally, and a minor difference financially—some fifty thousand dollars for me."[11]

Other horses remaining in the stable continued to be unimpressive. Desha told Henry that he had been to Louisville "racing for several days. At least . . . I had been going to the races, for the horses I ran did not do much racing." To his relative and fellow horseman Breckinridge Long of Missouri Desha sadly wrote that he had won practically nothing in 1925, and the next year he continued the tale of woe. Horses not worth "a tinker's damn" had won only "six or eight" races. And, fittingly, he had had his pocket picked at the Derby so he could not bet there. In 1927 his horses won only $3,625 on Kentucky tracks. He ended a letter to Long saying that there was little news from the Kentucky Breckinridges, for "the annals of the poor and humble are brief and simple."[12]

Breckinridge's chief contribution to racing lay away from the track. In 1906 he and several interested men employed two attorneys to draft a proposal creating a state racing commission. Parimutuel betting would replace the system then used, in which bookmakers set odds. With Governor Beckham's approval the bill became law. Though a director of the Thoroughbred Horse Association, Desha declined appointment to the racing commission. Greatly tempted to accept the post, he refused from "the fear that whatever influence we might have through the written word would be discounted by some because of our acceptance of any appointive position." He continued his close ties with racing interests, however.[13]

Despite Kentucky's rich racing tradition, in the twenties the sport Breckinridge so loved came near extinction in the state. The growing power of the unbridled Kentucky Jockey Club united with a moral repugnance toward pari-mutuel betting to bring increased attacks. Through the efforts of men such as Helm Bruce and J.C.W. Beckham (who had reversed his earlier stand), a bill was introduced that would abolish pari-mutuel betting. Breckinridge reacted quickly. The bill fathered by Bruce and supported by Beckham would, Desha ominously predicted, decrease the value of Bluegrass lands, disrupt bank stability, and adversely affect many businesses. As a man whose forebears slept beneath the Bluegrass soil, he proclaimed, "I would feel ashamed to meet those who will come hereafter, if at this time I failed to raise my voice in defense of those who have gone before." Defeated that session, the proposal rose again in 1924 and passed the House by a 56–38 vote. The next day an editorial headed "A Move to Restore the Rule of the Book-Makers" said that a group of "adroit, ambitious and ruthless politicians" had duped the people into believing that the legislation favored good morals. Desha went to Frankfort to oppose the bill in a public hearing, and his newspaper, alone of the major state dailies, defended racing. In a nonpartisan vote the Senate refused to advance the House-passed bill to its first reading. While the Lexington *Leader* attacked the *Herald*'s "stubborn defense of the race-track gambling trust," the New York *Evening Telegram* reported that Breckinridge had "personally rescued racing in Kentucky." Though the *Telegram* overstated the case, Desha had been one of the keys to the successful defense of racing as it was then constituted.[14]

Emergence of the racing issue signified only one aspect of the change taking place in Kentucky politics in the 1920s. New issues, new coalitions, and new leaders caused Desha Breckinridge to reassess his chiefly independent stands of the previous two decades. The choices, however, did not grow easier. Factionalism among the Democrats continued, for instance. The old Beckham-Stanley antagonism cooled as other issues and other leaders brought about realignment. Beckham continued to be important, as did his cohort Haly, but a newcomer joined them to form a triumvirate. Robert Worth Bingham, a former North Carolina attorney who had been appointed acting mayor of Louisville by Beckham in 1907, had married into the wealthy Flagler family and later purchased the *Courier-Journal*. Bingham, Haly, Beckham—the publicist, the boss, the politician—viewed themselves as the reform element and made moral issues their chief target. In opposition stood a nebulous, headless group united chiefly by their opposition to the triumvirate. In addition to Stanley supporters, the alliance included those who supported racing as it existed in the commonwealth. Partially funded by the wealthy Jockey

Club, the "bipartisan combine" would play a major role in many elections.[15]

Throughout the decade the *Herald*'s owner made a perceptible shift away from Beckham and toward the horse-racing interests, but that meant distasteful alliance with some of the political bosses who were increasingly powerful in Kentucky. For a reformer, that move did not sit well, so at the same time Desha truculently attacked many of the "bosses" who furnished the combine its votes. Once again, he could not support either group with total devotion. Ally of the combine, yet often an opponent of its leaders, he suffered the indecision independence gave. Joy came more often from defeating opponents than from winning victories. The first test of his independence came in the Democratic gubernatorial primary of 1923, when a veteran member of the House, J. Campbell Cantrill, was challenged by a young upstart congressman named Alben W. Barkley, making his first statewide race.

Tall, raw-boned, his red hair and mustache emphasizing a thin, stern face, Cantrill for years had been a political enemy of the Breckinridges, although efforts by Desha and his old foe to bring about the creation and successful operation of the Burley Tobacco Growers Co-operative Association in 1921 helped heal the split. Now, Cantrill's chief support came from the Stanley Democratic wing.[16] Young, energetic, and already an iron man in political campaigning, Congressman Barkley represented the Beckham-Haly-Bingham faction in the 1923 contest. Though Desha had reluctantly supported Beckham in his unsuccessful Senate reelection bid in 1920, the editor still disliked the former senator for his strong opposition to women suffrage and for his association with political boss Haly. As party chieftain, the short, stoop-shouldered, sleepy-eyed Haly remained off public stage but was ever-present in Democratic decisions. To Breckinridge, he stood for all that was repugnant in "bossism." If all that were not enough, Barkley in his opening campaign speech called for a tax on coal deposits and for the ending of parimutuel betting. As Breckinridge had business interests in both coal and racing, that stand— together with Haly's backing of Barkley—persuaded Desha to support Cantrill. A parody sung by a young A. B. (Happy) Chandler was given full coverage in the *Herald*:

> Mr. Barkley says that betting is a crime
> He fights the races so
> I think he must have lost some dough
> That he bet upon a losing horse one time.[17]

Breckinridge had advised both Cantrill and Barkley not to run. His choice had originally been Bingham, whom he had praised in 1920 as a man of ability, political courage, and tact. Bingham, as one of the original members of the Jockey Club, had, with Breckinridge, spoken before a legislative committee in 1922 opposing a bill outlawing parimutuels. But in 1923 Bingham came out for Barkley—a stand that seemed treasonous to Breckinridge. The Louisville papers linked the *Herald* to "corrupt" coal and racing interests, and in response Breckinridge replied that they attempted to place on every individual who did not belong to the Beckham-Haly-Bingham clique the unholy brand of corruption. "Assuming to speak with the authority of the delphic oracle," the chameleon papers of Louisville had simply changed their stands at Haly's bidding, in Desha's view.[18]

Breckinridge's feud with Louisville went back many years, before Bingham arrived on the scene. Part of the dispute had even begun long before Desha's birth. For a century the two cities had been jealous rivals. Lexington, "the Athens of the West," was disliked for its claims to intellectual and social dominance; Louisville, "Gateway to the South," was disliked for its commercial prominence. Editors Watterson and W.C.P. Breckinridge, once allies, had parted ways in the 1890s and their successors did little to heal the wounds. Desha, for example, had been a member of the Kentucky State Fair Board of Control in 1905–06, when it selected Louisville over Lexington as the site of the State Fair. Within days, the *Herald* commented on the provincialism and arrogance of the "village" of Louisville (a city some eight times the size of Lexington).[19]

As the 1923 primary began, then, Breckinridge found himself supporting an old enemy and opposing the man he had once wanted to run. The "venomous" Democratic primary resulted in a Cantrill victory that featured a completely sectional vote. As a member of the seven-man campaign committee, Breckinridge began planning for the fall election. Then a ruptured appendix sidelined Cantrill. Despite reports of his expected recovery, he never rallied and died in September. A select group hurriedly chose Congressman William J. Fields, a former traveling salesman and farmer from Olive Hill, as the party nominee for November. Republican candidate Charles I. Dawson called Fields, "Dodging Bill, the Moses from Olive Hill, rescued from the bullrushes by the seven wise men." "Honest Bill" Fields in turn was advised by Breckinridge to refer to his opponent as "Changing Charley" because he had once been a Democrat. The rhetoric seldom rose above those levels. Fields' victory brought to office a man very unlike Breckinridge but the one governor who received his complete support. "I have never met a man who had higher political ideals, a man of more transparent honesty, nor," he added, "one whose highest ambition lay more directly in the path of service to his own state." Many of Breckinridge's contemporaries did not share his charitable view of "Honest Bill," but for the editor the governor's message to the legislature marked the beginning of a new era and was the most important message submitted by any governor of his generation.

The governor's proposed $75 million bond issue, financed by gasoline, automobile license, handgun, and book taxes, would fund new roads, penal and charitable institutions, and schools, and would retire the debt. Breckinridge, delighted with the proposal, spoke in its favor before a joint session of the General Assembly. Roads would unite the state, and "Kentucky would quickly regain the leadership that the Kentucky of old so nobly exercised." He later gave a fuller explanation of his support, concluding: "I want the day to come when the simple statement, 'I am a Kentuckian,' will be as proud an exclamation as in ancient days when 'I am a Roman Citizen' was the proudest boast of that civilization. All this can be done. . . . Kentucky will either march in the very vanguard or lag in the very rear of her sister states." The final decision was to be made by the voters in a referendum.[21]

Speaking before many civic and business groups, Breckinridge gave the bond issue his fullest support. "Far and away the most important question we of my generation in Kentucky have had to decide," it should be answered affirmatively. He told the Lexington Optimist Club: "For me the shadows are lengthening. I leave no children of my own." His purpose was not personal or selfish but for future generations, he declared.[22] Bingham opposed the measure, citing the heavy burden of taxation it would bring, and support for his course of action came from the Efficiency Commission. The governor, in open letters to both, angrily denied their conclusions. Eventually resorting to name-calling, he labeled Bingham "that carpetbagger from North Carolina." Breckinridge responded with his regrets that Governor Fields would even dignify the "nominal" editor of the *Courier-Journal* by addressing a letter to him. Boss Haly, "the Svengali of the Courier," controlled Bingham, "the present Trilby." Once the Louisville paper had been a "real Kentuckian, owned and edited by real men"; now it was the servant of one who was neither. Future generations would lavishly praise Bingham, Breckinridge facetiously predicted:

> We can see them now. Little children kneeling beside their bed at night in an humble home in a rural section, knowing that the next day if it rains they will be mud-bound and can not go to school. . . . The schools that they will go to are ill ventilated, poorly heated, crowded and poorly equipped. . . .
>
> In the prisons of the state hundreds upon hundreds are crowded into cells where no humane man would keep a horse or dog; in the asylums of the state . . . the blind, not only denied the right to see but denied by the miserly greed of their fellow men the right to provide for themselves. . . .
>
> We can hear them all as night is falling, a night symbolic of lack of progress, retrogression and decay. We can hear them in a plaintive murmur, an almost inarticulate cry toward heaven all of them in one broken voice thanking God again and again for Robert W. Bingham.[23]

Much alike in background, and in their papers' independence, Breckinridge and Bingham in reality desired similar ends but differed on the means. Breckinridge agreed that vital state needs overrode the need for financial conservatism. Bingham did not. Defeat of the bond issue in the fall of 1924 indicated that Kentuckians heard the Bingham voice loudest.[24]

In late 1926 Governor Fields and Jockey Club leader James B. Brown tried to persuade Desha Breckinridge to make the race for governor the next year. He seriously considered the idea, acknowledging that he would like to "get my ideas before the people." But the restricted powers of the office, the limits of "this infernal constitution," the costs, and the labor involved made the offer unattractive. Desha, almost sixty years old, wisely declined. He had only a weak political base and little public charisma. His support instead went to Fields' choice, whom Beckham promptly defeated in the Democratic primary. Republican nominee Flem Sampson quickly gained the support of the Jockey Club when Beckham made known his continued opposition to the parimutuel machines. The decision became one of Beckham or betting. While Sampson remained silent on the issue, the horsemen spent a rumored two million dollars to secure his election.[25]

Breckinridge's horse-racing interests vied with his strengthened devotion to the Democratic party and his dislike of Sampson. He announced he would vote the Democratic ticket "because it is the Democratic ticket, not because Mr. Beckham is the head of it." The election results could not have better pleased Breckinridge. Anti-Beckham Democrats had deserted the head of the ticket. Every Democrat save Beckham was elected. Unleashed from his support of Beckham, Breckinridge analyzed the campaign as one "begotten by greed, inspired by malice and waged with venom. It was in no sense a Democratic campaign. It was purely a Haly campaign." Now perhaps the state would be rid of "Halyism" once and for all. While Bingham was shooting on his game preserve or dallying on his yacht, the Louisville publisher had yielded control of his papers to Haly's forces—in Breckinridge's version—and lost all. Beckham had splintered his lance on the parimutuel windmill. The Democratic party would control the state—despite Republican Governor Sampson—and horse racing would not be threatened. It was the best of both worlds.[26]

The end of the 1927 political campaign allowed Desha to devote more time to social events. Increasingly his attention centered on the widowed Mary Frazer LeBus. Her husband, Clarence, had been the largest tobacco grower in Kentucky and at one time the president of the Burley Tobacco Society, before his death on 18 June 1928 after a long illness. Mrs. LeBus and Mrs. Breckinridge, co-workers in various endeavors, had been allies in the reform fight, and had each been injured in a serious car accident in 1919. Partly through the association of the two women, Desha and Mrs. LeBus were long-time, intimate friends. Their families had vacationed together; her interests in the Democratic party, in society, and in racing coincided with his. Very attractive—"the most celebrated of the Kentucky beauties of the day"—charming, likeable, gracious, Mary LeBus was very different from Madge McDowell. At noon on 27 July 1929, at her summer home of "Quanta" on Nantucket Island, the fifty-six-year-old Mary LeBus married Desha Breckinridge. In mid-August the couple returned to Lexington, eventually to live in her country home, "Hinata," on the outskirts of town. Both continued to be social leaders of Lexington.[27]

The year 1929 promised to be a good one in other ways as well. Breckinridge's racing hopes rose. The sixth horse for his stable was purchased at Saratoga (for $4,500) and named Colonel Henry. Another thoroughbred, Lord Braedalbane, turned in some good performances. Encouraged, Desha made what he correctly described as "a foolish bet." Fifty dollars at 200–1 odds and another $350 at 100–1 odds represented his faith in Lord Braedalbane's ability to win the Derby. After the race, he told a kinsman, "my whole damned stable seems to have gone on the blink." The next year he confided that his thoroughbreds had been neither a pleasure nor a profit. By 1931 Breckinridge's luck so disgusted him that he could write— with some truth—that he found the prospect of peace and quiet more attractive than the "hurley-burley" of the Kentucky Derby. His support for racing, however, remained strong.[28]

Thoroughbred breeder, bank director, owner of the *Herald*—in addition to those business interests Breckinridge invested heavily in stocks. In November 1928 he complained that he was "a damn fool" not to have taken advantage of the opportunities in the market, and with typical luck he determined in 1929 to remedy that; he purchased an additional 1,800 shares, chiefly of aircraft motor stock. At first the stock market crash that year did not hit him hard. Acting on "the homeopathic principle" he sold a thousand shares of Standard Brands, "a bunch" of Bethlehem Steel, some Electric Bond & Share, and another thousand shares of Anaconda. At that moment, "I did not think there was any need for me to worry," he told Long. Then Jouett Shouse, former *Herald* business manager turned Kansas congressman, Desha's partner in racing and good friend, talked him into buying some railroad securities expected to rise. Another friend's "authoritative" information led him to purchase Bendix stock as well. "I got in the whirlpool," Breckinridge acknowledged. Though not irreparable, his losses proved "damn disagreeable." Economy dictated selling Lord Braedalbane too cheaply. Once fairly wealthy, he had now lost significantly.[29]

As a result of the setbacks, Breckinridge began to pay more attention to his newspaper than he had for years. Looking at the *Herald*, its editor had much to be proud of. As Henry Breckinridge once told him, "the Herald is yourself." Desha perceived the relationship the same way and took a great personal interest in his paper. When leased in 1897, the

Herald, a four-page paper, had a paid circulation of under six hundred. Helped by being named the official printer for Lexington when Democrats controlled the city, the *Herald* absorbed the rival *Democrat* in December 1904. By 1916, Breckinridge's paper contained an average of twenty pages, went to nearly nine thousand subscribers, and was preparing to move into a new building.[30]

A series of capable business managers had helped strengthen the paper, and Thomas R. Underwood later relieved Desha of some of the editorial work and made a fine managing editor. Many young reporters from the university, such as future governor Keen Johnson, worked for the *Herald*. Such "cubs" stood in awe of their editor. Desha represented many of the stereotypes of the profession. He read "practically every word" of each day's paper, then in his almost unreadable handwriting, penned comments to the managing editor about the stories. As one of those young workers later recalled, "a typographical error was a major calamity" to Breckinridge. He told readers one time (perhaps apocryphally) how his term "Battle-scarred veterans" came out as "Battle-scared," then was corrected, only to appear in print as "Bottle-scarred." Though he could be scathing in criticism, he balanced this with almost fatherly protection of his reporters and workers. When managing editor Underwood married, Breckinridge's gift was generous, and, later, when the young couple wanted a build a house, he promised to see that it would be paid for. While the Depression temporarily slowed fulfillment of that promise, the Underwoods discovered, after Desha's death, that he had willed them enough to pay off the mortgage.[31]

The success of the *Herald* owed much also to those writers who contributed to its columns. Such well-known Kentuckians as Samuel Wilson, Charles Kerr, John Wilson Townsend, and Cora Wilson Stewart joined Madge, Sophonisba, and Henry Breckinridge as *Herald* columnists. No cause was ignored, nor was an unworthy opponent spared. Desha told his secretary, "I think I'm the best-hated man in Lexington." But opinions contrary to those of the editor were often given full prominence as well. Wanting his paper to be the "gentleman" that W.C.P. had sought, Desha tried to be fair to the other viewpoint, in his own way. His frequent vituperation resulted in only one lawsuit for libel in his long career, and that suit failed. Going into the depression, then, the *Herald*, with its circulation increased to nineteen thousand, stood as one of the largest and best Kentucky newspapers, and it had a national audience as well. Breckinridge determined to keep the paper afloat, and despite monthly losses as high as $1,500, the *Herald* survived.[32]

In contrast to his record in state politics, Breckinridge, and the *Herald*, had strongly supported the national Democratic ticket ever since 1920. As a delegate to the San Francisco convention that year he had favored James M. Cox. As a delegate in 1924 Desha voted for John W. Davis—thereafter advocating the Democrat over Calvin Coolidge, who was "as silent as the grave, as dumb as an oyster." Of all the candidates in the twenties, Alfred E. Smith in 1928 received Breckinridge's greatest approval. As one of Kentucky's "big eight" (at-large delegates) to the Houston convention, he gave strong support to Smith. The editor recognized the difficulties involved in trying to elect the New York governor, however. Because of Smith's "wet" stand, Breckinridge believed the Beckham faction would stay away from the polls, and strong "religious fanaticism" in Kentucky would cost the Catholic Smith votes also. Throughout the campaign Breckinridge objected to the use of the religious issue, particularly in Republican Governor "Flim-Flam Flem" Sampson's speeches. The Kentucky editor had accurately gauged the difficulty of the task, however: Hoover carried Kentucky by over 175,000 votes, the largest majority to that time.[33]

In 1932 the election would be vitally important. Breckinridge's own financial difficulties made him acutely aware of the need for someone to lead America to a quick recovery: "The Hoover wave of prosperity . . . is rather hard sledding," he noted. Unemployment, the state of business, and the president's policies all made Desha "gravely apprehensive" that if something was not done quickly "the lid will blow off." The frontrunner for the Democratic bid to forestall that occurrence, Franklin D. Roosevelt, did not attract either Desha or Henry Breckinridge. Instead, they supported Harry F. Byrd, and events at the Chicago convention strengthened Desha's anti-Roosevelt predilections. When F.D.R. supporters installed their man as permanent chairman over Breckinridge's friend Shouse, the Kentuckian grew angry. Roosevelt's nomination increased that anger. Had the delegates been free men, he told Byrd, "instead of such servient serfs of a vicious political oligarchy," they would have chosen the Virginian. But even as *Herald* editorials attacked Hoover rather than supporting the Democratic nominee, Breckinridge's admiration for the New Yorker was slowly growing. To Long (a strong Roosevelt supporter) he acknowledged that if F.D.R. could mold Congress into an effective party, "he will be ranked as one of the very greatest Presidents. . . . I feel that there must quickly come a radical economical reformation or there will come in the not distant future revolution." Roosevelt's victory message of thanks to Breckinridge surprised him, for his support had been tardy and less than strong. Nor was he in favor with the Barkley forces, who managed the Kentucky campaign. Yet Roosevelt's little personal touch pleased and affected the editor, who told Long that the victor "must be a man of real intuition, with a remarkable flair for popular leadership." His admiration increased, and, impressed that Roosevelt was doing something quickly, he highly praised the March inaugural address.[34]

Now determination rather than fear guided the nation. The "national vision" of the president had wrought unbelievable change. Saying "the spirit here really, on the whole, is very much better," Breckinridge defended the vast powers given F.D.R., asking rhetorically: "Is it better to authorize President Roosevelt to try and find the solution . . . or to let things go and risk the consequences?" In May 1933 he admitted that he had been wrong about Roosevelt, who had demonstrated "every quality of leadership." The president's appointment of Long as ambassador to Italy, and Breckinridge acquaintances William E. Dodd to Germany and Claude G. Bowers to Spain, pleased the Kentuckian, although Bingham's appointment to England left different feelings. By early 1934 Desha confessed to Henry Breckinridge, increasingly a bitter critic of the president, that he suppressed in print many of his own thoughts about the White House occupant. The initial glow of praise had dimmed, but the old progressive still remained a New Dealer in 1934.[35]

At the state level in the 1930s Breckinridge fought proposed tax reductions and endorsed the Democratic "ripper bills" opposing Governor Sampson. During "Bloody Harlan's" coal strike of the early 1930s he approved the harassing actions taken against writer Theodore Dreiser, a "mentally corrupt and physically obnoxious" person who had come only as a publicity-seeker. Illness blunted Breckinridge's criticisms, however, and slowed his pace. He had long lived—as a relative told him—as if he were "a spring chicken," though he was now in his mid-sixties. In April 1933 cancer and digestive problems required an operation. His condition had been so serious that his sister expected him to die. For a time afterwards his stomach was pumped daily, and in mid-May, a second operation was required. Though weighing less than 135 pounds now, he slowly recovered at Hinata. By July his wife wrote that she had never seen Desha so happy. He had just returned from speaking at Kentucky's Mountain Laurel Festival and was enjoying his improved health. "If I can stage a financial comeback anything like what I have so far staged in a physical comeback," he wrote, "life will be one grand sweet song."[36]

In early September 1934 Breckinridge picked up "a hell of a bug," and on 22 September he suffered a stroke while in New York. He recovered enough to be brought to Lexington ten days later. Though he could take occasional automobile rides, Desha never fully regained his speech, and poor eyesight bothered him. Friends knew that complete recovery was unlikely. To honor him they arranged for a testimonial dinner. "The Breckinridge Steaks" featured a taped replay of one of his horse's infrequent victories. Amidst his racing colors, and with tables set up to resemble a racetrack, speakers commented on his efforts to preserve racing. Keen Johnson—claiming he knew so little about horses that he would make a good handicapper—spoke for those assembled. Breckinridge had run the race of life, he told the large crowd, "like the thoroughbred he is." Shouse, with tears in his eyes, praised his friend's courage and courtesy. Too ill to attend, unable to see the decorations,

Breckinridge could only listen to the proceedings over his radio. Three months after the dinner, on the morning of 18 February 1935, he died at the age of sixty-seven.[37]

The tribute that best captured his career had been given not at the dinner but a year earlier when Henry Breckinridge told him: "You have championed every worthy cause. You have stood . . . against every corruption and unworthiness. . . . The measure of your work is not alone what the state is but what it might have been had it not been for your career." Desha had summed up his own goals and philosophy in a lengthy letter in 1932 to the editor of the *American Press*. Rather than tell the youth of the nation that all is well, said Desha,

> . . . why not tell our children to scrutinize the temple erected by our fore-bearers; to enter therein and go into the great hall, on the door of which is the word "Justice"; to determine whether justice is impervious to the power of gold. . . .
> Let those children determine for themselves whether our forebearers and we have so constructed the great temple into which their lives and our lives have been welded as to give protection to the weak and lowly and to women and children the fullest mead of the law and the fullest opportunity for development. . . .
> Every drop of blood in our veins comes from those who have been residents of this country for over two hundred years. We claim and shall exercise the right of every American whose people have helped in the building of this nation to criticize the temple that has been erected in the attempt to improve that temple. . . . We think it the duty of every American to endeavor to improve that which has been done for the benefit of those who may come hereafter.[38]

Though he himself had no children, Desha Breckinridge had lived and worked so that Kentuckians of the future would enter an improved temple.

SIX

MARY BRECKINRIDGE

1881-1965

JOHN B. BRECKINRIDGE

1913-1979

I saw a man pursuing the horizon
Round and Round they sped.
I was disturbed at this
I accosted the man.
"It is futile," I said,
"You can never—"
"You lie," he cried,
And ran on.

Stephen Crane

Seventeen

The Last Pioneer

THE YEAR was 1923. It could well have been one hundred thirty years earlier. In 1793 John Breckinridge had brought his family to Kentucky, and what he experienced then was not unlike what this rider through the Appalachian Mountains was now experiencing. John's route had been mostly by water; this lonely figure had fewer navigable streams for use than did he. His roads had been primitive but passable. These roads were little more than paths—frozen and slippery in the cold, muddy and almost impassable when wet. John Breckinridge's 1793 trek had ended in a vibrant, growing town, one soon celebrated for its cultural attainments. This explorer in 1923 encountered few towns that exceeded frontier Lexington in size, none that offered such advantages. At the end of the eighteenth-century trip, the Breckinridge family had found good homes, fine soils, numerous physicians, and contentment. Their twentieth-century counterpart saw mostly small, crude houses, little fertile land, few doctors, and disappointment.[1]

This mountain rider in 1923 knew of John's journey, was aware of the comparisons, and probably enjoyed them. After all, she too belonged to the family whose name he had borne. Mary Carson Breckinridge was searching also, just as earnestly as had her ancestor, but she sought not plenty but poverty, not population but isolation. In the Kentucky mountains she found all this.

Settlements had come later to these Kentucky mountains than to the central part of the state. It was the Bluegrass region that spawned the stories that attracted the frontier settler; the mountains' roughness turned away those first seekers of land. But soon the best Bluegrass land was taken; settlers began to notice that mountain-valley bottomland was attractive as well. For the first half of the nineteenth century, the Appalachian influx continued. In those years the absence of roads meant less than later, for transportation was difficult across all of America. Abundant game furnished necessary food. Life in the mountains, if not easy, did not differ significantly from that elsewhere along the frontier.[2] But conditions changed. As altered transportation systems and routes bypassed the state, they bypassed the Appalachian area even more. New lands and fortunes in the West now called. Immigration decreased while families expanded, and a quality of sameness appeared. Land divisions among patriarchs' offspring reduced moderate holdings to smaller ones. In an era of great technological and material change, little changed in the highlands.

All of this had become reality by about 1870, when accounts began what would become a flood of literature concerning the region. Over the next half-century more major articles would be written about eastern Kentucky than any other area of the state. And the stories usually told a similar tale—one of dingy log cabins, widespread poverty, violent feuds, a world whose people lived in an era long forgotten elsewhere. This extremely rural culture and archaic lifestyle shocked some writers, and they passed this sense of shock on to the city audiences. Only a few of these observers recognized the realities—the existence of various mountain classes, of quiet, peaceful villages, prosperous homes, satisfied citizens. The stereotypes did, however, contain elements of truth: violence existed; high illiteracy rates haunted the region; large, extended families were the norm; and tremendous isolation was prevalent.[3]

This was not a completely unappealing situation. While "barbarians," "aborigines," and "unreclaimed savages" to certain commentators, the mountain people were considered by others to be worthy of the uplifting graces of civilization—as they defined it. To some, these "marooned" highlanders represented not the dregs of society but rather the hope for its future. In a time when vast immigration to America was transforming the nation's visage, here stood the "uncontaminated," "purest" Anglo-Saxons, the people who had populated the United States during its early years of greatness, the kin of George Washington and Daniel Boone. These examples of "sound Americanism and pure Christianity" were simply "our contemporary ancestors." More than that, they had fought on the "right side" in the Civil War. Highlanders' wartime Union sympathies, their relative lack of slaveholding, their nonaristocratic make-up—as pictured in some of the accounts—meant that they resembled the North, in the eyes of the predominantly northern-based writers who described the region. The mountains became "the New England of the South," the beginning point for modernizing the defeated South into the northern model.[4]

Charitable, educational, and religious aid poured into the area. Settlement and mission schools, stimulated by motives similar to those that supported black schools in the Reconstruction Era, now grew up across Appalachia. Colleges, such as Berea and Lincoln Memorial, received large donations. In short, some of what has been called the northern missionary impulse was aimed at the Appalachian region, and great good resulted. But the settlement schools and the missionaries needed philanthropic support to keep their activities alive. To gain that aid meant perpetuating the stereotypes that had attracted attention in the first place. The mountain people became noble but needy, proud but poverty-stricken, hospitable but helpless. Ironically, at the same time that the newcomers' work was attacking each stereotype, at the moment when they were making great educational inroads, these private groups had to balance their achievements with reports of continuing, desperate need. To accomplish their positive goals they had to perpetuate an image that would long haunt the region.[5]

During this time parts of the region were experiencing their greatest change in history. Coal became the new king and, once crowned, would not abdicate. Its effect on the people proved widespread. Collectivism now competed with individualism, and urbanism with agrarianism. Quiet farming valleys almost overnight became great mining complexes. New forces arrived and new questions arose. The "broad-form deed," labor-management conflict, the company store—for some, these became the important matters for discussion. But in other parts of the region, the old ways continued. The society had many parts, following different paths to varied ends.[6]

Interest in the coal boom, coupled with the existing literature on the area, meant that Appalachia had received an enormous amount of attention in the half-century before the 1920s. Only a few writers had adequately portrayed the existing diversity, richness, and strengths. Clearly this was a territory of two worlds—one coal-oriented, the other not. By the 1920s the coal culture idea was gradually supplanting the earlier view, but the idea of a frontier world still predominated. A typical stereotype had people living in log cabins, eating poor food, having large families, doing little work (except moonshining and feuding), and existing as had their ancestors. They might show great hospitality, speak the English of Shakespeare's time, and exhibit other laudable traits, such as weaving and folksinging, but in the main these quaint, isolated people required modernizing. So ran the image.

Mary Breckinridge, a well-read woman, was aware of this image as she rode through the Kentucky mountains that summer of 1923. It had been one reason why she traveled these trails. Mary knew what she wanted to do, and knew that this was where she would attempt it. But the first two decades of Breckinridge's life had offered only a few hints of her future course. She had a fairly typical upper-class childhood, though somewhat more mobile than most. The record in the Carson family Bible revealed the simplicity of an old aristocracy: "Mary Carson Breckinridge born in Memphis Tenn. February 17th 1881." Above that entry was another, telling of her brother's birth four years earlier. But that was all. The Bible did not note that the newcomer was the daughter of twenty-eight-year-old Katherine Carson and thirty-four-year-old Clifton Rodes Breckinridge.[7]

It was because of her father's career that Mary's early life was so transient. Clifton Breckinridge, the son of the charismatic John Cabell Breckinridge, had followed his father's path early.[8] At age fifteen he had joined the Confederate forces, and after the final collapse of that cause his life became one of wandering, just as John's was during his overseas exile. Clifton sold merchandise for a time, went to what became Washington and Lee University, then was a cotton planter and commission merchant in Arkansas. In this latter role, he married kinswoman Katherine Breckinridge Carson on 21 November 1876, one day before his thirtieth birthday. Ten months later, their son James Carson was born in his mother's family home of Memphis. After Mary in 1881 came two more children: Susanna Preston Lees, born two years later, and finally Clifton Rodes, Jr., delivered by a midwife in 1895 while his mother was in Russia.

Like many of his family, planter Breckinridge could not long resist the lure of politics. In 1882 he was elected to represent Arkansas in Congress, and he served for most of the next dozen years, becoming a leading member of the Democratic party's low-tariff wing. The rather small (five feet, five inches tall), fair-skinned, quiet, and controlled Clifton, with his glasses and drooping mustache, looked and spoke more like a professor than a politician. As member of the Ways and Means Committee, as party spokesman, as Cleveland supporter, however, he commanded respect. But lack of attention to his district, identification with an increasingly unpopular president, and party factionalism contributed to his defeat in the 1894 primary. Recognizing his ally's talents, President Cleveland quickly appointed Breckinridge minister to Russia. He left that position in 1897, served on the Dawes Commission to the Indians for a time later, operated several Arkansas businesses, and became a leading figure in his home of Fort Smith. "The Major," as he was known, provided a positive example of service for his family, but his varied career made their life uneven and often uncertain.

As a result Mary seemed to be searching for some kind of stability in her early years. The family had no permanent residence until she was nearly twenty; even then, the house was a summer home more than a year-round one. Her happiest memories centered, instead, on long visits to the New York home of her wealthy great-aunt, Mrs. James Lees, or to Oasis Plantation in the Mississippi Delta, the home of an uncle, Joseph Carson. In the southern locale she encountered an area much like the early frontier. She learned to ride, hunted deer in the dense forests, observed around her other animals, including bears, and watched as man-made fires continued to clear the land. Black servants became an accepted part of her life there; so too did black midwives. In that long, low house amid the oak and pecan trees, she heard her elders talk of the old days with tears in their eyes. There she found freedom and security. She needed both.[9]

When the family moved to Russia in 1894 inward uncertainty continued to gnaw away at Mary. While close to brother Carson and sister Lees, she never felt a oneness with them. (Her mother had told Mary that she resembled her father and was not beautiful like Lees.) At St. Petersburg Mary found few playmates and fewer friends. She—like other children—discovered solace in a dream world. At night the young girl sat alone in her room, expressing her loneliness in a journal and penning poems and other works, including an 1896 manuscript called "A Paper-Doll Book Called Little Mischiefs." An admirer of Scott, Thackeray, Dickens, and Kipling earlier, Breckinridge soon turned to Milton. Later she would eagerly read Russian authors and Schiller. The books not only educated, they offered an escape. Mary recalled later how she invented a Lancelot, a hero "to come and take me away for adventures. . . . The plan seemed to be for us to travel back into the Middle Ages together and to live where nature was wildest. . . ." At another time, the teenager in Russia listed the world's problem areas and cried out, "For the first time in my life I would like to be a boy. Though only sixteen I could fight, and I remain idle here!"[10]

But reality always intruded into the dreams. Imagination could not take Breckinridge away from the "horror and mass suffering" all around her in Russia, and she grew more aware of the desperate needs of others. Nor could Mary's imaginary world substitute for the education, governesses, and boarding schools that made up an often disagreeable part of her life. Tutors in Washington were followed by French, German, and two Russian governesses in Europe. Later her mother placed Mary in a school in Lausanne, Switzerland, where she stayed for most of two years. Breckinridge learned well the French spoken there daily; other languages and other courses proved more difficult. Some friendships overcame the frequent spells of homesickness and doubt, but in January 1898, the family left Europe for America. The almost-seventeen-year-old had experienced and learned much, but Mary Carson Breckinridge remained very much the young southern lady."[11]

For most upper-class southern women of the late nineteenth century, careers outside the home were neither expected nor accepted. Limited education would be followed by a happy marriage, many children, and respected old age. Mary's mother, though a supporter of woman suffrage, still retained these ideals concerning her daughter's future. After a brief time at Miss Low's school in Stamford, Connecticut (where she edited the yearbook), Mary Breckinridge at age eighteen left conventional academic schooling behind. She heard her mother express disapproval over the course of cousin Willie's daughter Sophonisba, who had gone on

Mary Breckinridge. Courtesy Marvin Breckinridge Patterson

to college and a career. College would not be in Mary's future, at least in her parents' version of it.[12]

Marriage was. Mary had beaux for the first time only the year before, when at seventeen she had visited the family of another southern uncle. Of those early courtships Breckinridge recalled that "Southern men made love as easily as they breathed, with the utmost respect and no liberties whatever." The whole process was a carefully defined ritual. Daytime trips alone with a suitor, or to a party with him were permissible; any nighttime rendezvous required a chaperone. Young men usually addressed young women by "Miss" and their last names only and carefully avoided mentioning such subjects as babies or, for that matter, even bulls. Acceptable presents—books, flowers, candy—could be retained; all others had to be returned. Out of numerous friendships, loves developed.[13] In this atmosphere Mary Breckinridge surrendered to the romantic spell surrounding her and put aside other unspoken ambitions. In 1904 she married attorney Henry Ruffner Morrison of Hot Springs, Arkansas. The whole affair remains very much a mystery. In her memoirs Breckinridge does not mention her husband's name, nor does she write of their life together except to say "that it gave me all, and more than all, I had wanted in married friendship." The joys she obviously found in marriage lasted only briefly, for her husband of only two years died in 1906. A widow at age twenty-five, Mary could not turn away the memories that kept recurring. Over the next five years she would write him eight letters in her journal. The last entry told of her hurt and why, almost a half-century later, she could not bring herself to remember that part of her past:

> Across the darkness of my inner soul
> Thy spirit, oh, my darling, yearns to shine,
> Illuming its dull waste, throughout the whole
> Piercing superbly with a love divine,
>   Whisp'ring in trancèd breath
>   Across the night of death.[14]

The searching that Breckinridge had forgone for the stability of marriage she now resumed. Her article on women and literature appeared in the *Westminster Review* in 1907, but writing apparently did not satisfy her. A trip to the North Carolina mountains, where an aunt had supported a school, took some time, but finally, more than a year after her husband's death, the young widow entered a nursing class at St. Luke's Hospital in New York City. For three years she remained, determined to learn something that could be of service to others, but completion of the course of studies there did not solve Mary's conflicts. She yielded to what she called "the pull of my family" and returned to Fort Smith, where her father had finally built a comfortable home. Once again under the spell of the South,

Breckinridge retreated from her determination on a career. She fell into familiar patterns and in 1912 married again.[15]

Second husband and Kentucky native Richard Ryan Thompson gave Mary an outlet for her creative energies. As president of the two-year Crescent College and Conservatory in Eureka Springs, Arkansas, he agreed to let his wife teach French classes—"the most interesting ones in the school," a student remembered—then a new course in child welfare. Mary prepared for the latter offering by writing to noted educators such as John Dewey. She told Dewey of the women students' "ignorance of the fundamental laws of life. . . . They knew next to nothing about themselves." That she sought to change.[16] Teaching provided only one outlet for a suddenly energetic Mrs. Thompson. She served as president of the library association of the town, as secretary of the Eureka Springs Committee for Child Welfare Week, as corresponding secretary of the local Equal Suffrage Committee, as member of the board of directors of the State Public Health Association, and as appointee to a tuberculosis committee of the National Organization for Public Health Nursing. Mary also wrote a series of articles on "Motherhood—A Career," for the *Southern Woman's Magazine*.[17]

But these outside pursuits remained secondary to home life and family. On 12 January 1914 her first child, Clifton Breckinridge Thompson, was born. "Breckie" would become the focus of his mother's whole life. She recorded his progress almost daily and in a journal poured out her hopes for him: "Here is my life, . . . my longed-for baby, my despaired-of baby, my love-life, my great man in embryo, for whom high deeds are now preparing." He was to be the vehicle for realizing her own ambitions. He was to do what she could not. He was to be the next great Breckinridge. In 1915 Mary wrote, "If I am living in a backwater now I am rearing a man child who will emerge someday to lead the crisis of his age." Her "Great-Heart," this child with fair skin, ruddy cheeks, and curly yellow hair, she loved with all the love a mother could gather. With him, she could be happy at last. On 27 June 1916 she concluded in her journal: "I have security."[18]

Eleven days later her safe little Arkansas world began to dissolve. A second child, daughter Mary, was born prematurely and died within hours. The forlorn mother clipped a lock of the dead baby's hair and would keep it with her whenever possible. Mary would never forget "Polly," as she called her child, but at least she had Breckie. She now devoted even more attention to her son. His fourth birthday, on 12 January 1918, was a joyous occasion, but differed only in degree from the daily devotion given Breckie. Then, five days later, he became ill. An operation followed, but the boy's condition grew worse. After praising her "brave soldier," Mary heard her son say, weakly, "I twy to do wight."

As he lapsed into unconsciousness Mary bent over and whispered that she too would try to do right. On 27 January 1918 Breckie died.[19]

That same year, partially to make certain that she would not forget, partially to honor a worthy life, Mary wrote an almost-two-hundred-page memoir of Breckie's four years. A moving work, it told of her memories: "There is not a rod of ground within miles over which I walk where his little feet have not trudged, not a spring at which his sunny face was not turned to drink, not a creeping thing, hardly a stone or bush or tree, or puff of wind which does not recall the gallant-hearted child who fraternized with them. At night on his balcony I look at the moon and stars thinking: 'these perhaps we hold in common even yet.'" Although she symbolically ended a segment of her life when she burned her journals soon afterwards, Mary never tried to forget her Breckie. Even while a part of her worked among the living, another part was elsewhere, "playing with Breckie and his sister on that seashore of endless worlds where the children meet with shouts and songs and dances." For Mary, Breckie still lived, waiting for her.[20]

Mary's life-course was now changed. No more offspring would be born. Her husband's infidelity hastened a difficult decision for one of her class, and in 1920 the marriage which had been held together primarily by the love for children now gone was dissolved. After the divorce Mary reassumed the Breckinridge name. So much did she want to erase that part of her life that she asked friends to destroy any letters that bore her former married name. Large-scale modifications in Breckinridge's career matched those taking place in her private life. In May 1918 Mary told cousin Nisba her plans and motives: "My . . . parents are both willing for me to go to France for the duration of the war. Nurses who speak French are much needed—and of course the absolute difference in work and environment will probably operate to save my sanity. . . . The old life and its associations are unbearable since my baby died." That overseas move, however, would take some time to arrange, and in the interim, in the summer of 1918, Breckinridge spoke across the nation on the child welfare question. For nearly the first time she became aware of her enormously persuasive oratorical powers. The Chicago *Daily Tribune* noted an aspect of her life that she had seldom seen stressed before: "She comes of a family," the paper commented, "—the Breckinridges of Kentucky—noted for their oratory." Her appeals proved so successful that numerous friends and public officials asked her to remain in the United States.[21]

But Breckinridge was determined to help overseas. Work with victims of the 1918 influenza epidemic and an intensive six-week course at Boston's School of Public Health Nursing prepared her further. The war's end did not halt her plans. Through relatives, she met Anne Morgan, the daughter of J. Pierpont Morgan and chairman of the executive committee of the American Committee for Devastated France (or CARD, an acronym from the French name for the group). Soon the thirty-seven-year-old nurse was on her way to Europe. In late February 1919 she arrived in Vic-sur-Aisne, France, to begin working with CARD. Her own quarters were reasonably comfortable: from the windows of the damaged chateau on the banks of a river she could see a beautiful old town, or she could sit in a willow chair before a large wood fire and look at Breckie's picture on her mantle. But another, darker picture kept taking her away. Nearby battlefields told of the horrors left and the work required. As she looked over the jagged earth, furrowed with bomb craters and broken into huge crevices, Mary wrote, "Literally there is nothing, not a bush or a weed, not even ruins for a long distance." Back at Vic-sur-Aisne, she saw the French people slowly, hesitantly, returning to their homes, or what was left of them. And she saw the children.[22]

Breckinridge worked quickly and hard. Given virtually free rein, "Tompy"—as she was called then—began to meet the needs of a region where doctors and druggists lived long distances away. Mary, as director of CARD's Public Health Nursing Service in the region, expanded the area covered from one village to seventy-two, and her staff from one nurse to eleven—all in only a little more than a year. In a six-month period the group set up over 140 clinics and treated some 4,500 patients. Food and milk were distributed; prenatal care was given. French midwives (sages-femmes) continued to supervise the childbirths. From this experience Breckinridge learned a great deal. Much of her later work would come out of the French background. She saw the value of midwives in France but realized that no follow-up care was being done. The director discovered other, smaller lessons. The couriers, the uniforms, the motion picture publicity, the gathering of facts, the discipline, the American fund-raising activities—all this Breckinridge would remember later, as her own work unfolded.[23]

The most important effect of the French experience, however, was the driving will it gave Mary Breckinridge. She knew now that this was the field in which she could do real good. To her mother, Mary explained her motivation: "Always when I lose a baby, always while the fight for it is on, I seem conscious of another child in the room. The pale flicker of the lamp flame the other night seemed to shine like a halo above his yellow hair. When the baby died, I said, 'Here Breckie, take this little child. We have done all we could, now she goes to you.' Nor did I doubt the welcome on the other side for Breckie and I have a sort of partnership about babies." Mary did not know what "special thing" awaited her in America. She only knew that she had to return and fulfill, in some way, a desire to help young children. "I dream dreams . . . ," she told her mother, "and tens of thousands of children . . . are dancing always across the visions and the dreams. . . . I know that the way leads back over the ocean to the country where my own children were born and where they are buried. . . . America is home. Her I love as I love my dead." If Mary could not save her own children, she was determined to save hundreds of others.[24]

In October 1921 Breckinridge returned home from Europe. Within a month her mother died. Already mentally tired after the work in France, still recovering from the tensions of her divorce, Mary now had to face another tragedy. It proved almost too much to bear, and what was referred to as an almost "disastrous breakdown" followed. Recovery and subsequent toil demonstrated once again the strong will of Mary Breckinridge: whatever it was that drove her to achieve was so powerful that it could submerge all else. Rest at "The Brackens," the family's island home on the Muskoka Lakes in Ontario, Canada, helped restore Mary's health. It also brought her back in touch—directly and indirectly—with the brothers and sister she too seldom saw. Carson, the oldest, had served in the Spanish-American War and was assistant naval attache in Russia on the eve of World War I; he would later go to Scandanavia and China, and ultimately become the first lieutenant general of the Marine Corps. His marriage to Dorothy T. Thomson in December 1922 delighted Mary. Lees had served in France with the YMCA and had married George Warren Dunn. The youngest sibling, Cliff, still in his twenties, would eventually become an army colonel and marry Martha Rodes Estill Prewitt. Her family's support was an emotional restorative for Mary.[25]

As had been the case in the past, Breckinridge determined that she needed further training. After her first husband's death, she had gone to New York for schooling; after the loss of Breckie came France; now, after her mother's death, she went first to a course at Teachers College of Columbia University, then to the Kentucky mountains, and finally overseas again, this time to England. In the fall of 1923 Mary began to study midwifery at the British Hospital for Mothers and Babies, in the dockyard section of southern London. The four-month course featured no holidays, hard work, and the dampest place she had encountered "short of a frog pond." But it also trained her, and well. She went to Scotland in August 1924 to study the Highlands and Islands Medical and Nursing Service. There, in the remote highlands and Outer Hebrides islands, nurse-midwives traveled, often on bicycles, to provide medical care for those who could not otherwise receive it. The whole situation—the organization, the idea, the execution—appealed to Mary. After a postgraduate midwifery course back in London, Mary returned to the United States in early 1925 with definite plans on what she—at last—would do. As she wrote later, "It was time to begin."[26]

Eighteen

Midwifery in
the Mountains

BUT *where* to begin? An answer did not prove difficult. Breckinridge wanted to initiate her grand experiment in an almost inaccessible location, not only because success there could be duplicated anywhere, but also because it was simply "more sporting" that way. She also sought a suitable "native" population, one where positive results would translate into greater good. The remote Kentucky mountains with their "old American stock" met her requirements. Moreover, the Appalachian highlands appealed to her for the very reasons they did to others. Mary Breckinridge was a part of her times. Like the missionaries who preceded her, she was motivated by the prevalent images of the region. She sought to bring the twentieth century to what she called a people "left behind in the eighteenth," to a "last stronghold of the American frontiersman," to "the only self-sustaining people in our national life." More than that, as she told *Harper's* readers in 1931, America needed these highlanders' healthy offspring, because Nature "gives physical fertility in inverse ratio to mental and spiritual endowments." If upper-class native American classes produced few children, then the best youth of other "pure" American classes must balance the numerous lower-class immigrant births. The most important point was that Mary simply wanted to help.[1] She chose Kentucky over other areas, such as the Arkansas Ozarks, for several reasons. Despite some initial problems, the state health commissioner supported Breckinridge's concept and would aid in numerous ways. So too would numerous kin and friends. And, of course, in Kentucky, as Mary said, "my family name was known and I would be accepted without explanation, because I belonged."[2]

That was evident on 28 May 1925, when Breckinridge rose to speak in the Capital Hotel in Frankfort, at the initial meeting of her Kentucky Committee for Mothers and Babies. (In three years the name would be changed to the Frontier Nursing Service.) Those in attendance represented a cross-section of high society. Edward C. O'Rear, former Court of

Appeals justice and gubernatorial candidate, chaired the session and called the highlanders "the seed corn of the world." Editor Desha Breckinridge provided—and would continue to provide—extensive publicity. Kinsman Dr. Scott D. Breckinridge of Lexington agreed to serve on an executive committee that included prominent leaders. Several settlement workers joined the presidents of Berea College and the University of Kentucky as original members. Within a month a magazine appeared, and with it a motto taken from Isaiah: "He shall gather the lambs with his arm and carry them in his bosom and shall gently lead those that are with young." A beginning had been made.[3]

Real success would require hard work in the Kentucky mountains. There, in an area covering some seven hundred square miles over parts of several counties, the organization would succeed or fail. Activities centered in Leslie County, chosen, in Mary's words, "because nowhere are conditions more remote or more difficult." Hyden, the county seat for some three hundred people, did little to dispel that assertion. In the last century a minister had admitted his fear of going there, for the "people were so wild." A visitor in 1915 proclaimed that he had never seen "so dismal and desolate a haunt of human life." The very year the FNS began work in Hyden a sheriff was killed, a mob gathered, and troops had to be called in. The town's main street could not even be deemed a thoroughfare. Dirty, unpaved, uneven, full of holes, with pigs and cows roaming freely across it, it proved almost impassible in the rain, almost unbearable in the dry, choking, dust. No paved roads existed in or near the county; virtually everyone rode horses, for the county still had few automobiles. Amid the rocky, rural terrain, where every clearing was farmed, residences contained no electricity (and would have none, for the most part, until 1948). Almost nonexistent plumbing meant that only five bathtubs existed in the county—and the FNS owned two of those. A county sewage system would not be installed until 1969. Leslie had been a county for thirty-six years before a high school was organized in 1914. The city of Hyden had been incorporated for thirty-seven years before a nurse came. She left in 1923, four years later, and there were no doctors or nurses when the FNS organized.

Life in the county changed very slowly. A study conducted in 1950 of two communities revealed that of forty-five fathers, forty-two had been born in the county. Each household averaged 5.8 members, slightly above Leslie County's 5.1 average and far above the nation's 3.4. In that isolated community the fathers had gone to school an average of 7.2 grades, the mothers, 6.5 (compared to a national median of 9.3). Yearly income per family was $1,360, half the United States' median figure. Even by 1950 the people there had no running water or telephones, and fewer than one in two had electricity. Daily routine differed little from that of earlier times: the family arose by five, the mother cooked, the father fed the animals, the children carried in wood and coal. After the usual workday—inter-rupted perhaps by a neighbor's visit—the family would retire early, often by eight o'clock.[4]

Yet this picture of poverty and scarcity obscures many of the intangi-bles the people enjoyed. It was a homogeneous, supportive society, one that aided both neighbors and strangers in need. Divorce was almost nonexistent. Picturesque mountains and vast forests surrounded the homes and their occupants. Pollution, already a concern of the nation's cities by the 1920s, presented few problems here in the mountains. A sense of place was evident. In short, the society and its people gave two contradictory images, both based in fact—one of a secure, self-sufficient independence, the other of a poverty-stricken, unfulfilled existence. To Breckinridge's credit she saw both images, respecting the former, attack-ing the latter.[5]

Health and maternal care in the region was deplorable, and it would be in the area of maternal care that Mary Breckinridge would focus her efforts. Her solution to the existing problems—the use of nurse-mid-wives—would be a daring, innovative, and, as it turned out, farsighted one.[6]

For most of the western world's history midwives provided the only care at parturition. Childbirth remained a totally female rite, and males—whether husbands or physicians—were excluded from it. Only in the seventeenth century did change occur as doctors and surgeons began to break down traditional attitudes. While the Victorian era's increasing concern with modesty and sexual roles slowed the trend, that same age also moved toward a way of thinking that stressed professionalism and science. In this manner midwifery came under attack. Medical thought turned from childbirth as a natural process to a concept in which it was more mechanical. Instruments, treatments, and hospitals replaced home births. Technology would triumph over nature. Increasingly, Victorian middle- and upper-class women, despite the affront to "delicacy," chose doctors over "untrained" midwives. As late as 1910, however, midwives attended about one-half of all American births.[7]

Yet midwifery was under tremendous pressure. Unorganized, gener-ally uneducated, centered in lower-class families, midwives proved an easy target for highly organized physicians and other Progressive Era professionals. "Inveterate quacks," *Medical News* termed midwives in 1898. Writing in the *American Journal of Obstetrics* in 1912, two doctors proclaimed that "the field of the physician has been invaded": these often-alien midwives should be eliminated. Seven years later a similar attack called midwifery "unnecessary." Some defenders of the practice spoke up. They pointed to a 1912 survey indicating that the average medical student in obstetrics witnessed only one delivery before entering practice—a far cry from experienced midwives. Nor did general practitioners' success rate surpass the midwifery record. In 1917, for example, a Rhode Island study revealed infant mortality rates for midwives' deliveries far lower than for other deliveries.[8]

But the battle went to the obstetricians. In 1900 fewer than 5 percent of American women had delivered in a hospital; in 1929, 50 percent had. In New York City midwives attended 30 percent of live births in 1919; twenty years later the figure had shrunk to 2 percent. Only among the urban ethnic population and the rural poor did midwifery continue as an acceptable practice. When Mary Breckinridge proposed, then, to use nursemidwives in the Kentucky mountains, the very words raised red flags to many physicians and friends.[9]

Breckinridge had traveled some 650 miles that summer of 1923, all of it on horseback, most of it alone. She had located fifty-three midwives in the three counties visited and from interviews with them compiled a composite picture. All had been married at one time or another, and virtually all had had children—an average of 8.5 each. Fewer than a fourth of the midwives could read or write; about one fifth lived in "filthy" homes. Befitting their "granny" name, they had a median age of fifty-seven, but ranged from thirty to ninety. Not a single one had had any formal training, although some had attended conferences conducted by physicians and county health officers. Their real teacher was experience, and Breckinridge found that their methods varied from the unsafe to the unusual. All, for example, made pelvic examinations with greased (but unwashed) hands. It was an "almost universal" custom, Mary noted, that the patients delivered sitting on someone's knee or in a chair. The babies were literally caught, or "ketched," in such cases. The umbilical cord would be cut with unsterilized scissors and the navel covered with a "scorched rag." Normal births presented few problems, even under these conditions. But when hemorrhaging or other difficulties arose, the weakness of such midwives became evident. Methods for stopping severe bleeding, for instance, included putting an ax under the bed, or placing the patient on someone's dirty clothes, or simply giving the woman tea or some other concoction. Breckinridge planned to change all that by combining midwifery with professional nursing to provide pregnant women with a skilled and trained deliverer, the nurse-midwife. That crucial difference signaled success for the venture.[10]

Like the mountain babies they sought to save, the Frontier Nursing Service was born mostly with hope and nurtured chiefly with hard work. Yet it survived the rough beginnings and, in time, grew to become a nationally known concern. It never was easy. An organization based on the idea of nurse-midwives needed nurses trained in midwifery, and Breckinridge had to turn to her beloved England and Scotland, for few in the States had such combined training. Over time many Americans joined them to form an interesting mixture of tongues, ranging from high English to the Scottish brogue to the New England accent to the western drawl. But few of these nurses, even those who had overseas experience, were prepared for what they experienced in the Kentucky mountains. Merely to reach the offices of the Frontier Nursing Service in those early days meant a train trip from Lexington to an obscure station, then a horseback ride (by many who had never ridden) across seemingly endless creeks and rivers or, if the water was too high, over hills and mountains. As one nurse remembered, the roads "ran in the river bottom half the time, and the other half the time the river ran in the road." Another FNS worker firmly asserted, "I went across country that I know the last person there was Daniel Boone."[11]

Betty Lester, later assistant director, had an all-too-common introduction to the service. While training in England, Lester heard of the FNS and decided to join it. After an eight-day voyage to New York City, she took an all-night train to Lexington, boarded another train, and at six in the morning arrived in Krypton, at that time the nearest station to the FNS. "I was the only one getting off the train. . . . The train went off around the bend, and there I was, standing there, mountain on one side and a mountain on the other, and the river, and the railroad track going along. Not a soul in sight. . . . It was the most lonesome feeling to just be standing there in this strange land not knowing what was going to happen next." Shortly a nurse arrived, with an extra horse. Lester rode over steep, sometimes treacherous, mountains to an outpost nursing center, then, the following morning, went on to Hyden—crossing the river four times on the way. The next day she went to work.[12]

Nurse after nurse duplicated those experiences, with some variation. Coming to the FNS meant breaking away completely from old ties; it meant beginning anew in an unfamiliar environment. In some ways it resembled entering the army, and the difficult trip there provided basic training. Uniforms reinforced this feeling, for the nurse-midwives dressed in white shirts, black ties, sky-blue uniforms, and high boots, with capes and hoods patterned after those used by the Royal Canadian Mounted Police. Yet the FNS was more than just a regimented way of life. Unusual for the time, it was a world of women. Aside from a few male workers or visitors, women did everything. In such an atmosphere a special camaraderie existed. And nowhere was this more evident than in the "Big House."[13]

Mary Breckinridge's "Wendover" aroused a feeling of awe in those who first viewed it. Situated high on a mountain that overlooked the quiet Middle Fork of the Kentucky River, the massive, two-story log house, though partly hidden in trees, dominated the countryside like a medieval castle. Carefully constructed paths, a landscaped yard, an elaborate water system running here and there, together with barns for the animals and several smaller dwellings built over the years, all combined to form an impressive complex. It was also a strange little world unto itself. On the one hand, its log buildings amid the beech, sycamore, and mountain laurel trees attested to the remoteness; on the other, the interior provided respite, relaxation, and even a sense of urbanity. Every afternoon at four, "come hell or high water," all stopped working and tea was served. Then, with a huge fire warming them in winter and the shade and breezes from the mountains cooling in the summer, the nurses ceased talking "shop" and concentrated on other stories. The foreign-born might tell of their varied experiences in other parts of the world, or the Americans might discuss current events, or all might simply recite the trivial as a way to relax over a glass of sherry. Formal meals in the long dining room contributed to this special feeling. One visitor recalled that she "felt as if I was entering a king's palace: tables set with flawless linens, glistening glassware, and sparkling dishes." Another traveler there, in 1947, noted the Old World atmosphere in the New World frontier setting: "I could not help but think that this was the most beautiful and awe inspiring spectacle that I had ever seen."[14]

Reigning over this world was Mary Breckinridge. A journalist commented that she ran the FNS "as a colonel runs his regiment. She asks nothing that she herself cannot and will not do, but she is the commander, and duty is duty." A nurse who worked with Breckinridge for years noted this same quality: when Mary came into the room, her very presence made nurses feel as if they should salute. They had to obey. But they knew that a driving will, which expected the best from everyone at all times, made Mary the way she was. That realization did not make working for her any easier, however. "Autocratic," "very demanding," a "mania for perfection"—these and similar words were applied to Breckinridge. One secretary remembered, "I was scared to death of her really; the first year I was terrified. I would go back to my room and scream. I was so scared." Those in disagreement with Mary, whether on matters of nursing, history, or current events, received little understanding. A mountaineer, at his first meeting with her, found himself being "bawled out" for his ideas; nurses seldom won an argument; young couriers, lowest in the "pecking order," were often intimidated by her.[15]

Breckinridge displayed a second side, though. The same woman who called Mary "autocratic" and "biting" also pointed out that she could be "truly loving," deeply caring, and openly maternal. A worker of the late 1930s discovered in the FNS director a "warmth of spirit which I have never met in another woman in my entire life." Mary was determined to succeed at what she was doing, not only for herself but for the sake of the mountain children she was helping—and for Breckie. A will that could not be submerged created problems, but more often it held the organization together. Around her, nurses and other workers could not be afraid of outside forces. Described accurately as "a softly powerful person," Breckinridge inspired both confidence and respect.[16]

Mary Breckinridge's personality bore most heavily on the couriers. Generally young students from well-to-do homes, these girls served for periods of time that ranged from weeks to months. Their jobs required little skill but much work. One of them succinctly described her chores: "The humble courier cleans horses and exercises and massages and anoints and loses 'em and waits on 'em hand and foot, cleans tack, stokes fires, gets tea, hunts eggs, bathes dogs, plays postmistress [Wendover had its own post-office], does filing, . . . brings people in and out, . . . goes with nurses on deliveries, runs errands, and does any other little odd job." An inglorious position on the surface, the courier's job proved to be an important part of FNS success.[17]

The courier system not only provided needed free labor but, even more important, it gave Breckinridge a continuing supply of friends. The parents of couriers became FNS supporters; couriers in adult life became organizers themselves; in time the children of couriers came to the mountains and the circle continued. But why? What was so appealing about the seemingly thankless job? Part of the answer lies in the image developed around the FNS itself. A cult, an almost romantic mystique, grew up around the idea of "angels on horseback" helping others and saving lives in a dangerous, remote frontier. Mary Breckinridge said as much in a poem:

> At last you come to what's the pith
> A story to unfold
> Of gallant girls astride the horse
> Quite like the knights of old.[18]

Breckinridge was developing the image that she herself had dreamed when young. No outlet had then existed for her to fulfill such dreams. Now one did.

The couriers' own reasons for coming varied, but they always seem to hark back to the fact that the FNS appealed to their senses of adventure. "I was burning with desire to do something different and get out and work with people," a courier explained. One recruit had heard of the FNS in college, where a girl told her about the horses and forests "and primitive kind of ex-American experience similar to the Frontier days." Others sought to get away from home. By the early 1930s girls from Chicago's "Gold Coast" and elsewhere were flocking as couriers to the Appalachians, paying for the privilege to serve. To the lengthening waiting list upper-class newborns were added by their mothers. The FNS had become "the debutante's Foreign Legion." With the English nurses and tea, with the beautiful Big House, with the couriers and their image—was the Frontier Nursing Service really succeeding in the health care field?

The first difficulty Breckinridge had to overcome was with the mountain people themselves. Often unfairly portrayed, they had grown skeptical and suspicious of "outsiders" like Mary. Actually, Breckinridge never sought to become socially involved in the lives of those she served. A few square dances took place at Wendover, and the FNS distributed clothes and food at Christmas, but contact between the nurses and the people of the region was restricted. But the social distance did not extend to medical care, and quickly the people saw the benefits to be gained through association with FNS nurses. Although a few remained cautious, the vast majority in the area came to view Mary and her nurses almost as saints. Working long hours at a low salary, the nurse-midwife gained a heroic image, as a 1931 *New York Times* story attests: "Her uniform . . . is as dashing as the scarlet coat of the royal mounted policeman. . . . And with as little concern for her own safety as that gallant fellow would show, she leaps into her saddle at a moment's notice and rides wherever duty calls." Actually, if the overexuberance of the writer is discounted, the story portrayed rather accurately the commitment of the FNS nurse.[19]

The nurses, as part of a preventive health program, went into an area wracked by epidemics of typhoid, diphtheria, and smallpox, a region whose people were riddled with hookworm. Inoculations and careful attention to the details of prevention reduced those hazards considerably, but the primary focus remained on childbirth and postnatal care. The nurse-midwives, operating out of Wendover or the remote outpost nursing centers, made regular visits to give prenatal care in the homes to pregnant women. Yet when time came for delivery, dangers could arise. The husband might ride up to a center or to Wendover in the middle of the night with word that "it's time." On horseback, the nurse-midwife would leave quickly, even in inclement weather. Darkness compounded the winter's discomfort and could conceal dangers, as one nurse found out when her horse went into quicksand up to its shoulders. The interiors of the houses varied considerably, but all too often they resembled one described in 1944, a single room surrounded by log walls chinked with clay. A simple door provided the only light in daytime; there was none at night. Smoke from a cookstove with no pipe either hung in the room or, if the wind was right, went out a chimney. Into such places the nurse-midwife brought her forty-pound saddle-bags of equipment, a lantern or flashlight, and much patience. Eventually, after a successful birth, the nurse-midwife gave instructions for immediate care (including the breastfeeding the FNS advocated), and—finally—headed home. She would return periodically for examinations and care. In such ways a few dedicated professionals made a tremendous difference for large numbers of people.[20]

Thus, despite disagreements with Mary Breckinridge, despite the isolation, despite the rigorous routine, life in the mountains and at the FNS could be very satisfying for the couriers and nurses. They had survived a tough and demanding regimen and took pride in their accomplishment. Not only could they contribute in easily discernible medical ways, they could also find intangibles at Wendover. One, in 1933, told of quiet evenings reading, of simple and healthy work, of the absence of distractions and annoyances. Seven years later, a courier recorded in her diary how she could be alone—very alone—or with company, whichever she wanted: "It is a closely-knit community—yet made up of separate individuals and entities." The most dominant of those individuals, Mary Breckinridge, summed it up simply: "After all," she declared, "there is not much more in this life than something to eat, a roof to shelter you, and a friend to share it with." The FNS provided all three, but emphasized the last.[21]

The Frontier Nursing Service could not survive on achievement alone. Funding was vital, and almost every year Breckinridge ventured forth from the mountains to raise money. A 1936 foray, for example, lasted two months and included fifty major addresses, plus many more informal ones; on a similar four-week trip in 1944, Breckinridge ranged from Minneapolis to Cleveland. She did not dislike the travel, even though it took her from the security of Wendover. Mary was comfortable in both urban and rural worlds and, in fact, needed both to be happy. A member of New York's Cosmopolitan Club, she stayed there on visits, enjoyed the city's theater, and played contract bridge with friends. When the FNS director traveled, everything was meticulously planned—the schedule, the lodging, the people to be met. Breckinridge would sweep into her room, open her suitcase, from which she took pictures of Breckie and Polly, place them on a desk, and then prepare her talk for the evening. Local committees, frequently consisting of the "best" people, would have organized a suitable audience.[22]

This somewhat stooped figure, this small, plump woman with a roundish face, this undistinguished-looking person, presented a deceptive first appearance. But on the platform Mary Breckinridge became irresistible. Running her fingers through her greying, boyishly cut hair, she looked over an audience and her intense grey-blue eyes galvanized them. When she began to speak the total effect proved unforgettable. Her voice emitted qualities of leadership and certainty; it "enchanted . . . hypnotized"; it projected a "rare imagery"; it ranged from warm humor to high drama. In an accent alternately described as southern, English, or simply cultured, Mary's words were both soft and vibrant, forceful and sympathetic. As a great-niece recalled, "It's something if you've heard it once, it'll always come back to you."[23]

Breckinridge liked to shock audiences, and would on occasion show pictures of hookworms found in diseased children. At other times she would charm her eastern ladies by using mountain dialect to make a point. When emotional appeals were failing, she would turn to statistics and almost overwhelm with numbers. Sharp-witted and intelligent, Mary provided an answer—some answer—to questions. And she complemented her own oratory by presenting films. The first to go on the circuit, a silent movie entitled "The Trail of the Pioneer," stressed the frontier aspects of the region, showed Hyden almost as a western town, and included subtitles with words spelled in English fashion—"centre," "colour," and so on. Much more professional was "The Forgotten Frontier," made in 1928. With less melodrama, fewer frontier themes, and more of a story line, this motion picture made similar points. After the talk, film, and questions, meetings would end—but not with an appeal for funds. Though Mary did not ask for money directly, she seemed always to get the contributions she sought.[24]

There were other sources as well. Foundations funded such diverse items as record-keeping and laboratory work. The Ford Motor Company turned over its mineral rights to the land held by FNS; a wood-product company donated nearly one hundred acres of timber rights. Almost from the beginning, the Louisville and Nashville Railroad provided either free transportation or large rebates to the FNS as it took seriously ill children to better-equipped city hospitals. Charity benefits, cruises, contributions from organizations and individuals—in this way the FNS grew.[25]

Less than five years after its founding the FNS faced the beginnings of the Depression. At the same time, Kentucky experienced a severe drought. Mary fought for support for the mountain population she saw suffering all around her. She wrote articles, sent letters to politicians, and gave speeches, all stressing the need for relief. But more and more she simply had to fight to keep her own organization alive. In 1932 her $145,000 budget represented a decline of $10,000 from the previous year. In 1933, things were worse. Only twenty-two nurses—a loss of nine—remained at the FNS; salaries were reduced by one-third. Conditions improved only slowly; not until 1944 would receipts rise to the 1932 level. But the FNS had survived.[26]

The 1930s were difficult years for Breckinridge physically as well. In late 1931 her new horse, Traveller, threw Mary on some rocks, breaking her back. Bedridden at first, then restricted in movement, she could not visit the outpost nursing centers or ride on horseback for some seventeen months. During that period, on 3 December 1932, her father died. The Major had lived at Wendover for years, had helped plan its water system, had grown to know his "girls" there. Now Wendover would be lonelier for the woman who guided it.[27]

In 1939, when war broke out in Europe, the British nurse-midwives requested a release to return home. Trained nurse-midwives had to be found to replace them. Breckinridge's solution was the Frontier Graduate School of Midwifery located at the Hyden Hospital she had founded some eleven months earlier. The FNS would educate its own staff now, and in a school that provided almost unique training for the time. The few earlier midwifery schools in the nation typically had given little training or had survived only briefly. The best known of them, the Bellevue School for Midwives in New York, had closed its doors in 1935. Breckinridge thus not only filled an immediate void—the lack of trained nurse-midwives for the FNS—but she provided the needed facility to keep alive the idea of nurse-midwifery.[28]

With the war's end in Europe several overseas nurses returned to Wendover, and the rest of the decade would be a rebuilding one for the FNS. For Mary Breckinridge this security allowed her to reflect more on her past. She began writing, first a novel that appeared in 1948 and then her memoirs. Both revealed more than she intended; both concealed much. In her short novel, *Organdie and Mull*, Breckinridge in essence told of herself. The central figure, Cynthia (who had "no roots in her roving childhood"), has two suitors—Ronald Dark and Leigh Murchison. Dark is an older, quiet, courtly man, whose mountain-climbing adventures in far-off places gives him a special appeal. He represents, Mary wrote, "the longing to escape the claims of tradition and find risk and danger in remote and high places." The second man, Murchison, personifies the southern youth of Breckinridge's childhood. He is antebellum in outlook, persistent, bold, even reckless. The book has two endings; in one, Cynthia chooses Dark, in the other Murchison. But the writer's own sympathies are clear. Dark is more appealing, and even when Cynthia chooses the traditional southern beau, Mary has her think, "If I have a girl child . . . and she wants to break loose when she grows up, she shall."[29]

Completion of this novel apparently stimulated Breckinridge to further writing. By 1950 the director was sixty-nine years old and ready to write her memoirs. With typical energy and efficiency, she would rise at 4:30 in the morning, drink a cup of coffee, meditate for a time, then read her previous day's dictation until seven. After an hour's break, she would call her secretary up to the second-floor room and dictate the manuscript. At noon, the morning mail was read, and after lunch and one of her many cigarettes, Breckinridge would go out to enjoy her hobbies—caring for her favorite pets, especially dogs and geese, feeding the chickens, working in the garden. From about two to four every afternoon she went over earlier typescripts of the book and did research for the next section. Tea came at four o'clock, then supper, then sleep at eight. Still wearing a back brace, Breckinridge increasingly remained in a small room where, on occasion, she would gather friends or even young couriers around her.

Yet, though surrounded by people, she was lonely. A close associate remembers Breckinridge in those days as being "desperate" to have friends. "She used to say to me, 'You do love me, don't you'?"[30]

Publication in 1952 of her autobiography, *Wide Neighborhoods*, symbolically marked the end of another era in Breckinridge's life and that of the Frontier Nursing Service. Mary told a supporter that it was up to another generation to carry on now: "We who are older have tried to right the wrongs of the world. We did the best we could—some of us." The FNS's first era had closed in 1931, when Breckinridge's back injury slowed her mountain activities. Now, some two decades later, it was clear that the FNS and its people were changing. Some of the key early leaders had gone. Efficiency was replacing romanticism, as nurses began to make their rounds in jeeps rather than on horseback. While more effective (but more dangerous), this move had serious overtones that few recognized at the time. For as the horses left, so too did some of the romance, the spirit that had attracted so many to the FNS in the first place. Cavaliers did not ride in jeeps.[31]

Changes occurred in the entire region as well. A flood-control dam necessitated closing two of the outpost nursing centers. Better roads allowed more people to go to clinics or hospitals if sick or pregnant. In many areas a rural economy had been gradually superseded, in part at least, by a coal-based one. By 1960 nearly 50 percent of Leslie County workers toiled in the mines. Per capita income had risen 193 percent in the previous decade. Iroically, then, just at the time when the national mood was becoming more favorable to the idea of nurse-midwives, changing mountain conditions made survival more difficult for the pathbreaking midwifery organization in that area.[32]

By the 1960s Mary Breckinridge was growing old, and her Frontier Nursing Service was entering a fifth decade in which it had served eastern Kentucky. The FNS had been a great experiment, one which was supposed to be a model for similar undertakings in other areas of America and the world. The Kentucky experiment had succeeded, but few duplicated it. Overseas visitors—in one year from Bolivia, Canada, Finland, England, South Africa, the Philippines, China, and India—saw the achievement, and many of them did use the FNS model in their countries. But it was not so in America. A 1930 report noted that the Ozark Mountains were being studied as a possible site for a branch organization, but that move never materialized. The next year a *New York Times* story predicted that all in the mountains would soon be served. They never were. Nor had large numbers of American nurse-midwives been trained by the 1960s—only some eight hundred over three decades.[33]

Some critics pointed to what they saw as a second failure of Breckinridge's—that she did not involve herself sufficiently in other community needs and such questions as land-use, outside control of wealth, education, social well-being. But this criticism can be challenged. Breckinridge came to a traditional society, and, to her credit, she did not try to destroy an entire tradition in an effort to achieve her aims. Her concept of what community change was needed might have clashed so strongly with the realities that the region would not have been well served by broader activity. Other missionary and educational groups, for example, tried to mold the highlanders to their own image and in the process destroyed vital traditions.[34] Breckinridge focused instead on one area of need and worked within a traditional pattern. The statistics are telling in their testimony: after forty years, by 1965, the FNS nurse-midwives had delivered almost fifteen thousand babies—over eight thousand of them in homes—with only nine obstetrical-related deaths, none since 1954. The infant death rate of 11.0 for the first 10,000 deliveries was far better than the national rate of 36.3. Of the FNS's first one thousand births, doctors had been present in only fifty-two cases; forceps had been used but nine times. In the preventive health care area the FNS achieved similar results: in that same period some 57,000 patients had been treated, a quarter of a million inoculations given. The wartime year of 1943, for example, saw a small staff of nurses treat over eight thousand people, make over eighteen thousand home visits, and distribute Christmas candy and toys to more than five thousand children. Each life saved bore eloquent witness to the success of Mary Breckinridge's dream. A man from the area said it simply and well: "I think they was a awful lot of children that's growed up healthy that wouldn't have been done if they [the nurses] hadn't been here."[35]

Those children had been Mary Breckinridge's motivation—those and her own. She was eighty-four in 1965, needed a cane to walk, and had failing vision. Doctors had already removed malignant bladder tumors and were treating her for leukemia. But a sustaining faith kept her going. Early in life she had talked of "that love for Jesus Christ that has come to be a mainspring of my life." Always religious, Mary personally conducted Sunday afternoon chapel services and read from her Episcopal prayer book at Wendover. Yet her spiritual feelings went beyond that. Breckie and Polly were always a part of her makeup. Mary talked of them to friends, mentioned them prominently in her writings, kept items that had been theirs. More than that, she felt "a sense of communion with them that is almost continuous." "The next world," she wrote a relative, "is so much more real to me than this one." From her children, she said, she drew spiritual strength, and she firmly believed that she communicated directly with her Breckie. A member for a time of the London Spiritualist Alliance, she attended seances in that city and others. Her morning meditations at Wendover included her "Great Heart." She spoke to him and believed he answered. She heard his voice, she wrote, "in the lapping of the lake upon the shore, in the wind sighing softly in the cedar and hemlock trees; I feel it in the brave sunlight and the wide stretches of water and sky. . . . Perhaps they are the voices of our dead, the voices of little children and babies who cannot reach us through any other language until we too are free." On Sunday, 16 May 1965, Mary Breckinridge died, quietly, bravely, like her "little soldier," the one child she loved above all others, the one she believed would greet her, the one "Breckie." Now he could reach her, for she too was free at last.[36]

Nineteen

A White Knight Riding Alone

JOHN BAYNE BRECKINRIDGE was one of the few twentieth-century members of his family who pursued a political career. Nisba, Desha, Mary, the others—most had at times influenced the political sphere but few had placed themselves before the voters' critical gaze. In this, they were not unlike other patricians who found new and varied careers more appealing than some more traditional family ones. As befits a prolific clan, numerous Breckinridges performed their duties in the world and contributed in important ways to the civilization around them. But their influence in Kentucky lessened as mobility led more and more of them outside the state to seek their livelihood. In this sense John B. Breckinridge stood forth as an exception. He walked the political field, loved its aroma, and sought its rewards, understanding fully the implications and dangers such a course held in a rapidly changing world. But if the exception in his times, he was only carrying what had been the standard of his forebears. Breckinridge represented the lingering past as well as the appealing model for an unforeseen future.

On 29 November 1913 a future politician was born into the household of a nonpolitical family.[1] The father, thirty-one-year-old Scott Dudley Breckinridge, had only recently completed his medical internship in Washington, D.C., after earlier schooling at Lafayette College, the U.S. Military Academy, and Georgetown University. An expert collegiate fencer, Dr. Breckinridge continued that pursuit, becoming national foil champion twice and a member of the 1912 Olympic team. He was the head of an active household. His wife, Gertrude Ashby Bayne, was the daughter of a Washington surgeon; she bore three children—John Bayne, then Scott Dudley, Jr. (born 17 April 1917), and Gertrude Bayne (born 20 January 1922). The last child was born in Kentucky, unlike her parents and two brothers, for in September 1919 Dr. Breckinridge, five-year-old Johnny, and the rest of the family moved to the old ancestral haunts of Lexington. Over the next two decades the father would earn a reputation as a fine physician, one who was, in his son's words, "a good doctor in a small town and that is all he wanted to be."[2]

In this familiar Breckinridge atmosphere the young John B. Breckinridge grew to maturity. Like others before him he heard conversations that abounded with references to certain cousins or uncles—many of them famous—and learned in general ways about past family achievements. John's brother recalled that their father "knew that there were people in the family who had been prominent. I think he saw that as setting standards he should maintain." John's awareness of that past would grow over time. In fact, as an adult, he rather liked to downplay his knowledge of family history, though in truth his awareness transcended the surface comments, becoming almost something *felt* more than something *known*. John knew he was a Breckinridge; that meant something, but for a long time he did not know exactly what.[3]

From his father and mother John also learned certain attitudes toward life and society. The strong-willed but quiet Dr. Breckinridge would tell the family, for example, "This is a middle class society. . . . If you can abide by the standard of that society then that's really all you have to do." Believing in the stability, vitality, and high quality of that society, he offered advice not as a designing patriarch telling his children to lower themselves to gain the majority's support and votes, but rather as a man— almost a Jacksonian in spirit, though not in party—who believed in the strengths of what he might call the average people. If the family could gain the approval of such citizens, then the chances were good that their course and judgments were sound. In other ways, Scott Breckinridge's outlook more closely resembled those of the Republican party he supported. The traditionalist in him preferred the patrician approach of voluntary aid over governmental support. He gave time freely to community clinics and expected others of his class to respond similarly. Dr. Breckinridge placed his full faith in the private enterprise system and in the idea that, if the economy functioned well, so too did the country. The Depression of the 1930s altered the physician's outlook only little, as his fears of excessive governmental intervention and its possible results overcame troubling questions. He remained, in essence, a Hoover Republican.[4]

Not so his son John. He had a rather typical Breckinridge childhood— erratic and energetic—and like many children he both accepted and rejected diverse parts of his parents' teachings. The Breckinridge tradition of service, for instance, apparently was well inculcated. His father's political views were less so. Of the several reasons for the latter divergence, the most important was the Depression and its effect on an impressionable youth. Within the family circle few surface changes took place as a result of the national economic reverses. The father and mother consciously tried to prevent any feelings of insecurity by hiding their own financial problems from the children; Kentucky and its rural-based economy did not suffer, as a whole, as much as many other parts of the nation.

Yet the Depression left its mark on the teen-age Johnny. He attended various schools, including Massie Preparatory School in Versailles, Kentucky, where later political foe A.B. ("Happy") Chandler then coached, and then entered the University of Kentucky in 1932. During his second college semester Franklin Delano Roosevelt entered the White House. In the university setting John met new people with fresh ideas. This exposure, coupled with Democratic successes in changing the psyche of a people, were vital factors in the transformation of John Bayne Breckinridge, first to Independent, then to Democrat.[5]

Johnny's collegiate career was not marked by outstanding academic achievement, but those years represented more than just classwork. Social events proved a rewarding experience for one who already had some thoughts of entering public life. While active for a time in a military fraternity, the Pershing Rifles, he focused more attention on Theta chapter of Kappa Alpha fraternity; during the 1935-36 school year he served as president of the chapter. Other nonacademic activities are more difficult to trace. Tantalizing fragments ("Johnny Breckinridge isn't driving the green Pontiac any more. He prefers walking with Pat [terson] hall flashes, so they say") provide more gossip than substance. Evidently John Breckinridge's college years were rather typical.[6]

After the 4 June 1937 commencement exercises, at which *Courier-Journal* managing editor Mark Ethridge spoke on "A Rendezvous with Destiny," the new graduate entered the university's law school in the fall. There a more mature man emerged as Breckinridge began to take more interest in his chosen field. As staff member and contributor to the *Kentucky Law Journal*, he joined a group that produced a first-rate quarterly. Passing the bar exams in February 1940, Breckinridge was now an attorney facing his future. For a twenty-six-year-old in 1940, however, the present looked grim enough, the future, frightening. War in Europe was drawing closer daily. The center of activity in America, more than ever, was the nation's capital, and there Breckinridge went to seek his first job. After a stint as an automobile inspector in "Call Carl's" garage ("All I knew about cars was what I had learned from my stripped-down Model T and it wasn't much"), he was hired as an attorney in the Anti-Trust Division of the Department of Justice, a job much to his liking.[7]

The return to Washington had been a journey back to the home he had left at age five. Yet it was really an introduction to a different world, for Breckinridge had lived a sheltered life in a small town, and had gone to what was still a small university. Washington in 1940 was active with preparation for the war that grew nearer. A pathbreaking election was coming. Changes of major import had taken place over the last seven years; equally great changes lurked on the horizon. A bustling, crowded, exciting city that still held fast to its southern small-town cohesiveness welcomed John Bayne Breckinridge and quickly taught him much.

But John's stay was brief. On 1 April 1941 the United States army ordered the reserve first lieutenant to active duty. Eight months later he was at war. During the next five years the young officer would rise to the rank of colonel and take part in several important planning and policy-making decisions. First sent to Egypt in 1943 as a liaison officer, Breckinridge centered his subsequent activities on the Balkans. Later, in the midst of the Cold War, he would be credited with having been partially responsible for persuading leaders to keep forces in that area to slow "the Communist threat." As commander of the U.S. Military Liaison Headquarters in Albania, Colonel Breckinridge was an able adviser and planner; his experiences would prove useful in his subsequent career.[8]

In November 1946, just before his thirty-third birthday, Breckinridge left military service and returned to Kentucky. Seven months later he and his brother, Scott, opened their law offices on West Short Street. Scott D. Breckinridge, Jr., three-and-a-half years younger, brought to the practice a background almost identical to John's. He had entered the University of Kentucky three years after his brother, joined the same fraternity and followed John into law school. He too wrote an article on black rights for the law journal there (suggesting that separate but equal segregation statutes must fall). Completion of his course of study was followed closely by World War II and four years' service in the Navy. Six years after opening their practice, the two brothers went separate ways and they shared few career parallels thereafter. In mid-1953 Scott joined the Central Intelligence Agency, to serve that branch over the next twenty-six years. For his achievements there he twice received the Distinguished Intelligence Medal—a highly unusual honor in the CIA. In 1979 Scott returned to Lexington, bringing with him memories of long and rewarding governmental service and of traditions and trends in the family whose name he bore.[9]

Unlike Scott, John remained in Lexington and began a process designed to culminate in his own contribution to the Breckinridge tradition. His chosen field was political, and his course was rocky. At almost the same time John opened his law office, he formally joined the Democratic party and became involved in state politics. What he found was the usual chaos. Again, factionalism dominated Democratic circles, while Republicans capitalized on those divisions to keep their party alive in the state. The deaths of the leaders of the earlier Beckham-Haly-Bingham faction, the decline of the bipartisan combine, the fading of the power of the old boss system before the New Deal agencies, had left voids in the political universe. Coming out of the Beckham faction, young Happy Chandler soon developed a large personal following and became a new factional leader of the Democrats. By 1947, when John B. Breckinridge came to the political world, the second major leader, Earle C. Clements, was just beginning his rise. For the next two decades those two men and their forces dominated the Democratic party. In this maelstrom of swirling Democratic factionalism and infighting Breckinridge expressed his thoughts on politics in America and Kentucky, politics as they were and as they should be. In a campaign speech on behalf of the eventual loser of the Democratic primary, Harry Lee Waterfield, John warned of the dangers of centralized power and called for the election of "men of integrity." The issue, he wrote in two draft speeches, was simply "the search for that past and way of life whereby man can see the fruit of his life returned unto himself." Perhaps not consciously, but still in fact, John presented ideas that resembled closely those expressed two decades earlier by Desha Breckinridge:

> The name "Kentucky" became a word upon the lips of men and nations alike, and our leaders became the nation's leaders, taking their place in halls of progress and annals of liberty in tempests searing the world not too dissimilar from those which now beset us.
> But where do we find ourselves to-day . . . ? No longer are we that elysian field to which the ambitious transport themselves, in search of a new and fuller life; rather . . . we now find that we are exporting some thousand of our sons annually. . . . Kentucky is no longer in the vanguard of the nations leaders.[10]

Like his cousin Desha, John wanted to return the commonwealth to the prominence it had enjoyed a century earlier; he sought to revive that past time when the state had been powerful. Perhaps not coincidentally, it had been in that "golden era" that the Breckinridges had made their greatest political gains as well. But questions arose over whether something now gone for almost a century could be regained. Would the state have to look now not to past glories but to future realities?

Breckinridge's strong support of Waterfield resulted from his own crusading spirit; his work in the anti-trust division in 1941 now led to attacks on the opposition "machine" and its candidate's supposed ties to monopolies. But John's perceptions did not match those of the voters of Kentucky, for Clements won the primary by more than thirty thousand votes and went on to a convincing victory in the general election.[11]

The years between that 1947 campaign and 1955 were often difficult. John assisted in two unsuccessful local races entered by his brother, helped organize an independent but politically unsuccessful reform group called the "Friends of Fayette," and did some election work for a lieutenant governor candidate who eventually withdrew from the 1955 Democratic primary. Viewed somewhat as "radicals" in the Lexington context, the two law partners achieved little success: "We have experienced a 'leper' status in the community over the period of our first few years," John wrote in 1951. For that reason, he journeyed back to the nation's capital to assess job prospects. Disillusioned over the "lethargy" there, Breckinridge returned and told a friend, "I suppose that I went to Washington, in search of something that did not exist (I had to go, to know)." By 1953 he determined either to make a success of his practice or "seek my fortunes elsewhere."[12]

But financial solvency and another event, perhaps even more important to his career, made his decisions for him. In 1954 Breckinridge remarried. His first marriage, to Frances Knight Archibald, had ended in divorce and a prolonged struggle over custody of the two children, son John, Jr., and daughter Knight. The second Mrs. Breckinridge was Helen Congleton, the energetic and personable daughter of a former Lexington mayor. Helen, a graduate in the same college class as John, remembered her future husband from those days chiefly as a whirl of robes dashing up to the graduation line at the last minute before the procession began. Later they came to know each other through occasional political work. After marriage, over the next twenty-five years, Helen Breckinridge did a great deal of the organization required to run a campaign or an office and provided a positive, stabilizing force in John's often hectic life. Security and support would be important for a man entering politics, as Breckinridge was in 1955.[13]

John B. Breckinridge's decision to run for a vacant Kentucky House of Representatives seat surprised his wife, for he filed on the last day. Early, he had felt the tug of public office, and he had skirted along the political fringes ever since returning from the war. A chaotic personal life, an uncertain political base, a fledgling law practice—all had held him back. But now, at age forty-two, he was finally ready. This first race and the results of the attempt could be the key to whether he would become a public servant or remain a private fixture for the rest of his days.

Physically, the candidate was an attractive and appealing figure for the voters whose support he sought. Just over six feet tall, trim and robust, John always looked younger than his years. A full head of dark, wavy hair touched by a little gray later, and piercing eyes added to the impression. An erect posture, a vigorous, energetic manner—these he kept for most of his public career, and they served him well. Vitality characterized his actions. If the appearance impressed others favorably, his speeches left more varied feelings. At his best, Breckinridge could draw together diverse facts, tie them to complex concepts, and present the whole in a clear, at times extemporaneous, talk that won admiration. With his steel-gray eyes covering the crowd, his voice rising with wit and sarcasm, and his pleasing appearance softening the criticism, he could be an imposing political figure. On the other hand, a mood change, an uninteresting topic, a long day—these might result in a talk that did not impress listeners. Inclined to use statistics, as his great-uncle Willie

Breckinridge had been, John could present them to advantage on some days; at other times, that tactic was a burden to be overcome.[14]

In more private surroundings Breckinridge enjoyed the laughter and relaxation of parties. He moved smoothly through intimate gatherings; he won allies there. But he never fully displayed the kind of charismatic personality that gained instant friends. He liked his privacy too much, perhaps, to give all of himself to the public. For whatever reason, Breckinridge was liked, admired, respected—but seldom loved—by the masses. That particular emotion, however, was not as necessary to victory as in earlier times. John's era was moving away from the back-slapping, bombastic oratory of a Happy Chandler into a calmer, cooler form, partly because of the increasing use of television. Image became, in some ways, more important than the spoken word; while Breckinridge could do well in both worlds, his real strength lay in the image he projected. His family name and its positive connotations helped at first; his own actions strengthened that element. He avoided "political machine" implications, cultivated an image of integrity in government, and gained admiration for his independence.

One of the five candidates in a crowded primary field, John won a victory with 33 percent of the votes. In the fall he almost doubled that number, trouncing his little-known Republican opposition. As the new legislator entered the chamber where the first John, Robert, and John C. Breckinridge had all served, he knew that they had gone from there to greater things. It was an exciting time. But circumstances darkened the neophyte's joy. Democrat Happy Chandler, reelected to the governorship twenty years after his first term had begun, naturally sought to control both houses in order to enact legislation he favored. Always independent, Breckinridge had his own programs and bills. The two men's plans seldom coincided. Moreover, John now supported the Clements wing of the party and Happy had little use for those who gave their allegiance elsewhere. Chandler seemed all-powerful.[15]

In such an unpromising atmosphere Breckinridge began his legislative career. Generally frustrated in attempts to enact into law the twenty-three bills he introduced, the representative from District 49 nevertheless showed both his future interests and his present reform goals in those attempts. He hoped to aid the educational system his great-grandfather had served through a bill raising the allowable school-tax rate, one changing the composition of the Council on Public Higher Education, and a third setting up a statewide school board. All failed. In the area of voter reform John sought to provide for the secret election of precinct committeemen, to require votes to be counted within a week, and to authorize nonpartisan citizen groups to name election challengers. He was unsuccessful each time. He also fought for legislation extending coverage of the merit system and for an act requiring child-care centers to obtain permits.

Only the latter became law. Overall, however, the newcomer did reasonably well. Facing a hostile administration, he had gotten 21.7 percent of his bills passed (compared to the session's overall average of 30.1 percent). Breckinridge had not only survived but he had drawn attention to himself as a promising freshman in the halls of the capitol.[16]

Governor Chandler, faced with programs not yet enacted and a constitutional limitation of a sixty-day regular legislative session every two years, called four straight special sessions in an attempt to enact his legislation. The full-scale rebellion of John B. Breckinridge came to the fore. With Appalachian spokesman Harry Caudill, fellow Fayette Representative Foster Ockerman, and sixteen others, he voted in the minority to oppose Chandler's governmental reorganization plan. Then John introduced the other eight bills of the session, all of them predictably going nowhere. Much the same occurred in the second extraordinary session; in the third, he did not vote on the one bill presented; throughout the last session Breckinridge, Caudill, Ockerman, and rising politician Edward T. ("Ned") Breathitt again opposed "His Happiness'" proposals, again losing. When the regular legislature opened in 1958 most observers predicted that party factionalism and legislative independence would combine to produce a stormy session. Chandler, now a "lame duck" unable to succeed himself, sought to consolidate power behind his candidate in the gubernatorial election the next year. The Clements faction attempted to defuse just such a move. And still others simply wanted to secure legislation they viewed as more progressive than that offered by the governor. As it turned out, the elements merged in such a way that Breckinridge profited politically from it all.[17]

Breckinridge's legislative record in 1958 showed only one successful act in thirty-six attempts; over twenty of his bills died in committee. Yet the output obscured the role being played. Frequently the individuals opposing an administration receive more attention than those working to achieve a program; if the division is within the majority party, such notice can be magnified; when the internal fighting is part of a long pregubernatorial struggle, as in 1958, the focus becomes even more intense. John Breckinridge, conservative in some ways, seemed to revel in his rebelliousness. Not only in 1958, but throughout his career, he would never be stereotyped with a certain faction or particular outlook. That independence would help him rise but, in the end, it also kept him from achieving more. In 1958, however, Breckinridge was rising. His defeated bills spoke again of reforms: modifications in the election process (including required use of voting machines), extensions of the merit system, and constitutional authorization for annual legislative sessions. He introduced bills to abolish the politically active highway commission, to require open meetings of boards and commissions, to amend the constitution to allow city home rule, and to establish a constitutional revision commission to look at the state's outdated governing document. The fact that many of his proposals would later become law spoke for his foresight; their defeat showed his minority status in a Democratic administration.[18]

While gaining recognition for his proposals, especially from the powerful *Courier-Journal* (which also opposed Chandler), Breckinridge received more attention for his leadership in a group of self-styled rebels. These "young Turks," meeting periodically at a house near the capitol, supported what they saw as a reform plan. Their bloc voting on many issues in the 1958 legislature frustrated the Chandler forces, causing them to form a coalition with Republicans in order to win their victories—a tactic hurtful in the next canvass. Tightly organized, the rebels seemed to opponents to be only a further factionalism of party politics by an idealistic group; to supporters, they promised to blaze new political paths in Kentucky.[19]

But the roads led nowhere. The election of 1959 submerged plans, confused alliances, and eventually destroyed the group as a separate force in the state's future. Basically anti-Chandler, the "rebels"—Breckinridge among them—now faced a difficult choice. Two candidates vied for their support, former Court of Appeals judge Bert T. Combs, backed by the Clements faction, and a newcomer to the statewide scene, former reform mayor Wilson Wyatt of Louisville. Wyatt had the backing of independents like Breckinridge, of the Bingham family and their powerful papers, and of the Louisville voters generally. His opponent, Combs, however, had organization—the Clements faction and their western Kentucky ties plus Combs's own drawing power in his native eastern Kentucky. Combs had campaigned across the state four years earlier, building a base; Wyatt was almost unproven in that regard. Although each candidate proved attractive to voters, both drew from the same anti-Chandler constituency: divided opposition could bring primary victory to the third candidate, Chandlerite Harry Lee Waterfield. The solution seemed obvious but difficult to bring about. Breckinridge, in June 1958, talked to Clements of the need for a united ticket, and finally the bargain was struck, in terms similar to those Breckinridge had urged. Combs would run for governor, Wyatt for the second spot. In three years, the Clements-Combs forces would be expected to back Wyatt for a Senate seat.[20]

All this was of more than passing interest to Breckinridge. He had sought the lieutenant governorship himself, but, with the merger, he agreed to run instead for attorney general, the job another John Breckinridge had held so long ago. While not of the Clements "inner circle," the candidate for once was on the team. The entire slate swept to victory in the primary. Breckinridge won what a Louisville paper called a "surprisingly big victory," with 145,855 votes to 91,766 for his nearest competitor. The defeat of the Chandler forces marked the decline of Happy's power in Kentucky politics. In the general election, the results were similar, and John Breckinridge's climb up the political ladder continued without pause.[21]

    With his entry into the office of attorney general in 1960 Breckinridge began what may have been the happiest years of his public life. His new job gave satisfaction in many ways. He had a fairly small staff that could be managed reasonably well. No huge bureaucracy distracted him. On the other hand, little patronage could be distributed. For John the individual, that was to his liking; for John the politician, that allowed few debts to be paid or contracted from others. The attorney general found his position appealing because he was his own boss: while part of the governor's cabinet, Breckinridge had a reasonably free hand. He moved cautiously at first, for he had few real powers. The attorney general and his staff basically briefed criminal cases on appeal to the state's highest court, or gave legal opinions to officials and citizens of the commonwealth. Unlike its federal counterpart the state office could not prosecute criminals on its own, but the new attorney general used his investigatory and information-gathering powers to full capability.[22]

    In two particular cases this strategy made Breckinridge highly visible. The first instance began in 1960, when the state auditor uncovered what seemed to be widespread irregularities in the Carter County school system. The attorney general demanded that the state superintendent of public instruction move as quickly as possible to oust the local superintendent there. A running fight developed—one that included a National Education Association investigation, the discharge of the Carter County Board of Education, and numerous challenges by both sides. The second, even more sensational, and perhaps more dangerous, example came in 1961, when Breckinridge and his staff vigorously supported the prosecution of several law enforcement officials from Newport, a notoriously "open" town across the river from Cincinnati. Charges of corruption and mob payoffs filled the air; a former prostitute was only one of the witnesses involved. Appeals to the state's highest court, Breckinridge's appearance before the grand jury in the role of private citizen (in order to help the investigation), angry charges and countercharges, several Newport resignations—all this kept the story before the public.[23]

    Less dramatic labor also took time. Breckinridge served on the air and water-pollution commissions, toiled with the 1960 legislature to enact some of his pet programs, and, reflecting a key interest, chaired the Kentucky Advisory Committee on Nuclear Energy. His overworked staff brought action against numerous strip mine operators under what was then a weak law, initiated suits against firms and individuals in the water-pollution field, and pushed other such moves. All of this took its toll on the occupant of the office. Breckinridge wrote of himself in 1961, "I am a lousy correspondent under normal circumstances, but things at the office lately have been such as to make it even worse!" In March of the next year he recorded running weeks in arrears in his correspondence. On one occasion, John answered an Easter card in October.[24]

Yet the hard work and long hours were paying dividends, not only in accomplishments, but also in the attention given to the man behind it all. Breckinridge received for the most part a very favorable press, and he was increasingly pictured as a front-runner in the gubernatorial sweepstakes of 1963. In a vivid, eulogistic column in the August 1961 *Courier-Journal*, popular columnist Allan M. Trout wrote, under a headline that read "Have (Legal) Gun—Will Travel," "John Breckinridge is acquiring considerable stature. . . . His stand upon the principle of stern rectitude is like a fresh breeze in the state environs of sagging law and wilting order." The following January an editorial noted, "Wherever you find John Breckinridge, you will find political action." A western Kentucky newspaper praised his "drive and dedication." The Frankfort *State Journal*, in late January 1962, viewed him as the strongest candidate at that time.[25]

Speculation and a good press did not mean the governorship, however, and Breckinridge knew that. What was happening behind the public scene would be more important in the long run. The vital question was who would gain the support of a popular and powerful administration. In January 1962 the attorney general told an Owensboro ally that Governor Combs "has in effect advised would-be aspirants to try their spurs, in order that the public might help in his personal decision as to whom to support, and they are all hell bent for leather doing just that!" The hot race narrowed quickly, however, to two front-runners: Breckinridge and Ned Breathitt, a former legislative colleague, now a Public Service Commission member, whose grandfather had been a state attorney general and whose uncle had been lieutenant governor. Young Breathitt had important allies in his camp, and strong regional support. Breckinridge had an image, a reputation, a good record.[26]

This bid for the governorship may have been the crucial moment in Breckinridge's career. If he could gain the governor's support, chances were excellent that the primary victory would be his. Similar results in the fall election would elevate him to an office none of his ancestors had held. After that, perhaps the senatorship and a return to the nation's capital would be possible. John had been a "rebel" in Lexington, a "young Turk" in the legislature, a maverick in the administration. The attorney general clearly was his own man. If he could bring that image unblemished to a campaign, while still holding the administration's support, the combination might well be unbeatable. John, however, could not sacrifice enough to satisfy those whose support could elect him. Never overly popular with political professionals, he was perceived by them as a bit too independent, too unpredictable: Breckinridge was basically not a compromiser. By May 1962 the administration's clear choice was Breathitt. Breckinridge, realizing that his continued candidacy would split the administration forces and perhaps allow Chandler's faction to win, withdrew from the gubernatorial canvass. Still an attractive vote-getter, he aimed for the second slot on the ticket and hoped to use that avenue to victory.[27]

Administration forces found themselves in a dilemma. Clearly, a Breathitt-Breckinridge ticket was a strong one—the western Kentucky man balanced by the central Kentuckian. All the strengths of both camps would now be united. Breckinridge had the support of party liberals; he could be expected to do well in urban areas, Breathitt in more rural ones. it seemed a dream ticket, much like the Combs-Wyatt merger four years earlier. The only problem in all this was that some administration advisors bitterly opposed Breckinridge, and the candidate for lieutenant governor did not think so highly of Breathitt's selection over some other men, himself included. There were no "deals" made or exchanges of support, as had occurred earlier. That was not Breckinridge's style, for better or worse. An uneasy, almost unspoken, alliance resulted and went forth to attack the Happy Chandler–Harry Lee Waterfield dragon.[28]

Traveling much of the time by air, Breckinridge campaigned across the state, taking stands for government reorganization, a new state constitution, an open meetings law, an extended merit system, public disclosure of political spending, increased aid to education ("the key issue in this—or any other—campaign"), more park development, and new atomic energy plants. A positive image went with him. An editorial in a McLean County newspaper presented views prevalent in the state; it discovered "an intelligent, resourceful young man who is always found on the side of law, reason and morality."[29]

Not everyone, of course, held that opinion. An unfriendly story in the Louisville *Times* summarized attitudes that prevailed among many of the state's political figures: "Is he a Don Quixote tilting at political windmills or a Sir Galahad searching for the Holy Grail of good government?" The writer said that unnamed "veteran politicians" found Breckinridge a dedicated, dynamic, honest, sincere public servant, yet one whose judgment and administrative ability troubled them; Governor Combs reportedly liked his cabinet officer but doubted his political acumen; some praised his "streaks of genius" in the attorney general's office, while they questioned his administrative qualities there. Overall, the account did nothing to help a campaign already troubled by little money and less time. Editorial endorsement by the *Courier-Journal*, the black Louisville *Defender* (which praised his "liberal" race relations record), and other important papers helped overcome the disappointments, but Breckinridge knew that Democratic primary opponent Waterfield would be a formidable foe. John himself had found Waterfield's qualities admirable early in his career and realized the strengths this old campaigner brought with him.[30]

Election day brought victory to Breathitt as he won nearly 54 percent of the vote, beating Chandler by a margin of over sixty thousand. Newspapers commented that television, a more informed electorate, and new faces and theories had ended "a colorful chapter in Kentucky's political history." Chandler's defeat was, said an eastern Kentucky editor, "the end of an era." Widespread predictions of a "new politics" followed.[31]

Election night brought defeat to Breathitt's running-mate, however. Breckinridge lost to Waterfield by more than fifty thousand votes. Several papers noted that the lieutenant governor's race was closer than most had predicted. Others suggested that Breckinridge made "perhaps the best race of the major candidates," given the conditions he labored under. An Associated Press account pointed to his "surprisingly strong showing" against the favorite Waterfield. Yet such praise could not conceal what was a bitter defeat. Why had some fifty thousand voters cast their ballots for Breathitt, but not for his running-mate? The answer had been suggested during the campaign and the results confirmed it. Administration forces had not opposed Waterfield's candidacy in western Kentucky. Or, to put it another way: Breathitt ran with Breckinridge openly in the East and with Waterfield covertly in the West. The uneasy alliance had proved fragile, indeed. By election time it did not even exist.[32]

Openly, Breckinridge displayed little of the bitterness voiced by supporters who felt their candidate had been "sold out." He had chosen his path; he had known the dangers; he had rejected the alternatives. A newspaper had reported earlier in his campaign, "He rides swiftly. And alone." Now it was simply time to ride on to other fights.[33]

Twenty

In Pursuit of the Horizon

FOR THE next decade, beginning in 1963, Breckinridge moved in and out of the halls of political success. He debated running for United States senator in 1966 but wisely declined to challenge the incumbent. He ran for statewide office the next year, and in 1971 canvassed again for lieutenant governor. As in the past he spread his energies to other than political fields, as well. Service on committees, councils, and boards took much time away from his law practice, but he was not one who particularly cared for the daily grind such a practice required. Besides, John had a deep interest in many of the causes he served. In some cases, such as in the atomic energy issue, his contributions were sizable.[1]

State history attracted him as well. While never particularly well informed on all aspects of Kentucky's past, Breckinridge did know its importance in shaping not only himself but also the present-day government. He occasionally spoke at historical gatherings, and at one such talk in Georgia he concealed his knowledge: when introduced as a great-grandson of Confederate General John C. Breckinridge, he let the error pass. "I lacked the heart to advise that I was the grandson of Private Joseph Cabell Breckinridge, who . . . served . . . on the Union side!" As Kentucky Historical Society president from 1961 to 1963, however, he did much to advance the cause of Clio in the commonwealth. That service, and his awareness of the importance of preserving his own papers, indicate that the man who so often and so openly minimized the importance of history in his own career knew full well that he could not escape his past.[2]

In 1967 Breckinridge sought to repeat a part of his recent past by running for the office of attorney general. His tenure there earlier had been happy. Now he prepared to recapture that happiness after four hectic years away from office. The outlook for success was mixed. While victory in the primary came easily this time, the general election presented a real challenge. John's own opponent, Republican Lester Burns, might not be the catalyst for defeat, but that party's standard-bearer could be. Louie B. Nunn might carry others into office on his coattails. Barely defeated for governor four years earlier, the fifty-two-year-old former county judge had rebounded from that setback. In the Republican primary, the hard-hitting, rural-based, Protestant Nunn emerged as victor in an intense contest against an urban, Catholic candidate.[3]

The election brought Republicans the governorship but gave Nunn a divided administration, as over half the elected offices went to Democrats—including Wendell Ford as lieutenant governor and Breckinridge as attorney general. Once again Breckinridge had overcome odds, had gone it alone, and had gained the sought-after goal. Subsequent events proved predictable. Breckinridge soon found himself in the midst of controversy with the Republican administration. Nunn's firing of several thousand state employees supposedly protected by the merit system brought about an extended legal fight in which the courts eventually supported most of the stands taken by the attorney general and others. Further actions provoked similar criticisms of the governor—for raising the sales tax, for the state's conduct in an apartment building project, for supposed political assessments done on state time and property. All this brought a headline reminiscent of the first attorney general's term: "Breckinridge Rides White Horse Again."[4]

But actions in the political sphere did not obscure Breckinridge's role as chief law enforcement officer of the state. As attorney general, he toured Kentucky, expressing his opinions on crime both in his commonwealth and in America. Admitting that answers were complex, John presented two solutions to the rising crime rate. First of all, he suggested in July 1968, a respect for the law must be instilled early. Citizens must teach the "old-fashioned idea of doing right for right's sake—not for fear of getting caught." That conservative, moral stance he balanced, however, with a reform-oriented appeal for more scientific crime-prevention programs, while cautioning against "vigilante" groups, which had no place in modern society. Later that same year he added that criminal justice must pursue "the disease—not just the symptoms—by the programs of education and prevention."[5]

Still later, in the midst of riots and rising crime rates, surrounded by those who were crying out for "law and order" and those who cautioned patience, the attorney general spoke for both sides but more often counseled understanding. Acknowledging that he viewed these times of "ferment, turmoil, and confusion" as "insidiously inspired," Breckinridge at the same time warned against panicking into a totalitarian environment to control crime. He stressed connections between the larger society and the law, "which does not operate in a vacuum." What was required was "patience, understanding, intellectual concentration on this problem of disorder, and proper action." And by "proper action" he meant firm action—but not uncontrolled, reactionary retaliation. His was a moderating voice for both extremes.[6]

Crusades against crime and other notable actions that gained attention were soon accompanied by preparations for another lieutenant governor's race following the term. Within two and a half years after taking office, Breckinridge announced his candidacy for the state's second highest office, stressing his stands on pollution and the merit system. The *Herald* promptly described him as "a veteran lone-wolf campaigner," chronically short of funding and staff. It was 1963 revisited, and this time the candidate hoped for a different result. Compared with his earlier race, Breckinridge had advantages unavailable then. He was more experienced, he had been named the outstanding attorney general in the nation in 1968–69, and he knew the political situation better now. On the other hand, he did not have the same youthful, rising, political image; he was no longer a fresh face; his momentum had slowed. Another difficult race awaited, but Breckinridge hardly hesitated on entering the fray. He set up files for all counties, contacted old allies in each locale, chose youth, farm, veteran, and finance chairmen for each area, and then sent stickers, brochures, press releases, and other items to every headquarters.[7]

Throughout his long statewide tours the candidate stressed educational needs as "the number one problem" of Kentucky. He advocated expanded vocational education, better teacher-retirement funding, an appointed (not elected) superintendent of public instruction, and a professional negotiations law. More than that, he emphasized philosophical, moral questions as well. In a 13 March 1971 speech in Lexington he spoke out against "centralism," which held few answers to pressing problems, in his view. Instead, John wanted to return to what he called a simple principle—that all men, "even including women in that category," were equal in rights and had society's obligation to receive fulfillment of those rights. Problems existed, and had in each era. But, he added, "basically they're the same problems arising out of ignorance and prejudice and bias and selfishness and avariciousness. And every generation that comes along . . . will have in it that vanguard that will contain within it the seed of progress. . . . " He hoped that his own course was one that would justify his election slogan: "It does make a difference."[8]

But how much of a difference, was the question. Kentucky gubernatorial politics influenced his race, and victory, as usual, did not depend solely on Breckinridge's actions. The candidate's chief opposition in the Democratic primary was Julian M. Carroll, the forty-year-old Speaker of the Kentucky House. Carroll quickly aligned with former governor Bert Combs, who was seeking a second term as governor. Their ticket appeared strong. Opposing Combs was Wendell H. Ford, forty-six and fresh from party leadership as the Democratic lieutenant governor. Breckinridge and Combs had never been particularly close, and the former governor's action in John's first lieutenant governor's race had not changed their positions. With Carroll going to Combs, a Breckinridge-

Ford team seemed natural. As in earlier races, however, no alliance resulted. Instead, John pointed out his factional independence and asked for support from "all sides." Such a course of action nullified several of his advantages. In a race with otherwise equal factors, John should have beaten Carroll, who was less known on the state scene. But his opponent had the benefit of the statewide resources available to Combs, and Breckinridge did not. By April 1971 commentators rated the campaign even; by primary time that analysis had not changed.[9]

Ford's bold challenge of the former governor proved a successful gamble; he defeated Combs by more than forty thousand votes. Breckinridge, once again, did not profit. He lost his primary race by over twenty thousand. As had happened eight years earlier, the two factions split the state's two highest elective offices when the ticket won in November. After Ford entered the Senate three years later, Carroll became governor. It was a scenario in which Breckinridge might have played the leading role; as it was, he had tried and had been passed over again. Nor were the causes new or unexpected. In western Kentucky "Ford-Carroll" bumper stickers had appealed for support of the two men from that section, recalling the tactics used against John earlier. Regionalism in the state had contributed to his defeat in several ways, and Breckinridge's campaign itself had not been immune to such appeals: an advertisement in the central Bluegrass asked voters, "Who do you want for Lieutenant Governor? A lifelong resident of Central Kentucky . . . or a Western Kentuckian[?]" Unfortunately for him, their answer was softer than that spoken in the west. His independence had again failed to translate into political victory. John B. Breckinridge had made his last bid for statewide office.[10]

Breckinridge, fifty-eight, had been unable to advance in his two most important political races. Time dictated a return to private practice and to the confines of home and hearth. Over the years John had rested seldom. Always energetic, involved with several projects at once, he made it difficult for friends to keep pace. Yet there had always been times of sociability. At their Fincastle Road home, near Henry Clay's Ashland estate, John and Helen frequently entertained friends and relatives. At other times the scene shifted to nearby lakes and rivers, where the indomitable "S.S. Uslyss" (pronounced "useless") provided the setting for some of the happiest private moments. On a Sunday, for example, John would rise early, dress casually, and fix a bountiful breakfast, which often included eggs, sausage, fried tomatoes, molasses, and his "famous left-handed pancakes." He and Helen might leisurely read the newspaper, then go out for an afternoon ride in the countryside. During that time they would talk—and always about the future: "We never talked about the past. The past just didn't figure in his life. . . . He was always looking forward." That orientation meant that those pleasant, relaxing days would not last. For though the tranquility of the river appealed, the turbulence of political waters presented attractions that John could not resist.[11]

In the spring of 1971 the incumbent congressman of John's home district died. His almost twenty-year hold of that seat had long made it outside Breckinridge's reach. Still involved in his own lieutenant governor's race at first, John did not challenge the caucus choice for the vacancy. As a result, he did not run in the December 1971 special election that selected a successor to fill the term. But on 21 February 1972 John Bayne Breckinridge announced his candidacy for the United States Congress, and the incumbent declined to seek a full term.[12]

Endorsed by the deceased congressman's widow and law partner, unopposed by the state administration, supported by organized labor, Breckinridge took to the stump to gather further support in the Democratic primary. His chief opponent in a three-man race was young political novice Tom Ward, a farmer from a neighboring county. Ward's radio and television appeals asked voters to "Send a man, not a name" to Congress. Breckinridge, in turn, emphasized his residence in Fayette County (the district's largest county) and his long governmental experience. Results surprised few. Breckinridge won 57 percent of the primary vote, carrying all but four of the district's seventeen counties. He now faced a former classmate and Democratic colleague–turned Republican, fifty-eight-year-old Laban P. Jackson of Shelbyville.[13]

The fall election promised to be more difficult than the primary. First of all, the congressional race would be tied to the presidential election between George McGovern and Richard Nixon, and political polls suggested a landslide margin for the latter. Second, the Ashland district itself had been moving towards the Republicans, especially in Breckinridge's home county of Fayette, as urban voters increased in number; Nixon had carried the district four years earlier. Breckinridge seemed to recognize these trends and the dangers they posed. He either had grown more conservative over the years or had decided to emphasize conservative stands more often, for his oratory increasingly expressed that side of his political being. On the question of Southeast Asia, for example, the former army colonel stated that he would not limit the president's war powers nor favor a coalition government in Vietnam—"the first step in the staging of a Trojan horse takeover." This had the practical effect of reducing differences between him and Jackson; it also showed his distance from Democratic standard-bearer McGovern. At the same time, though, Breckinridge did not ignore his party ties. He took what were considered at the time as "liberal" stands on questions of women's rights, the environment, and consumer protection. Overall, he walked the middle ground.[14]

Important area newspapers approved his course. The Lexington *Her-*

ald, while disapproving Breckinridge's "hawkish" views on Vietnam, easily endorsed him over Jackson. The *Kentucky Post* in the northern part of the district dispersed praise, concluding that "his name and bearing bespeak congressional ability." But all this meant little if voters decided otherwise. Ticket-splitting dominated election day. Citizens of the Sixth District gave Republican Nixon 67 percent of their ballots; they supported a Democratic senator by a 50-percent to 48-percent margin; and they elected John Breckinridge to the U. S. House. His 76,185 votes (52 percent) outdistanced Jackson's 68,012 supporters. What had seemed the nadir of a political career only some eighteen months earlier had now been transformed into a fresh beginning in a new environment.[15]

On 3 January 1973 Breckinridge was sworn in as a United States representative, the seventh of the clan to sit in Congress. Nearly eight decades had elapsed since the last Breckinridge had stood where he did, and during that interval Congress had changed a great deal. For one thing, the Ninety-second Congress was involved in many more facets of national life than Willie Breckinridge's Fifty-third. Now its functions as investigative forum, as ombudsman, as clearing-house, dictated large congressional staffs. Congressman Breckinridge, like his peers, received an allotment of almost a quarter of a million dollars in salaries for aides to help him meet the demands. His expanded workload required more letters, more telephone calls, more complimentary publications for constituents. A neophyte's life in Congress was not necessarily easy.[16]

Washington had a habit of distracting its elected leaders. As Texas Democrat James C. Wright had declaimed a few years earlier, "I came here to make laws and what do I do? I send baby books to young mothers, listen to every maladjusted kid who wants out of the service, write sweet replies to pompous idiots who think a public servant is a public footstool, and give tours of the Capitol to visitors who are just as worn out as I am." A legislator's day included long hours at the office, listening to lobbyists and constituents, dictating correspondence, discussing legislation with other congressmen, and answering reporters' questions. In addition, the solon might attend committee meetings, floor sessions, and party caucuses, all the while trying to coordinate a far-flung staff. Nocturnal respites could be few: embassy receptions, state dinners, cocktail parties, the social circuit generally—all demanded attendance. In short, a congressman could easily find too much to do in too short a time. A good staff could help overcome these numerous diversions and duties; Breckinridge's however, never fulfilled the congressional ideal. As a *Guide to Congress* noted, "Staff aides multiply the member's arms, legs, eyes and ears. . . ." The Kentuckian's aides, as a rule, were talented, and he did not consciously misuse them. But administration was never his strong point. John had a mind for large matters but he found it difficult to focus properly on a lower level. Consequently, he never received the support he needed. Unsatisfied constituents, sporadic confusion, and occasional misunderstandings resulted.[17]

Further hindering the new congressman was the state of the nation, its parties, and its people. The psyche of the citizenry was shaken. Continuing anger and debate over Vietnam, Cambodia, and their legacy raised the specter of American defeat and guilt. Moreover, the aftermath of the November 1972 elections brought further chaos. Five days after Breckinridge's swearing in, seven men went on trial for their role in a break-in at the Watergate building in Washington, D.C., some six months before. With the executive branch in the hands of the Republicans while both houses remained Democratic, possibilities for conflict intensified. Added to this, in a little more than nine months after John took office, the vice-president of the United States resigned and pleaded no contest to an income tax–evasion charge. A growing "cancer" brought down the president less than a year later. It was not the most propitious time to begin a congressional career.

After a month in office Breckinridge determined that invitations to parties were too numerous, that real-estate values were too high, and that Congress was too slow. A year later, his opinions—especially on Congress—had changed little: "I'm doing more now than I've done," he told a reporter, "—but with less satisfaction." The antiquity of House procedures, the fragmented leadership, the constituent problems were all frustrating at times. Long committee meetings "virtually suffocated" him during the first six months. John continued to be optimistic, however; he still believed that one man could change the system.[18]

If so, that man must work hard. Typically Breckinridge rose early, ate a hearty breakfast, and had attended various functions by eight. A speech at a congressional prayer breakfast might be followed by an 8:30 State Department briefing on some foreign situation. A half-hour later John would meet with a special caucus, then hurry to his office to sign letters, greet visitors, and talk with a constituent about black-lung benefits. Then, at ten, two simultaneous committee meetings meant that he must divide his time until noon, when the bell summoned members to the House floor for a vote. Lunch was often omitted or forgotten. The afternoon presented a similar pattern. Finally, by 11:30 P.M., just before retiring for the evening, John would sign more letters, autograph some pictures, and end his day scanning a book-length reading file prepared by staff.[19]

As part of his intellectual baggage, Breckinridge carried to his new station a philosophy that contained diverse elements of conservative and liberal thought. That mixture produced a three-session record that made him hard to characterize. Kentucky's new congressman, for example, consistently supported a strong military force. References to "Soviet imperialism," "Soviet totalitarianism," and "totalitarian Communists"

Congressman John B. Breckinridge, speaking to a Frontier Nursing Service meeting in the Old Capitol at Frankfort. Copyright 1975, *Louisville Courier-Journal*. Reprinted with permission

had dotted his early Cold War speeches. Now, years later, he still sought to counter Russian expansion, though he feared the idea of a worldwide Communist movement somewhat less. This position, coming as it did in a time of increasing sentiment in the other direction, brought him immediate attention—much of it unfavorable. Alone of the state's Democrats John voted to sustain President Nixon's veto of an appropriation bill that included an amendment to halt American military operations in Indochina. In fact, in nine defense-related votes between January and July 1973 he supported the President on seven.[20]

Breckinridge's stance on American actions in Vietnam derived from his conviction that the chief executive should be given a relatively free hand on foreign policy. He thus opposed the war-powers limitation bill that essentially restricted a president's ability to commit forces to combat. More than that, though, John believed in the war and what was being done. To withdraw aid would dishonor America and result in a South Vietnamese defeat, he asserted. But by 1975 the Kentuckian increasingly stood alone, the only member of his state's Democratic delegation to approve continued military assistance to the area; of 238 members of his party voting in a caucus only 48 joined him in that stand. But, in John's view, that did not make his convictions wrong.[21]

While the Vietnam War faded as an issue, Soviet military strength and intentions grew increasingly prominent. In the extension-of-remarks section of the 1976 *Congressional Record* Breckinridge inserted page after page of a series entitled "the Balance(s) of Power." Based on a military analyst's report, the papers warned of Russian military superiority. So strongly did John feel on this point that it became his sole message in a bicentennial letter "To the Citizens of 2076." Replete with such references as "Communist imperialism" and "Communist aggression, subversion, and incursion," the two-page letter reiterated Breckinridge's firm belief that American institutions would bring peace, liberty, justice, and equality of opportunity; Soviet totalitarianism would result in war, restriction, and enslavement. As one who had seen Eastern Europe at the end of World War II, Breckinridge considered his message top priority; all else depended on the maintenance of security. Only then could the promise be fulfilled.[22]

Breckinridge's emphasis on a stronger defense posture would gain in popularity, but in the 1973–79 period it involved mostly conflict and some unfavorable publicity in his home district. Siding on the defense issue with Republicans Richard Nixon and Gerald Ford, John's first term votes more often supported Nixon than his own party. Yet John Breckinridge was far from being a Nixonphile. Aside from his support in the area of the military and on a few other issues widely supported by southerners, John actually opposed the president a great deal more vehemently than his early record indicates. On social and consumer issues, for example,

Breckinridge followed the Democratic pattern much more frequently. He joined the majority to defeat a reduction in a proposed minimum wage bill, voted nay on an antibusing amendment, and refused to sign a petition which would release an antiabortion amendment from a subcommittee. On energy-related issues, the Kentuckian opposed the chief executive on the Alaskan oil pipeline question, on urban mass transit reductions, and on weaker automobile emission standards.[23]

And the Democrat's words matched his votes. After slightly more than three months in Congress, John voiced concern over what he presented as the president's "studied and . . . determined and purposefully duplicitous attempt to mislead" American citizens. More than a year later, he offered a critical analysis of existing economic conditions, noting that "all the President's men seem to have different solutions . . . their house is divided." But of all the issues on which Breckinridge differed from Nixon, the one that brought forth the harshest words concerned a subject close to the Kentuckian's interests, one that raised key constitutional questions. The question focused on the president's attempt to impound funds authorized by Congress. As one of the founders and the first chairman of the bipartisan Congressional Rural Caucus—one of his major accomplishments—Breckinridge now saw Nixon using the impoundment tactic to halt support of cherished rural programs. The Kentuckian struck hard at what he perceived to be an "arrogant," unconstitutional action that "diverted, subjected and throttled" legislative intent. Victory eventually came to the congressional army on this and other issues as a retreating president folded his tents.[24]

With Nixon's resignation in August 1974 and the eventual decline of the Watergate question, Breckinridge could focus on his chief interests. On defense matters, he continued to support larger expenditures; on rural questions, he spoke out forcefully for the agricultural issues—tobacco, price supports, and others—that so affected Kentucky; and he grew increasingly interested in small businesses and the problems they faced. He considered his chairmanship of the House Small Business Subcommittee on Antitrust, Consumers, and Employment one of his most important tasks. In his view, economic concentration had grown at the expense of small business; this trend, he thought, signified the need for stronger anti-trust laws—an old cry from him—and aid for the smaller businesses, "the mainstay of our competitive system." He called for reduced inflation, a revised tax rate, and fewer regulations, as partial solutions. His subcommittee held numerous hearings on the question and eventually issued through the full committee a study entitled *The Future of Small Business in America.* Dedicated to Breckinridge and his "landmark hearings," the report quickly became the most popular publication the committee had ever issued.[25]

Congressman Breckinridge's stands on small business mirrored the divergent paths he followed on various questions. On that one issue he had been the reformer calling for further regulation of the economic giants he distrusted, yet also a voice harking back to an old Progressive Era ideal of America. So it was, too, on other matters, and, as a result, his overall congressional career showed sharp changes. The statistics tell only part of the story, but they reveal much. Breckinridge's support of Conservative Coalition stands—37 percent in 1973—placed him exactly where his state stood—a border between southern and northern Democrats. But he tended to move even further from those causes as time passed. A similar picture emerged on the question of his voting with his party's majority, which rose from one year to the next (his 72 percent in 1974 exceeded the House Democratic average). On environmental matters in 1975 John's score of 61 matched the Democratic national figure but far surpassed his state's overall rating of 44. Two years later, however, Ralph Nader's Public Citizen, a consumer-advocate organization, gave Breckinridge a score of only 40 percent, below his party's national average but almost exactly in the middle of Kentucky's House delegation. The next year another consumer group ranked John at 55, far above the House's overall average of 40. And on issue after issue the pattern, in its inconsistency, held consistent. John B. Breckinridge was still a non-doctrinaire independent.[26]

In August 1977 he reassessed his political future. Now in his third congressional term, the sixty-three-year-old representative had begun to experience health problems. He could easily step down and point to genuine accomplishment in the areas of rural and small business affairs, among others. He could take pride in his advocacy of programs that were now growing in popularity. And there were negative reasons for retirement, as well: Congress continued to annoy him, with its restrictive committee system, its disorganization, its seeming confusion. John complained of being "hemmed in," of having to vote without the needed information, of a "madhouse" atmosphere. More than that, though, for the first time he faced potentially strong opposition in the Democratic primary scheduled for May 1978.[27]

Breckinridge's past reelection races had been surprisingly easy. In 1974 his challenger in the primary suffered defeat by a five-to-one ratio, and in the fall election his little-known Republican opponent, Thomas F. Rodgers, III, received no party organizational support and was soundly defeated. Potential problems darkened the outlook in 1976 when the secretary of defense proposed to reduce by 2,500 the complement at the Lexington-Bluegrass Army Depot, a chief employer in Breckinridge's district. Studies, meetings, court tests, and other self-acknowledged "dilatory" tactics by Breckinridge all failed to stop the action. The angry congressman knew the unrest of the local electorate, but the expected rebellion never materialized. Breckinridge overcame virtually unknown opposition in May; in November his only challenge came from an equally obscure candidate of the American party. The Republicans had not even entered a slate. It had been almost too simple.[28]

That history made Breckinridge's decision even more difficult in 1977. The young candidate already on the campaign trail back in Kentucky might not provide any more resistance than had others before him, and one more term would allow John to complete several of his cherished projects. In the end, perceived duty overcame personal feelings. He told his wife, "I've got to run one more time."[29]

Breckinridge's opponent in the Democratic primary was no stranger. Tom Easterly, a thirty-seven-year-old state senator from Frankfort, had once served on John's election committee and had heard potential weaknesses discussed there. The two men knew and respected each other. Now an attorney, Easterly was a former Fulbright scholar fluent in several languages and an independent like his opponent. By July 1977—some eleven months before the election—the young state senator was already hard at work. He fully realized the odds which confronted anyone trying to unseat an incumbent.[30] Breckinridge's indecision further delayed a campaign already restricted by his House of Representatives work schedule. But once the decision was made, he began the reelection race in earnest, consulting with local hospital officials, lunching with citizens groups, visiting plant sites, addressing Rotary Clubs. All the while Easterly was waging an intense "grass-roots" campaign.

The race aroused relatively little interest. It was an off-year election, the state was gearing up for the 1979 gubernatorial canvass, and the outcome seemed predictable. On 23 May 1978 the voters went to the polls to decide Breckinridge's political fate one more time. Initial returns showed a surprising Easterly lead, built chiefly on his huge 3,800-vote margin in his native Franklin County. Two hours after the polls closed, the challenger had a nearly 2,500-vote edge. But it was dwindling. A half-hour later, the difference was less than a thousand; by the time the voting machines were all tallied—but not the absentee ballots—Breckinridge trailed by about five hundred. The count of absentees followed. A final accounting left the incumbent 495 short. Easterly had won.[31]

It was a shocking defeat for Breckinridge. Observers asked how the challenger could beat a man "whose name is almost as well known to Kentuckians as those of Boone, Lincoln and Barkley?" How indeed? Analysts noted the extremely low turnout throughout the district. Even in Franklin County, where the winner polled nearly three of every four votes, participation dropped to below 30 percent of the eligible voters. Elsewhere it fell much further—to 13 percent in Fayette County, for example. Voter apathy magnified the challenger's strengths: he needed fewer votes to win. But in other ways this low turnout could have aided Breckinridge, for an incumbent congressman should be able to mobilize enough organizational support to overcome one-man challenges. Getting out the vote, however, was not something John did well. Four years earlier he had admitted after his primary victory that he had made no effort to have campaign workers at each precinct in his home county. He had done much better in 1978, but the tendency still remained.[32]

A third factor in his defeat, to some observers, was the congressman's supposed inattention to his district. Commentators argued that Breckinridge preferred "to debate the details of Soviet tanks to the handling and processing of constituent complaints." They asserted that his office did not aid—in fact perhaps hindered—his efforts. In essence, such political surveyors faulted John for being too little the politician, for not using the powers of incumbency to full advantage. And, finally, still other analysts pointed to both the concrete—Easterly outspent Breckinridge $33,577 to $13,666—and the abstract—John simply was overconfident.[33]

Nationally in 1978, over 98 percent of all House incumbents won their races in the primary; 95 percent were successful in the general election.[34] Why did Breckinridge lose? He had known the race could be difficult, but he was not prepared for such a challenge. Reelection had been so easy to that point that some of the organization he needed in 1978 simply was not there, and could not be supplied at short notice. John did face a money problem, an 1 he did have some angry constituents. Yet in the end the defeat came basically because Breckinridge did not convince his supporters that he needed their votes badly. If he expected the race to be close, John should have articulated this to the district and modified his campaigning schedule accordingly. That he did not do this satisfactorily was his failure. It was ironical that Breckinridge, who devoted so much time in Congress to those issues that he deemed vitally important for America, working for what he saw as the nation's good, underestimated the work necessary for his own reelection. Thus the problems on which he wanted to spend one more term remained unsolved, and his personal promise remained unfulfilled.

Defeat produced disappointment but not despondency. As John told Helen, "I had to run, but I didn't have to win." He had lost before; he had always rebounded to run and win again. The optimist in him saw no cause to doubt that he would repeat the pattern and become victorious once more. It was simply a matter of time. Breckinridge left his options open as he talked with reporters. They speculated that he would run for attorney general again or that he would seek to regain his congressional seat in 1980 or that he would be given a federal appointment. In January 1979 John left Congress, where his successor was ironically not Easterly, but rather the conservative Republican who had defeated Easterly in the fall.[35]

Returning to Lexington, Breckinridge came to a city that was changing in ways other than political. The town of his ancestors had remained almost unchanged for a century. It had been a sleepy, slow-paced city that reveled in its horses, aristocracy, and past. Writer A. B. Guthrie, Jr., described it in 1965 as a place where people on Main Street "seldom let business interfere with a chat."[36] The charm of an old, passing way of life, however, now combined with the stimulus of an awakened new spirit. For the established leadership, the heritage of the past was a valuable commodity worth preserving. For some commercial interests and some of the state leadership, a fresh approach was required. They sought modernization, not preservation. Low-level, service-related industry advanced in the 1950s; then the city's central location on the interstate highway system made it an attractive site for offices; later, a coal-industry boom brought more money. Soon the growth became more spectacular than steady. Burgeoning suburban areas drew businesses away from Main Street. Appalachian migrants who once went to Ohio or Michigan for work increasingly stopped at the central Bluegrass instead. A new business class developed their own social circles. Yankees found the style of life in the Bluegrass to their liking, and new arrivals and different patterns began to change Lexington's long-stolid face.

The city exploded outward, taking rural lands for shopping malls and horse farms for housing sites. Confusion and unplanned growth conflicted with patterned development. Social conflicts between old and new elites were matched by modified conditions in race relations, labor, education, and business. The small-town atmosphere where old friendships and long-standing family ties predominated now was fading. A walk down Main Street by the late 1960s might reveal only strange faces and closed stores. But the old Lexington did not vanish. Many patrician patterns of the past persisted. The race track–country club set, the old elite, the established businesses, merged with the new to form a more cosmopolitan society. Eventually the symbolic death of old Lexington— the decay of downtown—was almost forgotten as new projects brought redevelopment. The Opera House, where Willie Breckinridge had cried out for forgiveness in 1894, now remodeled, stood as only one symbol of the city's link to a past it did not want to ignore, even in times of great growth.

John B. Breckinridge symbolized that heritage, while at the same time he began to represent Lexington's metamorphosis. He did not long enjoy the new city, however. On Sunday, 29 July 1979, Breckinridge returned to Lexington from a discussion at the state capital. That night he suffered a heart attack and was pronounced dead at 9:55 P.M.[37]

Praise for the man and his life came quickly and from diverse sources. The themes were similar: sincerity, honesty, dedication, courtesy, integrity, all had marked his actions. Congresswoman Barbara Jordan remembered her colleague as a dedicated man whom "one could count on when it really mattered." Speaker of the House Tip O'Neill told his fellow members that this unpretentious man "always kept his word." Breckinridge's one-time subcommittee counsel referred to him as "a man of great moral integrity, honesty, determination and a true gentleman." From Kentucky came similar sentiments, from both allies and opponents. Governor Julian Carroll, who had defeated Breckinridge in 1971, emphasized that "no opponent was ever more of a gentleman." To Tom Easterly, he was also an opponent one could never dislike or not respect. Declared former Governor Bert Combs, "John B. Breckinridge had as much integrity and intellectual honesty as any person I've ever known in public life." Newspaper editorials proclaimed similar evaluations: "Breckinridge, Man of Principle" headlined the *Courier-Journal*; "Breckinridge Served with Integrity," pronounced the *Herald*.[38]

John had discounted the family influence on his career. "History doesn't determine what you shall do," he once said; "you determine that yourself." To his own family he rarely mentioned anything about being a Breckinridge. Yet he—and they—understood the truth of the matter. So too did others. Former Governor Ned Breathitt noted that "Kentucky has grown to expect . . . high standards of conduct from a Breckinridge. . . . John did not disappoint us." Kentucky Congressman Carl Perkins acknowledged that the surname John bore was as old as the commonwealth, and that the latest Breckinridge "added distinction and luster to it."[39]

Breckinridge's own words explained his career perhaps better than any eulogy could. Leaders of the past were great, he had suggested once, "because they believed in and activated principles relating to the good of the whole human family." He told YMCA youth in 1969 that "to have my own code of ethics and to criticize practices not in accordance with this code had been my philosophy as a public servant." Live by principles, he advised, and when principles conflict with emotions, "let your principles prevail." That philosophy was both his strength and weakness. John B. Breckinridge never attained the heights many had predicted for him. He might have, had he been more of a politician, had he compromised, had he played the party tune. His integrity and honesty often meant that only in defeat could he remain true to his principles.[40]

For that, his ancestors would have been proud. He had carried well the banner and the burden of being a Breckinridge, had brought the name and its positive connotations once more before the public, and had borne the appellation with dignity and honor. His work, like that of others in the family before him, had fulfilled the dreams that had brought Alexander Breckinridge across the sea and another John Breckinridge across those mountains so long before. Moreover, his example had inspired new generations to dream their own dreams.

SEVEN

THE FAMILY
1728-1981

She [Mary Breckinridge] does not stand alone as an individual of the twentieth century, but seems backed and surrounded and placed by a long sequence of kinfolk, past and present. . . . Hence one has a sense that twentieth century descendants are encompassed by a crowd of witnesses to uphold their standards and back their plans and purposes.

Philadelphia Ledger, 26 February 1933

Twenty-one

Dreams and Realities

IT was a strange gathering, this meeting of the Breckinridge clan that took place near Lexington on 3 September 1884. The atmosphere seemed festive and light, yet a sense of somberness lay just below the surface mood. Servants left town first, to begin preparations for lunch; then came the main body in carriages. It was an impressive entourage. From St. Louis came judge and family historian Samuel Miller Breckinridge; from his distant army post arrived Major (and later General) Joseph Cabell Breckinridge and his family; from the Bluegrass livestock breeder Dr. William Warfield joined them; from Lexington came W.C.P. Breckinridge, who would go to Washington as congressman within months, and his family, including the young Desha and Nisba. Leaving town, the procession moved slowly toward the old plantation site and the past that lay there.

On this day those Breckinridges buried at the Cabell's Dale estate would be disinterred and reunited with other family members in the lot of Robert J. Breckinridge in the Lexington Cemetery. The family gathered and watched as grave after grave was opened—fifteen in all. They saw the first John Breckinridge's coffin, with its silver handles intact. Other names passed before them—John's mother, Lettice, who had been born in 1728; John's distinguished children—John, Cabell, and many of the others who had perished so young. But two caskets received particular attention. The indomitable Mary Hopkins Cabell Breckinridge—"Grandma Black Cap"—and her sister Elizabeth Cabell Lewis—"Aunt Lewis"—had died in the very cold winters of 1858 and 1856 and had been buried in heavy metal coffins with glass plates over the faces. Now their resting places were disturbed.

The family grew quiet, the children moved closer, the adults became reflective. The glass plate on one casket was cleared and those present viewed the almost perfectly preserved body. Men and women who knew "Aunt Lewis" recognized her immediately; those who did not were marshaled to study the figure within. Then these two coffins were placed with the others and were taken to the Lexington Cemetery.

Breckinridges who had known the two women had been deeply moved by the experience at the cemetery. They recalled the stories each had told of their youth, and turned to telling their own stories, as eager youngsters listened. They "could talk of nothing else the rest of the day," according to one who was there, "except of the past so strangely recalled." And then they returned home. Behind lay an estate no longer owned by the family. Although John Breckinridge's old law office, built of logs and covered with clapboards, still stood, it seemed to a relative "lonely and forlorn, like some forgotten relic of the past." John's home had long ago burned; the law office would shortly be gone as well. The cemetery's stone walls protected little now; the old iron gate stood open. Soon ground myrtle would cover the empty graves. Only memories remained.[1]

For other families in America, an event like the one at Cabell's Dale in 1884 might have been even more symbolic, representing an end to the era in which great families dominated. In the twentieth century few patrician families could match previous achievements. They changed, or the times changed, and past glories were never recaptured in the same way. But in the case of the Breckinridges, this was not so. Family members continued prominent in state, regional, and national affairs. For them, the disinterment in 1884 would be symbolic, but not because of the empty graves, or the movement from an agrarian setting to an urban one. The memories sparked by the gathering would be enduring incentives to their generation, and their own actions to the next, and on and on. The pilgrimage in 1884 represented not a break with the past, but a rededication to a heritage.

What was it, then, about the Breckinridges that caused them to become and remain leaders over an extraordinarily long time? Every generation produced leaders: John Breckinridge (1760-1806) served as U.S. senator and cabinet officer; his son Robert (1800-1871) rose to his church's highest position and chaired the convention renominating Abraham Lincoln; John C. Breckinridge (1821-1875) was the nation's youngest vice-president and was a presidential candidate, a U.S. senator, a Confederate general and cabinet officer; Robert's son W.C.P. Breckinridge (1837-1904) represented Kentucky in Washington for a decade as a congressman; Willie's daughter Sophonisba Breckinridge (1866-1948) became a leader in social work and national reform movements; her brother Desha (1867-1935), together with his wife Madge, led the Progressive Movement in Kentucky; Mary Breckinridge (1881-1965) pioneered in the field of midwifery; and, finally, John B. Breckinridge (1913-1979) filled several state offices before his election as congressman. Many other Kentucky members of the family contributed in other ways over the years.

Why this success story? Studies of other families of similar background have presented varied, and predictable, answers that range from

Disinterment at Cabell's Dale, 1884

almost genetic ones ("something . . . had altered the cells of the Adams brains") to environmental factors (the Lowells' cosmopolitan background through travel) to physical ones (a landed estate and manor house gave a sense of family identity) to social ones (the men married well) to various other explanations. In short, those writers who have considered the question agree generally on the importance of family, of tradition, and of heritage in producing leaders, but beyond that the factors are complex and obscure.[2] Some of these explanations are useful; others do not apply at all to the Breckinridges. The Kentucky family, for example, traveled overseas little, even less perhaps than others of their class in the commonwealth. Nor did they have the benefit of a landed estate and an old family home. After John Breckinridge died in 1806, not a single major member of the family lived his or her adult life in the same home as a parent. The evidence for other answers, such as the question of genetics, is too contradictory. In the end, the multigenerational positions of power achieved by the Breckinridges resulted from a combination of factors: a regional attitude that supported them, a family environment that shaped them, a historical sense that guided them, a Breckinridge identity that nourished them, and a group philosophy that reassured them.

The prevailing environment was favorable. Historians have long noted the South's deep sense of tradition. To the refrain that citizens of the region continue to live in the dead past, poet Miller Williams replies, "Not so, the past continues to live in southerners." Family was and remains important in the South and in Kentucky. In the Bluegrass the family's road to prominence offered few detours.[3]

Patrician families have generally been most influential in agrarian or early industrial situations. Kentucky's later poverty, its ruralness (not until 1970 was its population more urban than rural), its lack of industrial progress—the very things family members attacked over the centuries—ironically served to reinforce the Breckinridges' leadership. Lexington's homogeneity and relatively small population (until only recently) added to an intergenerational transfer of ideas. What was written about the New England Adamses of the 1700s applied to the Breckinridges well into the twentieth century: "The smallness of the community . . . made the process [of gaining a reputation] far easier and more rapid."[4]

More than that, some evidence suggests that parts of the commonwealth did in fact provide unusually strong support for the family elements the Breckinridges personified. A respected professor of English history who traveled and studied widely in Great Britain and who taught many years in Kentucky recently pointed out the numerous similarities between Georgian England and his adopted state. His stress on the existence of an agrarian ethos, of a rural-oriented government, and of landed families, reinforced what others had long said. The author of an 1881 travel account, for example, wrote that the central Bluegrass towns had little industry: "they make one think of villages in rural England." Kentucky writer and Breckinridge teacher James Lane Allen spoke over a decade later of a regional landed aristocracy: "One great honored name will do nearly as much in Kentucky as in England to keep a family in peculiar respect." Another scholar wrote to an English friend that Kentuckians represented "the highest type of rural life, . . . the only region which would remind you of the best parts of your own island." Whether or not Kentucky actually resembled Old England in its physical setting and in the mind-set of its people is of less importance than the fact that educated observers perceived an unusually strong inclination among citizens to favor certain traditional families.[5]

Solid and extensive kinship patterns and beliefs reinforced that inclination. To a Kentuckian, wrote Thomas D. Clark, history "centers on his family." In many cases "his family" involves a widespread network and important leaders. As one late-nineteenth-century commentator noted, with tongue only partly in cheek, "In Kentucky all who are not related to each other are in love with one another." Occasionally, they were both. The Breckinridges' ties to the Prestons and through them to other leading families of America was not unusual for Kentucky, except in degree.[6]

In the South intermarriage among upper class families was com-monplace—a North Carolina study indicated that 80 to 125 planter fam-ilies were "closely related." Kentucky showed a similar pattern. Nor should this be surprising, for in frontier society, few upper class families had existed. Thus the choices were narrowed to marriage outside one's class or marriage within a limited circle of supposed equals. All of this operated to the Breckinridges' advantage, as their own ties brought further distinguished connections. In a land where the bloodlines of horses were discussed daily, genetic bloodlines of humans apparently attracted similar interest. Missouri's long-time congressional leader Champ Clark had been born and educated in Kentucky in such an environment, and his opinions may have reflected those of others of his generation. He believed, he wrote in 1920, that not only talent and physical ability were passed down from generation to generation, but also even more tangible things—"manners, tastes, inclinations, and ap-titudes." A minister concluded that, in Kentucky, "as nowhere else on this soil, they hold family connection as almost divine heritage."[7]

Oliver Wendell Holmes, in his *Autocrat of the Breakfast Table*, wrote that "I go (always, other things being equal) for the man who inherits family traditions and the cumulative humanities of at least four or five genera-tions." In Kentucky all things did not have to be equal for similar results to take place. A Henry Countian met a voter who wanted him to tell congressional candidate W.C.P. Breckinridge "that he could not read all your writings but could read enough to know your name was Breckinridge." In the next century FNS founder Mary Breckinridge at-tended a meeting in a mountain county at which, she recalled later, the chairman said that he did not know her, "but that my people had held 'high office' in Kentucky, and none of them had betrayed a public trust." She was thus recommended to the audience. Even representative John Bayne Breckinridge, who once wrote that when he got a case because of his "good name," that was the first tangible reward he had received from his surname—even he discovered letters from supporters who indicated that the name itself was a positive factor. To be a Breckinridge meant instant advantages in public life.[8]

Limitless success was not assured, of course. Periodically critics would complain that "hero worship and the worship of certain families" must cease. Nor did the combination of deference and democracy always work smoothly for the family. Defeats and rejections did take place. Yet the Breckinridges were fortunate in several ways. Their state and par-ticularly their region within it contained the mixture of elements that made success easier for them. Many Kentuckians apparently attached a great deal of importance to family ties and tradition in the lives of public figures. A sense of the importance of history was regarded as useful for public servants. Additionally, both those who molded current opinion and those who analyzed the past gave the Breckinridges rather consistently favorable attention on the printed page. Nor was such a situation accidental.[9]

From the earliest years on, the Breckinridges provided aid and materials for historians of the commonwealth. In one of the first important works, Lewis Collins's *Historical Sketches of Kentucky* (1847), Robert J. Breckinridge and John C. Breckinridge contributed biographical studies. The favorable sketches therein—of John, Cabell, and the Reverend John Breckinridge—were probably the product of their descendants' pens. In Richard H. Collins's massive two-volume edition of the same work (1874), W.C.P. Breckinridge received acknowledgment for aid, and sketches of additional Breckinridges appeared. By the 1880s and certainly by the 1890s, a new wave of historical awareness was sweeping the nation. Historical and genealogical societies sprang up in unprecedented numbers; interest in the past rose perceptibly. When Nathaniel Southgate Shaler wrote his 1884 history of Kentucky he, like Collins, thanked W.C.P. Breckinridge for aid. Soon thereafter a Breckinridge relative, Thomas Marshall Green, penned his history of the family, and in 1893 *The Cabells and Their Kin*—funded in part by relatives—devoted a large portion of the book to the Breckinridges. In the early 1920s Charles Kerr edited an extensive history of the commonwealth; he had studied law under W.C.P. Breckinridge. Few major historical works in that seminal 1880–1920s period did not involve a Breckinridge or Breckinridge friend in their preparation.[10]

Often that involvement took the form of allowing historians the use of the extensive family manuscript holdings. Given the poor state of archival records in Kentucky, access to such holdings could mean the difference between a superficial history or a thorough one, a dull tome or an interesting work. Even after Sophonisba Breckinridge deposited the collection in the Library of Congress in 1905, for some time permission was needed to use it. To the family's credit, that permission came readily to interested scholars. The result—though not necessarily by design—was that the first serious historical studies of the commonwealth generally devoted more attention to the Breckinridges' role in Kentucky history than was in fact deserved, and the reliance on the family manuscripts usually resulted in a favorable analysis. Clio's followers viewed history through the rosy filter of the Breckinridge papers.[11]

All of this would be vitally important to the family, for it came at a crucial time. In 1894 W.C.P. Breckinridge was in disgrace; the memory of his Unionist father, Robert, stood out as a sore point for the pro-Confederates in the state. Desha and Nisba had only begun their careers. Mary remained out of the state. A period of decline appeared evident. But historians did not let the memories fade: new works on Kentucky—often written by friends or by historians using the family papers—kept the

Breckinridge name alive. The editor of the state's historical quarterly wrote in 1908, for example, "Much was to be expected of John C. Breckinridge by Kentuckians, who believe in blood, and inherited character and talent." Four years later, the author of a multivolume history of the state invited Madge Breckinridge to write a section of that study and then himself wrote that Robert was "able, eloquent and fearless, as a Breckinridge should be, and has always been."[12]

Desha's purchase of the Lexington *Herald* proved equally propitious for the family fortunes. In its pages he praised his ancestors, provided a forum for his articulate relatives, and presented his own thoughts to an almost captive audience. (For some four decades the supportive *Herald* was virtually the sole Democratic paper in a Democratic county.) The combination of favorable historical treatment, family control of the Democratic press, and regional attitudes toward family and tradition produced a special aura that surrounded those who carried the name Breckinridge.

Into such an atmosphere were born the Breckinridge offspring. As a rule they, like most Americans, entered a nuclear family rather than an extended one. Relatives were ever-present, to be sure, but did not usually form a permanent part of a specific household. The child's basic family consisted of father, mother, and siblings. High mortality rates and short life-spans characterized many early families. In the years before 1850, for example, nearly one in three Breckinridge children (32 percent) never reached the age of ten. The next half-century saw that reduced to one child in five (20.9 percent)—still a frightful death rate for a family that could afford the best medical care (although, given the state of early medicine, such care could be counterproductive to health).[13]

Few of the early Breckinridges lived long lives, if they survived childhood. Those born before 1820 who lived past age ten died at an average age of 46.8 years—below the average for the nation or for their class. Later family mean longevity rose to resemble American norms: those born in the two decades before 1860 lived, on the average, to age fifty-nine. Those born between 1880 and 1900 lived to sixty-five.

Statistically, those who survived to adulthood entered wedlock at approximately the same age as their contemporaries. And while they seemed to have large families—Robert sired fourteen children, his son Joseph thirteen—in fact, the overall family figures did not match the national means. While their averages more nearly approach those of others of their class and education, overall the 6.6 children (1780-1820) represented less than the 7.0 American average in 1800. The roughly 3 children per family (1840-1880) similarly fell below the national average of 4.2 in 1880.[14] Almost 57 percent of these offspring were male; and, of thirteen families headed by Breckinridges, all had surviving male issue.[15]

But beyond statistics were the complex human relationships that shaped each child within the home. The intimate ties of husbands and wives varied, marked by both deep affection and strong conflict. John Breckinridge and Polly showed tensions as both partners matured and changed, although, when apart, they wrote of the undivided love between them. Their son Robert had a strong marriage with first wife, Sophy, but it is doubtful that any person could have lived with "Old Bob" without conflict. His second wife, Virginia Shelby, considered the almost unspeakable antebellum act of divorce before her death. Willie Breckinridge expressed his growing love and concern for his wife Issa, but at the same time could not resist the attractions of Madeline Pollard, his mistress.

The effects of that scandal ran deep. Of Willie Breckinridge's four still unmarried children, two never married. A third, Desha, wed, but to a woman already crippled with disease, one who bore him no children. Willie's last son, Robert, the wayward one, would marry only much later, after his return from a self-imposed exile. Contemporary relatives of that generation found problems in their marriages as well: Mary, after an apparently happy but brief union ended in her spouse's death, concluded a second marriage with the now more accepted divorce. More recently, John B. Breckinridge's first marriage ended similarly. Only the 1843-75 marriage of John C. Breckinridge remained relatively clear of conflicts within, and his immediate offspring would not vary from the familiar pattern.

If Breckinridge children saw tensions in their household, they also witnessed love. Letters that passed between husbands and wives reveal affection, though the manner of expression varied over the generations. In the early national period, John and Polly Breckinridge wrote with reserve, but in a language that could not hide their emotions. By Robert's antebellum era, Romanticism prevailed. Feelings exploded into flowery phrases, excessive sentiment, and even passionate poetry. Willie Breckinridge's post–Civil War letters spoke with neither the reserve nor the excess of earlier family members. His communications reflected his own eloquence and could withstand scrutiny by modern-day standards. And then the record speaks no more: later private family letters were mostly destroyed or have been unavailable for other reasons. Fragments suggest that later family members experienced the deep emotions and the conflicts shared by Breckinridges of the early centuries.

That continuity of human emotions contrasted with the changing mortality and age patterns, and with a modified role for women in the family. Physically, the alterations did not seem great. Breckinridge marriages begun in the decade of the 1850s, for example, show that women had their first child, on the average, a little more than fifteen months after marriage. (Over time, in eight of every nine [88.8 percent], a birth occurred within two years of marriage.) Wives would continue to bear children over the next twelve years, ending their childbearing stage of life when 37.5 years old. A sample of the same number of Breckinridge marriages in the period before 1850 surprisingly reveals almost the same figures, although the woman bore one more child, on the average, in the same period. Marriages since the 1850s reflected the same patterns as well, except that the period of childbearing dropped from 12.2 years in the 1850s to 10.4 afterwards. This meant, simply, that women of the late nineteenth and twentieth centuries spent a somewhat briefer part of their lives bearing children. Since they bore fewer children in those same decades, life for Breckinridge women was freer as time passed.[16]

Some form of birth control could have changed the nineteenth-century pattern, of course, but studies of that controversial subject still disagree on when such information was available to Americans. The first John Breckinridge's lament at the birth of another child in 1806—"I hope he is the last"—speaks of the problem, but not the solution. Maternal lactation, of course, provided a form of birth control, making the birth interval generally twenty-four to thirty months. Given the rapidity and regularity with which Robert and his wife produced their eleven children—the intervals varied little from the twenty-four-month figure—such physical controls seem obvious. Writing later, Sophonisba P. Breckinridge, born in 1866, recalled of her childhood, "There was no doctrine of birth control or spaced child bearing prevalent at that time." The subject of birth control remains, however, like much family history, hidden and private.[17]

Marriage in their twenties, a child within two years, deaths of more than one in five children, a dozen years of childbearing, almost a lifetime with children in the home—this was the history of Breckinridge wives in the nineteenth century. They toiled many hours without the aid of long-absent husbands who rode the lawyer's circuit or went to Congress. They managed home life, estate affairs, and a work force of slaves, then servants. They confronted their strong-willed husbands. They raised equally willful—and intelligent—children. In fact, the women of the Breckinridge family, thought one of its products, "have, as a rule, been the most intellectual and brilliant members." Desha Breckinridge, writing in 1926, mirrored his own Bluegrass interests when he suggested that the brains of the family "have been more largely transmitted through the female than the male line. If they wrote of the family as they do of thoroughbred families, I think it would be known more as a great dam family than a great sire family."[18]

Desha was primarily referring to the ancestors of John Breckinridge, the man who had brought the Breckinridges to Kentucky. John's background had included the important Patton-Preston women. John's own wife, Mary Hopkins Cabell Breckinridge, presented an even clearer case of the maternal influence in shaping the children's future. "Grandma

Black Cap" dominated her family and their careers. Her grandson John C. Breckinridge, the most nationally prominent member of the clan, grew up with females all around. His father dead, in a family of sisters, with a strong-willed mother and grandmother, John C. felt and echoed the influence of women. Those Breckinridges who came into the most prominence after 1850, however, reflected the paternal influence more strongly. At almost the same time the women's movement in America was formally beginning, the Breckinridge wives moved in the opposite direction. Their husbands' deaths had forced independence on the early nineteenth-century Breckinridge women. Talented, they excelled under difficult circumstances. But as the century progressed the husbands lived longer and their spouses moved back into more traditional roles. Thus it was that when Sophonisba and Mary grew to maturity, in an era much more responsive to a greater role for women in public affairs, the most available models were their fathers. The mothers of both women spoke chiefly in long-familiar, traditional, domestic terms. The fathers gave advice on public questions, on how to succeed away from the home, on life outside marriage. The ambitions of the talented daughters in a changing time dictated that they—either consciously or subconsciously—reject their mothers' world. While loving both parents, the two women idolized the fathers, for it was they who met the daughters' needs at an important time. Not surprisingly, male members of the family developed in a similar pattern. The ties between Willie and his father, then between Desha and his father Willie, remained unbreakable. Civil War hatreds, a searing sex scandal, bitter personal conflicts—none of this could destroy the image each generation had formed.

Child-rearing practices could reveal much about how these images were shaped, but the extent of contacts between parents and their children and, more important, the nature of those intrafamily contacts, remain difficult to ascertain. In the Breckinridge case, extrapolations from limited evidence offer possible interpretations, but even here the answers vary widely, as often contradicting as explaining. A study of childhood in the 1700s noted that "one is often struck by how infrequent, brief, casual, and sometimes hard-hearted are the references made to children by eighteenth-century Americans." Yet John Breckinridge's letters late in that century speak of his children frequently, centrally, and kindly. Motivations for making a still-dangerous move to Kentucky included betterment of his children's welfare. His example supports those who argue that an affectionate family environment, with children as a focus of interest, was the late eighteenth-century norm.[19]

In the next century Breckinridge child-rearing practices varied from family to family. John's wife would send her children away to school, would rule with a strong hand at home, and would demand—rather than earn—respect. Her son Robert and his son Willie would follow similar patterns, but with significant variations. In Robert's case, for example, he ruled over the male offspring with a much harsher hand than he did the females; he expected more of his sons, and the old Calvinist governed accordingly. In Willie's instance, not sexual distinctions but individual characteristics caused him to treat Ella, his first-born, and Robert, his rebellious son, differently than he did Nisba and Desha, the ones who eventually excelled in public life. And Willie responded to his last-born, Curry, in yet another way, as her sister recalled: "From the day of her birth she was the darling of the family. Discipline had been exhausted in dealing with the older children, and the baby did as she pleased. . . . That she grew up a generous-hearted, unselfish, radiant person must have been because it was impossible to spoil her." Over time, few Breckinridge parents tried to apply—or succeeded in applying—the same child-rearing tactics to each youth.[20]

Given this, any generalizations remain full of exceptions. The high levels of affection present from the first John Breckinridge's time through Mary Breckinridge's "Breckie" in the twentieth century do not, for example, negate the existence of equally high levels of authority, as Fass has noted. Family wishes may not always have overridden individual desires, but they certainly were considerations not to be discarded lightly. A sketch written twenty years after the death of Polly Breckinridge noted that "even at the advanced age of ninety, her distinguished sons were obedient to her." That three of her four sons eventually became ministers—in a family that had no past ministerial tradition—suggests her strong influence. Robert, in the next generation, displayed extreme distress—"I would a hundred times rather have died"—when a son rejected the religious career his reverend father had planned. He had expected more obedience. By the late nineteenth century, familial expectations were more realistic. Willie—the object of his father's outburst regarding his choice of occupation—tried to guide his children into suitable professions, yet basically gave them more control. His generation had seized that control; his children's would be given it. But, saying this, the variations should again be noted. Another member of Willie's generation decided that one of his children should be a doctor, another an army officer. Each son made moves in the direction his father wished, indicating the lingering strengths of family wishes. (Ironically, each became what the other was supposed to be.) The emerging pattern extends to other areas: in three out of every four families, for instance, the order of marriage of sisters followed the birth sequence. Thus, some deferential conduct certainly existed, but continuing disharmony and power struggles underscored the constant struggle between the ideal of order and authority, and the reality.[21]

The Breckinridge family, like others, began immediately to shape character in ways both visible and hidden. It is the family, as Christopher

Lasch and Lawrence Cremin have noted, that first educates and implants the modes of thought and action that may in time become accepted behavior. Subsequent conduct results, in varying degree, from this socialization process. The family teaches values and duties, as defined not only by society, but by that family's particular expectations.[22]

The Breckinridges demanded much. Some members of the family found such levels of expectation extremely difficult to meet. They feared failure and worried over whether they could live up to the past ideals that compounded in each generation. For them, their family provided feelings not of stability and strength, but rather inadequacy and insecurity. Nor were such attitudes unique to the Breckinridges. David Musto, in writing of John Quincy Adams' youth, noted that Adams "could not bring down to reality the image of his father whom he was obligated to emulate and to succeed." Or, as a Kennedy explained more recently, "Having this name brings burdens as well as opportunities."[23]

Some Breckinridges could overcome and excel; others could not. Robert, John C., Willie, Nisba, Desha, and Mary felt an inadequacy early in their lives, but ultimately they acquired the confidence of successful leaders. Others were less fortunate. Robert J. Breckinridge's son Charles acknowledged feeling "how unfortunate I was to be a member of a family where all were so well endowed with mental abilities." Willie Breckinridge felt the stings when an opponent taunted him about the scandal, and said he would rather honor an obscure family than "have the distinction of bearing unworthily the name of a distinguished ancestry." In the twentieth century Mary Breckinridge's brother, as his wife described it, simply "O. D.'ed" on the family and had little to do with it. And it may be more than coincidental that many of the "problem" children were those who carried the added albatross of being namesakes. In a family that gave a parent's name to at least one member in almost 80 percent of the cases, such situations occurred often. Rebellion against authority and parents became almost commonplace. It did, and does, as a recent family member explained, take a "great deal" of patience to raise a Breckinridge. Frequently, after a stormy youth many of the children settled as young adults into established family patterns. For others, such as Willie's son Robert, who virtually disappeared for years, the process took longer. Some never overcame the burden of being a Breckinridge.[24]

There were many family members who never reached the highest levels of achievement but who recorded important acts in their particular communities. Their actions might not receive national attention or affect the lives of great numbers of people, but numerous almost forgotten members of each generation carried on the traditions. Many transcended the local level, of course, and became important state and national figures. Central to success was their family environment and its stress on a family tradition. Some historians have argued that, in essence, no such tradition exists. It is rather "upper-class prejudice," or simply values determined not in the family but elsewhere. They suggest that an emphasis on a family tradition is a retreat from the American ideal of the self-made man toward a view that the group—not the person—determines identity and behavior.[25] At certain levels of society, such an analysis may have some validity, but for the Breckinridges—and probably for most long-established, service-oriented patrician families—a family tradition did exist. It would be difficult indeed to read the thousands of family letters and come away without recognizing the presence of a distinct, particular, family outlook transmitted across generations. The tradition changed, of course; it was interpreted differently by new generations; it may not have been accepted by all. Yet, like the family's basic structure itself, the main points remained consistent.

Breckinridges grew to maturity aware of this tradition. Some internalized it much less than others, and some, almost in spite of themselves, became imbued with it. A tradition is, of course, an abstraction, and to youngsters its meaning might be obscure. But, slowly, they saw concrete evidence that increased their awareness and revealed what the tradition was expected to mean for them. In the home where Robert J. Breckinridge grew up, the somber portraits of family members looked down from the walls of a large reception hall, attracting the attention of even the youngest. His son Willie recalled that at age seven he traveled with his father the same road used by John Breckinridge when he first came to the Bluegrass State fifty years before; almost a half-century after his own trip, Willie still recalled the strong emotions resulting from that experience. The family letters were saved and made available for youngsters to read. Books shared the same experience: John Breckinridge's 1788 copy of the debates in Virginia on the federal Constitution, for example, was passed down to his son Robert, then to John C. Breckinridge, W.C.P., Desha (in 1921), Scott, and, in 1941, John Bayne Breckinridge. In many ways, those actions did more to develop a sense of tradition than any of the other physical actions.[26]

But primarily the Breckinridges learned from other family members, who told stories of past glories and present standards. To eager children, made a part of the adult world by the accounts, it mattered little whether some of what they heard was not altogether accurate. What was important was the story itself—an account filled with ancestors who did important things in an exciting way. The Breckinridge talent in oral presentations made it all even more interesting, as they sat around an open fire or on a vine-shaded veranda. From such narratives a cultural heritage was transmitted through the generations. One of Willie's daughters recalled that she would creep along, "making myself as small as possible, for fear of being noticed and sent away," and would listen to the grown-ups talk of the past. The very perceptive Sophonisba Breckinridge, in writing her autobiography, recognized the importance of such occasions. She discussed her ancestors, Nisba commented, "because they meant so much not only in the way of my inheritance but because they meant so much in my conscious experience."[27]

Others, outside the family, added to this awareness of family achievement. Desha Breckinridge, who died in 1935, recounted that he had talked once to some very elderly men whose eyes filled with tears as they told the young boy about his ancestors. A former slave related similar stories, stretching back nearly a century. Mary Breckinridge, whose death occurred three decades later than Desha's, was raised by the same black nurse who had reared her mother. Visitors to the household added to this sense of history. Breckinridge children saw some of America's leaders visit them, saw them converse with their parents as equals, saw them as men and women with their own frailties. Early associations taught the children that, like John C. Breckinridge, they too were "the peer of presidents." His granddaughter Mary remembered that her first childhood recollections were of discussions of national problems in her parents' home. With living examples to lead them, with past ones to guide further, the Breckinridges faced the public with a strong sense of confidence that emanated from a powerful childhood environment.[28]

With that confidence came a sense of history. History, to them, was alive and spoke to them directly. Characters in the historical pageant were seldom strangers. Breckinridge ancestors had been a part of the whole national fabric. Some attempted to go beyond all this and to write history as well. In his numerous writings Robert touched upon the subject. Willie, devoted to a memory, began a biography of his father, though he never completed it. Sophonisba—working at a time when "social science" was replacing "history" in the curriculum, and when it was thought necessary for subject matter to address social problems—worked diligently both to preserve the family papers and to write from them. She understood the forces shaping her own life and sought to learn more about herself by studying that past. Nisba, too, began a biography of her father and, later, an autobiography. Her brother Desha frequently gave talks of a historical nature and penned editorials critical of Kentucky's feeble efforts to preserve its "historic treasures." Mary Breckinridge, admitting that history was her favorite subject, also spoke on historical topics and told a friend in 1934, "We cannot understand our twentieth century, even a wee bit, without a profound study . . . of the 19th." In the 1960s John Bayne Breckinridge addressed the Kentucky Young Historians, a group he had helped to found, and warned of the national tendency to ignore state and regional history—that "which gives our Commonwealth its character." Nearly a decade later he made a similar plea for more teaching of history in the schools. The family knew the importance of history in their lives and sought to insure that other citizens would reap similar benefits.[29]

This sense of history combined with a sense of tradition to produce a multigenerational family identity. In 1822, at the age of twenty-two, Robert told an audience that what their forebears achieved "is ours to maintain." Posterity would demand that they transmit "unimpaired" the heritage they received. Later, in the midst of the Civil War, he attempted to dispel the stigma that his nephew—the "traitor" John C.—had attached to the family name. "The blood that I inherit and the name I bear," he emphasized, "render it wholly impossible that I could see my country suffer." After the war's end, shortly before his own death, Robert gave son Willie his opinion of five generations of the family: "In the aggregate they are equal to any thing." Clifton Breckinridge, son of a vice-president and himself later a congressman and diplomat, told parent John C.: "I desire— from ambition . . . to perpetuate the reputation of our family." To his dying father, he subsequently wrote: "None of us, my father, may bear your name with as much distinction as you have borne it; but we will try."[30]

"We are a believer in blood," Willie Breckinridge proclaimed. He placed faith (albeit qualified faith) in an intellectual heredity, in a "predisposition" to progress, in a tendency to advocate change. In 1902 he told Nisba that "the name has been connected with good intellectual work for some generations—for over a century;—you must preserve this connection for the next generation." Only months before his death the orator-editor suggested that "each one is a composite product of past ages and of all who have gone before." Desha wrote, "We are inheritors of the past, heirs of all its glory, joint tenants of all its achievements." References to John Breckinridge and others of the clan frequented his editorial columns. At almost the same time Mary's brother Carson Breckinridge wrote, "I have never forgotten that I must try to be what my Father and my Mother would have me be." Abundantly aware of who and what they were, they tried to achieve what was expected of them.[31]

The public recognized this Breckinridge attribute as well. The children upon maturity moved into the public arena and found that their associations with a name and a tradition gave instant advantages, ones which multiplied over the years. Thus, when Breckinridges made a plea for support, responses usually proved positive. Even when the opposition claimed that individuals did not measure up to their Breckinridge past, they nevertheless acknowledged the strength of that tradition. In a field of unknown competitors, before a people conscious of their history, such Breckinridge advantages could make the vital difference. Talent also had to be present, and family members recognized this. One relative wrote in the late nineteenth century that family influences were important "only so far as the public discerned in the individual the valuable characteristics common to his kindred." In 1902 Willie Breckinridge concluded that, in the end, "we make our own inner life and from this spring our outer deeds and our uttered words." Some seventy years later the next Breckinridge congressman told a reporter that his father had stressed the importance of a sense of responsibility to what the family stood for, but that "history doesn't determine what you shall do; you determine that yourself."[32]

In a sense, though, history gave them the strength to determine their own destiny. From their traditions and past, Breckinridges received motivation, guidance, and an advantageous political and public name. As an intimate friend noted of the family members she had known: "All were very conscious of their name and their heritage and were very proud and anxious to carry on . . . to the next generation the same ideas they grew up with. And their ideas of service—it wasn't light and frivolous—they really felt consciously they should carry on their ideas." Another friend wrote of Willie's daughter's work in the Appalachian mountains: "If you knew the love the members of the Breckinridge family have for Kentucky and if you knew well the utter desire Curry has to serve others in the name of Kentucky . . . you would not wonder that she is happy." And as John Bayne Breckinridge's brother expressed it, "There was a subconscious quality that you wanted to [and] had to do it." It is these attitudes and aspects of behavior that are so difficult to discern in records, but which are powerful forces in the family. Their existence would be vitally important for state and nation; those Breckinridges who attained success did not ignore Henry Clay's advice to John C. Breckinridge: "Be true to your name," wrote the Great Commoner. "Never forget that you are a Kentuckian and a Breckinridge."[33]

Out of that background, a family philosophy emerged and remained remarkably stable over decades, even centuries. What Henry Adams called "the family mind," what a recent scholar termed "the family myth," what the Breckinridges simply referred to as "blood"—this resulted in a confidence that gave family members the strength to achieve. The family philosophy grew across generations, was adapted to a changing environment, and emerged in restructured form, over the years. When young Breckinridges sought to understand the society around them, the family's basic philosophical outline stood ready to serve as at least a temporary instructor. Many adapted it for their own age, and the result was that in the family—an institution very resistant to change—a philosophy developed that proved equally enduring.[34]

Historian Bell I. Wiley once remarked that if the thousands of Civil War letters were tossed in the air and fell to the earth without identification, the sentiments, emotions, and thoughts would be so similar that one would not know whether the writer was Rebel or Yankee. The same confusion would ensue if Breckinridge manuscripts, from 1760 to 1980, suffered the same fate. The words would speak eloquently the philosophy all members could identify. What was written of the Lodges of Massachusetts applies also to the Breckinridges of Kentucky, and probably other families as well: "Change a few names here, an idiom or two there, and the speeches of his great-grandson . . . and those of his great-great-great-grandsons . . . echo the thought of the patriarch himself."[35]

In the Breckinridge papers the same images and phrases dot speeches and writings over the generations. Robert's disgust with "third rate politicians" found repetition in his son's attacks on William Goebel as a "third rate leader." John C.'s portrayal of Lincoln's "German mercenaries" was matched by Willie's talk of Goebel's Hessian mercenaries. Desha's plea that Kentucky's "mines must be opened, her mountains tunnelled" echoed his father's call for Kentucky to "dig into her mountain sides and develop her inexhaustible mineral wealth." From the first John through the last, able Breckinridges attacked the "negativism" of the opposition; the term might allude to John's Federalist enemies, John C.'s Republicans, Robert's "fanatics," Willie's Goebelites, Nisba's conservative opponents, Desha's state politicians of both parties, Mary's medical critics, or John B. Breckinridge's political ones.

But the family philosophy involved more than words. It was a world view that incorporated aspects of politics, religion, education, and the arts generally. Involvement in education, for example, went back to the basic belief that an educated citizen made the most intelligent choices, ones that served to better the community. An instructed public would support proper laws, would abhor violence and force, and would protect themselves from any attempt to usurp their rights. That Breckinridges believed those choices would necessarily involve selection of them to political and other public office did not slow their support, of course. But it went beyond that. They supported educational advancement because they sincerely believed in its benefits. In the 1790s John Breckinridge served on the Board of Curators of what is now Transylvania University; his son Cabell was on the board as well as the law faculty; another son, Robert, sat on the board and led the state's educational reforms as superintendent of public instruction. John C. Breckinridge also filled a position on Transylvania's board, while W.C.P. Breckinridge was a trustee, taught at the school, served on the Board of Visitors of what would become the University of Kentucky, and strongly supported education in his congressional votes; his daughter Sophonisba through her position on the faculty of the University of Chicago educated hundreds of social reformers; her brother Desha editorialized long and hard for better educational facilities in Kentucky; through the spoken rather than the written word, Congressman John Bayne Breckinridge did much the same thing. He argued in 1971, for example, that education was the primary issue in his election race.

Education was but one thread of several reform strands woven into the Breckinridge tapestry. Prison improvement, free speech, the ideal of public service over private gain—these and other causes enabled family members to march in support of change—if within the perceived bounds of their tradition. At other times, the same voices fought the forces of reform. "Radical" change, fomented by "demagogues" of negativism, became the Breckinridges' enemy as often as did the reactionaries whose fear of change they criticized. John's opposition to the more democratic second Kentucky constitution, John C.'s support for slavery, Robert's anti-Catholic and anti-immigrant attacks, Willie's equating the free-silver movement with communism, Desha's call for black disfranchisement, Mary's tacit acceptance of the Appalachian status quo—all amply demonstrate the Breckinridges' other side. Conservative strands introduced another weave into the fabric.

The resulting mixture of conservatism and reformism proved, however, to be an attractive blend for both the family and the citizens of their state and nation. American history, as Arthur Dudden has pointed out, has often incorporated two seemingly contradictory elements: the idea of progress and the search for stability, or as he called it, "a deep-running tide of *nostalgia*." Such elements appeared in the Revolutionary War period when a search for the old, English ways (as they were thought to exist) coupled with a quest for new forms to produce revolt. Similarly, the Civil War represented, at least in part, a struggle between both worlds. By the late nineteenth century, the idea of progress united with a longing for a simpler past time, in Robert Wiebe's "search for order." Similar cycles have marked this century's history.[36]

The Breckinridges benefited from this part of America's make-up. They could speak for the idea of progress, could call for change, yet still satisfy the urge for stability. Their past made them recognizable as the carriers of tradition, as safe, secure, sound, but seldom reactionary. Post–Civil War family members increasingly pictured the past glories of their nation and state, and wrapped their reforms in the clothes of nostalgia. Their actions were thus designed to recapture lost and past glories; they made reform appealing to both liberal and conservative elements. To follow a Breckinridge meant that Americans did not have to attack their past in order to progress into their future.

The overall pattern of the Breckinridges' philosophy was shaped by an optimistic view of the future tempered by a pessimism stemming from their religious and moral outlook—the Calvinism of their Presbyterian background. They spoke of a world of predestination and absolute standards. "That which we see," W.C.P. Breckinridge told a Presbyterian General Assembly in 1888, "and our fathers have seen, which we and our children are to see, was not produced by some blind chance. . . . All was . . . perfectly provided for." "There is no luck in the Divine economy, and no accident in the progress of events." Every human being was assigned to a peculiar place, to do his or her particular duty, and over this the person "had no control."[37] Not all Breckinridges held such views so strongly, but in varying gradations the attitude was present, even in those who appeared to reject it. And the step from such beliefs in a religious context to ones in secular areas was anything but long. "One absolute standard of right and wrong" to Breckinridges usually meant their standard. They seldom doubted themselves, and compromise could be difficult. A belief in a kind of predestination, however muted, could quickly lead to the conclusion that the course pursued was the course approved by the Almighty. A strict interpretation of the Bible could transfer easily to similar views about a Constitution seen as equally sacred. At the same time, as a Breckinridge relative wrote in 1889, Calvinism did much else: "Making all men lowly before Him, it renders them high and before kings. Extinguishing fear, making final triumph certain, . . . it gives strength." The political and social philosophies of the Breckinridges coincided with this religious philosophy, each to reinforce the other.[38]

This philosophical background alone would have doomed the Breckinridges. It needed a second element, the optimism many family members displayed. When John Breckinridge told his wife in 1806 to "view the bright side of things," he expressed an attitude that sustained the family for centuries. Calvinist Robert J. Breckinridge gazed at "stars that glimmer thro' the horrors of this Egyptian darkness, which may guide us along the dazzling pinnacle of fame." The next generation, though tested by the hatreds of war and the reconstruction of their society, proved even more hopeful. Willie Breckinridge predicted that the "river of human history" would always flow toward freedom—of the soul, of the will, of the intellect. In the 1890s, after going through the worst crisis of his life Willie still spoke boldly and optimistically. To a daughter who was on her way to becoming a major force in social reform he wrote, "You must not permit yourself to grow morbid, nor get into the habit of looking at the dark side of life. We will all pull together & all will come right." In the twentieth century, this same view prevailed. His wife said of John B. Breckinridge, "Nothing ever got him down."[39]

This belief in progress, in evolution, in an optimistic future, constantly grappled in Breckinridge minds and hearts with the feeling that this "vile world" might not move forward, or upward, after all. Pessimism sometimes tempered the optimism. Thus a sense of despair over "man's depravity" met head on this faith in the future. Individuals had to work to the end that the future would be better than the past. This was, after all, the duty of a Breckinridge. Such an outlook drove the family to pursue aims that few could oppose. Who would debate the view of John Breckin-

Direct descendants of the Breckinridges, Lexington, 1981. Photograph by J.N.E. Prichard

ridge, who wanted better lives for his children; of Robert J., who wanted a world free of racial and political slavery; of John C., who wanted a government of laws; of W.C.P., who wanted a world where children would see grander things than had their parents; of the childless Desha, who wanted an improved temple of democracy for future generations; of Sophonisba, who wanted fairness not just for the few but the many; of Mary, who wanted not death but health as the rule for the mountain families; and of John B., who wanted a secure nation that would be a guide for the world? While these visions might lead to errors or to delusions, they spoke for an optimistic, uplifting spirit, in which good works were done not only for concrete rewards but also for important abstractions—respect, honor, and family.[40]

Robert said in 1844, "There are three things which every human being may obtain: the favor of God, the approbation of conscience, and the applause of the good. With these life is truly glorious; without them it has neither dignity nor grace." John B. Breckinridge, some 127 years later, expressed the view for his generation: "They may change from generation to generation. But basically they're the same problems arising out of ignorance and prejudice and bias and selfishness and avariciousness. And every generation that comes along behind its predecessor will have in it that vanguard that will contain within it the seed of progress. . . . And each of us pursues that course which . . . circumstances impose and dictate without even knowing it."[41]

On 11 June 1981 the "Kentucky Homecoming of the Descendants of John and Mary Cabell Breckinridge" began in Lexington. Almost a hundred family members, from twenty states and Hong Kong, joined over a dozen guests to celebrate the gathering. Appropriately, they first went to a race track, where the uninitiated quickly learned—like Desha earlier—that a winning bet did not come automatically to a Breckinridge. The next day formal ceremonies began at Transylvania University with the dedication there of a Breckinridge Room. As in the past, historians of the family were honored by the family and, in turn, honored them. Lowell H. Harrison, biographer of John, Frank Heck and William C. Davis, chroniclers of John C., and even the author of a then-unpublished history of the family spoke of the past to both the young, who knew little, and the old, who sought more.

Lunch took place within sight of the old Cabell's Dale farm. A trip to Mt. Horeb Presbyterian Church placed family members in the sanctuary founded by their ancestors a hundred and fifty years before. Then they moved, like the caravan from Cabell's Dale almost a century earlier, to the Lexington Cemetery. There lay "Grandma Black Cap" and all the rest. In the quiet beauty of the site, the young peered at the graves, amused, confused, and, at times, awed. Their elders remembered some of the men and women buried around them and talked of the past. At the evening meal, the last speaker asked, "Is not that man successful also who by his valor, moderation, and courage, with all their associate virtues, presents to the world such a specimen of true manhood as his children and children's children will be proud to emulate?" He concluded, "You Breckinridges are not really of the blood of Kentucky; rather, Kentucky is of your blood. . . . It is an association which . . . will continue to . . . do enduring honor to you both."

The next morning buses and automobiles took family members to the Frontier Nursing Service headquarters and to Mary Breckinridge's partially restored Wendover. Even the cool of the shade and the breezes over a quiet river could not overcome the heat of a June day in the mountains, but the weather did not drive the visitors away. They lingered on, some to recall once more the memories the Big House held for them, others to imagine what it all had been like in those early days of the FNS. But finally it was back along the dirt road to the paved one, then to the interstate highway and on to the Bluegrass for the reunion's end. The family quickly scattered to their towns across America. Kentucky no longer was home for most. Nor were they involved in the same professions as in the past: among all living descendants only one minister and no elected official could be located.

But if the family had changed, it had also remained the same. The reunion stressed that unity. The people exhibited it, and the historians present understood it. Perhaps the most memorable event had occurred spontaneously, as the event was nearing its end. Just before the group went to hear the last speakers, an attorney rose to give an impromptu summation and appreciation to those involved. He quoted his former mentor, John Bayne Breckinridge, dead now some two years, a man known to many of those in attendance. He told how he once asked Breckinridge, after a defeat, why he continued to go on. "His answer was that in the last analysis it was all for family."[42]

It had not been all for family. Other motives operated as well. But without family it would have all been very different.

Appendix 1. Breckinridge Longevity and Child-Bearing

BRECKINRIDGE LONGEVITY
(for those over age 10)

Year Born	Age at Death (Mean)	No. in Sample
1780-1819	46.8	9
1820-1839	58.0	21
1840-1859	59.0	27
1860-1879	61.8	29
1880-1899	64.9	51

BRECKINRIDGE FAMILY SIZE

Year of Birth of Breckinridge Parent	No. of Children	No. in Sample
1780-1819	6.6	9
1820-1839	4.2[a]	22
1840-1859	2.9[b]	21
1860-1879	3.2	18
1880-1899	2.0	39
1900-1919	2.6	28
1920-1939	2.9	35

[a] Four of the 22 had no children. Those who had children averaged 5.1 children.
[b] Three of the 21 had no children. Those who had children averaged 3.4 children.

CHILD-BEARING IN BRECKINRIDGE FAMILIES

Family of	Wife's Child-bearing Years	Mean Months Between Births	Number in Sample
John Breckinridge	1786-1806	30.9	7
J. Cabell Breckinridge	1812-1824	28.8	5
Robert J. Breckinridge	1824-1844	23.9	10
William Breckinridge	1825-1849	26.4	9
John Breckinridge	1826-1832	32.0	2
Robert J. Breckinridge			
Marie Breckinridge (Handy)	1858-1873	23.0	7
W. C. P. Breckinridge	1860-1875	25.9	7
Joseph C. Breckinridge	1869-1890	20.6	11

Note: Incomplete data, in a few instances, resulted in estimates; e.g., a child was listed as being born in 1812, the next in July 1814.

Appendix 2. Abbreviated Breckinridge Genealogy

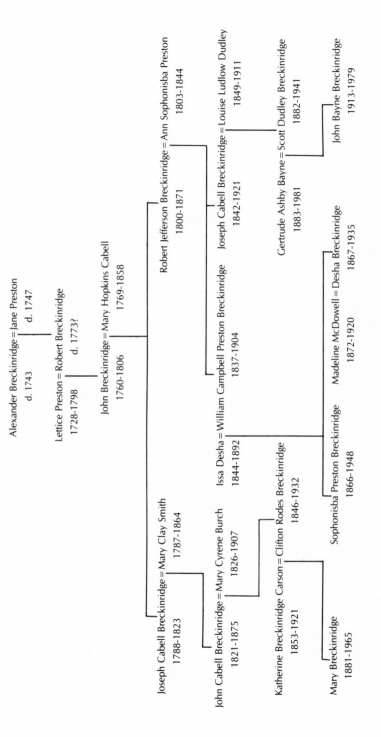

Alexander Breckinridge = Jane Preston
d. 1743   d. 1747

Lettice Preston = Robert Breckinridge
1728-1798   d. 1773?

John Breckinridge = Mary Hopkins Cabell
1760-1806   1769-1858

Robert Jefferson Breckinridge = Ann Sophonisba Preston
1800-1871   1803-1844

Joseph Cabell Breckinridge = Louise Ludlow Dudley
1842-1921   1849-1911

Gertrude Ashby Bayne = Scott Dudley Breckinridge
1883-1981   1882-1941

John Bayne Breckinridge
1913-1979

Joseph Cabell Breckinridge = Mary Clay Smith
1788-1823   1787-1864

John Cabell Breckinridge = Mary Cyrene Burch
1821-1875   1826-1907

Issa Desha = William Campbell Preston Breckinridge
1844-1892   1837-1904

Madeline McDowell = Desha Breckinridge
1872-1920   1867-1935

Katherine Breckinridge Carson = Clifton Rodes Breckinridge
1853-1921   1846-1932

Sophonisba Preston Breckinridge
1866-1948

Mary Breckinridge
1881-1965

Notes

Abbreviations

B.MSS	Breckinridge Family Papers, Manuscript Division, Library of Congress
DB	Desha Breckinridge (1867-1935)
FC	The Filson Club, Louisville
FCHQ	*The Filson Club History Quarterly*
Herald	The Lexington *Morning Herald* and *Herald*
JB	John Breckinridge (1760-1806)
JBB	John Bayne Breckinridge (1913-1979)
JCB	John Cabell Breckinridge (1821-1875)
KHS	Kentucky Historical Society, Frankfort
LC	Manuscript Division, Library of Congress
MB	Mary Breckinridge (1881-1965)
Register	*The Register of the Kentucky Historical Society*
RJB	Robert Jefferson Breckinridge (1800-1871)
SPB	Sophonisba Preston Breckinridge (1866-1948)
UK	Margaret I. King Library, University of Kentucky

Preface

1. *Biographical Sketch of Hon. John C. Breckinridge of Kentucky* (1860), 5; J. W. Brock to W.C.P. Breckinridge, 18 March 1884, vol. 332, Breckinridge Family Papers (hereinafter B.MSS) (Manuscript Division, Library of Congress [hereinafter LC]; Lexington *Herald*, 1 March 1914, 27 November 1920, 10 August 1955, 30 July 1979 (hereinafter *Herald*).

2. Stephen Hess includes the Breckinridges, for example, in his *America's Political Dynasties from Adams to Kennedy* (1966).

3. Ronald D. Cohen review of *The Randolphs of Virginia*, in *History* 1 (1973): 63 (first quotation); Peter N. Stearns, "Toward a Wider Vision: Trends in Social History," in Michael Kammen, ed., *The Past Before Us: Contemporary Historical Writing in the United States* (1980), 218; Edward N. Saveth, "The Problem of American Family History," *American Quarterly* 21 (1969): 312; Saveth, "Varieties of Family History," *Reviews in American History* 1 (1973): 345 (second quotation).

4. Christopher Lasch, "The Family and History," *New York Review of Books* (13 November 1975), 33. See John Demos, "The American Family in Past Time," *American Scholar* 43 (1974): 422-46; E. Anthony Wrigley, "Reflections on the History of the Family," *Daedalus* 106 (1977): 71-85; Maris A. Vinovskis, "From Household Size to the Life Course: Some Observations on Recent Trends in Family History," *American Behavioral Scientist* 21 (1977): 263-87; Lawrence Stone, "Family History in the 1980s: Past Achievements and Future Trends," *Journal of Interdisciplinary History* 12 (1981): 51-87.

5. James R. McGovern, *Yankee Family* (1975), i; Edward Pessen, "Some Critical Reflec-

tions on the New Histories," *South Atlantic Quarterly* 78 (1979): 482. One attempt to bridge the two historical approaches is Randolph Shipley Klein's good *Portrait of an Early American Family: The Shippens of Pennsylvania Across Five Generations* (1975).

6. Saveth, "Varieties of Family History," 343, writes: "One way [of solving problems of family history] is to cut and prune the family tree so that the history is limited to those members . . . who express . . . the most prominent feature of family identity. . . . [This] is admittedly arbitrary. But is it any more artificial than the historian arguing a thesis?"

7. Harold D. Woodman, "Class, Social Change, and Family History," *Reviews in American History* 11 (1983): 236.

8. Ferris Greenslet, *The Lowells and Their Seven Worlds* (1946), v.

1. Americans

1. John Breckinridge (hereinafter cited as JB) to James Breckinridge, 17 August 1788, vol. 5, B.MSS; JB to James Breckinridge, 10 February 1789, John Breckinridge Papers (UK).

2. Mary H. Breckinridge to Lettice Breckinridge, March 1789, vol. 5, B.MSS.

3. JB to Lettice Breckinridge, 7 May 1789, vol. 5, B.MSS; Lowell Harrison, *John Breckinridge, Jeffersonian Republican* (1969), 29.

4. JB to Lettice Breckinridge, 19 August 1792, vol. 8, B.MSS; JB to George Thompson, 29 March 1792, Thompson Papers (University of Michigan).

5. Malcolm J. Rohrbough, *The Trans-Appalachian Frontier: People, Societies, and Institutions, 1775-1850* (1978), 23, 18, 4; Johann David Schaepf, *Travels in the Confederation*, translated and edited by Alfred J. Morrison (1911; orig. pub. in 1788), 261; John Bakeless, *Background to Glory: The Life of George Rogers Clark* (1957), 31; Samuel Meredith to JB [1791], vol. 7, B.MSS.

6. Arthur K. Moore, *The Frontier Mind: A Cultural Analysis of the Kentucky Frontiersman* (1957), 23; William E. Connelley and E. Merton Coulter, *History of Kentucky*, 5 vols. (1922), 1:379.

7. William Gilmore Simms, "Daniel Boon; The First Hunter of Kentucky," *Southern and Western Magazine and Review* 1 (1845): 230; Otis K. Rice, *Frontier Kentucky* (1975), 122.

8. On the question of frontier democracy, see John D. Barnhart, "Frontiersmen and Planters in the Foundation of Kentucky," *Journal of Southern History* 7 (1941): 19-36, and his *Valley of Democracy: The Frontier Versus the Plantation in the Ohio Valley, 1775-1818* (1953); Thomas B. Abernethy, *Three Virginia Frontiers* (1940), 64-76, and his "Democracy and the Southern Frontier," *Journal of Southern History* 14 (1938): 7, 10-11; and Patricia Watlington, *The Partisan Spirit: Kentucky Politics, 1779-1792* (1972).

9. JB to Joseph Cabell, Jr., 23 July 1793 (copy), vol. 9, B.MSS; JB to Joseph Cabell, 10 May 1793, Breckinridge-Marshall Papers (FC); Lexington *Kentucky Gazette*, 6 April 1793 (hereinafter *Kentucky Gazette*).

10. "Journal of General Butler," *The Olden Time* 2 (1847) (entry of October 1785): 451; Mary Coburn Dewees, *Journal of a trip from Philadelphia to Lexington in Kentucky . . . in 1787* (1936), 15; *National Gazette* in Eugene L. Schwaab and Jacqueline Bull, eds., *Travels in the Old South*, 2 vols. (1973), 1:53; F. A. Michaux, "Travels to the West of the Allegheny Mountains . . . the Year 1802," in Reuben G. Thwaites, ed., *Early Western Travels, 1748-1846*, 32 vols. (1904), 3:195; Needham Parry's Diary, 3 June 1794, Kentucky Papers, Draper Collection, 14CC2 (State Historical Society of Wisconsin microfilm); André Michaux, "Journal of Travels into Kentucky: July 15, 1793–April 11, 1796," in Thwaites, *Early Western Travels*, 3:36; Harry Toulmin, *A Description of Kentucky in North America* (1793), 85-87.

11. William Russell to JB, 29 August 1792, vol. 8, B.MSS; Charles R. Staples, *History of Pioneer Lexington, 1779-1806* (1939), 93.

12. Richard C. Wade, *The Urban Frontier: The Rise of Western Cities, 1790-1830* (1959), 18-20, 142, 330-31, 140; Hazel Dicken Garcia, "A 'Great Deal of Money . . .': Notes on Kentucky Costs, 1786-1792," *Register* 77 (1979): 186-87; Toulmin, *Description of Kentucky*, 26.

13. JB to Joseph Cabell, Jr., 23 July 1793, vol. 9, B.MSS; JB to Joseph Cabell, 10 May 1793, Breckinridge-Marshall Papers.

14. To avoid confusion and numerous uses of *sic*, the varied spellings of the name have been changed in the text to "Breckinridge." For background on the name itself see "The Name and Family of Breckenridge or Breckinridge," B.MSS; Scott D. Breckinridge, "Breckinridge Family Memorandum" (copy in author's possession), 1-2; and George F. Black, *The Surnames of Scotland: Their Origin, Meaning, and History* (1946), 96.

15. Ethelbert Dudley Warfield, *The Kentucky Resolutions of 1798*, 2d ed. (1894), 50; Thomas Marshall Green, *A Sketch of the Breckinridge Family* (c. 1887-1904), 1.

16. James M. Breckenridge, *William Clark Breckenridge . . . His Life, Lineage and Writings* (1932), 116; W.C.P. Breckinridge to James M. Breckenridge, 13 December 1901, Breckenridge Family Papers (Joint Collection, University of Missouri-State Historical Society of Missouri); Lyman Chalkley, *Chronicles of the Scotch-Irish Settlement in Virginia*, 3 vols. (1912-13), 2:372; Green, *Sketch of Breckinridge Family*, 2-3; Howard M. Wilson, *The Tinkling Spring: Headwater of Freedom . . . 1732-1952* (1954), 418, 424; "Ancestry of Col. Wm. Campbell Preston Breckinridge," B.MSS boxes.

17. Clayton Torrence, comp., *Virginia Wills and Administrations, 1632-1800* (1930), 50; Green, *Sketch of Breckinridge Family*, 6; Chalkley, *Chronicles*, 2:377, 416; 1:33, 46, 70, 69, 77; F. B. Kegley, *Kegley's Virginia Frontier* (1938), 79-80, 299, 314-16, 542-43.

18. See Joseph A. Waddell, *Annals of Augusta County, Virginia* (1886), 81-83, 90-91, 95; "The Official Records of Robert Dinwiddie," *Collections of the Virginia Historical Society*, N.S., 4 (1884): 531n; Lewis P. Summers, *Annals of Southwest Virginia, 1769-1800* (1929), 300; John M. Brown, *Memoranda of the Preston Family* (1870), 5-7; John F. Dorman, *The Prestons of Smithfield and Greenfield* (1982), 1-6; Chalkley, *Chronicles*, 2:276; and Draper MSS, 16CC9. Lettice P. Breckinridge's gravestone in the Lexington Cemetery indicates she was born in 1728 in Ireland. Since Robert's father had probably married a Preston and his first wife's father had also, the ties were further entwined.

19. Chalkley, *Chronicles*, 1:306; Letitia Floyd (William Preston's daughter) to Rush Floyd, 22 February 1843, George Rogers Clark Papers, Draper MSS, 6J89-108; "List of Revolutionary Soldiers of Virginia (Supplement)," *Special Report of the Department of Archives and History for 1912* (1913), 43; John F. Dorman, comp., *Virginia Revolutionary Pension Applications* (1965), 10:1; A.C. Quisenberry, comp., *Revolutionary Soldiers in Kentucky* (1895), 1, 3, 7; Kentucky *House Journal*, 1st Sess.(1792), 3; 2nd Sess., 31; J. Stoddard Johnston, ed., *Memorial History of Louisville*, 2 vols. (1896), 1:124, 233; 2:44.

20. Letitia Floyd to Rush Floyd, 22 February 1843, Draper MSS; Robert J. Breckinridge sketch on early family history, May 1845, B.MSS.

21. Alexander Brown, *The Cabells and Their Kin* (1895), 256; Summers, *Annals*, 59-71; Waddell, *Annals*, 131-32.

22. Summers, *Annals*, 122; *Kegley's Virginia Frontier*, 385-86; bill of sale from David Ross, 16 August 1771, vol. 1, B.MSS.

23. Andrew Lewis to William Preston, 20 August 1772, Preston Papers, Draper MSS, 2QQ135; *Kegley's Virginia Frontier*, 508-10, has the will.

24. Letitia Floyd to Rush Floyd, 22 February 1843, Draper MSS; William Preston (surveyor of Montgomery County) nomination of John Breckinridge, 10 January 1780, vol. 1, B.MSS; "Calendar of Early Jefferson County, Kentucky, Wills," *FCHQ* 6 (1932): 202; John Brown to William Preston, 17 March 1780, Preston Papers, Draper MSS, 5QQ22.

25. JB to William Preston, 22 April 1781, Preston Papers, Draper MSS, 5QQ94.

26. JB to Lettice Breckinridge, 7 June 1781, vol. 1, B.MSS; Earl G. Swem and John Williams, *A Register of the General Assembly of Virginia, 1776-1918* (1918), 13-15.

27. JB to Lettice Breckinridge, 9 February and 28 May 1783, vol. 1, B.MSS.

28. JB to Lettice Breckinridge, 17 March, 16 May 1784, vol. 2, B.MSS; Harrison, *John Breckinridge*, 13.

29. MS entitled "What is the Best form of Government?" dated 6 January 1784, vol. 2, B.MSS.

30. "On the Impost," 9 February 1784, vol. 2, B.MSS.

31. "Rules of the Constitutional Society of Virginia," in Robert A. Rutland and others, ed., *The Papers of James Madison* (1962-), 8:71-72, 72n; "On Demand of the Governor of South Carolina," dated February, 3, 9 April 1784, vol.2, B.MSS.

32. Henry Steele Commager, "Leadership in Eighteenth-Century America and Today," *Daedalus* 90 (1961): 652-62; Charles S. Sydnor, *American Revolutionaries in the Making* (1965), 19, 74-75; Summers, *Annals*, 398; Brown, *Cabells and Their Kin*, 232, 236.

33. Albemarle County Personal Property Tax List, 1786, Virginia State Library; *Kegley's Virginia Frontier*, 546-47. In 1790 when Breckinridge held 10 bondsmen, the average number of slaves owned by slaveholding families in Virginia was 8.5. Sydnor, *American Revolutionaries*, 142n.

34. Alexander Breckinridge to JB, 3 November 1784; William Breckinridge to JB, 9 August 1784, vol. 2, B.MSS; Johnston, *History of Louisville*, 2:3; William Breckinridge to Lettice Breckinridge, 22 December 1784, vol. 2, B.MSS.

35. Certificate of Election of "John Brackinridge," dated February 1792, in William P. Palmer, ed., *Calendar of Virginia State Papers* (1885), 5: 499.

2. Kentuckians

1. JB to Mary Cabell, 26 April 1798 (copy), vol. 16, B.MSS; Fayette County Tax Books, 1794-97, 1799, 1801-02 (KHS microfilm).

2. Agreement between John Breckinridge and Robert Russell, 30 October 1804 (copy made in 1889), vol. 26, B.MSS.

3. Albemarle County Tax List, 1786; Fayette County Tax Books, 1793, 1806; *Kentucky Gazette*, 21 February 1798, 30 March 1801; Harrison, *John Breckinridge*, 123; agreement with "Capt. Banks," June 1801, vol. 20, B.MSS; Fayette County Tax Books, 1804; Jockey Club dues, 24 August 1804, B.MSS boxes; *Kentucky Gazette*, 23 July 1802.

4. "What is the best form of Government?" 6 January 1784, vol. 2, B.MSS; JB to James Breckinridge, 11 July 1790 (typed copy), Evans Papers (UK).

5. John D. Wright, Jr., *Transylvania: Tutor to the West* (1975), 8-32; "Records of the proceedings of the Board of Trustees for the Transylvania Seminary," 1793-1797 (Transylvania University); William Leavy, "Memoir of Lexington and Its Vicinity," Nina Visscher, ed., *Register* 41 (1943): 129; George W. Ranck, *History of Lexington, Kentucky* (1872), 194. Breckinridge's own children learned from tutors.

6. Harrison, *John Breckinridge*, 33, 50-52, has a fine discussion of Breckinridge's law practice and of the land problems of the time.

7. George M. Chinn, *Kentucky: Settlement and Statehood* (1975), 29, 426; W[illiam] D. G[allagher], "An Historical Sketch of the Early Settlements and Early Men of Kentucky," *The Hesperian* 2 (1838): 89-91.

8. *Reprints of Littell's Political Transactions In and Concerning Kentucky* . . . , Filson Club Publications Number 31 (1926), 62-64, 66-68, *passim*.

9. See Thomas D. Clark, *A History of Kentucky*, rev. ed. (1960), 80, 85; Stuart S. Sprague, "Senator John Brown of Kentucky, 1757-1837: A Political Biography" (Ph.D. dissertation, New York University, 1972), 76n.

10. James Breckinridge to JB, 13 June 1788, vol. 5, B.MSS; John Brown to Jefferson, 10 August 1788, in Julian P. Boyd, ed., *The Papers of Thomas Jefferson* (1950-), 13: 494. On the "Conspiracy" see *Littell's Transactions*; John M. Brown, *The Political Beginnings of Kentucky*, Filson Club Publications Number 6 (1890); Thomas M. Green, *The Spanish Conspiracy* (1891); William R. Shepherd, "Wilkinson and the Beginnings of the Spanish Conspiracy," *American Historical Review* 9 (1904): 490-506; Watlington, *Partisan Spirit*, 140-60; Arthur P. Whitaker, *The Spanish-American Frontier: 1783-1795* (1927, reprinted in 1962), 116-18; Deposition of John Means, vol. 22, Harry Innes Papers (LC).

11. *Kentucky Gazette*, 24, 31 August 1793.

12. James T. Flexner, *George Washington: Anguish and Farewell* (1972), 182.

13. Eugene P. Link, *Democratic-Republican Societies, 1790-1800* (1942), 73, 73n; E. Merton Coulter, "The Efforts of the Democratic Societies of the West to Open the Navigation of the Mississippi," *Mississippi Valley Historical Review* 11 (1924): 381, 388n; *Kentucky Gazette*, 16 November 1793.

14. Philip S. Foner, ed., *The Democratic-Republican Societies, 1790-1800* (1976), 363-66.

15. Flexner, *Washington*, 52; George Rogers Clark to [the French minister], 5 February 1793; General Clark's claims, Draper MSS, 55J35.

16. James White to Gayoso de Lemos, 1 February 1794, in Lawrence Kinnaird, ed., "Spain in the Mississippi Valley, 1765-1794," *Annual Report of the American Historical Association for the Year 1945*, 4 vols. (1946), 4:253; Flexner, *Washington*, 158; John Nicholas to JB, 15 July 1794, vol. 10, B.MSS.

17. JB to Samuel Hopkins, 15 September 1794, vol. 11, B.MSS.

18. JB to Monroe, 15 January 1796, Monroe Papers (LC, microfilm edition Series 1, Reel 1).

19. Executive Journal, 30 November 1797, Papers of the Governors of Kentucky: James Garrard (Public Records Division, Department for Libraries and Archives); *Kentucky Gazette*, 2, 16 December 1797; certificates of election, Executive Papers, Garrard's Papers; *Kentucky Gazette*, 2 May 1798.

20. JB to Monroe, 20 July 1798, Monroe Papers (copy in vol. 16, B.MSS); James Morton Smith, "The Grass Roots Origins of the Kentucky Resolutions," *William and Mary Quarterly*, 3d Series 27 (1970): 223; *Kentucky Gazette*, 8 August 1798.

21. Mary H. Breckinridge to JB, 26 August 1798, vol. 16, B.MSS; Jefferson to Joseph Cabell Breckinridge, 11 December 1821, vol. 43, B.MSS; Nicholas to JB, 10 October 1798, vol. 16, B.MSS; Nicholas to Jefferson, 4 October 1798, cited in Edward Channing, "Kentucky Resolution of 1798," *American Historical Review* 20 (1915): 333-36. Harrison, *John Breckinridge*, 75-84, has a fine discussion of the controversy.

His son Cabell's belief in his father's authorship caused his 1821 query to Jefferson (above). In 1877 one of John's grandsons told a questioner that Jefferson's "memory or his veracity was at fault," for John Breckinridge drafted them while the man from Monticello only changed the language of the original. W.C.P. Breckinridge to P. Donan, 3 May 1877, in *Weekly Maysville* [Ky] *Eagle*, 30 May 1877. John Breckinridge's wife never doubted her husband's authorship according to relative Ethelbert D. Warfield, "The Authorship of the Kentucky Resolutions of 1798," *Magazine of Western History* 3 (1886): 581.

22. Draft, mistakenly dated "[July 1799?]," Vol. 18, B.MSS; Frankfort *Palladium* 13, 20 November 1798; *Kentucky Gazette*, 14 November 1798. Paul L. Ford, ed., *Works of Thomas Jefferson* (1904) 8:458-79, has both the Jefferson draft and Breckinridge's version. See also Ethelbert D. Warfield, "John Breckinridge: A Democrat of the Old Regime," *Magazine of American History* 14 (1885): 197.

23. Warfield, *Kentucky Resolutions*, 163; Reuben T. Durrett, "The Resolutions of 1798 and 1799," *The Southern Bivouac* 1 (1886): 579; Smith, "Grass Roots Origins," 238-45; Jefferson to Nicholas, 29 November 1798, in Ford, *The Works of Thomas Jefferson* 8:483. See also James A. Van Kirk, "The Public Career of John Breckinridge" (Ph.D. dissertation, Northwestern University, 1937), 145n, 150.

24. JB to Tazewell, 2 December 1798 (copy), vol. 17, B.MSS.

25. *Kentucky Gazette*, 28 November 1799. Adrienne Koch and Harry Ammon, "The Virginia and Kentucky Resolutions," *William and Mary Quarterly*, 3d Series 5 (1958): 169-75, suggest that Breckinridge "was not the author," and Noble E. Cunningham, Jr., *The Jeffersonian Republicans: The Formation of Party Organization, 1789-1801* (1957), 136-37, argues for Jefferson as primary author. Harrison, *John Breckinridge*, 83-84, seems to support the view that his subject authored the document.

26. *Kentucky Gazette*, 28 November 1799.

3. Politician and Parent

1. Nathaniel Henderson Petition, 21 November 1778, in James R. Robertson, *Petitions of the Early Inhabitants of Kentucky to the General Assembly of Virginia, 1769 to 1792*, Filson Club Publications Number 27 (1914), 44-45; Winthrop D. Jordan, *White Over Black: American Attitudes Toward the Negro, 1550-1812* (1968), xii, 341, 429-38.

2. J. Winston Coleman, Jr., *Slavery Times in Kentucky* (1940), 4; John Bakeless, *Daniel Boone* (1939), 329; Charles Gano Talbert, *Benjamin Logan: Kentucky Frontiersman* (1962), 22; Chinn, *Settlement and Statehood*, 131; Census Bureau, *A Century of Population Growth . . . 1790-1900* (1909), 82, 222.

3. William Littell, *Statute Law of Kentucky*, 3 vols. (1809), 1:21-38; Asa Martin, *The Anti-Slavery Movement in Kentucky Prior to 1850*, Filson Club Publications Number 29 (1918), 13-17.

4. JB to Lettice Breckinridge, 18 March, 19 August 1972, vol. 8, B.MSS.

5. William Russell to JB, 29 August 1792, vol. 8, B.MSS; Albemarle County Personal Property Tax List 1786 (Virginia State Library); Fayette County Tax Books, 1793, 1795, 1799 (KHS microfilm); Fayette County Will Book A, Inventory of late John Breckinridge, April 1807 (UK microfilm), 419; *Century of Population Growth*, 135; JB to William Breckinridge, 10 September 1797, John Breckinridge Papers (UK).

6. Agreement between John Breckinridge and James Busby, 15 August 1793, vol. 9, B.MSS; *Kentucky Gazette*, 22 August 1795; Agreement dated 20 June 1801, vol. 20, B.MSS; Lowell H. Harrison, ed., "John Breckinridge's Bluegrass Plantation, Agreement to Operate, 1806," *FCHQ* 31 (1957): 104-14, original in vol. 30, B.MSS.

7. JB to Lettice Breckinridge, 14 June 1786, vol. 3; "Instructions for John Payne in my Absence—Oct. 18, 1806," vol. 30, both in B.MSS; George M. Fredrickson, *The Black Image in the White Mind: The Debate on Afro-American Character and Destiny, 1817-1914* (1971), 1-2, 43-70; James Breckinridge to JB, 19 February 1798, vol. 16; John Green to JB, 22 November 1802, vol. 22, both in B.MSS.

8. Robert McColley, *Slavery and Jeffersonian Virginia*, 2d ed. (1973), 204-5; Joan Wells Coward, *Kentucky in the New Republic: The Process of Constitution Making* (1979), 107.

9. *Kentucky Gazette*, 21 February 1798; JB to Samuel Meredith, 7 August 1796 (copy), vol. 14, B.MSS.

10. JB to Shelby, 11 March 1798, Isaac Shelby Papers, Reuben T. Durrett Collection (University of Chicago), copy in vol. 16, B.MSS.

11. "Sidney" in *Kentucky Gazette*, 9 May 1798, 11 April 1799. For the reaction to Breckinridge's attacks see 1798 broadsides, "To the Citizens of Fayette County," "A Tenant," and "Hampden" in Durrett Collection.

12. Frankfort *Palladium* and *Kentucky Gazette* of 16 May 1799; "Resolves," June 1799, vol. 17, B.MSS; Richard R. Beeman, *The Old Dominion and the New Nation, 1788-1801* (1972), 34, 222.

13. An excellent discussion of the convention is found in Coward, *Kentucky in the New Republic*, 124-61.

14. "Mem. of debates in the Convention which commenced 22nd July 1799," vol. 18, B.MSS; *Kentucky Gazette*, 1, 8 August 1799; Coward, *Kentucky in the New Republic*, 138-59.

15. *Kentucky Gazette*, 16 November 1793; *Laws of Kentucky* (1799), 11-27; Parry Diary, 10 June 1794; Harrison, *John Breckinridge*, 86-87; Kentucky *House Journal* (1797-98), 55, 61, 101.

16. *The Biography of Elder David Purviance . . . Written by Himself* (1848), 21; Frankfort *Palladium*, 25 November 1800.

17. JB to James Breckinridge, 25 January 1788, vol. 3, and 21 November 1800, vol. 19, both in B.MSS; *Kentucky Gazette*, 26 December 1799; "Memorandum of Suits Given to Clay by John Breckinridge," 20 February 1800, in James F. Hopkins, Mary W. M. Hargreaves, and Robert Seager II, eds., (*The Papers of Henry Clay* 1959-), 1: 22.

18. Warfield, *Kentucky Resolutions*, 70-71; Durrett, "Resolutions of 1798 and 1799," 764-65; Robert J. Breckinridge, "The Third Defense of Robert Breckinridge," *Spirit of the XIX Century* 2 (1843): 50; John Shane interview with Thomas Marshall, Draper MSS, 16CC239; William Allen, *A History of Kentucky* (1872), 59; Desha Breckinridge, "John Breckinridge," Lexington *Herald*, 9 December 1923; Purviance, *Biography*, 22; Dumas Malone, *Jefferson the President: First Term, 1801-1805* (1970), 112-20; *Annals of Congress*, 7th Cong., 1st Sess., 23-29, 97-99.

19. Monroe to JB, 15 January 1802, vol. 21, B.MSS; *Annals of Congress*, 7th Cong., 1st Sess., 179, 183, 1306.

20. *Kentucky Gazette*, 7 December 1802; James Garrard to Breckinridge and John Brown, 3 January 1803, vol. 23, B.MSS.

21. JB to Thomas Todd, 20 January 1803 (copy), vol. 23; JB to James Monroe, 9 July 1803 (copy), vol. 24; JB to Jefferson, 10 September 1803 (copy), vol. 24, all in B.MSS.

22. Jefferson to JB, 12 August 1803, Jefferson Collection (University of Michigan); Malone, *Jefferson*, 328.

23. *Annals of Congress*, 8th Cong., 1st Sess., 60, 65, 73.

24. Jefferson to JB, 24, 25 November 1803, vol. 25, B.MSS; *National Intelligencer*, 4 January 1804.

25. E. S. Brown, "Senate Debate on the Government of Louisiana, 1804," *American Historical Review* 22 (1917): 345-54; Brown, ed., *William Plumer's Memorandum of Proceedings in the United States Senate, 1803-1807* (1923), 129, 140.

26. *Kentucky Gazette*, 20 July 1803; Randolph to Monroe, 28 February 1804, Monroe Papers; Taylor to Nicholas, 15 March 1804, Edgehill-Randolph Papers (University of Virginia).

27. *Kentucky Gazette*, 22 May, 3, 10, 17 July, 21 August, 11 September 1804; JB to editor of the *Palladium*, 5 July 1804, vol. 26, B.MSS; JB to Monroe, 8 September 1804, Monroe Papers.

28. Jefferson to JB, 7 August 1805, vol. 28, B.MSS.

29. Leonard D. White, *The Jeffersonians: A Study in Administrative History* (1951), 336; Harrison, *John Breckinridge*, 188-91; Letters from and Opinions of Attorneys General, 1791-1811, Record Group 60 (National Archives); Brown, *Plumer's Memorandum*, 478-79 (8 April 1806); 474-75 (4 April 1806); Jefferson to JB, 10 April 1806; Abraham Baldwin to JB, 15 April 1806, vol. 30, B.MSS.

30. JB to Mary H. Breckinridge, quoted in Van Kirk, "John Breckinridge," 367.

31. "The Life and Time of Robert B. McAfee and His Family Connections," *Register* 25 (1927): 128; *Kentucky Gazette*, 14 December 1793, 4 January 1794; JB to James Breckinridge, 10 March 1794, vol. 10, B.MSS.

32. Brown, *Cabells and Their Kin*, 497, 500, 511, 236, 487; JB to James Breckinridge, 21 May 1800 (copy) (in possession of Mr. and Mrs. John Marshall Prewitt, Mt. Sterling, Ky.); JB to James Breckinridge, 23 August 1806, vol. 30, B.MSS; Fayette County Will Book A (1807), 420.

33. Mary H. Breckinridge to Lettice Breckinridge, March 1789; Mary H. Breckinridge to JB, 12 April 1789, vol. 5, B.MSS; Autobiography of General [James] Taylor (University of Chicago, microfilm copy in FC), 22.

34. Mary H. Breckinridge to JB, 14 September 1789, vol. 16; JB to Mary H. Breckinridge, 30 December 1803, vol. 25, both in B.MSS.

35. JB to Mary H. Breckinridge, 15 November 1804, vol. 27; JB to Mary H. Breckinridge, 6 February 1806, vol. 30, B.MSS.

36. JB to Mary H. Breckinridge, 20 February 1806, vol. 29, B.MSS.

37. *Ibid.*, 25 July 1806; JB to J. Cabell Breckinridge, 30 August 1806, both in vol. 30, B.MSS.

38. "Instructions for John Payne in my Absence—Oct. 18, 1806," vol. 30, B.MSS; John Shane interview with Thomas Marshall (Breckinridge's doctor), Kentucky Papers, Draper MSS, 16CC240; Mary Ann Castleman to Eliza Lewis, 29 July 1813, vol. 33, B.MSS, *Kentucky Gazette*, 15 December 1806.

4. The Jaws of Death

1. Unidentified clipping written by Ethelbert D. Warfield (great-grandson of Mary H. Breckinridge), located in the Kentucky Historical Society's copy of John Brown, *Memoranda of the Preston Family*; Elizabeth M. Simpson, *Bluegrass Houses and Their Traditions* (1932), 19; John Breckinridge Castleman, *Active Service* (1917), 21, 31; Ethelbert D. Warfield, *Joseph Cabell Breckinridge, Junior . . . A Brief Story of A Short Life* (1898), 6. Actually, Polly Breckinridge, sometime in the 1825-28 period, suffered a serious illness that resulted in the loss of three teeth, all of her hair, and some sight. See Mary H. Breckinridge to Patsy McDowell, 7 January [1825?], Breckinridge Family Papers (UK).

2. Robert Davidson, *History of the Presbyterian Church in the State of Kentucky* (1847), 361-64; "John Breckinridge," *Dictionary of American Biography;* clipping, Autograph Collection of Simon Gratz (Historical Society of Pennsylvania); James W. Alexander, "A Discourse in Memory of the Late Reverend John Breckinridge, D.D. . . . on the Last Day of January, 1842," *Spirit of the XIX Century* 1 (1842): 340; Robert J. Breckinridge (hereinafter RJB) to Rev. Stephen Williams, 5 August 1841, Robert Jefferson Breckinridge Collection (Chicago Historical Society).

3. "William Lewis Breckinridge," *Twentieth Century Biographical Directory of Notable Americans* (1904), vol. 1; Johnston, *History of Louisville,* 2:73, 156; Diary of Nancy Wilson Brown, 10 August 1863 (in the possession of Wilanna Brown of Waddy, Ky., in April 1978 and since destroyed by fire. Copy in my possession).

4. Brown, *Cabells and Their Kin,* 487-88, 497; Mary H. Breckinridge and Letitia P. B. Grayson to Eliza Meredith, 27 February [1818?] (copy), Evans Papers; Lexington *Reporter,* 14 February 1816.

5. William Breckinridge to RJB, 22 March 1841, vol. 91, B.MSS; JB to James Breckinridge, 21 May 1800 (copy), Prewitt Collection; John Shane interview with Richard Butler (September 1858), Kentucky Papers, Draper MSS, 15CC50, 16CC71.

6. Shane interviews with Robert J. Breckinridge, 1858, 16CC58-59; Dr. A. Young, 11CC234; and Dr. Louis Marshall, 16CC241; all in Draper MSS; questionnaire about Robert J. Breckinridge (circa 1878), B.MSS boxes; Benjamin B. Warfield, "R.J.B. Notes," Warfield Collection (in possession of Robert B. Warfield, Lexington); Henry Adams, *History of the United States of America During the Administration of Jefferson and Madison,* 9 vols. (1889-90), 1:192-93.

7. David Castleman (his guardian and brother-in-law) to RJB, 19 December 1817, vol. 36, B.MSS; Shane interviews with Abraham Van Meter, 1856 (11CC203); Dr. Elijah Stack (14CC27), and Robert J. Breckinridge (16CC58), all in Draper MSS; Edmund A. Moore, "The Earlier Life of Robert J. Breckinridge, 1800-1845" (Ph.D. dissertation, University of Chicago, 1932), 6-8.

8. "Various Memoranda—1830," B.MSS boxes.

9. J. Cabell Breckinridge to RJB, 15 August 1822, vol. 45, B.MSS; Lexington *Kentucky Reporter,* 31 March 1823. Cousin marriages occurred in over 12 percent of the cases in the South for this generation. See Catherine Clinton, *The Plantation Mistress* (1982), 233.

10. William B. Preston, *The Preston Genealogy* (1900), 141-217; Orlando Brown, *Memoranda of the Preston Family* (1842), 3-10; "The Preston Family," in J. Lewis Peyton, *History of Augusta County, Virginia,* 2d ed. (1953), 303-7.

11. "Various Memoranda—1830," boxes; RJB to Ann Sophonisba Preston Breckinridge (hereinafter Sophy), 16 May 1824, vol. 50, both in B.MSS.

12. "An Oration on the Formation of a National Character, to be delivered at the reception of the degree of A.M. . . . July 10th 1822" (FC).

13. Detailed surveys of this period appear in Frank F. Mathias, "The Turbulent Years of Kentucky Politics, 1820-1850" (Ph.D. dissertation, University of Kentucky, 1966); Wallace B. Turner, "Kentucky in a Decade of Change, 1850-1860" (Ph.D. dissertation, University of Kentucky, 1954); Clark, *History of Kentucky,* 144-54, 290-306; Robert M. Ireland, *The County Courts in Antebellum Kentucky* (1972).

14. RJB to Sophy Breckinridge, 21, 22 July 1825, vol. 52, B.MSS.

15. Arndt M. Stickles, *The Critical Court Struggle in Kentucky, 1819-1829* (1929), *passim.* Frank Mathias, "Turbulent Years," 75-79, notes that of the eight anti-relief counties that voted that way both in 1820 and 1824, seven voted Whig in the next seven gubernatorial races.

16. Lexington *Kentucky Reporter,* 18 July 1825; *Kentucky House Journal* (1825-26), 25, 152; Frankfort *Patriot,* 3 April 1826. See also Frankfort *Spirit of '76,* 28 April 1826.

17. Hunt to Jackson, 27 August 1827, in John Spencer Bassett, ed., *Correspondence to Andrew Jackson,* 6 vols. (1926-33), 3:379-80. Accounts also appear in Elizabeth O. Boggs to "brother," 10 August 1827, Lilburn W. Boggs Papers (Missouri Historical Society, St. Louis) and J. M. McCalla to RJB, vol. 91, B.MSS.

18. *Kentucky House Journal* (1828-29), 342-43.

19. Military Commission dated 16 May 1822, vol. 44; document dated 30 July 1822, vol. 45, both in B.MSS; Lewis and Richard H. Collins, *History of Kentucky,* 2 vols. (1874), 1:525-26.

20. Jefferson to John Adams, 17 May 1818, in Andrew A. Lipscomb, ed. *The Writings of Thomas Jefferson,* 20 vols. (1903), 15:168-69; Niels Henry Sonne, *Liberal Kentucky, 1780-1828* (1939), 160-261; Wright, *Transylvania,* 87-118.

21. "Various Memoranda," B.MSS boxes; Sophy Breckinridge to RJB, 28 April, 15, 24 December 1828, vol. 55, B.MSS.

22. Ann Breckinridge to RJB, 13 September 1823, vol. 49, "Various Memoranda," boxes. Sophy Breckinridge told her sister-in-law Letitia Porter on 31 May 1831 that she lost "both my other darlings in the absence of my husband." vol. 58, B.MSS. The first, Francis, died in Virginia on 27 July 1825. See RJB to John Mason Brown, 22 July 1869, B.MSS boxes.

23. "Various Memoranda," B.MSS boxes.

24. RJB to Sophy Breckinridge, 31 December 1829, vol. 56, B.MSS

25. John B. Boles, *The Great Revival, 1787-1805* (1972), 1-93; Boles, *Religion in Antebellum Kentucky* (1976), 16-30; Colin Brummitt Goodykoontz, *Home Missions on the American Frontier* (1939), 127.

26. Francis Butler Simkins and Charles Pierce Roland, *A History of the South,* rev. ed. (1972), 154-59; Boles, *Religion in Antebellum Kentucky,* 32, 142; Sonne, *Liberal Kentucky,* 9, 260-61.

27. The fullest studies of Robert J. Breckinridge's career are chiefly unpublished ones: Edgar C. Mayse, "Robert Jefferson Breckinridge: American Presbyterian Controversialist" (Ph.D. dissertation, Union Theological Seminary in Virginia, 1974); Moore, "The Earlier Life of Robert J. Breckinridge, 1800-1845"; Robert W. Miles, incomplete manuscript biography of Robert J. Breckinridge, Robert W. Miles Papers (UK); and Will D. Gilliam, "Robert J. Breckinridge: Conservative Non-Conformer" (manuscript, *ibid.,* copy in my possession). I am indebted to these studies for insights and interpretations much more than my footnotes indicate.

28. RJB, "A Discourse on the Formation and Developement [sic] of the American Mind . . . ," *Baltimore Literary and Relgious Magazine* 3 (1837): 497; RJB, "Politics and the Church," *Danville Quarterly Review,* 2 (1862), 614; RJB, "Some Thoughts on the Development of the Presbyterian Church in the U.S.A.," *Southern Presbyterian Review,* 2 (1848), 311-40; William Breckinridge to RJB, 14 January 1850; RJB to William Breckinridge, 21 January 1850, vol. 136, B.MSS.

29. RJB, *The Knowledge of God Subjectively Considered* (1859), 148, 317; Gilliam, "Robert Jefferson Breckinridge, Part I," *Register* 72 (1974): 220-21; Ernest Troeltsch, *The Social Teachings of the Christian Church,* trans. Olive Wyon, 2 vols. (1931), 2:589, 620. See also Ralph B. Perry, *Puritanism and Democracy* (1944), 252-53.

5. A Great Thing to Be a Kentuckian

1. David M. Potter, *The Impending Crisis, 1848-1861,* ed. and completed by Don E. Fehrenbacher (1976) *passim;* Allan Nevins, *Ordeal of the Union,* 2 vols. (1947), 1:34-112; 2:515-54.

2. Mayse, "Robert Jefferson Breckinridge," 11-15, 363n; Ralph Henry Gabriel, *The Course of American Democratic Thought* (1940), 14-38.

3. RJB, "A Discourse on the American Mind," 481-508.

4. *Baltimore Literary and Religious Magazine* 2 (1836): 2.

5. *Ibid.,* 1 (1835): 153.

6. Rev. John Breckinridge, *A Discussion of the Question Is The Roman Catholic Religion . . . Inimical to Civil or Religious Liberty* (1855, orig. pub. 1836), quotations on 60, 543. See also Alice Felt Tyler, *Freedom's Ferment* (1944), 368.

7. RJB, *Memoranda of Foreign Travel,* 2 vols. (1845), 2:125, 216-17, 229, 249, 200-201.

8. RJB, *Papism in the XIX Century, in the United States* (1841), 21, 25, 206; RJB, "An Address to the American People," *Baltimore Literary and Religious Magazine* 2 (1836): 148.

9. Sophy Breckinridge to Sarah H. Preston, 9 June 1836, vol. 72; RJB to Sophy Breckinridge, 3 October 1838, vol. 78, both B.MSS; RJB to John C. Breckinridge, 5 June 1843, vol. 106, B.MSS; RJB to Thornwell, 24 July 1846, in B. M. Palmer, *The Life and Letters of James Hensley Thornwell* (1875), 291; RJB to Thornwell, 16 March 1849, vol. 133, B.MSS. On the eve of many important occasions—such as his first law case and a crucial debate—Breckinridge displayed symptoms of illness, suggesting that his ailments may have been not always physically induced.

10. RJB to Mary Breckinridge, 16 April 1850, vol. 137; RJB to Sophonisba Breckinridge (daughter), 17 December 1851, vol. 143; RJB to Thornwell, 16 January 1852, vol. 144, all in B.MSS; RJB to [J.J.?] Bullock, 13 January 1854, Bullock Collection (UK); RJB to W. C. P. Breckinridge, 28 January 1856, vol. 181, and 27 November 1857, vol. 199, B.MSS; RJB to Sophy Breckinridge, 31 December 1829, vol. 56, B.MSS. See also Lewis O. Saum, "Death in The Popular Mind of Pre-Civil War America," *American Quarterly* 26 (1974): 477-95.

11. Moore, "The Earlier Life of Robert J. Breckinridge," 112.

12. The case can be followed in the *Baltimore Literary and Religious Magazine* 6 (1840): 17, 120, 182-89, 193-200; RJB to James H. Thornwell, 3 April 1843, vol. 104, B.MSS.

13. RJB to Sophy Breckinridge, 13 December 1837, vol. 75, 1 September 1841, vol. 93, RJB to William C. Preston, 24 January 1845, vol. 116, all in B.MSS; William L. Breckinridge, "In Memorandum . . . Mrs. Ann Sophonisba Breckinridge." The fourth child, John, had died on 25 July 1833. See John Wilson to James McDowell, 25 July 1833, Breckinridge Collection (UK).

14. RJB to Thornwell, 17 October 1842, vol. 101; RJB to B. M. Smith, 23 January 1843, vol. 103, B.MSS.

15. William Breckinridge to RJB, 14 December 1844, vol. 115; 4 February 1845, vol. 116; RJB to Sophy Breckinridge, 11 June 1843, vol. 106, all in B.MSS; *Catalogue of the Officers and Students of Jefferson College* (1846); Mary Breckinridge to RJB, 11 November 1845, vol. 119, RJB to S. R. Williams, 3 August 1847, vol. 128, B.MSS. Robert had been a candidate for the president's position at Transylvania University in 1840 (see RJB to Sophy Breckinridge, 31 January 1840, and John C. Breckinridge to RJB, 17 February 1840, vol. 84, B.MSS).

16. W. H. West to RJB, 30 December 1846, vol. 126; John C. Breckinridge to RJB, 20 February 1847; John C. Darby to RJB, 15 May 1847, both vol. 127; Board of Trustees Resolution, 8 June 1847, vol. 128; RJB to S. R. Williams, 9 October 1846, vol. 125, B.MSS.

17. The poems appear in vol. 121, B.MSS and the Grigsby Collection (FC). Virginia Shelby to RJB, 18 November 1845, vol. 119, B.MSS; RJB to a Colonel and Mrs. Thompson, 27 January 1846, Grigsby Collection.

18. RJB to Virginia Shelby, 26 February 1846, Grigsby Collection; Virginia Shelby to RJB, 11, 23 March 1846, vol. 122, B.MSS. See her letter to Robert, 15 April 1846 (vol. 122), B.MSS, and his of 27 July 1846, Grigsby Collection; Virginia Shelby to RJB, 22, 25 December 1846, vol. 126, 27 February 1847, vol. 127, 7, 12, January 1847, vol. 126, B.MSS; Draper MSS, 16CC369.

19. Virginia Shelby to RJB, 12, 30 January 1847, vol. 126, 16 March 1847, and 13 February 1847, vol. 127, B.MSS.

20. John C. Breckinridge to RJB, 8 April 1848, vol. 130; Mary Breckinridge to RJB, 13 April 1847, vol. 127; RJB to John Mason Brown, 22 July 1869, boxes; RJB to W. C. P. Breckinridge, 9 January 1857, vol. 191 and 18 January 1859, boxes; Virginia Shelby Breckinridge to RJB, 4 January 1849, vol. 133; RJB, "Memorandum of an Interview, with Col Grigsby . . . on the 20th 1856," boxes all in B.MSS; Virginia Breckinridge to J. Warren Grigsby, 27 September 1856, Grigsby Collection; RJB to John C. Breckinridge, 28 September 1856, vol. 187, B.MSS. See also Jane Turner Censer, " 'Smiling through the Tears': Ante-Bellum Southern Women and Divorce," *American Journal of Legal History* 25 (1981): 24-47.

21. Frankfort *Kentucky Yeoman*, 16 September 1847; Kentucky *House Journal* (1827-28), 351-52; Moses E. Ligon, *History of Public Education in Kentucky* (1942), 81-92; William H. Vaughan, *Robert Jefferson Breckinridge as an Educational Administrator* (1937), 40, 65-66, 41. Robert's niece Caroline Breckinridge had married the state's first superintendent, J. J. Bullock.

22. RJB to S. R. Williams, 29 September 1848, vol. 132, B.MSS; Vaughan, *Breckinridge as*

Educational Administrator, 68-70; Edsel T. Godbey, "The Governors of Kentucky and Education, 1780-1852," *Bulletin of the Bureau of School Service* [University of Kentucky] 32 (1960): 104, 108.

23. *Report of the Superintendent of Public Instruction . . . for the Year 1850*, in *Kentucky Documents*, 603, 629; *ibid.* (1852), 455; (1851), 84; Frankfort *Tri-Weekly Kentucky Yeoman*, 14 August 1851.

24. *Annual Report . . . for the Year 1848*, 561; *ibid.* (1853) in *Documents*, 455, 468. See also RJB, *A Plea for the Restoration of the Scriptures to the Schools* (1839), 8-9, 15; RJB, "Denominational Education," *Southern Presbyterian Review* 3 (1849): 1-19.

25. *Annual Report . . . for the Year 1848*, 574; *Report . . . for the Year 1852*, 452; *Annual Report . . . for the Year 1853*, 96; Barksdale Hamlett, *History of Education in Kentucky* (1914), 76, 60.

26. Robert W. Hartness, "The Educational Work of Robert Jefferson Breckinridge" (Ph.D. Dissertation, Yale University, 1936), 88; *Annual Report . . . for the Year 1853*, 9.

27. RJB to Joseph R. Underwood, 14 February 1851, Underwood Collection (Western Kentucky University); Ray A. Billington, *The Protestant Crusade: A Study in the Origins of American Nativism* (1939), 390.

28. *Compendium of the Seventh Census* (1854), 118, 243; Agnes G. McGann, *Nativism in Kentucky to 1860* (1944), 64.

29. Frankfort *Commonwealth,* 4 May 1855; RJB to John C. Breckinridge, 18 January 1855, vol. 174, B.MSS.

30. Wallace B. Turner, "The Know-Nothing Movement in Kentucky," *FCHQ* 28 (1954): 277-79; W. Darrell Overdyke, *The Know-Nothing Party in the South* (1950), 284; John C. Breckinridge to RJB, 26 October 1856, vol. 188, B.MSS.

31. Johnston, *History of Louisville* 2:291; Ranck, *History of Lexington* (see chap. 2, n. 5), 277; Robert Peter, *History of Fayette County, Kentucky* (1882), 120, 142; Victor B. Howard, "Sectionalism, Slavery and Education: New Albany, Indiana, versus Danville, Kentucky," *Register* 68 (1970): 292-310.

32. RJB, *The Knowledge of God Objectively Considered . . .* , preface; E. Brooks Holifield, *The Gentlemen Theologians: American Theology in Southern Culture, 1795-1860* (1978), 203.

33. Review of "The Knowledge of God Objectively Considered," *Biblical Repertory and Princeton Review* 29 (1857): 719-20; "Dr. Breckinridge's Work," *Presbyterian Expositor* 1 (1857); Thornwell review cited in Holifield, *Gentlemen Theologians*, 205.

34. Holifield, *Gentlemen Theologians*, 204-5, and Mayse, "Robert Jefferson Breckinridge," 519-26, 526n, have concise discussions of the controversy. RJB, *Knowledge of God Subjectively Considered*, 107, 127, 148; Thornwell review, in *Southern Presbyterian Review* 12 (1859): 604-23; statement to R. Carter & Bros (a New York publisher), 20 January 1860, vol. 207, B.MSS.

6. Ultimate Rather Than Present Glory

1. RJB, "An Address Delivered before the Colonization Society of Kentucky, at Frankfort, on the 6th day of January, 1831," *African Repository* 7 (1831): 176.

2. *Century of Population Growth*, 82, 140, 138.

3. James F. Hopkins, *A History of the Hemp Industry in Kentucky* (1951), 4; *Compendium of the Seventh Census* (1854), 82, 95.

4. Amelia Jones, Edd Shirley, and Peter Bruner interviews, in Federal Writers Project, Works Progress Administration, "Folk History of Slavery in the United States From Interviews with Former Slaves: Kentucky Narratives," 39, 23, 88-89; *Narratives of the Sufferings of Lewis and Milton Clarke* (1846), 16; Coleman, *Slavery Times*, 246-48; Boynton Merrill, Jr., *Jefferson's Nephews: A Frontier Tragedy* (1976), 256-74. For a summary of the WPA interviews see Lowell H. Harrison, "Memories of Slavery Days in Kentucky," *FCHQ* 47 (1973): 242-57.

5. Eli Johnson and J.F. White, quoted in Benjamin Drew, *The Refugee: A North-Side View of Slavery* (1969; orig. pub. 1855), 271, 238.

6. Wes Woods interview, "Slavery Narratives," 26; William Ruth and Aby. B. Jones, quoted in Drew, *Refugee*, 164.

7. William Birney, *James G. Birney and His Time* (1890), 131, 156; quoted in Lowell H. Harrison, *The Antislavery Movement in Kentucky* (1978); James Freeman Clarke, *Autobiography, Diary and Correspondence*, Edward Everett Hale, ed. (1891), 98; Clarke, "George D. Prentice and Kentucky Thirty-Five Years Ago," *Old and New* 1 (1870): 743; Seward quoted in William H. Townsend, *Lincoln and The Bluegrass* (1955), 118; Jared M. Stone to Thomas E. Thomas, 4 March 1836, in Alfred A. Thomas, ed., *Correspondence of Thomas Ebenezer Thomas* (1909), 8.

8. On Kentucky antislavery generally, see Harrison, *Antislavery Movement*; Martin, *Anti-Slavery Movement* (see chap. 3, n. 3); Jeffrey Brooke Allen, "Were Southern White Critics of Slavery Racists? Kentucky and the Upper South, 1791-1824," *Journal of Southern History* 44 (1978): 169-90; Allen, "Did Southern Colonizationists Oppose Slavery? Kentucky 1816-1850 as a Test Case," *Register* 75 (1977): 92-111; and Gordon E. Finnie, "The Antislavery Movement in the Upper South Before 1840," *Journal of Southern History* 35 (1969): 333-35.

9. Boles, *Religion in Antebellum Kentucky*, 105-6; William W. Sweet, *Religion on the American Frontier: The Presbyterians, 1783-1840* (1936), 2:112.

10. "List [of] Robert J. Breckinridge's Negroes, their ages & c. Jany. 1825"; "Various Memoranda—1830," both in B.MSS boxes; Fayette County Manuscript Slave Schedules, Eighth Census (1860) and Fayette County Tax Books, 1860-61 (KHS microfilm); Ruby Jo Taylor, "Robert J. Breckinridge: Views on Slavery to Emancipation" (thesis, Western Kentucky University, 1933), 23n. Some of these themes are suggested in Fredrickson, *Black Image in the White Mind*, 12-19 and Carl Degler, *The Other South: Southern Dissenters in the Nineteenth Century* (1974), 20-41.

11. The articles were reprinted as "Hints on Slavery," *Spirit of the XIX Century* 1 (1842): 433-58.

12. *Ibid.*, 458; Birney, *Birney and His Times*, 148.

13. Victor B. Howard, "The Anti-Slavery Movement in the Presbyterian Church, 1835-1861" (Ph.D. dissertation, Ohio State University, 1961), 19, 35.

14. RJB, "Address before Colonization Society," 162, 166-67, 174-75, 176, 178. On the Kentucky colonization movement generally see Charles Raymond Bennett, "All Things to All People: The American Colonization Society in Kentucky, 1829-1860" (Ph.D. dissertation, University of Kentucky, 1980).

15. "Signs in Kentucky," *African Repository* 7 (1831): 51; 8 (1832): 125.

16. Martin, *Anti-Slavery Movement*, 59n; Deed of Emancipation (copy), dated 14 January 1835; RJB to Sophy Breckinridge, 15 January 1835, both in vol. 68, B.MSS.

17. RJB, "Hints on Slavery and Abolition," *Biblical Repertory and Theological Review* 5 (1833): 287, 295.

18. Boston *Liberator*, 2, 9, 16, 23, and 30 August 1834; "Abolitionism," *Baltimore Literary and Religious Magazine* 1 (1835): 285, 287. Like most articles in the magazine, this was unsigned. Internal evidence can usually fix authorship.

19. William Lloyd Garrison, *Lectures of George Thompson . . . Also a brief History of His Connection with the Anti-Slavery Cause in England* (1969, orig. pub. 1836), iii, xxxiii; *Discussion on American Slavery Between George Thompson, Esq . . . and Rev. Robert J. Breckinridge . . .*, 2d. ed. (1836), 1-5, quotes on 35, 69, 23. See also RJB, *Letter to the Rev. Ralph Wardlow* (1839), 9-12.

20. *Thompson-Breckinridge Discussion*, 32, 56, 50, 57, 25, 29, 79.

21. *Ibid.*, 19, 6n, 7n, 10n; Garrison to Henry E. Benson, 21 August 1836, Garrison to Isaac Knapp, 23 August 1836, in Louis Ruchames, ed., *The Letters of William Lloyd Garrison* (1971), 2:165, 170.

22. RJB, "A Discourse On the American Mind," 505.

23. Jordan, *White Over Black*, 569; Fredrickson, *Black Image*, 12-19, 29; Mayse, "Robert Jefferson Breckinridge," 231, 260.

24. Hambleton Tapp, "The Slavery Controversy Between Robert Wickliffe and Robert J. Breckinridge Prior to the Civil War," *FCHQ* 19 (1945): 157-58; manuscript signed "Crito" and dated 26 October 1827, vol. 54, B.MSS; Earl Gregg Swem, ed., *Letters on the Condition of Kentucky in 1825* (1916), 21.

25. *Speech of Robert Wickliffe Delivered in The Court House, in Lexington . . . in Reference to the "Negro Law"* (1840), 12-19.

26. "Scrapbook, 1864-1879," B.MSS boxes; E. T. Baird, "Reminiscences of Rev. R. J. Breckinridge, D.D., L.L.D.," *Presbyterian Banner* (21 February 1883), 2-3; New York *Daily Times*, 31 May 1853; Castleman, *Active Service*, 41; Palmer, *Life and Letters of Thornwell*, 159-60.

27. *Speech of Robert J. Breckinridge Delivered in the Court-House Yard at Lexington . . .* (1840), 13, 24, 15.

28. *Speech of Robert Wickliffe in Reply to The Rev. R. J. Breckinridge* (1840), 4, 21-25, 49-51.

29. RJB to John C. Breckinridge, 13 February, 10 March 1841, vol. 90, B.MSS; *The Second Defense of Robert J. Breckinridge* (1841), 16, 19; *Reply of Robert Wickliffe to Robert J. Breckinridge* (1841), 3, 6, 31.

30. "Third Defense of Robert J. Breckinridge," 1, 86, 88.

31. Wickliffe, *A Further Reply*, 4, 5, 8, 9, 14, 41, 10.

32. *Ibid.*, 7, 6, 55-56, 62, 57. Milley (born in 1802) was a slave inherited from John Breckinridge's estate; Louisa (born in 1808) was purchased by Robert from his brother William. See "List of Breckinridge's Negroes," B.MSS boxes.

33. Clement Eaton, *The Freedom of Thought Struggle in the Old South*, rev. ed. (1964), 176-77, 114, 129; Cassius M. Clay to Z. Eastman, 24 August 1851, James Franklin Aldrich Collection (Chicago Historical Society); Degler, *Other South*, 79-85, 94-96.

34. Jean E. Keith, "Joseph Rogers Underwood, Friend of African Colonization," *FCHQ* 22 (1948): 117-32; David L. Smiley, "Cassius M. Clay and John G. Fee: A Study of Southern Anti-Slavery Thought," *Journal of Negro History* 42 (1947): 201-13; Will Frank Steely, "William Shreve Bailey, Kentucky Abolitionist," *FCHQ* 31 (1957): 274-81.

35. RJB to Samuel Steele, 17 April 1849, vol. 134; RJB to J. C. Coit, 10 January 1843, vol. 102, B.MSS. See Louisville *Weekly Courier*, 10 March 1849.

36. Lexington *Observer & Reporter*, 28 April 1849; Louisville *Examiner*, 28 April 1849; Martin, *Anti-Slavery Movement*, 130; Fayette County Tax Books, 1849-50 (KHS microfilm); Manuscript Slave Schedules, Seventh Census (1850); Louisville *Weekly Courier*, 5 May 1849.

37. Louisville *Examiner*, 5 May 1849; Frankfort *Commonwealth*, 1 May 1849.

38. Lexington *Observer & Reporter*, 30 June, 4 July 1849.

39. Hambleton Tapp, "Robert J. Breckinridge and the Year 1849," *FCHQ* 12 (1938): 142-43; Lexington *Observer & Reporter*, 7 July 1849; RJB to Richard Martin, 14 July 1849, vol. 135, B.MSS; Lexington *Observer & Reporter*, 27 June, 4 August 1849; Ruth E. Kelly, "Robert Jefferson Breckinridge: His Political Influence and Leadership During 1849 and the Civil War" (thesis, University of Kentucky, 1948), 42.

40. Frankfort *Commonwealth*, 14 August 1849; Martin, *Anti-Slavery in Kentucky*, 134-35; RJB to Virginia Shelby Breckinridge, 8 August 1849, Grigsby Collection.

41. RJB, *The Black Race* (1851), 7, 10; Lexington *Observer & Reporter*, 18 July, 24 November 1855.

42. RJB to Keiser, 13 November 1845, Keiser to RJB, 17 November 1845, vol. 114; Keiser to RJB, 24 December 1846, vol. 126; agreement between Theodore Elbert and RJB, for the year 1848, vol. 129, B.MSS; Fayette County Manuscript Agricultural Schedules, Seventh Census (1850), 429-30 (KHS microfilm); Fayette County Tax Books, 1850.

43. RJB to Robert J. Breckinridge, Jr., 2 March 1853, vol. 156; Mary C. Warfield to RJB, 11 June 1851, vol. 140; RJB to Robert J. Breckinridge, Jr., 13 December 1852, vol. 153; RJB to John C. Breckinridge, 14 December 1852, vol. 153; Robert J. Breckinridge, Jr. to RJB, 16 December 1852, vol. 153; *ibid.*, 6 June 1854, vol. 168; RJB to W. C. P. Breckinridge, 8, 13 February 1860, vol. 208, B.MSS.

44. Excellent descriptions of the farm by two visitors and by Breckinridge himself appear in "L.H.T.," "Braedalbane Farm," *The Country Gentleman* 8 (1856): 121-22; "A Day or Two in Fayette," *ibid.*, 345-46; and "What Kentucky Can Do!," *The Southern Planter* 17 (1857): 140-41. See also Richard L. Troutman, "Plantation Life in the Ante-Bellum Bluegrass Region of Kentucky" (thesis, University of Kentucky, 1955), 20; Eleanor Breckinridge Chalkley,

"Magic Casements," 11 (original in possession of Mrs. Lyssa Harper, Richmond, Va.); RJB to W. C. P. Breckinridge, 6 January 1860, vol. 207, B.MSS.

7. The Last, Cruel Decade

1. Collins, *History of Kentucky*, 1:59.
2. RJB to W. F. Warner, 20 October 1860 (copy), vol. 211; William Warfield to RJB, 14 December 1860, vol. 212; RJB to John C. Breckinridge, 9 January 1860, in Frankfort *Commonwealth*, 18 January 1860. See also Manuscript Slave Schedules, Fayette County, Kentucky, Eighth Census (1860); Fayette County Tax Books, 1860-61 (KHS microfilm)
3. RJB to W. C. P. Breckinridge, 15 November 1860, vol. 211, B.MSS; *Discourse of R. J. Breckinridge, D. D. Delivered at Lexington, Ky., January 4, 1861; The Day of National Humiliation* (1861); *Index Volume from 1825 to 1868* [*Princeton Review*] (1871), 115; James G. Blaine, *Twenty Years of Congress*, 2 vols. (1884-86), 2:517-18.
4. *Discourse of Breckinridge, 1861*, 5, 18-19. See also RJB to Charles Hodge, 19 January 1861, Charles Hodge Papers (Princeton Theological Seminary).
5. See John Fox, Jr., *The Little Shepherd of Kingdom Come* (1973, orig. pub. 1903), 153; Lowell H. Harrison, *The Civil War in Kentucky* (1975), 94-95; R. Delavan Mussey to Joseph H. Barrett, 26 July 1861, Lincoln Collection (University of Chicago); Will D. Gilliam, Jr., "Family Friends and Foes," in the Louisville *Courier-Journal Magazine: The Civil War in Kentucky*, 20 November 1960, 38, 41, 44.
6. Robert J. Breckinridge, Jr. to RJB, 4 July 1861, vol. 217; RJB to W. C. P. Breckinridge, 14 January 1862, vol. 219; W. C. P. Breckinridge to RJB, 15 July 1862, vol. 225, 27 October 1862, vol. 226, B.MSS; Hambleton Tapp, "Robert J. Breckinridge During the Civil War," *FCHQ* 6 (1937): 124-25.
7. RJB, "The Civil War: Its Nature and End," *Danville Quarterly Review* 1 (1861): 640; RJB, "The Secession Conspiracy in Kentucky and Its Overthrow," *ibid.* 2 (1862): 222; B. M. Palmer, "A Vindication of Secession and the South," *Southern Presbyterian Review* 14 (1861): 134-77.
8. John W. Finnell to John J. Crittenden, 26 April 1862, John Jordan Crittenden MSS (LC).
9. Quoted in Harrison, *Antislavery Movement*, 103; Kentucky *Acts* (1863), 392. See also Hambleton Tapp and James C. Klotter, eds., *The Union, The Civil War, and John W. Tuttle: A Kentucky Captain's Account* (1980), 33, 212n.
10. *Discourse of Breckinridge, 1861*, 3-23.
11. RJB, "Negro Slavery and the Civil War," *Danville Quarterly Review* 2 (1862): 670-713.
12. RJB, "An Inquiry into the True Doctrine of Human Society . . . With Special Reference to the State of Public Affairs in America," *Danville Quarterly Review* 3 (1863): 31; RJB, "The Nation and the Insurgents," *ibid.*, 642-84; Mrs. Chapman Coleman, ed., *The Life of John J. Crittenden*, 2 vols. (1871), 2:357-58; Cincinnati *Gazette*, 19 November 1863.
13. John David Smith, "The Recruitment of Negro Soldiers in Kentucky, 1863-1865," *Register* 72 (1974): 364-76; RJB, "The Loyalty Demanded by the Present Crisis," *Danville Quarterly Review* 4 (1864): 96, 110.
14. RJB to Clay, 18 March 1864, Brutus Junius Clay Papers (UK microfilm); RJB, "The Past Course and The Present Duty of Kentucky," *Danville Quarterly Review* 4 (1864): 428, 439.
15. C. M. Miles to RJB, 12 April 1864, vol. 234; "Memorandum," dated 14 May 1864, vol. 234; "Memorandum Left With Gen'l Fry at Camp Nelson" (copy), 19 July 1864, vol. 235, all in B.MSS; Collins, *History of Kentucky*, 1:148n; unidentified newspaper clipping, 1871, in Warfield Collection; RJB to Stephen G. Burbridge, 26 March 1864, S. G. Burbridge Correspondence (UK microfilm).
16. Bramlette to William Goodloe, 12 March 1864 (copy), vol. 233, B.MSS; Louisville *Daily Journal*, 14 March 1864; Hambleton Tapp, "Incidents in the Life of Colonel Frank Wolford," *FCHQ* 10 (1936): 91-92; "Statement of J. M. Kelley," vol. 233, B.MSS; Louisville *Daily Journal*, 17 March, 3, 16 April 1864; T. S. Bell to RJB, 7 April 1864, vol. 233, 9 April 1864,

vol. 234; "Memorandum Concerning the Two Proclamations of Gov. Bramlette," vol. 234, all in B.MSS; RJB to Stephen G. Burbridge, 26 March 1864, Burbridge Correspondence.

17. Lexington *National Unionist,* 19 April 1864; Cincinnati *Daily Gazette,* 13 April 1864.

18. Will D. Gilliam, Jr., "Robert J. Breckinridge: Kentucky Unionist," *Register* 69 (1971): 381-82; Temple Bodley and Samuel M. Wilson, *History of Kentucky,* 4 vols. (1928), 2:353; Lexington *National Unionist,* 12 July 1864; Blaine, *Twenty Years,* 1:518.

19. John G. Nicolay and John Hay, *Abraham Lincoln: A History,* 10 vols. (1890), 4:66; Bodley and Wilson, *History of Kentucky,* 2:355.

20. Collins, *History of Kentucky* 1:142. I have been unable to find this quotation reported elsewhere. N. S. Shaler in his *Kentucky: A Pioneer Commonwealth* (1884), 35ln, says that Collins' reporting of this "is entirely unfounded."

21. Louisville *Daily Journal,* 29, 30 September 1864.

22. RJB to John Breckinridge (son), 16 October 1864, vol. 237, B.MSS; Collins, *History of Kentucky,* 1:142, 148n; Bramlette to Lincoln, 22 November 1864, Jacob to Lincoln, 26 December 1864, J. Bates Dickson to Lincoln, 28 December 1864, Lincoln to Jacob, 18 January 1865, in Roy P. Basler, ed., *The Collected Works of Abraham Lincoln,* 9 vols. (1953) 7:120n, 183n, 222; George D. Mosgrove, *Kentucky Cavaliers in Dixie* (1895), 231; RJB to Lincoln, 25 July 1864, Preston Family Papers (Virginia Historical Society).

23. Issa Desha Breckinridge to John Desha, 18 October 1864; Burbridge to Lincoln, 24 October 1864, vol. 237, B.MSS.

24. RJB to Ewing, 9 December 1864; Speed to RJB, 14 December 1864, vol. 239, B.MSS.

25. RJB to Edwin M. Stanton, 16 September 1864, vol. 23, Edwin M. Stanton Papers (LC); Robert J. Breckinridge Compiled Service Record, Record Group 109 (National Archives); E. D. Townsend to Governor John Brough of Ohio, 24, 25 February 1865, in *The War of theRebellion: A Compilation of the Official Records of the Union and Confederate Armies,* 128 vols. (1880-1901), Series II, 8:302, 305 (hereinafter *O.R.*); John G. Prentice to W. T. Hartz, 12 May 1865 and Stanton to RJB, 14 May 1865, *O.R.,* 8:552, 555.

26. Lincoln to Orville H. Browning, 22 September 1861, in Basler, *Works of Lincoln,* 4:532. On the "Readjustment" period in Kentucky, see E. Merton Coulter, *The Civil War and Readjustment in Kentucky* (1926), 256-439; Ross A. Webb, "Kentucky: 'Pariah Among the Elect,' " in Richard O. Curry, *Radicalism, Racism and Party Realignment* (1969), 115-45; and Webb, *Kentucky in the Reconstruction Era* (1979).

27. RJB to Edwin M. Stanton, 22 October 1865, vol. 29, Stanton Papers.

28. Webb, *Kentucky in Reconstruction Era,* 6, 13, 26, 40; T. K. Noble, State Superintendent of Freedmen Schools to Rev. J. N. Alvord, 11 February, 8 July, 1 December 1867, 1 January, July, 10 September, 16 November 1868; Ben P. Runkle to Alvord, 24 January 1870, Records of the Educational Division of the Bureau of Refugees, Freedmen, and Abandoned Lands: Monthly Reports, Kentucky Record Group 105 (National Archives); Kentucky *Acts* (1865-66), 3; Cincinnati *Daily Gazette,* 31 July 1867; Frankfort *Commonwealth,* 30 August 1867; Lexington *Kentucky Statesman,* 9 August 1867.

29. Lewis G. Vander Velde, *The Presbyterian Churches and The Federal Union, 1861-1869* (1932), 244-71; *Minutes of the Synod of Kentucky* (1866), 2, 21; Records of West Lexington Presbytery, 9 September, 15 October 1868 (Presbyterian Historical Society).

30. RJB to "Miss Minnie," 9 June 1865, vol. 241; W. C. P. Breckinridge to RJB, 19 April 1868, vol. 260, B.MSS; Lexington *Kentucky Statesman,* 6 September 1867; Issa Desha Breckinridge to RJB, 31 March 1864; Mary C. Desha to W. C. P. Breckinridge, 3 August 1864, typescript copies, B.MSS boxes.

31. RJB to W. C. P. Breckinridge, 7 August 1867, vol. 253; W. C. P. Breckinridge to RJB, 28 November 1867, vol. 258, B.MSS.

32. RJB to W. C. P. Breckinridge, 20 February 1866, vol. 246; RJB to John Breckinridge (son), 24 January 1868, vol. 259, 14 February 1869, vol. 265, 24 May 1870, vol. 273; RJB to W. C. P. Breckinridge, 19 August 1870, vol. 274; and *passim,* B.MSS.

33. RJB to W. C. P. Breckinridge, 10 March 1866, vol. 246, 7 March 1867, vol. 253, B.MSS.

34. Margaret Breckinridge to Robert, Jr. and W. C. P. Breckinridge, 15 August 1869, vol.

268, B.MSS; Lexington *Kentucky Statesman*, 21 September 1869; RJB to W. C. P. Breckinridge; 18 November 1870, vol. 275, B.MSS; Gilliam, "Robert J. Breckinridge," 269.

35. See Garnet Duncan to W. C. P. Breckinridge, 29 February 1872, B. MSS boxes.

36. Young to RJB, 20 January 1852, vol. 144, B.MSS; E. T. Baird, "Reminiscences of Rev. R. J. Breckinridge, D.D., LL.D.," *Presbyterian Banner* (7 February 1883), 2-3; Lexington *National Unionist*, 7 June 1864.

37. Frankfort *Old Guard*, 4 April 1850; Lexington *Daily Press*, 13 February 1872.

8. A Son of Fortune

1. Castleman, *Active Service*, 31-32.

2. Lowell H. Harrison, "A Young Kentuckian at Princeton, 1806-1810: Joseph Cabell Breckinridge," *FCHQ* 38 (1964): 299, 304, 306, 308-11; Joseph Cabell Breckinridge to James Breckinridge, 11 May 1809, typescript of original, B.MSS boxes.

3. Cabell Breckinridge to Eliza Meredith, 20 September 1808, Evans Papers; Mrs. Harry K. McAdams, *Abstracts of Pioneer and Court Records* (1967), 243 (copied from J. Cabell Breckinridge's Bible entry); Brown, *The Cabells and Their Kin*, 489-90; Eliza Lewis to Mary C. Breckinridge, 16 April 1821, Mary H. Breckinridge to RJB, [1821], both in vol. 41, B.MSS.

4. Cabell Breckinridge to James Breckinridge, 2 February 1813, Prewitt Collection; Robert H. Bishop, *Another Voice from the Tomb: Being a Funeral Sermon Occasioned by the Death of Joseph Cabell Breckinridge, Esq. . . .* (1824), 13-14, 19; Ranck, *History of Lexington* (see chap. 2, n.5), 178; Lexington *Reporter,* 7, 14 August 1816; Kentucky House Journal (1817-18), 5.

5. "An Oration Pronounced before the Union Philosophical Society of Transylvania University, February 22, 1820, in Commemoration of the virtues and services of General George Washington, by Joseph Cabell Breckinridge, Esq.," *Western Review and Miscellaneous Magazine* 2 (1820): 91, 99.

6. Mary H. Breckinridge to RJB, 12 June 1821, vol. 41, B.MSS; Bishop, *Voice from the Tomb*, 21. See also William C. Davis' excellent *Breckinridge: Statesman, Soldier, Symbol* (1974), 8-10. I wish to thank Mr. Davis for helping me secure certain material for this chapter. My debt to his work and to Frank H. Heck's strong *Proud Kentuckian: John C. Breckinridge, 1821-1875* (1976) is greater than these notes indicate.

7. Bishop, *Voice from the Tomb,* 28; J. Cabell Harrison to RJB, 4 September 1823, vol. 49; David Castleman to RJB, 20 September 1823, vol. 49; Rev. John Breckinridge to RJB, 1, 23 September 1823, vol. 49; RJB to JCB, 12 January 1843, vol. 102, all in B.MSS; McAdams, *Pioneer Records,* 243.

8. JCB to RJB, 16 June 1840, vol. 86, B.MSS; Mary F. Taney, *Kentucky Pioneer Women* (1893), 75.

9. JCB to James G. Birney, 6 September 1858, Birney Papers (University of Michigan Library); Davis, *Breckinridge,* 13; Clifton R. Breckinridge Notebook (No. 2), 44; (No. 3), 14, Prewitt Collection; W. D. Green to JCB, 19 January 1842, vol. 96, Caroline L. Bullock to JCB, 3 March 1843, vol. 104; JCB to Mary C. Breckinridge, 24 June 1846 and Mary C. Breckinridge to JCB, 28 June 1846, vol. 123, all in B.MSS.

10. Townsend, *Lincoln and the Bluegrass,* 13; Lucille Stillwell, *John Cabell Breckinridge,* (1936), 18, 21; Brown, *Cabells and Their Kin,* 490-92.

11. Lexington *Intelligencer,* 12 October 1838; JCB to RJB, 17 February 1840, vol. 84, 20 April 1840, vol. 85, 16 June 1840, vol. 86, all in B.MSS; *Biographical Sketch of John C. Breckinridge,* 5.

12. Stillwell, *Breckinridge,* 18-19; Rev. John Breckinridge to JCB, 26 January 1841; JCB to RJB, 1 February 1841; certificate dated 26 February 1841, all in vol. 90, B.MSS.

13. Thomas J. McCormack, ed., *Memoirs of Gustave Koerner, 1809-1896,* 2 vols. (1909), 1:347; Ellis S. Chesbrough to H. W. Nelson, 9 December 1837, Nelson Collection (UK); Timothy Flint, *The History and Geography of the Mississippi Valley,* 2d. ed., 2 vols. (1832), 1:354; Charles A. Murray, *Travels in North America . . . ,* 2 vols. (1854), 1:185; James Stuart, *Three Years in North America,* 2 vols. (1833), 2:271; Lexington *Intelligencer,* 28 June 1829; Thomas D.

Clark, *The Kentucky* (1942), 88; Andrew Reed and James Matheson, *A Narrative of the Visit to the American Churches*, 2 vols. (1835), 1:129.

14. Julius P. B. McCabe, *Directory of the City of Lexington . . . for 1838 & '39* (1838), 29-30; William H. Perrin, *History of Fayette County Kentucky* (1882), 272; J. Winston Coleman, Jr., *Stage Coach Days in the Bluegrass* (1935), 234.

15. Robert Peter, *A Brief Sketch of the History of Lexington, Kentucky and of Transylvania University* (1854), 18; McCabe, *Directory,* 18-19; Flint, *History of Mississippi Valley,* 1:354; McCormack, *Koerner Memoirs,* 1:355, 361.

16. F. Garvin Davenport, *Ante-Bellum Kentucky* (1943), 2; Lexington *Intelligencer,* 28 June 1839; Reed and Matheson, *Narrative,* 1:129; *Sixth Census* (1840), 1:279; *Compendium of the Seventh Census* (1854), 236.

17. *Observer and Reporter,* 13 October 1838; Lexington *Intelligencer,* 3 August 1838.

18. "W. A." to JCB, 16 February 1841, vol. 90; James B. Townsend to JCB, 23 February 1841, vol. 90; "Catalogue of the books I have accurred [*sic*] from Hon. John J. Crittenden," dated 17 May 1841, vol. 92, all in B.MSS; Davis, *Breckinridge,* 19.

19. Henry L. Dawes, "Two Vice-Presidents," *Century Magazine* 1 (1895): 463; *Reminiscences of General Basil W. Duke* (1911), 193, 436-37; *New York Times,* 8 February 1859; Thomas Z. Morrow, *Recollections of an Old Democratic Mass Meeting* ([n.d.]), 13; Champ Clark, "Kentucky During the Civil War," in J. F. Cook, *Old Kentucky* (1903), 227-28; J. Stoddard Johnston, "Sketches of Operations of General John C. Breckinridge, No. 3," *Southern Historical Society Papers* 7 (1879): 392.

20. *Duke's Reminiscences,* 436, 193; H. H. Crittenden, comp., *The Crittenden Memoirs* (1936), 32.

21. Henry Watterson, *"Marse Henry": An Autobiography,* 2 vols. (1919), 1:151; Jacob R. Marcus, *Memoirs of American Jews, 1775-1865,* 3 vols. (1955), 3:81; Louisville *Courier-Journal,* 17 November 1887; "Memoirs of Henry V. Johnson of Scott County, Kentucky, 1852-1931" (Georgetown, Kentucky, Public Library), 16; James B. Townsend to JCB, 23 February 1841, vol. 90, B.MSS; Robert M. Myers, *The Children of Pride* (1972), 325.

22. Draft speech, "Gentlemen of the Frankfort Light Infantry," dated 4 July 1841, vol. 92, B.MSS.

23. Frankfort *Commonwealth,* 6 July 1841; Rev. John Breckinridge to JCB, 6 February 1841, vol. 90, JCB to RJB, 14 November 1841, vol. 94, 4 February 1842, vol. 96, all in B.MSS.

24. JCB to RJB, 29 May 1843, vol. 106; RJB to Sophonisba P. Breckinridge, 11 June 1843, vol. 106; JCB to RJB, 13 August 1843, vol. 106, 9 October 1843, vol. 108, 9 October 1843, vol. 108, 29 December 1843, vol. 110, all in B.MSS; JCB to James G. Birney, 6 September 1853, Birney Papers; Davis, *Breckinridge,* 29-30.

25. JCB to John S. Cunningham, 18 August 1855, John C. Breckinridge, Miscellaneous MSS (FC); J. W. Moore to JCB, 20 January 1857, vol. 191, B.MSS; Stillwell, *Breckinridge,* 68-69. For the state of law practices in Kentucky at that time see James W. Gordon, "Lawyers in Politics, Mid-Nineteenth Century Kentucky as a Case Study" (Ph. D. dissertation, University of Kentucky, 1980).

26. JCB to RJB, 4 January 1845, vol. 116, B.MSS; Brown, *Cabells and Their Kin,* 495-96; Laetitia Breckinridge to JCB, 5 September 1846, vol. 124, B.MSS; Lexington *Kentucky Statesman,* 20 March 1850.

27. Ranck, *History of Lexington,* 358-59; Joel T. Hart Diary, 20 July 1847, Joel Tanner Hart Papers, Durrett Collection; Commission dated 6 September 1847, vol. 126, B.MSS; *Report of the Adjutant General of the State of Kentucky: Mexican War Veterans* (1889), 82.

28. Charles F. Hinds, ed., "Mexican War Journal of Leander M. Cox," *Register* 55 (1957): 34, 45-47; C. R. Breckinridge Note, Prewitt Collection, 20-21; Frankfort *Weekly Kentucky Yeoman,* 5, 26 November 1847; JCB to RJB, 8 April 1848, vol. 130, B.MSS.

29. Davis, *Breckinridge,* 42; Mary C. Breckinridge to JCB, 21 May 1842; Young to JCB, 25 April 1842, both in vol. 98, B.MSS.

30. Frankfort *Commonwealth,* 14, 28 August 1849; Lexington *Observer and Reporter,* 8 August 1849.

31. Lexington *Observer and Reporter,* 2 January 1850; *Kentucky House Journal* (1849-50), 4-11, 51, 54, 103-4, 217-18, 385, 435.

32. Lexington *Kentucky Statesman*, 20 March 1850; Lexington *Kentucky Statesman*, 8, 15 January 1851; JCB to D. Howard Smith, 5 March 1854, Breckinridge Miscellaneous MSS; Wallace B. Turner, "Kentucky State Politics in the Early 1850's," *Register* 56 (1958): 132; Frankfort *Weekly Kentucky Yeoman*, 12 August 1847; *Biographical Sketch of John Breckinridge*, 7.

33. Davis, *Breckinridge*, 53-55; Castleman, *Active Service*, 44-45; Leeland Hathaway Recollections, VII, 36 (microfilm, Southern Historical Collection, University of North Carolina); Morrow, *Recollections*, 17; Frankfort *Commonwealth*, 2 September 1851.

34. Lexington *Kentucky Statesman*, 22 February, 5 April 1853; *Life of Cassius Marcellus Clay: Memoirs, Writings and Speeches* (1886), 215.

35. Julia S. Ardery, "The Rogers Family and Old Cane Ridge," *Register* 53 (1955): 245, 302; Bennett Young, "John Cabell Breckinridge," *Confederate Veteran* 13 (1905): 258.

36. Paris *True Kentuckian*, 7 July 1875.

37. Lexington *Kentucky Statesman*, 19 April, 3, 10, May, 5 August 1853; G. Glenn Clift, "Kentucky Votes, 1792-1894," 70 (KHS); *Congressional Quarterly's Guide to U.S. Elections* (1975), 593. Breckinridge received a suspiciously high vote: Owen County exceeded its qualified vote by 124. The other two counties he carried turned out all but 82 of their 3285 qualified voters.

38. *Cong. Globe*, 32nd Cong., 1st Sess., 47, 710-14, 9, 1964-65; 33rd Cong., 1st Sess., 318-19; Lazarus W. Powell to JCB, 5 January 1853, vol. 154, B.MSS; JCB to J. C. Dobbin, Secretary of the Navy,[undated], 19 August 1853, Charles J. and George E. Hoadley Collection (Connecticut Historical Society).

39. *Cong. Globe*, 33rd Cong., 1st Sess., *Appendix*, 439, 760-64; Louisville *Courier-Journal*, Mounted Clippings about John Cabell Breckinridge. Ben Perley Poore, *Perley's Reminiscences of Sixty Years in the National Metropolis*, 2 vols. (1886), 1:439-42, offers a slightly different version.

40. Davis, *Breckinridge*, 102-10; Robert W. Johannsen, *Stephen A. Douglas* (1973), 414-15; Alexander H. Stephens, *A Constitutional View on the Late War Between the States*, 2 vols. (1868-70), 2:274.

41. *Cong. Globe*, 33d Cong., 1st Sess., *Appendix*, 441-42; 32d Cong., 1st Sess., 384.

42. *Cong. Globe*, 33d Cong., 1st Sess., *Appendix*, 441-42; 32d Cong., 1st Sess., 774-75; New York *Day-Book*, 7 July 1860, clipping in Andrew McBrayer Sea Political Scrapbook, Sea Collection (FC).

9. A Lucky Steed Falters

1. Turner, "Kentucky Politics in 1850's," 138-39; JCB to D. Howard Smith, 5 March 1854, Breckinridge Miscellaneous Manuscripts; Lexington *Kentucky Statesman*, 7 August 1855.

2. Lexington *Kentucky Statesman*, 3 April 1855; Seventh Census (1850), Agricultural Schedules, 421-22; Ranck, *History of Lexington* (see chap. 2, n. 5), 133.

3. Mary C. Breckinridge to A. W. Venable, 28 January 1852, Abraham Watkins Venable Papers (Southern Historical Collection, University of North Carolina); Johannsen, *Douglas*, vii-viii, 482, 519; George F. Milton, *The Eve of Conflict: Stephen A. Douglas and the Needless War* (1934), 213; H. M. Rice to JCB, 23 January 1856; Charles G. McHatton to JCB, 24 January 1856, vol. 181, B.MSS.

4. *Lives of James Buchanan and John C. Breckinridge* (1856), 84-85; J. Stoddard Johnston to "Dear Aunt," 10 June 1856, typescript copy (in possession of Mrs. James C. Breckinridge, Summit Point, W. Va.); John C. Rives to JCB, 10 October 1856, vol. 188, B.MSS.

5. J. Stoddard Johnston to "Dear Aunt," 10 June 1856, Mrs. James C. Breckinridge MSS; Andrew Johnson to A. O. P. Nicholson, 27 June 1856, in Leroy P. Graf and Ralph W. Haskins, eds., *The Papers of Andrew Johnson* (1967), 2:388, 385; JCB to Ignatius Donnelley, 22 June 1856, Ignatius Donnelley Papers (Minnesota Historical Society microfilm); New York *Times*, 2, 9, 10 September 1856; Louisville *Times*, 11 July 1856.

6. Louisville *Times*, 5, 9 September 1856.

7. Buchanan to JCB, 20 June 1856, Breckinridge-Marshall Papers; JCB to A. O. P.

Nicholson, 18 November 1856, John Cabell Breckinridge Papers (New York Historical Society); New York *Times,* 8 February 1859.

8. J. Stoddard Johnston to his aunt, 26 November 1859, Josiah Stoddard Johnston Papers (UK); Collins, *History of Kentucky* (see chap. 4, n. 19), 1:81; *Substance of a Speech by Hon. John C. Breckinridge . . . December 21, 1859* (1860), 4-11.

9. *Breckinridge Speech of December 1859,* 11-13; Frankfort *Daily Commonwealth,* 26 December 1859.

10. Davis, *Breckinridge,* 237, 14, 17, 172; JCB to RJB, 11 January 1841, vol. 89, B.MSS; Kentucky Slave Schedules, 1850, Fayette County (KHS microfilm); C. R. Breckinridge Notebook (No. 4), 49-50; Fayette County Deed Book #3 (1856-1858), 390-410 (UK microfilm). The *Kentucky Statesman* (cited in Washington, D. C. *Constitution,* 21 August 1860) said that Breckinridge owned "several" slaves that year, a conclusion not reflected in the tax lists.

11. Davis, *Breckinridge,* 156, 163, 43, 33, 626-27; Kentucky *House Journal* (1849), 67; John W. Forney, *Anecdotes of Public Men* (1874), 1:41; Samuel Fishback to JCB, 20 February 1850 vol. 137, B.MSS; Lousiville *Times,* 5 September 1856; Lexington *Observer and Reporter,* 30 May 1849; *Speech of John C. Breckinridge Delivered at Lexington, Kentucky, September 5th, 1860* (1860), 3, 7.

12. William K. Scarborough, ed., *The Diary of Edmund Ruffin* (1972), 1:270; Buchanan to John B. Floyd, 5 August 1859, in Philip G. Auchampaugh, *James Buchanan and His Cabinet on the Eve of Secession* (1926), 57; JCB to RJB, 30 January 1860, in Dorothy G. Melzer, "Mr. Breckinridge Accepts," *Register* 56 (1958): 227; JCB to Theodore O'Hara, 19 January 1860, Fred M. Dearborn Collection (Harvard University); Johannsen, *Douglas,* 743; Robert Toombs to Alexander H. Stephens, 11 January 1860 in Ulrich B. Phillips, ed., *The Correspondence of Robert Toombs, Alexander H. Stephens, and Howell Cobb* (1913), 2:455; Emerson D. Fite, *The Presidential Campaign of 1860* (1911), 224.

13. New York *Herald,* 23 April 1860; Louisville *Courier-Journal,* 17 November 1887; William B. Hesseltine, ed., *Three Against Lincoln: Murat Halstead Reports the Caucuses of 1860* (1960), 30, 99; Roy F. Nichols, *The Disruption of American Democracy* (1948), 281.

14. Hesseltine, *Halstead Reports,* 103-4; Washington *Constitution,* 3 May 1860.

15. JCB to J. B. Clay, 9, 21 May 1860, Thomas J. Clay Papers (LC); Hesseltine, *Halstead Reports,* 185, 249, 265, 273-77; *Breckinridge Speech, 5 September 1860,* 1; JCB to Caleb Cushing, 6 July 1860, Container 87, Caleb Cushing Papers (LC).

16. JCB to J. B. Clay, 21 May 1860, Thomas J. Clay Papers; *Louisville Courier-Journal,* 17 November 1887; J. H. Smith to Stephens, 18 August 1860, Alexander H. Stephens Papers (LC).

17. John E. Helms to Andrew Johnson, 16 August 1860, in Graf and Haskins, *Papers of Andrew Johnson,* 3:658; J. H. Smith to Alexander H. Stephens, 18 August 1860, Stephen Papers; Jefferson Davis, *The Rise and Fall of the Confederate Government,* 2 vols. (1881), 1:52; Milton, *Eve of Conflict,* 487; Douglas to Charles H. Lamphier, 5 July 1860, in Robert W. Johannsen, ed., *The Letters of Stephen A. Douglas* (1961), 498.

18. Frank H. Heck, "John C. Breckinridge in the Crisis of 1860-1861," *Journal of Southern History* 21 (1955): 323; clipping in A. M. Sea's Political Scrapbook, Sea Collection; JCB to Caleb Cushing, 6 July 1860, Cushing Papers; New York *Times,* 17, 25, 26 July 1860.

19. New York *Times,* 28 August, 8, 10 September 1860; *Breckinridge Speech, 5 September 1860,* 3, 13-14; Davis, *Breckinridge,* 234-40; New York *Times,* 13 July 1860.

20. Varina Davis, *Jefferson Davis . . . A Memoir,* 2 vols. (1890), 1:685; Ollinger Crenshaw, *The Slave States in the Presidential Election of 1860* (1945), 71; *Cong Globe,* 36th Cong., 2nd Sess., 894.

21. Heck, "Breckinridge in the Crisis," 330; Heck, *Proud Kentuckian,* 64, 92; James E. Copeland, "Where Were the Kentucky Unionists and Secessionists?" *Register* 71 (1973): 357-60; Turner, "Kentucky in a Decade of Change" 84-85; Will D. Gilliam, Jr., "Party Regularity in Three Kentucky Elections and Union Volunteering," *Journal of Southern History* 16 (1950): 511-18.

22. Ollinger Crenshaw, "Urban and Rural Voting in the Election of 1860," in Eric F. Goldman, ed., *Historiography and Urbanization: Essays in American History in Honor of W. Stull Holt* (1941), 58-61; Seymour M. Lipset, *Political Man: The Social Bases of Politics* (1960), 347-49;

Ralph A. Wooster, *The Secession Conventions of the South* (1962), 261-64; Peyton McCrary, Clark Miller, and Dale Baum, "Class and Party in The Secession Crisis: Voting Behavior in the Deep South, 1856-1861," *Journal of Interdisciplinary History* 8 (1978): 450-52; quoted in Heck, "Breckinridge in the Crisis," 328.

23. Dawes, "Two Vice-Presidents," 464; *Cong. Globe*, 36th Cong., 2nd Sess., 894, 720, 1413, 1433; "Speech of Hon. J. C. Breckinridge . . . April 2, 1861 . . .," in *Southern Rights Doc. No. 1* (1861), 13, 17, 19-20.

24. *Cong. Globe*, 37th Cong., 1st Sess., 142, 377-79.

25. *Ibid.*, 36th Cong., 2nd Sess., 1467-69, 1510.

26. *Ibid.*, 37th Cong., 1st Sess., 261, 138-42, 377.

27. *Ibid.*, 275, 263, 378, 452.

28. Frankfort *Tri-Weekly Kentucky Yeoman*, 29 August 1861; Garrett Davis to Salmon Chase, 3 September 1861, in A. B. Hart, ed., "Letters to Secretary Chase from the South, 1861," *American Historical Review* 4 (1899): 346-47; *Cong. Globe*, 37th Cong., 1st Sess., 142, 376; Davis, *Breckinridge*, 281-82; Mary Breckinridge Maltby, "Recollections of Civil War Times in Kentucky," *Register* 45 (1947): 227.

10. Mount and Away

1. Broadside (UK).

2. *O.R.*, Ser. I, 4:455, 504, 552, 556; John Cabell Breckinridge Compiled Service Record, Record Group 109 (National Archives); Frank Moore, comp., *Rebellion Record* (1862), 3:102; Davis, *Breckinridge*, 293.

3. *O.R.*, Ser. I, 10, pt. 1, 382-84, 389, 395; pt. 2, 398-400, 433; George B. Hodge, "Sketch of the 1st Kentucky Brigade," *The Land We Love* 4 (1868): 400.

4. Ed. Porter Thompson, *History of the First Kentucky Brigade* (1868), 118-19, 131, 135; Diary of J. Stoddard Johnston, 14 August 1862, J. Stoddard Johnston Papers; John B. Pirtle, "Defense of Vicksburg in 1862: The Battle of Baton Rouge," *Southern Historical Society Papers* 8 (1880): 328; J. Stoddard Johnston, *Kentucky,* vol. IX of *Confederate Military History*, Clement A. Evans, ed., 12 vols. (1899), 77. The best history of Breckinridge's unit is William C. Davis' fine *The Orphan Brigade* (1980).

5. Johnston, *Kentucky*, 82; Theodore O'Hara to JCB, 16 January 1863, James Wilson to JCB, 20 January 1863, both in Papers of John Cabell Breckinridge (New York Historical Society); James Lee McDonough, *Stones River: Bloody Winter in Tennessee* (1980), 180-202; Thompson, *First Brigade*, 163, 189-91.

6. Lowell H. Harrison, "John C. Breckinridge: Nationalist, Confederate, Kentuckian," *FCHQ* 47 (1973): 134-35; Thompson, *First Brigade*, 206; Davis, *Breckinridge*, 385-93; James Lee McDonough, *Chattanooga—A Death Grip on the Confederacy* (1984), 184, 186, 205.

7. Johnston, *Kentucky*, 70; "Louisville Courier-Journal, Mounted Clippings about John Cabell Breckinridge" (UK); Castleman, *Active Service*, 46; J. Cabell Breckinridge Compiled Service Record, Record Group 109 (National Archives).

8. Thomas Jordan, "Notes of a Confederate Staff-Officer at Shiloh," in Robert U. Johnson and Clarence C. Buel, eds., *Battles and Leaders*, 4 vols. (1887), 1:601; Thompson, *First Brigade*, 307; Mercer Otey, "Story of Our Great War," *Confederate Veteran* 8 (1900): 342; *Duke's Reminiscences*, 193-94; C. Vann Woodward, ed., *Mary Chesnut's Civil War* (1981), 554.

9. Maltby, "Civil War Recollections," 225-26; Johnston Diary, 14 August 1862, 5 June 1863; Mary C. Breckinridge to JCB, 8 January 1863, 9 November, 5 December 1862, 1, 13, 14 June 1863, 31 October 1862, 18 February 1863, all in John C. Breckinridge Service Record.

10. Mary C. Breckinridge to JCB, 5 February 1862 (?), 4 February 1863, 9 November 1862, 1, 13, 14 June, 27 October 1863, all in John C. Breckinridge Service Record; Johnston Diary, 19 March 1863; Thompson, *First Brigade*, 104; Mary Breckinridge Maltby, *Mary Cyrene Breckinridge* (1910), n.p.

11. Thomas L. Connelly, *Autumn of Glory: The Army of Tennessee, 1862-1865* (1971), 53,

63-64, 273, 277; Davis, *Breckinridge*, 384 and passim; John B. Gordon, *Reminiscences of the Civil War* (1903), 192.

12. Grady McWhiney, "Controversy in Kentucky: Braxton Bragg's Campaign of 1862," *Civil War History* 6 (1960): 5-6; Thomas L. Connelly and Archer Jones, *The Politics of Command: Factions and Ideas in Confederate Strategy* (1973), xiii-xiv, 52, 57, 75, 65-66, 72.

13. JCB to Samuel Cooper, 31 March 1863 (copy), Breckinridge Papers (New York Historical Society); "Proceedings of the First Confederate Congress," *Southern Historical Society Papers* 48 (1941): 193, 211, 217-18.

14. Connelly and Jones, *Politics of Command*, 73; Gordon, *Reminiscences of the Civil War*, 193; B. L. Ridley, "Camp Scenes Around Dalton," *Confederate Veteran* 10 (1902): 68; Davis, *Breckinridge*, 331-32.

15. *O.R.*, Ser. I, 3, pt. 2, 745; Davis, *Breckinridge*, 394-97; 512n.

16. John S. Wise, *The End of An Era* (1899), 450-53.

17. Woodward, *Chesnut's Civil War*, 545; Johnston, *Kentucky*, 184, 188; JCB to W. H. Taylor, 19 October 1864, John Cabell Breckinridge Collection (Chicago Historical Society); J. Stoddard Johnston, "Sketches of Operations of John C. Breckinridge, No. 1," *Southern Historical Society Papers* 7 (1879): 258, 262.

18. Davis, *Breckinridge*, 422-32; John Echols, *Memorial Elegy on The Battle of New Market . . .* (1877), 6-13; Heck, *Proud Kentuckian*, 124; Johnston, "Sketches of Operations, No. 1," 261; Frank E. Vandiver, ed., *The Civil War Diary of General Josiah Gorgas* (1947), 110-11; J. Stoddard Johnston, "Sketches of Operations of General John C. Breckinridge, No. 2," *Southern Historical Society Papers* 7 (1879): 317; Douglas S. Freeman and Grady McWhiney, eds., *Lee's Dispatches* (1957), 216-17, 219; "Diary of Robert E. Park," *Southern Historical Society Papers* 1 (1876): 380, 385; Gordon, *Reminiscences*, 315.

19. William C. Davis, "Massacre at Saltville," *Civil War Times Illustrated* 9 (1971): 4, 45-46; Mosgrove, *Cavaliers in Dixie* (see chap. 7, n. 22), 206-8; Lee Smith, "Experiences of A Kentucky Boy Soldier," *Confederate Veteran* 20 (1912): 440; J. B. Clay, Jr. to Susan Clay, 16 October 1864, Thomas J. Clay Papers. Breckinridge reported the capture of some 200 prisoners. He also noted his men suffered from the "greatest fatigue and exposure I have seen borne during the war," a condition that may have been a factor in their actions. See report dated 3 January 1864, Breckinridge Collection (Chicago Historical Society).

20. J. B. Jones, *A Rebel War Clerk's Diary*, 2 vols. (1935), 2:394, 389, 412; Rembert W. Patrick, *Jefferson Davis and His Cabinet* (1944), 149.

21. William C. Davis, "Secretary of War John C. Breckinridge and Confederate Defeat" (paper presented at the Southern Historical Association Meeting, 1974); Edward Younger, ed., *Inside the Confederate Government: The Diary of Robert Garlick Hill Kean* (1957), 200; JCB to J. Stoddard Johnston, 23 February 1865, Johnston Papers (FC).

22. JCB to Jefferson Davis, 23 April 1865, "Letters Sent by Secretary of War," *Southern Historical Society Papers* 12 (1884): 101; JCB to J. E. Johnston, 24 April 1865, in "Last Letters and Telegrams of the Confederacy: Correspondence of General John C. Breckinridge," 98.

23. Lewis Shepherd, "The Confederate Treasure Train," *Confederate Veteran* 25 (1917): 258; H. G. Damon, "The Eyes of General Breckinridge," *ibid.* 17 (1909): 380.

24. A. J. Hanna, *Flight Into Oblivion* (1938), 105-76, 193; Davis, *Breckinridge*, 525-29; Mary E. Dickison, *Dickison and His Men: Reminiscences of the War in Florida* (1890), 225; Sherman, *Memoirs*, 353-54; New York *Times*, 1 May 1865.

25. The account of the escape is from John Taylor Wood, "Escape of the Confederate Secretary of War," *Century Magazine* 1057 (1893): 110-23, and JCB to Owen Breckinridge, 28 July 1865, Breckinridge Family Papers (UK). The latter document was published. See Alfred J. Hanna, ed., "The Escape of the Confederate Secretary of War John Cabell Breckinridge as Revealed by His Diary," *Register* 37 (1939): 323-33.

26. Cincinnati *Daily Enquirer*, 26 June 1865, 10 April 1868; New York *Herald*, 27 June 1865; G. G. Dibrell to William Preston Johnston, 9 April 1878, in Dunbar Rowland, ed., *Jefferson Davis, Constitutionalist* 10 vols. (1923), 8:163.

27. JCB to Owen Breckinridge, 28 July 1865, Breckinridge Family Papers (UK).

28. Diary of John C. Breckinridge, 8-30 August, 9, 12 September, 7 October 1866, 1

February, 1 April, 22 April, 27 September 1867; Nash K. Burger and John K. Bettersworth, *South of Appomattox* (1959), 103; Breckinridge diary, 13 November 1867-3 March 1868; Heck, *Proud Kentuckian*, 147; Mary C. Breckinridge to Ann Johnson, 13 December 1867, 31 May 1868, 15 July 1868, Mary C. Breckinridge MSS.

29. Prentice to James Speed, 17 October 1865; Prentice to JCB, 17 October 1865, both in Breckinridge-Marshall Papers; Greeley to George Shea, 8 April 1867, vol. 253; Kate Coyle to JCB, 30 August 1868, vol. 261, James B. Beck to JCB, 25 November, 11 December 1868, vol. 263, all in B.MSS.

30. "Charlie" to JCB, 17 February 1867, Breckinridge-Marshall Papers; Cincinnati *Daily Enquirer,* 10 April 1868.

31. Louisville *Courier-Journal,* 23, 24 February, 3, 9, 11 March 1869.

32. JCB to W. D. Porter, 22 April 1870, Breckinridge Miscellaneous Manuscripts; "Louisville Courier-Journal Clippings."

33. E. A. Ferguson to JCB, 3 August 1869, vol. 268, B.MSS; Leonard P. Curry, *Rail Routes South: Louisville's Fight for the Southern Market, 1865-1872* (1969); Watterson to JCB, 5 January 1870, vol. 271, B.MSS.

34. Curry, *Rail Routes South,* 74-76, 136, 128; Davis, *Breckinridge,* 602-3.

35. Frankfort *Commonwealth,* 25 March 1870; T. T. Crittenden to W. C. P. Breckinridge, 22 May 1875, vol. 294, B.MSS; Cassius M. Clay, *The Life of Cassius Marcellus Clay: Memoirs . . .* (1886), 220; Burger and Bettersworth, *South of Appomattox,* 106, 110; Davis, *Breckinridge,* 611-12; "Louisville Courier-Journal Clippings." Later, Owen became a state senator; Cabell, surveyor general of the Washington Territory; and Clifton, an Arkansas congressman.

36. Frankfort *Weekly Kentucky Yeoman,* 15 May 1875; "Scrapbook, 1863-1894," B.MSS boxes; JCB to W. C. Hardy, 29 June 1874, Breckinridge Miscellaneous MSS; Johnston, "Sketch No. 3," 392; "Louisville Courier-Journal Clippings"; Clifton Breckinridge to JCB, 13 May 1874; James Beck to JCB, 27 April 1874, both in Mrs. James C. Breckinridge Collection; William Preston to Henry Watterson, 5 November 1874, vol. 1, Henry Watterson Papers (LC).

37. Davis, *Breckinridge,* 619, 622-24, 638; "Louisville Courier Journal Clippings"; Castleman, *Active Service,* 40; Lexington *Kentucky Gazette,* 19 May 1875; Lexington *Weekly Press,* 23 May 1876. Mrs. Breckinridge died in 1907. *Herald,* 10 October 1907.

38. Davis, *Breckinridge,* 622-27; Louisville *Courier-Journal,* 17 November 1887.

11. The Ready Kindling of the Spirit

1. *Herald,* 17 July 1902. W. C. P. Breckinridge recalled much of his early life in later editorials. He early spelled his nickname "Willy," but the family usually spelled it "Willie."

2. W. C. P. Breckinridge (hereinafter WCPB) to RJB, 8 March 1864, vol. 233; WCPB to Issa Desha Breckinridge, 18 April 1864, vol. 234; and WCPB to Issa Breckinridge, 11 March 1864, vol. 233, B.MSS.

3. *Herald,* 17 July 1902; Fox, *The Little Shepherd of Kingdom Come* (1973; orig. pub., 1903), 247.

4. Sketches of W. C. P. Breckinridge's life appear in Brown, *Cabells and Their Kin,* 507-8; *National Cyclopaedia of American Biography,* 29 (1941): 42-43; *Dictionary of American Biography,* 20 vols. and supplements (1928-), 3:11-12; George Lee Willis, *Kentucky Democracy,* 3 vols. (1935), 1:188-92; *Biographical Directory of the American Congress, 1774-1971* (1971), 631; and Sister Mary E. Graves, "Contemporary Scenes as Found in the Writings of W. C. P. Breckinridge" (thesis, Catholic University, 1960), quotation from C. C. Moore, clipping from the *Courier-Journal,* in Breckinridge, Desha, and Chalkley Family Scrapbooks (UK).

5. "Private Journal and Account" (1851), vol. 143, B.MSS; *Congressional Record,* 49th Congress, 1st Session (13 May 1886), 4489; Castleman, *Active Service,* 24-27; *Herald,* 10 June 1902; M. G. Webb to WCPB, 8 September 1853, vol. 160; Sally Breckinridge to WCPB, 1 October 1853, vol. 160; W. Goodloe to WCPB, 25 September 1856, vol. 187; RJB to WCPB, 27 November 1857, vol. 199, B.MSS.

6. *Herald,* 1 April 1904; "Data of Activities, Hon. Wm. C. P. Breckinridge 1850-1884," B.MSS boxes; Alvin F. Harlow, *Weep No More My Lady* (1942), 177; *General Catalogue of Centre College of Kentucky . . . 1890* (1890); WCPB, *Address Before The Alumni Association of Centre College on June 17, 1885* (1885), 20.

7. "Scrapbook, 1863-1894"; WCPB to Issa Breckinridge, 27 February 1863, B.MSS boxes; Lexington *Kentucky Statesman,* 19 May 1857; RJB to WCPB, 8, 13 February 1860, vol. 208, B.MSS; WCPB, "Essays on Agriculture as Connected with Common Schools," *The Kentucky Farmer,* 1 (1859): 162-63.

8. Genealogical notes, circa 1867, Breckinridge Family Papers (UK); G. Glenn Clift, ed., "Kentucky Marriages and Obituaries," *Register* 38 (1940): 341; Lexington *Kentucky Statesman,* 8 May 1860; Sophonisba P. Breckinridge "Autobiography" (University of Chicago).

9. *Herald,* 21 July 1901; WCPB to Issa Breckinridge, 21 July 1861, [July] 1861, B.MSS boxes.

10. WCPB to Issa Breckinridge, 2, 24, 26 February 1861, B.MSS boxes.

11. WCPB to RJB, 15 July 1862; RJB to WCPB, 16 July 1862, vol. 225, B.MSS; *Herald,* 17 July 1900, 17 July 1901, 26 July 1925; Broadside (FC); W. C. P. Breckinridge Service Record, Record Group 109 (National Archives).

12. Issa Breckinridge to WCPB, 3 August 1863; WCPB to Issa Breckinridge, 20 October 1863; Issa Breckinridge to WCPB, 11 August, 17 November 1864, B.MSS boxes.

13. Issa Breckinridge to WCPB, 30, 15 July 1864, 11 October 1863, B.MSS boxes.

14. *Report of the Adjutant General of the State of Kentucky, Confederate Kentucky Volunteers, War, 1861-65,* 2 vols. (1918), 2:2-4; WCPB, "The Opening of the Atlanta Campaign," in Johnson and Buel, eds., *Battles and Leaders,* 4:277-81; WCPB report, 2 December 1864, in *O.R.,* Series I, 44:889, 922; WCPB to W. T. Walthall, 3 April 1878, in Rowland, *Jefferson Davis,* 8:152.

15. W. T. Lafferty, ed., "Civil War Reminiscences of John Aker Lafferty," *Register* 59 (1961): 1-15; *Herald,* 18 December 1900; *Confederate AG Report,* 2:5; Harrison, *Civil War in Kentucky* (see chap. 7, n.5), 95.

16. *Herald,* 28 August 1904; J. P. Austin, *The Blue and the Gray,* (1899), 87.

17. WCPB to Issa Breckinridge, 16 July 1864, vol. 235, Joseph C. Breckinridge diary, 24 July 1864, boxes, both in B.MSS; Joseph Wheeler, "Bragg's Invasion of Kentucky," in Johnson and Buel, eds., *Battles and Leaders,* 3:13n; RJB to WCPB, 1 September 1864, vol. 236, B.MSS; Joseph C. Breckinridge to Abraham Lincoln, 14 March 1865, *O.R.,* Series II, 8:390.

18. Austin, *Blue and Gray*, 63; Wheeler's report, 9 October 1864, *O.R.* Series I, 38, pt. 3, 961; *Herald,* 2 December 1904.

19. Basil W. Duke, "Last Days of the Confederacy," in Johnson and Buel, eds., *Battles and Leaders,* 4:766; WCPB to Issa Breckinridge, 9 June 1864, vol. 235 and 2 April 1865, vol. 240, B.MSS.

20. For period surveys see Hambleton Tapp and James C. Klotter, *Kentucky: Decades of Discord, 1865-1900* (1977); Coulter, *Civil War and Readjustment;* Webb, *Kentucky in the Reconstruction Era.* See also Arthur J. Wormuth, "The Development of the Democratic Party in Fayette County, Kentucky, 1864-1868" (thesis, University of Kentucky, 1971), 51-91, and Thomas L. Owen, "The Formative Years of Kentucky's Republican Party, 1864-1871" (Ph.D. dissertation, University of Kentucky, 1981).

21. Edward F. Prichard, Jr., "Popular Political Movements in Kentucky, 1875-1900" (senior thesis, Princeton University, 1935), 8-11; Tapp and Klotter, *Decades of Discord,* 29-36; Thomas L. Connelly, "Neo-Confederatism or Power Vacuum: Post-War Kentucky Politics Reappraised," *Register* 64 (1966): 257-69.

22. Lexington *Kentucky Statesman,* 5 July 1867; Cincinnati *Daily Gazette,* 31 July 1867; *Kentucky Statesman,* 13 August, 23 July 1867; Lexington *Observer and Reporter,* 27 October 1866, 13 April 1867 (hereinafter *Observer*). See also Melta M. Sublett, "The Role of the Confederate Veteran in the Industrial Development of Kentucky" (thesis, University of Wisconsin, 1945), 9, 19, 23, 96.

23. *Observer,* 17, 20 October 1866, 23 November 1867.

24. Paul M. Gaston, *The New South Creed* (1970); *Observer,* 5 September, 10 October, 1867, 4 January 1868.

25. WCPB to Issa Breckinridge, 2 April 1865, vol. 240, B.MSS; *Observer*, 7, 10, November 1866, 16 October 1867, 4 January 1868.

26. *Observer*, 10 November 1866, 4 December 1867.

27. *Ibid.*, 4 September 1867. On the controversy see Victor B. Howard, "The Black Testimony Controversy in Kentucky, 1866-72," *Journal of Negro History* 58 (1973): 140-65; Howard, "The Breckinridge Family and the Negro Testimony Controversy in Kentucky," *FCHQ* 49 (1975): 37-56.

28. "WCPB Activities, 1850-1884"; Lexington *Kentucky Statesman*, 21 September 1869; Lexington *Kentucky Gazette*, 1, 12 February, 8 April 1868; Joseph C. Breckinridge Diary, 8 April 1868.

29. C. E. W. Dobbs (a Richmond, Ky., minister in 1868) to the editor, *Century Magazine* 31 (1886): 478. See also *Herald*, 2 August 1925. Perhaps overstating his case, Breckinridge later told a northern audience, "The first line in favor of opening the witness box to every citizen, whether a white or colored man, was printed by me." *Ninth Annual Festival of the New England Society of Pennsylvania* . . . (1890), 53. A black leader, the Reverend S. E. Smith, supported that contention in 1905. See Lexington *Kentucky Leader*, 1 October 1905.

30. WCPB to RJB, 8 March 1868, vol. 259, B.MSS; Georgetown *Weekly Times*, 11 August 1869; Cincinnati *Daily Gazette*, 17 March 1868.

Robert J. Breckinridge, Jr., faced the same issue, with the same outcome, a year later. A former Confederate congressman, defeated in his bid for the state superintendent of public instruction nomination in 1867, he now won Democratic nomination for the state senate. His opponent, running as an independent, was Albert G. Talbott, a former Whig who made the Negro testimony question his chief issue. Talbott won and Robert later turned to a local office in 1876. He won a state senate seat later. See Howard, "Breckinridge Family," 44-54; *Documents for the Canvass of 1867* . . . *of the Democratic Party of Kentucky* (1867), 6, 9; Georgetown *Weekly Times*, 11 August 1869; Lexington *Kentucky Statesman*, 6, 10 August 1869; Paris *True Kentuckian*, 11 August 1869; B. M. Burdett to WCPB, 9 August 1869, vol. 268, B.MSS; clipping in Monthly Reports, Records of the Education Division of the Bureau of Refugees, Freedmen, and Abandoned Lands, 1865-1871, Record Group 105 (National Archives); and Sam C. Elliott, ed. *The Illustrated Centennial Record of the State of Kentucky* (1892), 60.

31. *Observer*, 27 August 1870; RJB to WCPB, 19 August 1870, vol. 274, B.MSS; *Prather's Directory of the City of Lexington* . . . *1875-6* (1875), 44; Lexington *Daily Press*, 17 February 1872; *Kentucky Acts* (1878), 454; *Kentucky University: Substance of the Argument of Col. W. C. P. Breckinridge* (n.d.), 19, 21, 23; James F. Hopkins, *The University of Kentucky: Origins and Early Years* (1951), 151.

32. Breckinridge, "Autobiography"; Issa Breckinridge to WCPB, 28 October 1867, vol. 257; WCPB to Issa Breckinridge, 27 October 1867, vol. 257; Issa Breckinridge to WCPB, 6 January 1870, vol. 271, 29 March 1870, vol. 272, B.MSS.

33. Brown, *Cabells and Their Kin*, 508; United States Census: Fayette County (1870); Issa Breckinridge to WCPB, 24 October 1884, vol. 336; WCPB to Issa Breckinridge, 14 May 1885, B.MSS boxes.

34. Collins, *History of Kentucky*, 1:246c; Louisville *Courier-Journal*, 2 November 1878; Midway *Blue-Grass Clipper*, 31 May 1878; Peter, *History of Fayette County*, 412-13; Herbert B. Adams to WCPB, 22 October 1884, vol. 336, B.MSS; "WCPB Activities, 1850-1884."

35. Frankfort *Tri-Weekly Kentucky Yeoman*, 11 May 1875; Louisville *Courier-Journal*, 3 May 1879; Louisville *Commercial*, 2 May 1879.

36. WCPB, *Address at the Dedication of the Monument of the Confederate Dead, Erected in the Battle-Grace Cemetery, Cynthiana, Ky.* . . . (1869), 5; WCPB, *A Plea for a History of the Confederate War* (1879), 8; WCPB, *Who Were the Confederate Dead?* (1887), 18, 37.

37. WCPB, *Address in Memory of the Confederate Dead* (1869), 5; WCPB, *Address before the Literary Societies of Washington and Lee University, Delivered June 27, 1877* (1877), 1, 4, 16, 8, 9.

38. WCPB to Cassius M. Clay [nephew of the emancipationist], 9 February 1884, Cassius Marcellus Clay Papers (UK); Midway *Blue-Grass Clipper*, 21 February 1884; Lexington *Daily Press*, 30 April, 25 July 1884; Lexington *Weekly Press*, 9 July, 12 November 1884.

12. A Man of Passion

1. Richmond *Kentucky Register*, 21 May 1880; John J. McAfee, *Kentucky Politicians: Sketches of Representative Corn-Crackers* (1886), 26; "Scrapbook concerning the death of W. C. P. Breckinridge, 1904" (UK); Hopkinsville *South Kentuckian*, 22 July 1879; Midway *Blue-Grass Clipper*, 21 February 1884; Frankfort *Capital*, 28 July 1891; Philadelphia *Daily Evening Telegram*, 10 March 1888; unidentified clipping, circa 18 May 1888 in Clipping Scrapbook of W. C. P. Breckinridge, Breckinridge Family Papers (UK); Washington *Post*, 12 January 1894.

2. Crittenden, *Crittenden Memoirs*, 468; Sherman cited in William Preston Kimball draft speech, 17 March 1909, Democratic Party Papers, Samuel Wilson Collection (UK); E. Polk Johnson, *A History of Kentucky and Kentuckians*, 3 vols. (1912), 1:191; *Duke's Reminiscences*, 486.

3. Lexington *Kentucky Leader*, 19 October 1888, 9 November 1890.

4. WCPB to Issa Breckinridge, 9 June 1864, vol. 235, B.MSS; Poore, *Perley's Reminiscences*, 2:512-13; Chalkley, "Magic Casements," 12; Isaac F. Marcosson, *Adventures in Interviewing* (1919), 211; J. M. Tanner, in "Scrapbook concerning the death of W. C. P. Breckinridge."

5. Woodrow Wilson, *Congressional Government* (1885), 255; James Bryce, *The American Commonwealth*, 2 vols. (1891 ed.), 1:197; John A. Garraty, *The New Commonwealth, 1877-1890* (1968), 223.

6. Morton Keller, *Affairs of State* (1977), 300, 311; *Cong. Record*, 52d Congress, 1st Session (3 February 1892), 820-21; George B. Galloway, *History of the House of Representatives* (1961), 132; Washington *Post*, 19 January 1888.

7. Neil Mac Neil, *Forge of Democracy: The House of Representatives* (1963), 119; James C. Klotter, "Sex, Scandal, and Suffrage in the Gilded Age," *Historian* 42 (1980): 225-43; Henry Adams, *Democracy* (1961; orig. pub. 1880), 26.

8. Quoted in Mac Neil, *Forge of Democracy*, 211.

9. Mark Twain and Charles D. Warner, *The Gilded Age, A Tale of To-Day* (1873); Vernon Louis Parrington, *Main Currents in American Thought: The Beginnings of Critical Realism in America*, 3 vols. (1930), 3:23; Garraty, *New Commonwealth*, 306.

10. Wilson, *Congressional Government*, 62. On Clifton Breckinridge see James F. Willis, "An Arkansan in St. Petersburg: Clifton Rodes Breckinridge; Minister to Russia, 1894-1897," *Arkansas Historical Quarterly*, 38 (1979): 3-31, and "Hon. Clifton R. Breckinridge," *Harper's Weekly* (2 June 1894), 509.

11. Wilson, *Congressional Government*, 79; *Cong. Record*, 49th Cong., 1st Sess. (7 January 1886), 538; Robert Kelley, "Presbyterianism, Jacksonianism and Grover Cleveland," *American Quarterly*, 18 (1966): 615, 622; WCPB, "Issues of the Presidential Campaign," *North American Review* 154 (1892): 273-77.

12. *Cong. Record*, 51st Cong., 1st Sess. (13 May 1890), 4631; 51st Cong., 2d. Sess. (28 February 1891), 3617; 52d Cong., 1st Sess. (29 January 1892), 677.

13. *Ibid.*, 50th Cong., 1st Sess. (8 October 1888), 9592.

14. Champ Clark, *My Quarter Century of American Politics*, 2 vols. (1920), 1:340-43. Mention of the disturbance was stricken from the *Congressional Record*.

15. *Cong. Record*, 49th Cong., 2d Sess. (31 January 1887), 1203-4; 51st Cong., 1st Sess. (6 January 1890), 407, (13 January 1890), 527; 52d Cong., 1st Sess. (7 January 1892), 203, (29 February 1892), 1578; Keller, *Affairs of State*, viii.

16. *Cong. Record*, 53d Cong., 2d Sess. (11 January 1894), 710; 49th Cong., 1st Sess. (2 April 1886), 3038; 53d Cong., 2d Sess. (11 January 1894), 710.

17. *Ibid.*, 53d Cong., 2d Sess. (11 January 1894), 710-12; New York *Times*, 2 November 1892.

18. R. Hal Williams, " 'Dry Bones and Dead Language': The Democratic Party," in H. Wayne Morgan, ed., *The Gilded Age* (rev. ed., 1970), 131, 146; Horace Samuel Merrill, *Bourbon Leader: Grover Cleveland and the Democratic Party* (1957), 186, 189.

19. Keller, *Affairs of State*, 195, 553; WCPB, "Free Trade or Protection," *North American Review* 150 (1890): 517, 513-14.

20. *Cong. Record*, 52d Cong., 1st Sess. (6 April 1892), 3019; 53d Cong., 2d Sess. (11 January 1894), 711-13.

21. *Ibid.*, 50th Cong., 1st Sess. (8 October 1888), 9592-93; 51st Cong., 1st Sess. (13 May 1890), 4633; Marion Miller, ed., *Great Debates in American History,* 14 vols. (1913), 12:252.

22. Arthur Wallace Dunn, *From Harrison to Harding: A Personal Narrative . . . 1888-1921,* 2 vols. (1922), 1:26-27; "Scrapbook concerning the death of W. C. P. Breckinridge"; Lexington *Kentucky Leader,* 10 November 1890; Hazel Green *Herald,* 8 July 1892; Lexington *Kentucky Leader,* 15 November 1892; New York *Times,* 28 January 1888; *Proceedings of the Celebration By the Pilgrim Society at Plymouth, August 1st, 1889* (1889), 103; *Ninth Annual Festival of the New England Society of Pennsylvania* (1890), 56; *Young Men's Democratic Association of Philadelphia Annual Banquet. Jackson's Day Thursday January 8th 1891* (1891), 7; *Union League Club, Chicago, Exercises in Commemoration of the Birthday of Washington, February 22, 1891* (1891), 28-51; New York *Times,* 29 October, 9 December 1892.

23. "Address to the Oberon Society," B.MSS boxes; Lexington *Press,* 11 June 1882.

24. [Anonymous], *The Celebrated Trial: Madeline Pollard vs. Breckinridge* (1894), [11-14], 18-21. This is basically a collection of newspaper accounts and has blank spaces throughout, representing "offensive" words withdrawn at the last minute. Fayette Lexington (pseud.), *The Celebrated Case of Col. W. C. P. Breckinridge and Madeline Pollard* (1894), has more of the author's comments and, like the above, is antagonistic to Breckinridge. Agnes Parker, *The Real Madeline Pollard* (1894), is a collection of letters from Parker to one of Breckinridge's lawyers ("x"). Parker was often with Pollard, and reported that Breckinridge offered Pollard a "liberal allowance," if she would drop the suit.

25. WCPB to R. E. Mehan, 12 March 1894, B.MSS boxes. She had several other aliases as a middle name or middle names, including Vinton and Vinton Breckinridge.

26. *Celebrated Trial,* [12], 75-77, 67; Washington *Post,* 17 March 1894.

27. *Celebrated Trial,* 46-47, 116, 37, 97; Parker, *Real Pollard,* 124. Breckinridge married Mrs. Wing secretly on 29 April 1893. See Washington *Post,* 17 March 1894, and WCPB to Preston Scott, 14 May 1893, Green Collection-Falls of Rough (Western Kentucky University).

28. WCPB to Desha Breckinridge, 25 September 1893, box 130, Craig Shelby papers (UK).

29. E. H. Hughes to [John T. Shelby?] [1893]; "Memorandum," 5 December 1893; "Memorandum of R. D. Wittington"; "Memorandum," 28 November 1893; "Memorandum" [1893], Craig Shelby Papers, box 130; *Celebrated Trial,* 135-43.

30. *Celebrated Trial,* 170-84; New York *Times,* 30 March 1894; Louisville *Courier-Journal,* 3 April 1894; Lexington (pseud.), *Celebrated Case,* 30.

31. *Celebrated Trial,* 176, 199, 216, 225-27, 209; Louisville *Courier-Journal,* 4 April 1894.

32. *Celebrated Trial,* 302, 307, 282-87; New York *Times,* 14 April 1894. A doctor offered Breckinridge the information that "every well-informed physician . . . knows that a woman who will have illicit sexual intercourse with one man will with another." James P. Parker to WCPB, [March] 1894, vol. 468, B.MSS.

33. *Celebrated Trial,* 319; Lexington *Kentucky Leader,* 15 April 1894.

34. Lexington (pseud.), *Celebrated Case,* 29; Tapp and Klotter, *Decades of Discord,* 337; *Celebrated Trial,* [3]; Lexington *Kentucky Leader,* 15, 7 April 1894.

35. Pivar, *Purity Crusade: Sexual Morality and Social Control, 1868-1900* (1973), 7, 210-11, 186, 146.

36. Lexington *Kentucky Leader,* 7 April, 26, 27 March, 6 April 1894; New York *Times,* 17 April 1894; Lexington (pseud.) *Celebrated Case,* 26.

37. Lexington *Kentucky Leader,* 15, 22 April 1894; *New York Times,* 30 April 1894; WCPB to Shelby, 17 April 1894 (copy), B.MSS boxes.

38. Lexington *Kentucky Leader,* 16 April 1894; New York *Times,* 15 September 1894; "Mt. Horeb Presbyterian Church, Fayette County, Kentucky Record Book," entries of 9 April 1894 through 3 February 1895 (UK microfilm); New York *Herald,* 16 September 1894; Lexington *Kentucky Leader,* 26 February 1894.

39. WCPB to Cassius M. Clay [nephew of the antislavery leader of the same name], 20 February 1884, Cassius Marcellus Clay papers (UK).

40. H. Levin, ed., *Lawyers and Lawmakers in Kentucky* ([1897]), 572-74; Prichard, Jr., "Popular Political Movements," 149; Midway *Blue-Grass Clipper,* 14 February 1884; Louisville

Post, 23 August 1882; WCPB to John E. Holman, 15 February 1894, B.MSS boxes; John W. Rodman to WCPB, 19 August 1893, box 130, Craig Shelby Papers; *Leader,* 12 March 1894.

41. *Biographical Cyclopedia of the Commonwealth of Kentucky* (1896), 502; Lexington *Kentucky Leader,* 15 May 1894; unidentified clipping and clipping from Lexington *Press,* 1894, vol. 465, B.MSS.

42. Louisville *Courier-Journal,* 6 May 1894; Lexington *Kentucky Leader,* 5 May 1894; New York *Times,* 6 May 1894; "Scrapbook Concerning Death"; Joseph M. Tanner, "Lexington and Its Institutions, 1875-1925" (UK).

43. Desha Breckinridge to WCPB, 15 May 1894, vol. 472, B.MSS; Desha to George Grady, 22 May 1897 (copy), box 146, Shelby Papers; Lexington *Kentucky Leader,* 15 July 1894; clipping in "Scrapbook, 1863-1894," B.MSS boxes; Lexington *Press,* 28 August 1894; Samuel B. Rodgers to WCPB, 9 April 1894, vol. 469, B.MSS.

44. Washington *Post,* 27 August 1894; Rev. William E. Knight, *The Wm. C. P. Breckinridge Defense* (1895), 20.

45. See WCPB letter dated 11 May 1894 (copy), box 146, Craig Shelby Papers. For other information on the matter see a letter to WCPB, dated 24 February 1894, and Robert J. Breckinridge, Jr. to WCPB, 10 October 1893, B.MSS boxes; WCPB to Desha Breckinridge, 26 February 1894, vol. 466, and a letter from WCPB dated 28 February 1894, B.MSS boxes. Certain names have been intentionally omitted in this footnote.

46. Lexington *Kentucky Leader,* 21, 6, 11 May 1894; F. C. Riddell to WCPB, 21 May 1894, vol. 473, Shelby to WCPB, 17 April 1894, vol. 470, B.MSS; New York *Times,* 15 May 1894; Susan B. Anthony to Laura Clay, 21 September 1894, Laura Clay Papers (UK); unidentified clipping in Mary Desha Papers (UK); WCPB to Henry A. Bond, 23 April 1894 (copy), vol. 470, B.MSS. A good sketch of the women's role is Paul E. Fuller, "Congressman Breckinridge and the Ladies," *Adena* 2 (1977): 1-13.

47. *United States Census: Agriculture* (1890), 64, 79; unidentified clipping in "Scrapbook, 1879-"; Midway *Blue-Grass Clipper,* 20 September 1888; Paris *Kentuckian-Citizen,* 15 August 1888.

48. Lexington *Kentucky Leader,* 6 September, 15 July 1894.

49. *Ibid.,* 22, 16 September 1894; *Herald,* 9 September 1896; *Appleton's Annual Cyclopaedia . . . 1894* (1895), 396; Samuel Duncan to WCPB, 17 September 1894 and A. Curtis to WCPB, 19 September 1894, vol. 476, B.MSS.

50. Washington *Post,* 17 September 1894; Cincinnati *Enquirer,* 16 September 1894; New York *Herald,* 16 September 1894; Lexington *Kentucky Leader,* 18 September 1894; Los Angeles *Times,* 16 September 1894; Atlanta *Constitution,* 16 September 1894.

51. Los Angeles *Times,* 16 September 1894; New York *Herald,* 16 September 1894; Cincinnati *Enquirer,* 16 September 1894; Fuller, "Congressman Breckinridge," 11; Lexington *Kentucky Leader,* 17 September 1894.

13. Rising Suns & Lengthening Shadows

1. The preceding paragraphs are drawn from Tapp and Klotter, *Decades of Discord;* James C. Klotter, *William Goebel: The Politics of Wrath* (1977), 10-25; Connelley and Coulter, *History of Kentucky* 2:906-1008; Gaye Keller Bland, "Populism in Kentucky, 1887-1896" (Ph.D. dissertation, University of Kentucky, 1979).

2. *Herald,* 4 September 1896; *Proceedings of the National Democratic Party . . .* (1896), 40-49, 42.

3. *Herald,* 21 October 1896; 2 October, 24 May, 8 June, 19, 23 May 1897; 15 September 1896; 14 July, 17 May 1897.

4. *Ibid.,* 5, 8 November 1896; *Congressional Quarterly's Guide to U. S. Elections* (1975), 678; *Herald,* 15 April 1917; "Scrapbook Concerning the death of W. C. P. Breckinridge, 1904" (UK).

5. WCPB to W. H. Mackoy, 15 November 1897, Mackoy Family Correspondence and Papers (UK); *Herald,* 25 July 1898, 7 November 1897.

6. On Goebel see Klotter, *Goebel;* R. E. Hughes, F. W. Schaefer, and E. L. Williams, *That Kentucky Campaign* (1900); and Urey Woodson, *The First New Dealer: William Goebel* (1939).

7. *Herald,* 12, 14, 20, 27, February 1898.

8. Klotter, *Goebel,* 126-28; Paducah *Sun,* 17 July 1899; Lexington *Kentucky Gazette,* 29 July, 5 August, 1, 4, November 1899.

9. WCPB to W. H. Mackoy, 17 July 1899, Mackoy Family Papers; *Herald,* 29 July 1899.

10. *Herald,* 18, 22, 19 August, 9 March, 28 October 1899.

11. *Herald,* 13 November 1899; Louisville *Courier-Journal,* 10 November, 13 December 1899; Louisville *Commercial,* 12 December 1899; *Herald,* 15 November 1899.

12. *Herald,* 11, 13 January 1900; William S. Taylor to WCPB, 6 January 1900, vol. 505, B.MSS; Willis, *Kentucky Democracy* 1: 383-84; WCPB to Sophonisba P. Breckinridge, 29 January 1900, vol. 506, B.MSS; Stanley J. Folmsbee, Robert E. Corlew, and Enoch L. Mitchell, *Tennessee: A Short History* (1969), 403.

13. *Herald,* 11 January 1900; Louisville *Courier-Journal,* 27 January 1900; *Herald,* 25 February 1898.

14. Klotter, *Goebel,* 100-108; McKenzie R. Todd Testimony, Examining Trial of Caleb Powers, March 1900, 1295, 1352-63, Goebel Papers (KHS); Taylor Interrogation, 21 June 1909, William S. Taylor Papers (UK); WCPB to Sophonisba P. Breckinridge, 8 February 1900, vol. 506, B.MSS.

15. George Denny and WCPB form letter, 16 March 1900, Arthur Younger Ford Papers (FC); Hughes, Schaefer, and Williams, *That Kentucky Campaign,* 265; Chicago *Record,* 10 February 1900, Goebel clippings (in possession of Charles Atcher, Lexington); WCPB to Sophonisba P. Breckinridge, 11 February 1900, vol. 506, B.MSS.

16. Taylor & C. v. Beckham, & C., 108 *Kentucky Reports* 278-321; *Herald,* 11-12 March 1900.

17. *Herald,* 17 August, 1 November, 26 November 1900; Lexington *Argonaut,* 21 September 1896.

18. WCPB, *Virginia State Bar Association Annual Address* (1891), 19; *Herald,* 1 November 1898, 15 November 1897; Lexington *Daily Leader,* 16 October 1899.

19. *Herald,* 15 June 1897, 17-18 February, 19-20 March, 9, 8, 21 April 1898.

20. *Ibid.,* 18 April 1898, 4 May 1897, 4 August, 11 July 1898; 23 June 1900, 24 April, 18 October 1898. Christopher Lasch in his "The Anti-Imperialists, The Philippines and The Inequality of Man," *Journal of Southern History* 24 (1958): 323, 319, concludes that "not a single expansionist proposed the privileges of citizenship be extended to the Philippines" and that southerners felt Asiatics "could not be assimilated." See also Jack T. Kirby, *Darkness at the Dawning: Race and Reform in the Progressive South* (1972), 115-16.

21. WCPB to Francis W. Dawson, 11 January 1889, Francis Warrington Dawson, I and II, papers (Duke University); *Herald,* 12 May 1900; *Twelfth Census: Population* (1900), 540, cxix; Kentucky *Senate Journal* (1891-92), 623; C. Vann Woodward, *The Strange Career of Jim Crow,* 3d. rev. ed. (1974), 71-96.

22. *Herald,* 17 June 1904; WCPB, "The Race Question," *The Arena* 2 (1890): 48; *Herald,* 2 January 1898, 12 October 1900; WCPB "The Old South and The New South," in Hamilton W. Mabie, *The Memorial Story of America* (1894), 805-10; *Herald,* 8 July 1901, 8 June 1902.

23. *Herald,* 30 July 1901, 19 November 1898, 27 May, 24 July 1901, 31 May 1900, 25 April 1901, 12 May 1900, 9 November 1901; 16 November 1897, 31 May 1900, 20 May 1901, 2 January 1898.

24. *Ibid.,* 16-17 July 1903, 7-9 July 1897; William H. H. Hart to WCPB, 21 March 1894, vol. 468; WCPB to Carroll D. Wright, 29 January 1894 (copy), B.MSS boxes; Cincinnati *Enquirer,* 16 September 1894; *Herald,* 11 May 1897, 20 April 1900. For a more reserved estimation of DuBois, see WCPB to Sophonisba P. Breckinridge, 27 July 1903, vol. 513, B.MSS.

25. Degler, *Other South,* 311; Charles E. Wynes, ed., *Forgotten Voices: Dissenting Southerners in an Age of Conformity* (1967), 3-7.

26. "Account Ledger, 1884-1917"; "Letters Pertaining to Various Railroad Companies 1891-1896," box 145, Craig Shelby Papers; *Herald,* 9 June 1904, 17 August 1900; WCPB to

Huntington, 4 October 1884, vol. 336, B.MSS; *Herald,* 26 May 1899, 11 April, 29 January 1899, 27 March 1897.

27. *Herald,* 3 April 1899, 5 February 1903, 2 February 1904, 2 July 1897.

28. *Ibid.,* 7, 14 May, 2 July 1901, 11 December 1897, 6 January 1898, 9, 15 January, 28 July 1902, 20 November 1897. Quotations from 1 April 1897, 25 August, 1 January 1902.

29. "The Running Turf in America," *Harper's Monthly Magazine* 41 (1870): 252; Noble L. Prentis, *Southern Letters* (1881), 12-15; Louisville *Post,* 12 September 1882; William H. Bishop, "Among the Blue-Grass Trotters," *Harper's Magazine* 67 (1883): 715-19; James Lane Allen, *Blue Grass Region of Kentucky* (1892), 28-37, 142-45, 184-88; H. L. Wilhelm, ed., *Will B. Moore Letters, Scenes in The Sunny South* (1900), 14; Alexander K. McClure, *The South: Its Industrial, Financial and Political Condition* (1886), 251.

30. *Prather's Directory of the City of Lexington . . . (1895),* 25; Breckinridge "Autobiography"; New York *Times,* 5 May 1898, 1, 2 February 1889; Warfield, *Joseph Cabell Breckinridge, Junior,* 9-22; J. C. Breckinridge, "Our National Folly and Its Victims," *North American Review* 167 (1898): 428-33; Graham A. Cosmas, *An Army for Empire: The United States Army in the Spanish American War* (1971), 271, 294; Lexington *Kentucky Leader,* 2 July 1903. The third Mrs. Breckinridge died in 1920. See *Herald,* 29 April 1920.

31. Breckinridge "Autobiography"; *Herald,* 15 June 1904, 16 April 1911; New York *Times,* 26 January 1897; Eleanor Chalkley Diary, Lyman Chalkley Papers (UK).

32. *Lexington Directory, 1898-9,* 342; Lucy Furman, "Katherine Pettit: A Pioneer Mountain Worker," *Mountain Life & Work* 12 (1936): 18; WCPB to Sophonisba P. Breckinridge, 6 July 1899, vol. 503, B.MSS.

33. Robert J. Breckinridge (son) to WCPB, 14 March 1890, B.MSS; New York *Times,* 15 November 1891; Lexington *Morning Transcript,* 23 March 1893; Breckinridge "Autobiography"; Robert J. Breckinridge to Issa D. Breckinridge, 3 September 1891, vol. 425; WCPB to Sophonisba P. Breckinridge, 13 March 1893, B.MSS boxes; New York *Times,* 22 September 1894; WCPB to Sophonisba P. Breckinridge, 8, 12, 16 December 1897, B.MSS boxes.

34. "Scrapbook Concerning Death"; Hazel Green *Herald,* 22 March 1899; Stanford *Interior Journal,* quoted in *Herald,* 22 July 1897; Washington *Post,* quoted in Lexington *Kentucky Leader,* 20 July 1900; "An Ardent Admirer" to WCPB, 28 March 1900, vol. 507, B.MSS; *Herald,* 27 July 1902.

35. WCPB to Sophonisba P. Breckinridge, 20 September, 25 October, 15 November 1904, vol. 515; 11 November 1904, B.MSS boxes; Lexington *Kentucky Leader,* 20 November 1904.

36. Quoted in *Herald,* 30 November 1904. A month after his death, blacks of The Emancipation Proclamation Association also praised him (*ibid.,* 10 December 1904) and a black sculptor was selected to design his bust. Lexington *Kentucky Leader,* 25 September, 1 October 1905.

37. M. A. Cassidy and William Myall in "Scrapbook Concerning Death"; *Herald,* 5 December 1900, 27 April, 5 September 1897; Atlanta *Constitution,* quoted in *Herald,* 22 July 1900; Edgar DeWitt Jones, *Lords of Speech* (1937), 176; *Address before the Literary Societies of Washington and Lee University,* 19.

14. Nisba

1. Steven J. Diner, *A City and Its Universities: Public Policy in Chicago, 1892-1919* (1980), 29. On Breckinridge's career at the University of Chicago see Richard L. Popp to author, 5 November 1984. No full published biography of Sophonisba Breckinridge exists. Sources include Christopher Lasch, "Sophonisba Preston Breckinridge," in Edward T. James, ed., *Notable American Women, 1607-1950,* 3 vols. (1971), 1:233-36; Allen F. Davis, "Sophonisba Preston Breckinridge," in John A. Garraty and Edward T. James, eds., *Dictionary of American Biography: Supplement Four, 1946-1950* (1974), 106-7; Margaret S. Vining, "Sophonisba Preston Breckinridge and the Graduate School of Public Welfare Administration at the University of

Chicago" (M.A. Thesis, George Washington University, 1982); Mary Jo Deegan, "Sopho-nisba Preston Breckinridge," in Lina Mainiero, ed., *American Women Writers*, 4 vols. (1979), 1:219-23; Anthony R. Travis, "Sophonisba Breckinridge, Militant Feminist," *Mid-America* 58 (1976): 111-18; Helen R. Wright, "Three Against Time: Edith and Grace Abbott and Soph-onisba P. Breckinridge," *Social Science Review* 28 (1954): 41-53; and sketches of her in *Social Science Review* 22 (1948): 417-50.

2. Breckinridge "Autobiography." This frank, unorganized document of over one hundred generally unnumbered pages is the most revealing source for her motivations and thoughts.

3. *Ibid.*

4. *Ibid.*

5. WCPB to Issa Desha Breckinridge, 27 October 1867, vol. 257; Issa to WCPB, 30 March 1870, vol. 272, 28 October 1867, vol. 257, B.MSS; "Autobiography"; "Report of Nisba Breckinridge . . . May 9th, 1873," B.MSS boxes.

6. Anne Firor Scott, *The Southern Lady: From Pedestal to Politics, 1830-1930* (1970), 4-21, quotation on 4; Margaret Ripley Wolfe, "The Southern Lady: Long Suffering Counterpart of the Good Ole' Boy," *Journal of Popular Culture* 2 (1977): 22.

7. Hopkinsville *South Kentuckian*, 28 October 1879; Frankfort *Daily Kentucky Yeoman*, 27 April 1880; Laura Clay, "Kentucky," in Elizabeth Cady Stanton, Susan B. Anthony, Matilda Joslyn Gage, and Ida H. Harper, eds., *The History of Woman Suffrage*, 6 vols. (1888-1922), 4:671; Helen Deiss Irvin, *Women in Kentucky* (1979), 96, 99-100; Paul E. Fuller, *Laura Clay and the Woman's Rights Movement* (1975), 39-40.

8. Fuller, *Laura Clay*, 22-29, 16; Clay, "Kentucky," 4:665-66.

9. "Autobiography."

10. Wooster (Ohio) *Voice*, 11 February 1893, in B.MSS boxes; *Herald*, 24 October 1901, 28 September 1898, 21 January, 3 October 1902.

11. State of Kentucky Matriculators Book (1869-89), 106, 122, 136, 156 (microfilm, Public Records Division, Department for Libraries and Archives, Frankfort); State College to Richard C. Stoll, 31 March 1900, vol. 506, B.MSS; John P. Rousmaniere, "Cultural Hybrid in the Slums: The College Woman and the Settlement House, 1889-1894," *American Quarterly* 22 (1970): 51; Issa Desha Breckinridge to Sophonisba P. Breckinridge (hereinafter SPB), 20 September, 2 December 1884; Issa to Fanny Barnes, 17 October 1884, B.MSS boxes.

12. Issa Desha Breckinridge to SPB, 19 September 1884, B.MSS boxes; "Autobio-graphy"; SPB to Issa, 17 May [1885?], B.MSS boxes.

13. WCPB to SPB, 20 September, 3, 8 October 1884, 30 March, 10 May 1885, B.MSS boxes. Many of these 1884-85 letters appear in Helen L. Horowitz, " 'With more love than I can write': A Nineteenth Century Father to His Daughter," *Wellesley* 65 (1980): 16-20.

14. "Autobiography"; SPB to Issa Desha Breckinridge, 1 April 1885, 15 September 1886, B.MSS boxes; Edith Abbott, "Sophonisba Preston Breckinridge: A Supplementary Statement," *Social Science Review* 23 (1949): 94; SPB to Issa Desha Breckinridge, undated (spring 1885) undated (1885), undated (November 1885?); undated (fall 1885), SPB to WCPB, 22 January 1885, B.MSS boxes.

15. SPB to WCPB, 1 November 1886; SPB to Issa, 2 [January?] 1887; SPB to WCPB, 13 February 1887, 1 November 1886; SPB to Issa Desha Breckinridge, 12, 18 January, 1 February 1887, 1 March 1887; SPB to WCPB, 20 March 1887, all in B.MSS boxes.

16. SPB to WCPB, 9 March, 10 June 1887, B.MSS boxes; "Autobiography."

17. Alice Stone Blackwell to Mary Barr Clay, 28 June 1888, Cassius Marcellus Clay Papers (FC).

18. "Autobiography." According to Isabelle M. Pettus, "The Legal Education of Wo-men," *Journal of Social Science* 38 (1900): 239-40, Boston Law School opened its doors to women in 1872, but few others had by 1890.

19. "Autobiography"; New York *Times*, 29 November 1892; Abbott, "Breckinridge: Supplementary Statement," 94; Lexington *Kentucky Leader*, 19, 26, 31 October 1890; Eugenia D. Potts, "Woman's Work in Kentucky," *Illustrated Kentuckian* 2 (1894): 254; "Autobiogra-phy"; "Tom" to SPB, 15 November 1884 and undated [1880s]; WCPB to SPB, 19 July 1891; Robert W. Woolley to Edith Abbott, 30 July 1948, B.MSS boxes.

20. "Autobiography." A story in the 28 January 1897 *Herald* disputed the suggestion that Nisba was the first female admitted to the Kentucky bar, saying that Flora U. W. Tibbits was examined earlier in 1892. I have not seen evidence, however, supporting that claim. New York *Times*, 29 November 1892, 26 January 1897. Some later sources, beginning with one quoted in Abbott, "Breckinridge: Supplementary Statement," 94, said that Nisba used tears to overcome parental objections to her career in law. None of Breckinridge's own recollections support this assertion, which does not seem compatible with her father's other actions. See for example, WCPB to SPB, 6 July 1899, vol. 503, B.MSS.

21. "Autobiography"; WCPB to John T. Shelby, 14 September 1893, vol. 459, B.MSS; Lexington *Kentucky Leader*, 22, 27 March 1894.

22. Clarke A. Chambers and Andrea Hinding, "Charity Workers, the Settlements, and the Poor," in *Who Spoke for the Poor? 1880-1914* (1968), 21; Louise C. Wade, "The Heritage from Chicago's Early Settlement Houses," *Journal of the Illinois State Historical Society* 60 (1967): 416; John D. Buenker, John C. Burnham, and Robert M. Crunden, *Progressivism* (1977), 75; "Autobiography."

23. WCPB to SPB, 7 March 1894 (copy), 24 January, 6 February 1898, B.MSS boxes; "Autobiography"; WCPB to SPB, 2 April 1899, vol. 502, 31 August 1899, vol. 504, B.MSS; Lexington *Daily Leader*, 15 October 1900; *Herald*, 15 June 1904; Ray Ginger, *Altgeld's America: The Lincoln Ideal versus Changing Realities* (1958), 237; WCPB to SPB, 17 June 1904, vol. 515, and 1 November 1904, B.MSS boxes.

24. Desha Breckinridge to SPB, 24 February 1906, 30 October, 30 November 1907, 24 August 1927, B.MSS boxes; SPB to John T. Shelby, 15 May 1917, box 45, Craig Shelby Papers (UK); *Herald*, 20 February 1914, 28 January 1907, 1 December 1912; Desha Breckinridge to SPB, 3 February 1905, B.MSS boxes; Desha Breckinridge to SPB, 5 October 1914, Chalkley Papers; *Herald*, 16 April 1911.

25. The preceding sketch comes in part from Louise C. Wade's excellent *Graham Taylor: Pioneer for Social Justice* (1964), 1, 55-71; Bessie Louise Pierce, *A History of Chicago*, vol. 3, *The Rise of a Modern City, 1871-1893* (1957); Henry F. May, *The End of American Innocence: A Study of the First Years of Our Own Time, 1912-1917* (1959), 101-3; Helen L. Horowitz, *Culture & the City: Cultural Philanthropy in Chicago from the 1880s to 1917* (1976), ix; Richard Hofstadter, *The Age of Reform: From Bryan to F. D. R.* (1955), 326; and Ginger, *Altgeld's America*, 133.

26. Allen F. Davis, *Spearheads for Reform: The Social Settlements and the Progressive Movement, 1890-1914* (1967), 33-35, 27, 245; Arthur A. Ekirch, Jr., *Progressivism in America: A Study of the Era from Theodore Roosevelt to Woodrow Wilson* (1974), ix, 13; Robert H. Wiebe, *The Search for Order, 1877-1920* (1967), 198; Carl N. Degler, *Out of Our Past: The Forces That Shaped Modern America* (1959), 370; Hofstadter, *Age of Reform*, 205.

27. "Autobiography"; Jill Conway, "Women Reformers and American Culture," *Journal of Social History* 5 (1971-72): 167-68, 174; Ginger, *Altgeld's America*, 123, 117, 136; Lynn Gordon, "Women and the Anti-child Labor Movement in Illinois, 1890-1920," *Social Service Review* 51 (1977): 233, 246; David Potter, "American Women and the American Character," in John A. Hague, ed., *American Character and Culture* (1964), 69.

28. Dorothy G. Becker, "Social Welfare Leaders as Spokesmen for the Poor," in *Who Spoke for the Poor?*, 11.

29. SPB, "The Unshackled Spirit," *Survey* (27 November 1915), 222; *The Crisis* 9 (1915): 308; Travis, "Militant Feminist," 117; SPB, "The Color Line in the Housing Problem," *Survey* (1 February 1913), 575-76; Steven J. Diner, "Chicago Social Workers and Blacks in the Progressive Era," *Social Service Review* 44 (1970): 408; James C. and Freda Campbell Klotter, "Mary Desha, Alaskan Schoolteacher of 1888," *Pacific Northwest Quarterly* 71 (1980): 78, 86; "Autobiography." Both Nisba and Curry Breckinridge refused to see Mary Desha after 1894, however, since she had been active in opposition to their father in the Pollard affair.

30. SPB to Laura Clay, 29 October 1911; Clay to SPB, 1 November 1911 (copy), SPB to Clay, 3 November 1911, Box 6, Laura Clay Papers.

31. SPB, "Legislative Control of Women's Work," *Journal of Political Economy* 14 (1906): 107-9; SPB, "Political Equality for Woman and Women's Wages," in James P. Lichtenberger, ed., *Women in Public Life* (1914), 122-33. See also Edith Abbott and SPB, "Employment of Women in Industries: Twelfth Census Statistics," *Journal of Political Economy* 14 (1906): 14-40;

SPB, "The Home Responsibilities of Women Workers and the 'Equal Wage,' " *ibid*. 31 (1923): 521, 543; SPB, *Women in the Twentieth Century; A Study of Their Political, Social and Economic Activities* (1933), 103-5, 344. See also SPB, "Widows and Orphan's Pensions in Great Britain," *Social Service Review* 1 (1927): 249-57; SPB, "Separate Domicil for Married Women," *ibid*. 4 (1930): 37-52; and SPB, "The Activities of Women Outside the Home," in *Recent Social Trends in the United States . . .* (1933), 709-50.

32. Robert H. Bremner, *From the Depths: The Discovery of Poverty in the United States* (1956), 140; SPB and Edith Abbott, "Housing Conditions in Chicago, III: Back of the Yards," *American Journal of Sociology* 16 (1911): 457.

33. Wade, "Chicago's Settlement Houses," 420; SPB and Edith Abbott, "Chicago's Housing Problem: Families in Furnished Rooms," *American Journal of Sociology* 16 (1910): 293-94; SPB and Abbott, "Back of the Yards," 450, 468; SPB and Abbott, "Chicago Housing Conditions, IV: The West Side Revisited," *American Journal of Sociology* 17 (1911): 33; SPB and Abbott, "Chicago's Housing Conditions, V: South Chicago at the Gates of the Steel Mills," *ibid.*, 176; Bremner, *From the Depths*, 161, 201-3.

34. SPB, "Education for the Americanization of the Foreign Family," *Journal of Home Economics* 11 (1919): 188-89; SPB, *New Homes for Old* (1921), 3-5.

35. SPB, "The Community and the Child," *Survey* (4 February 1911), 785-86; Gordon, "Anti-child Labor Movement," 235. See also SPB and Edith Abbott, *The Delinquent Child and the Home* (1912), 175-77; SPB, "Family Budgets," in *Standards of Child Welfare: A Report of the Children's Bureau Conferences . . .* (1919), 34-43; SPB, "Summary of the Present State Systems for the Organization and Administration of Public Welfare," *Annals of the American Academy of Political and Social Sciences* 105 (1923): 93-103; SPB, *The Family and the State* (1934); and SPB, "Government's Role in Child Welfare," *Annals of the American Academy of Political and Social Science* 212 (1940): 42-50.

36. Eleanor K. Taylor, "The Edith Abbott I Knew," *Journal of the Illinois State Historical Society* 70 (1977): 178-79. Abbott, in an interesting admission, told John C. Baker in a 26 November 1948 letter that she enjoyed Nisba not only for her gifted and quick mind, but also because "she was so lovely to look at." Copy, Papers of Edith and Grace Abbott (University of Chicago). See also Lela B. Costin, *Two Sisters for Social Justice: A Biography of Grace and Edith Abbott* (1983).

37. Wright, "Three Against Time," 41-42; Sophonisba P. Breckinridge Passport, 10 April 1928, B.MSS boxes; Abbott, "Breckinridge: Supplementary Statement"; Abbott, "The Debt of the School of Social Service Administration," *Social Science Review* 22 (1948): 448; Taylor, "Abbott I Knew," 182-83; Edith Abbott, "Sophonisba Preston Breckinridge Over the Years," *Social Science Review* 22 (1948): 420, 422. On her ideas on the social welfare profession, see SPB, "Frontiers of Control in Public Welfare Administration," *Social Service Review* 1 (1927): 84; SPB, "Public Welfare Organizations with Reference to Child Welfare Activities," *ibid*. 4 (1930): 376-419; and SPB, "The New Horizons of Professional Education for Social Work," *ibid*. 10 (1936): 437-49.

38. Unidentified clipping, circa 1933, B.MSS boxes; Taylor, "Abbott I Knew," 182; Edith Abbott, "Sophonisba Breckinridge over the Years," *Social Science Review* 22 (1948): 417; *Chicago Daily News*, 8 June 1946; Charles E. Merriam, "A Member of the University Community," *Social Science Review* 22 (1948): 424; Katherine F. Lenroot, "Friend of Children and of the Children's Bureau," *ibid*. 427, 429. Abbott, "Breckinridge Over the Years," 421.

39. [Marguerite Woolley?] to Robert W. Woolley, 2 August 1948, Robert W. Woolley Papers (LC); Edith Abbott to W. H. Courtney, 6 April, 10 July 1948, Abbott Papers. Breckinridge's estate totalled $10,418.

15. The Patrician as Progressive

1. *Herald*, 19 November 1906, 17 January 1918, 19 November 1907; Desha Breckinridge (hereinafter DB) to SPB, 12 January 1905, 21 March 1920, B.MSS boxes, There are no biographies of or scholarly articles on Desha Breckinridge. Sketches of his life appear in the

Dictionary of American Biography, Supplement I, and Willis, *Kentucky Democracy* (see chap. 11, n. 4), 2:200-203.

2. *Herald*, 19 February 1935. His name is pronounced "Da-shaỳ."

3. *Herald*, 12 March 1911, 17 February 1931, 5 March 1911, 2 July 1908; Chalkley, "Magic Casements," 12-16, 20, 73.

4. *Herald*, 14 January 1905, 12 April 1906, 28 January 1917.

5. *Ibid.*, 19 February 1935; State of Kentucky Matriculates Book, 1869-89; J. C. Mac-Kenzie to WCPB, 28 March, 20 June 1884; DB to WCPB, 2 March 1884, vol. 332, B.MSS.

6. DB to Henry Breckinridge, 11 July 1933; DB to Issa D. Breckinridge, 24 November 1885, 16, 6 October, B.MSS boxes.

7. DB to SPB [undated], 28 September, 15 November 1884; DB to Helm Bruce 10 June 1921 (copy); DB to Issa D. Breckinridge, 17 November 1886, B.MSS boxes; *Herald*, 3 July 1927; DB to Issa D. Breckinridge, 21 November 1886, B.MSS boxes.

8. DB to Issa D. Breckinridge, 2 November 1885, B.MSS boxes; *Herald*, 7 February 1924.

9. *Herald*, 12 March 1912, 13 March 1911; WCPB to Curry Breckinridge, 29 May 1891, WCPB to Curry Breckinridge and SPB, 9 May 1891; WCPB to Nisba, 5 August 1891; Issa D. Breckinridge to Curry Breckinridge, 3 January 1892, B.MSS boxes; Louisville *Times*, 29 November 1921.

10. Lexington (pseud.), *Celebrated Case* (see chap. 12, n. 24), 42.

11. DB to Roberts, 18, 23 November 1893, vol. 461, B.MSS; *New York Times*, 10 June 1894; Unidentified speech, 1894, B.MSS boxes.

12. Lexington *Leader*, 22 September 1894; *New York Times*, 22 September 1894.

13. *Herald*, 26 July 1908; Agreement between S. G. Boyle and DB, 19 January 1897; WCPB to Nisba, 2 February 1898, B.MSS boxes.

14. Desha Breckinridge's view of his ancestors is drawn from numerous *Herald* editorials covering the 1904-1935 period.

15. Allen, *Blue-Grass Region*, 11, 19, 34, 40; Thomas D. Clark, introduction to Mary C. Browning, *Kentucky Authors: A History of Kentucky Literature* (1968), x-xii.

16. Browning, *Kentucky Authors*, xii, 255; Fox, *Little Shepherd of Kingdom Come*, 87-88, 139.

17. New York *Times*, 14 June, 23 August 1894; SPB, "Madeline McDowell Breckinridge: Herald of Community Service," in Howard W. Odum, ed., *Southern Pioneers in Social Interpretation* (1925), 199; "Autobiography"; SPB, *Madeline McDowell Breckinridge: A Leader in the New South* (1921), x, 4, 10-11, 13, 19-20; Margaret W. Preston Diary, 4, 17 July 1910, 25 January 1911, box 40, Preston-Johnston Papers (UK); author's interview with Florence Cantrill, Lexington, 31 January 1975. Mrs. Cantrill was a cousin of Madge Breckinridge and a niece of John T. Shelby, and she married the half-brother of Congressman J. Campbell Cantrill.

18. SPB, *M. M. Breckinridge*, 15; Bessie W. Haskell to SPB, 16 April 1921, B.MSS boxes; Louisville *Courier-Journal*, 16 March 1913; *Illustrated Kentuckian* 1 (1893): 188; Frederick Eberson, *Portraits: Kentucky Pioneers in Community Health and Medicine* (1968), 9; Melba Porter Hay, "Madeline McDowell Breckinridge: Kentucky Suffragist and Progressive Reformer" (Ph.D. dissertation, University of Kentucky, 1980), 6-8; "A. P. C.," "Madeline McDowell Breckinridge," typescript dated 17 August 1962 (FC); Cantrill Interview; "Autobiography."

19. WCPB to SPB, 29 May 1898, B.MSS boxes; *Herald*, 16, 18 November 1898.

20. Cantrill interview; author's interview with Mrs. Thomas R. Underwood, Lexington, 24 January 1975 (Mrs. Underwood worked for Breckinridge during and after World War I and married eventual managing editor Thomas Rust Underwood). "Autobiography"; *Herald*, 22 February 1935.

21. Cantrill and Underwood interviews; *Herald*, 5 December 1920, 20 February 1923; Hay, "Madeline McDowell Breckinridge," viii, 23; SPB, "Herald of Community Service," 188; Louisville *Courier-Journal*, 23 January 1910; SPB, *M. M. Breckinridge*, 29; SPB, "Herald of Community Service," 191-95; Melba D. Porter, "Madeline McDowell Breckinridge: Her Role in The Kentucky Woman Suffrage Movement, 1908-1920," *Register* 72 (1974): 343; Louisville *Courier-Journal*, 16 March 1913; *Herald*, 1 December 1912, 26 March 1914.

22. SPB, *M. M. Breckinridge*, 45; Scott, *Southern Lady*, 219, 219n; *Herald*, 24 October 1911; "Autobiography."

23. *Herald*, 7 January 1905; Harriet T. Upton to Clay, 30 November 1906, box 3, Laura Clay Papers; *Herald*, 7 January 1907, 8 August 1909.

24. Porter, "M. M. Breckinridge," 347-48; *Herald*, 4 March, 17 February 1910, 14 April 1912.

25. Porter, "M. M. Breckinridge," 345; *Herald*, 15 November 1915; Madeline M. Breckinridge, "Another Reason For Granting School Suffrage . . . III, IV," Madeline McDowell Breckinridge Papers (UK); Harrodsburg *Republican*, quoted in *Herald*, 5 November 1911; clipping in James Campbell Cantrill Papers (UK microfilm); SPB, *M. M. Breckinridge*, 201; Hay, "Madeline McDowell Breckinridge," 160; Laura Clay to M. M. Breckinridge, 9 October 1918 (copy), box 11, Laura Clay Papers; Fuller, *Laura Clay*, 144, 147-54; *Herald*, 13 March, 3 June, 14-19, February 1919.

26. *Herald*, 7 January 1920; SPB, *M. M. Breckinridge*, 236-37.

27. *Herald*, 17 January, 18 March 1905; *Abstract of the Thirteenth Census [1910]* (1913), 23; *Herald*, 16 September 1908.

28. *Herald*, 31 January 1906, 6 June, 7 June, 14 February 1919, 10 February 1905.

29. *Ibid.*, 3 January 1906, 5 May 1912; Otis L. Graham, Jr., *An Encore for Reform: The Old Progressives and the New Deal* (1967), 67; G. Edward White, "The Social Values of the Progressives: Some New Perspectives," *South Atlantic Quarterly* 70 (1971): 64, 72-73.

30. *Herald*, 14 December 1904, 29 January 1905, 14 March 1906, 29 August 1919, 3 May 1906; Hortense Flexner, "Social Legislation in Kentucky," *The Survey* 28 (1912): 697.

31. *Herald*, 5 April 1912, 26 October 1924; *Annual Report of the Board of Prison Commissioners . . . 1905* (1905), 9, 12, 38-40; *Herald*, 25 August 1909, 27 June 1911, 9 September 1919.

32. *Herald*, 20 May 1912, 30 March 1916, 16 September 1908, 17 December 1904, 14, 15 January 1905, 9 September 1907, 5 June 1911; 12 June, 10 September, 28 March 1912.

33. *Ibid.*, 26 January 1906, 9 August 1912, 22 April 1913, 8 June 1911; New York *Age*, 20 April 1905, 16 March 1915; George W. Forbes, "President Wilson, Trotter and the American People," *A. M. E. Church Review* 31 (1915): 313-15; *The Crisis* 7 (1913): 333; 9 (1915): 125-26; *Herald*, 27 April 1919, 5-6 March 1926.

34. *Herald*, 17 February 1905, 10 November 1911, 15 December 1908; Fredrickson, *Black Image in the White Mind*, 296; John Higham, *Strangers in the Land: Patterns of American Nativism, 1860-1925* (1955), 140-44, 173-75; Ekirch, *Progressivism in America*, 8-9, 84; *Herald*, 3 January 1904; 29 November 1906; 7 November, 1907.

35. *Herald*, 5, 8, November 1909; 11 November 1910; Dewey W. Grantham, Jr., "The Progressive Movement and the Negro," *South Atlantic Quarterly* 54 (1955): 461-77.

36. *Herald*, 5 May 1912.

37. *Herald*, 28 November 1906, 4 January 1917.

38. Chalkley, "Magic Casements," 113.

39. For the political situation in the 1900-20 period, see Thomas H. Appleton, Jr., "Like Banquo's Ghost: The Emergence of the Prohibition Issue in Kentucky Politics" (Ph.D. dissertation, University of Kentucky, 1981); Nicholas C. Burckel, "From Beckham to Mc-Creary: The Progressive Record of Kentucky Governors," *Register* 76 (1978): 285-306; John H. Fenton, *Politics in the Border States* (1957), 14-46; Robert K. Foster, "Augustus E. Willson and the Republican Party of Kentucky, 1895-1911" (thesis, University of Louisville, 1955); Glenn Finch, "The Election of United States Senators in Kentucky—The Beckham Period," *FCHQ* 44 (1970): 38-50; Thomas W. Ramage, "Augustus Owsley Stanley: Early Twentieth Century Kentucky Democrat" (Ph.D. dissertation, University of Kentucky, 1968); *Herald*, 21 August 1907, 4 August 1915; Arthur Krock, *Myself When Young: Growing Up in the 1890's* (1973), 174-75; "Campaign Hand Book of the Republican Party, 1915," 6, 24, in Ollie Murray James Papers (UK); *Herald*, 21, 28 September 1919.

40. *Herald*, 8 July 1908, 9 August 1912, 5 March 1905, 29 April 1906, 18 September 1910; Lexington *Leader*, 12 July 1911; Woodrow Wilson to Henry Watterson, 29 June 1911, vol. 11, DB to Watterson, 2 August 1911, vol. 12, Henry Watterson Papers.

41. DB to Robert W. Woolley, 4 December 1912, 15 May 1913, Woolley to DB, 11 January 1913, box 2, Woolley Papers; clippings in Cantrill Papers, "Scrapbook, April 3, 1913-July 27,

1913"; *Herald,* 5 October 1911; DB to William H. Taft, 6 May 1909, DB to William F. Combs, 2 April 1913, DB to Wilson, 3 May 1913, William G. McAdoo to Wilson, 7 May 1913, all in Woodrow Wilson Papers (LC); Arthur S. Link, *Woodrow Wilson and the Progressive Era, 1910-1917* (1954), 29, 29n; Link, *Wilson: The New Freedom* (1956), 153, 161.

42. Lexington *Herald,* 26 July 1914, 13 June 1915; Link, *Wilson and Progressive Era,* 107-24, 124n; *Herald,* 14 May, 21, 25 April 1914. See also William E. Leuchtenburg, "Progressivism and Imperialism: The Progressive Movement and American Foreign Policy 1898-1916," *Mississippi Valley Historical Review* 39 (1952): 483,496.

43. *Herald,* 12 March, 9 May, 25 June 1916; DB to Robert Woolley, 26 June 1916, box 2, Woolley Papers.

44. *Herald,* 22 February 1906, 1, 6 September, 4 April, 7 August 1914, 14 November 1915 (quotation); 16 March 1916 (last quotation).

45. *Ibid.,* 27 April, 15 October, 12 March 1916; DB to Curry Breckinridge, 12 March 1917, B.MSS boxes.

46. *Herald,* 2 March 1917, 30 March, 16 February, 6, 14 April 1918.

47. *Ibid,* 28 March 1917, 4 February 1919.

48. *Ibid.,* 27, 28 January 1917, 2, 5 January, 5, 6 March 1919. See also N. Gordon Levin, Jr., *Woodrow Wilson and World Politics: America's Response to War and Revolution* (1968), 104, 109, 187.

49. *Herald,* 9 May 1919, 21 March 1920.

50. *Ibid.,* 1 February, 15, 13 August 1920; DB to Breckinridge Long, 4 May 1933, Breckinridge Long Papers, box 100 (LC); Robert P. Browder, *The Origins of Soviet-American Diplomacy* (1953), 31, 52, 72, 172.

51. *Herald,* 23 July 1907, 7 August 1906; Preston Diary, 5 August, 30 May 1913, 30 March 1917, 17 October 1907, 22 August 1908, 31 January, 27 November 1913, 10 December 1908, 31 December 1913; Cantrill interview; Madeline M. Breckinridge to SPB, 27 July 1914, B.MSS boxes; *Herald,* 31 March 1912.

52. DB to Curry Breckinridge, 20 December 1914, Chalkley Papers; Cantrill and Underwood interviews; "Autobiography"; Chalkley, "Magic Casements," 17; DB to Curry Breckinridge, 2, 6 June 1916; Ella Breckinridge to Curry Breckinridge, 31 July 1916, B.MSS boxes.

53. Lexington *Daily Leader,* 7 October, 1 September 1900, 10 January 1901; Furman, "Katherine Pettit," 18; "Autobiography"; [Mary Breckinridge], "The Vocation of Nursing," *Quarterly Bulletin of Frontier Nursing Service* 29 (Summer 1953): 53-54; DB to Curry Breckinridge, 23 February 1915, Chalkley Papers; Linda Neville to Carolyn Van Blarcom, 30 September 1917, Group I, box 11, Linda Neville Papers (UK); *Herald,* 24 June 1918.

54. Graham, *Encore for Reform,* 156-63; William E. Leuchtenburg, *The Perils of Prosperity, 1914-32* (1958), 120-27; Eric F. Goldman, *Rendezvous With Destiny,* rev. ed. (1956), 224-25; Otis L. Graham, Jr., *The Great Campaigns: Reform and War in America, 1900-1928* (1971), 117-19, 121, 130, 138, 152; Herbert F. Margulies, "Recent Opinion on the Decline of the Progressive Movement," *Mid-America* 45 (1963): 265; May, *End of American Innocence,* 393-98.

16. Transformation of Desha Breckinridge

1. SPB, *M. M. Breckinridge,* 56, 125; DB to Curry Breckinridge, 26 August 1916, B.MSS boxes.

2. *Herald,* 26 November, 5 December 1920.

3. *Herald,* 1 January 1922. It was widely rumored that Desha Breckinridge had long been having an affair with one of his wife's friends. Whether true or not, Breckinridge "in his own way" had continued to show affection and respect for Madge. His editorial words reflected accurately his feelings of loss. For a discussion of the rumored affair, see Hay, "Madeline McDowell Breckinridge," viii, 177-79.

4. *Herald,* 1 July 1923.

5. *Ibid.,* 1 May, 8 August 1924, 31 January 1932, 19 March 1926, 1 May 1923; George B.

Tindall, "Business Progressivism: Southern Politics in the Twenties," *South Atlantic Quarterly* 42 (1963): 93-95.

6. *Herald*, 17 August 1919, 5 September 1923, 5 February 1922.

7. *Ibid.*, 3 March 1922, 31 July 1931, 11 October 1923.

8. *Herald*, 2 August 1923, 12 August 1924, 27 January 1930, 16 August 1924; DB to Alben Barkley, 18 May 1923, Political File, box 2, Barkley Papers.

9. *Herald*, 21 March 1926; 5, 21 January, 19, 26 February, 8, 11 March 1930; "Cumberland Falls Saved," *Survey* (15 April 1930), 68; George W. Robinson, "Conservation in Kentucky: The Fight to Save Cumberland Falls, 1926-1931," *Register* 81 (1983): 48-53; Virginius Dabney, *Liberalism in the South* (1932), 410.

10. *Herald*, 5 February 1922; Agreement between C. B. Lowry and Desha Breckinridge, 31 May 1897; "Last Will and Testament of Mr. Desha Breckinridge, 1898" (copy), both in B.MSS boxes.

11. *Herald*, 8 April, 5, 6 May, 20 September, 5 May, 12 June 1923, 28 September 1924, 16, 17 May 1925; clipping from Louisville *Post*, B.MSS boxes; Madisonville *Messenger*, 19 February 1935, clipping in Thomas R. Underwood Papers (UK); DB to Henry Breckinridge, 9, 19 May 1925, B.MSS boxes.

12. DB to Henry Breckinridge, 28 October 1925, B.MSS boxes; DB to Long, 9 November 1925, box 30, 19 May, 30 July, 10 December 1926, box 82, all in Long Papers; *Herald*, 3 August 1927.

13. *Herald*, 8 May 1908, 5 February 1922, 13 May, 26 January, 1923. See Ralph W. Clark, "The Legal Regulation of Organized Racing in Kentucky" (thesis, University of Kentucky, 1941), 18-62.

14. *Herald*, 5 February 1922, 14-15, 21, 22 February, 20 March 1924, 8 November 1934; Lexington *Leader* 28 October 1924. Breckinridge reacted to the *Leader's* criticism by calling on them to refuse to print racing news, if they opposed the sport so.

15. For 1920-35, see Robert F. Sexton, "Kentucky Politics and Society, 1919-1932" (Ph.D. dissertation, University of Washington, 1970); Jasper B. Shannon, "The Political Process in Kentucky," *Kentucky Law Journal* 45 (1957): 413-17; Glenn Finch, "The Election of United States Senators in Kentucky: The Barkley Period," *FCHQ* 45 (1971): 286-304; and James B. Skaggs, "The Rise and Fall of Flem Sampson" (thesis, Eastern Kentucky University, 1976).

16. Press release dated 6 January 1922, Cantrill Papers.

17. *Herald*, 20 February, 12 June 1923; Arthur Krock, *Myself When Young: Growing Up in the 1890's* (1973), 178-79; George W. Robinson, "The Making of a Kentucky Senator: Alben W. Barkley and the Gubernatorial Primary of 1923," *FCHQ* 40 (1966): 127-29; *Herald*, 20 February, 12 June 1923.

18. *Herald*, 8 May 1923, 16 November 1920, 22 January 1922; 13 May, 21-22 July 1923. See also DB to Robert W. Bingham, 8 August 1918, and Bingham to DB, 10 November 1920 (copy), Robert Worth Bingham Papers (FC).

19. Hay, "Madeline McDowell Breckinridge," 147; Paducah *Weekly News-Democrat*, 19 July 1906; *Herald*, 22 July 1906.

20. DB to Breckinridge Long, 6 August 1923, Long Papers, box 71; *Herald*, 24, 29 August, 3, 9 September, 25, 26 October 1923, 11, 9 January 1924.

21. *Herald*, 15 January, 25 February 1924; DB to Henry Breckinridge, 7 January 1924, B.MSS boxes.

22. *Herald*, 27 July 1924.

23. *Herald*, 22 February, 30 August, 26, 28 February, 7 September 1924.

24. Robert Worth Bingham to DB, 19 November 1920 (copy), Robert Worth Bingham Papers. (LC).

25. DB to Breckinridge Long, 1 January 1927; DB to Leon P. Lewis, 5 January 1927 (copy), Long Papers, box 85; Louisville *Kentucky Irish-American*, 8 January 1927; Louisville *Herald-Post*, 31 December 1926; "Kentucky to Choose Between Beckham and Betting," *Literary Digest* (27 August 1927). See T. Harry Williams, *Romance and Realism in Southern Politics* (1961), 62, and Frances S. Wagner, "The Kentucky Gubernatorial Election of 1927" (thesis, University of Kentucky, 1969), 49-50.

26. *Herald*, 9 October 1927, 10, 12, 14 November 1927. Sampson won by 32,133 votes;

the Democratic nominee for lieutenant governor won by 159 votes. *Herald*, 22 November 1927.

27. James O. Nall, *The Tobacco Night Riders of Kentucky and Tennessee, 1905-1909* (1939), 141; J. C. Cantrill to J. B. Simpson, 12 May 1922 (copy), Cantrill Papers; *Herald*, 20 June 1928, 14 March 1919. Preston Diary, 24 April 1913, 15 April 1910; Cantrill, Underwood interviews; Krock, *Myself When Young*, 131; DB to Breckinridge Long, 24 February 1928, Long Papers, box 88; Lexington *Herald-Leader*, 12-13 June 1949; *Herald*, 28 July 1929; *New York Times*, 28 July 1929; Cantrill interview. See also DB to Breckinridge Long, 6 August 1923, Long Papers, box 71; DB to Henry Breckinridge, 22 August 1925, B.MSS boxes.

28. DB to Henry Breckinridge, 12 January, 4 February 1929; clipping from *Daily Racing Form*, 22 March 1929 in B.MSS boxes; DB to Breckinridge Long, 12 April 1929, 24 June 1929, box 91, 28 May 1930, box 93, 7 March 1931, box 95, all in Long Papers.

29. *Herald*, 11 January 1928; DB to Breckinridge Long, 28 November 1928, Long Papers, box 88; DB to Henry Breckinridge, 12 January 1929, B.MSS boxes; DB to Long, 16 November 1929, Long Papers, box 91.

30. DB to Breckinridge Long, 21 November 1931, Long Papers, box 95; Henry Breckinridge to DB, 4 May 1921 (copy), B.MSS boxes; *Edward P. Remington's Annual Newspaper Directory for 1898* (1898), 100; *Herald*, 1 November 1916.

31. *Herald*, 5 August 1914, 1 January 1922, 25 March 1923; Willard Rouse Jillson, "Governor Keen Johnson," *Register* 38 (1940): 2; *Herald*, 2 June 1907; Underwood interview.

32. interview with Mrs. A. E. Oram, 27 May 1980 (Mrs. Oram, who was 87 in 1980, was Breckinridge's secretary during the later 1910s); *Herald*, 3 January, 15-19 June 1926, 27 November 1931; DB to Cassius M. Clay, 1 April 1900, Cassius M. Clay Papers (UK); DB to Mary E. Flanery, 12 June 1926, Mary Elliott Flanery Correspondence, box 1 (UK); DB to Henry Breckinridge, 18 June 1934, B.MSS boxes.

33. *Herald*, 16 October 1924, 24 June 1928; New York *Times*, 7, 6 September 1928; DB to W. H. Claggett, 1 May 1928 (copy), DB to Breckinridge Long, 20 June, 10 July, 3, 14 September 1928, all in Long Papers, box 88; *Herald*, 28 November 1928.

34. DB to Breckinridge Long, 21 November 1931, Long Papers, box 95; *Herald*, 22 July 1931, 12 June, 12 January, 7, 26, 29 June 1932; DB to Howard P. Ingels, 1 February 1932 (copy), DB to Byrd, 13 July 1935 (copy), B.MSS boxes; DB to Breckinridge Long, 10 October 1932, Long Papers, box 97; DB to Fred Vinson, 13 May 1932, Political File, box 110, Fred M. Vinson Collection (UK); DB to Breckinridge Long, 23 November 1932, Long Papers, box 97.

35. *Herald*, 12, 15, 21 March, 30 April 1933; DB to Henry Breckinridge, 25 March 1933, B.MSS boxes; DB to Long, 4 May 1933, 23 October 1933, box 100; 31 August 1929, box 91, Long Papers; William E. Dodd, Jr. and Martha Dodd, eds., *Ambassador Dodd's Diary, 1933-1938* (1941), 95; DB to W. E. Dodd, 30 October 1911, William E. Dodd Papers, box 8 (LC); DB to Henry Breckinridge, 27 December 1933, 20 January 1934, B.MSS boxes. Henry Breckinridge, like his close friend and client Charles Lindbergh, moved to the right, attacking what he called the president's "anti-collectivism," appeals to class hatreds, and anti-constitutional moves. Henry Breckinridge died on 2 May 1960. See Henry Breckinridge to Harry F. Byrd, 7 December 1933, 20 August 1934, Harry F. Byrd Papers (University of Virginia Library); Henry Breckinridge, *Excerpts, 1935-1936* (1938), 5.

36. *Herald*, 14, 17 March, 15, 29 January, 5, 19 February, 1930; DB to Robert W. Woolley, 28 May 1934, Woolley Papers, box 2; Breckinridge Long to DB, 3 December 1923 (copy), box 71; Mary Breckinridge to Long, 14 April 1933, box 100, both in Long Papers; SPB to Henry Breckinridge, 14 April 1933, DB to Thomas McG. Lowry, 3 April 1933 (copy), B.MSS boxes; Mary Breckinridge to Long, 9 July 1933, Long Papers, box 100; Pineville *Sun*, 21 February 1935, clipping in Underwood Papers; DB to Henry Breckinridge, 6 June 1933, B.MSS boxes. "Ripper bills" reorganized state agencies, necessitating new appointments.

37. DB to Henry Breckinridge, 8, 10 September 1934, B.MSS boxes; *Herald*, 19 February 1935; Underwood interview; *Herald*, 8 November 1934, 19, 22 February 1935; New York *Times*, 19 February 1935.

38. Henry Breckinridge to DB, 26 October 1933 (copy), B.MSS boxes; *Herald*, 10 January 1932.

17. The Last Pioneer

1. Generalizations on Appalachia in this period come from James C. Klotter, "The Black South and White Appalachia," *Journal of American History* 66 (1980): 832-49, and from material in the footnotes cited therein; Ronald D Eller, *Miners, Millhands and Mountaineers: Industrialization of the Appalachian South, 1880-1930* (1982); Henry D. Shapiro, *Appalachia on Our Mind: The Southern Mountains and Mountaineers in the American Consciousness, 1870-1920* (1978); John C. Campbell, *The Southern Highlander & His Homeland* (1969; orig. pub. 1921); and Cratis D. Williams, "The Southern Mountaineer in Fact and Fiction," (Ph.D. dissertation, New York University, 1961).

2. On this pre-1870 settlement, see Henry P. Scalf, *Kentucky's Last Frontier*, 2d ed. (1972), 92-231; Virginia Clay McClure, "The Settlement of the Kentucky Appalachian Highlands" (Ph.D. dissertation, University of Kentucky, 1933); Gary S. Foster, "Appalachian Isolation in Perspective," *Appalachian Heritage* 8 (1980): 34-47.

3. Eller, *Miners and Mountaineers*, xviii. See also James C. Klotter, "Appalachian Feuds: An Overview," *FCHQ* 56 (1982): 290-317; D. H. Schockel, "Changing Conditions in the Kentucky Mountains," *Scientific Monthly* 3 (1916): 22; and Hal S. Barron, "A Case for Appalachian Demographic History," *Appalachian Journal* 4 (1977) 211.

4. Young E. Allison, "Moonshine Men," *Southern Bivouac* 2 (1887): 528; New York *Times*, 30 November 1878, 9 July 1885; Samuel T. Wilson, *The Southern Mountaineers* (1914), 9, 193; William G. Frost, "New England in Kentucky," *Advance* (6 June 1895), 1285; Ellen Churchill Semple, "The Anglo-Saxons of the Kentucky Mountains . . . ," *Bulletin of the American Geographical Society* 42 (1910): 566; Julian Ralph, *Dixie; or Southern Scenes and Sketches* (1896), 312; Raymond Fuller, "Old Time American Stock," *The Mentor* 16 (1928): 15; Frost, "Our Contemporary Ancestors in the Southern Mountains," *Atlantic Monthly* 83 (1899): 311; William G. Frost, "Appalachian America," *Ladies Home Companion* 23 (1896): 4.

5. Klotter, "Black South and White Appalachia," 842-48; Richard B. Drake, "The Mission School Era in Southern Appalachia, 1880-1940," *Appalachian Notes* 6 (1978): 1-8; David E. Whisnant, *Modernizing The Mountaineer* (1980), 3-8. See also James M. McPherson, *The Abolitionist Legacy: From Reconstruction to the NAACP* (1975), 143, 161, 240.

6. See Judge Watson, "The Economic and Cultural Development of Eastern Kentucky From 1900 to the Present" (Ph.D. dissertation, Indiana University, 1963) and Bruce Crawford, "The Coal Miner," in W. T. Couch, ed., *Culture in the South* (1934), 361-73.

7. Carson Family Bible, photostat, B.MSS boxes.

8. The following sketch of Clifton Breckinridge is from Louisville *Courier-Journal*, 4 December 1932; *Who's Who in America (1920-21)*, 341; "Clifton R. Breckinridge of Arkansas," *American Industries* (30 December 1893), 1; Henry Loomis Nelson, "Hon. Clifton R. Breckinridge," *Harper's Weekly* (2 June 1894), 309; David W. Hacker, "Dealing with the Russians," Little Rock *Arkansas Gazette Sunday Magazine*, 3 July 1955; John H. Page, "Political Reminiscences," newspaper clipping in Prewitt Collection; "Clifton Rodes Breckinridge," *National Cyclopaedia of American Biography* 8 (1925): 191; Dorsey D. Jones, "Breckinridge: An Arkansan at the Court of the Tsar," *Arkansas Historical Quarterly* 1 (1942): 193-205; and James F. Willis, "An Arkansan in St. Petersburg: Clifton Rodes Breckinridge, Minister to Russia, 1894-1897," *ibid.* 38 (1979): 3-31.

9. Mary Breckinridge, *Wide Neighborhoods: A Story of the Frontier Nursing Service* (1981; orig. pub. 1952), 44, 3-7; "Description of a Rural Community Known to Me," paper for a Columbia University education course, 1923, Mary Breckinridge Papers (UK); Florence B. Carson, "Memories of 'Oasis' Plantation, Miss.," Breckinridge Family Papers (Southern Historical Collection, University of North Carolina Library). Since Breckinridge apparently destroyed many of her papers, her autobiography, *Wide Neighborhoods*, is the best available source on her early life. Later in life, she told a friend to destroy letters sent by her and told how she would destroy her girlhood journals, "lest there be any chance of strangers reading it after I am dead." Mary Breckinridge (hereinafter MB) to "Pansy" [Mrs. Jesse Turner], 20 December 1951 (copy), Frontier Nursing Service Administrative Records (on deposit, UK).

10. Transcript of tape-recorded interviews with Julia Breckinridge Davis, 24 April 1980, and with Grace Reeder, 25 January 1979, both in Frontier Nursing Service Oral History

Project (Frontier Nursing Service, Hyden, Kentucky and copies at UK); "A Paper-Doll Book Called Little Mischiefs or Dot and Bill" (1896), Mary Breckinridge Papers; *Wide Neighborhoods*, 5, 7, 10, 12, 14, 20, 13, 25.

11. *Wide Neighborhoods*, 15 (quotation), 5, 9, 20-28; three-page typescript life of Mary Breckinridge in John Bayne Breckinridge Papers.

12. *Wide Neighborhoods*, 30-37; *Year Book . . . of Miss Low's School* (1898), 44, 53.

13. *Wide Neighborhoods*, 30-37, 31.

14. *Herald*, 26 November 1904; Little Rock *Arkansas Gazette Magazine*, 27 October 1935; *Wide Neighborhoods*, 49, 52, 50.

15. *Wide Neighborhoods*, 52-58, 59; Mary Breckinridge Morrison, "The Women of Thackeray: A Tribute," *Westminster Review* 168 (1907): 299-303 and her later "The Poetry of the Southern United States," *ibid*. 176 (1911): 61-72; Little Rock *Arkansas Gazette Magazine*, 27 October 1935.

16. On Thompson, see *Who's Who in America, 1922-1923*, 3047; *ibid., 1942-43*, 2172. Born in 1878, he married Breckinridge on 8 October 1912. Thompson later served as Democratic state senator and remarried in 1927. Emily Sangman to "Miss Lewis" (Agnes Lewis?), 3 August 1965, B.MSS boxes; MB to John Dewey, 28 August 1917 (copy); John Dewey to MB, 4 October 1917; "Report of a course in Child Welfare instituted at Crescent College, Eureka Springs, Arkansas, 1917-18 . . . " (typed MS), all in Mary Breckinridge Papers.

17. Eureka Springs *Daily Times-Echo*, 26 November 1915, 3, 31 March 1917; Little Rock *Arkansas Gazette*, 13 January 1918; MB to Murray Averback, 16 September 1917 (copy); Mary C. Nelson to MB (copy) [1917]; and MB to Marie T. Durning, 25 November 1917, all in Mary Breckinridge Papers; Mary Breckinridge Thompson, "Motherhood—A Career," *Southern Woman's Magazine* (January through June 1917).

18. *Herald*, 8 February 1914; Mary Breckinridge Thompson, *Breckie: His Four Years, 1914-1918* (1918), 5, 29, 73, 62, 57.

19. Thompson, *Breckie*, 58-59, 187-88; *Wide Neighborhoods*, 66, 73.

20. Thompson, *Breckie*, 195, 192; *Wide Neighborhoods*, 60.

21. *Who's Who, 1942-1943*, 383; Thompson, *Breckie*, 57; Interviews with Marvin Breckinridge Patterson, 13 May 1978, and Helen E. Browne, 27 March 1979, both in FNS Oral History Project (transcript); MB to "Pansy" [Mrs. Jesse Turner], 20 March 1952 (copy), FNS Records; MB to SPB, 23 May 1918 (copy), Mary Breckinridge Papers; Chicago *Daily Tribune*, 20 August 1918.

22. *Wide Neighborhoods*, 75-77; Mary Beard and Gracy O'Bryan to Chairman, C.A.R.D., 15 January 1919, Mary Breckinridge Papers; Anne G. Campbell, "Mary Breckinridge and the American Committee for Devastated France: The Foundations of the Frontier Nursing Service" *Register* 82 (1984): 257-76; MB to Lees Breckinridge Dunn, 23 February 1919; MB to Katherine Carson Breckinridge, 11 November 1920, 30 March 1919 (quotation), 24 February 1919, Mary Breckinridge Papers.

23. MB to Katherine Carson Breckinridge, 22 January 1920; "Child Welfare Work: Quarterly Report of Public Health Nursing, Vic s/ Aisne Center" (1 January 1920), 1, Mary Breckinridge Papers; *Six Months Report of the Five Centers of the American Committee for Devastated France . . .* ([1920]), 1-2; Mary Breckinridge and Evelyn Walker, *Annual Report of the Department of Public Health Nursing, American Committee for Devastated France* (1921), 2-3; January 1920 "Report," 4; *Wide Neighborhoods*, 85, 81, 109; MB, "Our Work in Child Hygiene in Devastated France," *"Under Two Flags": A Weekly Bulletin of the Work in France and America* (6 September 1919), 1; MB to Katherine Carson Breckinridge, 18, 31 May 1919, Mary Breckinridge Papers; *"Under Two Flags"* (17 April 1920), 1.

24. *Wide Neighborhoods*, 104-5, 100; MB to Katherine Carson Breckinridge, 17 October 1920, Mary Breckinridge Papers.

25. *Wide Neighborhoods*, 110, 99, 113, 115, 77; MB to Katherine Carson Breckinridge, 28 March 1921, 23 July 1919; MB to Anne Morgan, 10 January 1922; Elizabeth Scarborough to MB, 20 December 1921; Carson Breckinridge to Clifton Rodes Breckinridge, 15 December 1931, Mary Breckinridge Papers; *Herald*, 3, 4, 6 March 1942; *Who's Who, 1942-43*, 383; "James Carson Breckinridge, U.S.M.C.," FNS Administrative Records.

26. "A few papers of M.B. at Teachers College, Columbia," 4 January 1923, Mary

Breckinridge Papers; *Wide Neighborhoods*, 124, 157, "Private Record," 18 August - 9 October 1924 and "Note Book," 9 October 1924 - January 1925, Mary Breckinridge Papers.

18. Midwifery in the Mountains

1. "Introduction," *Kentucky Committee for Mothers and Babies*, 1 (June 1925), 2. (The name of this journal varied over the years and hereinafter will be cited as *FNS Bulletin*.) MB, "A Frontier Nursing Service," *FNS Bulletin* 24 (Autumn 1948): 17; MB, "Where the Frontier Lingers," *The Rotarian* 47 (1935): 12; MB, Introduction to Caroline Gardner, *Clever Country; Kentucky Mountain Trails* (1931), 5; Breckinridge, "Frontier Nursing Service," 18; MB, "Is Birth Control the Answer?" *Harper's Magazine* 163 (1931): 161. See also MB, "Maternity in the Mountains," *North American Review* 226 (1928): 768. Breckinridge seems to have generally opposed birth control for the mountain people, but she later relented and finally allowed doctors to introduce the then-new birth control pill to the area. For a recent interpretation of the FNS see Nancy Dammann's good *A Social History of the Frontier Nursing Service* (1982).
   2. MB to "Molly, Laetitia, Cabell" (Bullock?), 7 January 1922; *Wide Neighborhoods*, 157-58
   3. Breckinridge, "Introduction" (*FNS Bulletin*), 3 (quotation), 6-8.
   4. Mary Breckinridge, "An Adventure in Midwifery," *The Survey* (1 October 1926), 26; W. T. Price, *Without Scrip or Purse; or "The Mountain Evangelist," George O. Barnes* (1883), 287; William A. Bradley, "Hobnobbing with Hillbillies," *Harper's Monthly Magazine* 132 (1915): 94; Jackson (Ky.) *Times*, 20 November 1925; "The Trail of the Pioneer," videotape of a 1927 silent motion picture, filmed by Elizabeth Perkins and Sophia Smith (UK); interviews with Fredricka Holdship, 25 March 1979, Hallie Maggard, 20 November 1978, James Parton, 25 May 1979, Mardi Bemis Perry and Susan Morse Putnam, 25 January 1979, Mary Brewer, 10 August 1978, all in FNS Oral History Project (transcripts): Juanetta M. Morgan, ed., "Old Courier News," *FNS Bulletin* 47 (Spring 1972): 19; *Wide Neighborhoods*, 187; Mary T. Brewer, *Rugged Trail to Appalachia: A History of Leslie County, Kentucky, and Its People . . . 1878-1978* (1978), 4, 37, 40; *Thirty Years Onward: Frontier Nursing Service 1925-1955* (1955), 3; Mary Ann Stillman Quarles, "A Comparison of Some Aspects of Family Life Between Two Areas of Leslie County, Kentucky" (thesis, University of Kentucky, 1952), 41, 31, 43, 45, 48-49, 74-75; *Census of Population: 1950*, vol. 2, part 1, 97, 96, 104, part 17, 25.
   5. Eller, *Miners and Mountaineers*, 6-39; interview with Gertrude Isaacs, 15 November 1978, FNS Oral History Project (transcript); *The Fifteenth Census of the United States; 1930, Population*, vol. 3, part 1, 917, shows that 99.6 percent of Leslie County's population was native-born white.
   6. It is possible that Mary Breckinridge's ideas and the FNS' organizational name may have evolved from a comment in Campbell's *Southern Highlander*, 221. In this well-known 1921 work, he wrote: "A 'pioneer nursing corps' could revolutionize existing conditions. . . . "
   7. Carl Degler, *At Odds: Women and the Family in America from the Revolution to the Present* (1980), 56; Richard W. and Dorothy C. Wertz, *Lying-In: A History of Childbirth in America* (1977), 2, 4, 42, 46-47, 67-69; Jane B. Donegan, *Women & Men Midwives: Medicine, Morality, and Misogyny in Early America* (1978), 3, 17-20, 141-96; Judy Barrett Litoff, *American Midwives: 1860 to the Present* (1978), 10, 27; Litoff, "Forgotten Women: American Midwives at the Turn of the Twentieth Century," *Historian* 40 (1978): 235.
   8. Nancy Schrom Dye, "History of Childbirth in America," *Signs* 6 (1980): 104; Litoff, *American Midwives*, 23; Arthur B. Emmons and James L. Huntingdon, "The Midwife: Her Future in the United States," *American Journal of Obstetrics and Diseases of Women and Children* 65 (1912): 394; Charles V. Chapin, "The Control of Midwifery," in *Standards of Child Welfare: A Report of the Children's Bureau Conference May and June 1919* (1974; orig. pub. 1919), 163, 157; Frances E. Kobrin, "The American Midwife Controversy: A Crisis of Professionalization," *Bulletin of the History of Medicine* 40 (1966): 351-52.
   9. Wertz and Wertz, *Lying-In*, 133; Hattie Hernschemeyer, "Midwifery in the United States," *American Journal of Nursing* 39 (1939): 1182; Litoff, *American Midwives*, 58, 77, 82. See

also Nancy Schrom Dye, "Mary Breckinridge, The Frontier Nursing Service and the Introduction of Nurse-Midwifery in the United States," *Bulletin of the History of Medicine* 57 (1983): 485-507.

10. MB, "Midwifery in the Kentucky Mountains: An Investigation" (typescript), 7, 20, Mary Breckinridge Papers. See also Sadie W. Stidham, *Trails Into Cutshin Country: A History of the Pioneers of Leslie County, Kentucky* (1978), 39, 148, and John W. Raine, *The Land of Saddle-Bags: A Study of the Mountain People of Appalachia* (1924), 215.

11. *Wide Neighborhoods*, 188-89; interview with Brooke Alexander, 24 September 1979, FNS Oral History Project (transcript); Michelle Marder Kambi, "Nursing," *RF Illustrated* 5 (1980): 13; interview with Martha Prewitt Breckinridge (Mary Breckinridge's secretary, later her sister-in-law), 30 March 1979, FNS Oral History Project (transcript).

12. Interview with Betty Lester, 27 July 1978, FNS Oral History Project (transcript). See also Betty Lester, "The Experiences of a Midwifery Supervisor in the Kentucky Hills," *American Journal of Nursing* 31 (1931): 573-77.

13. Lester interview; *Herald*, 21 December 1931; *Wide Neighborhoods*, 284; interview with Allyn Johnson Shepherd, 18 January 1979, FNS Oral History Project (transcript). A one-time FNS nurse asserted, to a leading question, that if "you look through the staff, you will find few who really like men" (Reeder interview).

14. Jack Hall, "Mary Breckinridge at Wendover," *Mountain Review* 4 (1978): 26; Louisville *Courier-Journal & Times*, 18 May 1975; Reeder and Shepherd interviews; interview with Kate Ireland, 1 November 1979, and Carrie M. Parker, 29 September 1979, both in FNS Oral History Project (transcripts); Georgia Ledford, "Memories of Mary Breckinridge and the Big House," *FNS Bulletin* 56 (Winter 1980): 9 (quotation); Hall, "Mary Breckinridge," 26 (last quotation).

15. John F. Day, *Bloody Ground* (1941), 261; Lester interview; Martha Breckinridge interview; interviews with Helen Hifner Fortune and Carl D. Fortune, 6 October 1978, Ed Morgan, 7 July 1978, Dorothy Caldwell, 18 January 1979, all in FNS Oral History Project (transcripts); Perry/Putnam and Reeder interviews.

16. Isaacs, Browne (II), and Martha Breckinridge interviews; interviews with Mary Wilson Neel, 1 December 1979, FNS Oral History Project (transcript); Margaret McDowell, "Letters from Wendover," *FNS Bulletin* 23 (Spring 1948); Shepherd interview.

17. Mary Grover Littover to "Aunt Eda," 27 February 1933, in "Letter to the Editor . . . ," *FNS Bulletin* 56 (Spring 1981): 25.

18. Louisville *Courier-Journal & Times*, 18 May 1975; Gardner, *Clever Country*, 32; Dorothy Miles, "Heroines on Horseback," *Collier's* 31 (August 1946); Katherine E. Wilkie and Elizabeth R. Moseby, *Frontier Nurse: Mary Breckinridge* (1969); and Ernest Poole, *Nurses on Horseback* (1932) all illustrate the theme. Quotation from MB, "Of Making . . . Books there is no End," *FNS Bulletin* 26 (Spring 1951): 27.

19. Perry interview; interview with Carolyn Booth Gregory, 31 March 1979, FNS Oral History Project (transcript); Ireland interviews; Louisville *Courier-Journal*, 13 May 1932; T. S. Hyland, "The Fruitful Mountaineer," *Life* (26 December 1949), 65; Shepherd interview; *Herald*, 18 November 1928; Louisville *Courier Journal & Times*, 18 May 1975; Morgan interview; Stidham, *Cutshin Country*, 159-60; interview with Charlie Rice, 30 October 1978, FNS Oral History Project (transcript); New York *Times*, 18 January 1931.

20. Louisville *Courier-Journal*, 17 January 1932; MB, "Frontier Nursing in the United States," *St. Luke's Alumnae Bulletin* 20 (February and March 1930); clipping dated 1926, in James Parton Scrapbook (UK); MB to "My dear two chiefs [Anne Dike and Anne Morgan]," 3 August 1926, Mary Breckinridge Papers; Louisa Chepman, "A Cadet in Scalf Hollow," *FNS Bulletin* 20 (Summer 1944): 41; Ruth E. Alexander, "A Cadet on Leatherwood," *ibid.*, 49-50; Reeder and Parton interviews; Lexington *Herald-Leader*, 16 November 1975; *Wide Neighborhoods*, 327; MB, "Frontier Nursing Service," 22.

21. Littover, "Letter to the Editor," 28; Patricia Pettit, "Diary of a Courier," *FNS Bulletin* 20 (Winter 1945): 26; Breckinridge quoted in Helen Worden, "She Nurses Her Patients for a Dollar a Year," *American Magazine* 112 (December 1931): 108.

22. *Herald*, 4 March 1936; [Mary Breckinridge], "Town and Plane," *FNS Bulletin* 25 (Autumn 1949): 43-55; interview with Patsy Lawrence and Sue Grandin, 26 January 1979,

FNS Oral History Project (transcript); Caldwell interview; MB to Dorothy Breckinridge, 11 January 1943, B.MSS boxes; "Mary Breckinridge," in Durward Homes, ed., *American Women . . . 1935-36* (1935), 66; Arpee Interview.

23. This sketch of Breckinridge is from the Davis, Parton, Martha Breckinridge, and Arpee interviews; interviews with Nancy N. Porter, 5 March 1979; Ann D. Mulhauser, 17 January 1979, both in FNS Oral History Project (transcripts); Hall, "Mary Breckinridge," 26; *Herald*, 29 March 1926; Eureka Springs *Times-Echo*, 8 June 1917; and "Saving Lives on the Last Frontier," *Literary Digest* (2 February 1935), 22. The quotations, in order, are from Fortune interview; *Herald*, 5 July 1931; and Davis interview.

24. Carol Crowe-Carraco, "Mary Breckinridge and the Frontier Nursing Service," *Register* 76 (1978): 187; Arpee, Fortune and Fortune, and Lawrence/Grandin interviews; "Trail of the Pioneer"; "The Forgotten Frontier," videotape of a 1928 motion picture, filmed by Marvin Breckinridge (UK); Marvin Breckinridge Patterson, "Foreword" to *Wide Neighborhoods*, xvi; MB to Katherine Arpee, 26 September 1949 (copy), FNS Records.

25. Louisville *Courier-Journal*, 15 November 1931; *Herald*, 30 May 1934; [Mary Breckinridge], "Field Notes," *FNS Bulletin*, 24 (Winter 1949): 74; *ibid.*, 25 (Spring 1950): 66; *Wide Neighborhoods*, 211, 257, 279-82.

26. *FNS Bulletin* 6 (Summer 1930): 2; *ibid.*, (Winter 1931): 3; *ibid.*, (Spring 1931): 1-3; MB, "The Corn-Bread Line," *The Survey* (15 August 1930), 422-23; *Wide Neighborhoods*, 268-70, 291, 301; *Herald*, 19 January 1932; 2, 25 June 1933.

27. *Wide Neighborhoods*, 283-86, 346, 325. DB to Breckinridge Long, 26 December 1931, Long Papers, box 97.

28. Wertz and Wertz, *Lying-In*, 217-18; Litoff, *Midwives*, 52-108; Litoff, "Forgotten Women," 241-43; *Wide Neighborhoods*, 324-26.

29. MB, *Organdie and Mull* (1948), 26, 32-33, 40. See also MB to Nadine Laughton, 30 September 1948 (copy), FNS Records.

30. [Mary Breckinridge], "Field Notes," *FNS Bulletin* 26 (Summer 1950): 59; *ibid.* (Autumn 1950): 45; Patterson "Foreword," xiv; Louisville *Courier-Journal*, 22 May 1938; Patterson, Neel, Harper, and Browne (II) interviews.

31. Margaret S. Dudley, "One of the Least of These," *To Dragma* (Fall 1951): 21; Davis interview.

32. *Today and Tomorrow*, 3; interview with Alden Gay, 1 September 1978, FNS Oral History Project (transcript); "Economic Program Facts, Leslie County," John B. Breckinridge Papers; Joe Creason, "Horseback to Jeep," Louisville *Courier-Journal Magazine*, 11 June 1961.

33. "Summary of Annual Report," *FNS Bulletin* 25 (Summer 1953): 13; Louisville *Courier-Journal*, 19 November 1930; New York *Times*, 18 January 1931; Vera Keane, "The Role of the Nurse-Midwife in the United States Today," in *The Midwife in the United States* (1968), 96; Crowe-Carraco, "Mary Breckinridge," 189.

34. See Day, *Bloody Ground*, 198-99, and *Wide Neighborhoods*, 346-48, for examples of Breckinridge's involvement. See also David E. Whisnant, *All That Is Native and Fine* (1983).

35. "Fortieth Annual Report . . . ," *FNS Bulletin* 41 (Summer 1965): 15; "Metropolitan Life Insurance Company Tabulations of FNS Midwifery Records," in FNS Administrative Papers; Crowe-Carraco, "Mary Breckinridge," 191; "Annual Report of the Frontier Nursing Service, Inc., May 1, 1943 to April 30, 1944," *FNS Bulletin* 20 (Summer 1944): 8, 12; Morgan interview.

36. Parker interview; MB, "Beyond the Mountains," *FNS Bulletin* 40 (Winter 1965): 46-47; "From 12th M.B. Journal . . . (November 12, 1901)," in Mary Breckinridge Papers (quotation); Harper and Caldwell interviews; Perry/Putnam and Lawrence/ Grandin interviews; MB to "Molly, Laetitia, Cabell [Bullock?]" 7 January 1922, Mary Breckinridge Papers; MB to Laura B. Ten Eyck, 18 October 1944 (copy), FNS Records; interview with Ann Winslow, 25 September 1979, and with Ruth Huston (n.d.), both in FNS Oral History Project (transcripts); Reeder and Neel interviews; *Who's Who in America, 1942-43*, 383; Elizabeth Agard to MB [1925-26], Mary Breckinridge Papers; Alexander interview; Thompson, *Breckie*, 64; Betty Lester, "The Trumpets Sounded," *FNS Bulletin* 40 (Spring 1965): 304; Browne interview. As Breckinridge wished, pictures of both her children and a lock of Breckie's hair were buried with her.

19. White Knight Riding Alone

1. No biography or scholarly article on John B. Breckinridge has yet appeared in print. Sketches of his life can be found in the *Congressional Directory, 94th Congress, First Session* (1975), 72-73; "Biographical Sketch Attorney General John B. Breckinridge" (in author's possession); "John B. Breckinridge" biographical sketch (in author's possession); and Paducah *Sun-Democrat*, 7 January 1962. General information on his career can be found in these sources. It should be noted that several statements concerning Breckinridge are based on informal conversations by the author with members of the Lexington community.

2. "Scott Dudley Breckinridge," *National Cyclopaedia of American Biography* 31 (1944): 235-36; Citizens Historical Association, "Scott D. Breckinridge, Physician," typed manuscript, biography files (KHS); *Herald*, 2 August 1941, 5, 6 February 1981; interview by author with Scott D. Breckinridge, Jr., 22 May 1980.

3. Scott Breckinridge interview, 22 May 1980.

4. *Ibid.*; Scott D. Breckinridge, Jr., to the author, 17 August 1980 (hereinafter referred to as Scott Breckinridge letter); and Louisville *Courier-Journal*, 4 January 1973.

5. Scott Breckinridge interview and letter; Paducah *Sun-Democrat*, 7 January 1962; interview by author with Mrs. Helen Breckinridge, 18 February 1981 (hereinafter referred to as Helen Breckinridge interview, II); *Herald-Leader*, 28 January 1979.

6. *The 1933 Kentuckian* (1933), 106, 203; *The Kentuckian of 1937* ([1937]), 303; *The 1936 Kentuckian* (1936), 172-73, 281.

7. *University of Kentucky Seventieth Annual Commencement Exercises, Nineteen Hundred and Thirty-Seven Friday, June the Fourth* ([1937]), 2-3 (UK Archives); *The Kentuckian . . . 1938* ([1938]), 290; *Avenues of Beauty: Kentuckian Nineteen Thirty-Nine* ([1939]), 196, 272-74; *Kentucky Law Journal* 26 (1938): 359; John B. Breckinridge, "Autobiography" (eighteen page incomplete manuscript, copy in possession of Mrs. Helen Breckinridge, Lexington); Paducah *Sun-Democrat*, 7 January 1962. His two publications in this period were: "Public Utilities: The Influence of Nebbia v. People in State Regulation," *Kentucky Law Journal* 27 (1939): 323-31, and "Constitutional Law—Fourteenth Amendment—Racial Segregation for the Purposes of Education," *ibid.*, 335-38.

8. Louisville *Courier-Journal*, 4 January 1973; Paducah *Sun-Democrat*, 7 January 1962; JBB, "Autobiography"; Harry T. Fultz to JBB, 5 September 1953, JBB Papers, UK.

9. On Scott D. Breckinridge, Jr. see Scott Breckinridge interview; *Kentuckians* of 1936-39; clipping dated "6-22-47" in John B. Breckinridge folder, Alumni-Biographical File (University Archives, UK); and Scott D. Breckinridge, Jr., "Effect of *Mitchell* vs. *United States* on the Duty of the Common Carrier in Kentucky Toward the Negro Passenger," *Kentucky Law Journal* 30 (1942): 247-50.

10. *Herald-Leader*, 28 January 1979; speech of JBB for Waterfield, 1947; two untitled draft speeches, circa July 1947, all in JBB Papers, UK. See also William Clark Spragens, "The 1947 Kentucky Gubernatorial Election" (thesis, University of Kentucky, 1952).

11. Malcolm E. Jewell, *Kentucky Votes*, 3 vols. (1963), 2:31, 35.

12. *Herald-Leader*, 3 August 1952; Scott Breckinridge interview; draft statement, "Friends of Fayette," 9 February 1949; "Articles of Incorporation of Fayette Committee for Citizenship, Inc." (copy), 8 December 1949; Henry Ward to JBB, 5 May 1955, all in JBB Papers, UK; JBB to Joseph L. Intemaggio, 5 March 1951 (copy); JBB to Henry Breckinridge, 8 February 1951 (copy); JBB to Earl Brennan, 7 February 1951 (copy); JBB to Homer W. Davis, 13 February 1951 (copy); JBB to Gertrude Breckinridge, 7 January 1953, all in Helen Breckinridge Papers.

13. See JBB letters (all copies in Helen Breckinridge Papers) to Homer W. Davis, 13 February and 15 November 1951; to Gertrude Breckinridge, 23 April 1951; to John T. Vance, 28 December 1953; to Anne Mattingly, 13 July 1953; and to Perry J. Stevenson, 3 March 1955; plus Charles M. Bellum to JBB, 5 October 1953, JBB Papers, UK; interview with Mrs. Helen Breckinridge, 27 February 1980 (hereinafter Helen Breckinridge interview, I); Helen Breckinridge interview, II; Scott Breckinridge interview and letter to the author, 11 December 1979; interview with Robert Montague, III, 3 August 1981. Montague was an assistant attorney-general under Breckinridge.

14. Helen Breckinridge interview, I; Scott Breckinridge interview and letter; Montague interview; Paducah *Sun-Democrat*, 7 January 1962; Calhoun (Ky.) *McLean County News*, 6 December 1962; Libby Hunt to Helen Breckinridge, 3 August 1979, Helen Breckinridge Papers; Wini Mastin to Editor, *Herald*, 11 February 1974; Louisville *Times*, 23 May 1963; Wilson Wyatt to Helen Breckinridge, 3 [July] 1979, Helen Breckinridge Papers.

15. Pierce, *Border South States*, 218, 231; *Herald*, 5, 7, 9 August, 9 November 1955. John's opponent in November was Carroll W. Jacobs, Jr., who received 6,261 to the Democrat's 12,249.

16. JBB to Mrs. Joseph Grable, 12 September 1956 (copy), JBB Papers, UK; Kentucky *House Journal* (1956), ii-xxxix.

17. Kentucky *House Journal, First Extraordinary Session* (1956), 51-54; *Second Extraordinary Session* (1956), 91, 138-39, 161; *Third Extraordinary Session* (1956), 220; *Fourth Extraordinary Session* (1956), 33, 349; JBB to Homer W. Davis, 17 September 1956 (copy), Helen Breckinridge Papers; JBB to William A. Young, 11 September 1956 (copy), JBB Papers, UK. Breckinridge won reelection with 10,962 votes to Republican Jack R. Wilkinson, Jr.'s 7,306. *Herald*, 6 November 1957.

18. Kentucky *House Journal* (1958), vi-xv.

19. On the "Rebels," see *Courier-Journal*, 20 August 1961; Author's talk with Lon Carter Barton (a 1958 "rebel"), 25 June 1980; Pat Tanner to Barry Bingham, 2 January 1959 (copy); agenda of JBB for WKYT television program of 4 January 1959; Alton Moore and JBB to "Dear Rebel," 7 January 1959 (copy); JBB to "Dear Reb," 12 January 1959 (copy), all in JBB Papers, UK; and Madisonville (Ky.) *Messenger*, 28 March 1959.

20. See Harry Lee Waterfield, "Recollections," in Robert A. Powell, *Kentucky Governors* (1976), 8-11; Robert L. Riggs interview, Earle C. Clements Oral History Project, UK, 13 November 1975 (transcript), 17; JBB to Scott Breckinridge, 28 June 1958 (copy), JBB Papers, UK; George W. Robinson, ed., *The Public Papers of Governor Bert T. Combs, 1959-1963* (1979), 4. As it turned out, by 1962 Clements had broken with Governor Combs, and refused to support Wyatt, who lost his senate race to Thruston Morton.

21. Scott Breckinridge to JBB, 4 July 1958, JBB Papers, UK; Madisonville (Ky.) *Messenger*, 18 March 1959; Louisville *Times*, 28 May 1959; Jewell, *Kentucky Votes*, 2:49-51.

22. JBB to Ray Corns, 2 February 1964 (copy), JBB Papers, UK; Scott Breckinridge interview; *Courier-Journal*, 20 August 1961; Montague interview.

23. *Courier-Journal*, 28 February 1960; National Commission on Professional Rights and Responsibilities of the NEA . . . , *Report of an Investigation, Carter County, Kentucky* (1963); Bert T. Combs to the Secretary of State, 7 December 1961 Executive Order (copy); John L. Davis to Bert T. Combs, 22 November 1961; "Report of Special Grand Jury," Campbell Circuit Court, 16-21 August 1961, all in JBB Papers, UK; Montague interview.

24. Lexington *Kentucky Kernel*, 1 November 1972; Montague interview; JBB to Rapp Brush, 25 October 1961 (copy); JBB to Mr. and Mrs. Charles D. Milliken, 6 March 1962 (copy); JBB to Billy Clyde Burnett, 27 October 1961 (copy), all in JBB Papers, UK.

25. *Courier-Journal*, 20 August 1961, 24 January 1962; Paducah *Sun-Democrat*, 7 January 1962; Frankfort *State Journal*, 28 January 1962.

26. JBB to R. Douglas Ford, 25 January 1962 (copy), JBB Papers, UK; Louisville *Times*, 3 August 1962; Frankfort *State Journal*, 10 January 1962; Powell, *Kentucky Governors*, 106; G. Glenn Clift, "Governor Edward Thompson Breathitt, Jr.," *Register* 62 (1964): 1-3.

27. Morganfield (Ky.) *Union County Advocate*, 10 February 1966; Louisville *Times*, 23 May 1963; Scott Breckinridge interview.

28. Edward T. Breathitt, Jr. interview on "Bywords" program, 16 March 1981, Kentucky Educational Television; Henderson (Ky.) *Gleaner and Journal*, 11 May 1962; *Herald*, 22 November 1962; Cincinnati *Enquirer* (Kentucky edition), 30 November 1962; Frankfort, *State Journal*, 28 November, 2 December 1962; unidentified clipping, "6-16-62," JBB Papers, UK.

29. "Outline of Program," JBB Papers, UK; Calhoun (Ky.) *McLean County News*, 6 December 1962.

30. Louisville *Times*, 23 May 1963; Elizabethtown *News*, 24 May 1963; Louisville *Defender*, 23 May 1963. One late-breaking question was Breckinridge's charge that Happy

Chandler's son Dan had offered the candidate some $35,000 if he would withdraw from the race. See state newspapers of 22-25 May 1963.

31. *Courier-Journal*, 23 June, 30 May 1963; Pikeville *Pike County News*, 30 May 1963.

32. Clay City (Ky.) *Times*, 27 June 1963; Owensboro *Messenger and Inquirer*, 30 May 1963; *Herald*, 23 May 1963; Lexington *Leader*, 27 May 1963; Irvine (Ky.) *Estill County Herald*, 30 May 1963; Adairville (Ky.) *Enterprise*, 30 May 1963; Russellville (Ky.) *News-Democrat*, 31 May 1963.

33. Arlie Decker and A. L. Wood to JBB, 8 March 1966, JBB Papers, UK; Louisville *Times*, 23 May 1963.

20. *In Pursuit of the Horizon*

1. Helen Breckinridge interview, II; *Herald*, 16 April 1966.

2. JBB to Laurence K. Gould, Jr., 23 May 1961 (copy), JBB Papers, UK; "News and Notes," *Register* 60 (1962): 160-61; Informal Club speech, JBB Papers, UK; Helen Breckinridge interview, I. Also see *Report of the President, 1961-1963*, Kentucky Historical Society (1963).

3. Powell, *Kentucky Governors*, 108; Robert F. Sexton, ed., *The Public Papers of Louie B. Nunn, 1967-1971* (1975), 3.

4. Notes for merit system speech; notes for speech; both circa 1968-69, JBB Papers, UK; Louisville *Courier-Journal*, 6 August 1971; *Herald*, 3 June 1970. See also *Courier-Journal*, 6 August 1971; *Herald*, 3 June 1970. See also *Courier-Journal*, 17 January 1971.

5. "Crime and the Commercial Conscience" speech, 29-30 July 1968 (copy); "The Administration of Criminal Justice—The Challenge and the Responsibilities" speech, 25 September 1968, JBB Papers, UK.

6. "Prevention and Control of Civil Disorders and Riots" speech, circa 1968-70, *ibid.* See also "Crusader vs. Crime" speech, 29 March 1971, *ibid.*

7. *Herald*, 9 June 1970; memorandum from "G&B" to JBB, 9 February 1971 (copy); "County Chairmen & Co-Chairman" list, both in JBB Papers, UK.

8. Lexington speech, 13 March 1971, *ibid.*; *Herald-Leader*, 14 March 1971; *Courier-Journal*, 11 May 1971; Lexington *Leader*, 24 May 1971.

9. Powell, *Kentucky Governors*, 104, 110, 112; Frankfort *State Journal*, 5 May 1971; *Courier-Journal*, 19, 29 April, 22 May 1971.

10. *Herald*, 17 June 1971; Richmond (Ky.) *Madison County Newsweek*, 20 May 1971.

11. Scott D. Breckinridge, Jr. to author, 11 December 1979; Scott Breckinridge interview; JBB to Gertrude Breckinridge, 7 August 1956 (copy); JBB to Mrs. M. D. Knight, 14 June 1953 (copy), both in Helen Breckinridge Papers; Helen Breckinridge interviews, II, I.

12. *Herald* and *Courier-Journal*, 22 February 1972; JBB to Loyal Jones, 15 November 1971 (copy), JBB Papers, UK. In March 1972 the incumbent, William P. Curlin, Jr., made his announcement. *Courier-Journal*, 19 July 1972.

13. *Herald*, 22 February 1972; *Courier-Journal*, 22 February 1972; *Herald*, 4 May 1972; Lexington *Leader*, 22 April 1972; Tom Ward television ad, 22 April 1972; Michael Barone, Grant Ujifusa, and Douglas H. Matthews, *The Almanac of American Politics . . . 1974* (1973), 381-82; *Herald*, 24 May 1972; "Laban Phelps Jackson," in Hambleton Tapp, ed., *Kentucky Lives: The Blue Grass State Who's Who* (1966), 273-74; *Herald*, 6 November 1972.

14. *Herald*, 13 June, 16, 19 October (quotation) 1972; Lexington *Kentucky Kernel*, 27, 17 October, 1 November 1972.

15. *Herald*, 28 October, 6 November 1972; *Almanac of Politics*, 381-82; Ralph Nader Congress Project, *Statistical Supplement to Congressional Profiles*, 10 vols. (1974), 10:359.

16. Herbert B. Asher, "The Changing Status of the Freshman Representative," in Norman J. Ornstein, ed., *Congress in Change: Evolution and Reform* (1975), 229; Robert A. Diamond and Patricia Ann O'Connor, eds., *Congressional Quarterly's Guide to Congress*, 2d ed. (1976), 463, 466-77.

17. *Congressional Quarterly's Guide*, 457, 459; *Courier-Journal*, 2 February 1973; Helen Breckinridge interview, I; Scott Breckinridge letter; *Herald*, 18 July 1973.

18. *Courier-Journal*, 2 February 1973, 3 January 1974. For a critique of the House in this period, see Donald M. Fraser and Iric Nathanson, "Rebuilding the House of Representatives," in Orstein, ed., *Congress in Change*, 288-89.

19. *Herald-Leader*, 1 February 1976.

20. *Courier-Journal*, 28 June, 15 July 1973.

21. *Ibid.*, 3 January 1974, 18 November 1973; Lexington *Kentucky Kernel*, 7 April 1975; *Congressional Roll Call, 1973: A Chronology and Analyses of Votes in the House and Senate* (1974), 12-13; *Herald*, 16 May 1973; 14 March 1975; *Congressional Roll Call 1974* (1974), 5, 13; *Almanac of Politics*, 382.

22. *Congressional Record*, 94th Cong. 2d Sess. (17 March 1976), 6980-81; (31 March 1976), 8938-39; (12 May 1976), 13735-36; (24 August 1976), 27558-60; (31 August 1976), E4785; (8, 27 September 1976), 29416-17, 32803-5; *Herald-Leader*, 24 July 1977; JBB to "The Citizens of 2076," 29 December 1976, copy in author's possession. Also, JBB, "Special Introduction" to John M. Collins, *American and Soviet Military Trends Since the Cuban Missile Crisis* (1978), xi.

23. Nader Project, *Congressional Profiles*, 10:359, 360; *Congressional Roll Call, 1973*, 37, 10-13; *Courier-Journal*, 19 May 1974; *Herald*, 12 November 1973.

24. *Cong. Record*, 93d Cong., 1st Sess. (18 April 1973), 13186; 2d Sess. (24 July 1974), 25057-58; Iowa representative Berkley Bedell to Winthrop Rockefeller Award Trustees, 11 September 1979, Helen Breckinridge Papers; *Herald*, 17 May 1974; *Courier-Journal*, 3 February 1975.

25. *Herald*, 17 July 1973, 10 December 1975; *Courier-Journal and Times*, 12 October 1975; *Cong. Record*, 94th Cong., 1st Sess., Index, 161, 14093; Helen Breckinridge interview, I; Scott Breckinridge interview; JBB, "The Future of Small Business: Clouded," *Successful Business* (1979): 66; Jere W. Glover to William Cox, 30 November 1979, Helen Breckinridge Papers; House of Representatives Committee on Small Business, *Future of Small Business in America* (1979), iii.

26. Nader Project, *Congressional Profiles*, 10:359; *Courier-Journal*, 10 August, 18 May 1975, 29 November 1977; *Congressional Roll Call, 1974*, 25, 35; *Congressional Roll Call, 1973*, 30-33. See also *Courier-Journal*, 31 October 1976.

27. Helen Breckinridge interviews I and II; *Herald*, 30 July 1979; Scott Breckinridge interview and letter; Lexington *Leader*, 29 July 1979.

28. *Herald*, 29 May 1974; *Courier-Journal*, 3, 6 November 1974; Lexington *Kentucky Kernel*, 17 January 1975; *Herald-Leader*, 15 March, 23 August 1975; *Courier-Journal*, 23 August 1975; *Herald*, 27, 7 August 1975; *Courier-Journal*, 31 October, 3 November 1976.

29. Helen Breckinridge interviews I and II.

30. Helen Breckinridge interview, I; *Herald*, 18 August 1977; *Courier-Journal*, 29 August 1977.

31. *Courier-Journal*, 29 August 1977, 24 May 1978; *Herald-Leader*, 11 June 1978.

32. *Courier-Journal*, 25, 24 May 1978; *Herald*, 25 May 1978; *Herald-Leader*, 11 June 1978; Scott Breckinridge interview; *Herald*, 29 May 1974.

33. *Courier-Journal*, 25 May 1978; 5 August 1979; 24 May 1978; Hazel Sanderman to Helen Breckinridge, 1 August 1979, Helen Breckinridge Papers; *Herald-Leader*, 11 June 1978; *Herald*, 25 May 1978.

34. William J. Keefe, *Parties, Politics, and Public Policy in America*, 3d ed. (1980), 38.

35. Helen Breckinridge interview, I; *Herald*, 9 August 1978; *Courier-Journal*, 20 August 1978; *Herald-Leader*, 28 January 1979. Initial Republican candidate Mary Louise Foust withdrew following Breckinridge's defeat, stronger candidate Larry Hopkins replaced her, and he defeated Easterly.

36. Guthrie quoted in John W. and Dorothy Townsend, *Kentucky in American Letters*, 3 vols. (1913 and 1976), 3:142-43. See W. E. Lyons, *The Politics of City-County Merger: The Lexington-Fayette County Experience* (1977), 18-19; Helen Breckinridge interview, II; John D. Wright, Jr., *Lexington: Heart of the Bluegrass* (1982), 193-225.

37. Scott D. Breckinridge to Stansfield Turner, 13 August 1979 (copy), Helen Breckinridge Papers; *Herald*, 30, 31 July 1979.

38. Barbara Jordan to Helen Breckinridge, 10 January 1980, Helen Breckinridge Papers; *Cong. Record*, 96th Cong., 1st Sess. (30 July 1979), 6831; Jere W. Glover to Raymond P. Shafer, 10 September 1979 (copy), Helen Breckinridge Papers; *Herald*, 30, 31 July 1979; *Courier-Journal*, 30 July 1979; Tom Easterly to Helen Breckinridge, 30 July [1979], Helen Breckinridge Papers; *Courier-Journal*, 31 July 1979.

39. *Courier-Journal*, 4 January 1973; Helen Breckinridge interview, I; *Herald*, 8 August 1979; *Cong. Record*, 96th Cong., 1st Sess. (30 July 1979), 6831.

40. "Prevention and Control of Civil Disorders and Riots"; "Ethics in Politics," 30 March 1969; "What is Happiness?" 4 December 1970, all speeches in JBB Papers, UK.

21. Dreams and Realities

1. This account is taken from Lexington *Press*, 7 September 1884; Castleman, *Active Service*, 40; Chalkley, "Magic Casements," 28; Ethelbert D. Warfield to Reuben T. Durrett, 26 March 1886, Durrett Collection; Louisville *Courier-Journal*, 5 April 1886.

2. James Truslow Adams, *The Adams Family* (1930), 12; Greenslet, *Lowells and Their Seven Worlds*, 114; Klein, *Portrait of an Early American Family*, 4, 49; James A. Ramage, "The Hunts and Morgans: A Study of a Prominent Kentucky Family" (Ph.D. dissertation, University of Kentucky, 1972).

3. Charles P. Roland, "The Ever-Vanishing South," *Journal of Southern History* 48 (1982): 12.

4. Edward N. Saveth, "Class," in Saveth, ed., *American History and the Social Sciences* (1965), 206; McGovern, *Yankee Family*, 39; Adams, *Adams Family*, 17.

5. Carl B. Cone, "The English Connection," *Louisville Courier-Journal Magazine*, 1 August 1976; Prentis, *Southern Letters*, 13; Allen, *Blue-Grass Region*, 36; Nathaniel S. Shaler, *Autobiography* (1909), 277.

6. Thomas D. Clark, "Kentuckians," in Federal Writers' Project, *Kentucky: A Guide to the Bluegrass State* (1939), 4; Pattie French Witherspoon, *Through Two Administrations: Character Sketches of Kentucky* (1897), 67.

7. Jane Turner Censer, *North Carolina Planters and Their Children, 1800-1860* (1984), 7; "Memoirs of Henry V. Johnson . . . 1852-1931" (Georgetown, Ky., Public Library), 65; Clark, *My Quarter Century*, 2:227; Knight, *The Wm. C. P. Breckinridge Defense*, 30.

8. Holmes quoted in David F. Musto, "Continuity Across Generations: The Adams Family Myth," in Allan J. Lichtman and Jean R. Challinor, eds., *Kin and Communities: Families in America* (1979), 79; George H. Mitchell to WCPB, 26 February 1884, B.MSS boxes; Mary Breckinridge, *Wide Neighborhoods*, 158; JBB to Jos. L. Intemaggio, 5 March 1951, Helen Breckinridge Papers.

9. Lexington *Leader*, 16 May 1894.

10. Lewis Collins, *Historical Sketches of Kentucky* (1847), iv, 138, 214, 280; Collins, *History of Kentucky*, 1:477-79, 2:xiii-ix, 98-100, 198; George Allen Hubbel, "Kentucky in the New Nation, 1865-1909," in Julian A. C. Chandler, ed., *History of the Southern States* (1909), 1:326-27; Wiebe, *Search for Order*, 44; Shaler, *Kentucky*, viii; Green, *Sketch of the Breckinridge Family* (see chap. 1, n.15); Brown, *Cabells and Their Kin*, 486-515; Alexander Brown to Edward C. Cabell, 25 October 1893, Warfield Family Collection; Connelley and Coulter, *History of Kentucky*.

11. See WCPB to Reuben T. Durrett, 22 September 1885, Durrett Collection; SPB to Herbert Putnam, 9 January 1905 (copy); Worthington C. Ford to SPB, 23 March 1905, B.MSS boxes.

12. Jennie C. Morton, "General John C. Breckinridge," *Register* 6 (1908): 11; E. Polk Johnson, *A History of Kentucky and Kentuckians*, 3 vols. (1912), 1:177.

13. Barbara Laslett, "The Family as a Public and Private Institution: An Historical Perspective," *Journal of Marriage and the Family* 35 (1973): 482; Rudy Rod Seward, *The American Family: A Demographic History* (1978), 78, 101, 144, 173, 176. All chapter statistics are taken from Brown, *Cabells and Their Kin*, 486-515 (which is reasonably thorough through the 1870s), Helen C. Breckinridge, *Descendants of John and Mary Cabell Breckinridge* (1980), and notes from the family papers. Censer in her *North Carolina Planters*, 28, found that at least 25 percent of the children born to these North Carolina families did not reach the age of five. In Kentucky in 1880, one in six children died before reaching the age of one (versus one in eighty

presently). See Thomas R. Ford, "Kentucky in the 1880s: An Exploration in Historic Demography," *Kentucky Review* 3 (1982): 57.

14. John Moddell, Frank F. Furstenberg, and Douglas Strong, "The Timing of Marriage in the Transition to Adulthood: Continuity and Change, 1860-1975," in John Demos and Sarane Spence Boocock, eds., *Turning Points: Historical and Sociological Essays in the Family* (1978), 122-43; John J. Waters, "Family, Inheritance, and Migration in Colonial New England: The Evidence from Guilford, Connecticut," *William and Mary Quarterly* 3d ser. 39 (1982): 64-86; Peter Laslett, *Family Life and Illicit Love in Earlier Generations: Essays in Historical Sociology* (1977), 218; Daniel Scott Smith, "Family Limitation, Sexual Control, and Domestic Feminism in Victorian America," in Mary S. Hartman and Lois Banner, eds., *Clio's Consciousness Raised: New Perspectives on the History of Women* (1974), 122-23; Yasukichi Yasuba, *Birth Rates of the White Population in the United States, 1800-1860* (1962), 45. See also Philip J. Greven, Jr., "The Average Size of Families and Households in the Province of Massachusetts in 1764 and in the United States in 1790: An Overview," in Peter Laslett and Richard Wall, eds., *Household and Family in Past Time* (1972), 551, and Daniel Blake Smith, "The Study of the Family in Early America: Trends, Problems and Prospects," *William and Mary Quarterly* 3d ser. 39 (1982): 10.

15. Waters, "Family, Inheritance, and Migration," 80, for example, found 67 percent of the East Guilford taxpayers had male heirs. (The figure perhaps should read twelve of thirteen had male issue. One John Cabell Breckinridge, a wealthy great-grandson of John C. Breckinridge, apparently underwent a sex-change operation in Denmark in the 1950s and became known as "Bunny" Breckinridge. See San Francisco *Chronicle*, and Chicago Daily *Tribune* of 5 May 1954, and undated clipping, Name Files [KHS]. The book *Myra Breckinridge* may have been based in part on these and other accounts.)

16. Stephanie Grauman Wolf, in her *Urban Village: Population, Community, and Family Structure in Germantown, Pennsylvania, 1683-1800* (1976), 262n, found 80 percent of the couples studied produced a live child within two years of marriage. The Breckinridge statistics are:

	Months between marriage and first child's birth	Number of years spent in childbearing
Pre-1850s	21.9 (15.4)	12.7
1850s	15.4	12.2
Post-1850s	19.7 (16.0)	10.4

The 15.4 months and 16.0 months figures in parentheses reflect a truer picture, for in each case an unusual example skews the mean. Discarding those cases produces the second mean. One pre-1850s marriage, for example, produced no children for 84 months.

A study of Quaker marriages of the eighteenth century, for example, indicates that wives spent 17.4 years in childbearing, and the median age of mothers at the birth of their last child was 37.9 years. The author notes that wives born in the decades of the 1880s had a median length of childbearing some six years shorter—11.3 years. See Robert V. Wells, "Demographic Change and the Life Cycle of American Families," in Theodore K. Rabb and Robert I. Rotberg, *The Family in History: Interdisciplinary Essays* (1971), 88.

17. Daniel Blake Smith, *Inside the Great House: Planter Life in Eighteenth-Century Chesapeake Society* (1980), 27; SPB "Autobiography."

18. *Herald*, 12 July 1903; DB to Breckinridge Long, 1 March 1926, box 82, Long Papers.

19. John F. Walzer, "A Period of Ambivalence: Eighteenth Century American Children," in Lloyd de Mause, ed., *The History of Childhood* (1974), 358; Smith, *Inside the Great House*, 22, 286.

20. Chalkley, "Magic Casements," 35.

21. Paula S. Fass, *The Damned and the Beautiful: American Youth in the 1920s* (1977), 86; *Biographical Encyclopedia of Kentucky*, 19; RJB to WCPB, 13 February 1860, vol. 208, B.MSS; Scott Breckinridge letter; Daniel Scott Smith, "Parental Power and Marriage Patterns: An Analysis of Historical Trends in Hingham, Massachusetts," *Journal of Marriage and the Family*

35 (1973): 425. The percentages of Breckinridges who married before their father's death (55.5 percent) almost exactly corresponds with Censer's figure for North Carolina planters (55.8 percent). Jane Turner Censer, "Parents and Children: North Carolina Planter Families, 1800-1860" (Ph.D. diss., Johns Hopkins Univ., 1980), 196n.

22. Lasch, "The Family and History" 33; Lasch, *Haven in a Heartless World: The Family Besieged* (1977), 3-4; Lawrence A. Cremin, "The Family as Educator: Some Comments on the Recent Historiography," *Teachers College Record* 76 (1974): 262; Kirk Jeffrey, "Varieties of Family History," *American Archivist* 38 (1975): 521.

23. Saveth, *American History and the Social Sciences*, 155; Ruth S. Cavan, *The American Family* (1953), 136; David F. Musto, "The Youth of John Quincy Adams," *Proceedings of the American Philosophical Society* 113 (1969): 271; *Time* (31 May 1976), 18.

24. Charles Breckinridge to RJB, 8 February 1865, vol. 240, B.MSS; New York *Times*, 8 May 1894; Martha Prewitt Breckinridge interview; author's notes of a conversation with Mr. and Mrs. John Marshall Prewitt and Mrs. Martha Breckinridge, 28 November 1973. In Helen Breckinridge's family genealogy she lists 17 people who carried the name "John Breckinridge," 12 Marys, 10 Williams, 7 Joseph Cabells, and 5 Robert J's. My own study of 94 Breckinridge-related families indicates that in 83.8 percent of the early families at least one member bore a parent's name, while 73.7 percent of later ones did. The decrease resulted chiefly from a decline on the feminine side.

25. This viewpoint is summarized in James A. Hijiya, "Roots: Family and Ethnicity in the 1970s," *American Quarterly* 30 (1978): 548-56. Reuben Hill, in his *Family Development in Three Generations: A Longitudinal Study of Changing Family Patterns of Planning and Achievement* (1970), 44, finds a "high" transmission of value orientations from generation to generation.

26. Castleman, *Active Service*, 32; Louisville *Courier-Journal*, 6 May 1894; *Debates . . . of The Convention of Virginia . . .* (1788, copy at UK).

27. Nicholas Perkins Hardeman, *Wilderness Calling: The Hardeman Family in the American Westward Movement, 1750-1900* (1977), 300; Chalkley, "Magic Casements," 1; SPB, "Autobiography."

28. Desha Breckinridge speech, December 1923, in JBB Papers; *Herald*, 5 March 1911; Mary Breckinridge, "Description of a Rural Community Known to Me," Breckinridge Papers; Mary Breckinridge, "Is Birth Control the Answer?", 157.

29. Unidentified clipping, "Scrapbook, 1864-1879," B.MSS boxes; SPB notes, *ibid.*; *Herald*, 2 March 1914; MB to Dorothy Breckinridge, 16 June 1942, B.MSS boxes; MB to "Pansy" [Mrs. Jesse Turner], 18 August 1934, FNS Records; "Notes for Speech to Young Historians Convention," JBB Papers; Frankfort *State Journal*, 12 November 1970.

30. "An Oration on 'The Formation of a National Character' to be delivered . . . July 10th 1822," Robert J. Breckinridge Miscellaneous MSS; Lexington *National Unionist*, 19 April 1864, RJB to WCPB, 23 August 1867, vol. 256, B.MSS; Clifton R. Breckinridge to JCB, 23 March 1867, 13 May 1874, in Mrs. J. C. Breckinridge Collection.

31. *Herald*, 25 September 1900, 12 July 1903; WCPB to SPB, 16 November 1902, vol. 513, B.MSS; *Herald*, 3 April 1904; draft speech in Underwood Papers; Carson Breckinridge to Clifton R. Breckinridge, 15 December 1931, Mary Breckinridge Papers.

32. Thomas Marshall Green, *Historic Families of Kentucky* (1889), 290; cited in *Herald*, 1 January 1914; Louisville *Courier-Journal*, 4 January 1973.

33. Mrs. Thomas R. Underwood interview; Linda Neville to Carolyn Van Blarcom, 30 September 1917, Linda Neville Papers, Group I, Box 11; Scott D. Breckinridge, Jr., interview; Clay quotation in William C. Davis, "John C. Breckinridge (1821-1875)," 5 (paper presented at the Southern Historical Association, 15 November 1979).

34. Earl N. Harbert, *The Force So Much Closer Home: Henry Adams and the Adams Family* (1977), ix; Musto, "Continuity Across Generations," 87; David F. Musto, "The Adams Family," *Proceedings of the Massachusetts Historical Society* 93 (1981): 42; Lasch, *Haven in a Heartless World*, 4.

35. Wiley cited in Edward Pessen, "Antebellum North and South in Comparative Perspective: A Discussion," *American Historical Review* 85 (1980): 1166; Alden Hatch, *The Lodges of Masssachusetts* (1973), 1.

36. Arthur P. Dudden, "Nostalgia and the American," *Journal of the History of Ideas* 22

(1961): 516; Wiebe, *Search for Order*, 44. See also Paul Goodman, "Ethics and Enterprise: The Values of a Boston Elite, 1800-1860," *American Quarterly* 18 (1966): 437; Rush Welter, "The Idea of Progress in America: An Essay in Ideas and Method," *Journal of the History of Ideas* 16 (1955): 404-5; and Clarke A. Chambers, "The Belief in Progress in Twentieth-Century America," *ibid.* 19 (1958): 199, 224.

37. Reprinted in *Herald*, 24 May 1925, 22 February 1931.

38. Green, *Historic Families of Kentucky*, 292.

39. JB to Mary H. Breckinridge, 20 February 1806, vol. 29, B.MSS; "Formation of a National Character," Robert J. Breckinridge Miscellaneous MSS; *Herald*, 24 May 1925; WCPB to SPB, 28 December 1896, B.MSS boxes; Helen Breckinridge interview, I.

40. RJB to JCB, 28 December 1846, vol. 126, B.MSS.

41. RJB to J. B. Bittiner, *et al*, 16 January 1844 (copy), Helen Breckinridge Papers; speech, 13 March 1971, JBB Papers.

42. William C. Davis, "John C. Breckinridge: The War Years and After" (transcript of talk delivered at the Kentucky Homecoming of the Descendants of John and Mary Cabell Breckinridge, Lexington, 12 June 1981); Montague interview.

Bibliographical Note

A full essay on the sources might read like a historiographical discussion of Kentucky, Southern, or American history, given the long time frame and numerous subject areas examined; a complete listing of all sources cited in the notes would be too involved (over 350 books and some 90 separate manuscript collections, for instance). For a limited listing of the sources, see James C. Klotter, "The Breckinridges of Kentucky: Two Centuries of Leadership" (Ph.D. dissertation, University of Kentucky, 1975) and the notes in Klotter, "Clio in the Commonwealth: The Status of Kentucky History," *Register of the Kentucky Historical Society* 80 (1982): 65-88 (hereinafter *Register*). More extensive notes to the manuscript appear in an earlier draft, now on deposit at the University of Kentucky.

Among the manuscripts used, the Breckinridge Family Papers at the Library of Congress (hereinafter LC) furnished the basis for this book. There are few sources of American history richer than that collection, which consists of over 200,000 items in 515 bound volumes and some 350 additional boxes. Only small portions have been microfilmed.

The bound volumes span the years 1752 to 1904, with over half of them covering the last four decades of that period. Thirty volumes deal with the first John Breckinridge, for example. Robert J., John C., and W.C.P. Breckinridge are the primary focus of the remaining bound volumes. The rest of the collection is divided among: Henry Breckinridge (19 containers); General Joseph C. Breckinridge (143 containers); Madeline McDowell Breckinridge (31 containers); Robert J. Breckinridge (an additional 26 containers); Sophonisba P. Breckinridge (39 containers, mostly microfilmed); W.C.P. Breckinridge (an additional 41 containers); plus some 45 containers on other family members, including Mary and Desha Breckinridge.

The current condition of the papers varies considerably from the situation when I first examined them in 1973. At that time all the material now processed and arranged in the some 350 boxes was in a virginal archival state, untouched by human hands, it appeared, since being deposited in the Library of Congress. No guide existed; I literally went into the stacks and picked out the material I needed to study. My notes abounded with rather obscure references to "Add. b," "Box 10" (of which there were two), and "small trunk." Although dusty, frustrating, and time-consuming, it was also an exciting, fruitful work of discovery, and the Library of Congress staff aided me in that search.

By 1978 this mass of material was finally processed—some of it almost seven decades after deposition—and a useful guide prepared. That part of the collection remains somewhat difficult to use, since several Breckinridges bearing the same surname may be included erroneously as one in a single folder, and since the arrangement often appears to be by letter recipient rather than author. Thus a thorough search for all letters written by Robert J. Breckinridge, Jr., for example, theoretically would require a researcher to survey not only that person's folder but many of the 350 other containers.

This presented a real problem, for most of my notes were taken from the unprocessed mass. After a reexamination of many of the newly arranged boxes, I have traced the current location of many of these documents. Others remain, however, in places yet unsearched. While scholarly use would be facilitated by my updating all notes in this book to correspond with the present state of arrangement, such a project would contribute neither to my mental well-being nor speedy completion of the book. Therefore, I have simply cited the material as "B. MSS boxes." Those wishing the original citation or, in some cases, present abode of these documents so cited are welcome to inquire of the author.

Other manuscripts proving particularly valuable on the family include the wide-ranging Breckinridge Family Papers, the less-revealing Madeline McDowell Breckinridge Papers, the newly organized Mary Breckinridge Papers, and the sizable (and mostly official) John Bayne Breckinridge Papers, all at the University of Kentucky (hereinafter UK). Unorganized and incomplete, but very revealing, is Sophonisba P. Breckinridge's manuscript autobiography at the University of Chicago; her sister's more polished recollections of their early life appear in Eleanor Breckinridge Chalkley, "Magic Casements," in the possession of her daughter, Lyssa Harper of Richmond, Virginia. Also in private hands are extensive materials focusing on John C. Breckinridge (held by Dorothy Breckinridge of Summit Point, West Virginia), John C., Clifton, and Mary Breckinridge (in possession of Katherine Breckinridge Prewitt of Mt. Sterling, Kentucky), and John Bayne Breckinridge (with Helen Breckinridge of Lexington).

While specific and general material on the Breckinridges appears in many collections, the most useful include the Evans Papers, the Craig Shelby Papers, and the Frontier Nursing Service Administration Records (all at UK), the Grigsby Collection at the Filson Club, Louisville, the Draper Collection at the State Historical Society of Wisconsin, the Reuben T. Durrett Collection (University of Chicago), the Breckinridge Long Papers (LC), and the John Cabell Breckinridge Compiled Service Record, Record Group 109 (National Archives). Surprisingly, this last source contains letters that passed between husband and wife during wartime. Given the mass of family material that remains available, it is evident that the Breckinridges—fortunately for historians—were not successful records managers. They seem to have kept everything.

Scholars have used much of this material to tell, over the years, the stories of individual Breckinridges. James A. Van Kirk's "The Public Career of John Breckinridge" (Ph.D. dissertation, Northwestern University, 1937) gave his subject rather pedestrian treatment; over three decades later that was remedied by the publication of Lowell H. Harrison's definitive *John Breckinridge: Jeffersonian Republican* (1969). Robert J. Breckinridge has received more detailed attention than perhaps any other member of the family, yet students of his life seem too overwhelmed by the diversity of the man to complete and publish a full biography. Edgar C. Mayse, "Robert Jefferson Breckinridge: American Presbyterian Controversialist" (Ph.D. dissertation, Union Theological Seminary in Virginia, 1974) and Will D. Gilliam, "Robert J. Breckinridge: Conservative Non-Conformer" (manuscript biography, UK) both represent excellent studies which concentrate on the religious man, for instance; William H. Vaughan, *Robert Jefferson Breckinridge as an Education Administrator* (1937) and Robert W. Hartness, "The Educational Work of Robert Jefferson Breckinridge" (Ph.D. dissertation, Yale University, 1936) stress the educational side; while Edmund A. Moore, "The Earlier Life of Robert J. Breckinridge, 1800-1845" (Ph.D. dissertation, University of Chicago, 1932) and Robert A. Miles, in an incomplete manuscript biography (UK), examine only the early portion of his life. A full biography is needed.

The best-known of the family members, John C. Breckinridge, is fortunate in having three published biographies. Lucille Stillwell, *John Cabell Breckinridge* (1936), starts on the wrong foot by giving her subject an incorrect birthdate but, overall, presents an adequate, brief portrayal. Much sounder interpretations and much fuller details are in William C. Davis's well-written *Breckinridge: Statesman, Soldier, Symbol* (1974). Also excellent is Frank H. Heck's concise *Proud Kentuckian: John C. Breckinridge, 1821-1875* (1976), which offers some interpretations that vary from Davis's. If on the losing side in war, John C. Breckinridge has been very successful in attracting winning biographers.

After John C. Breckinridge, the biographical fires begin to flicker, however. Only Mary E. Graves' very limited "Contemporary Scenes as Found in the Writings of W.C.P. Breckinridge" (thesis, Catholic University, 1960) examines "Willie" in any depth, and Desha Breckinridge and John Bayne Breckinridge have attracted little earlier historical attention. Desha's wife, the reformer Madeline McDowell Breckinridge, was the subject of sister-in-law Sophonisba P. Breckinridge's scholarly but friendly *Madeline McDowell Breckinridge: A Leader in the New South* (1921). Almost six decades later, Melba Porter Hay researched "Madge" and gave a full and fair interpretation in her first-rate "Madeline McDowell Breckinridge: Kentucky Suffragist and Progressive Reformer" (Ph.D. dissertation, University of Kentucky, 1980). Sophonisba P. Breckinridge, active in so many fields, is mentioned in numerous Progressive Era works, but aside from the articles cited in the notes and Margaret S. Vining's thesis, "Sophonisba Preston Breckinridge and the Graduate School of Public Welfare Administration at the University of Chicago" (George Washington University, 1982), little detailed work has appeared. She, too, awaits a biographer. Mary Breckinridge has been the subject of a biography written for children; the best insights into her life still come from her autobiography, *Wide Neighborhoods: A Story of the Frontier Nursing Service* (1952), and her sad but revealing account of the son who died: *Breckie: His Four Years, 1914-1918* (1918). Virtually all the Breckinridges wrote articles that were published in their lifetimes; some, such as Sophonisba, produced several books, while others, such as Robert, John C., and W.C.P., also had speeches printed in article or pamphlet form. Between 1897 and 1935 the Lexington *Herald* provided an outlet for Breckinridge philosophy and thoughts, as did the official journals of the

United States Congress and the Kentucky House and Senate, for the appropriate years.

Providing information on the family's early history are Thomas Marshall Green, *A Sketch of the Breckinridge Family* (n.d., circa 1887-1904), James M. Breckenridge, *William Clark Breckenridge . . . His Life, Lineage and Writings* (1932), and Helen Congleton Breckinridge, *Cabell's Dale: The Story of a Family (1760-1876)* (1983). The genealogical background so needed both to keep everyone straight in a researcher's mind and to give raw data for statistical reconstructions can be found in Alexander Brown, *The Cabells and Their Kin* (1895) and in Helen C. Breckinridge, *Descendants of John and Mary Cabell Breckinridge* (1980). Stephen Hess includes a discussion of the family in his *America's Political Dynasties from Adams to Kennedy* (1966).

To understand the Breckinridges fully requires involved research in state, regional, and national history. Obviously this bibliographical note is not the place to discuss all these kinds of sources, for whole books exist on that subject. They range from editors Arthur S. Link and Rembert W. Patrick's dated *Writing Southern History* (1965) to the more recent Michael Kammen, ed., *The Past Before Us: Contemporary Historical Writing in the United States* (1980). Dozens of excellent books and articles survey specific aspects of the national scene, with an emphasis on politics. Those most useful for my particular purposes include Noble E. Cunningham, Jr., *The Jeffersonian Republicans: The Formation of Party Organizations, 1789-1801* (1957); Cunningham, *Republicans in Power: Party Operations, 1801-1809* (1963); David M. Potter, *The Impending Crisis, 1848-1861*, edited and completed by Don E. Fehrenbacher (1976); James M. McPherson, *Ordeal by Fire: The Civil War and Reconstruction* (1982); Morton Keller, *Affairs of State: Public Life in Late Nineteenth Century America* (1977), a fine study; and Arthur S. Link, *Wilson: The New Freedom* (1956).

Numerous other works provided their own strengths in more specific areas. On the question of race relations, for example, Winthrop D. Jordan's superb *White Over Black: American Attitudes Toward the Negro, 1550-1812* (1968), George M. Frederickson's *The Black Image in the White Mind: The Debate on Afro-American Character and Destiny, 1817-1914* (1971), Claude H. Nolen's *The Negro Image in the South: The Anatomy of White Supremacy* (1967), and John David Smith's thorough *An Old Creed for the New South: Proslavery Ideology and Historiography, 1865-1918* (1985) all provide insights into the white mind regarding blacks in America. Similarly, on the background of midwifery see Richard W. and Dorothy C. Wertz, *Lying-In: A History of Childbirth in America* (1977), Jane B. Donegan, *Women & Men Midwives: Medicine, Morality, and Misogyny in Early America* (1978), Judy Barrett Litoff, *American Midwives: 1860 to the Present* (1978), and Frances E. Kobrin, "The American Midwife Controversy," *Bulletin of the History of Medicine* 40 (1966): 350-63. For the background on other subjects, again, the notes should be consulted.

Turning to the regional context, numerous works provide fine background materials there as well. A half-dozen books cover the last 150 years of southern history and politics in an exemplary manner: William J. Cooper, *The South and the Politics of Slavery, 1828-1856* (1978); Emory M. Thomas, *The Confederate Nation: 1861-1865* (1979); C. Vann Woodward, *Origins of the New South, 1877-1913* (1951)—dated, and the subject of revisionism and re-revisionism, but still insightful;

Dewey M. Grantham, *Southern Progressivism: The Reconciliation of Progress and Tradition* (1983); George B. Tindall, *The Emergence of the New South, 1913-1945* (1967), indispensable for that period; and Charles P. Roland, *The Improbable Era: The South Since World War II* (1975), readable and path-breaking. Carl N. Degler attacks the idea of a monolithic South in his *The Other South: Southern Dissenters in the Nineteenth Century* (1974), which additionally provides the context in which Robert and W.C.P. Breckinridge operated.

The field of Kentucky history remains fertile ground for scholars. The best one-volume history continues to be Thomas D. Clark, *A History of Kentucky*, published in 1937 and updated periodically since then but never fully revised. Clark's *Kentucky: Land of Contrast* (1968) is a well-written, shorter, and more interpretive look at the commonwealth, while Steven A. Channing, *Kentucky: A Bicentennial History* (1977), even briefer but also well-written, is the most recent examination. The fullest study of Kentucky, now sadly dated, appeared in 1922. Still, William E. Connelley and E. Merton Coulter's *History of Kentucky* (5 vols., three of them biographical sketches) has held up well.

Covering the chronological sweep of Kentucky history unfortunately involves references to many works, for few large-scale surveys of a long timeframe exist. Beginning in the early period of Kentucky history, Otis K. Rice's *Frontier Kentucky* (1975) is a brief overview, strong on the international setting. Much more interpretive, Arthur K. Moore's *The Frontier Mind* (1957) should be considered one of the classic studies dealing with the state. The political and constitutional evolution of early Kentucky emerges from Patricia Watlington's *The Partisan Spirit: Kentucky Politics, 1779-1792* (1972), which, despite a flawed argument, is an excellent survey with superior character sketches; and from Joan Wells Coward's *Kentucky in the New Republic: The Process of Constitution Making* (1979), a work that skillfully shows the interplay of society and the Constitution. John B. Boles's concise *Religion in Antebellum Kentucky* (1976) and F. Garvin Davenport, *Ante-Bellum Kentucky* (1943) provide the kind of social and intellectual background necessary to understanding Breckinridge actions.

The political sphere has not been the subject of much of the analysis of the "new" history; Harry A. Volz's "Party, State and Nation: Kentucky and the Coming of the American Civil War" (Ph.D. dissertation, University of Virginia, 1982) represents one of the first attempts to use that approach and it does it well. Together a trio of works cover the 1830-1860 period and give a full summary of the events, as well as a flavor of the times: Frank F. Mathias, "The Turbulent Years of Kentucky Politics, 1820-1850" (Ph.D. dissertation, University of Kentucky, 1966), Wallace B. Turner, "Kentucky in a Decade of Change, 1850-1860" (Ph.D. dissertation, University of Kentucky, 1954), and Albert D. Kirwan, *John J. Crittenden: The Struggle for the Union* (1962). Articles by Mathias and by Turner, based on their respective dissertations, have appeared in the *Register* and the *Filson Club History Quarterly*. A part of Richard P. McCormick's *The Second American Party System: Party Formation in the Jacksonian Era* (1966) focuses specifically on Kentucky and its political place in the nation.

Wartime Kentucky, 1861-1865, has been the subject of much study, some of it full of sound and fury. However, Lowell H. Harrison's tight, well-researched, and cogently argued *The Civil War in Kentucky* (1975) provides an excellent account and should be the starting place for those who wish further study on the Brothers' War. E. Merton Coulter's *The Civil War and Readjustment in Kentucky* (1926) is a surprisingly good survey, given the fact that it was written when only limited sources were available and when the author's biases quickly dated many of the conclusions. Ross A. Webb's succinct *Kentucky in the Reconstruction Era* (1979) revises many of the Coulter themes and uses fresh material to do so. Thomas L. Connelly, "Neo-Confederatism or Power Vacuum: Post-War Kentucky Politics Reappraised," *Register* 64 (1966): 257-69, offers still another interpretation, one stressing the regionalism of the state. A work that looks not only at politics, but also social life, education, and the arts is Hambleton Tapp and James C. Klotter, *Kentucky: Decades of Discord, 1865-1900* (1977). Edward F. Prichard, Jr.'s "Popular Political Movements in Kentucky, 1875-1900" (senior thesis, Princeton University, 1935) and Gaye Keller Bland's "Populism in Kentucky, 1887-1896" (Ph.D. dissertation, University of Kentucky, 1979) portray the outlook of those so hated by W.C.P. Breckinridge, as does James C. Klotter's *William Goebel: The Politics of Wrath* (1977).

In the twentieth century, political history continues to be a patchwork affair, for a full survey requires bringing together diverse sources. The resulting historiographical quilt does cover the subject, however. Paul E. Fuller's *Laura Clay and the Woman's Rights Movement* (1975) offers a fine beginning by showing the conflicting currents of Progressivism. Focusing more directly on the politics of the first decade of the century is Thomas H. Appleton, Jr., " 'Like Banquo's Ghost': The Emergence of the Prohibition Issue in Kentucky Politics" (Ph.D. dissertation, University of Kentucky, 1981), while Robert F. Sexton contributes by far the fullest survey of the 1920s in his "Kentucky Politics and Society, 1919-1932" (Ph.D. dissertation, University of Washington, 1970). Also useful is John Fenton, *Politics in the Border States* (1957). More recent analyses of the political world known as Kentucky appear in Malcolm E. Jewell and Everett W. Cunningham, *Kentucky Politics* (1968) and Neal R. Pierce, *The Border South States* (1975). The Pierce essay is always readable, often one-sided, and sometimes insightful. A profile of John B. Breckinridge's congressional district can be found in the Ralph Nader Congress Project, *Statistical Supplement to Congressional Profiles*, 10 vols. (1974). For background on the urban area in which most of the Breckinridges operated, see Richard C. Wade, *The Urban Frontier: The Rise of Western Cities, 1790-1830* (1959), Bernard Mayo, *Henry Clay: Spokesman of the New West* (1937), and John D. Wright, Jr., *Lexington: Heart of the Bluegrass* (1982).

Mary Breckinridge worked in a different environment much of her adult life. For a good historical view of that world as she found it, see Ronald D. Eller, *Miners, Millhands, and Mountaineers: Industrialization of the Appalachian South, 1880-1930* (1982); for an interesting but impressionistic view, see John F. Day, *Bloody Ground* (1941). Perhaps the best sources on Appalachia and the Frontier Nursing Service (FNS) are the interviews in the FNS Oral History Project at the University of Kentucky Library. Also there are videotapes of early FNS films, which give a valuable perspective. Among interviews I did for this book, those with Florence Cantrill, Eliza Underwood, Helen Breckinridge, and Scott Breckinridge contributed most to understanding my subject.

Finally, as the notes to chapter 21 should indicate, *The Breckinridges of Kentucky, 1760-1981* has sought to place the family in the intellectual context of the

"New Social History," while retaining much of the physical approach of the older style. Essays by Edward N. Saveth, "The Problem of American Family History," *American Quarterly* 21 (1969): 311-29, and Lawrence Stone, "Family History in the 1980s: Past Achievements and Future Trends," *Journal of Interdisciplinary History* 12 (1981): 51-87, offer some thoughts on the problems of this kind of plan. Jane Turner Censer in her *North Carolina Planters and Their Children, 1800-1860* (1984) gives a good analysis of another state's leadership class, while David F. Musto, "The Adams Family," *Proceedings of the Massachusetts Historical Society* 92 (1981): 40-58, presents a discussion of "the family mind." In my own study of the minds of the Breckinridges, I have been also influenced by the approaches taken by Allen F. Davis, *American Heroine: The Life and Legend of Jane Addams* (1973), Drew Gilpin Faust, *James Henry Hammond and the Old South* (1982), and Arthur P. Dudden, "Nostalgia and the American," *Journal of the History of Ideas* 22 (1961): 515-30.

Index

ing, received a letter from Ella Chambers, she is going to come here to school. I see that I have some little influence. I got acquainted with her while teaching in their district. Answered her letter, and now am going to sow at the little girls bonnets. Yesterday evening instead of lecture, Dr. McFadden tried chemical experiments, exploded some powder on land, and some under water, had quite a time in getting the rope across the stream.[5]

November 18, 1858 I see it is quite a while since I last wrote in my journal. Miss Chambers is here now, we three room together, that is Mary,[ii] Miss C, and I, hope we will get along well. Cousin Isaac[6] is with us now, he thinks of giving one lecture before he leaves, he wants me to go home with him, wish I could. Last Friday I was elected secretary in literary society. I am afraid I won't fill the chair well, well I guess I can do as well as I can, Saturdy night M. Miller and I sat up with a sick girl, sowed nearly all night. I have to read in "public" in a week from Saturday, those public exercises do take me down dreadfully, wish it was over.[7]

November 27, 1858 This was the day for our Monthly rhetorical exercises. It commenced snowing in the morning and snowed all day. I had hard work to get my essay finised. got through just in time, the snow was so deep that we could scarcely get down to the chapple. After the exercises, all those that read went to Proffessor

---

functioned as joint-stock library associations, providers of entertainment, debating and composing teams, and proto-fraternities and sororities. Much of the extracurricular college life available to students like Rachel was organized by and around these societies. Thomas S. Harding, *College Literary Societies: Their Contribution to Higher Education in the United States, 1815–1876* (New York, 1971).

5. Thomas McFadden, M.D., educated at Dickinson College in Carlisle, Pennsylvania, had been appointed professor of natural sciences and scientific agriculture and horticulture in 1858. He resigned from the faculty during the Civil War to become an army surgeon with the 46th Ohio, then returned to Otterbein as professor of natural sciences in 1866. He occupied that chair until his death in 1883. Garst, *Otterbein*, pp. 113–26, 184–86. Otterbein was not only teaching natural sciences, but offering its students rudimentary laboratory work and geology field trips (see May 18, 1859). On the important role of small schools like Otterbein in the dissemination of modern knowledge see Colin B. Burke, "The Quiet Influence: The American Liberal Arts Colleges and Their Students, 1800–1860," forthcoming, New York University Press.

6. Probably Isaac L. Bowman (1830–1893), youngest son of Rachel's father's brother John B. Bauman and his wife Nancy Bechtel Bauman. Isaac was a prominent educator in the public school system of Waterloo Township, Canada West. *BHWI*, II, 25.

7. The public recitation of original essays was a standard pedagogical technique in nineteenth-century colleges.

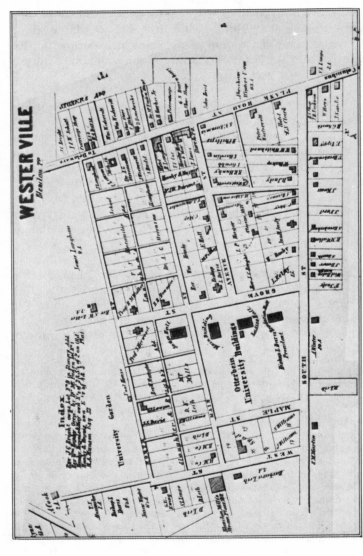

Westerville, Ohio, in the late 1850s. Rachel (B. B. Bowman) lived directly across Grove Street from Saum Hall. The homes of many of the people Rachel mentions can be located on this map. Detail from John Graham, *Map of Franklin County, Ohio, from Actual Survey and Records* (Philadelphia, 1856). Maps Division, LC.